Varieties of English 2
The Americas and the Caribbean

Varieties of English 2

The Americas and the Caribbean

Edited by
Edgar W. Schneider

Mouton de Gruyter · Berlin · New York

Mouton de Gruyter (formerly Mouton, The Hague)
is a Division of Walter de Gruyter GmbH & Co. KG, Berlin.

♾ Printed on acid-free paper which falls within the guidelines of the
ANSI to ensure permanence and durability.

Library of Congress Cataloging-in-Publication Data

The Americas and the Caribbean / edited by Edgar W. Schneider.
   p. cm. − (Varieties of English ; 2)
   Includes bibliographical references and index.
   ISBN 978-3-11-019636-8 (pbk. : alk. paper)
   1. English language − Dialects − America.   2. English language
Variation − America.   3. English language − Dialects − Caribbean
Area. 4. English language − Variation − Caribbean Area.   I. Schnei-
der, Edgar W. (Edgar Werner), 1954−
   PE2841.A775   2008
   427'.97 − dc22

2007045283

Bibliographic information published by the Deutsche Nationalbibliothek

The Deutsche Nationalbibliothek lists this publication in the Deutsche Nationalbibliografie;
detailed bibliographic data are available in the Internet at http://dnb.d-nb.de.

ISBN 978-3-11-019636-8

Cover design: Martin Zech, Bremen.
        Imagery provided by Google Earth/TerraMetrics, NASA.
Typesetting: Dörlemann Satz GmbH & Co. KG, Lemförde.
Printing and binding: AZ Druck und Datentechnik GmbH, Kempten (Allgäu).
Printed in Germany.

Contents

Phonology

Morphology and Syntax

Contents of volume 1

Morphology and Syntax

Contents of volume 3

Phonology

Morphology and Syntax

Contents of volume 4

Morphology and Syntax

Abbreviations

AAVE	African American Vernacular English
AbE/C/P	(Australian) Aboriginal English / Creole / Pidgin
AfBahE	Afro-Bahamian English
AfkE	Afrikaans English
AmE	American English
AnBahE	Anglo-Bahamian English
AppE	Appalachian English
AusE/VE/C	Australian English/Vernacular English/Creoles
BahE	Bahamian English
Baj	Bajan (Barbadian Creole)
BelC	Belizean Creole
BIE	Bay Islands English (Honduras)
BrC	British Creole
BrE	British English (= EngE + ScE + WelE)
ButlE	Butler English (India)
CajE	Cajun English
CAmC	Central American Creoles (Belize, Miskito, Limón, etc.)
CamP/E	Cameroon Pidgin/English
CanE	Canadian English
CarE	Caribbean English
Car(E)C	Caribbean (English-lexicon) Creoles
CFE	Cape Flats English
ChcE	Chicano English
ChnP	Chinese Pidgin English
CollAmE	Colloquial American English
CollSgE	Colloquial Singapore English
EAfE	East African English
EMarC	Eastern Maroon Creole
EngE	English English
EModE	Early Modern English
ME	Middle English
OE	Old English
ESM	English in Singapore and Malaysia
FijE	Fiji English
GhE/P	Ghanaian English/Pidgin
GuyC	Guyanese Creole
HawC	Hawaii Creole

HKE	Hong Kong English
IndE	Indian English, Anglo-Indian
InlNE	Inland Northern (American) English
IrE	Irish English
JamC/E	Jamaican Creole / English
KenE	Kenyan English
KPE	Kru Pidgin English
LibC/E	Liberian Creole/English
LibSE	Liberian Settler English
LibVE	Liberian Vernacular English
LimC	Limonese Creole (Costa Rica)
LonVE	London Vernacular English
LnkE	Lankan English
MalE	Malaysian English
NEngE	New England English
NfldE	Newfoundland English
NigP/E	Nigerian Pidgin / English
NZE	New Zealand English
NYCE	New York City English
OzE	Ozarks English
PakE	Pakistani English
PanC	Panamanian Creole
PhilE	Philadelphia English
PhlE	Philippines English
RP	Received Pronunciation
SAfE	South African English
BlSAfE	Black South African English
CoSAfE	Coloured South African English
InSAfE	Indian South African English
WhSAfE	White South African English
SAmE	Southern American English
SAsE	South Asian English
SEAmE	South Eastern American English enclave dialects
ScE	Scottish English, Scots
ScStE	Scottish Standard English
SgE	Singapore English
SLVE	St. Lucian Vernacular English
SolP	Solomon Islands Pidgin
StAmE	Standard American English
StAusCE	Standard Australian Colloquial English

StAusFE	Standard Australian Formal English
StBrE	Standard British English
StE	Standard English
StGhE	Standard Ghanaian English
StHE	St. Helena English
StIndE	Standard Indian English
StJamE	Standard Jamaican English
SurC	Suriname Creoles
TanE	Tanzanian English
TobC	Tobagonian Creole
Trad-RP	Traditional Received Pronunciation
TrnC	Trinidadian Creole
T & TC	Trinidadian & mesolectal Tobagonian Creoles
TP	Tok Pisin, New Guinea Pidgin, Neomelanesian
WAfE/P	West African English/Pidgin
WelE	Welsh English
WMwE	Western and Midwestern American English
ZamE	Zambian English

More abbreviations

ESL	English as Second Language
EFL	English as Foreign Language
EIL	English as International Language
ENL	English as Native Language
L1	First Language
L2	Second Language
P/C	Pidgins and Creoles

List of features: Phonology and phonetics

Edgar W. Schneider

Please indicate whether or to what extent the following features / variants occur in the variety that you have discussed by inserting A, B or C in the left-most column as follows:

A   occurs normally / is widespread
B   occurs sometimes / occasionally, with some speakers / groups, in some environments
C   does not normally occur.

If you have covered more than one variety, please give your set of responses for each of them, or give a summary assessment for a group of related varieties as specified.

Elements in parentheses (../..) are optional; ">" suggests a direction of movement.

Please note that the variants suggested for a single item (e.g. lexical set) are meant to be relatively exhaustive but not necessarily mutually exclusive.

Phonetic realization: vowels (lexical sets)

1.   KIT [ɪ]
2.   KIT raised / fronted, > [i]
3.   KIT centralized, > [ə]
4.   KIT with offglide, e.g. [ɪə/iə]
5.   DRESS half-close [e]
6.   DRESS raised, > [i]
7.   DRESS half-open [ɛ]
8.   DRESS backed, > [ʌ/ɐ]
9.   DRESS with centralizing offglide, e.g. [eə]
10.   DRESS with rising offglide, e.g. [eɪ]
11.   TRAP [æ]
12.   TRAP raised, > [ɛ/e]
13.   TRAP lowered, > [a]
14.   TRAP with offglide, e.g. [æə/æɛ/æɪ/ɛə]
15.   LOT rounded, e.g. [ɒ]
16.   LOT back unrounded, e.g. [ɑ]

17.   LOT front unrounded, e.g. [a]
18.   LOT with offglide, e.g. [ɒə]
19.   STRUT [ʌ]
20.   STRUT high back, > [ʊ]
21.   STRUT central [ə/ɐ]
22.   STRUT backed, > [ɔ]
23.   FOOT [ʊ]
24.   FOOT tensed [u]
25.   FOOT back, lower, e.g. [ʌ]
26.   BATH half-open front [æ]
27.   BATH low front [a]
28.   BATH low back [ɑ]
29.   BATH long
30.   BATH with offglide, e.g. [æə/æɪ/ɛə]
31.   CLOTH rounded [ɔ/ɒ]
32.   CLOTH back unrounded [ɑ]
33.   CLOTH front unrounded [a]
34.   NURSE central [ɜ:/ɚ]
35.   NURSE raised / fronted / rounded, e.g. [ø]
36.   NURSE mid front [ɛ/e(r)]
37.   NURSE [ʌ(r)] (possibly lexically conditioned, e.g. WORD)
38.   NURSE backed, e.g. [o/ɔ]
39.   NURSE diphthongal, e.g. [əɪ/ɔɪ]
40.   FLEECE [i:]
41.   FLEECE with centralizing offglide, e.g. [iə]
42.   FLEECE with mid/central onset and upglide, e.g. [əɪ/ei]
43.   FLEECE with high onset and upglide, e.g. [ɪi]
44.   FLEECE shortened, e.g. [i/ɪ]
45.   FACE upgliding diphthong with half-close onset, e.g. [eɪ]
46.   FACE upgliding diphthong with half-open or lower onset, e.g. [ɛɪ/æɪ]
47.   FACE upgliding diphthong with low / backed onset, e.g. [a(:)ɪ/ʌɪ]
48.   FACE upgliding diphthong with central onset, e.g. [əɪ]
49.   FACE monophthong, e.g. [e:]
50.   FACE ingliding diphthong, e.g. [ɪə/ɪɛ]
51.   PALM low back [ɑ(:)]
52.   PALM low front [a(:)]
53.   PALM with offglide, e.g. [ɑə/ɒə]
54.   THOUGHT [ɔ(:)]
55.   THOUGHT low [a:/ɑ:]
56.   THOUGHT with offglide, e.g. [ɔə/ʊə]

57. GOAT with central onset, e.g. [əʊ/əʉ]
58. GOAT with back rounded onset, e.g. [oʊ/ou]
59. GOAT with low or back unrounded onset, e.g. [a(:)u/aʉ/ʌʊ/ʌʉ]
60. GOAT with relatively high back onset [ʊu]
61. GOAT ingliding, e.g. [ʊə/uɔ/ua]
62. GOAT monophthongal, e.g. [o(:)]
63. GOOSE [u:]
64. GOOSE fronted, > [ʉ(:)]
65. GOOSE gliding, e.g. [ʊu/ɪu/ə(:)ʉ]
66. PRICE upgliding diphthong, e.g. [aɪ/ɑɪ/ʌɪ]
67. PRICE monophthong [a:] before voiced C
68. PRICE monophthong [a:] in all environments
69. PRICE with raised / central onset, e.g. [əɪ/ɜɪ]
70. PRICE with backed onset, e.g. [ɔ(:)ɪ/ɒɪ]
71. PRICE with mid-front offglide, e.g. [ae/aɛ]
72. CHOICE [ɔɪ]
73. CHOICE with low onset [ɒɪ]
74. CHOICE with central onset [əɪ/əi]
75. MOUTH [aʊ/ɑʊ]
76. MOUTH with raised and backed onset, e.g. [ʌu/ɔʊ]
77. MOUTH with raised onset [əʊ] only before voiceless C
78. MOUTH with raised onset [əʊ] in all environments
79. MOUTH with fronted onset, e.g. [æʉ/æʊ/æo/ɛo]
80. MOUTH low monophthong, e.g. [a:]
81. MOUTH mid/high back monophthong, e.g. [o:]
82. NEAR [ɪə(r)]
83. NEAR without offglide, e.g. [ɪr]
84. NEAR with tensed / raised onset, e.g. [i(:)ə]
85. NEAR with half-closed onset [e(:/ə/r)/ea]
86. NEAR with half-open onset [ɛ(:/ə/r)]
87. NEAR high-front to low glide, e.g. [ia]
88. SQUARE with half-open onset [ɛə]
89. SQUARE with half-closed onset [eə/ea]
90. SQUARE with high front onset [ɪə]
91. SQUARE with relatively open onset, possibly rising [æə/æɪ]
92. SQUARE half-closed monophthong, [e(:/r)]
93. SQUARE half-open monophthong, [ɛ(:/r)]
94. START low back unrounded, e.g. [ɑ(:/r)]
95. START central, e.g. [ɐ(:/r)]
96. START low front, e.g. [a(:/r)]

97. START front, raised, e.g. [æ(:/r)]
98. START with offglide, e.g. [ɑə/ɒə)]
99. NORTH half-open monophthong [ɔ(:/r)]
100. NORTH half-closed monophthong [o(:/r)]
101. NORTH [ɒ]
102. NORTH with offglide, e.g. [ɒə/oa]
103. FORCE half-open monophthong [ɔ(:/r)]
104. FORCE half-closed monophthong [o(:/r)]
105. FORCE ingliding, e.g. [ɔə(r)/oə(r)/oa]
106. FORCE with upglide, e.g.[oʊ(r)]
107. CURE [ʊə/ʊr]
108. CURE with tensed / raised onset, e.g. [u(:)ə/ur]
109. CURE lowered monophthong, e.g. [o:/ɔ:]
110. CURE with upglide, e.g. [oʊ(r)]
111. CURE low offglide, e.g. [ua/oa(r)]
112. happY relatively centralized, e.g. [ɪ]
113. happY central, e.g. [ə]
114. happY tensed / relatively high front, e.g. [i(:)]
115. happY mid front, e.g. [e/ɛ]
116. lettER [ə]
117. lettER (relatively) open, e.g. [a/ʌ]
118. horsES central [ə]
119. horsES high front [ɪ]
120. commA [ə]
121. commA (relatively) open, e.g. [a/ʌ]

Distribution: vowels

122. homophony of KIT and FLEECE
123. homophony of TRAP and BATH
124. homophony of *Mary* and *merry*
125. homophony of *Mary*, *merry* and *marry*
126. homophony of TRAP and DRESS before /l/
127. merger of KIT and DRESS before nasals (*pin = pen*)
128. homophony of DRESS and FACE
129. homophony of FOOT and GOOSE
130. homophony of LOT and THOUGHT
131. homophony of LOT and STRUT
132. homophony of NEAR and SQUARE

133. vowels nasalized before nasal consonants
134. vowel harmony / cross-syllable assimilation phenomena in some words
135. vowels short unless before /r/, voiced fricative, or in open syllable (SVLR)
136. commA/lettER (etc.): [ɑ/ɛ/i/ɔ/u], reflecting spelling

Phonetic realization and distribution: consonants

137. P/T/K-: weak or no aspiration of word-initial stops
138. -T-: lenisation / flapping / voicing of intervocalic /t/ (*writer* = *rider*)
139. -T: realization of word-final or intervocalic /t/ as glottal stop
140. K-: palatalization of velar stop word-initially: e.g. kj-/gj-in *can 't/ garden*
141. B-: word-initial *bw-* for b-: e.g. *bw-* in *boy*
142. S-/F-: voiceless initial fricatives voiced: [z-/v-]
143. TH-: realization of word-initial voiced TH as stop, e.g. *dis*, 'this'
144. TH-: realization of word-initial voiceless TH as stop, e.g. *ting, 'thing'*
145. TH-: realization of word-initial voiced TH as affricate [dð]
146. TH-: realization of word-initial voiceless TH as affricate [tθ]
147. WH-: velar fricative onset retained, i.e. *which* is not homophonous with *witch*
148. CH: voiceless velar fricative [χ/x] exists
149. h-deletion (word-initial), e.g., *'eart* 'heart'
150. h-insertion (word-initial), e.g. *haxe* 'axe'
151. L-: palatal (clear) variant in syllable onsets
152. L-: velar variant in syllable onsets
153. –L: palatal variant in syllable codas
154. "jod"-dropping: no /j/ after alveolars before /u:/, e.g. in *news, tune*
155. deletion of word-initial /h/ in /hj-/ clusters, e.g. in *human, huge*
156. labialization of word-central voiced -TH-, e.g. [-v-] in *brother*
157. labialization of word-final / word-central voiceless –TH, e.g. [-f] in *mouth, nothing*
158. intervocalic /-v-/ > [b], e.g. in *river*
159. W: substitution of labiodental fricative /v/ for semi-vowel /w/
160. word-final consonant cluster deletion, monomorphemic
161. word-final consonant cluster deletion, bimorphemic
162. deletion of word-final single consonants
163. simplification of word-initial consonant clusters, e.g. in *splash, square*
164. non-rhotic (no postvocalic –r)

165. rhotic (postvocalic –r realized)
166. phonetic realization of /r/ as velar retroflex constriction
167. phonetic realization of /r/ as alveolar flap
168. phonetic realization of /r/ as apical trill
169. /r/ uvular
170. intrusive –r–, e.g. *idea*-r-*is*
171. post-vocalic –l vocalized
172. neutralization / confusion of liquids /l/ and /r/ in some words
173. realization of velar nasals with stop: -NG > [-ŋg]
174. velarization of some word-final nasals, e.g. /-ŋ/ in *down*

Prosodic features and intonation

175. deletion of word-initial unstressed syllables, e.g. *'bout, 'cept*
176. stress not infrequently shifted from first to later syllable, e.g. *indi'cate, holi'day*
177. (relatively) syllable-timed rather than stress-timed
178. HRT (High-Rising Terminal) contour: rise at end of statement
179. tone distinctions exist

List of features: Morphology and Syntax

Bernd Kortmann

The features in the catalogue are numbered from 1 to 76 (for easy reference in later parts of the chapter) and provided with the short definitions and illustrations. They include all usual suspects known from survey articles on grammatical properties of (individual groups of) non-standard varieties of English, with a slight bias towards features observed in L1 varieties. The 76 features fall into 11 groups corresponding to the following broad areas of morphosyntax: pronouns, noun phrase, tense and aspect, modal verbs, verb morphology, adverbs, negation, agreement, relativization, complementation, discourse organization and word order.

Pronouns, pronoun exchange, pronominal gender

1. *them* instead of demonstrative *those* (e.g. *in them days, one of them things*)
2. *me* instead of possessive *my* (e.g. *He's me brother, I've lost me bike*)
3. special forms or phrases for the second person plural pronoun (e.g. *youse, y'all, aay', yufela, you ... together, all of you, you ones/'uns, you guys, you people*)
4. regularized reflexives-paradigm (e.g. *hisself, theirselves/theirself*)
5. object pronoun forms serving as base for reflexives (e.g. *meself*)
6. lack of number distinction in reflexives (e.g. plural *-self*)
7. *she/her* used for inanimate referents (e.g. *She was burning good* [about a house])
8. generic *he/his* for all genders (e.g. *My car, he's broken*)
9. *myself/meself* in a non-reflexive function (e.g. *my/me husband and myself*)
10. *me* instead of *I* in coordinate subjects (e.g. *Me and my brother/My brother and me were late for school*)
11. non-standard use of *us* (e.g. *Us George was a nice one, We like us town, Show us* 'me' *them boots, Us kids used to pinch the sweets like hell, Us'll do it*)
12. non-coordinated subject pronoun forms in object function (e.g. *You did get he out of bed in the middle of the night*)
13. non-coordinated object pronoun forms in subject function (e.g. *Us say 'er's dry*)

Noun phrase

14.   absence of plural marking after measure nouns (e.g. *four pound, five year*)
15.   group plurals (e.g. *That President has two Secretary of States*)
16.   group genitives (e.g. *The man I met's girlfriend is a real beauty*)
17.   irregular use of articles (e.g. *Take them to market, I had nice garden, about a three fields, I had the toothache*)
18.   postnominal *for*-phrases to express possession (e.g. *The house for me*)
19.   double comparatives and superlatives (e.g. *That is so much more easier to follow*)
20.   regularized comparison strategies (e.g. in *He is the regularest kind a guy I know, in one of the most pretty sunsets*)

Verb phrase: Tense & aspect

21.   wider range of uses of the Progressive (e.g. *I'm liking this, What are you wanting?*)
22.   habitual *be* (e.g. *He be sick*)
23.   habitual *do* (e.g. *He does catch fish pretty*)
24.   non-standard habitual markers other than *be* and *do*
25.   levelling of difference between Present Perfect and Simple Past (e.g. *Were you ever in London?, Some of us have been to New York years ago*)
26.   *be* as perfect auxiliary (e.g. *They're not left school yet*)
27.   *do* as a tense and aspect marker (e.g. *This man what do own this*)
28.   completive/perfect *done* (e.g. *He done go fishing, You don ate what I has sent you?*)
29.   past tense/anterior marker *been* (e.g. *I been cut the bread*)
30.   loosening of sequence of tense rule (e.g. *I noticed the van I came in*)
31.   *would* in if-clauses (e.g. *If I'd be you, ...*)
32.   *was sat/stood* with progressive meaning (e.g. *when you're stood* 'are standing' *there you can see the flames*)
33.   *after*-Perfect (e.g. *She's after selling the boat*)

Verb phrase: Modal verbs

34.   double modals (e.g. *I tell you what we might should do*)
35.   epistemic *mustn't* ('can't, it is concluded that... not'; e.g. *This mustn't be true*)

Verb phrase: Verb morphology

36. levelling of preterite and past participle verb forms: regularization of irregular verb paradigms (e.g. *catch-catched-catched*)

37. levelling of preterite and past participle verb forms: unmarked forms (frequent with e.g. *give* and *run*)

38. levelling of preterite and past partiple verb forms: past form replacing the participle (e.g. *He had went*)

39. levelling of preterite and past partiple verb forms: participle replacing the past form (e.g. *He gone to Mary*)

40. zero past tense forms of regular verbs (e.g. *I walk* for *I walked*)

41. *a*-prefixing on *ing*-forms (e.g. *They wasn't a-doin' nothin' wrong*)

Adverbs

42. adverbs (other than degree modifiers) have same form as adjectives (e.g. *Come quick!*)

43. degree modifier adverbs lack *-ly* (e.g. *That's real good*)

Negation

44. multiple negation / negative concord (e.g. *He won't do no harm*)

45. *ain't* as the negated form of *be* (e.g. *They're all in there, ain't they?*)

46. *ain't* as the negated form of *have* (e.g. *I ain't had a look at them yet*)

47. *ain't* as generic negator before a main verb (e.g. *Something I ain't know about*)

48. invariant *don't* for all persons in the present tense (e.g. *He don't like me*)

49. *never* as preverbal past tense negator (e.g. *He never came* [= he didn't come])

50. *no* as preverbal negator (e.g. *me no iit brekfus*)

51. *was–weren't* split (e.g. *The boys was interested, but Mary weren't*)

52. invariant non-concord tags, (e.g. *innit/in't it/isn't* in *They had them in their hair, innit?*)

Agreement

53.   invariantpresenttenseformsduetozeromarkingforthethirdpersonsingular (e.g. *So he show up and say, What's up?*)
54.   invariant present tense forms due to generalization of third person *-s* to all persons (e.g. *I sees the house*)
55.   existential/presentational *there's, there is, there was* with plural subjects (e.g. *There's two men waiting in the hall*)
56.   variant forms of dummy subjects in existential clauses (e.g. *they, it,* or zero for *there*)
57.   deletion of *be* (e.g. *She ___ smart*)
58.   deletion of auxiliary *have* (e.g. *I ___ eaten my lunch)*
59.   *was/were* generalization (e.g. *You were hungry but he were thirsty*, or: *You was hungry but he was thirsty*)
60.   Northern Subject Rule (e.g. *I sing* [vs. **I sings*], *Birds sings, I sing and dances*)

Relativization

61.   relative particle *what* (e.g. *This is the man what painted my house*)
62.   relative particle *that* or *what* in non-restrictive contexts (e.g. *My daughter, that/what lives in London,…*)
63.   relative particle *as* (e.g. *He was a chap as got a living anyhow*)
64.   relative particle *at* (e.g. *This is the man at painted my house*)
65.   use of analytic *that his/that's, what his/what's, at's, as'* instead of *whose* (e.g. *The man what's wife has died*)
66.   gapping or zero-relativization in subject position (e.g. *The man ___ lives there is a nice chap*)
67.   resumptive / shadow pronouns (e.g. *This is the house which I painted it yesterday*)

Complementation

68.   *say*-based complementizers
69.   inverted word order in indirect questions (e.g. *I'm wondering what are you gonna do*)
70.   unsplit *for to* in infinitival purpose clauses (e.g. *We always had gutters in the winter time for to drain the water away*)

71.   *as what / than what* in comparative clauses (e.g. *It's harder than what you think it is*)
72.   serial verbs (e.g. *give* meaning 'to, for', as in *Karibuk giv mi*, 'Give the book to me')

Discourse organization and word order

73.   lack of inversion / lack of auxiliaries in *wh*-questions (e.g. *What you doing?*)
74.   lack of inversion in main clause *yes/no* questions (e.g. *You get the point?*)
75.   *like* as a focussing device (e.g. *How did you get away with that like? Like for one round five quid, that was like three quid, like two-fifty each*)
76.   *like* as a quotative particle (e.g. *And she was like "What do you mean?"*)

General introduction

Bernd Kortmann and Edgar W. Schneider

This book, together with its three companion volumes on other world regions, derives from the *Handbook of Varieties of English*, edited by Kortmann, Schneider et al. (2004). To make the material compiled in the *Handbook* more easily accessible and affordable, especially to student pockets, it has been decided to regroup the articles in such a way that all descriptive papers on any of the seven major anglophone world regions distinguished there are put together in a set of four paperback volumes, and accompanied by the CD-ROM which covers data and sources from all around the world. In this brief introduction we are briefly revisiting and summarizing the major design features of the *Handbook* and its contributions, i.e. information which, by implication, also characterizes the articles in the present volume.

The all-important design feature of the *Handbook* and of these offspring paperbacks is its focus on structure and on the solid description and documentation of data. The volumes, together with the CD-ROM, provide comprehensive up-to-date accounts of the salient phonological and grammatical properties of the varieties of English around the world. Reliable structural information in a somewhat standardized format and presented in an accessible way is a necessary prerequisite for any kind of study of language varieties, independent of the theoretical framework used for analysis. It is especially important for comparative studies of the phonological and morphosyntactic patterns across varieties of English, and the inclusion of this kind of data in typological studies (e.g. in the spirit of Kortmann 2004).

Of course, all of this structural information can be and has to be put in perspective by the conditions of uses of these varieties, i.e. their sociohistorical backgrounds, their current sociolinguistic settings (not infrequently in multilingual societies), and their associated political dimensions (like issues of norm-setting, language policies, and pedagogical applications). Ultimately, all of the varieties under discussion here, certainly so the ones spoken outside of England but in a sense, looking way back in time, even the English dialects themselves, are products of colonization processes, predominantly the European colonial expansion in the modern age. A number of highly interesting questions, linguistically and culturally, might be asked in this context, including the central issue of why all of this has happened, whether there is an underlying scheme that has continued to drive and motivate the evolution of new varieties of English (Schneider 2003, 2007). These linguistic and sociohistorical background issues will be briefly addressed in the regional introductions and in some of the individual chapters, but it should be made clear that it is the issue of structural description and comparison which is at the heart of this project.

The chapters in the four paperbacks are geared towards documenting and mapping the structural variation among (spontaneously spoken) non-standard varieties of English. Standard English is of course that variety, or set of closely related varieties, which enjoys the highest social prestige. It serves as a reference system and target norm in formal situations, in the language used by people taking on a public persona (including, for example, anchorpersons in the news media), and as a model in the teaching of English worldwide. Here, however, it is treated as is commonplace in modern descriptive linguistics, i.e. as a variety on a par with all other (regional, social, ethnic, or contact) varieties of English. Clearly, in terms of its structural properties it is not inherently superior to any of the non-standard varieties. Besides, the very notion of "Standard English" itself obviously refers to an abstraction. On the written level, it is under discussion to what extent a "common core" or a putatively homogeneous variety called "International English" actually exists: there is some degree of uniformity across the major national varieties, but once one looks into details of expression and preferences, there are also considerable differences. On the spoken level, there are reference accents like, for example, Received Pronunciation for British English, but their definition also builds upon abstractions from real individuals' performance. Thus, in the present context especially the grammar of (written) Standard English figures as no more than an implicit standard of comparison, in the sense that all chapters focus upon those phenomena in a given variety which are (more or less strikingly) different from this standard (these being perceived as not, note again, in any sense deficient or inferior to it).

The articles in this collection cover all main national standard varieties, distinctive regional, ethnic, and social varieties, major contact varieties (pidgins and creoles), as well as major varieties of English as a Second Language. The inclusion of second-language varieties and, especially, English-based pidgins and creoles may come as a surprise to some readers. Normally these varieties are addressed from different perspectives (such as, for example, language policy, language pedagogy, linguistic attitudes, language and identity (construction), substrate vs. superstrate influence), each standing in its own research tradition. Here they are primarily discussed from the point of view of their structural properties.

This will make possible comparisons with structural properties of, for example, other varieties of English spoken in the same region, or second-language or contact varieties in other parts of the English-speaking world. At the same time the availability of solid structural descriptions may open new perspectives for a fruitful interaction between the different research traditions within which second-language and contact varieties are studied. The boundaries of what is considered and accepted as "varieties of English" has thus been drawn fairly widely. In accepting English-oriented pidgins and creoles in the present context, we adopt a trend of recent research to consider them as contact varieties closely related to, possibly to be categorized as varieties of, their respective superstrate languages (e.g. Mufwene 2001). Creoles, and also some pidgins, in many regions vary along a continuum from acrolectal forms, relatively close to English and used by the higher sociolinguistic strata in formal contexts, to basilects, "deep" varieties maximally different from English. Most of our contributions focus upon the mesolects, the middle ranges which in most creole-speaking societies are used most widely.

For other varieties, too, it may be asked why or why not they have been selected for inclusion in this collection. Among the considerations that led to the present selection, the following figured most prominently: amount and quality of existing data and research documentation for the individual varieties, intensity of ongoing research activities, availability of authors, and space constraints (leading, for example, to the exclusion of strictly local accents and dialects). More information on the selection of varieties will be given in the regional introductions.

While in the *Handbook* there is one volume each for phonology and grammar (i.e. morphology and syntax), this set of paperbacks has been arranged by the major world regions relevant for the discussion of varieties of English: the British Isles; the Americas and the Caribbean; Africa, South and Southeast Asia; and the Pacific and Australasia. Each of the volumes comprises all articles on the respective regions, both on phonology and on grammar, together with the regional introductions, which include accounts of the histories, the cultural and sociolinguistic situations, and the most important data sources for the relevant locations, ethnic groups and varieties, and the regional synopses, in which the editors summarize the most striking properties of the varieties of English spoken in the respective world regions. Global synopses offering the most noteworthy findings and tendencies on phonological and morphosyntactic variation in English from a global perspective are available in the two hardcover Handbooks and in the electronic online version. In addition, there is a list of "General references", all of them exclusively book publications, which are either globally relevant or central for for individual world regions.

What emerges from the synopses is that many of the features described for individual varieties or sets of varieties in this Handbook are not unique to these (sets of) varieties. This is true both for morphology and syntax and for phonology.

As a matter of fact, quite a number of morphosyntactic features described as salient properties of individual varieties may strike the reader as typical of other varieties, too, possibly even of the grammar of spoken English, in general. In a similar vein, it turns out that certain phonological processes (like the monophthongization of certain diphthongs, the fronting, backing or merging of some vowels, and some consonantal substitutions or suprasegmental processes) can be documented in quite a number of fairly disparate language varieties – not surprisingly, perhaps, given shared underlying principles like constraints of articulatory space or tendencies towards simplification and the reduction of contrasts.

The distributions of selected individual features, both morphosyntactic and phonological, across varieties world-wide is visualized by the interactive world maps on the accompanying CD-ROM. The lists of these features, which are also referred to in some contributions, especially the regional synopses, are appended to this introduction. On these maps, each of a set of selected features, for almost all of the varieties under discussion, is categorized as occurring regularly (marked as "A" and colour-coded in red), occasionally or only in certain specified environments (marked as "B" and represented by a yellow circle) or practically not at all ("C", black). These innovative maps, which are accompanied by statistical distribution data on the spread of selected variants, provide the reader with an immediate visual representation of regional distribution and diffusion patterns. Further information on the nature of the multimedia material accompanying these books is available on the CD itself. It includes audio samples of free conversations (some of them transcribed), a standard reading passage, and recordings of the spoken "lexical sets" which define and illustrate vocalic variation (Wells 1982).

The chapters are descriptive survey articles providing state-of-the-art reports on major issues in current research, with a common core in order to make the collection an interesting and useful tool especially from a comparative, i.e. cross-dialectal and cross-linguistic, point of view. All chapters aim primarily at a qualitative rather than quantitative perspective, i.e. whether or not a given feature occurs is more important than its frequency. Of course, for varieties where research has focused upon documenting frequency relationships between variants of variables, some information on relevant quantitative tendencies has been provided. Depending upon the research coverage in a given world region (which varies widely from one continent to another), some contributions build upon existing sociolinguistic, dialectological, or structural research; a small number of other chapters make systematic use of available computerized corpora; and in some cases and for some regions the chapters in this compilation provide the first-ever systematic qualitative survey of the phonological and grammatical properties of English as spoken there.

For almost all varieties of English covered there are companion chapters in the phonology and morphosyntax parts of each paperback volume. In these cases it is in the phonology chapter that the reader will find a concise introductory section on the historical and cultural background as well as the current sociolinguistic situation of the relevant variety or set of varieties spoken at this location.

In order to ensure a certain degree of comparability, the authors were given a set of core issues that they were asked to address (provided something interesting can be said about them in the respective variety). For the phonology chapters, this set included the following items:

- phonological systems
- phonetic realization(s) and (phonotactic) distributions of a selection of phonemes (to be selected according to salience in the variety in question)
- specific phonological processes at work in the relevant variety
- lexical distribution
- prosodic features (stress, rhythm)
- intonation patterns
- observations/generalizations on the basis of lexical sets à la Wells (1982) and Foulkes/Docherty (1999), a standard reading passage and/or samples of free conversation.

It is worth noting that for some of the contributions, notably the chapters on pidgins and creoles, the lexical sets were not sufficient or suitable to describe the variability found. In such cases authors were encouraged to expand the set of target words, or replace one of the items. The reading passage was also adjusted or substituted by some authors, for instance because it was felt to be culturally inappropriate.

This is the corresponding set for the morphology and syntax chapters:

- tense – aspect – modality systems
- auxiliaries
- negation
- relativization
- complementation
- other subordination phenomena (notably adverbial subordination)
- agreement
- noun phrase structure
- pronominal systems
- word order (and information structure: especially focus/topicalizing constructions)

– selected salient features of the morphological paradigms of, for example, auxiliaries and pronouns

Lexical variation was not our primary concern, given that it fails to lend itself to the systematic generalization and comparability that we are interested in in this project. However, authors were offered the opportunity to comment on highly salient features of the vocabulary of any given variety (briefly and within the overall space constraints) if this was considered rewarding. The reader may find such information on distinctive properties of the respective vocabularies in the morphology and syntax chapters. Especially for a student readership, short sets of exercises and study questions have been added at the end of all chapters in the four paperback volumes.

In the interest of combining guidance for readers, efficiency, and space constraints, but also the goal of comprehensiveness, bibliographic references are systematically divided between three different types of reference lists. As was stated above, in each paperback a "General references" list can be found which compiles a relatively large number of books which, taken together, are central to the field of world-wide varieties of English – "classic" publications, collective volumes, particularly important publications, and so on. It is understood that in the individual contributions all authors may refer to titles from this list without these being repeated in their respective source lists. Each of the individual chapters ends with a list of "Selected references" comprising, on average, only 15–20 references – including the most pertinent ones on the respective variety (or closely related varieties) beyond any others possibly included in the General references list, and possibly others cited in the respective article. In other words, the Selected references do not repeat any of the titles cited in the list of General references. Thirdly, a "Comprehensive bibliography", with further publications specifically on the phonology and morphosyntax of each of the varieties covered, for which no space limitations were imposed, is available on the CD-ROM. The idea behind this limitation of the number of references allowed to go with each article was to free the texts of too much technical apparatus and thus to increase their reader-friendliness for a target audience of non-specialists while at the same time combining basic guidance to the most important literature (in the General References list) with the possibility of providing comprehensive coverage of the writings available on any given region (in the Bibliographies on the CD-ROM). It must be noted, however, that at times this rule imposed limitations upon possible source credits allowed in the discussions, because to make the books self-contained authors were allowed to refer to titles from the General and the Select References lists only. In other words, it is possible that articles touch upon material drawn from publications listed in the CD-ROM bibliographies without explicit credit, although every effort has been made to avoid this.

A publication project as huge as this one would have been impossible, indeed impossible even to think of, without the support of a great number of people devoted to their profession and to the subject of this Handbook. The editors would like thank the members of their editorial teams in Freiburg, Regensburg, and Cape Town. We are also much indebted to Elizabeth Traugott, for all the thought, support and feedback she gave to this project right from the very beginning of the planning stage, and to Jürgen Handke, who produced the rich audio-visual multimedia support on the CD. Furthermore, we have always benefitted from the support and interest invested into this project by Anke Beck and the people at Mouton de Gruyter. Finally, and most importantly, of course, the editors would like to thank the contributors and informants for having conformed to the rigid guidelines, deadlines and time frames that we set them for the various stages of (re)writing their chapters and providing the input material for the CD-ROM.

This collection truly represents an impressive product of scholarly collaboration of people from all around the globe. Right until the end it has been an exciting and wonderful experience for the editors (as well as, we would like to think, for the authors) to bring all these scholars and their work together, and we believe that this shows in the quality of the chapters and the material presented on the CD-ROM. We hope that, like the *Handbook*, it will be enjoyed, appreciated and esteemed by its readers, and treasured as the reference work and research tool it was designed as for anyone interested in and fascinated by variation in English!

References

Kortmann, Bernd (ed.)
    2004   *Dialectology meets Typology: Dialect Grammar from a Cross-Linguistic Perspective.* Berlin/New York: Mouton de Gruyter.
Kortmann, Bernd, and Edgar W. Schneider, with Kate Burridge, Rajend Mesthrie, and Clive Upton (eds.)
    2004   *A Handbook of Varieties of English.* Vol. 1: *Phonology.* Vol. 2: *Morphology and Syntax.* Berlin/New York: Mouton de Gruyter.
Schneider, Edgar W.
    2003   "The dynamics of New Englishes: From identity construction to dialect birth." *Language* 79: 233-281.
Schneider, Edgar W.
    2007   *Postcolonial English: Varieties Around the World.* Cambridge: Cambridge University Press.

General references

The following is a list of general reference works relevant across the world regions covered in the Handbook and for individual of these world regions. The list consists exclusively of book publications. Those monographs, dictionaries and collective volumes in the list which are referred to in the chapters of the four paperbacks will not be separately listed in the selected references at the end of the individual chapters.

Aceto, Michael and Jeffrey Williams (eds.)
　　2003　*Contact Englishes of the Eastern Caribbean*. (Varieties of English around the World, General Series 30.) Amsterdam/Philadelphia: Benjamins.
Aitken, Jack and Tom McArthur (eds.)
　　1979　*The Languages of Scotland*. Edinburgh: Chambers.
Algeo, John
　　2006　*British or American English? A Handbook of Word and Grammar Patterns*. Cambridge: Cambridge University Press.
Algeo, John (ed.)
　　2001　*The Cambridge History of the English Language, Volume VI: English in North America*. Cambridge: Cambridge University Press.
Allen, Harold B.
　　1973
　　–1976　*Linguistic Atlas of the Upper Midwest*. 3 Volumes. Minneapolis: University of Minnesota Press.
Allen, Harold B. and Gary Underwood (eds.)
　　1971　*Readings in American Dialectology*. New York: Appleton-Century Crofts.
Allen, Harold B. and Michael D. Linn (eds.)
　　1997　*Dialects and Language Variation*. New York: Academic Press.
Alleyne, Mervyn C.
　　1980　*Comparative Afro-American: An Historical-Comparative Study of English-Based Afro-American Dialects of the New World*. (Linguistica Extranea 11.) Ann Arbor: Karoma.
Allsopp, Richard (ed.)
　　1996　*Dictionary of Caribbean English Usage*. Oxford: Oxford University Press.
Anderson, Peter M.
　　1987　*A Structural Atlas of the English Dialects*. London: Croom Helm.
Anderwald, Lieselotte
　　2002　*Negation in Non-standard British English: Gaps, Regularizations, Asymmetries*. (Routledge Studies in Germanic Linguistics 8.) London/New York: Routledge.
Atwood, E. Bagby
　　1953　*A Survey of Verb Forms in the Eastern United States*. (Studies in American English 2.) Ann Arbor: University of Michigan Press.

Avis, Walter S., Charles Crate, Patrick Drysdale, Douglas Leechman and Matthew H.
    Scargill
    1967   *A Dictionary of Canadianisms on Historical Principles*. Toronto: Gage.
Bailey, Beryl Loftman
    1966   *Jamaican Creole Syntax*. Cambridge: Cambridge University Press.
Bailey, Richard W. and Jay L. Robinson
    1973   *Varieties of Present-Day English*. New York: Macmillan.
Bailey, Richard W. and Manfred Görlach (eds.)
    1982   *English as a World Language*. Ann Arbor: University of Michigan Press.
Bailey, Guy, Natalie Maynor and Patricia Cukor-Avila (eds.)
    1991   *The Emergence of Black English: Text and Commentary*. (Creole Language
            Library 8.) Amsterdam/Philadelphia: Benjamins.
Baker, Philip and Adrienne Bruyn (eds.)
    1998   *St. Kitts and the Atlantic Creoles: The Texts of Samuel Augustus Mathews
            in Perspective*. (Westminster Creolistics Series 4). London: University of
            Westminster Press.
Bamgbose, Ayo, Ayo Banjo and Andrew Thomas (eds.)
    1997   *New Englishes – A West African Perspective*. Trenton, NJ: Africa World
            Press.
Baugh, John
    1983   *Black Street Speech: Its History, Structure, and Survival*. Austin: University
            of Texas Press.
Baumgardner, Robert J.
    1996   *South Asian English: Structure, Use, and Users*. Urbana, IL: University of
            Illinois Press.
Bell, Allan and Koenrad Kuiper (eds.)
    2000   *New Zealand English*. (Varieties of English around the World, General
            Series 25.) Amsterdam/Philadelphia: Benjamins and Wellington: Victoria
            University Press.
Bernstein, Cynthia, Thomas Nunnally and Robin Sabino (eds.)
    1997   *Language Variety in the South Revisited*. Tuscaloosa: University of
            Alabama Press.
Bickerton, Derek
    1975   *Dynamics of a Creole System*. Cambridge: Cambridge University Press.
    1981   *Roots of Language*. Ann Arbor: Karoma.
Blair, David and Peter Collins (eds.)
    2001   *English in Australia*. (Varieties of English around the World, General
            Series 26.) Amsterdam/Philadelphia: Benjamins.
Bliss, Alan J.
    1979   *Spoken English in Ireland 1600–1740*. Dublin: Dolmen Press.
Bolton, Kingsley
    2003   *Chinese Englishes. A Sociolinguistic History*. Cambridge: Cambridge
            Univeristy Press.
Bolton, Kinglsey and Braj B. Kachru (eds.)
    2006   *World Englishes: critical concept in linguistics*. 6 vols. London:
            Routledge.

Bolton, Kingsley (ed.)
2002   *Hong Kong English: Autonomy and Creativity*. Hong Kong: Hong Kong University Press.
Britain, David (ed.)
2007   *Language in the British Isles*. Cambridge: Cambridge University Press.
Burchfield, Robert (ed.)
1994   *The Cambridge History of the English Language, Volume V: English in Britain and Overseas: Origins and Development*. Cambridge: Cambridge University Press.
Carrington, Lawrence D., Dennis Craig and Ramon Todd Dandare (eds.)
1983   *Studies in Caribbean Language. Papers Presented at the 3rd Biennial Conference of the Society for Caribbean Linguistics Held in Aruba, Netherlands Antilles from 16–20 Sept 1980*. St. Augustine, Trinidad: Society for Caribbean Linguistics.
Carver, Craig M.
1987   *American Regional Dialects: A Word Geography*. Ann Arbor: University of Michigan Press.
Cassidy, Frederic G.
1961   *Jamaica Talk: 300 Years of the English Language in Jamaica*. London: Macmillan.
Cassidy, Frederic G. (ed.)
1985
–2002   *Dictionary of American Regional English*. 4 Volumes to date. Cambridge, MA/London: The Belknap Press of Harvard University Press.
Cassidy, Frederic G. and Robert B. LePage (eds.)
1967   *Dictionary of Jamaican English*. Cambridge: Cambridge University Press.
Chambers, J.K.
2003   *Sociolinguistic Theory: Linguistic Variation and its Social Significance*. 2nd edition. (Language in Society 22.) Oxford: Blackwell.
Chambers, J.K. and Peter Trudgill
1998   *Dialectology*. 2nd edition. (Cambridge Textbooks in Linguistics.) Cambridge: Cambridge University Press.
Chambers, J.K. (ed.)
1975   *Canadian English: Origins and Structures*. Toronto: Methuen.
Chambers, J.K., Peter Trudgill and Natalie Schilling-Estes (eds.)
2002   *The Handbook of Language Variation and Change*. (Blackwell Handbooks in Linguistics.) Malden, MA: Blackwell.
Cheshire, Jenny L. (ed.)
1991   *English Around the World: Sociolinguistic Perspectives*. Cambridge: Cambridge University Press.
Cheshire, Jenny L. and Dieter Stein (eds.)
1997   *Taming the Vernacular: From Dialect to Written Standard Language*. Harlow: Longman.

Christian, Donna, Nanjo Dube and Walt Wolfram
  1988   *Variation and Change in Geographically Isolated Communities: Appalachian English and Ozark English.* (American Dialect Society 74.) Tuscaloosa: University of Alabama Press.
Christie, Pauline, Lawrence Carrington, Barbara Lalla and Velma Pollard (eds.)
  1998   *Studies in Caribbean Language II. Papers from the Ninth Biennial Conference of the SCL, 1992.* St. Augustine, Trinidad: Society for Caribbean Linguistics.
Clarke, Sandra (ed.)
  1993   *Focus on Canada.* (Varieties of English around the World, General Series 11.) Amsterdam/Philadelphia: Benjamins.
Collins, Peter and David Blair (eds.)
  1989   *Australian English: the Language of a New Society.* St. Lucia: University of Queensland Press.
Corbett, John, J. Derrick McClure and Jane Stuart-Smith (eds.)
  2003   *The Edinburgh Companion to Scots.* Edinburgh: Edinburgh University Press.
Crystal, David
  2003   *The Cambridge Encyclopedia of the English Language.* 2nd edition. Cambridge: Cambridge University Press.
D'Costa, Jean and Barbara Lalla
  1989   *Voices in Exile: Jamaican Texts of the 18th and 19th Centuries.* Tuscaloosa/ London: University of Alabama Press.
Davis, Lawrence M.
  1983   *English Dialectology: An Introduction.* University, Alabama: University of Alabama Press.
Day, Richard R. (ed.)
  1980   *Issues in English Creoles: Papers from the 1975 Hawaii Conference.* (Varieties of English around the World, General Series 2.) Heidelberg: Groos.
De Klerk, Vivian (ed.)
  1996   *Focus on South Africa.* (Varieties of English around the World, General Series 15.) Amsterdam/Philadelphia: Benjamins.
De Wolf, Gaelan Dodds
  1992   *Social and Regional Factors in Canadian English. Study of Phonological Variables and Grammatical Items in Ottawa and Vancouver.* Toronto: Canadian Scholar's Press.
DeCamp, David and Ian F. Hancock (eds.)
  1974   *Pidgins and Creoles: Current Trends and Prospects.* Washington, D.C.: Georgetown University Press.
Devonish, Hubert
  1989   *Talking in Tones: A Study of Tone in Afro-European Creole Languages.* London/Barbados: Karia Press and Caribbean Academic Publications.
Eckert, Penelope (ed.)
  1991   *New Ways of Analyzing Sound Change.* (Qualitative Analyses of Linguistic Structure 5.) New York/San Diego: Academic Press.

Edwards, Viv
   1986   *Language in a Black Community.* (Multilingual Matters 24.) Clevedon: Multilingual Matters.
Edwards, Walter F. and Donald Winford (ed.)
   1991   *Verb Phrase Patterns in Black English and Creole.* Detroit: Wayne State University.
Ellis, Alexander J.
   1869
   –1889   *On Early English Pronunciation.* 5 Volumes. London: Trübner.
Fasold, Ralph W.
   1972   *Tense Marking in Black English: A Linguistic and Social Analysis.* (Urban Language Series 8.) Arlington, VA: Center for Applied Linguistics.
Fasold, Ralph W. and Roger W. Shuy (eds.)
   1970   *Teaching Standard English in the Inner City.* (Urban Language Series 6.) Washington, D.C.: Center for Applied Linguistics.
   1975   *Analyzing Variation in Language. Papers from the Second Colloquium on New Ways of Analyzing Variation.* Washington, D.C.: Georgetown University Press.
Ferguson, Charles and Shirley Brice Heat (eds.)
   1981   *Language in the USA.* Cambridge: Cambridge University Press.
Filppula, Markku
   1999   *The Grammar of Irish English: Language in Hibernian Style.* (Routledge Studies in Germanic Linguistics 5.) London/New York: Routledge.
Foley, Joseph A. (ed.)
   1988   *New Englishes – The Case of Singapore.* Singapore: Singapore University Press.
Foley, Joseph A., Thiru Kandiah, Bao Zhiming, Anthea F. Gupta, Lubna Alasgoff, Ho Chee Lick, Lionel Wee, Ismail S. Talib and Wendy Bokhurst-Heng
   1998   *English in New Cultural Contexts: Reflections from Singapore.* Singapore: Oxford University Press.
Foulkes, Paul and Gerard Docherty (eds.)
   1999   *Urban Voices: Accent Studies in the British Isles.* London: Arnold.
Francis, W. Nelson
   1958   *The Structure of American English.* New York: Ronald Press.
Frazer, Timothy C. (ed.)
   1993   *'Heartland' English: Variation and Transition in the American Midwest.* Tuscaloosa: University of Alabama Press.
García, Ofelia and Ricardo Otheguy (eds.)
   1989   *English across Cultures, Cultures across English: A Reader in Cross-Cultural Communication.* (Contributions to the Sociology of Language 53.) Berlin/New York: Mouton de Gruyter.
Gilbert, Glenn (ed.)
   1987   *Pidgin and Creole Languages: Essays in Memory of John E. Reinecke.* Honolulu: University of Hawaii Press.

Gordon, Elizabeth and Tony Deverson
1998   *New Zealand English and English in New Zealand.* Auckland: New House
        Publishers.
Gordon, Matthew J.
2001   *Small-Town Values and Big-City Vowels: A Study of the Northern Cities
        Shift in Michigan.* (Publication of the American Dialect Society 84.)
        Durham: Duke University Press.
Görlach, Manfred (ed.)
1985   *Focus on Scotland.* (Varieties of English around the World, General
        Series 5.) Amsterdam/Philadelphia: Benjamins.
Görlach, Manfred and John A. Holm (eds.)
1986   *Focus on the Caribbean.* (Varieties of English around the World, General
        Series 8.) Amsterdam/Philadelphia: Benjamins.
Green, Lisa
2002   *African American English: A Linguistic Introduction.* Cambridge: Cam-
        bridge University Press.
Guy, Gregory, John Baugh, Crawford Feagin and Deborah Schiffrin (eds.)
1996   *Towards a Social Science of Language, Volume 1: Variation and Change
        in Language and Society.* Amsterdam/Philadelphia: Benjamins.
1997   *Towards a Social Science of Language, Volume 2: Social Interaction and
        Discourse Structures.* Amsterdam/Philadelphia: Benjamins.
Hackert, Stephanie
2004   *Urban Bahamian Creole. System and Variation.* Amsterdam/Philadelphia:
        Benjamins.
Hancock, Ian F., Morris Goodman, Bernd Heine and Edgar Polomé (eds.)
1979   *Readings in Creole Studies.* Ghent: Story-Scientia.
Hewitt, Roger
1986   *White Talk, Black Talk: Inter-Racial Friendship and Communication
        amongst Adolescents.* Cambridge: Cambridge University Press.
Hickey, Raymond
2004   *The Legacy of Colonial English: Transported Dialects.* Cambridge:
        Cambridge University Press.
2005   *The Sound Atlas of Irish English.* Berlin/New York: Mouton de Gruyter.
Holm, John A.
1988
–1989   *Pidgins and Creoles.* 2 Volumes. Cambridge: Cambridge University
        Press.
2000   *An Introduction to Pidgins and Creoles.* Cambridge: Cambridge University
        Press.
Holm, John A. and Peter Patrick
forthcoming   *Comparative Creole Syntax: Parallel Outlines of 18 Creole
        Grammars.* London: Battlebridge.
Holm, John A. (ed.)
1983   *Central American English.* (Varieties of English around the World, Text
        Series 2.) Heidelberg: Groos.

Huber, Magnus and Mikael Parkvall (eds.)
  1999   *Spreading the Word: The Issue of Diffusion among the Atlantic Creoles.*
          London: University of Westminster Press.
Hughes, Arthur and Peter Trudgill
  1996   *English Accents and Dialects: An Introduction to Social and Regional*
          Varieties of English in the British Isles. 3rd edition. London: Arnold.
Hymes, Dell H. (ed.)
  1971   *Pidginization and Creolization of Languages: Proceedings of a Conference,*
          Held at the University of the West Indies Mona, Jamaica, April 1968.
          Cambridge: Cambridge University Press.
James, Winford and Valerie Youssef
  2002   *The Languages of Tobago. Genesis, Structure and Perspectives.* St. Au-
          gustine, Trinidad: University of the West Indies.
Jones, Charles (ed.)
  1997   *The Edinburgh History of the Scots Language.* Edinburgh: Edinburgh
          University Press.
Kachru, Braj B.
  1983   *The Indianization of English: The English Language in India.* Delhi:
          Oxford University Press.
Kachru, Braj B. (ed.)
  1982   *The Other Tongue: English Across Cultures.* Urbana: University of Illinois
          Press.
Kachru, Braj B. (ed.)
  2005   *Asian Englishes. Beyond the Canon:* Hong Kong: Hong Kong University
          Press.
Kachru, Braj B., Yamuna Kachru and Cecil L. Nelson (eds.)
  2006   *The Handbook of World Englishes.* Oxford: Blackwell.
Kachru, Yamuna and Cecil L. Nelson
  2006   *World Englishes in Asian Contexts.* Hong Kong: Hong Kong University
          Press.
Kautzsch, Alexander
  2002   *The Historical Evolution of Earlier African American English. An Em-*
          pirical Comparison of Early Sources. (Topics in English Linguistics 38.)
          Berlin/New York: Mouton de Gruyter.
Keesing, Roger M.
  1988   *Melanesian Pidgin and the Oceanic Substrate.* Stanford: Stanford
          University Press.
Kirk, John M. and Dónall P. Ó Baoill
  2001   *Language Links: The Languages of Scotland and Ireland.* Belfast: Cló
          Olscoill na Banríona [Queen's University Press].
Kirk, John M., Stewart Sanderson and John D.A. Widdowson (eds.)
  1985   *Studies in Linguistic Geography: The Dialects of English in Britain and*
          Ireland. London et al.: Croom Helm.
Kortmann, Bernd, Tanja Herrmann, Lukas Pietsch and Susanne Wagner
  2005   *A Comparative Grammar of British English Dialects: Agreement, Gender,*
          Relative Clauses. Berlin/New York: Mouton de Gruyter.

Kortmann, Bernd (ed.)
  2004   *Dialectology Meets Typology: Dialect Grammar from a Cross-Linguistic Perspective.* Berlin/New York: Mouton de Gruyter.
Krapp, George P.
  1925   *The English Language in America.* 2 Volumes. New York: Century.
Kretzschmar, William A. and Edgar W. Schneider
  1996   *Introduction to Quantitative Analysis of Linguistic Survey Data: An Atlas by the Numbers.* (Empirical Linguistics Series.) Thousand Oaks, CA: Sage.
Kretzschmar, William A., Virginia G. McDavid, Theodore K. Lerud and Ellen Johnson (eds.)
  1993   *Handbook of the Linguistic Atlas of the Middle and South Atlantic States.* Chicago: University of Chicago Press.
Kurath, Hans
  1949   *A Word Geography of the Eastern United States.* Ann Arbor: University of Michigan Press.
Kurath, Hans and Raven I. McDavid, Jr.
  1961   *The Pronunciation of English in the Atlantic States. Based upon the Collections of the Linguistic Atlas.* (Studies in American English 3.) Ann Arbor: University of Michigan Press.
Kurath, Hans (ed.)
  1939
  –1943   *Linguistic Atlas of New England.* Providence: Brown University Press.
Labov, William
  1966   *The Social Stratification of English in New York City.* (Urban Language Series 1.) Washington, D.C.: Center for Applied Linguistics.
  1972a   *Language in the Inner City: Studies in the Black English Vernacular.* (Conduct and Communication 3.) Philadelphia: University of Pennsylvania Press.
  1972b   *Sociolinguistic Patterns.* (Conduct and Communication 4.) Philadelphia: University of Pennsylvania Press.
  1980   *Locating Language in Time and Space.* (Quantitative Analyses of Linguistic Structure.) New York: Academic Press.
  1994   *Principles of Linguistic Change, Volume 1: Internal Factors.* (Language in Society 20.) Oxford/Malden, MA: Blackwell.
  2001   *Principles of Linguistic Change, Volume 2: Social Factors.* (Language in Society 29.) Oxford/Malden, MA: Blackwell.
Labov, William, Richard Steiner and Malcah Yaeger
  1972   *A Quantitative Study of Sound Change in Progress: Report on National Science Foundation Contract NSF-GS-3278 University of Pennsylvania.* Philadelphia: University of Pennsylvania Regional Survey.
Labov, William, Sharon Ash and Charles Boberg
  2006   *Atlas of North American English: Phonetics, Phonology and Sound Change.* (Topics in English Linguistics 41.) Berlin/New York: Mouton de Gruyter.

Lalla, Barbara and Jean D'Costa
  1990   *Language in Exile: Three Hundred Years of Jamaican Creole.* Tuscaloosa: University of Alabama Press.
Lanehart, Sonja L. (ed.)
  2001   *Sociocultural and Historical Contexts of African American English.* (Varieties of English around the World, General Series 27.) Amsterdam/ Philadelphia: Benjamins.
Leitner, Gerhard
  2004a   *Australia's Many Voices. Australian English – The National Language.* Berlin/New York: Mouton de Gruyter.
  2004b   *Australia's Many Voices. Ethnic Englishes, Indigenous and Migrant Languages. Policy and Education.* Berlin/New York: Mouton de Gruyter.
LePage, Robert B. and Andrée Tabouret-Keller
  1985   *Acts of Identity: Creole-based Approaches to Language and Ethnicity.* Cambridge: Cambridge University Press.
Lim, Lisa (ed.)
  2004   *Singapore English. A Grammatical Description.* Amsterdam/Philadelphia: Benjamins.
Lindquist, Hans, Maria Estling, Staffan Klintborg and Magnus Levin (eds.)
  1998   *The Major Varieties of English: Papers from MAVEN 97, Växjö 20–22 November 1997.* (Acta Wexionensia: Humaniora; 1.) Växjö: Växjo University.
Matthews, William
  1938   *Cockney Past and Present: A Short History of the Dialect of London.* London: Routledge.
McArthur, Tom
  1992   *The Oxford Companion to the English Language.* Oxford: Oxford University Press.
  2002   *Oxford Guide to World English.* Oxford: Oxford University Press.
McMillan, James B. and Michel B. Montgomery
  1989   *Annotated Bibliography of Southern American English.* Tuscaloosa/ London: University of Alabama Press.
McWhorter, John H. (ed.)
  2000   *Language Change and Language Contact in Pidgins and Creoles.* (Creole Language Library 21.) Amsterdam/Philadelphia: Benjamins.
Mehrotra, Raja Ram
  1998   *Indian English – Text and Interpretation.* (Varieties of English around the World, Text Series 7.) Amsterdam/Philadelphia: Benjamins.
Melchers, Gunnel and Philip Shaw
  2003   *World Englishes.* London: Arnold.
Mencken, Henry
  1963   *The American Language: An Inquiry into the Development of English in the United States. With the Assistance of David W. Maurer.* New York: Knopf.

Mesthrie, Rajend (ed.)
   1995   *Language and Social History: Studies in South African Sociolinguistics.*
            Cape Town: David Philip.
   2002   *Language in South Africa.* Cambridge: Cambridge University Press.
Milroy, James
   1981   *Regional Accents of English: Belfast.* Belfast: Blackstaff.
Milroy, James and Lesley Milroy (eds.)
   1993   *Real English: The Grammar of English Dialects in the British Isles.* (Real
            Language Series.) London: Longman.
Montgomery, Michael B. and Guy Bailey (eds.)
   1986   *Language Variety in the South: Perspectives in Black and White.* University,
            AL: University of Alabama Press.
Montgomery, Michael B. and Thomas Nunnally (eds.)
   1998   *From the Gulf States and Beyond. The Legacy of Lee Pederson and LAGS.*
            Tuscaloosa, AL/London: University of Alabama Press.
Mufwene, Salikoko S.
   2001   *The Ecology of Language Evolution.* (Cambridge Approaches to Language
            Contact.) Cambridge: Cambridge University Press.
Mufwene, Salikoko S., Guy Bailey, John Baugh and John R. Rickford (eds.)
   1998   *African-American English. Structure, History and Use.* London:
            Routledge.
Mufwene, Salikoko S. (ed.)
   1993   *Africanisms in Afro-American Language Varieties.* Athens: University of
            Georgia Press.
Mühleisen, Susanne
   2002   *Creole Discourse: Exploring Prestige Formation and Change across
            Caribbean English-Lexicon Creoles.* (Creole Language Library 24.)
            Amsterdam/Philadelphia: Benjamins.
Mühlhäusler, Peter
   1997   *Pidgin and Creole Linguistics.* (Westminster Creolistic Series 3.) London:
            University of Westminster Press.
Murray, Thomas and Beth Lee Simon (eds.)
   2006   *Language Variation and Change in the American Midland: A New Look at
            "Heartland" English.* Amsterdam/Philadelphia: Benjamins.
Muysken, Pieter and Norval Smith (eds.)
   1986   *Substrata versus Universals in Creole Genesis. Papers from the Amsterdam
            Creole Workshop, April 1985.* (Creole Language Library 1.) Amsterdam/
            Philadelphia: Benjamins.
Myers-Scotton, Carol
   2002   *Contact Linguistics: Bilingual Encounters and Grammatical Outcomes.*
            (Oxford Linguistics.) Oxford: Oxford University Press.
Nagle, Stephen J. and Sara L. Sanders (eds.)
   2003   *English in the Southern United States.* (Studies in English Language.)
            Cambridge: Cambridge University Press.

Neumann-Holzschuh, Ingrid and Edgar W. Schneider (eds.)
  2000   *Degrees of Restructuring in Creole Languages.* (Creole Language Li-
            brary 22.) Amsterdam/Philadelphia: Benjamins.
Nihalani, Paroo, Priya Hosali and Ray K. Tongue
  1989   *Indian and British English: A Handbook of Usage and Pronunciation.*
            (Oxford India Paperbacks.) Delhi: Oxford University Press.
Noss, Richard B. (ed.)
  1984   *An Overview of Language Issues in South-East Asia: 1950–1980.*
            Singapore: Oxford University Press.
Orton, Harold (ed.)
  1962
  –1971   *Survey of English Dialects: The Basic Material.* 4 Volumes. Leeds:
            Arnold.
Orton, Harold, Stewart Sanderson and John Widdowson (eds.)
  1978   *The Linguistic Atlas of England.* London: Croom Helm.
Parasher, S.V.
  1991   *Indian English: Functions and Form.* (Sell-series in English Language
            and Literature 19.) New Delhi: Bahri.
Parkvall, Mikael
  2000   *Out of Africa: African Influences in Atlantic Creoles.* London: Battle-
            bridge.
Patrick, Peter L.
  1999   *Urban Jamaican Creole: Variation in the Mesolect.* (Varieties of
            English around the World, General Series 17.) Amsterdam/Philadelphia:
            Benjamins.
Pederson, Lee (ed.)
  1986
  –1992   *The Linguistic Atlas of the Gulf States.* 7 Volumes. Athens, GA: University
            of Georgia Press.
Plag, Ingo (ed.)
  2003   *Phonology and Morphology of Creole Languages.* (Linguistische Arbeiten
            478.) Tübingen: Niemeyer.
Platt, John, Mian Lian Ho and Heidi Weber
  1983   *Singapore and Malaysia.* (Varieties of English around the World, Text
            Series 4.) Amsterdam/Philadelphia: Benjamins.
  1984   *The New Englishes.* London: Routledge and Kegan Paul.
Poplack, Shana and Sali Tagliamonte
  2001   *African American English in the Diaspora.* (Language in Society 30.)
            Oxford/Malden, MA: Blackwell.
Poplack, Shana (ed.)
  2000   *The English History of African American English.* (Language in Society 28.)
            Oxford/Malden, MA: Blackwell.
Preston, Dennis R. (ed.)
  1993   *American Dialect Research: An Anthology Celebrating the 100th
            Anniversary of the American Dialect Society.* (Centennial Series of the
            American Dialect Society.) Amsterdam/Philadelphia: Benjamins.

Rampton, Ben
   1995   *Crossing: Language and Ethnicity among Adolescents.* (Real Language
            Series.) London: Longman.
Rickford, John R.
   1987   *Dimensions of a Creole Continuum: History, Texts, and Linguistics
            Analysis of Guyanese Creole.* Stanford: Stanford University Press.
   1999   *African American Vernacular English: Features, Evolution, Educational
            Implications.* (Language in Society 26.) Oxford/Malden, MA: Blackwell.
Rickford, John R. and Suzanne Romaine (eds.)
   1999   *Creole Genesis, Attitudes and Discourse: Studies Celebrating Charlene
            J. Sato.* (Creole Language Library 20.) Amsterdam/Philadelphia: Ben-
            jamins.
Roberts, Peter A.
   1988   *West Indians and their Language.* Cambridge: Cambridge University
            Press.
Romaine, Suzanne
   1988   *Pidgin and Creole Languages.* (Longman Linguistics Library.) London/
            New York: Longman.
Schmied, Josef J.
   1991   *English in Africa: An Introduction.* (Longman Linguistics Library.)
            London: Longman.
Schneider, Edgar W.
   1989   *American Earlier Black English. Morphological and Syntactical Variables.*
            Tuscaloosa, AL/London: University of Alabama Press.
Schneider, Edgar W. (ed.)
   1996   *Focus on the USA.* (Varieties of English around the World, General Se-
            ries 16.) Amsterdam/Philadelphia: Benjamins.
   1997a   *Englishes Around the World, Volume 1: General Studies, British Isles,
            North America: Studies in Honour of Manfred Görlach.* (Varieties of
            English around the World, General Series 18.) Amsterdam/Philadelphia:
            Benjamins.
   1997b   *Englishes Around the World, Volume 2: Caribbean, Africa, Asia, Australasia.
            Studies in Honour of Manfred Görlach.* (Varieties of English around the
            World, General Series 19.) Amsterdam/Philadelphia: Benjamins.
   2007   *Postcolonial English.* Cambridge: Cambridge University Press.
Sebba, Mark
   1993   *London Jamaican: Language Systems in Interaction.* (Real Language
            Series.) London: Longman.
   1997   *Contact Languages – Pidgins and Creoles.* (Modern Linguistics Series.)
            London: Macmillan.
Singh, Ishtla
   2000   *Pidgins and Creoles – An Introduction.* London: Arnold.
Singler, John V. (ed.)
   1990   *Pidgin and Creole Tense-Mood-Aspect Systems.* (Creole Language Li-
            brary 6.) Amsterdam/Philadelphia: Benjamins.

Spears, Arthur K. and Donald Winford (eds.)
  1997   *The Structure and Status of Pidgins and Creoles. Including Selected Papers from the Meetings of the Society for Pidgin and Creole Linguistics.* (Creole Language Library 19.) Amsterdam/Philadelphia: Benjamins.
Spencer, John (ed.)
  1971   *The English Language in West Africa.* (English Language Series.) London: Longman.
Thomas, Erik R.
  2001   *An Acoustic Analysis of Vowel Variation in New World English.* (Publication of the American Dialect Society 85.) Durham: Duke University Press.
Thomason, Sarah G.
  2001   *Contact Languages.* Edinburgh: University of Edinburgh Press.
Thomason, Sarah G. and Terrence Kaufman
  1988   *Language Contact, Creolization and Genetic Linguistics.* Berkeley: University of California Press.
Tristram, Hildegard, L.C. (ed.)
  1998   *The Celtic Englishes.* (Anglistische Forschungen 247.) Heidelberg: Winter.
  2000   *The Celtic Englishes II.* (Anglistische Forschungen 286.) Heidelberg: Winter.
  2003   *The Celtic Englishes III.* (Anglistische Forschungen 324.) Heidelberg: Winter.
Trudgill, Peter
  1974   *The Social Differentiation of English in Norwich.* (Cambridge Studies in Linguistics 13.) Cambridge: Cambridge University Press.
  1986   *Dialects in Contact.* (Language in Society 10.) Oxford: Blackwell.
  1999   *The Dialects of England.* 2nd edition. Oxford: Blackwell. also: *The Dialects of England.* 2nd edition. Oxford: Blackwell.
Trudgill, Peter and Jean Hannah
  2002   *International English: A Guide to Varieties of Standard English.* 4th edition. London: Arnold.
  1994   *International English: A Guide to Varieties of Standard English.* 3rd edition. London: Arnold.
  1985   *International English: A Guide to Varieties of Standard English.* 2nd edition. London: Arnold.
  1982   *International English: A Guide to Varieties of Standard English.* London: Arnold.
Trudgill, Peter (ed.)
  1978   *Sociolinguistic Patterns in British English.* London: Arnold.
  1984   *Language in the British Isles.* Cambridge: Cambridge University Press.
Trudgill, Peter and J.K. Chambers (eds.)
  1991   *Dialects of English: Studies in Grammatical Variation.* (Longman Linguistics Library.) London/New York: Longman.
Upton, Clive, David Parry and John D.A. Widdowson
  1994   *Survey of English Dialects: The Dictionary and Grammar.* London: Routledge.

Viereck, Wolfgang (ed.)
1985   *Focus on England and Wales.* (Varieties of English around the World, General Series 4.) Amsterdam/Philadelphia: Benjamins.
Wakelin, Martyn
1981   *English Dialects: An Introduction.* London: Athlone Press.
Wakelin, Martyn F. (ed.)
1972   *Patterns in the Folk Speech of the British Isles. With a Foreword by Harold Orton.* London: Athlone Press.
Watts, Richard and Peter Trudgill (eds.)
2002   *Alternative Histories of English.* London: Routledge.
Wells, John C.
1982   *Accents of English.* 3 Volumes. Cambridge: Cambridge University Press.
Williamson, Juanita and Virginia M. Burke (eds.)
1971   *A Various Language. Perspectives on American Dialects.* New York: Holt, Rinehart and Winston.
Winer, Lise
1993   *Trinidad and Tobago.* (Varieties of English around the World, Text Series 6.) Amsterdam/Philadelphia: Benjamins.
Winford, Donald
1993   *Predication in Carribean English Creoles.* (Creole Language Library 10.) Amsterdam/Philadelphia: Benjamins.
2003   *An Introduction to Contact Linguistics.* (Language in Society 33.) Malden/ Oxford/Melbourne: Blackwell.
Wolfram, Walt
1969   *A Sociolinguistic Description of Detroit Negro Speech.* (Urban Language Series 5.) Washington, D.C.: Center for Applied Linguistics.
Wolfram, Walt and Ralph W. Fasold
1974   *The Study of Social Dialects in American English.* Englewood Cliffs, NJ: Prentice Hall.
Wolfram, Walt and Donna Christian
1976   *Appalachian Speech.* Arlington, VA: Center for Applied Linguistics.
Wolfram, Walt and Natalie Schilling-Estes
2005   *American English: Dialects and Variation.* (Language in Society 25.) 2nd ed. Malden, MA/Oxford: Blackwell.
Wolfram, Walt, Kirk Hazen and Natalie Schilling-Estes
1999   *Dialect Change and Maintenance on the Outer Banks.* (Publication of the American Dialect Society 81.) Tuscaloosa, AL/London: University of Alabama Press.
Wolfram, Walt and Erik R. Thomas
2002   *The Development of African American English.* (Language in Society 31.) Oxford/Malden, MA: Blackwell.
Wolfram, Walt and Ben Wards (eds.)
2006   *American Voices: How Dialects Differ from Coast to Coast.* Oxford: Blackwell

Wright, Joseph
1898
–1905   *The English Dialect Dictionary*. Oxford: Clarendon Press.
1905   *The English Dialect Grammar*. Oxford: Frowde.

Introduction: varieties of English in the Americas and the Caribbean

Edgar W. Schneider

1. Introduction: One region?

Dealing with the Americas and the Caribbean jointly, in a single volume and chapter, is a decision that requires some discussion, perhaps justification. Of course, in a global geographical perspective it comes natural, focusing upon a continent that is separated from other world regions by the globe's largest oceans on both sides. History also justifies such a perspective, with roughly similar population movements having occurred at similar times. All parts of the American continent were originally populated by Native Americans. After the "discovery" of the continent by Columbus and during the period of colonial expansion the indigenous tribes were subdued and cruelly decimated by European settlers, who, in turn, forced millions of Africans to be transported to the region, with the descendants of these, plus some smaller groups of later arrivals, making up for the major population segments. Close economic connections have prevailed to the present day, and substantial migration in both directions has occurred (and provided for mutual linguistic influences). On closer examination, however, there are of course also fundamental differences to be discerned in their economic, social, demographic and cultural make-up. North American settlers were attracted by the prospect of religious freedom and economic prosperity, while for a long time the Caribbean was not deliberately settled but rather exploited mainly as the site of the mass production of cash crops, most notably sugar cane, resulting in plantation societies which rested upon the infamous institution of slavery. Hence, while the descendants of Europeans predominate in North America, those of Africans constitute the majority throughout the Caribbean. Politically and socially, the Caribbean was much more fragmented and disputed by several European colonial powers, while on the North American continent the British secured their predominance (with the exception of remaining French enclaves and, around the Gulf of Mexico, Spanish traces and neighbors). Most importantly in the present, linguistic perspective, different settlement patterns have resulted in North American varieties of English being characterized by dialect transmission (with some degree of koinéization but also innovation) as against Caribbean forms of English being shaped by processes of creolization.

2.   Historical background

Disregarding Sir Walter Raleigh's late-sixteenth century "Lost Colony" of Roanoke, permanent English settlement in North America started early in the seventeenth century, and the fact that the earliest settler groups tended to be religious dissenters predominantly from southern parts of England has resulted in the fact that the dialects of the regions where they established their bridgeheads (1607: Jamestown, Virginia; 1620: the Pilgrim Fathers landing on Plymouth Rock in Massachusetts) have retained higher degrees of similarity to southern forms of British English. Later streams of settlers, migrating from landing sites in or near Pennsylvania into the interior North, the Midlands and the Upper South in search of new lands, brought their northern English or Scottish-derived forms of English and caused these to diffuse, thus giving them a particularly strong role in the evolution of distinctly American ways of speaking. The first two centuries of British settlement (and the French and Indian War of 1756–1763) secured English as the language of the Atlantic seaboard and beyond, the area occupied by the thirteen original colonies that declared their independence in 1776. As a consequence of relatively homogeneous settler groups and long-standing stability in this eastern region along the Atlantic coast, regional dialect differences have been found to be stronger there than further to the West. The Louisiana Purchase of 1803 opened up the continent for further exploration and settlement expansion throughout the nineteenth century, invigorated by the California Gold Rush after 1848 and the construction and completion (in 1869) of the transcontinental railway. Linguistically speaking, these processes resulted in even more dialect mixing and relatively higher degrees of linguistic homogeneity. At the same time, for centuries Africans had been brought to the South forcedly as slaves. Emancipation after the Civil War, in 1865, gave them freedom but did not prevent social segregation, which to some degree has persisted to the present day – developments which have resulted in and are reflected by the emergence and evolution of African American Vernacular English and Gullah and which in some respects may be taken to have resulted in a linguistic bridge between inland varieties and the Caribbean. In Canada, the British possession of Newfoundland dates back to the 16th century, caused it to be settled by people from Ireland and southwestern England, and has left a distinctive dialect there. On the other hand, Canadian English in general is said to have been characterized by a tension between its British roots (reinforced by loyalists who opted for living in Canada after America's independence) and the continuous linguistic and cultural pressure (or attractiveness, for that matter) exerted by its big southern neighbor. Furthermore, varieties of American English comprise accents forged by immigrant groups from a host of countries of origin, including southern and eastern Europeans, Asians, and South and Central Americans: Today, the most important of these are certainly the forms of English created by contact with Mexican Spanish.

In the Caribbean, the British entered the stage more than a century after the Spanish had established themselves; and the struggle for superiority and influence between these two and a few more European powers (most importantly, the French and the Dutch) shaped the ragged history of the region for centuries. The agents of these struggles were not primarily settlers but buccaneers, planters, and slaves, and many islands changed hands repeatedly (31 times, it is reported, in the case of Tobago). Such political turnovers and other activities resulted in high rates of cross-migration and mutual influences, also linguistically (Holm 1983). The earliest British possessions in the region were St. Kitts (1624; said to have been highly influential in the shaping and dispersal of Caribbean language forms: Baker and Bruyn 1998) and Barbados (1627). Jamaica, the largest and most important stronghold of Caribbean English (and Creole), became British in 1655. Suriname, located on the South American continent but culturally a part of the Caribbean in many ways, presents an exceptional and also linguistically extraordinary case: An English colony for only 16 years (from 1651 to 1667, when it was exchanged for New Amsterdam, which thus became New York), it has retained the English-related creole of its founder years, now called Sranan, and its maroon descendant forms of the interior to the present day, thus being the site of the most conservative and radical creoles in the region. In Trinidad, English and English-based creole replaced French creole only in the course of the nineteenth century. Finally, various historical incidents (minor settlement migrations, like from the Caymans to the Bay Islands of Honduras; logwood cutting, buccaneering and even shipwrecks in Belize and Nicaragua; economic activities, like railroad construction in Costa Rica and the building of the canal in Panama) established pockets of English creoles throughout central America.

3. Research coverage and main topics of investigations

All of these processes have resulted in a diverse range of varieties of English, which have attracted the attention of observers and scholars for centuries. Early accounts tended to be anecdotal records or short literary representations by native users or outside observers (except for sketchy dictionaries and grammars produced by missionaries, notably for Sranan, which is therefore historically uniquely well researched). Serious and systematic scholarly investigation of these varieties began with the launching of dialect geography in North America in the late 1920s. As a consequence, regional varieties of American English (as well as some degree of social variation), based upon data from the 1930s to the 1970s, are thoroughly documented by a series of regional atlas projects, most importantly the *Linguistic Atlas of New England* (Kurath 1939–43), the *Linguistic Atlas of the Middle and South Atlantic States*, directed first by Kurath, then by Raven McDavid, and now by William Kretzschmar (Kretzschmar 1994; see the web site with data for downloading at <us.english.uga.edu>) and the *Linguistic Atlas of the Gulf States* (Pederson et al. 1986-92), along with several others (see Davis 1983 for a survey). These projects were analyzed in several studies, three of which, covering the levels of vocabulary, morphology and pronunciation, respectively, count as classics, having established the conventional division of American English into three main regions – North, Midland, and South (Kurath 1949; Atwood 1953; Kurath and McDavid 1961). Carver (1987) later challenged this division and proposed to consider the northern Midlands and southern Midlands as divisions of extended North and South regions, respectively – a recategorization which is less dramatic than it might look at first sight. Since the 1990s the second major project of investigating the regional dialects of all of the US, Labov's Telsur survey, has been under way; it looks into phonological differences and analyses ongoing sound changes (Labov, Ash and Boberg fc.). This project has grown out of the second major discipline that has investigated variation within and varieties of American English, sociolinguistics, founded by Labov in the 1960s (Labov 1966, 1972). Employing conversational interviews and quantitative techniques of analysis, sociolinguists have investigated patterns of variation and change in many different cities and communities (Chambers 2003), including, most importantly, African American Vernacular English (AAVE) and, in recent years, dialect enclaves. The 1960s also saw the growth of creole studies as a distinct paradigm of linguistic investigation, with many of its early classics being concerned with the English-based creoles of Jamaica (Bailey 1966) and Guyana (Bickerton 1975; Rickford 1987). In addition to many important book-length studies of individual varieties (listed in the general bibliography and referred to in the individual articles of this book), many collective volumes, reflecting a variety of research activities, have been published, including Williamson and Burke (1971), Allen and Underwood (1971), Allen and Linn (1997), Preston (1993) and Schneider (1996) on North American varieties in general, Montgomery and Bailey (1986), Bernstein, Nunnally and Sabino (1997), Montgomery and Nunnally (1998) and Nagle and Sanders (2003) on Southern English, Frazer (1993) on the Midwest, as well as Carrington, Craig and Dandare (1983), Christie (1998), several volumes of the "Creole Language Library" series published by Benjamins, and, most recently, Aceto and Williams (2003) on Caribbean creoles and dialects.

Schneider (1996a), in a volume that uniquely unites dialectologists, sociolinguists and creolists, surveys ongoing research activities on North American Englishes, both quantitatively and qualitatively. Updating and supplementing these observations a little, we can observe the following major trends of ongoing research:

- computational and statistical procedures applied to dialect atlas data (Kretzschmar and Schneider 1996 and other work by Kretzschmar and, more recently, John Nerbonne);
- the study of variation and change of specific variables in select communities (for broad surveys, see Chambers 2003; Chambers, Trudgill and Schilling-Estes 2002), in particular
- investigations of enclave communities and their trajectories of change (Wolfram, Hazen and Schilling-Estes 1999 and other work by Wolfram and associates in North Carolina, and work by Cukor-Avila in Texas);
- investigations of ongoing sound changes in AmE (work by Labov and associates, most notably Labov 1994; Labov, Ash and Boberg fc.; Gordon 2001; Thomas 2001);
- investigations of ethnolinguistic differences, in particular cultural and pedagogical implications of the uses of AAVE (Mufwene et al. 1998; Rickford 1999; Lanehart 2001);
- historical investigations of regional varieties (in particular, Southern English: Nagle and Sanders 2003);
- improved diachronic documentation and interpretation of pertinent sources on the history of AAVE (Schneider 1989; Bailey, Maynor and Cukor-Avila 1991; Poplack 2000; Poplack and Tagliamonte 2001; Kautzsch 2002; Wolfram and Thomas 2002).

In a similar vein, it is also possible to survey the major research fashions, recurrent themes and basic concerns, in the investigation of the Caribbean English creoles. These include the following:

- the genesis of creoles (the perennial issue of universalism vs. substratism; cf. Alleyne 1980; Bickerton 1981; Muysken and Smith 1986) and the diffusion of creole forms (Huber and Parkvall 1999; Baker and Huber 2001)
- a search for historical documentation of earlier stages of Caribbean creoles (to provide improved empirical evidence for the aforementioned discussion; cf. for Jamaica D'Costa and Lalla 1989; for Guyana Rickford 1987; for Barbados Rickford and Handler 1994)
- acceptance of the fact that creoles come in different "degrees of creoleness", i.e. that differences between "deep / radical" creoles on the one hand and

"lighter" creoles with few basilectal features, sometimes called "semi-cre-oles" or "creoloids", exist and blur the very category of "creole languages" (Schneider 1990; Neumann-Holzschuh and Schneider 2000; Holm 2004), and increased emphasis on the importance of mesolects (Patrick 1999);

– consequently, the questioning of the distinctness of creoles as a language type altogether, thus regarding them as varieties of their lexifiers rather than distinct languages (Mufwene 2001; but cf. McWhorter 1998, 2000) and ul-timately the recognition of language contact as the appropriate overarching topic and field of study (Thomason and Kaufman 1988; Thomason 2001; Myers-Scotton 2002; Winford 2003)

– increased emphasis on empirical documentations, primarily with respect to relatively "minor", hitherto underinvestigated varieties (Aceto and Williams 2003; James and Youssef 2002) but also in association with typological and sociolinguistic thinking (e.g. Winford 1993; Hackert 2004).

– the emergence of an increasingly positive attitude toward creoles in public discourse, recognized as carriers of regional identities and gradually en-croaching into the public domain (Shields-Brodber 1997; Mühleisen 2002).

4.   Parameters of variation by language levels

The varieties of English in the Americas, like everywhere else, correlate with the parameters of region, social class, and style, and in most cases it is impos-sible to draw clear-cut, qualitative distinctions. Typically, select features tend to occur more frequently in certain varieties than in others; hardly ever are there any uncontroversial shibboleths to be observed (for instance, even the prototypically Southern pronoun *y'all* has been shown to be spreading outside of the South; Tillery, Wikle and Bailey 2000). Nevertheless, it is possible to state some broad tendencies which as such are of interest.

Broadly speaking, phonology tends to vary regionally while grammar varies socially in the first place. Pronunciation differences delimit dialect regions of North American English most clearly and consistently, and the contributors to the pronunciation papers point out local, regional and supraregional phono-logical or phonetic features. Of course, accents go by social class as well, but the standard assumption for American English is that even educated speak-ers, from certain regions at least (most notably New England and the South), at times use regional pronunciation characteristics and thus speak "with an accent"; hence, despite the persistent belief in a homogeneous "General American" accent or notions like "network English" there is in fact no single American norm of pronunciation that corresponds to RP in England, being a non-regional class dialect. (Kretzschmar, in this volume, defines a "Standard American English" as an accent deliberately held free of features associated with particular regions.) In contrast, the phonologies of Caribbean varieties of English are underresearched – the strong focus of the discipline upon creole genesis, reflected in the grammar of creoles, has made this a Cinderella of creole studies (Plag 2003 deliberately sets out to remedy this situation). Clearly there are both supra-regional features and tendencies and regional or local forms of pronunciation, but no systematic survey of such similarities or differences is available to date.

Unlike phonology, in North American English grammatical variation is primarily socially determined. This is perhaps less true for nonstandard morphology (like irregular nonstandard verb forms or noun plurals), where dialectological research has identified some regional correlations (Atwood 1953), and a small number of minor syntactic patterns may be pinned down to specific regions; but basically using nonstandard grammar betrays a speaker's social class background, not his or her regional whereabouts. Many of these patterns (like multiple negation, left dislocation, or intonation-marked but uninverted questions) are not even distinctly American but constitute elements of informal English, presumably British-derived, in many countries around the globe. Quantitative distinctions from one dialect to another exist in America (i.e. some features occur more frequently in certain regions or contexts than others), but basically it is the particular configuration, the specific sub-set of such forms and patterns available in a given region or community, that identifies and distinguishes individual varieties of North American English.

This particular aspect, the uniqueness of the mixture of forms at a given location rather than a diagnostic role of any individual variant, can be stated for the Caribbean situation as well, although the creole continua found there provide for quite different, and certainly no less complex, linguistic ecologies. As is well known, creole grammars are characterized first and foremost by the use of preverbal markers for categories of tense, mood and aspect, in addition to several other "characteristically creole" features (e.g. specific copula uses, the functional conflation of pronoun forms, or serial verb constructions), while, conversely, they display very little inflectional morphology on verbs, nouns, or other word classes. Some of these forms characterize certain sub-regions (most importantly, a few forms appear to mark off the eastern as against the western Caribbean), but the most important parameter of variation here is the class and style stratification that is captured by the notion of a creole (or "post-creole") continuum, the systematic variation between acrolectal (or near-standard), mesolectal and basilectal ("deep creole") choices. Bickerton (1975), following de-Camp (1971), described this variation as "implicational scales", with both lects (distinct "grammars") and their features arranged in such a tabular format that the presence of certain forms in certain lects predicts the presence of all other "more basilectal" forms in all other "more basilectal" lects. On the other hand, several aspects of this model have been challenged in recent years, including its monodimensionality and its diachronic implications (the assumption that creoles started out as basilects and have "decreolized", i.e. exchanged basilectal creole forms by corresponding acrolectal English forms, in the course of time). In fact, the scholarly concentration upon the putatively pure, basilectal creole has led to the paradoxical situation that basilects are at the center of creole studies even if no one has ever documented a pure basilectal creole, while mesolects, the forms that are really in use, have only recently begun to be the objects of scrupulous investigation (Patrick 1999).

Words, finally, vary readily and mostly by region, with the range of their spread extending from the strictly local through the regional to the quasinational domain. Variation in the lexicon is considerably more resistent to systematic investigation – which is why the contributions to this handbook project cover regional vocabulary only incidentally or not at all. Regional lexicography identifies the ranges and conditions of the uses of individual words (Kurath 1949; Carver 1987), and in the present context the main dictionaries to be consulted are the *Dictionary of American Regional English* for North America (Cassidy et al. 1985-) and the *Dictionary of Caribbean Usage* (Allsopp 1996) for the Caribbean.

5.   Chapters selected for this volume

The general considerations outlined above, in particular with respect to the existence of distinct dialectal forms, have guided the selection of individual varieties for coverage in this volume. Their arrangement roughly follows geographical and historical patterns, with the US and Canada followed by the Caribbean and varieties being strung together according to their geographical proximity (moving from north to south and east to west in most instances) and their historical patterns of diffusion.

The first part covers phonological variation. For American English, Kretzschmar's paper describes a baseline "Standard" variety, devoid of distinctly regional traces; this is followed by papers which focus upon the most distinctive regional varieties: New England (Nagy and Roberts), the staging cities of the East Coast and the urban dialects of the interior North, including the ongoing change known as the "Northern Cities Shift" (Gordon), the South (with Thomas documenting the richness of rural Southern pronunciations and

Tillery and Bailey discussing ongoing changes in the wake of urbanization), and the West and Midwest (Gordon, again). Boberg covers Canadian English, and Clarke describes the Newfoundland dialects. Ethnic varieties of AmE include AAVE (Edwards), Gullah (Weldon), Cajun Vernacular English (Dubois and Horvath), and Chicano English (Santa Ana and Bailey). In the Caribbean, the varieties represented are the Bahamas (Childs and Wolfram), Jamaica (with Devonish and Harry describing both English and Creole), smaller islands of the Eastern Caribbean (Aceto), Barbados (Blake), Trinidad and Tobago (Youssef and James), and Suriname (Smith and Haabo).

The morphosyntax part also starts with a baseline paper, covering structural phenomena which occur widely in colloquial AmE (Murray and Simon). Regionally distinctive grammatical variation in North America has been investigated in a small number of salient locations, including the Appalachians (presented in the chapter by Montgomery), enclave communities in the Southeast (discussed by Wolfram), and Newfoundland (documented by Clarke). The primary topics of grammatical research have been ethnic varieties, most notably AAVE (its urban form, discussed by Wolfram; its historical evolution, described by Kautzsch; and the extant creole form of Gullah, studied by Mufwene), but also Chicano English (see the chapter by Bayley and Santa Ana). For the Caribbean, on the other hand, regional differences from one island or region to another are obvious enough to justify such an arrangement, so there are papers on the Bahamas (Reaser and Torbert), Jamaica (Patrick), eastern islands (Aceto), Trinidad and Tobago (James and Youssef), Suriname (Winford and Migge), as well as Central America with special emphasis on Belize (Escure). Coverage of Barbadian Creole (Bajan) and Guyanese Creole would have been desirable, but, regrettably, papers commissioned on these topics failed to materialize.

Every selection of this kind requires decisions and categorizations, of course; I trust that the decisions made reflect the directions and intensity of ongoing research activities. This applies in the few cases where the commissioned papers for phonology and grammar do not match, for instance: Investigations of Cajun English have taught us much about the dialect's phonology but little about its grammar; conversely, an extensive debate on the emergence of AAVE has been concerned with grammar almost exclusively; and many writings on Caribbean creoles have discussed grammatical but not primarily phonological features (hence the coverage of Belize plus Central America, focussing on grammar only). Of course, other considerations also applied, including space restrictions and the amount of existing research documentation: a survey like the present one requires a certain degree of comprehensiveness and systematicity of earlier investigations of specific varieties, which is not available in many cases. It would have been very interesting to include papers on native American or

Asian forms of English, for instance, but publications and research on these dialects have been eclectic so far; a great many facts are either unknown or assumed to be largely similar to "mainstream" forms of AmE. Space constraints and the fact that our project set out to describe "major" varieties exclude strictly local dialects, like, for example, those spoken by the Texas Seminoles in Bracketville (Hancock 1980), on small islands like the Caymans (Washabaugh 1983), or in the city of Americana, Brazil (Montgomery and Melo 1990). The same applies to Falkland Islands English (Sudbury 2001) and, of geographically uncertain association with any continent, the dialect of Tristan da Cunha – well documented and interesting in the light of dialect contact (Schreier 2002, 2003) but spoken by less than three hundred people. Finally Hawai'i, even if politically a part of the US, is discussed in the volume on the Pacific and Australasian varieties of English, in line with its geographical location.

Selected references

Baker, Philip, and Magnus Huber
    2001   Atlantic, Pacific, and world-wide features in English-lexicon contact languages. *English World-Wide* 22: 157–208.
deCamp, David
    1971   Toward a generative analysis of a post-creole speech continuum. In: Hymes (ed.), 349–370.
Hancock, Ian
    1980   *The Texas Seminoles and Their Language*. Austin: University of Texas.
Holm, John
    1983   The spread of English in the Caribbean area. In: Görlach and Holm (eds.), 1–22.
    2004   *Languages in Contact. The Partial Restructuring of Vernaculars*. Cambridge: Cambridge University Press.
McWhorter, John
    1998   Identifying the Creole prototype: vindicating a typological class. *Language* 74: 788–818.
    2000a Defining 'creole' as a synchronic term. In: Neumann-Holzschuh and Schneider (eds.), 85–123.
Montgomery, Michael, and Cecil Ataide Melo
    1990   The phonology of the lost cause: The English of the Confederados in Brazil. *English World-Wide* 11:195–216.
Rickford, John, and Jerome Handler
    1994   Textual evidence on the nature of early Barbadian speech, 1676–1835. *Journal of Pidgin and Creole Languages* 9: 221–255.

Schneider, Edgar W.

1990 The cline of creoleness in English-oriented creoles and semi-creoles of the Caribbean. *English World-Wide* 11: 79–113.

1996a Introduction: Research trends in the study of American English. In: Schneider (ed.), 1–12.

Schreier, Daniel

2002 Terra incognita in the anglophone world: Tristan da Cunha, South Atlantic Ocean. *English World-Wide* 23: 1–29.

2003 *Isolation and Language Change: Contemporary and Sociohistorical Evidence from Tristan da Cunha English.* Houndsmills, New York: Palgrave Macmillan.

Shields-Brodber, Kathryn

1997 Requiem for English in an "English-speaking" community: The case of Jamaica. In: Schneider (ed.), 57–67.

Sudbury, Andrea

2001 Falkland Islands English: a southern hemisphere variety? *English World-Wide* 22: 55–80.

Tillery, Jan, Tom Wikle, and Guy Bailey

2000 The nationalization of a Southernism. *Journal of English Linguistics* 28: 280–294.

Washabaugh, William

1983 Creoles of the off-shore islands: Providencia, San Andrés and the Caymans. In: Holm (ed.), 157–179.

Phonology

Standard American English pronunciation

William A. Kretzschmar, Jr.

1.   Introduction

The idea that there should be a "standard" form of a language is a relatively recent development in western culture, at least in the way that "standard" is usually understood in this usage today. People seem always to have noticed language variation, for instance the *shibboleth* story in the Bible about recognition of spies, and the uses of language variation for more comic effect by Greek and Roman dramatists. However, our modern sense of a "standard language" emerged only during the Neo-Classical period, during the seventeenth century in parts of Europe (as for the Encyclopedists in France) and during the eighteenth century in England. The first citation for the collocation *standard English* in the *Oxford English Dictionary* comes even later, from the nineteenth century.

The word *standard* possesses a set of meanings related to criteria for measurement. The original fifteenth-century literal sense of objects, such as standard weights used to compare to working scale weights to enable fair commercial transactions, still survives, but today more emphasis falls on attributive or metaphoric senses in which there is comparative measurement of qualities. In actual use in American English as demonstrated in corpus evidence, *standard(s)* most frequently refers to a general level of quality, not to a particular authoritative statement of criteria for evaluation. The attributive use of the word in the collocation *Standard English* may therefore raise the expectation for some people that there must be a perfect and exemplary state of the language, just as there are perfect exemplars for a one-ounce weight or for a measure of length such as a yardstick. The way that most people interpret the collocation, however, will be as a general level of quality. Thus *Standard English* may be taken to reflect conformance to a set of rules, but its meaning commonly gets bound up with social ideas about how one's character and education are displayed in one's speech.

The term "General American" is sometimes used by those who expect for there to be a perfect and exemplary state of American English (see below). However, in this essay the term "Standard American English" (StAmE) is preferred; it designates the level of quality (here of pronunciation) that is employed by educated speakers in formal settings. StAmE pronunciation differs from region to region, even from person to person, because speakers from different circumstances in and different parts of the United States commonly employ regional and social features to some extent even in formal situations.

2.   Demographics and education in the development of a standard

The American attitude towards StAmE developed from two different forces, demographics and public education.

2.1.   Colonial settlement

The first settlement of America occurred in the seventeenth century within the different original colonial hearth areas (see Kretzschmar 2002 for a more detailed treatment of what follows). Travel was difficult enough so that the separate colonies developed cultural differences early on, including linguistic differences. No colony was settled exclusively from any single region of England; early settlers in every colony came from a variety of areas in England, and thus brought with them various regional English speech characteristics. Kretzschmar (1996) suggests on the basis of dialect evidence that the word stock of the different colonies was largely shared, but preserved differently in each place; in similar fashion, pronunciations characteristic of different parts of England were available in every colony. Out of the pool of language characteristics available in each colony there emerged, within a few generations, the particular set of features that would form the characteristic speech of the colony. No colony sounded too much like any particular area of England because of the mixture of settlers, and for the same reason the different American colonies sounded more similar to each other than to the speech of the old country. At the end of the seventeenth century settlers began to arrive in larger numbers from non-English-speaking places in Europe and Africa, but by then English was well established in most areas of the colonies by the English founder population (for this term see Mufwene 2001), and the later arrivals needed to fit themselves into English-speaking communities. The new settlers brought their own language characteristics, and some of these later became established in the speech of the communities that they entered. Of course there were also Native Americans in the colonies before the English founders and features from their languages did and do survive, particularly place names and the names for the flora and fauna of the New World (see Marckwardt 1960 for contributions from various languages to American English, particularly the lexicon).

The first standardizing effect to be seen in the colonies, then, was the establishment of English as a common community language, out of the welter of languages spoken by the Native Americans and the different settlers. The appearance of a new American English, relatively shared between the colonies when viewed in comparison with the different British regional varieties of the time, does not come from the imposition of a standard, or from the recovery of some basic, essential variety of English from which the British dialects had diverged, but instead from the demographic conditions – mixed settlement – of the founding population that formed communities in each colony. The new American English was also not the same as the emerging standard for English in Britain (see Upton, British Isles volume), and was criticized on those grounds at the time, as for example by John Witherspoon, the first president of Princeton University (Mathews 1931). At the same time, American English and the need of new settlers to learn it became a hallmark of the American experience, part of the voluntary social movement that Crevecoeur (1782) described in "What is an American."

Along with the formation of new political and social practices in the new American communities came a new commitment to public education. So-called "common schools" were created throughout the states, more quickly and completely in the North but also in the agrarian South. The one-room schoolhouse became an icon of American community action, and whenever the population and resources became dense enough, more elaborate "graded" schools and academies sprang up as well. Basic education in reading and writing began to have an effect on American English from the beginning.

2.2.   Westward expansion and urbanization

As the United States expanded, the speech habits of the hearth colonies were carried along with the settlers. Settlement generally proceeded from east to west, and so the influence of colonial speech was carried from east to west. Kretzschmar (1996) shows that the linguistic characteristics of several eastern inland towns are most similar to the characteristics of the coastal cities directly to their east. This fact is not a result of influence of an emerging standard language, but instead a consequence of the economic dominance of the coastal cities over the hinterlands (see McDavid 1948), again a matter of demographics. The younger sons and daughters of the population that occupied the coast moved west in search of more land and opportunity, and they carried their speech with them. New immigrants also often spent time in coastal embarkation areas before they moved west to the frontier (see, e.g., the story of Andrew the Hebridean in Crevecoeur 1782), and so began to acquire American English from established colonial models on the coast. Inland speech, however, was never exactly the same as the speech of coastal cities, because the effects of population mixture, and thus the creation of and selection from a pool of linguistic features, operated inland as it had on the coast.

Coastal cities did become wealthy, and so did develop a social hierarchy which allowed for the emergence of sociolinguistic differences. McDavid (1948) carefully separates the loss of postvocalic *r* in Charleston (which is associated with demographic factors) from nonstandard verb forms and other features that mark socially dispreferred speech. In America just as in England, increasingly during the eighteenth century the notion of a standard began to be associated with social status, so that Swift, Johnson, and other highly cultivated authors came to prefer the usage of the "best" authors over the common parlance. Such preferences became entrenched in the first prominent English grammars, like those by Lowth and Murray. The same attitude is expressed by Anne Royall, a social columnist who often wrote about—pilloried—varieties of American pronunciation that she did not find to be socially acceptable (Mathews 1931). The continuing prevalence of public education extended the influence of such grammars, including Webster's in America, and thus social preferences in speech became teaching standards. A prime example is the influence of Webster's "blue-backed speller", which became one of the most successful textbooks of all time through wide use in American public schools. It thereby succeeded in the creation of particular American habits of spelling (e.g. –er instead of –re, -or instead of –our, and so forth), and a particular American habit of spelling pronunciation, i.e. of attempting to pronounce a sound for every letter in the spelling of a word. The American educational system abetted the social hierarchy in the maintenance of qualitative linguistic preferences by the creation and promulgation of rules of grammar, spelling, and other matters of linguistic propriety. The prevalence of common schools ensured that the emerging idea of a linguistic standard was widely accepted, but it is also the case that citizens with the means to obtain better educational opportunities for their children, or to allow their children to spend more time in the educational system rather than going to work at an early age, were better able to enact the standards in their own speech. Thus was created a cycle that still operates today for the establishment and maintenance of language standards in linkage to the social hierarchy.

Continuing westward settlement in the nineteenth century followed essentially the same patterns, but the connection with eastern colonial speech ways became more diffuse the further west the frontier. West of the Mississippi River, settlement is still not dense enough and is still too recent to have allowed for very extensive development of the local speech patterns characteristic of eastern areas. Continuing urbanization added more ethnic neighborhoods, but again the essential pattern remained the same. Each of the main regional variants of American English – Northern, Midland, and Southern, as described by Kurath (1949) and Kurath and McDavid (1961) – had its own linguistic characteristics, and each region had its own socially preferred models of pronunciation prevalent among the socially prominent and more educated population.

2.3.   Twentieth-century changes

The twentieth century brought different demographic movements and associated linguistic change. Initial settlement of the western part of the country by homesteading was essentially complete, and demographic change then occurred by internal migration. In the first half of the century Southerners both black and white left the untenable agricultural conditions of their region and looked for new opportunities in the North and West. In the second half of the century Northerners sometimes moved away from the Rust Belt in search of opportunities in emerging industries in the South. These population movements often created speech islands in the regions to which the migrants traveled, such as African American or Southern White neighborhoods in Northern cities.

The greater change, however, stemmed from an essential change in the urban demographic pattern from residential neighborhoods within cities to the model of an urban core surrounded by suburbs. Suburban housing changed the essential interactions of the community, because people no longer lived with the people they worked with: in sociolinguistic terms, suburban social networks often became characterized by weak ties (i.e., the density and multiplexity of linguistic interactions decreased; see, e.g., J. Milroy (1992) for discussion of social network issues). In addition, because American suburban housing has most often been economically stratified, the social networks that did develop were more likely to be class-bound, unlike the situation in older cities where there was more mingling on a daily basis between people of different economic registers.

At the same time that suburban residential patterns were developing, improvements in transportation (highways, airlines) created a super-regional marketplace for the highly educated. While the American population has always been mobile, the most highly educated segment of the population has become nationally mobile to a much greater extent than the working and lower-middle class population, which tends to move around locally, often within the same metropolitan area or the same state. This change has led to the growth of the notion that highly educated speech should not show evidence of regional affiliation. Highly educated speakers in formal settings tend to suppress their regional features (to the extent that they have them in the first place, owing to suburban housing patterns; see Milroy and Milroy (1999) for the idea of suppression of variation). The typical speech of national news broadcasters is symptomatic – not a cause of the change, as many suppose.

The contemporary situation for StAmE pronunciation, then, is that the most highly educated speakers in formal settings tend to suppress any linguistic features that they recognize as marked, i.e., regionally or socially identifiable. Many educated speakers therefore think that language variation in America is decreasing. On the other hand, the economically-stratified suburban residential pattern promotes the continued existence, even expansion of local varieties (cf. Labov and Ash 1997: 508), though perhaps varieties with fewer strongly marked characteristics than were maintained before in the previous era of stronger, denser ties in social networks. American English, paradoxically, in some ways has more local variation than ever before, at the same time that in other ways it has less variation than before. The linkage between demographic trends and education remains the central fact for any discussion of standards in American English: those with the resources to proceed the furthest in the educational system have the greatest commitment to and investment in the idea of linguistic standards, now expressed particularly through their suppression of marked regional and social characteristics, while those with fewer resources and less investment in the educational system generally accept the idea of formal educational standards but do not routinely enact them in their own linguistic behavior. That said, it is of course true that many educated speakers value their regional affiliations and refuse to suppress, or even take pride in the display of, their regional speech characteristics, while some speakers without a high level of educational achievement may choose to suppress their regional features.

2.4.   "General American"

The term "General American" arose as a name for a presumed most common or "default" form of American English, especially to be distinguished from marked regional speech of New England or the South. "General American" has often been considered to be the relatively unmarked speech of "the Midwest", a vague designation for anywhere in the vast midsection of the country from Ohio west to Nebraska, and from the Canadian border as far south as Missouri or Kansas. No historical justification for this term exists, and neither do present circumstances support its use. While population mixture did make the different colonial varieties of American English more similar to each other than to any form of old-world British English, and there remain some relatively common pronunciation (and other) features that continue to justify use of the term "American English" in opposition to other national terms for English varieties, there has never been any single best or default form of American English that might form the basis for "General American". Take for example the state of Ohio, often seen as a model for "General American": the state is divided by Kurath's major Northern/Midland dialect boundary, and Labov's more recent Telsur field work yields a map in which no fewer than five boundaries criss-cross the state (Labov, Ash and Boberg 2006). Even Ohio's educated speakers, speaking in formal settings, tend to make different pronunciation choices. For example, Cleveland speakers might routinely pronounce a common word like *on* as [ɑn], while the speakers from Columbus might routinely pronounce the word as [ɔn]. No particular notice of the difference would be taken, because these pronunciations are not marked regional or social variants; neither pronunciation needs to be suppressed in order to achieve a StAmE level of quality. Thus a term like "General American" does not represent the condition of American English with respect either to StAmE or to regional and social varieties, because it implies that there is some exemplary state of American English from which other varieties deviate.

On the contrary, StAmE can best be characterized as what is left over after speakers suppress the regional and social features that have risen to salience and become noticeable. Decisions about which features are perceived to be salient will be different in every region, even different for every speaker, depending on local speech habits and the capacity of speakers to recognize particular features out of their varied linguistic experience. Some speakers are better than others at suppression of regional features, and some listeners are more subtle than others at detection of non-local features. The result of such decisions and perceptions is a linguistic continuum for American English in which no region or social group has pride of place (except for Southern American English, which is commonly singled out as a dispreferred variety by speakers from other regions), and a relative level of quality for StAmE that varies from place to place and person to person. When speakers travel outside of their native region, aspects of their pronunciation that are perfectly standard at home can be recognized by local speakers as being out of conformance with local StAmE preferences. This is just as true when Northerners travel South as when Southerners travel North, and people recognized as outsiders because of their speech must face the social consequences.

3.   StAmE pronunciation

The model for StAmE pronunciation presented here is composed of features that most highly educated speakers would not recognize as regionally or socially identifiable. For application of the model to particular words, the *Oxford Dictionary of Pronunciation for Current English* (*ODP*; Upton, Kretzschmar and Konopka 2001) will be a useful reference. ODP features both British and American English transcriptions for comparison by readers, and offers many phonotactic (but not recognizably regional or social) variants. To these features may be added those characteristics that commonly occur in educated speech in different regions of the country, generally unnoticed and preferred by educated speakers within the region but often noticed and sometimes stigmatized by educated speakers from other regions. Table 1 lists general features first ("unmarked"), and some regional standard features in a second group ("marked").

Table 1.   Unmarked and marked vowel pronunciation (lexical sets)

word	unmarked pronunciation	marked pronunciation	word	unmarked pronunciation	marked pronunciation
KIT	ɪ		CHOICE	ɔɪ	
DRESS	ɛ		MOUTH	aʊ	æʊ
TRAP	æ		NEAR	ɪɚ, ɪɚ	
LOT	ɑ	ɔ	SQUARE	ɛɚ	
STRUT	ʌ		MARRY	ɛ	æ
FOOT	ʊ		MERRY	ɛ	
BATH	æ	a	MARY	ɛ	e
CLOTH	ɔ, ɑ		START	ɑɚ	
NURSE	ɚ	ɜ	NORTH	ɔɚ	
FLEECE	i		FORCE	ɔɚ	oɚ
FACE	eɪ		ORANGE	ɔ	ɑ, o
PALM	ɑ	ɔ	CURE	jʊɚ	
THOUGHT	ɔ, ɑ		happY	i	ɪ
GOAT	oʊ		lettER	ɚ	
GOAL	oʊ		horsES	ə, i	
GOOSE	u		commA	ə	
PRICE	ɑɪ				

3.1.   StAmE phonological patterns

Kurath and McDavid (1961) distinguished four different phonological patterns for cultivated speakers of American English in the Atlantic States: I: Upstate New York, Eastern Pennsylvania, and the South Midland; II: Metropolitan New York, the Upper South, and the Lower South; III: Eastern New England; and IV: Western Pennsylvania. All of these sets held the high and central front vowels and the high back vowels in common /i, ɪ; eɪ, ɛ; æ; u, ʊ/, with some variation in the low vowels. The same patterns exist today, with the American West generally following the pattern Kurath and McDavid described for Western Pennsylvania. Discussion of three ongoing sound changes by Labov (1981, 1991, 1994), called the Northern Cities Shift, the Southern Shift, and Western Merger (for details see the sections elsewhere in this volume that report on these regions), has focused on working and lower-middle class speakers, and so it is difficult to estimate the extent to which these changes have penetrated StAmE.

KIT, DRESS, TRAP

These so-called "checked" vowels are not invariant in StAmE, although they are usually represented as such. They may be realized with glides or extra length by different speakers. More prominent use of glides, sometimes with changes in vowel height as well, may be recognized as part of Labov's Southern Shift.

LOT, CLOTH, PALM, THOUGHT

The low-back vowels are historically unstable in StAmE. The /ɑ~ɔ/ merger is said by Labov to be characteristic of the speech of the West, but instability in these vowels also characterizes Eastern New England (in which one also hears fronted pronunciations, as [a]) and Western Pennsylvania. "Merger" may be too strong a term here; there is some evidence that words historically with /ɑ/ retain it in some areas (so that a pronunciation with [ɔ] might be recognized as "different"), while words historically with /ɔ/ more freely show alternation within the /ɑ~ɔ/ range. The [ɔ] pronunciation in *palm* may be related to the American spelling pronunciation that inserts unhistorical [l], to yield [pɑm, pɔlm]. *ODP* represents words of the historical /ɑ/ class with [ɑ], and words of the historical /ɔ/ class with both sounds [ɑ, ɔ].

STRUT, FOOT

StAmE does not share the British tendency to raise the vowel of *strut* towards [ʊ] (this vowel is represented with [ə] in *ODP*). However, StAmE has a long history of alternation of the vowel in *roof, root* (but not *foot*) as [u, ʊ], with the short vowel more common in the North. The same is true, through with [u] in the North and [ʊ] in the South, for *coop*. *Route* is another word with alternation, this time commonly between [u] and [aʊ]. These alternations do not apply across the entire word class of [ʊ] words, although there is some evidence that there used to be more words that showed the alternation (e.g. *gums*).

BATH

New England preserves the [a] pronunciation in words of the *half, glass* class, and has [ɑ] in *aunt*. These pronunciations are sometimes heard from educated speakers in other regions of the country, possibly as a consequence of the historical importance of New England in American education.

NURSE

Loss of postvocalic *r* is receding in StAmE, even in its historical urban strongholds in Boston, New York, and the plantation South. One is most likely to hear *r*-less pronunciations from older educated speakers from these regions, while younger speakers commonly employ pronunciations with *r*. That said, it has always been true that a wide range of realizations of *r* after vowels has been and still is employed, even in StAmE, ranging from fully constricted [r] to different levels of constriction (so-called "*r*-coloring") to compensatory lengthening of the vowel to vocalization of the *r* to create a diphthong. Pronunciations similar to [nɔɪs], which used to qualify as StAmE in New York, Charleston, and New Orleans, are now stigmatized, as in the pronunciation of the cartoon character Bugs Bunny.

FLEECE, FACE, GOAT, GOAL

These long vowels differ characteristically by environment in StAmE: they are longest and most likely to be diphthongal before juncture, next most likely to be long and/or diphthongal before voiced consonants, and most likely to be realized without added length and without glides before unvoiced consonants. Thus in word sets like the following there may be graded variation in the vowel: *flee, feed, fleece* [flɪi, fⁱid, flis]; *fay, fade, face* [feɪ, feⁱd, fes]; *go, goad, goat* [goʊ, goᵁd, got]. Monophthongized variants in all environments are characteristic of educated speakers from the Upper Midwest.

GOOSE

This high back vowel has a relatively wide range of realizations in StAmE, from somewhat lowered pronunciations more likely in the North, such as [gʊs], to fully raised and fronted realizations in the South, such as [gʏs]. Still, words of the *goose* class are not recognized as having regular alternants like *root, roof, route* (for which see above, under *strut, foot*).

PRICE, CHOICE
Educated speakers in the South commonly pronounce these vowels with weakened glides. The pronunciations are affected by environment: /aɪ/ is more likely to show glide reduction before voiced consonants, as in possible graded variation in the series *rye, rice, ride* [raɪ, ra^{ı}s, rad]. /ɔɪ/ is more likely to show reduction before [l], as in *boil, oil*.

MOUTH
This diphthong has a long history of pronunciation as [æʊ] by some educated speakers, especially those from the Midland region, and this pronunciation seems to be on the increase.

NEAR, SQUARE, START, NORTH
The loss of postvocalic *r* is recessive, as indicated for *nurse*. With these vowels, before juncture, it is common for educated speakers to insert a schwa glide before the r-coloring, such as *square* [skwɛɚ]. However, when the *r* is intervocalic, for example when a participial ending is added, then the schwa glide typically does not appear, yielding pronunciation pairs like *near, nearing* [nɪɚ, nɪrɪŋ].

MARRY, MERRY, MARY
While these words have become homophones for a great many StAmE speakers, some or all of them are still distinguished in some regions by educated speakers. The pronunciation with [ɛ] for the set of words has spread from the North and North Midland regions. In the South, educated speakers still pronounce *Mary* with [e], and in the mid-Atlantic region educated speakers commonly pronounce words like *marry, carry* with [æ]. In the New York metropolitan area, educated speakers still commonly distinguish all three words.

FORCE, ORANGE
Historically the *horse/hoarse* pair was distinguished by pronunciations with [ɔ] and [o], respectively. Now most educated speakers no longer make the distinction, but the [o] pronunciation is still sometimes heard, primarily from older speakers. This vowel is particularly unstable before intervocalic *r*, so that words like *orange, forest* may still be heard not only with [ɔ] and [o] but also with [ɑ].

CURE

Words like *cure* not only show the effects of varying realizations of postvocalic *r*, but the palatal onset for the vowel also seems to create instability and a wide range of realizations [u~ʊ~ə]. A somewhat narrower range of realizations occurs in educated speech in similar words without the palatal, as *poor* [u~ʊ].

happY

The word-final sound is now commonly pronounced with [i], but older [ɪ] may still be heard, especially from educated Southern speakers.

lettER, horsES, commA

Vowels in unstressed final syllables vary between [ɪ~ə], often in harmony with the preceding vowel in suffixes like *–ness, -ity, -es*. This yields pairs of possible pronunciations like [-nəs, -nɪs; -əɾi, -ɪɾi; -əz, -ɪz], where the [ə]-form occurs after most vowels and the [ɪ]-form occurs after high-front vowels. That said, vowel harmony is only suggestive, not controlling, in such situations. Unstressed final *–er* and *–a* are of course distinguished by r-coloring in StAmE.

3.2.   StAmE consonants

There are only a few notable StAmE consonantal practices aside from the issue of postvocalic *r* already covered with the vowels in the previous section. The most prominent concern /t/. Intervocalic *t* is most often realized as a tap or flap, frequently with voicing, so that *latter/ladder* are homonyms for educated Americans, as [læɾɚ]; this pronunciation is transcribed as [lædər] in *ODP*, because the dictionary uses a restricted symbol set that does not include the ɾ or ɚ. /t/ is also frequently voiced prevocalically in consonant clusters such as –kt–, –pt–, –ft–, and –rt–. /t/ is typically deleted from –nt– clusters between vowels (unless separated by stress), for example making homonyms of the words *winter/winner*. The palatal glide /j/ remains firmly in place in words like *cure, music*, but in other words like *Tuesday, coupon, neurotic* it is frequently lost. Postvocalic /l/ is vocalized more and more often by educated speakers, except before juncture, to yield pronunciations like *alcohol, milk* [æʊkəhɔl, mɪᵁk]. Educated speakers sometimes voice other consonants as well, such as [ɛks-, ɛgz-] as variant pronunciations of the *ex-* prefix.

3.3.   StAmE stress patterns

As clearly exemplified in the transcriptions in *ODP*, StAmE pronunciation shows a different pattern of stress from British English. StAmE pronunciation tends more to preserve secondary stress, and thus more fully-realized vowels, than British English, as in StAmE [ˈsɛkrəˌtɛri] versus British English [ˈsɛkrɪtri]. This results in a characteristically different rhythm for StAmE pronunciation as compared to British and other world English varieties. Educated Southern speakers tend to prefer strong initial stress (and are recognized for it) in words like *insurance, police, Thanksgiving, umbrella*, while other Americans place strong stress on the second syllable of these words. It is possible that a general American tendency towards strong initial stress is responsible for vowel alternations between the use of stressed and unstressed vowel forms in the weakly-stressed initial syllables of many words, such as *electric* [əˈlɛktrɪk, iˈlɛktrɪk] or *retain* [rəˈteɪn, riˈteɪn].

4.   Conclusion

Because StAmE pronunciation is characterized negatively, by the suppression of identifiable regional and social variants, instead of positively by a collection of its own features, there is less to say about StAmE than about positively-defined varieties from different regions. It is clearly the case, however, that StAmE pronunciation is not somehow a perfect or correct exemplar of American English pronunciation, from which American regional and social varieties are deviant offshoots. StAmE pronunciation is the product of demographic factors, just as American regional and social varieties are. In common usage StAmE refers not to any set of "correct" pronunciations, but to a level of quality in pronunciation that corresponds to the degree of suppression of marked regional and social features.

Exercises and study questions

1. How is the idea of a standard language related to other kinds of standards, for example in weights and measures?

2. What does it mean to say that establishment and maintenance of American language standards is linked to the social hierarchy?

3. Is the American English spoken by newscasters and other media personalities a symptom or a cause of language standards in America?

4. Has the emergence of standard American English led to the loss of local variation in American speech?

5. Among what group is the use of standard American English most common, and why?

6. Explain how standard American English can best be defined in negative terms, as the absence of other features.

7. How does pronunciation of the consonants /r/ and /t/ help to define American English among world varieties of English?

8. How does pronunciation of words like PRICE help to define standard American English, both within the US and among world varieties of English?

Selected references

Please consult the General references for titles mentioned in the text but not included in the references below. For a full bibliography see the accompanying CD-ROM.

Bronstein, Arthur J.
  1960   *The Pronunciation of American English*. Englewood Cliffs, NJ: Prentice Hall.
Crevecoeur, J. Hector St. John
  1782 (1981) *Letters from an American Farmer*. Ed. by A. Stone. Harmondsworth: Penguin.
Kretzschmar, William A., Jr.
  1996   Foundations of American English. In: Schneider (ed.), 25–50.
  2002   American English: Melting Pot or mixing bowl? In: Katja Lenz and Ruth Möhlig (eds), *Of Dyuersitie & Chaunge of Langage: Essays presented to Manfred Görlach*, 224–239. Heidelberg: C. Winter.
Labov, William
  1981   Resolving the Neogrammarian controversy. *Language* 57: 267–309.
  1991   The three dialects of English. In: Eckert (ed.), 1–44.
Labov, William, and Sharon Ash.
  1997   Understanding Birmingham. In: Bernstein, Nunnally and Sabino (eds), 508–573.

Mathews, Mitford
  1931   *The Beginnings of American English*. Chicago: University of Chicago Press.
McDavid, Raven I., Jr.
  1948   Postvocalic /-r/ in South Carolina: A social analysis. *American Speech* 23: 194–203.
Marckwardt, Albert
  1960   *American English*. New York: Oxford University Press.
Milroy, James
  1992   *Linguistic Variation and Change*. Oxford: Blackwell.
Milroy, James, and Lesley Milroy
  1999   *Authority in Language*. 3rd ed. London: Routledge.
Upton, Clive, William A. Kretzschmar, Jr, and Rafal Konopka
  2001   *Oxford Dictionary of Pronunciation for Current English*. Oxford: Oxford University Press.

New England: phonology[*]

Naomi Nagy and Julie Roberts

1.   Introduction

The six states that make up New England (NE) are Vermont (VT), New Hampshire (NH), Maine (ME), Massachusetts (MA), Connecticut (CT), and Rhode Island (RI). Cases where speakers in these states exhibit differences from other American speakers and from each other will be discussed in this chapter. The major sources of phonological information regarding NE dialects are the *Linguistic Atlas of New England* (*LANE*) (Kurath 1939-43), and Kurath (1961), representing speech patterns from the first half of the 20th century; and Labov, Ash and Boberg (2006); Boberg (2001); Nagy, Roberts and Boberg (2000); Cassidy (1985) and Thomas (2001) describing more recent stages of the dialects.

There is a split between eastern and western NE, and a north-south split within eastern NE. Eastern New England (ENE) comprises Maine (ME), New Hampshire (NH), eastern Massachusetts (MA), eastern Connecticut (CT) and Rhode Island (RI). Western New England (WNE) is made up of Vermont, and western MA and CT. The lines of division are illustrated in figure 1. Two major NE shibboleths are the "dropping" of post-vocalic r (as in [ka:] *car* and [ba:n] *barn*) and the low central vowel [a] in the BATH class, words like *aunt* and *glass* (Carver 1987: 21). It is not surprising that these two features are among the most famous dialect phenomena in the region, as both are characteristic of the "Boston accent," and Boston, as we discuss below, is the major urban center of the area. However, neither pattern is found across all of NE, nor are they all there is to the well-known dialect group. We present a brief description of the settlement of the region as a whole and give examples of past and current pronunciation patterns to illustrate both how NE differs from the rest of the country and what region-internal differences exist. The material is rather thin in some areas, due to a dearth of recent research on NE English. Nevertheless, the resulting pattern is one that reflects the richness and diversity of the region itself.

2.   European settlement of New England

Our story begins with the European settlement of a region that was previously populated by a variety of indigenous peoples. There has been no systematic study of the possible influences of the indigenous languages on English, but

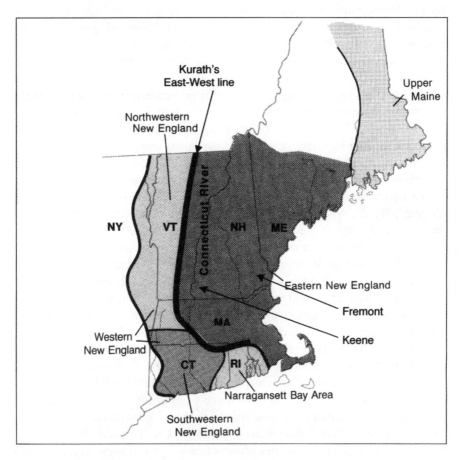

Figure 1.   Eastern and Western New England according to Carver (1987: 31). Reprinted with permission from the University of Michigan Press

we can see their influence in local toponyms, for example the Piscataqua River in NH, the Kennebec River in ME, Lake Memphremagog in VT, and Contacook, a town in Rhode Island, as well as the word Massachusetts.

European settlers in ENE came primarily from Boston, on the Massachusetts Bay, and were of English stock. This coastal area, originally home to indigenous groups, was settled by English immigrants in the early 1600's and became one of the country's cultural hearths. In search of better farm land, some of these original European settlers moved west from the coast and settled the Lower Connecticut River Valley in central CT. They were joined soon after by new immigrants from eastern and southern England, and later from Italy, Scotland and Ireland, among other places. Settlement spread, generally along river valleys, into NH, VT, ME, and RI (Carver 1987: 7).

WNE was settled by migration from central MA and central and western CT, including Hartford, Springfield, and New Haven, towns originally settled in the 1630s (Boberg 2001: 4). Following this movement, Eastern and Western NE remained isolated from each other until the early 18th century (Rosenberry 1962: facing 70; Kurath 1972: 42, cited in Boberg 2001: 4). Western VT was settled in the late 18th century by English-speaking migrants from western CT and MA (Kurath 1939-43: 104, cited in Boberg 2001: 5) and from NY (Rosenberry 1962: 136, cited in Boberg 2001: 5), as well as some settlers from east of the Green Mountains (NH, ME, and RI) (Kurath 1939-43: 103-4, cited in Boberg 2001: 5). WNE, in turn, was "the staging ground for the initial English-speaking settlement of the Inland North" (Boberg 2001: 9).

WNE also "received a considerable admixture of Scotch-Irish in the half century preceding the Revolution [early 18th century]" (Kurath 1928: 391, cited in Boberg 2001: 9), though they did not form a sizeable percentage of the population at any time. Also present in NE are Franco-Americans who moved south from French-speaking parts of Canada, and large Irish and Italian groups. Upper ME (north of Penobscot Bay) is quite distinct from the rest of the region, due to ties with New Brunswick, Canada (Carver 1987: 31).

Boston, the largest NE city, is still known as the *hub*, hearkening back to its position as the center from which settlements radiated in NE. Much of the rest of NE, however, is more rural, with many farms, forests, and undeveloped areas surrounding small towns and cities. Like many rural communities, NE is undergoing changes including increased highways, in-migration from other dialect areas, and change from small family farms to agribusiness (Frazer 1983; Labov 1994). The rural, regional dialects appear threatened with obsolescence due to the decrease in agriculture and increase in in-migration by speakers from other states. This loss evokes mixed reactions within the communities, where it may be seen as a sign of progress and increasing sophistication as well as a loss of cultural identity (Ring 1997).

3. New England dialect regions

The *Linguistic Atlas of New England* (Kurath 1939-43) divides the area into Eastern (ENE) and Western (WNE) (divided by the Green Mountains of VT in the north, the Berkshires in the middle, and the Connecticut River in the south), with seven subregions dictated by settlement patterns (Carver 1987). However, today there is little in the way of linguistic markers of these sub-regions, aside from some distinctive characteristics of ENE. *A Word Geography of the Eastern United States* (Kurath 1949) divides New England into only three regions (Northeastern, Southeastern, and Southwestern), better representing current linguistic differences.

As table 1 demonstrates, the English of NE is in many ways similar to that heard in many other regions of the United States. In the following section, we will discuss the ways in which NE English may be different from other regions.

4. Vowels

Table 1. New England vowels — summary

KIT	ɪ	FACE	eɪ	START	aː(ɹ) ~ ɑː(ɹ)		
DRESS	ɛ	PALM	aː ~ ɑː	NORTH	ɔ(ɹ) > ɒə		
TRAP	æ > ɛə	THOUGHT	ɑ ~ ɔ	FORCE	ɔ(ɹ)		
LOT	ɑ ~ ɒ	GOAT	əo > ɔ	CURE	jʊə(ɹ)		
STRUT	ə	GOOSE	u ~ ʊuː	happY	i		
FOOT	ʊ	PRICE	ɑɪ > əɪ	lettER	ə(ɹ)		
BATH	æ > ɛə > a	CHOICE	ɔɪ	horsES	ə > ɪ		
CLOTH	ɑ	MOUTH	aʊ>əʊ	commA	ə(ɹ)		
NURSE	ə(ɹ)	NEAR	iə(ɹ)	kittEN	ən ~ n̩		
FLEECE	iː	SQUARE	ɛə(ɹ)	aunt	ɑnt		

In discussing the vowel patterns, we begin with the elements considered essential as points of departure for the phonological analysis of North American English dialects, according to Labov (1991: 21). The lack of a merger between low, back, unrounded /ɑ/ (LOT) and mid, back, rounded, lengthened /ɔ/ (THOUGHT) and the behavior of low front /æ/ (TRAP/BATH) as a unified phoneme (rather than split into tense and lax classes) is seen as essential conditions for the Northern Cities Chain Shift (NCCS), a major ongoing change in American phonology. The presence of these two phonemic patterns is necessary for the onset of the NCCS: TRAP/BATH raises, leaving a space for LOT to move forward and maintain its distinction from THOUGHT (Boberg 2001: 11; Labov 1994: 184; Gordon, this volume), thus initiating a chain shift.

4.1.   TRAP, BATH, HAPPY and DANCE

At the time of the *LANE* fieldwork, both BATH and TRAP comprised a unified low front vowel across New England (Kurath 1939–43: Maps 150 *sack*, 344 *pantry*, and 371 *dad*, cited in Boberg 2001: 13). Laferriere's (1977: 102–3) findings from urban Boston show a less uniform picture. She reported for BATH a non-productive backing: lexicalized and categorical before many /f/ and /θ/ words and in some /n/ words (e.g., *half, rather, aunt*) and lexicalized but variable before /s/ and in other /n/ words (e.g., *last, dance*). Supporting evidence comes from Calais, ME, where a majority of speakers report saying [ant] for *aunt*. Some speakers report [ɑnt], but none report [ænt]. This differs from much of the US, where [ænt] is used (Miller 1989: 124). Our NH speakers use [æ] for all of these word classes except *aunt*, which is [ɑ].

Laferriere (1977) also reports a productive, phonological process raising TRAP and BATH to [ɛə], demonstrated by her younger speakers. As this process was found to affect both TRAP and BATH vowels, it thus encroaches on the lexical BATH class that had been subjected to backing.

A more recent study of WNE found raising of the nucleus in TRAP and BATH in all environments and tensing (as well as raising) before nasals (DANCE) (Boberg 2001: 17–19). A small sample of telephone survey data (Labov, Ash and Boberg 2006) showed this to be the case across WNE with exception of the very northern city of Burlington, Vermont. Words like *bad* and *stack* are pronounced with [eə], and words like *stand* and *can* are pronounced [ɛə].

Labov (1991: 12) suggests that unified raising of TRAP/BATH/DANCE is a pivot condition for the NCCS. Boberg (2001: 11) further argues that the NCCS may thus have had its beginnings in northwestern NE. The existence of this raising pattern is surprising if one accepts the reported lack of BATH-raising in the *LANE* data (Kurath 1939–43), especially given that Labov, Ash and Boberg (2006) does not show this to be an incipient vigorous change: older speakers show more raising than younger speakers in Hartford, CT, Springfield, MA, and Rutland, VT (Boberg 2001: 19).

4.2.   LOT, CLOTH and THOUGHT

There was a major split within NE as early as the 1930s at which point ENE did not have a distinction between LOT and THOUGHT, while WNE had two distinct phonemes, (Kurath 1939-43, discussed in Boberg (2001: 13). ENE pronounced both LOT- and THOUGHT-type words with [ɒ], while virtually all of WNE used [ɑ] and [ɔ:] respectively, resembling NYC.

One modern exception to this pattern is Providence, RI, where the two vowels are distinct (Labov 2000: Map 1). Another may be Calais, ME, where no speakers reported a merger in Miller (1989: 101). More recent data (Labov, Ash and Boberg 2006) presents a strikingly different picture for the LOT/THOUGHT merger. While all western CT speakers keep the two values clearly distinct, resembling the Inland North pattern, seven of eight VT speakers have completely merged the two vowels. One older northern VT woman did not merge these vowels, suggesting that the merger is more recent in VT than CT (Boberg 2001: 20). This trend is supported by unpublished data from the McGill-Vermont-New Hampshire Survey (Nagy, Roberts and Boberg 2002) which shows most New England speakers report merging these two vowels. Our two recorded NH speakers produced LOT, CLOTH and THOUGHT with [ɑ]. One of them also produced PALM with this vowel.

Boberg (2001: 22) attributes the presence of the merger in VT to lack of contact with the Inland North (due to the barrier of Lake Champlain) combined with contact over the Green Mountains with the merged speakers of NH. In contrast, CT speakers have more contact with NY and thus retain the distinction. Geographically located between CT and VT, western MA speakers exhibit an intermediary variable pattern. In our data, however, MA has the highest rate of merger. Interestingly, Burlington, VT speakers show a tendency to merge LOT and THOUGHT in low back position, similar to the ENE merger (and to the Canadian merger just north of them), whereas the two Rutland speakers, 67 miles south, show a merger in low-central position (like that of southwestern NE) (Boberg 2001: 24), providing a gradual transition between the northern and southern WNE patterns.

To summarize, with respect to the LOT/THOUGHT merger and BATH/TRAP/DANCE raising, ENE has full merger of LOT/THOUGHT (except RI) and no BATH/TRAP/DANCE raising, except for that reported in Boston by Laferriere (1977). WNE is more complex:

> The CT portion of the lower Connecticut Valley (the Hartford area) is a pure Northern [NCCS] system, with raised [bath/trap] and centralized [lot], distinct from mid-back [thought]. Northwestern VT (Burlington) is a pure "third dialect" system, not unlike the Canadian systems to the north of it [with no bath raising and a lot/thought

merger]. Between Burlington and the lower Connecticut Valley are two transitional types. Springfield, and perhaps western MA in general, is basically Northern [NCSS] but shows a reduction of contrast between the low-back vowels, which may be tending toward merger among the youngest speakers in that area. Southwestern VT (Rutland) shows a solid merger of the low-back vowels but in the phonetic position characteristic of [lot] in western MA and CT (Boberg 2001:25-6).

4.3.   FACE and FLEECE

In general, there is nothing remarkable about these tense front vowels. However, Duckert (1986: 141) reports diphthongs in words like [maʃi'jan] *machine* and [dreijan] *drain* as a feature of rural New England dialects. Laferriere (1979: 431) lists the variable pronunciation of FACE as [iə] or [eə] as a marker of Boston speech.

4.4.   GOAT

Avis (1961) described a complex pattern involving GOAT in ENE. Reporting on the data from *LANE*, Avis argues that there are, in fact, two phonemes: an upgliding phoneme that appears word-finally, and another phoneme in which alternation can be found between monophthongal [o] and one with a fronted inglide [əo]. Avis (1961: 552) also notes that the monophthongal vowel is more likely to be found in "dialectal" speech than in words "learned in school". Avis does not report on this vowel in WNE. Roberts (1997) indicates that GOAT is produced as a lowered, lax vowel with either no glide or a shortened upglide in VT. All older and younger adult speakers produce low, lax GOAT, overlapping with their productions of FORCE.

　　Laferriere (1977: 431) reports GOAT as [ɒ] as a feature of Boston English.

4.5.   GOOSE

Kurath (1939-43) found that both a tense ([u]) (as in *too*) and a lax ([ʊ]) (as in *took*) production of GOOSE occurred in NE, but we hear only [u] or [ʊu] today.

4.6.   PRICE and MOUTH

Miller (1989: 110) reports Canadian raising (the production of PRICE and MOUTH before voiceless vowels as [əʊ] and [əɪ] respectively) in Calais, ME –not surprising as this town is on the border of Canada. Raising was reported in Calais in *LANE* (Map 354, vol. II, Part 1; Map 481, vol. II, Part 2; Map 53, vol. I, Part 1, cited in Miller 1989: 110), but not in neighboring towns. Kurath and McDavid (1961: 109-10, cited in Miller 1989: 112) cited patterns similar to Canadian raising for coastal ME and southern NH. However, Canadian raising has not been reported elsewhere in NE. Our NH speakers do not produce raised nuclei in these diphthongs.

A pattern that may be seen as similar to Canadian raising, however, has been reported in Vermont for some time. Kurath (1939–43) reported a fronted, raised nucleus of MOUTH was being overtaken by a fronted, but low production in VT. He also found that change in progress was occurring with PRICE, in that the raised nucleus was receding in favor of a lowered, more "standard" pronunciation. Work by Amblo and Roberts (1997) notes the continuation of this trend in VT in that women and younger speakers are pronouncing these vowels in a more standard-sounding way than older rural men.

4.7.   START

Some variation between the central and back variants is seen for this vowel in NH. Our older male western NH speaker produced START with the central [a], while the younger female eastern NH speaker produced it with [ɑ]. The vowel /ɑ/ before /ɹ/ appears as [ɑ] even along the ME/New Brunswick border, in spite of the contact with Canadian [ɔr] pronunciations (Miller 1989: 88). Examples include *tomorrow*, *sorry* and *borrow*. This pattern was also reported in *LANE* (Kurath 1939–43: Map 72, vol. I, Part 1 and Map 564–5, vol. III, Part 1). However, all of Miller's sixteen speakers report [ɔɹɪndʒ] for *orange* (*Miller* 1989: 89), while *LANE* (Map 273, vol. II, Part 1) reported [ɒɹɪndʒ] for this area.

4.8.   NORTH/FORCE

ENEers traditionally made a distinction between pairs like *for* and *four*, or *horse* and *hoarse*, which is not heard in most of the rest of the U.S. As a result of this distinction, combined with r-dropping, a Boston pronunciation of *short* rhymes with *shot*; *north* rhymes with *moth*. This distinction may be disappearing among young people (Labov, Ash and Boberg 2006). Our NH speakers have merged these two vowels.

Laferriere (1979: 428) defines the vowel in *short* and *forty* (NORTH) as [ɒə], in contrast to the standard [oə(ɹ)]. The words that have this vowel in standard American English are divided (apparently arbitrarily, cf. McCarthy 1999) into two classes in the Boston dialect, some of which allow this alternation and some of which use only [oə] (Laferriere 1979: 429).

4.9.   BOTHER and FATHER

Bostonians and Northern New Hampshirites generally maintain a distinction between the vowels in the first syllables of *bother* [ɑ] and *father* [a], while many residents of VT and southern NH, especially younger people, have merged those vowels (Nagy 2001). Miller's respondents (Miller 1989: 124) report that *father* and *bother* do not rhyme in Calais, ME.

4.10.   Mary, merry and marry

Many speakers in eastern MA and northern NH have three distinct pre-rhotic front vowels, differentiated in the triplet *Mary* [e:] ~ *merry* [ɛ] ~ *marry* [æ], while those in VT and southern NH pronounce the three words alike (Nagy 2001; Nagy and Roberts 1998). Miller (1989: 99) reports that most speakers in Calais, ME, have a two-way merger: for 80% of the speakers, *Mary* and *marry* are [meri] and *merry* is [mɛri]. 13% of the speakers surveyed have merged all three. (7% have slightly different two-way mergers.) This indicates a marked change from *LANE*, where a three-way distinction was maintained across NE (Miller 1989: 100).

4.11.   Mergers before L

Pre-lateral mergers that occur in other parts of the U.S. are documented as *not* occurring in NE in Labov, Ash and Boberg (fc). These include the following tense and lax vowel pairs before /l/: /i/ and /iɪ/ (*pill* and *peel*), /u/ and /uʊ/ (*pull* and *pool*), and /e/ and /eɪ/ (*well* and *wail*).

5.   Consonants

5.1.   T, D

Several types of substitutions involving the alveolar stops /t/ and /d/ appear in the New England area. These include both substitutions of spirantized variants for alveolar stops as well as alveolar stops substituting for interdental fricatives. Glottal stop replacement of /t/ (e.g., [mɪʔn̩] *mitten*, [vəɹmã̃ʔ] *Vermont*, [ɹəɪʔ ɑn] *Right on!*) in VT appears to be a robust dialect phenomenon. Although considered to be a traditional rural phenomenon most common to older male speakers, these glottal forms are found in speakers of all ages in VT. Children produced at least as many glottal stop forms as their parents, with girls producing more /ʔ/ than boys (Roberts 2001). These findings demonstrate that dialect obsolescence, common in rural areas, does not necessarily mean a change toward

"Standard English." In this case, girls appear to be leading a change toward a resurgence of glottal stop replacement. Similar findings have been reported in the United Kingdom where research on the glottal stop has been going on for years (cf. Milroy et al. 1994; Foulkes, Docherty and Watt 1999).

Nagy and Ryback-Soucy (2000) indicates the frequent use of alveolar stops /t/ and /d/ in place of interdental fricatives /θ/ and /ð/ among speakers who self-identify as members of the Franco-American community of Manchester, NH.

Finally, Miller (1989: 104) reports categorical flapping in *butter* for the speakers he surveyed in ME. *LANE* also reports flapping for most of NE (Map 496, vol. III, Part 1, cited in Miller 1989: 105). This is in keeping with the general pattern of northern AmE: categorical post-tonic flapping for all speakers (Strassell 1997).

5.2. Word-initial H

The Franco-American speakers studied in Manchester, NH, who substitute [t,d] for /θ, ð/, also variably omit word-initial H and insert an initial 10 H in underlyingly vowel-initial words (e.g., [oli hɛndʒəl aɪ] *Holy Angel High*). Interestingly, several of these speakers are monolingual Anglophones, so this is not a case of mother tongue interference in a second language, but rather a marking of cultural identity.

5.3. W/HW distinction

The distinction between word initial <wh> and <w> words, as in *which* and *witch,* is retained to some extent in parts of NH, VT, and MA (Labov 2000). This pattern was reported in *LANE* (Map 163, vol. I, Part 2, and Map 179, vol. I, Part 2, cited in Miller 1989: 108). However, the distinction was not maintained by Miller's ME speakers. Kurath and McDavid (1961: 178) mention this merger as occurring "in a narrow coastal strip of NE extending from Boston to the Kennebec in Maine."

5.4. Ju (JOD-DROPPING)

Our survey data (Nagy and Roberts 1998) show the continuing presence, mostly among older speakers, of a palatal glide or jod between alveolar consonants and [u] in words such as *new* [n(j)u] and *Tuesday* [t(j)uzdeɪ]. This was also noted by Duckert (1986: 141) as a feature of rural NE speakers. Interestingly, *LANE* shows a preference for the jod-less pronunciation even among the oldest speakers (Kurath 1939-43: Map 4, vol. I, Part 1). Sixteen speakers from Calais,

ME, surveyed in the late 1980's showed no use of the jod in either relevant survey question (the pronunciation of *during* and *reduce*) (Miller 1989:86).

5.5.   R vocalization and intrusive R

Finally, a frequently noted feature of ENE, also exhibited by speakers in the Virginia and North Carolina hearth areas, is the vocalization (popularly referred to as "dropping") of /ɹ/ in post-vocalic position. People talk about "New Hampsha" and "Woosta" for *New Hampshire* and *Worcester*. Similarly, Laferriere (1979: 431) indicates that the R-less production of START with [a:] is a marker of Boston speech. Linking R is produced: if the following word begins with a vowel, the R is rhotic (*hear it*). A related NE pattern is the appearance of inter-vocalic /ɹ/ where the standard spelling does not indicate it, referred to as intrusive R, as in [sa:ɹ ɪt] *saw it*.

According to Labov (1966), "the vocalization of /ɹ/ is eroding under the influence of the post World War II convention that constricted /ɹ/ is the appropriate standard for careful speech." However, all three Boston speakers included in Labov (2000) show some vocalization of /ɹ/, and one Bostonian shows 50%. In contrast, most of WNE shows consistent [ɹ].

Our recorded NH speakers vocalize /ɹ/ in reading the word list, in words such as CURE, LETTER, FORCE, NORTH, START, SQUARE, and NEAR. Variable vocalization is also evident in the recorded and transcribed narratives.

6.   Compound word stress

Duckert (1986: 141) reports a tendency for stress to appear on the second element of compound words such as *maple TREE*, *band CONCERT*, *polar BEAR*, and *battle FIELD* in rural NE speech. We are not sure if this pattern is constrained to NE.

7.   Summary

As we have shown, NE presents a complex linguistic profile. There are a number of both consonantal and vowel patterns that preserve the distinction between NE English and other varieties present in the U.S. Some of these features are uniformly distributed across NE, while others illustrate the maintenance of distinct dialect subregions. It appears that, as people more frequently move into the area from all over the country, New Englanders increasingly sound like other AmE speakers. However, some local features remain. Many New Englanders still "drop their r's," though no longer as consistently or in as many words as they used to. Others substitute glottal stop for T, and many retain a variety of fairly subtle vowel differences. Thus, much as found by the scholars who documented the linguistic patterns of this region in the early 20th century, both the NE dialect and its regional subdialects operate as relevant markers of NE identity today.

This chapter is an extended version of a paper written by Nagy, Roberts and Boberg for *American Language Review* (2000). We are very grateful to Charles Boberg for sharing his large bank of knowledge about American dialects with us. We are also grateful for the assistance of Joleen Hansen and Denis Jobin who recorded and transcribed the two New Hampshire speakers.

Exercises and study questions

1. What is the main division within the New England dialect? What are some of the phonological patterns that differ across this isogloss?

2. What are some similarities between New England English and other varieties? What are some differences? You might compare geographically close dialects or dialects that you have reason to believe should be similar, perhaps due to migration patterns.

3. Choose three dialects of English, including New England. Compare the production of post-vocalic /r/ across these three dialects. How are they similar? How do they differ?

4. Make a list of the words in the reading passage that have a low, front vowel. Listen to the recording and transcribe the actual pronunciation of the words you listed. Do they follow the generalizations about raising and tensing of TRAP/BATH/DANCE that are given in the chapter? Why or why not?

5. Listen to the reading passage word lists. Focus on the words with underlying /t/. For each /t/, transcribe how it is actually pronounced. You may hear [t], [ɾ], [θ], [ʔ], or [ʔt]. What patterns can you see in the distribution of these allophones?

6. Listen to the reading passage. Pay particular attention to word-initial /h/. When is the /h/ pronounced and when is it deleted? Hint: Do you see a relationship between sentence-level stress and h-deletion?

7. Listen to the word list. Which of the words in the list below share the same vowel sound? What vowel do they share? How many different vowels do you hear?
   LOT
   CLOTH
   PALM
   THOUGHT
   START
   NORTH
   FORCE

8. Do you hear any words with this/these vowel(s) in the reading passage?

9. There are three words that sound the same for some speakers: *Mary*, *merry*, and *marry*. Make up two sentences containing each word. Given the sentences you created, what clues do speakers use to distinguish these three words? Do you think that speakers who pronounce these words the same have trouble conveying their meaning? (Hint: Think about the lexical category of each word.)

Selected references

Please consult the General references for titles mentioned in the text but not included in the references below. For a full bibliography see the accompanying CD-ROM.

Amblo, Rebecca and Julie Roberts
    1997   Change and obsolescence in rural Vermont: /aw/, /ay/, and /uw/ in younger and older speakers. Paper presented at NWAV (New Ways of Analyzing Variation) Conference. Laval, Université Laval.
Avis, Walter
    1961   The New England short o: A recessive phoneme. *Language* 37: 544–558.
Boberg, Charles
    2001   The phonological status of Western New England. *American Speech* 76: 1–29.
Duckert, Audrey A.
    1986   The speech of rural New England. In: Allen and Linn (eds.), 136–141.
Foulkes, Paul, Gerry Docherty, and Dominic Watt
    1999   Tracking the emergence of structured variation. *Leeds Working Papers in Linguistics and Phonetics*. Leeds, University of Leeds: 1–25.

Frazer, Timothy C.
  1983   Sound change and social structure in a rural community. *Language in Society* 12: 313–328.
Kurath, Hans
  1928   The origin of the dialectal differences in spoken American English. *Modern Philology* 25: 385–95.
Labov, William
  1991   The three dialects of English. In: Eckert (ed.), 1–44.
Laferriere, Martha
  1977   Boston short *a*: Social variation as historical residue. In: Fasold and Shuy (eds.), 100–107.
  1979   Ethnicity in phonological variation in change. *Language* 55: 603–617.
McCarthy, John
  1999   The dialects of Eastern New England. Linguistics 402 course handout. http://www-unix.oit.umass.edu/~jjmccart/ling402f01/11-Boston%20Vowels.pdf
Miller, Corey
  1989   The United States-Canadian border as a linguistic boundary: The English language in Calais, Maine and St. Stephen, New Brunswick. Undergraduate thesis, Linguistics Department. Cambridge, MA, Harvard University.
Milroy, Lesley, James Milroy, Sue Hartley, and David Walshaw
  1994   Glottal stops and Tyneside variation: Competing patterns of variation and change in British English. *Language Variation and Change* 6: 327–357.
Nagy, Naomi
  2001   'Live free or die' as a linguistic principle. *American Speech* 76: 30–41.
Nagy, Naomi and Julie Roberts
  1998   Yankee doodles in dialectography: Updating New England. Paper presented at NWAV (New Ways of Analyzing Variation) Conference University of Georgia.
Nagy, Naomi, Julie Roberts and Charles Boberg
  2000   Yakking with the Yankees. *American Language Review* 5: 40–43.
  2002   *McGill-VT-NH Dialect Survey*. Unpublished research instrument.
Nagy, Naomi and Wendy Ryback-Soucy
  2000   Exploring the dialect of the Franco-Americans of Manchester, New Hampshire. *Journal of English Linguistics* 28: 249–264.
Ring, Wilson
  1997   Time erodes all including traditional Vermont accent. *The Caledonian Record*: 2/15/1997: 1A, 12A.
Roberts, Julie
  1997   /ow/ movement and chain shift: An example from rural Vermont speech. Paper presented at NWAV (New Ways of Analyzing Variation) Conference, Laval, Canada.
  2001   An American variable? A continuing study of glottal stop in Vermont. Paper presented at NWAV (New Ways of Analyzing Variation) Conference, North Carolina State University, Durham, NC.

Rosenberry, Lois Kimball Mathews
    1962   *The Expansion of New England.* New York: Russell and Russell.
Strassell, S.
    1997   Variation in American English flapping. In Claude Paradis, Diane Vincent,
                Denis Deshaies and Marty Laforest (eds.), *Papers in Sociolinguistics -
                NWAVE-26 à l'Université* Laval, 125–35. Quebec: Nota bene.

New York, Philadelphia, and other northern cities: phonology

Matthew J. Gordon

1. Introduction

This chapter describes characteristic features of accents heard in some of the largest cities in the United States. The discussion considers two eastern cities, New York and Philadelphia, as well as the area around the Great Lakes which includes Chicago, Detroit, Cleveland, and Buffalo. In terms of the traditional dialectological classification, these locations represent a mixture of dialects (Kurath 1949). Philadelphia is squarely within the Midland region, while New York City is grouped as part of the North but is seen as constituting its own subregion. The Great Lakes area represents the core of the Inland North, a subregion of Northern speech that stretches from western New England to roughly the Mississippi River.

Compared to other varieties in the U.S. and elsewhere, the dialects discussed here have been studied quite extensively by linguists. This is particularly true in the case of New York which has attracted regular dialectological interest since Babbitt's 1896 report (e.g., Hubbell 1950; Thomas 1942). Much of the research on New York speech, as well as on that of Philadelphia and the Inland North, has focussed on the kinds of traditional features studied by dialect geographers. This information is valuable, but a description of contemporary speech patterns will also benefit from a more dynamic perspective, one that considers changing usage of older features as well as adoption of recent innovations. For this reason, much of the description here relies on sociolinguistic research, especially the work of William Labov who has written on New York City (1966), Philadelphia (2001), and the changes operating in the Inland North (Labov, Ash and Boberg 2006). Sociolinguistic research of this type is particularly well suited to the investigation of the speech of large urban areas because it examines a broad spectrum of the community of speakers rather than concentrating on any one segment of society. Still, even the best sociolinguistic studies cannot fully consider the rich social diversity of the populations of major cities like those discussed here. As a general caveat, therefore, it should be noted that the features described below characterize the speech of some, but certainly not all, people of these areas.

2.   Historical overview

Current dialect patterns often reflect historical trends. Among the forces shaping the American dialect landscape, particular attention is often paid to early settlement history. In the present case, settlement history can shine some light on the current dialect situation, at least on the general patterns if not on the occurrence of particular linguistic features. Some of the broad outlines of that history are sketched here.

During the colonial period, New York and Philadelphia came to represent economic hubs in the "Middle Colonies". They got their start as English colonies somewhat later than Massachusetts and Virginia. New York was a Dutch possession until 1664, and Pennsylvania was founded in 1680. From the earliest days, emigration to the Middle Colonies attracted a diverse population. This was especially true in Pennsylvania where the Quaker ideals of founder William Penn promoted religious and ethnic tolerance. In the colonial period and into the nineteenth century the most significant immigration, in addition to the British, was from Ireland and Germany. Toward the end of the nineteenth century, New York and Philadelphia (like other American cities) saw increasing immigration from southern and eastern Europe. Immigrants often settled in ethnically segregated neighborhoods such as the Irish neighborhood of Kensington in Philadelphia or New York's Little Italy. The ethnic character of many of these areas remains evident today, and studies have demonstrated that the sociolinguistic effect of ethnic identity endures as well (see Labov 1966, 2001). Even more sociolinguistically salient is the ethnic diversity contributed by the influx of African Americans from the South and, especially in New York, of Puerto Ricans and other Caribbeans in the twentieth century, though a description of the unique features of the accents of these groups is not attempted in this chapter.

With the exception of Upstate New York, the area of the Inland North was not heavily settled by Americans until after the establishment of the United States. Federal ordinances in 1785 and 1787 set into motion a process which eventually carved the "Northwest Territory" into the states of Ohio, Indiana, Michigan, Illinois, and Wisconsin. Many of the immigrants to the northern half of this region came from New England. Settlement of the area received a great boost from the opening of the Erie Canal in 1825 which connected the Hudson River with Lake Erie. The canal served not only to bring settlers from the East to the Inland North, but also to bring grain and other agricultural goods from the Inland North to markets in the East and abroad. In fact, the canal contributed greatly to New York City's rise to prominence as the business capital of America. Along the Great Lakes, cities like Milwaukee, Chicago, Detroit, and Cleveland grew rapidly in the nineteenth century, helped in part by foreign immigration as was the case in Philadelphia and New York. Curiously, the urban centers of the Inland North display little regional linguistic variation; the same basic accent features are heard from Buffalo to Milwaukee. By contrast, distinctive dialect features are found in New York and Philadelphia as well as in many of the cities of the Midland region including Pittsburgh, Cincinnati, and St. Louis. It is possible that the relative uniformity of speech in the Inland North stems from the original settlement, consisting mainly of New Englanders, but it may also be related to the rapid growth of the cities and their economic interdependence which could have promoted a leveling of dialect differences through the spread of a regional standard.

From these brief historical notes, we turn to a description of the accents. We consider first New York City before moving on to Philadelphia, then the Inland North.

3. New York City

The speech of New York City holds a special place in American public consciousness. New York together with the South top most Americans' lists of places with the most recognizable accents. Unfortunately for speakers of these accents, this salience comes from stigmatization. For outsiders, New York speech is often associated with toughness, lack of education, and "street smarts". This is the stereotype conveyed by the popular label "Brooklynese", which, in keeping with other cultural stereotypes, situates "true" New York speech outside Manhattan. The label raises the issue of potential differences across the five boroughs of the city. Some locals claim to be able to distinguish a Bronx speaker from a Brooklynite or a Staten Islander. The linguistics literature on New York speech does not recognize any consistent interborough differences though, in truth, the question has not been studied thoroughly. Of course, New York City does not lack for linguistic variation of other types. Indeed, with a socially diverse population of over eight million people, it is clearly a fiction to talk of *a* New York accent. The discussion of accent features below includes some comments about sociolinguistic variation, but readers are reminded of the earlier caveat about the diversity of accents in a city of this size.

3.1. Lexical incidence

With many of the traditional regional markers of pronunciation, New York City shows a mix of influences – not a particularly surprising finding given its location on the border between the Northern and Midland dialect regions. For example, using data from the Linguistic Atlas projects and therefore representing speakers born in the late 19th century, Kurath and McDavid (1961) report a roughly even mixture of /i/ and /ɪ/ in *creek* for New Yorkers. For *root*, the Midland (and Southern) /u/ was more common than the Northern /ʊ/. On the other hand, *on* normally shows /ɑ/ for New Yorkers as it does generally in the North. For the highly variable class of "short *o*" words with /g/, New Yorkers tend to have /ɑ/ in *hog*, *frog*, *fog*, and *log*, but /ɔ/ in *dog*. Among the more geographically restricted items, Kurath and McDavid (1961) note the pronunciation of *won't* with /u/ as a feature of New York City (as well as the Eastern Shore of Maryland and the Carolina coast). They note a tendency for "cultured" speakers to avoid the /u/ variant, and the form is apparently less common today. Another lexical peculiarity, the use of /ʌ/ in *donkey*, continues to be heard from New Yorkers.

3.2.   Vowels

New York speech was historically non-rhotic but has become increasingly r-pronouncing over the last half century (see below). The presence or absence of postvocalic /r/ typically has profound effects on vowel quality in dialects of English. In New York City, however, these effects seem to be less significant. For example, the inglides that are typical of non-rhotic speech (e.g., [nɪə] *near*; [skwɛə] *square*) may remain in New York speech even among rhotic speakers (e.g., [nɪəɹ] *near*; [skwɛəɹ] *square*) (Wells 1982: 506). In this overview whatever differences of vowel quality exist between rhotic and non-rhotic speakers are ignored and interested readers may refer to the specialist literature for further details.

KIT	ɪ	PALM	ɑə ~ ɒə	FORCE	o ~ ɔə
DRESS	ɛ	THOUGHT	ɔ ~ ɔə ~ ʊə	CURE	ʊə
TRAP	æ ~ æə ~ ɛə ~ɪə	GOAT	oʊ	happY	i
LOT	ɑ ~ ɑə	GOAL	oʊ	lettER	ə
STRUT	ʌ	GOOSE	ʊu ~ u: ~ ɪu	horsES	ɪ ~ ɨ ~ ə
FOOT	ʊ	PRICE	ɑɪ ~ ɒɪ	commA	ə
BATH	æə ~ ɛə ~ɪə	CHOICE	ɔɪ	TOMORROW	ɑ
CLOTH	ɔ ~ ɔə ~ ʊə	MOUTH	aʊ ~ æʊ	ORANGE	ɑ
NURSE	ɜ	NEAR	ɪə	MARRY	æ
DANCE	æə ~ ɛə ~ ɪə	SQUARE	ɛə	MERRY	ɛ
FLEECE	ɪi ~ i:	START	ɑə ~ ɒə	MARY	e ~ ɛ ~ɛə
FACE	eɪ ~ ɛɪ	NORTH	o ~ ɔə		

TRAP, BATH, DANCE

In New York City, and elsewhere in the Mid-Atlantic region, the historical "short *a*" vowel class is split into two phonemes. The complicated distribution of these phonemes, labeled here lax /æ/ and tense /æə/, is defined by phonological, morphological, and lexical patterns. The lax /æ/ occurs consistently before voiceless stops, /tʃ/, and /l/ (e.g., *cat, lap, back, match, pal*). The tense /æə/ generally occurs before voiced stops, /dʒ/, voiceless fricatives, and front nasals (e.g., *bad, badge, bath, ham, dance*). If, however, the vowel is followed by an unstressed syllable, the choice of phoneme depends on the morphological status of that syllable. The tense vowel appears when the syllable is a separate morpheme as in the case of an inflectional suffix (e.g., *badges, dragging*). The lax vowel appears when the unstressed syllable is part of the root morpheme (e.g., *clamor, dragon*). Function words such as *an, am, can* and *had* are exceptions to the phonological rule as they occur with lax phoneme. Thus, the auxiliary *can* and the noun *can* (as in the metal container) form a minimal pair for the lax/tense contrast. In the environments of a following voiced fricative or /ŋ/ (e.g., *jazz, bang*) the occurrence of /æ/ and /æə/ is variable. Before /v/, for example, the lax phoneme predominates, but *avenue*, in which /æə/ is usual, stands as a lexical exception. More details about the patterning of these phonemes can be found in Labov (1994: 335) and Labov, Yaeger, and Steiner (1972: 48–52).

Phonetically the tense phoneme is distinguished from the lax by lengthening and raising. The vowel often appears as an ingliding diphthong with the nucleus varying in height from [æ] to [ɪ]. Labov (1966) found the height of this vowel to vary sociolinguistically. The higher variants (i.e., [ɪə] ~ [ɛə]) occur more commonly among speakers from the lower end of the socioeconomic hierarchy and in less formal speaking styles.

LOT

As in other American dialects, the vowel in these items is most often [ɑ]. However, a subset of LOT items features a lengthened and diphthongized variant, [ɑə]. This variant may appear before a word final voiced stop, /dʒ/, or /m/ (e.g., *cob, cod, cog, lodge, bomb*). It also occurs variably before voiced fricatives (e.g., *bother*), /ʃ/ (e.g., *wash*), and in the words *on, John*, and *doll* (Wells 1982: 514).

CLOTH, THOUGHT

One of the more distinctive features of New York speech involves the raising of the vowel in the THOUGHT and CLOTH classes. Labov (1966) describes this pattern as varying on a scale from [ɔ] to [ʊ]. An inglide typically accompanies

higher variants, giving [oə] or [ʊə]. Labov (1994) has suggested that this raising may form part of a chain shift with the backing and raising of the PALM
vowel. The sociolinguistic patterning seen with /ɔ/ is less consistent than in the
case of /æ/ tensing. Labov's (1966) data on casual speech style show raising of
/ɔ/ to be more prevalent among middle and working class New Yorkers than
among the lower class, but the pattern is reversed in more formal contexts. Still,
there are similarities between the sociolinguistic distribution of the THOUGHT/
CLOTH variation and that of TRAP/DANCE. These similarities combined with
the fact that phonetically the changes present a mirror image suggest that they
may arise out of a kind of parallelism.

NURSE
One of the stereotypes of New York speech is the use of a front-rising diphthong in NURSE words. This stereotype is popularly represented in stock phrases like 'toity toid' for *thirty third*. The phonetic reality of this variant is near
[ɜɪ]. The variant may also appear in the CHOICE class, resulting in *verse* and
voice as homophones. The diphthongal variant in NURSE is highly stigmatized.
Labov's data from the mid-1960s indicated the form was recessive then. Only
2 of his 51 speakers under age 20 used the form as compared with those over
age 50 of whom 23 out of 30 used the form. CHOICE items may occur with [ɜɹ]
(e.g., [tɜɹlət] *toilet*), apparently as a result of hypercorrection.

FACE
The usual realization of this vowel is [eɪ] though a lax variant, [ɛɪ], has been
reported in words with a following /l/ (e.g., *sailor*).

GOOSE
The usual vowel in this class is either the monophthong [uː] or the diphthong
[ʊu]. Some speakers appear to have a separate phoneme, /ɪu/, in words such
as *tune*, *news*, *duke* (historically a separate class). The phonemic status of this
vowel is marginal. For example, Labov (1966) reports that New Yorkers may
contrast [duː] *do* with [dɪu] *dew* though they may also have [dɪu] *do*. Still, *dew*
is always [dɪu] and never [duː].

PRICE, MOUTH
The diphthongs in these items exhibit the tendency toward nucleus-glide differentiation, a pattern common in many varieties of English. The nucleus of the
back-gliding vowel in MOUTH is fronted while that of the front-gliding PRICE
is backed. The sociolinguistic evidence (Labov 1966) suggests that both of

these developments are active changes. The fronted nucleus in MOUTH and the backed nucleus in PRICE are more common among younger speakers, women, and the working and lower middle classes.

NORTH, FORCE

The historical distinction between these vowels has been lost in New York speech as is increasingly the case in other American dialects. Indeed, the Mid-Atlantic region was one of the areas in which the Linguistic Atlas researchers recorded this merger, a fact that suggests the merger has characterized New York speech since at least the late 19th century. The merged vowel is often recorded as [ɔə] but recent acoustic evidence suggests it may be closer to [oə] or even higher. Labov (1994) suggests it forms the second stage in a chain shift spurred by the backing and raising of START.

START, PALM

The vowel of these items is variously transcribed as [ɑ], [ɑ:], [ɑə], or [ɒə]. It is generally treated as phonemically distinct from the LOT class. Thus, even among non-rhotic speakers *cart* and *cot* remain distinct. The START/PALM vowel is often backed and may be raised as well. Labov (1994) suggests it operates as part of a chain shift with the raising of CLOTH/THOUGHT and NORTH/FORCE.

TOMORROW, ORANGE

In both of these sets, the usual vowel is the unrounded [ɑ]. In the case of ORANGE, this pronunciation distinguishes New York speech from that of other American dialects in which the NORTH/FORCE vowel is heard.

MARRY, MERRY, MARY

New York speech shows either a two- or three-way contrast among /æ/, /ɛ/, and /e/ before intervocalic /r/. MARRY is generally distinct with a low [æ]. MERRY and MARY may be merged at [ɛ] or the latter may remain distinct either as [e] or something like [ɛə].

3.3.   Consonants

R

One of the most salient stereotypes of New York City speech is *r*-lessness. The pattern resembles that heard in eastern New England as well as in southern England. Non-prevocalic /r/ is vocalized, yielding pronunciations such as [hɪə] *here* and [kɑət] *cart*. Word final /r/ is pronounced when the following word begins with a vowel (e.g., [hɪəɹ ɪn] *here in*). Also, non-etymological, "intrusive" /r/ may appear and is especially common in *idea* and *law*.

The non-rhotic status of the New York accent was noted by the Linguistic Atlas researchers and other early observers. *R*-lessness was characteristic of New Yorkers of all social levels through roughly the first half of the twentieth century. At some point, however, non-rhotic speech became stigmatized, and *r*-fulness appeared in the speech of many New Yorkers. By the time of Labov's study in the mid-1960s, /r/ had become a strong class marker with *r*-lessness being more common among the lower and working classes. Today, /r/ continues to divide New Yorkers along class lines though the trend toward rhoticity appears to be progressing.

TH

As in many other dialects, the interdental fricatives /θ/ and /ð/ are often realized as stops, [t] and [d] or affricates [tθ] and [dð]. Labov (1966) found this alternation to vary by class with the non-fricative forms appearing more regularly in lower and working class speech. Unlike the reported changes with /r/, the variation with /θ/ and /ð/ appears to be stable.

Alveolars

The alveolar consonants /t/, /d/, /n/, and /l/ may be articulated with the tongue blade rather than the tip. Wells (1982) indicates that this articulation may, in some cases, also involve affrication, producing [ts] and [dz]. With /t/, glottalization is reported to be more common in New York speech than in other American dialects, appearing, for example, before syllabic /l/ (e.g., *bottle* [baʔl̩]).

NG

In addition to the ubiquitous alternation of [ŋ] and [n] in *–ing* endings, the speech of some New Yorkers shows [ŋg] as a variant of /ŋ/. This variant is another salient stereotype of the New York accent and is commonly mocked in the pronunciation [lɔŋgaɪlənd] *Long Island*.

WH

The historical distinction between /hw/ and /w/ (e.g., *which* vs. *witch*) has been lost in New York as throughout much of the US. The merger seems to have taken hold in the Mid-Atlantic region relatively early as this area was reported as merged by the Linguistic Atlas researchers.

HJU

In words like *human* and *huge*, which begin with an /hj/ cluster, the /h/ is commonly deleted giving [jumən] and [jud͡ʒ].

L

Vocalization of /l/ is common in New York though it is perhaps not as pervasive as in other dialects. Like its fellow liquid /r/, it may be vocalized when appearing in non-prevocalic contexts (e.g., [sɛo] sell, [mɪok] milk).

4.   Philadelphia

The speech of Philadelphia has not attracted the kind of public awareness (outside the local area) that New York City has. Among linguists, however, Philadelphia is known for a number of intriguing speech features. Much of the city's linguistic notoriety is due to the work of William Labov, who, with the help of his students at the University of Pennsylvania, has been studying the great diversity of Philadelphia speech over the last three decades. Indeed, it is fair to say that Philadelphia is the most richly documented and thoroughly studied speech community certainly in the U.S. and probably in the world. The discussion here presents an overview of several important aspects of the Philadelphia accent; interested readers can find much more complete accounts in the specialist literature (Labov 2001; Tucker 1944).

4.1.   Lexical incidence

According to the traditional dialect geography of Kurath (1949), Philadelphia is located squarely in the Midland area, and in many ways it fits well into this neighborhood. For example, /u/ is commonly the vowel of *root*. It does, however, show exceptions to the usual Midland forms in a number of cases. For example, the Linguistic Atlas records suggest /ɑ/ is the usual vowel in *frog*, *hog*, and *fog* with /ɔ/ in *dog* – a pattern resembling that of the North. Also, Philadelphia has been noted as exceptional in featuring, at least among some speakers, the Northern /ɑ/ in *on* as opposed to the /ɔ/ that is heard in the Midland and the South (Kurath and McDavid 1961). The use of /ʌ/ as the stressed vowel in *donkey*, a pronunciation noted for New Yorkers, is also found in Philadelphia. Finally, regarding the well known pattern of consonant variation between /s/ and /z/ in *grease* and *greasy*, Philadelphia was identified as a transitional area between the generally Southern /z/ and the generally Northern /s/.

4.2.   Vowels

The vowels in Philadelphia speech show a remarkable degree of volatility. Labov's extensive research has identified changes affecting over half of the vowel phonemes. In regional terms, Philadelphia shows an interesting mixture of Southern and Northern patterns.

KIT	ɪ ~ ɪ̞	PALM	ɑ	FORCE	o ~ ʊ
DRESS	ɛ ~ ɛ̞	THOUGHT	ɔ ~ ɔ̝ə ~ oə	CURE	ʊ
TRAP	æ ~ æə ~ ɛə~ ɪə	GOAT	oʊ ~ ɜʊ	happY	i
LOT	ɑ	GOAL	oʊ	lettER	ə
STRUT	ʌ ~ ʌ̞	GOOSE	uː ~ ʉu	horsES	ɪ ~ ɨ ~ ʌ̵
FOOT	ʊ ~ ü	PRICE	aɪ ~ ʌe	commA	ə
BATH	æə ~ ɛə ~ ɪə	CHOICE	ɔɪ ~ ʊɪ	TOMORROW	ɑ
CLOTH	ɔ ~ɔ̝ə ~ oə	MOUTH	aʊ ~ æɔ ~ ɛɔ	ORANGE	ɑ
NURSE	ɜ	NEAR	iə	MARRY	æ
DANCE	æə ~ ɛə ~ ɪə	SQUARE	ɛə	MERRY	ɛ ~ʌ
FLEECE	iː	START	ɑ ~ ɒ ~ ɔ	MARY	e ~ ɛ
FACE	e ~ eɪ̞ ~ ɪ̞ɪ	NORTH	o ~ ʊ		

KIT, DRESS

Labov's research has indicated a tendency toward lowering of the lax vowels in KIT and DRESS. This pattern is not yet well established and is labeled by Labov as an "incipient" change.

TRAP, BATH, DANCE

Philadelphia shows the same split of the historical "short a" class described above for New York City, though the conditioning of the tense phoneme differs somewhat, appearing in a more limited set of phonological contexts. In Philadelphia the tense /æə/ occurs regularly only before /m/, /n/, /f/, /θ/, and /s/. Thus, one of the ways of distinguishing the New York pattern from the Philadelphia one is in the context of a following voiced stop. Items such as *cab*, *sad*, *bag*, and *badge* have the tense phoneme in New York but the lax phoneme in Philadelphia. There are, however, three lexical exceptions: *mad*, *bad*, and *glad* appear with the tense vowel in Philadelphia. As in New York, tensing is sensitive to morphology. The tense vowel normally appears only in closed syllables but does occur in open syllables resulting from inflectional suffixes. For example, *manner* has the lax vowel but *manning* (e.g., *Who is manning the store?*) has the tense phoneme as does *man*. Also, the tense vowel does not appear in function words (e.g., *an*, auxiliary *can*). Phonetically the tense class shows the same realizations here as in New York, varying in height to the high front position and typically diphthongized with an inglide.

STRUT

The STRUT vowel may show raised and backed variants. In some cases the vowel is in the high, back corner of vowel space near /u/. This is reportedly a recent development and is one more common among male speakers.

FOOT

The vowel of FOOT is sometimes fronted though not to the degree seen with the GOAT and GOOSE classes.

CLOTH, THOUGHT

Another speech feature shared by Philadelphians and New Yorkers is the raising of /ɔ/ to [o] or even higher. The raised variants often appear as diphthongs with a centering glide. Labov's research suggest that this pattern of raising is essentially complete in Philadelphia and seems no longer to be an active change.

FLEECE

Early descriptions of Philadelphia speech indicate lowered and/or laxed variants of FLEECE were common. The recent sociolinguistic evidence indicates a reversal of this trend such that the vowel is now commonly raised and fronted. This raising is heard primarily in "checked" contexts; i.e., when the vowel is followed by a consonant (e.g., *eat*).

FACE

The Linguistic Atlas researchers recorded lax variants of the FACE vowel near [ɛɪ]. As with FLEECE, recent research suggests this trend is being reversed by raising and fronting of the vowel often to a position well beyond [e]. This raising occurs primarily in "checked" contexts (e.g., *ate*).

GOAT, GOOSE

One of the features that Philadelphia shares with Southern dialects (and one absent from New York speech) is the fronting of the GOAT and GOOSE vowels. Generally greater degrees of fronting are heard when the vowels appear in "free" positions (i.e., without a following consonant) than in "checked" positions (i.e., with a following consonant). Fronting does not occur in the context of following liquids leading to significant separation of, e.g., the GOAT and GOAL classes. The fronting of GOAT and GOOSE is well established in Philadelphia, though cross-generational data show that it remains an active change.

PRICE

The diphthong of PRICE may begin with a nucleus of mid or even higher position. The raising appears only before voiceless obstruents, and thus resembles the process known as "Canadian Raising" (see Boberg, this volume). The sociolinguistic evidence suggests this raising is a fairly recent addition to Philadelphia speech.

MOUTH

Fronted nuclei in the diphthong of MOUTH are well established in Philadelphia speech as in New York. More recent research has noted a tendency among Philadelphians to raise the vowel, resulting in [ɛɔ].

START, NORTH, FORCE

Many Philadelphians use a rather high and back vowel in START, something near [ɔ]. The NORTH and FORCE classes are merged and typically appear with a mid to high back vowel. As noted in the discussion of New York, these tendencies toward backing and raising of START and NORTH/FORCE may constitute a chain shift. The evidence suggests the movement of START began this shift, and this vowel is relatively stable today, while generational differences are heard in the shifting of NORTH/FORCE.

TOMORROW, ORANGE

For Philadelphians, as for New Yorkers, the usual vowel in both these sets is the unrounded [ɑ].

MARRY, MERRY, MARY

The Linguistic Atlas records reported a two-way contrast for these vowels with /æ/ in MARRY and /ɛ/ in MERRY and MARY. More recent evidence indicates that MERRY and MARY remain separate in Philadelphia. Further supporting these reports of a contrast is the observation that MERRY items often appear with something like [ʌ], which results in a merger (or close approximation) of *merry ~ Murray, ferry ~ furry*, etc.

4.3.   Consonants

R

Philadelphia is situated in the middle of the only traditionally rhotic area of the Atlantic states. This area runs from Pennsylvania and New Jersey down to Delaware and Northern Maryland, and remains r-pronouncing today.

STR-

In word-initial clusters involving /str/ (e.g., *street*), the /s/ may be realized as a hushing sibilant, approaching [ʃ] in some cases.

TH

As in other areas, the interdental fricatives /θ/ and /ð/ are often realized as stops, [t] and [d] or affricates [tθ] and [dð] in Philadelphia speech. This variation appears to be a stable class-stratified feature with the non-fricative forms appearing more commonly in working class speech.

NG

Philadelphians display the usual variation between [ŋ] and [n] in *–ing* forms. As elsewhere, [n] appears more frequently in casual speech and does not appear to be undergoing change.

L

Vocalization of /l/ is quite pervasive in Philadelphia speech. Phonetically it may be realized as something like [o] or a velar or labio-velar glide, [ɰ] or [w], or the consonant may be deleted altogether. Among Philadelphians, as in other dialects, vocalization occurs quite frequently in word-final and pre-consonantal contexts (e.g., *mill, milk*). In a more unusual development, vocalization also may occur intervocalically in Philadelphia. This tendency is more common when /l/ appears following low vowels bearing primary word stress (e.g., *hollow*). This variable also shows some lexical conditioning, appearing, for example, with exceptionally high frequency in the pronunciation of the name of the city (Ash 1997).

WH

As in New York and elsewhere, the historical distinction between /hw/ and /w/ (e.g., *which* vs. *witch*) has been lost in Philadelphia.

5.   The Inland North

Many Americans might assume a description of Inland Northern speech to be unnecessary since in popular consciousness this region is known for its supposed lack of distinctive accent features. Together with the rest of the Midwest and West it represents the home of the "General American" accent. This label originally served to mark an accent lacking the features of the South and the Northeast. Dialectologists today have largely rejected the grouping of the area from Pennsylvania across the Great Lakes and the Midwest and westward to the Pacific as a single dialect, noting rightly the great diversity in speech habits within the region. Still, the notion of a General American dialect remains active in folk perceptions of American speech and represents a norm, a way of speaking that is unmarked regionally and socially. In fact, Inland Northern speech was actively promoted as a national standard. It is the variety described by John Kenyon in his popular textbook *American Pronunciation*, first published in 1924 (with multiple editions following). The dialect also became a model for the broadcast media, serving as the basis for the *NBC Handbook of Pronunciation* which first appeared in 1943. This sense that their speech represents a national standard remains strong today among Northerners despite the introduction there of a number of pronunciation features that distinguish Inland Northern voices from those heard in the national media.

5.1.   Lexical incidence

The Linguistic Atlas researchers identified a number of pronunciations as characteristic of the Northern dialect region. Many of these retain some currency in the Inland North today. One of the best known of these is the use of /ɑ/ in *on* as opposed to the Midland and Southern /ɔ/. The unrounded /ɑ/ also appears in *hog, fog,* and *frog,* while *dog* and *log* generally have /ɔ/. In *root* and *roof,* many Northerners use /ʊ/ though /u/ is also heard. The use of /ɪ/ in *creek,* traditionally very common in the North, has largely given way to /i/, and the lax vowel usage is often stigmatized.

5.2.   Vowels

The most significant vocalic features of the Inland North are those patterns of variation associated with the Northern Cities Shift. This phenomenon affects the KIT, DRESS, TRAP/BATH/DANCE, LOT/PALM, STRUT, and CLOTH/THOUGHT classes. The Shift is discussed in a separate section below. Considered here are other characteristics of the Northern vowels.

KIT	ɪ ~ ɪ̯ ~ ɪ̱	PALM	ɑ ~ ɑ̟ ~ a	FORCE	o
DRESS	ɛ ~ ɛ̝ ~ ɛ̱ ~ ɐ	THOUGHT	ɔ ~ ɒ ~ ɑ	CURE	ʊ
TRAP	æ ~ æə ~ ɛə ~ ɪə	GOAT	oʊ ~ öʊ ~ oː	happY	i
LOT	ɑ ~ ɑ̟ ~ a	GOAL	oʊ ~ o̝ː	lettER	ə
STRUT	ɜ ~ ʌ ~ ɔ	GOOSE	uː ~ ʉ	horsES	ɪ ~ ɨ ~ ə
FOOT	ʊ ~ ü	PRICE	aɪ ~ ɜɪ	commA	ə

BATH	æ ~ æə ~ ɛə ~ ɪə	CHOICE	ɔɪ ~ ɔɪ	TOMORROW	ɑ
CLOTH	ɔ ~ ɒ ~ ɑ	MOUTH	aʊ ~ ɜʊ	ORANGE	o ~ ɔ
NURSE	ɜ	NEAR	i	MARRY	ɛ
DANCE	æ ~ æə ~ ɛə ~ ɪə	SQUARE	ɛ	MERRY	ɛ
FLEECE	iː	START	ɑ ~ ɑ̟ ~ a	MARY	ɛ
FACE	eɪ ~ eː	NORTH	o ~ ɔ		

FOOT, GOAT, GOAL, GOOSE
As elsewhere in American English, these back vowels may undergo fronting. However, in the Inland North this fronting is generally less extreme than in other varieties. Acoustic data suggest GOOSE is more advanced than either GOAT or FOOT. Fronting is not usual in the context of following liquids, e.g., GOAL. In some areas, GOAT and GOAL appear with long monophthongs as they do in the Upper Midwest (see Gordon, this volume) and Canada (see Boberg, this volume).

FACE
Parallel with GOAT/GOAL, the mid front vowel of FACE may be produced as a long monophthong [eː].

PRICE, MOUTH
The pattern known as "Canadian Raising" is often heard in the Inland North. This results in mid nuclei of the diphthongs, near [ɜɪ] and [ɜu], in the context of following voiceless obstruents. Raised forms appear to be more geographically widespread in PRICE than in MOUTH.

NORTH, FORCE
The Linguistic Atlas researchers (Kurath and McDavid 1961) identified the North as an area that maintained the contrast between /ɔr/ NORTH and /or/ FORCE. This historical distinction is now largely gone with a vowel near [o] appearing in both classes.

MARRY, MERRY, MARY
As in most varieties of American English outside the Atlantic coast, the MARRY, MERRY, and MARY classes are pronounced with the same vowel, something near [ɛ].

The Northern Cities Shift
The most significant characteristic of Inland North speech today is the set of pronunciations associated with the Northern Cities Shift (NCS). The NCS de-

scribes a series of sound changes affecting six vowel phonemes. These changes are:

- KIT: /ɪ/ is backed and/or lowered to approach [ə] in extreme cases.
- DRESS: /ɛ/ is backed and/or lowered resulting in forms such as [ɚ], [ɜ], or [ɐ].
- STRUT: /ɜ/ ~ /ʌ/ is backed and may also be rounded resulting in [ɔ].
- TRAP/BATH/DANCE: /æ/ is fronted and raised to a mid or high position and is often produced with an inglide; i.e., [ɛə] or [ɪə]. Phonetically these variants resemble those described above for tense /æə/ in New York and Philadelphia.
- LOT/PALM: /ɑ/ is fronted to near /a/.
- CLOTH/THOUGHT: /ɔ/ is lowered and/or fronted, often with unrounding, to something near [ɑ].

The changes in the NCS are often represented as in figure 1 where the arrows indicate the main trajectories of the shifting vowels.

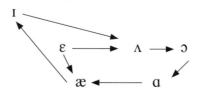

Figure 1.   The Northern Cities Shift

The NCS appears to be a fairly recent addition to the speech of the Inland North. Linguists first noticed the pattern in the late 1960s though the dialect literature provides evidence that some of the individual changes had been active for at least several decades earlier. For example, the Linguistic Atlas researchers noted the fronting of /ɑ/ as a feature of the Inland North, and studies of college students in the 1930s reported /æ/ raising and /ɛ/ centralization as characteristics of Upstate New York (Thomas 1935–37). Regardless of when the NCS began, it seems clear that it underwent a great expansion, geographically and phonologically, in the second half of the twentieth century.

The order in which the individual pieces of the NCS appeared is a matter of some debate, but it seems clear that the changes to /æ/, /ɑ/, and /ɔ/ are older than the others. One scenario holds that the shift started with the fronting and raising of /æ/, which drew /ɑ/ forward, which in turn drew /ɔ/ down and forward. The shifting of /ɛ/ and /ɪ/ began later and their centralizing movement may have sparked the final piece, the backing of /ɜ/ ~/ʌ/. The chronology of these changes is of great theoretical interest because they appear to form a chain shift. Chain shifting describes a series of related changes in which movement of one vowel causes movement in another. Representations like figure 1 make clear the apparent interactions among the shifting vowels. The scenario sketched here for the low vowels describes a "drag chain" where a vowel moves into an empty space vacated by a neighboring vowel. The alternative is a "push chain" where a vowel shifts into another's space causing the latter to shift to avoid crowding. The interaction between DRESS and STRUT appears to illustrate a push chain.

The changes associated with the NCS operate unconditionally in the sense that the vowels may be shifted in any phonological context. By way of comparison, we might recall that in New York and Philadelphia, for example, the TRAP/BATH/DANCE vowel undergoes raising only in particular environments. In the NCS, by contrast, all instances of this phoneme are potentially subject to raising. Nevertheless, phonological context does play a role in shaping the NCS variation. For each of the shifting vowels, there are some phonological environments that favor the change and others that disfavor the change. Raising of /æ/, for example, is generally favored by following nasals or palatals (e.g., *man, cash*) and disfavored by following /l/ (Labov, Ash, and Boberg 2006). This does not mean that raised forms do not appear before /l/, only that raising is less common or less advanced (i.e., [æ] vs. [ɪə]) in these items. The details of the phonetic conditioning of the NCS can be found in the specialist literature (e.g., Labov, Ash and Boberg 2006; Eckert 2000; Gordon 2001). Interestingly, studies of the NCS have not always found consistent patterns of conditioning across various communities. For example, Labov, Yaeger and Steiner (1972) found a following velar stop to be a disfavoring context for /æ/ raising in Detroit and Buffalo whereas it seemed to have the opposite effect in Chicago. More recently, in a study of rural Michiganders Gordon (2001) identified following /l/ as a leading promoter of /æ/ raising, a finding that runs counter to the effects reported by studies of urban speakers.

As the name implies, the NCS is associated with urban speakers from the traditional Northern dialect region. The most advanced forms of the shift are heard in the cities on and near the Great Lakes including Rochester, Buffalo, Cleveland, Detroit, Chicago, and Milwaukee. The national survey conducted by Labov and his colleagues (see Labov, Ash and Boberg 2006) finds evidence of the NCS (or at least some pieces of the Shift) in a vast stretch of the northern U.S. from Vermont, western Massachusetts, and Connecticut, across upstate New York and the Great Lakes region, and westward into Minnesota, northern Iowa and the Dakotas. In Ohio, Indiana, and Illinois the NCS is generally heard only in the northern counties; that is, in those areas included in the traditional Northern dialect region. This pattern is intriguing given that this dialect boundary, which divides the North from the Midlands, was established on the basis of older dialect forms collected over half a century ago. One major exception to the usual geographic restriction is seen in the appearance of NCS pronunciations in the Chicago-to-St. Louis corridor which takes the changes into the traditional Midland region.

The origins of the NCS may lie in the cities, but the changes are certainly no longer limited to urban speech. In Michigan, for example, quite advanced forms of the shift are heard even in small towns and rural areas (see Gordon 2001; Ito 1999). The changes appear to follow a pattern of hierarchical diffusion, spreading across large cities, then to smaller cities, and eventually to small towns (Callary 1975).

A number of studies have examined the sociolinguistic distribution of the NCS. This research has often found significant differences across gender lines with women's speech displaying more advanced forms of the shift. Such a finding is consistent with the common sociolinguistic tendency of women to be in the vanguard of language change. Sociolinguistic studies have also found that the NCS is generally characteristic of white speech; for the most part African Americans and Latinos do not participate in these changes.

Among other sociolinguistic effects, we might also expect to find class-based differences. The results on this score have been variable. Early research along these lines from a survey of Detroit suggested the changes are especially prevalent among the working and lower middle classes, or at least among women of these classes. Men showed very little class differentiation. A similar interaction of class and gender was also found in a later study by Eckert (2000) who conducted ethnographic research in a suburban Detroit high school. Eckert found that some of the changes in the NCS functioned primarily as markers of gender difference while others appeared to have associations with the class-based distinction of the Jocks and the Burnouts, the two main rival groups of students. Today the NCS can be heard in the speech of all social classes and even in the local broadcast media.

As a final sociolinguistic observation, it should be noted that the NCS has acquired very little social awareness in the areas where it has become established. For the most part, speakers with the NCS do not recognize it as a distinctive feature of their region, though the NCS pronunciations are readily noticed by listeners from other areas. The lack of salience of these very distinctive vowel shifts among the native speakers of the Inland North may be related to the traditional position of the dialect as a kind of national norm in the form of "General American" (see above). The belief that their speech is "accentless" remains very common among Northerners (especially Michiganders) today.

5.3. Consonants

Few distinctive consonantal features have been reported for the Inland North. The speech of the region has been and remains rhotic. The distinction between /hw/ and /w/ may be heard from some speakers but is clearly recessive. Alternations between the interdental fricatives, /θ/ and /ð/, and stops, /t/ and /d/, characterize the speech of some urban speakers, and the choice of /ŋ/ and /ɪn/ in –*ing* forms operates as a stylistic variable throughout the area. In addition to these features, which are common to many dialects, we note a pattern with a more restricted distribution: the devoicing of final obstruents in Chicago. This feature is a stereotype of working-class Chicago speech and is commonly illustrated by referring to the local football team as [də bɛrs] "the Bears", a stock pronunciation popularized by a television skit. The extent to which this devoicing occurs in less self-conscious usage has not been thoroughly studied.

Exercises and study questions

1. In some ways Philadelphia speech resembles Southern speech and in other ways it resembles Northern speech, especially New York. Identify some of the linguistic features Philadelphians have in common with Southerners and those they have in common with New Yorkers. Also, what features appear to be unique to Philadelphia?

2. New York City speech is one of the most salient accents in American English; that is, when Americans are asked to name places with distinctive accents, New York usually appears near the top of most lists. Which features of New York speech are most salient in people's perceptions? Ask several people to imitate a New York accent and listen to the features they use. How accurate are the stereotypical renditions of New York speech? Why are some features more salient than others?

3. Philadelphia speech is, and apparently has always been, rhotic, while New York has recently gone from solidly non-rhotic to increasingly r-full. How might you account for these differing treatments of /r/? Why were Philadelphia and New York historically different and why is the latter now experiencing change?

4. Compare the treatment of /æ/ in Philadelphia, New York, and the Inland North. It might be helpful to construct a list of words that could be used to distinguish representative speakers from each of the three areas.

5. With some exceptions, the Northern Cities Shift does not spread southward into the traditional Midland dialect region. What explanations can you offer for this geographic pattern? Consider linguistic as well as sociohistorical factors.

6. The Northern Cities Shift sometimes causes perceptual confusion. For example, a boy named Ian [iən] may be asked why his parents gave him a girl's name. How do you account for this confusion? List some other possible misunderstandings that might result from the Northern Cities Shift.

Selected references

Please consult the General references for titles mentioned in the text but not included in the references below. For a full bibliography see the accompanying CD-ROM.

Ash, Sharon
    1997   The vocalization of intervocalic /l/ in Philadelphia. In: Allen and Linn (eds), 330–43.
Babbitt, E.H.
    1896   The English of the lower classes in New York City and vicinity. *Dialect Notes* 1: 457–64.
Callary, R.E.
    1975   Phonological change and the development of an urban dialect in Illinois. *Language in Society* 4: 155–70.
Eckert, Penelope
    2000   *Linguistic Variation and Social Practice*. Oxford: Blackwell.
Gordon, Matthew J.
    2001   *Small-Town Values and Big-City Vowels: A Study of the Northern Cities Shift in Michigan*. Durham, NC: Duke University Press.
Hubbell, Allan F.
    1950   *The Pronunciation of English in New York City: Consonants and Vowels*. New York: King's Crown Press, Columbia University.
Ito, Rika
    1999   Diffusion of urban sound change in rural Michigan: A case of the Northern Cities Shift. Unpublished Ph.D. dissertation, Michigan State University.
Thomas, C.K.
    1935–7 Pronunciation in Upstate New York. *American Speech* 10: 107–12, 208–12, 292–97; 11: 68–77, 142–44, 307–13; 12: 122–27.
    1942   Pronunciation in Downstate New York. *American Speech* 17: 30–41, 149–57.
Tucker, R. Whitney
    1944   Notes on the Philadelphia dialect. *American Speech* 19: 37–42.

Rural Southern white accents

Erik R. Thomas[*]

1.   Introduction

If the "South" and "South Midland" dialect areas, as defined by Kurath (1949) and Kurath and McDavid (1961), are lumped as "Southern", rural white southern accents can be said to occur over a broad expanse of the United States. They occur throughout the southeastern part of the United States, excepting southern Florida, at least as far north as southern Maryland, central West Virginia, Kentucky, southern Missouri, and eastern and southern Oklahoma and perhaps as far west as western Texas and parts of eastern New Mexico. The exact limits are subject to disagreement; some researchers include northern West Virginia and the southern sections of Ohio, Indiana, and Illinois, while others exclude western Texas.

Southern English has received extensive attention from dialectologists, and a large number of sources, many of them gleaned from McMillan and Montgomery (1989), were consulted for this overview. Because of space limitations, few in-text citations are included and those that are included emphasize sources listed in the selected references. The full list of sources is given in the comprehensive bibliography, available on the CD accompanying this volume.

2.   Sociohistorical background

Within the vast territory in which Southern English is found, there is a considerable amount of dialectal diversity, especially in the South Atlantic states. The origins of this diversity are closely connected with the sociohistorical background of the region. Most of the Atlantic coastal sections were initially settled in the 17th and early 18th centuries by English colonists. Two areas, the Delmarva Peninsula and the Pamlico Sound area of North Carolina, remained relatively isolated from inland areas until the 20th century and show several dialectal features in common: rhoticity, failure of BATH and THOUGHT to diphthongize, backing of the nucleus of PRICE/PRIZE, and fronting of the glide of MOUTH/LOUD, among others. Two other coastal regions, one comprising the Tidewater and Piedmont sections of Virginia and adjacent counties in Maryland and North Carolina and the other consisting of the "Low Country" of the South Carolina and Georgia coastal plain, were settled mainly by the English and by African slaves and also show dialectal similarities to each other. These similarities include non-rhoticity and production of higher nuclei in MOUTH and PRICE than in LOUD and PRIZE. Each has (or had) its own features, though: for example, Virginia showed mutation of FACE to [ɛ] in some words (e.g., *make* and *afraid*) and *home* pronounced with the FOOT vowel, while the Low Country showed ingliding forms of FACE and GOAT.

During the 18th century, various non-English European groups began to settle the South. Numerous groups, including French Huguenots, Welsh, Highland Scots, Germans, Swiss, and Jews, clustered in limited areas. The major influx, however, was of Ulster Scots (Scotch-Irish). Large numbers of Ulster Scots migrated from Pennsylvania through the Great Valley of the Shenandoah River in Virginia or sailed to Charleston, South Carolina, mixing and, by the mid-19th century, intermarrying with English settlers who were moving inland and fanning out throughout the Piedmont and Appalachian regions. This mixture was aided by changes in religious affiliation because the organizational constraints of the older Presbyterian (Scottish) and Anglican/Episcopalian (English) denominations were too rigid to function well on the frontier and new denominations, mainly the Baptists and Methodists, attracted adherents from both backgrounds. In Piedmont sections, the Ulster Scots eventually adopted features such as non-rhoticity from their neighbors, and some adopted the plantation culture. In the southern Appalachians, though, the mixed Ulster Scot and English populations, who tended to live as hardscrabble farmers, maintained rhoticity. Much later, other features, such as glide weakening of PRICE (not just of PRIZE) developed in the Appalachians.

During most of the 18th century, plantations concentrated on growing tobacco in Virginia and North Carolina and rice and indigo in the Low Country. Tobacco growing spread to Kentucky and Tennessee as those states were settled in the late 18th century, but in other areas, such as the Delmarva Peninsula, it was replaced by wheat culture, which was less reliant on slaves. Although tobacco plantations depended on slaves, slave holdings tended to be largest in the Low Country. In parts of the Low Country, whites made up less than 20% of the population. The invention of the cotton gin in 1793 brought drastic changes, creating a new plantation culture centered on cotton and allowing plantation agriculture (and slavery) to expand westward through the Gulf States during the early 19th century. The westward spread was aided by the forced removal of Native Americans to Oklahoma on the infamous "Trail of Tears" in 1838. Plantation areas typically showed certain dialectal features, particularly intrusive [j] in *car* [cʰjɑː], *garden*, etc. and non-rhoticity. Plantations occupied the better farmland, such as the Mississippi valley and the "Black Belt" of central Alabama, while poor white farmers predominated in less arable regions, such as the rugged terrain of northern Alabama and the sandy "Piney Woods" region that stretched from southern Georgia and northern Florida to southern Mississippi, with a disjunct area in western Louisiana and eastern Texas. One distinctive area was southern Louisiana, with its French influence and its sugar cane- and rice-based agriculture, but it is covered in a separate paper in this volume by Dubois and Horvath.

West of the Mississippi, the plantation culture was largely restricted to the Mississippi valley and delta and the more fertile portions of eastern and southeastern Texas. Appalachian farmers, largely from Tennessee, settled the Ozarks. Germans settled parts of the Missouri and Mississippi valleys near St. Louis, and Kentuckyans and Virginians settled the "Little Dixie" region of Missouri north of the Missouri River. Various settlers, mostly from Tennessee and Arkansas, settled northern and central Texas, with a subsequent influx of Germans in central Texas. In southern Texas, these settlers encountered the already established Spanish-speaking Tejanos, though Anglo settlement of southern Texas was sparse until an agricultural boom occurred in the 1920s (Jordan 1984). Much of Oklahoma remained the "Indian Territory" until it was opened to white settlement in 1889, after which time settlers from Texas and Arkansas dominated its southern and eastern sections.

The Civil War (1861-65) put an end to slave-based plantation agriculture in the South, leading to the tenant and sharecropper systems on farms (in which owners divided profits from crops with tenants or sharecroppers) and ultimately to the establishment of mills for processing cotton and tobacco (see, e.g., Woodward 1951; Cobb 1984). Textile mills appeared in numerous towns, especially in Piedmont areas from Virginia to Alabama, and many of these towns grew into cities. Cotton growing declined in that same region, shifting in large part to the Mississippi valley and Texas. The invention of cigarette machines and the introduction of flue-cured tobacco led to large tobacco mills, primarily in North Carolina and Virginia, and a southward expansion of tobacco farming. Northern entrepreneurs also made timber a major industry throughout the South. Coal mining became a major industry in the Appalachians and mining towns sprang up there. Other industries, such as steel in Alabama, appeared locally. Expansion of railroads facilitated the growth. A demographic effect of these new industries was that it helped to inspire considerable migration of white workers toward mill towns. In addition, Texas received large numbers of migrants from other Southern states seeking new farmland after the Civil War, and not only did cotton expand there but extensive cattle ranches also covered much of western and southern Texas. It is possible that these movements played a role in the spread of several sound changes that previously occurred only locally, including the PIN/PEN merger, glide weakening of PRIZE, fronting of GOOSE, rounding of the nucleus of START, and, after 1900, lowering of the nuclei of FACE and GOAT.

Until World War II, the South generally showed net out-migration. This trend was spurred by persistent, widespread poverty and also by specific events, such as boll weevil infestation and the Great Depression. Migration from some regions, especially Appalachia, continued after World War II, but a counter-trend began. The oil industry in Texas, Louisiana, and Oklahoma; the establishment of numerous military bases; the growth of businesses attracted by cheap labor; and the appearance of resort and retirement communities all attracted migrants from other parts of the United States (see, e.g., Cobb 1984). This contact with non-Southerners may have influenced some sound changes, such as the decline of [j] in words such as *tune* and *news*, the FORCE/NORTH merger, the spread of [oɚ] in the ORANGE class, and the decline of triphthongization (a correlate of the "Southern drawl") in MOUTH/LOUD, DRESS, and other classes. However, the growth and in-migration has been concentrated in urban centers, and rural areas have continued to struggle economically. In fact, the economic gap between urban and rural areas is still widening today. Rural areas now show traditionally Southern dialectal features to a greater degree than urban areas.

Another event that may have influenced Southern dialectal patterns was the civil rights movement, particularly desegregation, which was accompanied by turmoil in the South from the 1950s through the 1970s. The civil rights struggle seems to have caused both African Americans and Southern whites to stigmatize linguistic variables associated with the other group. It coincides with the sudden spread among whites of GOAT fronting, which African Americans avoid, as well as with the reversal in which non-rhoticity changed from a prestigious to an unprestigious feature among whites. The latter change was probably also promoted by the influx of non-Southerners.

3.   Phonological systems

The phonological inventory is essentially the same as in other forms of North American English. Many Southerners distinguish the TRAP and BATH classes, though this distinction is disappearing. A number of distinctions, most notably those between NORTH and FORCE, between MARY and MERRY, and between w and HW (as in *witch* and *which*), persisted longer in the South than in most other parts of North America. The prosody of white Southern English follows patterns similar to that of white English in other parts of North America, albeit with a few special, interrelated features collectively called the "Southern drawl."

Table 1. "Typical" rural white Southern vowels–summary

	Older	Younger
KIT	ɪ~iə>ï	ɪ~iə
DRESS	ɛ~eə~ e̞iə	ɛ~eə
TRAP	æ~æɛæ̞	æ
LOT	ɑ	ɑ
STRUT	ɜ>ʌ	ɜ
FOOT	ü~ʏ	ü~ʏ
BATH	æ̞ɛ	æ
DANCE	æ̞ɛ	eə
CLOTH	ɔo~ɑɒ	ɑɒ
NURSE	ɚ>ɐɚ>ɜɪ	ɚ>ɐɚ
FLEECE	i̞i~ɪi	i̞i~ɪi
FACE	ɛi~æ̞i	ɛi~æ̞i
PALM	ɑ>æ	ɑ~ɒo
THOUGHT	ɔo~ɑɒ	ɑɒ
GOAT	ɔ̞u~ɒu	ɜy~ɜu>æ̞u
GOOSE	ʉu̞~yʉ	ʉu̞~yʉ~ʉy~yy
PRICE	ai~aːæ~aː~ɑːe	ai~aːæ~aː
PRIZE	aːɛ~aːæ~aː	aːɛ~aːæ~aː
CHOICE	oi~ɔoi>oːɛ~oːə	oi
MOUTH, LOUD	æɔ~æɒ~æɛɒ>aɒ>æɑ	æɔ~æɒ>aɒ
NEAR	i̠ɚ~iə	i̠ɚ
SQUARE	æɚ~æə~ɛiɚ~ɛiə~ e̞ɚ	e̞ɚ
START	ɒɚ~ɒː	ɒɚ>ɑɚ
NORTH	ɔɚ~ɔə~ɔoɚ~ɔoə~ɔo	oɚ

Table 1. (continued)   "Typical" rural white Southern vowels–summary

	Older	Younger
FORCE	oɚ~oə~ouɚ~ouə~ou	oɚ
CURE	uɚ~uə~ʊɚ~ʊə>oɚ	uɚ>ɚ
FIRE	aæɚ~aæə~aːɚ~aːɐ>ɒɚ	aæɚ~aːɚ
POWER	æɔɚ~æɔə>ɒɚ	aɔɚ
*happ*Y	ɪ~i	i
*lett*ER	ɚ~ə	ɚ
*hors*ES	ɪ~ï	ɪ~ï
*comm*A	ə	ə
HAND	æ~æɛæ	eə
PIN/PEN	ɪ~iə	ɪ~iə
THINK, LENGTH	ɪ>ɛi~æi	ɪ~ɪi
GOING	ɔu̜~o̜u	ɔu̜~o̜u
GOAL	ɔu̜~o̜u	ɔu̜~o̜u
POOL	ʉ~u	ʊ̝~u
PULL	ʊ	ʊ̝~u
FEEL	i̝i	ɪ~iə~i̝i
FILL	ɪ~iə	ɪ~iə~ï
FAIL	ɛi~æi~ei	ei~ɛ
FELL	ɛ~ei	ɛ
MARRY	æ	e̝
MERRY	ɛ	e̝
MARY	ei~ɛ	e̝
MIRROR/NEARER	ɪ~i̝	i̝
TOMORROW	ɑ~ɒ	ɑ~ɒ
ORANGE	ɑ~ɒ	ɑ~ɒ~o

3.1. Prosodic features

Two prosodic features of rural Southern English are commonly remarked upon: the "Southern drawl" and the tendency to place stress to the initial syllable of particular words. The Southern drawl is defined variously, and it has even been dismissed by some as nothing more than a stereotype. It is probably best described as prolongation of certain stressed vowels and diphthongs, often accompanied by breaking of and exaggerated pitch rises in those vocoids. Although the phenomenon has not been studied as extensively as it could have been, there seems to be adequate evidence that it exists. It is widespread in Southern white English. Nevertheless, it seems to be more observable in the speech of Southerners born before 1960 than in the speech of those born afterward, though published evidence for such a trend is lacking.

The exaggerated pitch peaks that have been noted as a correlate of the Southern drawl are the main intonational feature noted for white Southern English. These peaks occur in heavily stressed syllables. In other respects, Southern intonation patterns seem to be similar to those in other forms of American English, though little research on them has been carried out.

The other oft-noted aspect of Southern prosody, placement of primary stress on initial syllables, occurs for some speakers in words such as *cement, police, hotel, pecan, July, December, Detroit*, and *Monroe* for which other varieties of English do not show primary stress on the initial syllable. This feature has become a stereotype of Southern English, both white and African American. As a result, it is recessive for most words, but for at least one, *insurance*, it has become a marker of Southern identity and is still common. In a number of additional words, such as *theater* and *peanut*, many Southerners show a secondary stress that is absent in other varieties of English. This tendency is also stereotyped and recessive.

Other features of stress and rhythm, such as the relative degree of stress timing and syllable timing, have not been investigated in Southern English. Dialect-specific voice quality features also deserve some attention.

3.2. Lexical distribution

A large number of words show a phonemic incidence that is associated with Southern English. Many such words are discussed in Kurath and McDavid (1961) and the *Linguistic Atlas of the Gulf States* (Pederson *et al.* 1986-92, henceforth *LAGS*). For some of these words, the pronunciation is widespread but is stereotypically associated with the South; examples are *get* pronounced [gɪt] and *just* pronounced [dʒɪst]. Other cases are pronunciations that were once widespread but have receded and are now – in North America at least – largely restricted to the South. Examples are *rather* as [ɹʌðɚ], *further* as [fʌðɚ], *radish* as [ɹɛɾɪʃ], *kettle* as [kʰɪtɬ], *drain* as [dɹin], *sumac* as [ʃumæk], and *haunt* as [hænt]. This group, as a rule, occurs mostly among older, less-educated speakers. There are also variants whose primary distribution has long been the South, though many of them once had some currency elsewhere. The viability of these items varies. Some are highly recessive, e.g., *put* as [pʰʌt], *coop* and *Cooper* as [kʰʊp] and [kʰʊpɚ/ə] respectively, *shut* as [ʃɛt], and *pasture* pronounced to rhyme with *master*. Others are still used by many younger speakers, such as *grease* (verb) and *greasy* as [gɹiz(i)], *naked* as [nɛkɪd], *can't* rhyming with *faint*, *on* pronounced as *own*, and perhaps *Mrs.* as [mɪz(ɪz)], though these usages are probably receding slowly.

Lexical incidence in certain groups of words has attracted particular attention from dialectologists. One is a group of words that vary between the LOT and THOUGHT classes. Southerners who distinguish LOT and THOUGHT consistently produce *on* with the THOUGHT or GOAT vowels, not with the LOT vowel. *Long* and words rhyming with it formerly grouped with LOT in parts of Virginia and North Carolina but with THOUGHT elsewhere, though the THOUGHT variant has probably encroached on the LOT island. For words spelled *–og*, *dog* consistently groups with THOUGHT but other words (*fog, hog, log*, etc.) vary, generally grouping with LOT in coastal plain areas and with THOUGHT in inland areas. Among words spelled *wa-*, *want* with the THOUGHT vowel is particularly associated with the South. *Swamp, wasp*, and, in coastal plain areas, *water* also typically show THOUGHT (Kurath and McDavid 1961) but are less stereotyped than *want* with THOUGHT. Some younger speakers may be substituting the LOT vowel in these words.

In addition, there are a few function words (*was, what, of, anybody, nobody, somebody*, and *everybody*) that have been shifting in North American English from LOT to STRUT. In *was, what*, and *of* and possibly in *-body* words, the LOT pronunciation has survived longer in the South than elsewhere, though it is giving way now. Similarly, *because* is shifting from THOUGHT to STRUT, though the THOUGHT form is still common in the South.

3.3.   Vowels

Virtually every vowel class shows distinctive variants in rural white Southern English. A number of processes, such as triphthongization, glide weakening of PRIZE and PRICE, upgliding forms of THOUGHT and BATH, and the PIN/PEN merger, have become more or less stereotypical of Southern speech. One assemblage of vowel shifts, dubbed the *Southern Shift*, has attracted prominent attention recently; see especially Labov (1991, 1994) and Labov, Ash and Boberg (2006). It consists of several different shifts that are associated with each other. PRIZE, and often PRICE as well, undergo glide weakening to [aːɛ~aː] or, as in the Pamlico Sound region, become backed to [ɑːe~ɒːe]. The tense/lax front vowel pairs switch places: the nuclei of FACE and FLEECE become non-peripheral and fall, while KIT and DRESS become peripheral and rise toward [i] and [e], respectively. The nucleus of GOAT may fall, and GOAT and GOOSE become fronted. Finally, THOUGHT is either diphthongized to something like [ɔo] or raised toward [o]. It should be noted that the different components of the Southern Shift have not spread through the South at the same time. Shifting of THOUGHT may date from the late 18th or early 19th centuries and glide weakening of PRIZE apparently dates from the late 19th century, while fronting of GOAT spread mostly after World War II.

The following descriptions discuss the different variants that occur in various parts of the South, giving their general distributions across time, space, and social groups. Social distribution is poorly known for many of these forms, though some information is available in LAGS and various smaller-scale studies. Traditionally, the glides of upgliding diphthongs have been transcribed with lax vowel symbols, e.g., [ɪ] and [ʊ]. Acoustic measurements, however, show that upgliding diphthongs normally glide toward the periphery of the vowel envelope; see Thomas (2001). Hence these glides are usually transcribed here with tense vowel symbols. Similarly, acoustic measurements indicate that what have traditionally been called "ingliding" diphthongs actually glide both inward and downward, so that a form denoted as [eə] is probably better described as [eɛ] or [eæ]. Much of the information discussed below is taken from Thomas (2001) or from sources referenced therein.

KIT
Realizations of KIT vary. In the Southern shift, KIT may be tensed and raised to [i], usually with an inglide, i.e., [iə]. This process is most common in heavily stressed syllables. Under weak stress, a value of [ɪ] is usual. The tensing/raising is uncommon in some regions, such as Texas. In older Southern speech, centralized forms, i.e., ['ɨ], were common in certain words, such as *sister*, *thistle*, and *ribbon*, in which a schwa was present in the following syllable. See below under PIN/PEN and THINK for developments before nasals.

DRESS
This vowel shows some variation related to the Southern Shift. Considerable variation between the widespread form [ɛ] and the Southern Shift form [e] occurs, the latter often with an inglide. Under heavy stress, particularly before

/d/, as in *dead*, middle-aged and older speakers often show a triphthongal form, [eiə]. For the development of this vowel before nasals, see below under PIN/ PEN and LENGTH.

TRAP

An unshifted form, [æ], is common, but the Southern drawl results in triphthongal forms such as [æɛæ], especially before /d/ and /n/. Speakers born between the World Wars may also show some raising of TRAP to [ɛ]. For other raising, see below under DANCE/HAND.

Both the triphthongization and the raising are subsiding among young Southern whites. A few younger speakers from, e.g., Texas, who show the LOT/ THOUGHT merger have TRAP shifted toward [a], but this retraction is not yet as common as in some non-Southern regions (e.g., California and Canada), though it is increasing in parts of the Midwest on the margins of the South (e.g., central Ohio).

LOT

This vowel is among the most stable in rural Southern white English, being realized as low back unrounded [ɑ]. Rounded [ɒ] variants were reported for old-fashioned South Carolina Low Country speech. In some areas, THOUGHT is being merged into LOT (see below under THOUGHT).

STRUT

The most common realization is the [ɜ] that predominates in most North American English. In former plantation areas, a more backed form, [ʌ], is common among middle-aged and older speakers, but it appears to be recessive. Fronting to [ɛ] is sometimes reported. Raising to [ə] occurs for occasional speakers.

FOOT

This vowel varies on a gradient from central [ʉ] to fronted [ʏ]. The full range of variants occurs within most age groups and social levels. The degree of fronting of FOOT is usually correlated with the degree of fronting of GOOSE and GOAT.

BATH, DANCE

Most younger Southerners make no distinction between BATH and TRAP. White Southerners born before World War II, however, often do distinguish the two classes, though in a way unique to the American South. For such speakers, BATH shows an upglide. The most common realization is [æɛ], but variations such as [æe] and [aæ] occur. Some speakers who show these forms also show lowering of the FACE vowel; they distinguish pairs such as *pass* and *pace* by the height of the glide, which is mid for BATH words and high for FACE words. Many Southerners produce the same [æɛ] diphthong in the DANCE class (i.e., words in which RP shows [ɑː] before a nasal/obstruent cluster). Upgliding BATH and DANCE forms are widespread in the South Atlantic states, but are absent in three areas: around the Chesapeake Bay, around the Pamlico Sound, and in the Low Country of South Carolina. In the Gulf states, they occur everywhere–except perhaps southern Louisiana–but are most common in the Appalachian and Ozark Mountains and in the Piney Woods belt.

In a number of BATH and DANCE words – today usually only *aunt* or *rather* but in former times many others, such as *pasture* – some speakers show the vowel of START (in non-rhotic varieties) or LOT. This tendency most likely originated as an imitation of fashionable British usage rather than as a trait inherited from the earliest settlers. It is most prevalent in eastern Virginia.

CLOTH
This class is always merged with THOUGHT (see below).

NURSE
White Southern speech is increasingly rhotic, and stressed syllabic /r – i.e., NURSE – is the most likely context for rhoticity in syllable rhymes. The details of /r/ articulation are discussed below under R in the section on consonants. In older white Southern speech, though, non-rhotic forms of NURSE occurred. From South Carolina to Texas and north to eastern Arkansas and the southern edge of Kentucky, an upgliding form, [ɜɪ], once predominated, but very few speakers born after 1930 show it and it is thus nearly obsolete. A few Southerners from the same region, usually from high social strata, showed a monophthongal [ɜ]. The monophthongal form also occurred in eastern Virginia and adjacent parts of Maryland and North Carolina, but a weakly rhotic variant was more common there.

For rhotic speakers, a different diphthongization of NURSE can appear in which the variants [ɜɚ~ɐɚ] occur. This widening tends to co-occur with widening of the FACE and GOAT diphthongs.

FLEECE
Unless it is truncated–as would happen with weak stress or rapid speech–the FLEECE vowel is slightly diphthongal. In white Southern speech, diphthongal forms vary from the [ii] form that predominates in other parts of North America to wider [ɪi] forms. The latter are most common in areas in which the

FACE nucleus is strongly lowered, especially eastern Tennessee and much of Alabama (Labov, Ash and Boberg 2006). Variants that are even wider, such as [əi], are rare.

FACE

This vowel shows more variation in the South than in any other part of North America. In the past, a monophthongal form, [e̞ː], occurred inconsistently in plantation areas. In the Low Country of South Carolina/Georgia, the monophthong occurred in pre-pausal position and ingliding [e̞ə] occurred in other contexts. These forms are now nearly obsolete, though the nucleus of FACE has remained higher in the Low Country than in other parts of the South. Today, lowering and/or retraction of the nucleus are widespread in rural white Southern speech. The shift may be moderate–i.e., [ɛi] – or more extreme – i.e., [æi~ɜi]. The more extreme forms are found largely in areas in which PRICE is monophthongal in all contexts, which include the southern Appalachians, the Ozarks, Texas, the Piney Woods belt, and parts of the North Carolina coastal plain. The more moderately shifted forms tend to occur where PRICE remains diphthongal before voiceless consonants.

PALM

In contemporary Southern English, these words are nearly always merged with LOT or, with the *l* pronounced (as a spelling pronunciation), with THOUGHT– e.g., [pʰpɔɫm]~[pʰpɒm] (the latter with vocalized *l*). In the past, PALM was commonly merged with the TRAP or BATH classes, and occasional survivals of this usage, such as the term *slick ca'm* 'unrippled water,' persist locally. In the South Carolina Low Country, even *pa* and *ma* were once produced with [æ]. Merger of PALM with START in non-rhotic areas, especially eastern Virginia, also occurred sporadically.

THOUGHT

Upgliding forms of THOUGHT/CLOTH, [ɔo~ɒo~ɑɒ], are stereotypically associated with Southern speech in general. The actual picture, of course, is more complicated. There are a few Atlantic coastal areas – the eastern shore of the Chesapeake Bay, the Pamlico Sound area, and the South Carolina/Georgia Low Country–in which upgliding forms did not traditionally occur; instead, raised, monophthongal [ɔ] occurred. In the rest of the South, upgliding forms predominate, but there have always been many speakers who used monophthongal forms exclusively, and raised monophthongs are common after [w], as in *want* and *water*. In older speech, raised, upgliding forms, [ɔo], were common, though some speakers showed wider diphthongization, such as [ɒo] or even [ɑo]. During the 20ᵗʰ century there was apparently a trend toward lower variants, and today the most common form is [ɑɒ].

Merger of THOUGHT/CLOTH with LOT has been spreading recently in the South, especially in two areas: an Appalachian area including West Virginia, western Virginia, and eastern Kentucky and a western area extending from Texas and Oklahoma east through Arkansas, middle and western Missouri, and the vicinity of Memphis, Tennessee. Occasional speakers elsewhere show it as well. The result is a realization as [ɑ]. A possible stigma against upgliding variants may promote the merger.

GOAT

GOAT shows several different developments. Analogously with FACE, monophthongal [o̞ː] once occurred inconsistently in plantation areas, and the monophthong alternated with ingliding [o̞ə] in the South Carolina/Georgia Low Country. As with the corresponding variants of FACE, these forms have nearly disappeared. Lowering of the nucleus and fronting of both the nucleus and glide of GOAT have become widespread over the past century. Lowered but unfronted forms, [ɔu~ɒu], became common in the early 20ᵗʰ century and are still found among many older speakers. Fronted forms apparently originated in northeastern North Carolina during the 19ᵗʰ century and spread slowly at first. This fronting affected both the nucleus and the glide, yielding [ɜy]. Fronting only of the nucleus also spread slowly from Pennsylvania into Maryland, West Virginia, and southern Ohio. Since World War II, fronting has spread rapidly. Fronting of the nucleus is now found throughout the South among young whites. In combination with lowering, it yields forms as extreme as [æu], though [ɜu] is more common. Fronting of the glide is common as far west as Tennessee and Alabama but is less frequent west of the Mississippi River and quite rare in Texas; its northern limits are uncertain. It is possible that both fronting processes, at least in certain areas, are more prevalent among females than among males.

In certain contexts the GOAT vowel is not usually fronted; see below under GOAL and GOING.

GOOSE

When fully stressed, the GOOSE vowel is slightly diphthongal in Southern English. Some degree of fronting is associated with the nucleus of GOOSE in virtually all forms of white Southern English. The nucleus may vary from a central to a front position. Fronting of the glide also occurs and is more common in the eastern half of the South. Variants include [ʉu~yʉ] (without fronting of the glide) and [ʉy~yy] (with fronting of the glide).

PRICE, PRIZE

Monophthongization of PRICE (i.e., /ai/ before voiceless consonants) and, especially, PRIZE (i.e., other phonetic contexts of /ai/) is stereotypically associated with the American South. However, *glide weakening* is a more accurate term because it encompasses both monophthongal forms and variants with a glide that is only partly truncated, both of which are perceived as "flattened" by outsiders. Both forms are common and widespread.

Glide weakening has, since the late 19th century, occurred throughout the South except for a few Atlantic coastal areas, and even there it has shown signs of encroaching recently. Where weakening occurs, it consistently affects contexts before liquids most strongly and those before voiceless consonants least strongly, but the relative strength of the effects of following pauses, nasals, and voiced obstruents is a matter of dispute. Weakening produces forms such as [aːɛ~aːæ], leading ultimately to monophthongal [aː]. Some speakers show forms such as [æː] and [ɑː], but [aː] is more usual.

Weakening before voiceless consonants (PRICE) is geographically and socially restricted. It is found mainly in Appalachia (south to northern Alabama), Arkansas, Oklahoma, Texas, the Piney Woods Belt, and parts of the North Carolina coastal plain, but some working class speakers elsewhere show it. It has long been associated with working-class speech, and hence many upper-middle class speakers avoid it. Weakening in any context (PRICE or PRIZE) is apparently declining around the margins of the South, such as in Maryland and Oklahoma. Speakers with aspirations of upward white-collar mobility often avoid it, though such avoidance is not as prevalent in rural areas as in urban areas.

Glide weakening was traditionally absent on the eastern shore of the Chesapeake Bay, around the Pamlico Sound, and in the Low Country of South Carolina and Georgia. In the former two areas, backing of the nucleus occurred instead in all contexts. Forms such as [ɑːe] were usual, with [ɒːe] and [ɐɑe] occurring sporadically. Backing occurred for PRIZE in the Low Country. Such backing also occurs widely in the South before voiceless consonants (PRICE) where that context remains diphthongal. Another variation reported from older speech in Tidewater and Piedmont Virginia and the South Carolina/Georgia Low Country for contexts before voiceless consonants is [ɐi], with a higher nucleus. Acoustic analyses indicate that only some speakers from those areas showed [ɐi].

CHOICE

Although the widespread [oi~ɔi] forms are common in the South, two mutations occur in the South but not elsewhere in North America (except in varieties with Southern roots, such as African American English). The first is breaking, which results in triphthongs such as [ɔoi] and [ɒoɨ]. The second is lowering and/or weakening of the glide, resulting in forms such as [oːɛ] and [oːə]. The latter process is found most often in former plantation areas. Both processes occur mainly for speakers born before 1960. However, before /l/, as in *boil*, glide weakening is widespread among all age groups and monophthongization to [o] is common. The alternation in which certain CHOICE words derived from Middle English /ui/, e.g., *join* and *poison*, show the PRIZE vowel is highly recessive except in *hoist/heist*.

MOUTH, LOUD

Fronting of the nucleus and lowering of the glide, resulting in [æɔ~æɒ] and, in some areas, [æɑ], are widespread in white Southern English. Not all speakers show the fronting, and most speakers show [aɒ] under weak stress. In two areas – the South Carolina/Georgia Low Country and southern Louisiana – fronting was traditionally absent. Many speakers born before 1960 show breaking, resulting in triphthongal [æɛɒ].

Two local variations occurred in traditional dialects, though both are recessive today. In the Tidewater and Piedmont sections of Virginia and adjacent parts of Maryland and North Carolina, as well as in the South Carolina/Georgia Low Country, positional variation developed. Before voiced consonants and word-finally (LOUD), the variants described above occurred. Before voiceless consonants (MOUTH), both the nucleus and the glide were higher. The glide also tended to be fronted, with the result of [ɜʉ~ɜy]. On the Delmarva Peninsula and around the Pamlico Sound, fronting of the glide occurred with low nuclei in most contexts. The nuclei tended not to be much fronted. Common variants there were [aɵ~aø~aɛ].

NEAR

The common variants are [iɚ] and [iə]. In some areas, [jɚ] was once a common alternant in certain words, e.g., *beard*. In old-fashioned South Carolina/Georgia Low Country speech, NEAR and SQUARE were merged to [eə], but contact with other Southern dialects has reversed this merger.

SQUARE

A wide variety of variants occur in older Southern speech. Lowering of the nucleus, resulting in [æɚ] for rhotic speakers and [æə] for non-rhotic speakers, was once widespread, though today it is mainly heard among middle-aged and older speakers in regions far from urban centers, such as the Pamlico Sound area and the southern Appalachians. It never occurred in the South Carolina/

Georgia Low Country, however, where [eə] was usual. Breaking was common as well, especially in non-rhotic areas, where forms such as [ɛiə] and even [æiæ] could be heard. Young white Southerners have abandoned this diversity and uniformly show a quality of approximately [e̞ɚ].

START

Southern English, both rhotic and non-rhotic, shows a marked tendency toward rounding of the nucleus of START, resulting in values of [ɒɚ] or [ɒː]. This process is probably a 19th century development. There may be some stigma against the rounding today, as some young whites seem to be moving toward unrounded nuclei.

NORTH

NORTH remained distinct from FORCE in most parts of the South until recently. Usual pronunciations were [ɔɚ~ɔɔɚ] in rhotic speech and [ɔə~ɔɔə~ɔɔ] in non-rhotic speech. In certain areas–the Delmarva Peninsula, parts of the Mississippi and Ohio valleys, and Texas–many speakers merged NORTH with START as [ɒɚ]. On the Delmarva Peninsula, this merger dates from the 19th century and may have been a majority variant, but in Texas, it mainly comprises speakers born between the World Wars and was never a majority variant. Its demographics in the Mississippi and Ohio valleys are unclear. Over the course of the 20th century, the NORTH/FORCE merger gradually spread throughout the South. Very few Southerners born after World War II distinguish NORTH and FORCE. The result of this merger is a value of approximately [oɚ].

FORCE

In older Southern speech, FORCE could show variable diphthongization, i.e., [oɚ~ouɚ] in rhotic varieties and [oə~ouə~ou] in non-rhotic ones. Younger white rural Southerners seldom show upgliding in FORCE, the usual variant being [oɚ]. See above on the merger of FORCE and NORTH.

CURE

Merger of the vowels of CURE and FORCE became a stereotype for some older rural Southern speech, especially in Appalachia. As a result, most Southerners came to avoid it except for words spelled *–oor* (e.g., *poor, boor, Moore*), for which usage varies. Thus [uɚ~ʊɚ] predominates, especially in words such as *tour*. After palatals, as in *cure* and *sure*, and in non-final syllables, as in *tournament* and *Missouri*, merger with the NURSE class is common among young speakers in some areas, such as Texas and Missouri. Such speakers follow a pattern increasingly common in other parts of North America. This CURE/

NURSE merger tends to show considerable style shifting; many speakers who show the merger in casual speech pronounce CURE words with [uɚ~ʊɚ] when their attention is drawn to it.

FIRE

For a large number of speakers, FIRE follows the pattern of PRICE/PRIZE, with glide weakening resulting in [aæɚ~aːɚ] in rhotic varieties and [aæɐ~aːɐ] in non-rhotic ones. Many speakers, however, show merger of FIRE with START, resulting in [ɒɚ~aɚ~ɒː~aː]. This merger is highly stereotyped and, consequently, is most typical of older, working-class, and less educated speakers. Some speakers show hypercorrection of glide weakening for FIRE, resulting in [ajɚ].

POWER

For most speakers, power follows the same pattern as MOUTH/LOUD. Some speakers show loss of the glide before /r/, resulting in [æɚ], especially in the word *our*. *Our* is more commonly merged into the START class – in fact, this variant of *our* is quite general in North America – but for other words merger of POWER with START occurs infrequently, mostly among the same groups who merge FIRE with START.

*happ*Y

Although [ɪ] in *happ*Y persisted longer in the South than in other parts of North America, the shift to [i] is now essentially complete and only speakers in a few isolated communities (such as islands in the Chesapeake Bay) and some older speakers elsewhere still show [ɪ]. The final vowels of many other words, such as *borrow*, *soda*, *okra*, and *Sarah*, were once commonly pronounced with [ɪ~i] in the rural South, especially among speakers with less education, but this process is now highly recessive.

*lett*ER

The general distribution of rhotic and non-rhotic varieties and the wholesale shift to rhoticity in white Southern speech are discussed below under R. Unstressed syllables are the most likely contexts for non-rhoticity, and some varieties that show consistent rhoticity in other contexts show variable non-rhoticity in unstressed syllables. In older speech, the *comm*A vowel, both historical, as in *idea*, and derived from GOAT, as in *hollow*, is commonly produced as [ɚ].

*hors*ES

A value of [ɪ], perhaps better described as central [ɨ], is usual. However, the exact quality is highly affected by coarticulation with neighboring segments.

*comm*A

This vowel tends to be lower than the *hors*ES vowel, closer to [ə], but, like *hors*ES, it is strongly affected by context. On the production of some *comm*A words with [ɪ~i], see above under *happ*Y; on production as [ɚ], see above under *lett*ER.

HAND

Younger white Southerners follow the widespread North American trend of raising /æ/ before nasals to something like [eə]. This process includes words of the DANCE class, whose earlier development is discussed above. Older Southerners often showed triphthongal [æɛæ] forms.

PIN/PEN

The merger of the KIT and DRESS vowels before nasals, as in *pin* and *pen*, is strongly associated with Southern speech, though it also occurs among some whites in the southern Midwest and California and among African Americans everywhere. The resulting merged vowel is usually closer to [ɪ] in quality, though a few speakers have it closer to [ɛ]. The merger apparently grew from a sporadic feature of a few speakers to a majority feature during the late 19th century and continued to spread during the 20th century. Today, however, some Southerners, largely under the influence of schools, have begun to distinguish PIN and PEN.

THINK, LENGTH

Before [ŋ], as in *think* and *thing*, some Southerners diphthongize the KIT vowel and lower the nucleus to yield [ɛi~æi]. The same process may apply to LENGTH, which otherwise is usually pronounced with [ɪ].

GOING

In hiatus positions, as in *going, go out, so is*..., etc., fronting of the GOAT vowel does not occur for many speakers who otherwise front. The same may be true for GOOSE, as in *do it*. Fronting may also be blocked before nasals, as in *grown* and *don't*.

GOAL

The back vowels are seldom fronted before /l/, especially by younger speakers. Thus, GOAL is rarely if ever fronted. Common realizations are [ɔu~ɒu].

POOL, PULL

Although many older white Southerners show fronting of POOL, younger Southerners almost never do. PULL consistently remains backed. POOL and PULL are commonly merged by younger speakers throughout the South; the resulting vowel is [ʊ~ʉ].

FEEL, FILL

These two classes are also merged by many younger Southerners, ordinarily to [ɪ] or to a quality intermediate between [i] and [ɪ].

FAIL, FELL

Merger of these two classes also occurs, though less often than that of the other two pre-/l/ pairs. The resulting vowel is usually [ɛ].

MARRY, MERRY, MARY

These classes were once kept distinct by most Southerners, with qualities of [æ], [ɛ], and [ei~e], respectively. Younger Southerners have shown a whole-sale trend toward merging all three into the SQUARE class. Merger of MARY with MERRY has proceeded faster than merger of MARRY with the other two classes.

MIRROR/NEARER

Published evidence on this opposition is scarce for Southern English. Young white Southerners, in general, appear to merge them.

TOMORROW, ORANGE

The stressed vowel in these classes was formerly produced with [ɑ~ɒ], the LOT or START vowel, throughout the South. It still is for words in which the /r/ is followed by a vowel in an open syllable, such as *tomorrow* and *sorry*. However, for words in which the /r/ is followed by a vowel in a closed syllable, such as *orange*, *foreign*, and *horrible*, there is a trend toward [o], the FORCE/NORTH vowel. This trend appears stronger in some areas (e.g., Texas and Virginia) than in others (e.g., the Carolinas).

3.4.   Consonants

R

/r/, when it is articulated in the South, is articulated much as in other North American Englishes. The ordinary form is the "bunched-tongue *r*," produced with constrictions by the tongue root (in the pharynx), the tongue dorsum (to the velum or palate), and – in syllable onsets – the lips as well. The currency of the competing variant, the "retroflex *r*" (produced with the pharyngeal constriction and with retroflection of the tongue tip) is difficult to assess but seems far less common. Production of the bunched-tongue *r* often results in latent retroflection. One other variant, the tap [ɾ], may have occurred in some older Southern speech after [θ], as in *three*, but the evidence is unclear.

Postvocalic /r/ is the most heavily studied consonantal variable in Southern English, and it shows rich contextual, geographical, socioeconomic, diachronic, ethnic, and stylistic conditioning. It also shows continuous gradation from fully rhotic to fully non-rhotic variants. In terms of phonetic context, non-rhoticity is most frequent in unstressed syllables; see above on the *lett*ER class. Non-rhoticity may occur variably in this context in areas such as the Pamlico Sound region and Appalachia that are otherwise rhotic, and, as rhoticity has increased recently, unstressed syllables are often the last context to become rhotic. The next most frequent environment for non-rhoticity is in syllable codas, whether word-finally (*four*, *here*) or pre-consonantally (*hard*, *fourth*). Linking *r*, as in *here is* [hiɚ ɪz], has historically been absent for a large number of Southerners, though some speakers showed it, often variably. Intrusive linking *r* in other hiatus positions, as in *saw-r it*, is virtually unknown in the South, in part because intrusive *l* may occur in such contexts. Rhoticity tends to be more frequent after front vowels (e.g., *here*, *there*) than after back vowels (*four*, *hard*). Stressed, syllabic *r*, the NURSE class, is more likely to be rhotic than *r* in syllable codas; see above under NURSE. Some older Southerners are also variably non-rhotic in intra-word intervocalic contexts, as in *carry* [kʰæi]. Deletion of *r* occurs as well for some speakers between [θ] and a rounded vowel in *throw* and *through* and after a consonant in some unstressed syllables, e.g., the initial syllable of *professor*.

Deletion of *r* in certain words before coronal consonants, as in the widespread forms *bust*, *cuss*, and *gal* for *burst*, *curse*, and *girl*, respectively, and *ass* and *bass (fish)* for earlier *arse* and *barse*, as well as dialectal forms such as *futher*, *catridge*, and *passel* for *further*, *cartridge*, and *parcel*, is not properly considered to be non-rhoticity, since it arose earlier from assimilation. Nor is the dissimilation that results in deletion of the first *r* in words such as *surprise*, *governor*, *temperature*, *veterinarian*, and *caterpillar* properly considered non-rhoticity. Both processes are common in the South, though forms such as *passel* are recessive.

Geographically, non-rhoticity is strongly correlated with former plantation areas. Non-rhoticity formerly predominated in Tidewater and Piedmont Virginia and adjacent parts of southwestern Maryland and northern North Carolina; in a band stretching from South Carolina across the Georgia Piedmont through central Alabama and central Mississippi; throughout the Mississippi River lowlands as far north as Kentucky, extending to include the western two thirds of Kentucky and western and north-central Tennessee, and thence west to include Gulf coastal plain sections of Texas; and in some coastal communities in Georgia and the Gulf states. Much of North Carolina and parts of central and even western Texas showed mixed patterns. The principal rhotic sections were the Delmarva Peninsula; the Pamlico Sound region of North Carolina; the southern Appalachians, extending to northern Alabama; the Ozarks, Oklahoma, and northern Texas; and the Piney Woods region of the southern parts of Georgia, Alabama, and Mississippi, northern Florida, western Louisiana, and eastern Texas. None of these areas was monolithic, however, and the Piney Woods region, especially, showed mixture.

The socioeconomic and diachronic aspects of rhoticity in the South are intertwined. Various studies, notably McDavid (1948), Levine and Crockett (1966), Harris (1969), and Feagin (1990), have suggested that rhoticity has undergone a shift in prestige. Before World War II, non-rhoticity was prestigious, appearing most frequently among higher social levels and spreading (except, perhaps, in NURSE words). Afterward, rhoticity became prestigious and non-rhoticity became most common among lower social levels. Females have forged ahead of males in this change. Today, even in areas that were once strongholds of non-rhoticity, young white Southerners are rhotic, especially females. Predictably, rhoticity increases with stylistic formality. It should be noted that the dramatic increase in rhoticity applies only to white Southerners; African Americans remain largely non-rhotic except in the NURSE class, and, as discussed previously, social polarization of the two ethnicities magnified during the civil rights movement may be related to the divergence in rhoticity.

L

Although American English is often reported to show a "clear" [l] in syllable onsets and a "dark," or velar, [ɫ] in syllable codas, articulatory evidence suggests that American English shows a velar form in syllable onsets, and Southern English follows this pattern. In syllable codas, vocalization occurs. The term *vocalization* has been used loosely. It has been applied to what would be better referred to as *deletion*, as in [wʊf] for *wolf*. This deletion may occur before labials (except [b]), and the forms [hɛp] for *help*, [sɛf] in *-self* compounds, [tʰwev] for *twelve*, and [houp] for *holp* (old preterit of *help*) are stereotypically Southern. True vocalization of syllable-coda *l* is widespread in North American English and seems to be particularly common in the South. The result is a phone with the value of [o] or [w], as in *fill* [fɪo]. This phone is sometimes described as [ɯ] but is normally rounded. The acoustic similarity between [ɫ] and [w] has made vocalization of *l* difficult to study, and hence details of its distribution are unavailable.

Linking [ɫ] is apparently common in hiatus positions, as in *sell it* [sɛoɫɪʔt]. Intrusive [ɫ], as in *saw it* [sɑɒɫɪʔt], is known to occur irregularly. However, vocalization can also occur in hiatus.

Older Southern speech did show a truly "clear" [l] in one context: between front vowels, as in *silly*, *Billy*, and *Nelly*. Some elderly Southerners still show this variant.

KJAR, GJAR

During the 19ᵗʰ century, insertion of [j] in such words as *car* [cʰjɑː~ cʰjɑɚ], *garden*, and *Carter* was widespread in coastal plain and Piedmont sections of the South, though perhaps less so in the Appalachians. This variation probably began to decline in the late 19ᵗʰ century and has now entirely disappeared.

JU

In words with historical [iu~ju] after coronal stops, as in *tune*, *duke*, and *news*, [j] has persisted in the South longer than in any other part of the United States (though it still appears elsewhere as an affectation). Kurath and McDavid (1961), whose sample consisted almost entirely of speakers born in the 19ᵗʰ century, showed [ju] and its variants ([iu], [dʒu], [tʃu]) as nearly universal in the Southern states. Since World War II, however, a steady movement toward loss of [j] in the South has occurred. The loss has been slower in common words than in infrequent words. Findings differ on whether males or females lead in this change.

TH

Rural white southern English shows all of the mutations of /θ/ and /ð/ that African American speech is better known for, but they generally do not occur as often. Thus /θ/ may be realized as [t~tθ], usually by lower-status speakers, or, in syllable codas (e.g., *both*, *birthday*), occasionally as [f]. The [f] variant is much rarer in white speech than in African American speech. Mutations of /ð/ are more common. Realizations of /ð/ as [d~dð] may be increasing among young white males, though more study is needed. Assimilation of /ð/ to a preceding consonant, as in *in nere* for *in there* or *up pat hill* for *up that hill*, is fairly common. None of these variants can be described as a strictly Southern phenomenon.

SHR

In words such as *shrimp*, *shrink*, and *shrub*, many white Southerners produce [sɹ] instead of [ʃɹ]. Early reports of this feature were from the South Atlantic states, especially Virginia. In the Gulf States, LAGS found it to be widespread but most heavily concentrated in the Piedmont and Piney Woods regions. Surprisingly, LAGS found little correlation of [sɹ] with sex, age, education, or social status.

ZN, VN

Before *n*, voiced fricatives often undergo assimilation and become voiced stops. The result is forms such as *idn't*, *wadn't*, and *bidness* for *isn't*, *wasn't*, and *business*, respectively, and *sebem* and *elebem* for *seven* and *eleven* (with assimilation of /n/ to the labial place of articulation as well). Theoretically, this process might also affect /ðn/, as in *heathen*. The assimilation is most frequent in common words. It is sometimes reported as being specifically Southern, but in fact is far more widespread.

TAPS and FLAPS

Like other North Americans, Southerners produce intervocalic coronal stops as a tap or flap [ɾ]. This process normally occurs when the stop falls after any vowel or [ɚ] and before a heterosyllabic vowel or [ɚ], as in *batty* [bær.i], *sit out* [sɪɾ.æɔʔt], *Ida* [aːɾ.ə], *hardy* [hɒɚɾ.i], and *inner* [ĩɾ.ɚ]. It does not occur before a tautosyllabic vocoid, e.g., *attain* [ə.tʰɛin], *go tell* [gɝʉ.tʰɛo], and *a tamale* [ə.tʰəmɑɬi], except for unstressed *to* and *don't*, e.g., *go to* [gɝʉ.ɾə] and *I don't* [aː.ɾõnʔt]. It also affects *nt* clusters, as in *Santa* [sẽɚ̃ɾ.ə] and *enter* [ĩɾ.ɚ]. Technically speaking, a tap occurs after a vowel and a flap after [ɚ] or a tap + vowel (e.g., in *additives*, in which the <dd> is tapped and the <t> flapped). Some Southerners extend tapping/flapping to one additional context: before unstressed /n/. They produce *important* as [ɪm.pʰoɚ̃ɾ.ɪnʔt] and *get in a* as [gɪɾ.ĩɾ.ə] instead of as the more widespread pronunciations [ɪm.pʰoɚ̃ʔt.n̩ʔt] and [gɪʔt.n̩.ə], respectively. This process does not affect all pre-nasal examples, e.g., *button* [bʌʔt.n̩]. Outright deletion of the tap/flap is common in casual speech, e.g. *pretty* [pʰɹʷɪ.i], *little* [ɬɪ.o].

W

Deletion of *w* often occurs, mainly for *one* and *was*, as in *younguns* 'children,' *little 'un*, and *he 'uz* 'he was.' At one time, it apparently occurred in other words, e.g., *Edward*.

HW, HJ

The sequence *wh*, as in *which*, was formerly widely pronounced as [hw] (or [ʍ]) in the South; Kurath and McDavid (1961) found it in all parts of the South except the Low Country and part of Maryland. Nearly all young Southerners today produce it as [w], however. LAGS found that better-educated speakers were more likely to distinguish *wh*.

Pronunciation of the /hj/ sequence, as in *huge* and *Houston*, as /j/ occurs sporadically; most published reports of it are from Texas.

Intrusive T

A few words, notably *once, twice, across,* and *cliff,* may show an intrusive [t] after the final fricative, e.g., [wʌnst]. This process is not limited to the South but is especially common in older rural Southern white speech. Intrusive [t] is also reported in other words, e.g., *sermont* for *sermon.*

Other consonantal variables

Three other consonantal variables that have attracted extensive sociolinguistic attention are simplification of final consonant clusters (as in *last* and *raised*), unstressed final *-ing* (as in *looking* and *something*), and realization of nasal consonants in syllables codas only as vowel nasalization (as in [dõũ] for *don't*). As with other varieties of English, simplification of final consonant clusters is infrequent before vowels, common before consonants, and intermediate before pauses, as well as being more frequent in monomorphemic words (*last*) than in bimorphemic words (*raised*). Forms such as [pʰousɪz], [wɔsɪz], and [dɛsɪz] as the plurals of *post, wasp,* and *desk,* respectively, which were common in older African American speech, occurred only rarely in older Southern white speech. Forms such as [pʰoustɪz], [wɔspɪz], and [dɛskɪz] were more common in white speech but are now quite recessive and are currently most prevalent in Appalachia. Unmarked plurals or plurals such as [pʰousː] are still fairly common in white Southern speech, but they are widespread elsewhere, too.

Unstressed final *-ing* may occur as [ɪn] at higher rates in white Southern speech than in other white North American English, but otherwise it shows the same social and stylistic conditioning (i.e., [ɪn] is more frequent among lower socioeconomic groups, among males, and in less formal styles). Hypercorrection, e.g., *mounting* and *chicking* for *mountain* and *chicken*, was once common in the South, especially in writing. Realization of nasals in codas as vowel nasality is widespread as a sandhi-form.

Yet another consonantal variation, merger of /w/ and /v/ to [ʋ], once occurred around the Pamlico Sound and perhaps elsewhere but has now disappeared (Wolfram and Thomas 2002).

4.   Current issues

The most pervasive issue in studies of rural Southern white accents has been their relationship to African American vernaculars. This issue includes several more specific questions. Did African American vernacular speech arise from an earlier rural Southern white vernacular, or have they always differed? Did African American speech influence Southern white speech, and if so, how? Has rural Southern white speech been moving away from or toward African American norms in recent decades? What sorts of features have spread across ethnic lines, and which ones have not? At present, there is no consensus on any of these controversies. For example, it has been suggested that non-rhoticity spread from slave speech to white speech in the South, a contention supported by early accounts of white children adopting accents from slave children, by the concentration of non-rhoticity in former plantation areas, and by the consistently higher incidence of non-rhoticity in African American speech (Feagin 1997). However, others have argued that non-rhoticity emerged as an imitation of British usage, largely because Southerners of means often sent their children to England to be educated (e.g., Johnson 1928). The fact that Southerners with sufficient wealth to send their children to school tended to be slaveholders might explain why non-rhoticity was concentrated in plantation areas. A third explanation for non-rhoticity is that the original English settlers brought it, but rhotic regions in English-settled areas, such as the Pamlico Sound region, would seem to militate against that possibility (though settlers could have brought non-rhoticity in unstressed syllables). At any rate, while it appears clear that whites borrowed some morphological processes from African Americans, it is nearly impossible to prove or disprove that phonological borrowing occurred.

Similarly, the contemporary relationship between African American and Southern white vernaculars is open to dispute. There is ample evidence that African Americans in the South are not participating or barely participating in several aspects of the "Southern Shift" that typify the speech of Southern whites, such as GOOSE and GOAT fronting and FACE lowering. Whether this division reflects African American reaction against white norms, white reaction against African American norms, or a combination is not entirely clear. Even though the two ethnic groups have been diverging for those vowel quality features, the possibility that they may borrow other features from each other, such as pre-/l/ mergers, deserves some scrutiny.

Other issues have received less attention. The origins of white Southern English have sparked some inquiry, and some evidence suggests that many defining features of Southern speech, such as glide weakening of PRIZE, may not have spread widely until the late 19th or early 20th centuries (Bailey 1997). Another issue is what effects the recent population movements of the South, especially the heavy in-migration of Northerners, are having on Southern speech. It appears that these movements have made more of an impact on urban centers than on rural areas. However, it is difficult to say how impervious rural areas are to such changes. Rural areas may be intensifying Southern dialectal features in reaction to the cities, or they may eventually succumb to urban influences. The status of individual features has garnered considerable attention. Two of the most intensively studied changes are the spread of rhoticity and the disappearance of [j] in words such as *tune*. The speed of these changes and the reasons for them have been debated. Among other issues, the Southern drawl is still poorly defined and it has not been determined whether the vowel quality changes associated with the Southern Shift are still spreading or have begun to retreat. The disappearance of certain local features, such as the ingliding forms of FACE and GOAT in the Low Country, has attracted some research.

Clearly, the extensive research conducted on rural white Southern speech in the past has not exhausted the potential research topics on this group of dialects. Future work can be expected to address the issues noted above and open new questions. The intricacies of ethnic relations, population movements, shifts in prestige, and linguistic structure, as well as the historical differences that set the South off from the rest of the United States, combine to make the South a fertile ground for linguistic inquiry.

*   I wish to thank Walt Wolfram and Kirk Hazen for their comments on earlier drafts of this paper. I also wish to thank Guy Bailey, who introduced me to a number of the ideas articulated here, such as the importance of the growth of mill towns, some years ago. Finally, I would like to thank the speakers who contributed their voices to the speech samples on the CD.

Exercises and study questions

1. Four of the six speakers on the audio sample (all but the two youngest) show some non-rhoticity. Describe the pattern of their non-rhoticity. In what contexts are they rhotic and non-rhotic? How consistent is the pattern for each speaker?

2. Describe the pattern of glide weakening of PRICE/PRIZE for each speaker on the audio sample, categorizing the tokens according to the following phonetic context.

3. In what ways is the "Southern drawl" realized for each speaker on the audio sample?

4. Linguistic atlas records of speakers born in the mid-19th century show that whites were less likely to show monophthongal variants of FACE, GOAT, THOUGHT, FLEECE, and GOOSE than African Americans (Dorrill 1986). What implications does this have for understanding the historical relationship between Southern white and African American English? Does it prove anything?

5. Population movement has been a constant in the South. Compare and contrast the linguistic effects of a) the westward movement before the Civil War, b) the movement toward mill towns between the Civil War and World War II, and c) the migration toward the Sunbelt since World War II.

6. Population stability has also characterized parts of the South. The notion of isolation and preservation of old linguistic features has been applied to the Delmarva peninsula, the Pamlico Sound area, the Appalachians, and various other locales, such as Spicewood, Texas (Klipple 1945); the label "Elizabethan English" is often applied to dialects of such places in the popular press. To what degree do these areas really preserve older linguistic features?

Selected references

Please consult the General references for titles mentioned in the text but not included in the references below. For a full bibliography see the accompanying CD-ROM.

Bailey, Guy
    1997   When did Southern English begin? In: Schneider (ed.), 255–75.
Cobb, James C.
    1984   *Industrialization and Southern Society, 1877–1984*. Lexington: University of Kentucky Press.
Dorrill, George T.
    1986   *White and Black Speech in the South: Evidence from the Linguistic Atlas of the Middle and South Atlantic States*. New York: Peter Lang.
Feagin, Crawford
    1997   The African contribution to Southern States English. In: Bernstein, Nunnally and Sabino (eds.), 123–39.
Harris, Maverick Marvin
    1969   The retroflexion of postvocalic /r/ in Austin. *American Speech* 44: 263–71.

Johnson, H. P.
    1928   Who lost the Southern "r?" *American Speech* 3: 377–83.
Klipple, Florence Carmelita
    1945   The speech of Spicewood, Texas. *American Speech* 20: 187–91.
Labov, William
    1991   The three dialects of English. In: Eckert (ed.), 1–44.
Levine, Lewis, and Harry J. Crockett, Jr.
    1966   Speech variations in a Piedmont community. *Sociological Inquiry* 36: 204–26.
McDavid, Raven I., Jr.
    1948   Postvocalic /-r/ in South Carolina: A social analysis. *American Speech* 23: 194–203.
    1958   The dialects of American English. In: Francis, 480–543.
Woodward, C. Vann
    1951   *Origins of the New South, 1877–1913.* Baton Rouge: Louisiana State University Press.

The urban South: phonology

Jan Tillery and Guy Bailey[*]

1. Introduction

The single most important social fact about the American South since 1880 has been the urbanization of its population. Much of the current social fabric of the region, including increased educational levels, the existence of a substantial middle class, and both the Jim Crow laws that formalized racial segregation after 1890 and the Civil Rights movement that eliminated those laws after 1964, developed in part because of the emergence of Southern towns and cities. Urbanization has had profound linguistic consequences as well, initially forging a number of local vernaculars into the regional dialect we know of as Southern American English (SAmE) and later reshaping and transforming that dialect. A brief overview of urbanization in the South will illustrate how this process could factor in both the formation and the transformation of a dialect. A review of some phonological features of the urban South (and a comparison with the features of rural Southern phonology outlined in Thomas [this volume]) will illustrate the extent of the transformation.

2. Urbanization in the South

The urbanization of the South has taken place in two phases. Lasting from about 1880 to the beginning of World War II, the first phase saw the emergence of towns and small cities, with most of the new urban population coming from the surrounding countryside. The second phase, which began during World War II and continues today, has seen the development of large metropolitan areas, with the population coming not only from the surrounding countryside, but also from other areas of the United States. Both phases were rooted in larger economic forces, but their demographic and linguistic consequences were different.

2.1.   Late 19th century urbanization

The immediate impetus for the first phase of urbanization was the rapid and widespread expansion of general stores after the Civil War.

> While some general stores had grown up at junctions on Southern railroads in the 1850s, the clientele and impact of those stores remained small. Slaves could buy nothing, and small farmers, who spent most of their energy for their household or local market, had little currency and little need for credit ... The situation changed rapidly after emancipation with the rapid emergence of country stores in the late 1860s and 1870s. National laws written during the Civil War put most banks in the North and left stores to dispense the vast majority of credit [something which Southern farmers desperately needed because of the devastation of the war], with unplanted crops [serving] as collateral (Ayers 1992: 13).

The general store, then, served as the link between Northern bankers and Southern farmers and over the course of the last quarter of the 19th and early part of the 20th centuries "increasingly stood at the center of the rural economy" (Ayers 1992: 86). As a result of their importance to the rural economy, the growth in the number of stores during the last quarter of the 19th century was stunning: "by the turn of the century, the South contained 150,653 stores" (Ayers 1992: 81).

General stores not only played an essential role in the post-bellum Southern economy, but they also formed the nucleus of an emerging urban system in the

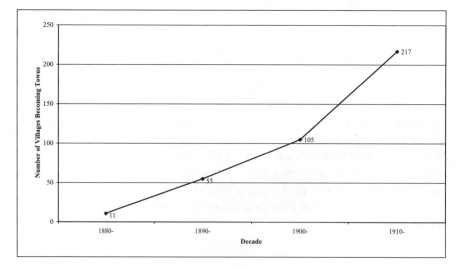

Figure 1.   Number of villages crossing the urban threshold (reaching populations of 2,500) between 1880 and 1910 (Source: Ayers 1992)

South. Because stores also supplied furnishings for an increasingly less self-sufficient farm population, loose clusterings of houses frequently grew up near them. With the construction of cotton gins, churches, schools, and railroads, these loose clusters often grew into the villages (settled places with populations under 2,500) that began to dot the Southern countryside after 1880. Some of these further evolved into towns (settled places with populations greater than 2,500 – the U. S. Census Bureau's definition of an urban area) and thus formed the first phase of urbanization in the South. The growth in the number of villages and towns was as stunning as the growth in the number of stores was: "the number of villages doubled between 1870 and 1880 and then doubled again by 1900 (Ayers 1992: 20). Literally "thousands of villages came into existence during the last quarter of the 19th century, and (as figure 1 shows), hundreds more passed over the line into official 'urban' status …" (Ayers 1992:55).

The end result of the rapid growth of villages and towns was a widespread redistribution of the Southern population. At the beginning of the Civil War only 10% of the Southern population lived in urban areas, and most of them were concentrated in only 22 cities and towns (four with populations greater than 25,000 and 18 with populations between 5,000 and 25,000). As late as 1880 urban residents represented only 12% of the Southern population, but after 1880 the urban and village population of the South expanded rapidly.

> The village and town population of the South grew by more than five million people between 1880 and 1910. The growth came fastest in the 1880s, slowed in the 1890s, and then accelerated again in the first decade of the new century. Villages … accounted for about a quarter of that increase. In 1900, about one of every six Southerners – in some regions, one of every four – lived in a village or town (Ayers 1992: 55).

Drawn largely from the surrounding countryside, the urban population of the South (the population living in communities of at least 2,500) reached 18% in 1900 and stood at 37% in 1940.

Two other factors were important in the first phase of urbanization in the South. First, even as the number of villages and towns grew as a consequence of the development of general stores, the emergence of the textile, lumber, tobacco, and mining industries provided the South with an incipient industrial base and an impetus for further urban growth. The incipient industrial base was especially important in the development of larger towns and cities. As a result, by 1910 the South included 33 cities with populations greater than 25,000 and 140 towns with populations greater than 5,000.

Second, the rapid expansion of the rail system paralleled the growth in the number of villages and towns and provided a mechanism that linked the entire urban network in the South. The parallel growth of the rail system meant that "from their very beginning, the villages, towns, and cities of the New South worked as parts of complicated and interdependent networks" (Ayers 1992: 20). This interconnected grid of population clusters stood in stark contrast to the self-sufficient, isolated farms and plantations of the antebellum South.

2.2.   Post-1940 urbanization (metropolitanization)

The first phase of urbanization proceeded steadily from 1880 until the advent of World War II. Mobilization for the war, however, led to a rapid accelera-tion of urban growth, to significant changes in the paths of urbanization, and ultimately to another substantial redistribution of the Southern population. Urbanization occurred at an astonishing pace during this second phase, and because it was focused primarily on the larger cities of the South, is probably better termed "metropolitanization". In 1940 just over a third of all Southern-ers lived in urban areas; 30 years later more than two thirds lived in towns and cities. However, whereas urbanization during the late 19th century involved the creation of villages and towns and migration to towns and small cities from the surrounding countryside, post-1940 urbanization involved migration to large cities and metropolitan areas and involved inter-regional migration as well as migration from the immediate area.

Urbanization during this second phase was initially triggered by the expan-sion of military installations in the South and the gearing up of industry to meet war needs. After the war, both the rapid mechanization of Southern agriculture, along with the consequent reduction in the number of family farms, and also Southern industrial development led to continued growth of the urban popula-tion, again primarily in large cities. Further, for the first time in the history of the South, the number of rural residents (as opposed to just the proportion) began to decline.

During the 1970s these trends received new impetus from the "Sunbelt Phe-nomenon", which was spurred by rapidly expanding economic development in the South and the decay of industry in the North. After 1970, however, urban growth occurred almost exclusively in metropolitan areas. Rural areas, towns, and even small cities began to stagnate and lose population as Southerners increasingly moved to the largest cities in the region. Again, the rate of the mi-gration to metropolitan areas is stunning. By 2000, some 78% of the Southern population lived in 119 metropolitan areas, all but four of which had more than 100,000 residents, while 43% of the population was concentrated in 19 met-ropolitan areas with populations greater than 1,000,000. These figures include Virginia residents, but not Maryland residents or residents of other states in the Washington, D. C. metropolitan area. Even if this area and other fringe areas of the South (e.g. Miami) were eliminated, the conclusions outlined above would still hold. The growth of Southern metropolises after 1970 was fueled not only by migration from the surrounding countryside, but also by migration from the North. The latter reversed a long-standing pattern, begun with the advent of World War I, that saw massive numbers of Southerners moving to Northern cities for work. Although the reversal of the South-to-North migration pattern was initially a white phenomenon, by the 1990s African Americans had begun to return to the South as well. The large-scale migration of African Americans out of the South continued through the mid-1970s, but during the 1990s African Americans began to move southward at a rate that closely paralleled their earlier exodus.

In the space of 120 years, then, what was once an agrarian society comprised primarily of isolated, self-sufficient farms, with almost nine of ten people living in rural areas, became a commercial-industrial society organized around large, interconnected metropolises, with almost eight of 10 people residing in just 119 metropolitan areas. The transformation of the demographic landscape has had an enormous impact on Southern culture and language. Like the process of urbanization, however, the linguistic transformation of the South has been complex and has taken place in two distinct stages.

3.   Phonology of the urban South

The half-century following 1880 was a period of extraordinary activity for SAmE phonology. During that time, many of the most distinctive features of the SAmE vowel system either first appeared or became widespread (e.g., monophthongization of the vowel in the PRIZE and PRICE classes, the merger of the vowels in the PEN and PIN classes, the vowel rotations known as the Southern Shift, and probably the Southern Drawl [see Bailey 1997; Feagin 1996; and Thomas 2001]). These are illustrated below. At the same time, some older hallmarks of rural SAmE began gradually to disappear (e.g., the long offglide in words like DANCE [dæɪnts]) and the "loss" of stressed syllabic and, to a lesser extent, postvocalic *r* in words like *third* [θɜd] and NORTH [nɔəθ ~ nɔθ]). In fact, Bailey (1997) argues that what we now think of as SAmE is largely a product of developments of this half-century. The kind of data that would indicate decisively whether or not these linguistic developments emerged first in urban areas and then spread elsewhere does not exist. The correlation of their spread with the initial period of urbanization, however, suggests that both the dialect contact that was a consequence of town and city building and also the expanded communication networks among villages, towns, and cities provided the impetus for the formation of a regional dialect from what was earlier a number of local vernaculars.

The regional dialect that was formed during the first phase of urbanization has been substantially transformed during the second phase. As non-Southerners have moved into the Southern cities in large numbers, many stereotypical features of SAmE, including some of those that emerged during the first period of urbanization, have begun to disappear in Southern metropolitan areas, especially during the last 30 years. As a consequence, the current metropolitan-rural distinction that has developed since the 1970s forms a major axis of variation in SAmE (see Thomas 1997), rivaling ethnicity as a correlate of language differences.

3.1.   Merger and the evolution of the SAmE phonological system

The last 30 years have seen significant shifts in the phonological inventory and in the sets of phonological contrasts in urban SAmE, especially in the largest cities and in the southwest. Historically, SAmE was one of the U.S. varieties that distinguished the vowels in words like LOT (pronounced with a low back unrounded vowel [ɑ]) from those in words like THOUGHT (pronounced with a low back rounded, often upgliding vowel [ɔ ~ ɔo]). Since World War II, and especially since the 1970s, however, the vowels in these two classes have increasingly become merged in Southern metropolises, with both realized as [ɑ]. The precise reason for the development of the merger after World War II is not clear, but three factors have likely played a role:

(1) extensive in-migration from the Midwest, where the THOUGHT/LOT distinction was often not maintained,

(2) the rapid growth of the Hispanic population, a group that does have the contrast, in the Southwest and in Florida, and

(3) the mild stigma that has begun to be attached to upgliding allophones of /ɔ/ (and more generally to anything resembling the Southern Drawl).

Once the upglide is eliminated, the vowels of the THOUGHT and LOT classes are so close in phonological space that the difference is difficult to maintain. The merger of the THOUGHT and LOT classes, of course, eliminates one of the most distinctive features of traditional SAmE—upgliding [ɔo] in the THOUGHT class—and aligns the vowel system of urban SAmE more closely with that of the American West in some respects.

The inventory of vowels before *r* and *l* is also changing rapidly in urban SAmE. Older rural Southern varieties often had a three-way distinction among the vowels in words like MARY, MERRY, and MARRY and typically maintained the distinction between vowels in the NORTH and FORCE classes (as [ɔ] and [o] respectively). Beginning after 1880 and accelerating rapidly after World War II, however, the distinction between the MARY and MERRY class began to disappear; currently both are typically pronounced with [ɛ] as the stressed vowel. Over the last quarter century, this merged MARY/MERRY class has begun to merge with the MARRY class as well. When all three are merged, either [ɛ] or [æ] can be the stressed vowel.

The time frame for the merger of the FORCE and NORTH classes parallels that of the MARY/MERRY merger; in the urban South, both FORCE and NORTH are now typically pronounced with close [o], though [ɔ] can also appear in both classes. The ultimate consequence of these mergers, of course, is a reduction in the set of vowel contrasts in SAmE. In stressed syllables, the most advanced varieties of urban SAmE include only two front vowels before tautosyllabic *r* ([i ~ ɪ] and [ɛ ~ æ]), two back vowels ([o] and [u ~ ʊ]), and one low central/back vowel [ɑ], along with a rhotic central vowel of course.

Traditional Southern dialects also maintained distinctions between tense and lax vowels before tautosyllabic *l*, but these distinctions have increasingly been lost over the last half-century too. As a result, vowels in the FEEL and FILL classes are often merged (usually as [ɪ]), as are vowels in the FAIL and FELL classes (usually as [ɛ]). Even more frequent is the merger of vowels in the POOL and PULL classes (usually as [ʊ]). This merger, like the THOUGHT/LOT merger, eliminates one of the hallmarks of earlier SAmE—upgliding or monophthongal [ʊu ~ u] in the POOL class. Finally, among some younger Southerners in urban areas, the stressed vowels in words like *hull* and *Tulsa* ([ʌ] in traditional SAmE) are merged with the vowel that results from the POOL/PULL merger, again usually as [ʊ]. As a result, in stressed syllables the most advanced urban varieties of SAmE include three front vowels before *l* ([ɪ],[ɛ], and [æ]), two back vowels ([ʊ] and [o]), and a low central/back vowel [ɑ ~ ɔ].

Finally, even as both the merger of the vowels in the THOUGHT and LOT classes and also the pre-*r* and pre-*l* mergers have rapidly expanded in Southern cities, one of the hallmarks of SAmE that developed during the period between 1880 and 1940, the merger of vowels before nasals in words like PEN and PIN (almost always as [ɪ]), has begun to recede. Although the PEN/PIN merger became one of the most distinctive features of SAmE after 1880, is still thriving throughout the rural South, and is even expanding in some areas contiguous to the South, in the largest Southern metropolises (areas such as Dallas and Atlanta) it is disappearing. The end result of all of these developments is widespread change in the set of vowel contrasts that affect urban SAmE and a substantial realignment of its phonological system. Table 1 summarizes the vowel mergers that currently affect urban SAmE.

Table 1.   Vowel mergers and their status in urban SAmE

Merged classes	Phonetic realization	Type of merger	Environment	Time frame	Status
PEN/PIN	[pɪn]	Conditioned	Pre-nasal	Post 1880	Contracting
MARY/MERRY	[mɛɚi]	Conditioned	Pre-*r* Front vowel	Post 1880	Expanding
MERRY/MARRY	[mɛɚi ~ mæɚi]	Conditioned	Pre-*r* Front vowel	Post WWII	Expanding
NORTH/FORCE	[noɚθ]	Conditioned	Pre-*r* Back vowel	Post 1880	Expanding
FEEL/FILL	[fɪɫ]	Conditioned	Pre-*l* Front vowel	Post WWII	Expanding
FAIL/FELL	[fɛɫ]	Conditioned	Pre-*l* Front vowel	Post WWII	Expanding
POOL/PULL	[puɫ]	Conditioned	Pre-*l* Back vowel	Post WWII	Expanding
Tulsa/PULL	[tuɫsə]	Conditioned	Pre-*l* Back vowel	Post 1970	Expanding
THOUGHT/LOT	[θɑt]	Unconditioned	———	Post WWII	Expanding

3.2.   Prosodic features

The gradual disappearance of the two most prominent features of traditional SAmE prosody, the Southern Drawl and the shift of primary stress to front syllables, parallels the changes in the set of vowel contrasts. The Southern Drawl typically involves two phonological processes: the extreme lengthening of stressed vowels and the development of ingliding diphthongs with lax vowels that are lengthened. Thus in Drawled speech, MOUTH might be pronounced [mæːoθ], *bid* might be pronounced [bɪːəd], and *bad* might be pronounced as [bæːɛd]. The Drawl is quite recessive in the urban South, confined largely to people born before World War II. Likewise, the shift of primary stress in words like *police*, *Detroit*, and *pecan* to the first syllable is quite rare among younger Southerners in urban areas, although initial syllable stress in *insurance*, *defense*, and in some cases *umbrella* still persists.

Little research exists on other features of SAmE prosody, but one feature of juncture deserves further comment – the syllabification of medial *r* and *l*. In earlier SAmE, medial *r* in words such as MARY and MERRY was grouped with the second syllable. Some time after 1880, the syllabification of medial *r* began to change so that *r* was grouped with the first syllable. This development, which entailed a change in the phonetic realization of *r* from [ɹ] to [ɚ], seems to have been the triggering event in the merger of the vowels in the MARY and MERRY classes (and latter the MARRY class) discussed above.

The situation with medial and post-vocalic *l* presents some interesting similarities and some striking contrasts to *r*. As indicated above, the set of contrasts before tautosyllabic *l* has been reduced in urban SAmE, just as it had earlier before tautosyllabic *r*. The syllabification of medial *l*, however, has not changed. In sets such as *mealy*/*Millie* and *Bailey*/*belly*, *l* usually remains grouped with the second syllable and the tense/lax contrast remains intact.

3.3. Other vowel features

3.3.1. Glide shortening in diphthongs (monophthongization)

The shortening of the offglides of diphthongs in words of the OIL class and of the PRIZE and PRICE classes (especially in the former) is one of the most noticeable features of SAmE. Words like *oil* are pronounced [ɔəɫ] in older and rural varieties of SAmE, while words in the PRIZE class typically have [aːɛ ~ aːə ~ aː] as stressed vowels. Although the history of glide shortening in the *oil* class is unclear, the shortening of offglides in PRIZE/PRICE classes (and in many cases the loss of the glide altogether) began during the last quarter of the 19th century and expanded rapidly thereafter. By the middle of the 20th century, glide-shortened and monophthongal variants of the PRIZE/PRICE classes were prevalent throughout most of the South, especially in voiced environments.

   Glide shortening (or monophthongization) has always been constrained both phonologically and socially, however. A following *r* or *l* has always been the phonological environment that favors monophthongs the most, with following nasals and other voiced obstruents also quite favorable. Before voiceless obstruents, monophthongs have always been less common and more restricted both regionally and socially. Although in voiceless environments [aːɛ~ aːə~aː] occurs throughout the South to some extent and even among African Americans sometimes, these realizations are most common in the Southern Appalachians and contiguous areas and in a broad area of Texas running west of Fort Worth through Lubbock (see Labov, Ash and Boberg 2006). Likewise, monophthongs in the PRICE class are also far more common among whites than blacks. In spite of its widespread geographic and social provenance, however, glide shortening in both the PRIZE and PRICE classes, like the PEN/PIN merger, is receding in the largest cities of the urban South. Increasingly, young Southerners in metropolises like Dallas, Houston, and Atlanta have full diphthongs in all environments, although monophthongs still frequently appear before *l* and *r*. In these same areas, full offglides are becoming the norm in pre-*l* environments for vowels in the *oil* class as well.

3.3.2. Vowel shifts

Like glide shortening, the vowel changes collectively known as the "Southern Shift" all either emerged during the last quarter of the 19th century or began to expand rapidly during that time. Although there is some debate about what exactly comprises the Southern Shift, the following processes have been included as part of it at one time or another:

(1)   the fronting of the vowels in the GOOSE class to [ʉ ~ y] and in the FOOT class to [ɵ ~ ʏ],
(2)   the fronting of the nucleus in the MOUTH class to [æo ~ ɛo],
(3)   the fronting or fronting and lowering of the vowels in the GOAT class to [ɜy ~ ɜʉ ~ æʉ],
(4)   the lowering and retraction of vowels in the FACE class to [ɛɪ ~ æɪ], and
(5)   in parts of the South, the lowering and retraction of the vowels in the FLEECE class to [ɪ > i].

By the middle of the 20th century these developments had become defining characteristics of the SAmE vowel system in most areas of the South. Since World War II, the fronting of back vowels and of the nucleus of the diphthong in the MOUTH class has continued in urban SAmE, even surpassing the fronting in non-urban varieties, and has expanded to include the vowels in the STRUT class sometimes, which can be realized as [ɜ]. The lowering and retraction of the front vowels, however, is receding in the largest metropolitan areas. For many urban Southerners born after 1970, the vowels in the FACE and FLEECE classes are as high as or higher than the vowels in the DRESS and KIT classes, and the tense member of the pair is often further to the front as well.

3.3.3. Consonants

Although it is clearly most different from other American dialects in its vowel system, SAmE also includes some distinctive consonant features. Unlike many other varieties of American English, traditional SAmE preserved *h* before *w* in words like *which* and *white*, maintained *j* after alveolar stops and nasals in words like *Tuesday*, *due*, and *news*, and had unconstricted *r* in postvocalic position. However, over the last 120 years, and particularly since World War II, all of these have begun to disappear in the urban South. In initial clusters, *h* is now usually lost before *w* and sometimes before *j*, so that *which* is typically [wɪtʃ] and *Houston* sometimes [ju:stn]. Likewise, among younger Southern urbanites, *j* is generally lost after alveolars so that *do* and *due* are homophones (both are usually realized as [dʉu]).

The situation with *r* is somewhat more complicated. Although the Southern mountains and piney woods have always been rhotic, in the plantation areas of the South, earlier varieties of SAmE had unconstricted *r* in four environments:

(1)   when *r* followed a vowel (as in *fire, four, ford*, and *far*),
(2)   when it functioned as a stressed syllabic (as in *first* and *fur*),
(3)   when it functioned as an unstressed syllabic (as in *father*), and

(4)   occasionally when it occurred in intersyllabic position (as in MARY and MERRY).

Present-day urban SAmE, however, generally has constricted *r* in all of these environments. The expansion of constricted *r* began first in intersyllabic and stressed syllabic environments before World War II. Since that time constricted variants have become the norm in Southern metropolises not only in inter-syllabic and stressed syllabic environments, but increasingly in postvocalic environments (after front vowels initially and then after back vowels) and in unstressed syllabic contexts as well. In fact, over the last quarter century, the expansion of rhotic variants has been so extensive among white Southerners that non-rhotic forms are now associated primarily with African Americans.

Three other features of traditional SAmE, however, have been preserved in urban SAmE to a greater extent. First, as in rural varieties, post-vocalic *l* is frequently vocalized; the vocalized *l* is often transcribed as [ɤ] in linguistic atlas records, but there is usually some lip rounding with vocalized *l*. Second, again as in rural varieties, medial *z* often undergoes assibilation before *n* so that *isn't* is pronounced [ɪdn] and *wasn't* pronounced [wʌdn]. (Note, however, that urban SAmE differs from rural varieties in that *v* is rarely assibilated in words like *seven*.) Finally, especially in rapid speech, final nasals are still sometimes realized only as vowel nasality; this accounts for the fact that *don't* can be pronounced as [dõʊ]. Other consonant features of traditional SAmE phonology, such as intrusive *t* in words like *once* and the unusually high rate of consonant cluster simplification, have largely disappeared from urban SAmE.

4.   Some issues for further research

Although recent research sheds considerable light on the urbanization of SAmE, a number of issues remain unresolved. For instance, the correlation between ur-banization and widespread phonological change is clear, but the motivations for innovations and their paths of diffusion are not clear. Bailey, Wikle, Tillery and Sand (1993) show that innovations may have traveled along a variety of paths of diffusion (i.e., either up or down the urban hierarchy or "contagiously"). However, whether different types of innovation correlate with different types of diffusion remains unclear and is an important topic for future research.

The triggers for linguistic innovation in urban SAmE are less clear than the paths of diffusion. Recent work on vowel–consonant transitions is promising, though. For example, Tillery, Bailey, Andres, Miller and Palow (2003) sug-gest that vowel-consonant transitions between diphthongs and a following *r* or *l* may have triggered glide shortening in words of the PRIZE/PRICE classes. They marshal linguistic atlas evidence to show that glide shortening probably occurred first in words like *file* and *fire*, then spread to other voiced environments, and finally diffused to voiceless environments in some areas. The development of monophthongs in the PRIZE/PRICE classes, in turn, created the phonetic context that allowed for the lowering and retraction of vowels in the FACE class, one of the major features of the Southern Shift (Labov, Ash, and Boberg 2006). The emergence of several of the most distinctive characteristics of SAmE, then, may have been triggered simply by the transition from vowels to a following *r* or *l*. While these are hypotheses that still must be confirmed, they do point to phonetic contexts as an important locus for studying the motivation for phonological change in SAmE. Fortunately, both the formation and the transformation of urban SAmE has occurred recently enough (within the last 125 years) that its history is well documented. The existence of such documentation (much of it on tape recordings) provides an unusual opportunity for studying the diffusion of linguistic innovations and the motivations for language change.

The transformation of urban SAmE is still a work in progress. Both in-migration and metropolitanization continue to be major forces in the South. In the United States, net gains in domestic migration between 1995 and 2000 were limited almost exclusively to the South and the Intermountain West. Domestic migration in some areas, though, now pales in comparison to migration from other countries. In Texas, for instance, net domestic migration between 1995 and 2000 was 148,000. Foreign migration during just the two-year span between 2000 and 2002, however, was more than 360,000. While most other Southern states have not yet experienced migration from abroad to this extent, the foreign population in states such as North Carolina and Georgia is growing at a rapid pace and is creating an ethnic complexity heretofore unknown. How the continuing transformation of the Southern population and its increasing ethnic complexity will affect SAmE is an important question for future research.

The concentration of the new Southerners in the largest cities of the region also creates new opportunities for social fissures in SAmE. The Sunbelt migration after 1970 and the rapid growth of the population in the largest metropolitan areas have already created significant new sociolinguistic dimensions. In the American Southwest, rurality and nativity now have more important consequences for linguistic variation than such factors as social class and gender do, and the emerging rural/urban split seems to be producing a dichotomy much like the earlier Southern/South Midland distinction. This emerging dichotomy provides an important venue for studying mechanisms of dialect creation.

Although African Americans returning to the South are now a significant part of the migration to the region, precisely how they will either impact or be impacted by the SAmE of whites is an open question. The relationship between African American Vernacular English (AAVE) and various white vernaculars, of course, has been an on-going controversy for more than 30 years. It is increasingly clear, however, that both a significant part of the distinctiveness of AAVE and also its relative uniformity across the United States is a consequence of the African American population's movement to and concentration in the inner-city areas of large metropolises. Future research on urban SAmE should examine whether African Americans maintain these national AAVE norms or whether they adopt local norms as they return to the South. The impact of African Americans on white speech also deserves consideration. Before they began leaving the South during World War I, African Americans had a significant influence on rural SAmE. Whether or not they influence urban SAmE as they return to the South is an important question for future research.

Because of its distinctiveness, SAmE has long been the most widely studied regional variety of American English. While the metropolitanization of SAmE is eroding some of that distinctiveness, it certainly has not eliminated it. Perhaps more important, metropolitanization has created new dimensions of language variation that should make SAmE fertile ground for research for years to come.

*   We wish to thank Erik Thomas for his insights into the development of the urban/rural-dichotomy in the South.

Exercises and study questions

For technical reasons, the audio files from the urban South referred to here (two reading passages) are not available on the CD-ROM. They can be obtained from the publisher's website.

1. The two speakers reading "The North Wind and the Sun" were born 30 years apart in urban Texas. In what ways did the population of the American South change during those thirty years?

2. In what linguistic environments was sound change most active during that time?

3. Does either of the people reading the passage have the "Southern Drawl"? If so, what words illustrate it?

4. Listen carefully to the words *then* and *obliged*. Do you hear any differences between the two speakers? If so, what are they?

5. Listen again to the passage and identify any instances of the "Southern Shift" that you hear. Do both speakers have the Shift? What words illustrate the shift?

Selected references

Please consult the General references for titles mentioned in the text but not included in the references below. For a full bibliography see the accompanying CD-ROM.

Ayers, Edward L.
   1992   *The Promise of the New South: Life After Reconstruction*. Oxford: Oxford University Press.
Bailey, Guy
   1997   When did Southern English begin? In: Schneider (ed.), Vol. 1, 255–275.
Bailey, Guy, Tom Wikle, Jan Tillery and Lori Sand
   1991   The apparent time construct. *Language Variation and Change* 3: 241–264.
   1993   Some patterns of linguistic diffusion. *Language Variation and Change* 5: 359–390.
   1996   The linguistic consequences of catastrophic events: An example from the Southwest. In: Jennifer Arnold, Renée Blake, Brad Davidson, Scott Schwenter and Julie Solomon (eds.), *Sociolinguistic Variation: Data, Theory, and Analysis*, 435–451. Stanford: Center for the Study of Language and Information.
Feagin, Crawford
   1996   Peaks and glides in Southern short -*a*. In: Guy, Baugh, Feagin and Schiffrin (eds.), 135–160.
Fridland, Valerie
   2000   The Southern Shift in Memphis, Tennessee. *Language Variation and Change* 11: 267–285.
Labov, William
   1991   The three dialects of English. In: Eckert (ed.), 1–44.
Thomas, Erik R.
   1997   A rural/metropolitan split in the speech of Texas Anglos. *Language Variation and Change* 9: 309–332.
Tillery, Jan
   1997   The role of social processes in language variation and change. In: Bernstein, Nunnally and Sabino (eds.), 434–446.
Tillery, Jan, Guy Bailey, Claire Andres, Jeff Miller and Naomi Palow
   2003   Monophthongal /ai/ in the American South: Evidence from three linguistic surveys. Southeastern Conference on Linguistics, Washington DC, 13 April.

The West and Midwest: phonology

Matthew J. Gordon

1. Introduction

This chapter offers a phonological sketch of the varieties of English spoken across the midwestern and western United States. The area covered can be visualized as a fairly narrow band that stretches from western Pennsylvania across central sections of Ohio, Indiana, and Illinois and widens at the Mississippi River to include Missouri, Iowa, and Minnesota and eventually the Great Plains and the western states as it continues to the Pacific coast. To be sure, this vast territory is by no means linguistically homogenous; indeed almost all of the speech characteristics described here occur variably across the regions considered and across speakers within any given region. Nevertheless, there are traits that can be heard throughout this broad territory and that serve to distinguish it from neighboring areas. The region seems also to have some coherence in popular perceptions of American dialects. The speech of this region generally lacks features that are salient markers of place to the ears of most Americans, a tendency that contributes to the perception that the region is "accentless". This sense of the region is encoded in the notion of a "General American" dialect, a term that was used by observers of American English such as H.L. Mencken before Kurath's tripartite division (North, Midlands, South) became received wisdom among dialectologists. General American was typically distinguished from Southern and Eastern speech and was defined negatively as a dialect that lacked the regionally distinctive features of the other two. Some linguists still employ the General American label though they are quick to add that it does not designate a monolithic accent.

2. Sociohistorical background

The territory under consideration here includes lands that came into the possession of the United States over a period of roughly 70 years. The eastern edge of this region (western Pennsylvania) stood as the western frontier during the colonial period. This frontier was expanded in the 1780s with the opening of the Northwest territories which included Ohio, Indiana, and Illinois. The

Louisiana Purchase in 1803 extended the U.S. holdings across the plains and into the Rocky Mountains. An 1846 settlement with Great Britain brought the Oregon Country under sole control of the U.S., thereby stretching the border to the Pacific. The final stages in this American expansion came after war with Mexico, which led to the cession of California and the rest of the Southwest to the U.S. in 1848, an acquisition that was extended southward in 1853 by the Gadsden Purchase of land that became part of Arizona and New Mexico.

This review of territorial expansion paints the broad strokes of the picture of American settlement of the region. The sections of the Old Northwest that are of concern here were settled mainly by two streams of emigrants from the Atlantic states: one coming west across Pennsylvania and the other coming north from the Mountain South. These settlers generally established themselves south of the Great Lakes which contributed to a cultural and linguistic divide with the northern lands which were settled primarily by New Englanders.

West of the Mississippi River the same general pattern held: northern states like Minnesota and the Dakotas tended to attract emigrants from western New York and New England while states like Iowa and Missouri were settled primarily by Midlanders with many of the new Iowans coming from Pennsylvania and Ohio and many of the Missourians coming from Kentucky and Tennessee (Hudson 1988). As American settlement moved west, the population became much more mixed in origin. For example the gold rush that began in 1848 drew people from across the US to California and helped to establish San Francisco as a cosmopolitan urban center. Further north in Oregon, migration in the mid-nineteenth century "drew about equally from the Free States and from the Slave States of the Border South" (Meinig 1972: 165). An exception to the usual diversity found in western settlement is seen in the relative homogeneity of the Mormon population that settled in Utah beginning in 1847.

The preceding account has focussed on settlement by English-speaking emigrants from the eastern US. These emigrants were, of course, moving into lands populated by speakers of other languages. It is probably fair to say that the hundreds of American Indian languages spoken across the West have had little if any impact on the phonology of the dialects of English spoken by Anglos. On the other hand, the legacy of Spanish in the Southwest has had a much greater impact on the English spoken in this area (see Santa Ana and Bayley, this volume). Also significant has been the linguistic influence of numerous European immigrants. Many of these immigrants settled in urban areas such as Pittsburgh and St. Louis, establishing ethnic neighborhoods. There was also a tremendous push to attract immigrants to farming areas in order to build the agricultural economy. Many Germans responded to this call and settled throughout the Midwest. Scandinavians also contributed to the westward flow.

In the last quarter of the nineteenth century an estimated one-fifth of the population of Norway and Sweden emigrated to the States, many of them settling in Minnesota and other areas of the Upper Midwest.

The central lesson to be taken from this sociohistorical overview is that the story of English in the American Midwest and West, while fairly short, nevertheless involves a diverse cast of characters. Given the mix of people from varied origins that settled the region, we might consider the relative uniformity of speech heard here – speech represented in the popular notion of the General American dialect – to be the result of dialect leveling. The process of dialect leveling can be useful in understanding the phonological characteristics discussed below because it accounts for not only the elimination of highly localized features but also the diffusion of innovations across a large region (e.g., Watt and Milroy 1999).

3. Phonetic realizations

3.1. Vowels

Table 1. Common vowel realizations in the American West and Midwest

KIT	ɪ	FLEECE	iɪ ~ iː	NEAR	i		
DRESS	ɛ	FACE	eɪ > eː	SQUARE	ɛ		
TRAP	æ	PALM	ɑ ~ ɑ̲ > ɒ	START	ɑ		
LOT	ɑ ~ ɑ̲ > ɒ	THOUGHT	ɑ ~ ɑ̲ ~ ɒ > ɔ	NORTH	o > ɔ > ɒ		
STRUT	ɜ	GOAT	oʊ ~ ɵʊ > oː	FORCE	o > ɔ		
FOOT	ʊ ~ ü	GOAL	oʊ > oː	CURE	ju > jə		
BATH	æ	GOOSE	uʊ ~ uː ~ ʉ	*happ*Y	i		
CLOTH	ɑ ~ ɑ̲ ~ ɒ > ɔ	PRICE	aɪ > əɪ	*lett*ER	ɜ		
NURSE	ə	CHOICE	ɔɪ > oɪ	*hors*ES	ɪ ~ i > ə		
DANCE	æ̜	MOUTH	aʊ > æʊ > əʊ	*comm*A	ə		

Comments on vowels:

LOT, CLOTH, PALM, THOUGHT: For many of the speakers in this region, the phonemic distinction between /ɑ/ and /ɔ/ has been lost. The geographic distribution and status of this merger is discussed in more detail below. The phonetic realization of the merged vowel varies regionally as well as according to phonological context. Most commonly the result is an unrounded back vowel near [ɑ] or slightly backer [ɑ̠]. The rounded [ɒ] appears to be more geographically restricted and is heard among some speakers in western Pennsylvania and neighboring West Virginia. The Northern Cities Shift (see Gordon, this volume) occurs to a limited extent in central Illinois and St. Louis. As a result, THOUGHT and CLOTH items may appear with a low and often unrounded back vowel, and LOT items may appear with a fronted vowel near [a]. In some parts of the Upper Midwest (e.g., Minnesota), the Northern Cities Shift appears to be moving into areas where the merger of /ɑ/ and /ɔ/ has already taken hold with the result that both LOT and THOUGHT/CLOTH items can appear with fronted vowels. PALM items generally pattern with LOT, and the [l] is frequently realized as an apparent example of spelling pronunciation.

DANCE: Raised allophones, [æ] or higher, are common for /æ/ before nasal consonants across much of the western US. The phonemic split of tense and lax /æ/ found in Middle Atlantic dialects such as Philadelphia and New York (see Gordon, this volume and Labov 1994) does not occur in the regions described here, though a similar phenomenon is heard in Cincinnati as discussed below.

FLEECE, GOOSE: As elsewhere in the US, variation between diphthongal and monophthongal forms appears to be dependant on phonetic length with the diphthongs more common in longer realizations (Thomas 2001). Fronted variants of GOOSE are discussed below.

FACE, GOAT, GOAL: Monophthongal variants of the mid vowels are common in the Upper Midwest. Fronted variants of GOAT are quite widespread throughout the entire region. Both of these features are discussed below.

PRICE, MOUTH: Centralized variants of these diphthongs before voiceless obstruents are heard especially in the northern areas of this region and are apparently an extension of the pattern known as "Canadian Raising" (see Boberg, this volume). Fronting in MOUTH is discussed below.

NORTH, FORCE: The historical distinction between /oɹ/ (e.g., *hoarse*) and /ɔɹ/ (e.g., *horse*) has been lost throughout most of the region. The resulting vowel is most commonly [o]. The low back [ɒ] is restricted to varieties affected by a different merger of /ɑɹ/ and /ɔɹ/ (see below).

3.2.   Consonants

As is true of other areas in North America, there is relatively little salient variation in the realization of consonants, or at least very little consonantal variation
has attracted the attention of linguists. Features worth noting include:

- NG: The variation between [ɪŋ] and [ɪn] that is heard throughout the English-speaking world in verbal <-*ing*> endings is also common here with the
  alveolar form associated with relatively informal styles.

- R: Postvocalic /ɹ/ is practically universal across the region though its actual
  realization may vary. For example, Hartman (1985) characterizes /ɹ/ as involving less retroflexion across a wide area of the West. The words *wash* and
  Washington are often produced with an "intrusive" /ɹ/, thus [wɑɹʃ] or [wɔɹʃ].
  This pronunciation is more common in the traditional Midland dialect areas
  from western Pennsylvania across the central sections of Ohio, Indiana, and
  Illinois and into Iowa, Missouri, and Nebraska. It appears to be more common among rural speakers and is often socially stigmatized – a trend that
  may contribute to its declining use among younger speakers.

- L: As in other parts of the U.S., /l/ may be vocalized or deleted altogether in
  a number of phonological contexts. Realizations such as [hɛp] ~ [hɛwp] ~
  [hɛop] for *help* or [pɪw] ~ [pɪo] for *pill* are more common in the traditional
  Midland areas. For example, the Linguistic Atlas of the Upper Midwest records them in the speech of several Iowans but only a single Minnesotan.
  They are also reported to be characteristic of Pittsburgh speech.

- WH: The distinction between /w/ and /ʍ/ as in *witch* ~ *which* may still be
  heard among some speakers though it is clearly under threat as younger
  speakers tend to merge these in favor of the voiced form, /w/.

3.3.   Suprasegmental features

No suprasegmental features serve as distinctive markers of this region.

4.   Discussion of features showing broad regional currency

This section offers further descriptions of some features that are widespread
across the region under discussion. While none of these features is unique to
this region, their co-occurrence here does serve to distinguish the region from
others.

4.1.   The low back merger

The phonemic contrast between /ɑ/, LOT, and /ɔ/, THOUGHT, has been lost for many speakers in the area described here. This development is the result of an uncondi-tional merger (i.e., one that applies across the board to every phonological context) and creates homophones of pairs such as *cot* and *caught, Don* and *dawn*, and *Polly* and *Paulie*. As noted above, the phonetic value of the merged vowel varies between the poles of the historical sources, /ɑ/ and /ɔ/, but is commonly unrounded, low and quite back. Some sources have treated the merger as a simple shifting of /ɔ/ into [ɑ], but evidence of misunderstandings between merged and unmerged speakers suggests that the phonetic result is more intermediate between [ɔ] and [ɑ]. Hearers who maintain the contrast may perceive a merged speaker's THOUGHT words as members of the LOT class (e.g., *Dawn* heard as *Don*), but the reverse also happens (e.g., *copy* heard as *coffee*).

The low back merger has been well known to dialectologists as a feature of eastern New England, where it tends to show a rounded vowel (Kurath and McDavid 1961). It is also well established across Canada (see Boberg, this vol-ume). For the region covered in this chapter, the early linguistic atlas records show the merger in western Pennsylvania and extending westward on either side of the Ohio river. More recent research has shown the merger to be char-acteristic of the western states (see, e.g., Metcalf 1972; Hartman 1985; Labov, Ash, and Boberg 2006). In an early statement about the merger, Labov (1991: 31) suggested it was a "nonurban" feature, and he noted its absence in Los An-geles and San Francisco. His more recent Telsur project shows the merger to be common in Los Angeles though many San Franciscans still maintain a contrast (see Labov, Ash, and Boberg 2006).

In fact, the low back merger appears to be a relatively new development in the West. Johnson (1975) compares Los Angeles natives who were interviewed in 1953 for the Linguistic Atlas of the Pacific Coast with speakers from his own study twenty years later. He found minimal evidence of the merger among the linguistic atlas speakers while in his sample he observed a steady increase in the adoption of the merger across the generations. Labov's Telsur findings generally confirm this trend and furthermore suggest the merger is spreading geographically into the Upper Midwest as far as Minnesota and into central states such as Kansas and Nebraska. In Missouri, the merger is relatively more common in the western part of the state (e.g., Kansas City) than in the eastern part, though it can be heard in the speech of some younger speakers in St. Louis. The evidence suggests, therefore, that the low back merger is a change in prog-ress and one that is expanding its geographical range.

4.2.   Fronting of /u/, /ʊ/, and /o/

The back vowels /u/, /ʊ/, and /o/ are commonly fronted to a central or nearly front position in vowel space resulting in variants whose nuclei might be transcribed as [ʉ] ~ [y], [ü] ~ [ʏ] and [ɵ] ~ [ø]. Like the low back merger, this is a feature that was identified by earlier dialectological research. The linguistic atlas records show fronted variants of /u/ and /ʊ/ to be fairly common in the South and South Midland while fronting of /o/ appeared to be more geographically restricted and was common in northeastern North Carolina and the Delaware River valley including Philadelphia. Fronting of both /u/ and /o/ was also shown as characteristic on western Pennsylvania (Kurath and McDavid 1961).

More recent evidence suggests that fronting of these back vowels has become very widespread geographically (see Thomas, this volume for a description of the situation in the South). For example, Lusk (1976) found fronting of all three of the vowels among her Kansas City speakers, and Luthin (1987) reports on similar developments in the speech of Californians. Thomas (2001) provides acoustic evidence of fronting of the vowels in several speakers from central and southern Ohio. The Telsur project has examined the position of /u/ and /o/ on a national level and uses acoustic measurements to distinguish various degrees of fronting (Labov 2001: 479; Labov, Ash, and Boberg 2006). For /u/, the most extreme fronting outside of the South is recorded in St. Louis though the rest of the Midland and West also show significant fronting. For /o/, Labov and his colleagues found extreme fronting in Pittsburgh and across central sections of Ohio, Indiana, and Illinois as well as in various locations in Missouri and Kansas. Less extreme fronting was recorded across most of the West including in Denver, Portland, Fresno, and Tucson. The backest (least fronted) variants of both /u/ and /o/ were generally dominant only in extreme northern areas including Montana, the Dakotas, and Minnesota (as well as in the Inland North and New England).

Fronting of these vowels is not normally found in the context of following liquids (i.e., /l/ and /ɹ/). Thomas (2001) plotted separate means for pre-/l/ tokens such as *pool*, *pull*, and *pole*, and his acoustic portraits show that these means generally remain along the back wall of vowel space even in the case of speakers with extreme fronting of the vowels in other contexts. In terms of their relative progression, /u/ fronting seems generally to lead fronting of /ʊ/ and /o/ (Labov 1994: 208; Thomas 2001: 33).

4.3.   Mergers and near mergers before liquids

The liquid consonants /ɹ/ and /l/ are well known for their tendency to influence the quality of adjacent vowels. A number of phonemic contrasts are neutralized in this environment. An example of this is the well established pattern in the West and Midwest whereby the distinctions among /æ/, /ɛ/, and /e/ are lost before /ɹ/. The resulting vowel is typically closest to [ɛ] so that *marry, merry,* and *Mary* are all pronounced as [mɛɹi].

The phoneme /l/ is also contributing to the reduction or loss of several phonemic contrasts across much of the US. Among the most important patterns for the region discussed here are conditioned mergers of /i/ and /ɪ/, /u/ and /ʊ/, and /e/ and /ɛ/ in the context of a following /l/. These mergers result in homophones for pairs such as *feel* and *fill, fool* and *full,* and *fail* and *fell.* The phonetic quality of the merged vowel approximates to the lax member of each pair; i.e., [ɪ], [ʊ], [ɛ] (Thomas 2001: 50).

Compared to the features described above, awareness of these mergers among dialectologists has come relatively recently. Labov, Yaeger, and Steiner (1972) identified mergers of /ul/ ~ /ʊl/, /il/ ~ /ɪl/ and /el/ ~ /ɛl/ among speakers from Albuquerque and Salt Lake City. Labov's more recent investigations through the Telsur project show these mergers to be widespread across almost all of the US though they are distributed quite sparsely in many regions. Their geographical patterning among the Telsur respondents bears some resemblance to that seen with the fronting of /o/: they are relatively more common across the Midland and in southern regions of the West than in the Northwest and Upper Midwest. This similarity in regional distribution is not surprising given that the pre-L mergers, like the fronting of back vowels, are also common in the South (see Thomas, this volume).

The pre-L mergers appear to be a fairly recent development and moreover active changes in progress, at least in some areas. Thomas' (2001) acoustic data suggest, for example, that /ul/ and /ʊl/ are merged for most younger Ohioans, those born after 1963, while older speakers maintain a clear separation in vowel space. Similar generational differences were found among Utahns by Di Paolo and Faber (1990). This latter study also established that these developments do not necessarily result in a complete merger of the vowels. Di Paolo and Faber found that even when the vowels overlap in phonetic space (as shown by acoustic measurements), speakers may preserve a distinction through phonation differences (e.g., creaky voice). One of the most intriguing aspects of these types of changes, which Labov (1994) labels 'near mergers,' is the finding that speakers may perceive no contrast between the sounds even when they consistently produce a distinction phonetically.

4.4.   "Southern" features

Many features that are characteristic of southern accents are heard throughout the Midwest and West as well though their occurrence is more scattered than the items discussed above. In terms of the traditional dialectological divisions, many of these pronunciations are associated with the South Midlands (or Upper South) rather than with the South proper. More background and information about the distribution of these features in the South can be found in Thomas (this volume).

One of the most common of these southern features is the fronting of the nucleus of /aʊ/ to something like [æʊ] often with a lowering of the glide to [æɔ]. Despite its Southern associations, this feature is heard well north of the Ohio river across roughly the lower halves of Ohio, Indiana and Illinois. It can also be heard across most of Missouri and Kansas and into Iowa and Nebraska. Linguistic atlas records (Allen 1973-76) document this pronunciation as far north as Minnesota, and the Telsur project shows that it is also heard throughout the West.

Also widespread in the Midwest and West is the merger of the vowels of KIT and DRESS before nasal consonants, a feature known as the *pin/pen* merger. The geographical distribution of this merger resembles that of /aʊ/-fronting though the merger's occurrence seems to be more spotty. The Telsur data suggest the merger is scattered across Ohio and Illinois and is more common in Indiana. Telsur also recorded several speakers in Missouri, Kansas and Nebraska with the merger. In the West, the *pin/pen* merger appears less common among Telsur informants, but it is documented throughout the region including the Pacific Northwest and California. The fact that the Telsur project concentrated on urban speech may have resulted in its underrepresenting the appearance of this merger. For example, studies of rural speech in Ohio indicate the merger is much more common than the Telsur sample suggests. Similarly, none of the Los Angeles informants for Telsur gave clear evidence of the merger, but Metcalf (1972) reports the merger to be quite common further inland in Riverside, CA.

The distributions of other southern features in the West and Midwest are less well documented. These include variants of /ɔ/ as upgliding diphthongs, that is [ɔu] or [ɔɔ]. These variants are particularly common in the context of a following /g/ as in *dog* or *log*. They have been recorded in Ohio, Indiana, Illinois, and Missouri and can certainly be heard elsewhere in the Midwest as well. The same can be said for monophthongal variants of /aɪ/. In the South monophthongized /aɪ/ appears before obstruents (e.g., *side*, *prize*), but here such variants are generally heard only before resonants (e.g., *time*, *tire*).

The appearance of "Southern" features in Midwest and West is clearly a result of the settlement patterns discussed above. Many of the early American settlers to this region came from states like Tennessee, Kentucky, and North Carolina. In central states such as Missouri and Illinois, these Southerners, being the first Americans to homestead there, came to occupy the prime farming lands, while Northerners, who arrived later, often settled in towns. Thus, the fact that many of the features discussed in this section are more common among rural speakers is no doubt a reflection of such early settlement tendencies.

5.   Discussion of features with localized distributions

It comes as no surprise that within an area so vast as the one treated in this chapter there are a number of pronunciation features that distinguish one region or city from others. The features described in this section illustrate some of the local phonological flavor to be heard in the West and Midwest. This list is not intended to be exhaustive, and interested readers can learn more about particular locations by consulting the specialist literature including the linguistic atlas projects.

5.1.   Monophthongal mid vowels in the Upper Midwest

For most speakers in the West and Midwest (as in other areas), the vowels of GOAT and FACE involve an upgliding diphthong; i.e., [oʊ] and [eɪ]. In the Upper Midwest, however, these vowels are often produced as monophthongs, sometimes with lengthening: [o] ~ [oː] and [e] ~ [eː]. Data from the Linguistic Atlas of the Upper Midwest (Allen 1973-76) suggest that monophthongal variants are more common in GOAT items than in FACE items, and also that they are more common in *coat* than in *ago* or *road*, which may indicate phonological conditioning.

Regionally, monophthongal mid vowels are more common in the northern tier of states. Linguistic Atlas records show them to be frequent in Minnesota and the Dakotas but much rarer in Iowa and Nebraska. The appearance of monophthongs in this region is sometimes explained as a consequence of the high degree of Scandinavian and German immigration to these northern states in the late nineteenth century. Thomas (2001) argues that these monophthongs are the product of language contact and notes that other areas where they occur are places where speakers of other languages have had an influence such as the Pennsylvania "Dutch" region. An alternative account posits that these monophthongal variants represent historical retentions. Diphthongization of the mid vowels seems to have been a relatively recent phenomenon, appearing within the last few centuries, and did not affect all dialects in the U.K. The monophthongs heard in the Upper Midwest may stem from the influence of Scots-Irish or other British dialects that maintain such forms. The fact that the monophthongs also appear in Canadian English may lend support to this account since Scots-Irish speech is known as an important influence in Canada.

5.2. Lowering of lax front vowels in California

In California, the vowels of KIT and DRESS may undergo lowering, and the vowel of TRAP may undergo both lowering and backing which results in realizations near [ɛ], [æ], and [a] respectively. Impressionistic descriptions of this trend suggest *six* sounds like *sex*, *sex* like *sax*, and *sax* like *socks*. This lowering appears to be a recent development and may be a change in progress. It was not noted in earlier studies of California English and seems to have come to the attention of linguists only in the mid-1980s. It is reported to be especially characteristic of the speech of young urban women—a pattern that is consistent with its interpretation as an active change. The geographical extent of this lowering is not known, but it has been documented in both Southern California and the San Francisco Bay area (see Hagiwara 1997; Luthin 1987).

   The behavior of the lax front vowels in California bears a striking resemblance to a pattern heard north of the border and known as the Canadian shift (see Boberg, this volume). Dialect contact is unlikely to be responsible for this similarity. Rather, the lowering in both varieties seems to stem from a common structural motivation. Both in California and across Canada, the LOT and THOUGHT vowels are merged, and, as described above, the resulting vowel is typically low and quite back. This merger thus provides /æ/ with greater freedom to shift since it can be lowered and retracted into the low central area of vowel space without encroaching on the territory of the LOT/THOUGHT vowel. When /æ/ shifts, this creates an opening into which /ɛ/ may be lowered, which in turns creates an opening into which /ɪ/ may lower. In this sense, the development of the lax vowels appears to be a chain shift, specifically a drag chain (see Labov 1994).

5.3. /aʊ/ monophthongization in Pittsburgh

One of the more unusual characteristics of Pittsburgh speech is the monophthongization of /aʊ/ to [aː]. Unlike the case of /aɪ/, monophthongization of /aʊ/ is rare in American English and has not been reported outside of Western Pennsylvania. Locally, social awareness of this feature is high, and it is commonly exemplified by spelling *downtown* as "dahntahn". Monophthongization occurs in a variety of phonological contexts including following nasals (e.g., *downtown*), liquids (e.g., *fowl, hour*), and obstruents (e.g., *house, out, cloudy*). It is not found, however, word finally (e.g., *how, now*). Monophthongization appears to be especially characteristic of white working class speakers. Its origins are not well documented, but it seems to have arisen in the late nineteenth or early twentieth centuries during a period of rapid industrial growth for the city. At that time Pittsburgh saw a great influx of immigrants speaking other dialects as well as other languages, and monophthongal /aʊ/ is likely a product of that dialect contact.

5.4.   Tensing of /æ/ in Cincinnati

The vowel of TRAP, BATH, and DANCE, known as "short-a", serves as a distinguishing feature of several American dialects. As noted above, the pattern found throughout most of the West and Midwest involves moderate raising of the vowel in the context of a following nasal. In Cincinnati, /æ/ is raised in this environment as well as before fricatives (e.g., *have, path*) and /d/ (e.g., *bad*). Phonetically, the raised variants are described as "tensed" because they typically involve a peripheral nucleus with an inglide; i.e., [eə]. Similar forms are heard in the Great Lakes region as part of the Northern Cities Shift and along the Atlantic Coast including the cities of Philadelphia and New York (see Gordon, this volume). However, the Cincinnati pattern is distinct from the others in terms of its conditioning. The tense forms appear in a wider range of contexts in Cincinnati speech than in the Mid-Atlantic dialects. Raising before voiced fricatives, for example, is very restricted in the East. On the other hand, tensing does not occur in all contexts, a fact that distinguishes Cincinnati speech from that affected by the Northern Cities Shift. Speakers in the Inland North, for example, will typically have raised forms before voiceless stops (e.g., *cat*) and /l/ (e.g., *pal*) while such items appear with a lax [æ] in Cincinnati. Actually, the Cincinnati pattern described here is today largely restricted to older speakers and appears to be undergoing change. Younger Cincinnatians seem to be moving toward the general Western pattern in which raising of /æ/ occurs only before nasals.

5.5.   Merger of /ɑɹ/ and /ɔɹ/ in St. Louis

As noted above, across most of the region discussed here the vowel of NORTH (historically /ɔɹ/) merges with that of FORCE (historically /oɹ/). In the St. Louis area and perhaps elsewhere, however, an alternative merger occurs in which

NORTH merges with START and so pairs such as *for ~ far, lord ~ lard*, and *born ~ barn* become homophones. The usual phonetic outcome of this merger is a back vowel near [ɒ] or [ɔ]. This feature carries a high degree of social awareness and is stereotypically represented in the pronunciation of the local highway *forty-four* as [fɒɹifoɹ]. Research on this merger is limited, but it is reported to be most common among working class St. Louisans and is heard with decreasing frequency as one moves up the socioeconomic ladder. The merger appears to be recessive as younger St. Louisans tend to exhibit the more widespread pattern that merges NORTH with FORCE.

6.   Concluding remarks

In popular perception, the speech of the American Midwest and West is largely uniform and unremarkable. When asked to imitate the speech of a Southerner or a New Yorker, most Americans can comply even if they manage to offer only a stock phrase such as "Yall come back now, y'hear?" Asked to imitate the speech of someone from Kansas City or Denver or Portland, however, they are likely to reply with blank stares. The speech of these places does not draw comment, in part, because it is accepted as a kind of national norm. The accents of the West and Midwest tend to lack features that Americans perceive as regionally distinctive such as *r*-lessness. The fact that such regionally marked features are also very often avoided in the broadcast media contributes to this sense that "normal" speech is found in the West and Midwest. The label "General American" has been used to capture this notion of an unmarked accent that is heard across the nation outside of the South and the Atlantic Coast. Thus, the area originally associated with General American included not only those parts of the Midwest and West that are considered here but also the Great Lakes region. Nevertheless, with recent sound changes such as the Northern Cities Shift (see Gordon, this volume), the latter area, known to dialectologists as the Inland North, has grown more regionally distinctive and therefore has more difficulty passing for General American.

The description provided in this chapter serves to counter the popular sense of a monolithic General American accent. The speech of the West and Midwest is richly variable. We have discussed features that vary from one region to another as well as features that vary from one group of speakers to another within a given region. Many of these features involve active sound changes. Changes such as the low back merger or the fronting of back vowels, which already have a widespread distribution, appear to still be spreading. At the same time many localized features such as /æ/ tensing in Cincinnati or the merger of /ɔɹ/

and /ɑɹ/ in St. Louis are on the decline. These trends are characteristic of dialect leveling, a process that leads to the reduction of regional variation. It might appear, then, that the monolithic General American accent of popular perception will eventually become reality. However, the wheels of language change will keep turning, and new trends will emerge that will continue to contribute to the variable linguistic landscape.

Exercises and study questions

1. Even though many Americans think of the Midwest and West as "accentless", there are a number of pronunciation features that distinguish this region. List some of the features that you believe are most noticeable to outsiders.

2. Is it correct that Americans do not have strong stereotypes of Midwestern or Western speech? Test this claim by surveying several people. Ask them how people from Kansas City, Omaha, Denver, and Portland sound? Are there places in the Midwest or West that Americans do have linguistic stereotypes of? Ask about Los Angeles, San Francisco, or other well-known cities. Try to survey people from various parts of the country. Why do linguistic stereotypes exist for some places and not others?

3. How is the speech of Midwesterners and Westerners represented in literature or in the media? You could look at novels, television shows, or movies set there. The film genre of the Western might be a rich source of material. Compare the features used by the characters to the features discussed here.

4. The speech of the West and Midwest has often been approached as a mix of the features found in Eastern dialects. How many of the features discussed here are also associated with other American dialects?

5. Which speakers in the audio sample have the low back merger of LOT and THOUGHT? Which words provide the evidence on this question? How is the merged vowel realized; i.e., what is its phonetic quality?

Selected references

Please consult the General references for titles mentioned in the text but not included in the references below. For a full bibliography see the accompanying CD-ROM.

Di Paolo, Marianna and Alice Faber
    1990   Phonation differences and the phonetic content of the tense-lax contrast in
            Utah English. *Language Variation and Change* 2: 155–204.
Hagiwara, Robert
    1997   Dialect variation and formant frequency: The American English vowels
            revisited. *Journal of the Acoustical Society of America* 102: 655–658.
Hartman, James W.
    1985   Guide to pronunciation. In: Cassidy (ed.), xli-lxi.
Hudson, John C.
    1988   North American origins of middlewestern frontier populations. *Annals of
            the Association of American Geographers* 78: 395–413.
Johnson, Lawrence
    1975   Sound change and mobility in Los Angeles. *Linguistics* 143: 33–48.
Labov, William
    1991   The three dialects of English. In: Eckert (ed.), 1–44.
Lusk, Melanie M.
    1976   Phonological variation in Kansas City: A sociolinguistic analysis of three-
            generation families. Ph.D. dissertation, Department of English, University
            of Kansas.
Luthin, Herbert
    1987   The story of California (ow): The coming-of-age of English in California.
            In: Keith Denning, Sharon Inkelas, Faye McNair-Knox, and John Rickford
            (eds.), *Variation in Language: NWAV-XV at Stanford,* 312–324. Stanford,
            CA: Department of Linguistics, Stanford University.
Meinig, D.W.
    1972   American Wests: Preface to a geographical interpretation. *Annals of the
            Association of American Geographers* 62: 159–184.
Metcalf, Allan A.
    1972   Directions of change in Southern California English. *Journal of English
            Linguistics* 6: 28–34.
Watt, Dominic, and Lesley Milroy
    1999   Patterns of variation and change in three Newcastle vowels: Is this dialect
            levelling? In: Foulkes and Docherty (eds), 25–46.

English in Canada: phonology

Charles Boberg

1. Introduction

As recently as 1948, Morton Bloomfield (1948: 59) was justified in remarking that very little research had been devoted to Canadian English, especially in comparison to American or British English. The projected Linguistic Atlas of the United States and Canada, which produced groundbreaking studies of dialect variation along the Atlantic seaboard of the United States, was never extended to Canada, beyond a few scattered informants in New Brunswick, Ontario, and Manitoba, interviewed in connection with studies of American English across the border. Since the 1950s, however, research on Canadian English has proliferated. It now comprises a substantial body of material focused on four major themes:

1) the historical origins of Canadian English;
2) alternation among American and British words, pronunciations, and usage in Canada;
3) the documentation of relic areas and traditional regional enclaves; and
4) Canadian Raising, the articulation of the diphthongs /aʊ/ and /aɪ/ with non-low nuclei when they occur before voiceless consonants, which became a standard example of the need for ordered rules in generative phonology.

Overviews of the research in these areas can be found in Avis (1973), Bailey (1982) and Chambers (1979, 1991). The present chapter will focus on the sound of Canadian English, and in particular on those phonological and phonetic variables that are most useful for distinguishing Canadian English from other varieties, and for identifying regional varieties within Canada.

The origins of Canadian English have been studied in light of the history of the settlement of Canada and will be briefly addressed in 2.1, below. The contributions of traditional dialectological research to determining the status of Canadian English in relation to American and British English will be the subject of 2.2. Section 3 will discuss three phonological features of Canadian English, while Section 4 will identify some phonetic patterns found in Canada. These sections will deal exclusively with vowels, as the author is not aware of any consonantal variables that show unique patterns in Canada. Finally, Section 5 will summarize the role of the U.S.-Canada border as a linguistic iso-gloss, and offer some comments on what the future may hold for Canadian English.

2. History and status of Canadian English

2.1. Origins: Settlement and influences

Apart from Newfoundland, which is the oldest English-speaking colony in North America (founded 1583), the earliest substantial European settlement of what is today Canada was dominated by French rather than English colonists. French colonies were well established in eastern Canada by the mid-17th century, a period when the region was practically empty of English speakers. In the mid-18th century, however, the outcome of the struggle between France and England for control of North America was decided in favor of England, and the former French territories became British possessions by the Treaty of Paris (1763). English-speaking settlement followed, leading to the bilingual status of modern Canada, with two official languages. By the 19th century, English-speakers outnumbered French, and the dominance of English in Canada has continued to increase ever since. Today, of the Canadian population of 30 million people, French speakers account for less than a quarter, and these are mostly found in the province of Quebec, which is 81% French-speaking. Outside Quebec – and neighboring parts of New Brunswick and eastern Ontario, which are bilingual – Canada is generally English-speaking.

The important exception to this is the large cities, where, as in the United States, the English-speaking population has been augmented by immigrants whose mother tongues come from every corner of the world. The four and a half million people of Toronto, for example, are about 59 per cent English-speaking, one per cent French-speaking, and 40 per cent native speakers of other languages, like Chinese (8%), Italian (4%), and Portuguese (2%). Vancouver, with close to two million people, is 61 per cent English-speaking, one per cent French-speaking, and 38 per cent 'other', with Chinese (15%) and Punjabi (5%) accounting for the biggest non-English groups. Montreal's 400,000 English-speakers (12% of the population) are outnumbered not only by speakers of French, the majority language (69%), but also by speakers of non-official languages, who now account for 19 per cent of the population. In total, only 59 per cent of Canadians – some 17 million people –are native speakers of English (Statistics Canada 2001). On the other hand, Canadian English is generally not divided like American English along racial lines; with a few local exceptions, all native speakers of English in Canada share a common variety.

Two inescapable facts have dominated previous discussions of Canadian English. The first is that, in spite of Canada's being a British colony until 1867 and enjoying close cultural ties with Britain for many decades thereafter, Canadian English is fundamentally a North American variety. The second is that, with the obvious exception of Newfoundland, which was a separate British colony until 1949 and remains to this day linguistically distinct from the rest of Canada, Canadian English is remarkably homogeneous from one end of the country to the other. This is particularly true in the broad stretch of territory extending almost 3,000 miles (4,500 km) from Ottawa and Kingston, Ontario, in the east, to Vancouver and Victoria, British Columbia, in the west, including all the major cities of central and western Canada. While traditional enclaves remain in a few places, modern, urban Canada does not exhibit anything approaching the dialect diversity of the United States, let alone that of Britain. Instead, one type of English, with minor regional variations, is spoken across most of the country, and central and western Canadians are generally incapable of guessing each other's regional origins on the basis of accent or dialect. These two facts have been explained in terms of Canada's settlement history, which comprises three distinct stages.

The first major English-speaking settlement of Canada came not directly from Britain but from the British colonies in what are today the United States (Avis 1973: 44–47). First to arrive were thousands of migrants from Eastern New England in the early 1760s, who took up land in Nova Scotia that had been abandoned by French-speaking Acadians expelled by the British government. Next came thousands of "United Empire Loyalists", known as "Tories" in the United States: American colonists loyal to the British crown in the American Revolution. The Loyalists joined the New Englanders in Nova Scotia and became the first large and permanent group of English-speaking settlers in three other regions: New Brunswick (especially the city of Saint John); the "Eastern Townships" of Quebec (south of the St. Lawrence River); and Ontario (the Kingston and Niagara regions on either end of Lake Ontario). "Late Loyalist" migration from the U.S. to Canada continued for several decades after the Revolution, so that by 1812, when Britain and the U.S. fought their last territorial conflict, Ontario (then called Upper Canada) had a population of around 100,000 that was predominantly American; people who had immigrated directly from Britain constituted a small minority of about 5,000 (Avis 1973: 46). In the late 19th and early 20th centuries, Americans also played a major role in settling Western Canada, along with other groups (Avis 1973: 48–49). The result was that, in almost every region of Canada except Newfoundland, Americans predominated or were an important element among the earliest settlers and must have had a significant influence on what later emerged as local speech.

Avis (1954: 14) and Bloomfield (1948: 62) argue that these facts explain the overwhelmingly North American sound of Canadian English, despite large-scale subsequent immigration from Britain and elsewhere: American speech patterns were already in place when the British settlers arrived. The recent arrivals, like immigrants elsewhere and in other times, found themselves adapting to these patterns rather than imposing new ones from abroad. The exceptions to this development are the areas where new settlements were made by relatively homogeneous groups of immigrants arriving directly from Britain in large numbers and in specific locations in the 19th century. These survive today as the traditional enclaves of regional speech referred to above: Newfoundland; Cape Breton (northern Nova Scotia); and the Ottawa Valley of eastern Ontario.

A different view of the origins of Canadian English is advanced by Scargill (1957), who chooses to emphasize the importance of the second major stage in the settlement of Canada: direct immigration from Britain, which reached a peak in the mid-19th century. Scargill points out that Bloomfield's "Loyalist theory" of the origins of Canadian English is flawed in two crucial respects (1957: 611–612). First, it ignores the numerical superiority of British over American settlement. British immigration is measured not in the tens but in the hundreds of thousands. Scargill finds it improbable that these much greater numbers could all have adapted their speech perfectly to a rigid model laid down by a comparatively small number of original American settlers. Second, Scargill warns against using comparisons between Canadian English and modern standard Southern British English (Received Pronunciation) as evidence of the American character of Canadian English, since this was not the variety spoken by the majority of British immigrants to Canada. He points out that many of the features of Canadian English that the incautious observer might automatically attribute to American influence could just as well have their origins in the regional speech of Northern or Western Britain, which predominated among 19th century British immigrants.

If we grant that Loyalist speech had at least some influence on the future development of English in Canada, this settlement history lends to the study of Canadian English an additional interest to scholars of American English, since Canadian speech may preserve features of colonial American English that have since been erased by subsequent linguistic change in the U.S. (Bloomfield 1948: 65–66). In Nova Scotia, American settlement came mostly from Eastern New England. In New Brunswick and Ontario, by contrast, it came mostly from Vermont, New York State, New Jersey, and Pennsylvania (Avis 1973: 46). American settlement in western Canada came from a much wider range of places, including the American Midwest; moreover, some of these settlers were recent European immigrants to the U.S., so that the extent to which they carried identifiable regional American dialects into Canada is questionable.

The third stage in the settlement of Canada came largely from non-English-speaking countries, producing the linguistic diversity in major cities referred to above. This wave of immigration began in the late 19th century and peaked in the decades after the Second World War, drawing mostly on southern, central, and eastern Europe. It continues today, though in recent decades its sources have shifted increasingly away from Europe to Asia and Latin America. Apart from the contribution of loan words, this last stage of immigration has had little effect on Canadian English, except where large, linguistically homogeneous concentrations of immigrants live in relatively segregated communities where they predominate numerically. Examples of the latter would be religiously-based communities of German-speakers in the rural West, like Mennonites in southern Manitoba, and certain ethnic enclaves in large cities, like Italians and Jews in Montreal and Toronto; in these cases, immigrant language substrates may be heard to varying degrees in the local varieties of Canadian English.

2.2.   Status: British vs. American identity; place in a taxonomy of North American dialects

The status of Canadian English with respect to American and British English has been a primary concern of many linguists studying Canadian English, and of commentators and critics outside academic circles. As Scargill asserted, the large number of British immigrants in the 19th century, together with the use of British English for official purposes during the colonial period and to some extent beyond, had a significant impact on Canadian English, which today shows the effect of a standard Southern British superstratum having been imposed on a North American variety. As a result, modern Canadian usage varies between standard British and American forms on a long list of variables concerning phonemic incidence, morphosyntax, lexicon, and general usage. Spelling has traditionally followed British practice in many respects (e.g., *colour* and *centre* rather than *color* and *center*), though spelling too shows American influence, which has recently increased. Very few if any Canadians would write *tyre*, *gaol*, or *kerb* for *tire*, *jail*, or *curb*, and many now write *color* and *center* as well.

Studying the alternation among British and American words, pronunciations, and usage in Canada has been the main preoccupation of the largest body of research on Canadian English. Beginning in the 1950s (Avis 1954–56), this tradition employed written surveys to investigate variables such as whether *missile* sounds like *mile* or *thistle*; whether *progress* (the noun) has /oʊ/ or /ɒ/ in the first syllable; whether *dived* or *dove* is the past tense of *dive*; and whether people say *tap* or *faucet*, *trousers* or *pants*, and *in hospital* or *in the hospital*. It culminated in a nationwide postal survey representing 14,000 participants (secondary school students and their parents) from every province of Canada, divided by age and sex, and covering a wide range of variables at every level of grammar, except of course phonetics (Scargill and Warkentyne 1972). The tradition has recently been renewed, with a sociolinguistic perspective and some methodological innovations, under the name of Dialect Topography (Chambers 1994). The general finding of these surveys has been to confirm what might be predicted from settlement and cultural history and from the present cultural dominance of the United States: that Canadian English exhibits a mix of American and British forms, varying slightly from one region to another, which is gradually shifting towards increasing use of American forms among younger Canadians. The Americanization of Canadian English at these levels has been a popular topic in both academic and popular circles.

While many early students of English in Canada sought to promote its affinities with either British or American English, a growing sense of Canadian identity in the decades after the Second World War produced a third view of the status of Canadian English, which preferred to emphasize a small but significant set of features that are uniquely Canadian. This position was espoused by Scargill (1957: 612), and was the motivation behind the compilation of the *Dictionary of Canadianisms on Historical Principles* (Avis et al. 1967). However, apart from a few items like the well-worn example of *chesterfield* for *couch* (which is strongly recessive and practically extinct among younger Canadians), these unique Canadianisms draw too heavily on the obvious categories of words connected with traditional, obsolescent occupations and with local flora, fauna, and topographic features, to make a very convincing case for a unique Canadian lexicon. In the more important domain of general vocabulary, Canadian usage inclines overwhelmingly toward the American variants of pairs like *chemist/drugstore*, *chips/fries*, *lift/elevator*, *lorry/truck*, *petrol/gas*, *spanner/wrench*, and *torch/flashlight*.

The questionnaire tradition has tended to overstate the British element in Canadian English, insofar as it concentrates by necessity on phonemic incidence and the lexicon, where British superstratal influence was strongest, exercised through schools, dictionaries, the media, and other institutions. The smaller amount of work done in descriptive phonetics and phonology, together with the component of the usage surveys that deals with phonological inventory, shows a clear preponderance of non-Southern British variants. The vocalization of /r/ and the split of Middle English /a/ (TRAP vs. BATH) have never had any currency in vernacular Canadian speech, and younger Canadians now flap intervocalic /t/ and delete the glide in words like *news* and *student* pretty much to the same extent and in the same environments as most Americans do (De Wolf 1992; Gregg 1957: 25–26). Combined with the merger of /ɒ/ and /ɔ: – the vowels of LOT and THOUGHT, or *cot* and *caught* – which is nearly universal in Canada, and of a maximal number of vowels before /r/ (both discussed in Section 3, below), these phonological features cause Canadian English to sound very similar to the North Midland and Western varieties of American English that underlie the popular conception of "General American" speech.

One exception to this assessment is Canadian Raising, which will be discussed below in Section 4.1. Another, much less well-known and studied but equally pervasive and distinctive, is the Canadian Shift, involving most notably a backing of /æ/ to [a], which will be the concern of Section 4.4. Phonetic variables of this type are of course beyond a written survey's powers of observation, but are the principal focus of the present chapter. It is therefore to the phonology and phonetics of Canadian English that we now turn.

3.   Phonological features of Canadian English

3.1.   The low-back merger (the LOT and THOUGHT sets)

The most significant defining feature of Canadian English at the phonological level is the general consistency across the country of the merger between /ɒ/ and /ɔ:/, the vowels of *cot* and *caught* (or LOT and THOUGHT), in the low-back corner of the vowel space. While this merger is by no means unique to Canada, being shared with neighboring areas of Eastern New England, Western Pennsylvania, and the Western United States and thereby causing Labov (1991) to include Canada with these regions in his "Third Dialect", it is nevertheless a unifying feature of English across Canada with important phonetic ramifications, to be discusssed below in relation to the Canadian Shift. For virtually all native speakers of Canadian English today, the pairs *cot* and *caught*, *sod* and *sawed*, *stock* and *stalk*, *Don* and *dawn*, and *collar* and *caller* are homophones.

The dialectological literature on this merger suggests that it is well entrenched in Canadian English and is at least several generations old. For example, Scargill and Warkentyne (1972: 64) record an average of 85% of Canadians responding 'yes' to a survey question that asked whether *cot* and *caught* rhyme. Since this was a written survey in which spelling may have influenced responses, it seems safe to speculate that the real rate of merger was very close to 100%. Indeed, a generation earlier, Gregg (1957: 22) reported an exceptionless merger among Vancouver university students. Avis (1973: 64) and the limited data on Canada in Labov (1991: 32) also suggest a consistent merger across Canada, as do more recent data from Labov, Ash, and Boberg (2006).

In Newfoundland, the same merger can be observed, but the merged vowel is produced further forward in the mouth, in low-central position. At a phonetic level, this means that a Newfoundlander's production of a word like *cod* will be very close to that heard in the "Northern Cities" of the Inland Northern or Great Lakes region of the United States: something like [kɑd]. At the phonological level, of course, the two dialects differ. In Newfoundland, *caught* would have the same low-central vowel as *cod*, whereas in the American Inland North, *caught* represents a distinct phonemic category, with a higher, backer vowel. This is one of many distinctive features of Newfoundland English that reflect its origins in southwestern England and southeastern Ireland. Others include a centralized pronunciation of /ɑr/ (see below), a back pronunciation of /ʌ/, and a spirantized articulation of post-vocalic /t/.

3.2.   Mergers before /r/

A conditioned merger of several vowels before intervocalic /r/ also character-izes Canadian English from coast to coast (with one important exception be-yond the usual case of Newfoundland) and unites it with other North American varieties, in this case all of those dialects that were not affected by the vocaliza-tion of /r/. In Canada, /eɪ/, /ɛ/ and /æ/ are all merged before intervocalic /r/ at approximately [ɛ], a lower-mid to upper-mid front quality, so that *Mary, merry* and *marry* all sound like a slightly lengthened version of *merry*. This was first noted by Gregg (1957: 82) in Vancouver, though he suggests it was a change in progress when he collected his data. Apart from some variability in Newfound-land, the important exception to this pattern is Montreal, where /æ/ remains distinct from the other two vowels before /r/: *carry* does not rhyme with *berry*, but *berry* rhymes with *dairy*.

In addition to this merger of front vowels, most Canadians have lost the distinction between several pairs of mid and back vowels before /r/. Like most standard varieties of English, Canadian English does not distinguish /ɔː/ and /oʊ/ in this environment (*for* and *four*, *horse* and *hoarse*), and as in the Mid-western and Western U.S., /ʌ/ and /ə/ (*hurry* and *her*) are also not distinct, both having the sound of [ə], or simply of a syllabic [ɹ]. A noteworthy feature of Canadian English, which might be expected from the general merger of /ɒ/ and /ɔː/, is that the merger of these vowels before /r/ is virtually complete, and does not exclude the residue of unmerged forms that is found in phonologically sim-ilar American dialects. In Canada, even the common words *borrow, sorry*, and *tomorrow* usually have the vowels of *bore, sore*, and *more*, whereas in most American speech they retain a low, unrounded articulation similar to that of the /ɑr/ class, even where less common words like *forest, historical*, and *orange* have merged with *four*, *store*, and *oar*. The Canadian pronunciation of *sorry* with a lower-mid-back vowel is particularly striking to many American ears.

3.3.   The Canadian pattern for foreign (a) words

The phonological adaptation or nativization of loan words can be a source of variation in any language. In English, one of the most remarkable examples of this variation concerns the nativization of foreign words containing the letter <a>, usually representing a low-central vowel quality in the source language, e.g. *falafel*, *karate*, *llama*, *macho*, *nirvana*, *pasta*, *plaza*, *souvlaki*, *taco*, etc. Such words are usually nativized with either /æ/ (TRAP) or /ɑː/ (PALM) as their stressed vowel, but each major national variety of English has developed its own pattern of assignment. British English tends to use /æ/, except where spelling and other factors conspire to suggest that the syllable should be treated as open, in which case /ɑː/ must occur, given the restriction on /æ/ in stressed open syllables. Thus *pasta* has /æ/, while *llama* has /ɑː/. American English, by contrast, prefers to use /ɑː/: both *pasta* and *llama* have /ɑː/ (which is not distinct from /ɒ/ [LOT] in most American dialects). The traditional Canadian pattern, however, is to use /æ/ in almost all foreign (a) words, even when both British and American English agree on /ɑː/. The only regular exception to this is in final stressed open syllables (*bra*, *eclat*, *faux pas*, *foie gras*, *spa*, etc.), where /æ/ cannot appear. While many younger Canadians are beginning to follow the American pattern in some instances (relatively few young people still use /æ/ in *macho* or *taco*), most Canadians retain /æ/ in both *pasta* and *llama*, and even in older loan words like *drama*, *garage*, and *Slavic*, where it may sound odd to speakers of other varieties (Boberg 2000).

4.   Phonetic features of Canadian English

A general view of the phonetic quality of Canadian English vowels can be obtained from Table 1, which gives an approximate phonetic transcription of each of the keywords used to represent Wells' lexical sets. These transcriptions are necessarily approximate, because small degrees of regional, social, and inter-speaker variation do of course exist, even in the largely homogeneous context described above. With this limitation, they can be taken to represent the general character of the vowels of Standard Canadian English. A more detailed view of the most distinctive aspects of Canadian pronunciation is given below.

Table 1. Phonetic transcription of typical Canadian pronunciations of the keywords in
Wells' lexical sets.

KIT	ɪ	PALM	ɒː	STAR	ɑɹ > ɐɹ
DRESS	ɛ	THOUGHT	ɒ	START	ʌɹ > ɐɹ
TRAP	æ ~ a	GOAT	ɵʊ	NORTH	ɔɹ
LOT	ɒ	GOOSE	ʉu	FORCE	ɔɹ
STRUT	ʌ	PRIZE	ɑɪ	CURE	jəɹ > jʊɹ > jɵɹ
FOOT	ʊ	PRICE	ʌɪ ~ ɜɪ ~ ɐɪ	happY	i
BATH	æ ~ a	CHOICE	ɔɪ	lettER	əɹ
CLOTH	ɒ	COW	aʊ ~ ɑʊ	horsES	ə
NURSE	əɹ	MOUTH	ʌʊ ~ ɜʊ	commA	ɐ
FLEECE	ii	NEAR	ɪɹ		
FACE	eɪ	SQUARE	ɛɹ		

4.1.   Canadian Raising (the PRICE and MOUTH sets)

Canadian Raising, the pronunciation of the diphthongs /aɪ/ (PRICE) and /aʊ/
(MOUTH) with non-low nuclei when they occur before voiceless consonants,
was first systematically analyzed by Joos (1942), who noticed that raising
interacts with flapping to produce apparently phonemic oppositions between
raised and unraised vowels in pairs like *writer* vs. *rider*, at least in some
varieties of Canadian English. Chambers (1973) showed how these patterns
could be accounted for in a generative framework by means of variable rule
ordering. Canadian Raising is by no means unique to Canada, even within
North America. Raised nuclei in one or both diphthongs have been documented in eastern Virginia (Kurath and McDavid 1961), Martha's Vineyard,
Massachusetts (Labov 1972a), Philadelphia (Labov 1994), and the Inland
North. Moreover, not all Canadians exhibit Canadian Raising: urban varieties in particular display considerable social variation in this regard, with
some speakers raising less than others, or not at all. However, if it does not
uniquely or consistently characterize all speakers of Canadian English, Canadian Raising nevertheless continues to be a reliable and distinctive identifier
of Canadian speech in most of the country and is the basis of the most popular American stereotype of Canadian speech, if only as it applies to /aʊ/.

Even among those Canadians who show consistent Canadian Raising, its
phonetic implementation is not uniform across Canada. Most Canadians have
two principal allophones of /aɪ/ (raised to lower-mid position before voiceless
consonants and low-central or low-back elsewhere) and three of /aʊ/ (raised
before voiceless consonants, fronted to [aʊ] or [æʊ] before nasals, and low-

central elsewhere). One of the few phonetic variables that divides Canadians regionally is the articulation of the raised allophone of /aʊ/. In Ontario, it tends to have a mid-central or even mid-front articulation, sometimes approaching [ɛʊ], while in the West and Maritimes a more retracted sound is heard, closer to [ʌʊ]. Among some speakers on the Prairies and in Nova Scotia, the retraction is strong enough to cause some tokens of raised /aʊ/ to merge with /oʊ/, so that *couch* and *coach* sound the same, and *about* sounds like *a boat* (though never like *a boot*, as in the American stereotype of Canadian Raising).

4.2.   Raising of /ɑːr/ (the START set)

Canadian pronunciation of words in the START set commonly involves a non-low nucleus, especially as a result of nuclear shortening before voiceless consonants. As with Canadian Raising, the relative advancement of the raised nucleus is a regional indicator. A striking feature of Atlantic Canadian speech (the Maritimes and Newfoundland) is a nucleus that approaches the front region of the vowel space, accompanied by strong rhoticity, ranging from [ɜɹ] to [ɐɹ]. Western Canadian speech has a much more retracted articulation with a longer non-rhotic portion, approaching a mid-back quality, [ɵɹ] (though there is no tendency toward a merger with NORTH/FORCE). Articulation of START in Ontario is in a position midway between the Atlantic and Western values.

4.3.   Raising of /æ/ before nasals and /g/

Unlike in many American English dialects, /æ/ remains a low-front vowel in most environments in Canadian English. Raising along the front periphery of the vowel space is restricted to two environments – before nasal and voiced velar consonants – and varies regionally even in these. Ontario and Maritime Canadian English commonly show some raising before nasals, though not as extreme as in many American varieties. Much less raising is heard on the Prairies, and some ethnic groups in Montreal show no pre-nasal raising at all. On the other hand, some Prairie speech exhibits raising of /æ/ before voiced velars (/g/ and /ŋ/), with an up-glide rather than an in-glide, so that *bag* sounds close to *vague*.

4.4.   The Canadian shift (the KIT, DRESS, and TRAP sets)

Labov (1991) proposed a three-dialect model of North American English based on two key phonological variables and their consequent phonetic developments. In this model, Canadian English was classified with several other dialects that appeared to show relative phonetic stability, compared to the complex patterns of chain-shifting that characterized the Northern and Southern dialects. A few years later, Clarke, Elms, and Youssef (1995) published a report on what they called the Canadian Shift, asserting that, far from being phonetically stable, Canadian English was involved in its own set of phonetic shifts, primarily affecting /ɪ/, /ɛ/, and /æ/, the KIT, DRESS, and TRAP sets. The young Ontario speakers they studied showed a retraction of /æ/ to [a] (filling the low-central space made available by the low-back, LOT-THOUGHT merger), a lowering of /ɛ/ toward /æ/, and a lowering of /ɪ/ toward /ɛ/. The most salient aspect of this chain shift, especially in the larger North American context, is the retraction of /æ/. The resulting quality is similar to that heard in the TRAP and BATH sets in Northern British English, in contrast with the fully fronted and often raised quality of /æ/ in much of the United States, and in particular in the American varieties spoken in the Inland Northern region along the border with central Canada. In fact, the Canadian Shift and the Northern Cities Shift (Labov 1991, 1994) involve directly opposite developments of the low vowels, so that the TRAP class in much Canadian speech has virtually the same vowel quality as the LOT class in the Great Lakes region of the U.S. The productions [hat] and [kap] would designate items of headwear in Ontario, but would be the opposite of *cold* and an informal term for a police officer across the border in southeastern Michigan or Western New York.

4.5. The fronting of /uː/ (the GOOSE set)

Another change in progress in Canadian English, part of a continental trend affecting many North American varieties, is the fronting of /uː/, whereby the nucleus of /uː/ moves forward to high-central or even high-front position, directly behind /iː/. There is a wide allophonic dispersion in the GOOSE set, extending over most of the high region of the vowel space. Most advanced are tokens of /uː/ in free position after coronals (*do, too*); behind these are tokens in syllables closed with coronals (*boots, food, soon*), then tokens before non-coronals (*goof, soup*); remaining in back position are tokens of /uː/ before /l/ (*cool, pool, tool*). Unlike in some British speech, Canadian English does not show any fronting or unrounding of the glide of /uː/, and most Canadians show no parallel centralization of /oʊ/, which generally remains in back position, except in Cape Breton and Newfoundland.

5.   Summary and conclusions

5.1.   The phonetic and phonological status of the U.S.-Canada border

Avis (1954–56) and Chambers (1994), among others, have shown how the international boundary between Ontario and the U.S. is a sharp linguistic isogloss for a wide range of variables at different levels of grammar, even though Avis (1954: 13) suggests that, from a broader perspective, the differences between Ontario speech and adjacent parts of the United States are minimal. However, these studies have generally dealt with non-phonetic data. The question of the linguistic significance of the U.S.-Canada border at the level of phonetics and phonology – and especially at the level of the vowel sounds that make up our primary impression of the regional character of someone's speech – has only now begun to be systematically investigated (Labov, Ash, and Boberg 2006; Boberg 2000).

In general, phonological and phonetic data indicate a border effect that diminishes in importance from east to west. In the east, the completely different phonological systems of Eastern New England and Maritime Canada are directly opposed across the international border. Though both regions share a low-back merger and a conservative treatment of /uː/ and /oʊ/, eastern Canada was not affected by the Southern British innovations – vocalization of /r/ and the split of Middle English /a/ – that shaped modern Eastern New England speech. This fact helps in the dating of these changes in New England, since Nova Scotia was settled by New Englanders: it seems likely that the changes became general after the emigration of New Englanders to Canada in the mid-18th century.

In the middle of the continent, the border between Canadian speech in Ontario and Inland Northern speech on the other side of the Great Lakes is remarkably sharp. It separates two different phonological systems, along with the phonetic developments that follow from them. On the Canadian side, a low-back merger has produced a backing of /æ/ in the Canadian Shift; on the American side, a low-back distinction has been preserved by a raising of /æ/ and a centralization of /ɒ/ in the Northern Cities Shift. Boberg (2000) showed that there was no sign of phonetic or phonological interference across the Detroit River between Detroit, Michigan, and Windsor, Ontario, despite the prediction of current models of geolinguistic diffusion that Windsor would be linguistically assimilated to its much larger American neighbor, not to speak of the importance of American settlement in the origins of Ontario English.

In western North America, however, the international boundary no longer represents a coherent bundle of isoglosses, with the exception that it marks the southern extent of Canadian raising (especially of /aʊ/) and of more extreme versions of the Canadian shift. Western North America, to a large extent, shares a common phonological system and very similar phonetics. The blurring of linguistic boundaries in the West, a well-established fact in American dialectology, is not merely a feature of American English, but of the continent as a whole, reflecting relatively sparse and recent settlement from a mixture of sources. People living in Saskatchewan and North Dakota, Alberta and Montana, or British Columbia and Washington can certainly hear a difference between their own speech and that of their neighbors across the border, but this difference would seem very small indeed to someone from outside the region.

Notwithstanding the varying border effects discussed above, it must be admitted that certain changes in North American English seem to be diffusing rapidly over most of the continent, including Canada. One of these, discussed above, is the fronting of /uː/. Others include the loss of /j/ in /juː/ after coronals (*news*, *student*, *tube*, etc.), the merger of /hw/ and /w/ (*whether* vs. *weather*, etc.), and the spread of *be like* as a verb of quotation (*I was like, what's up with that?*). Moreover, the mass media, which are essentially common to all of North America, spread lexical innovations rapidly across the border, thereby further leveling the differences between Canadian and American English. It remains to be seen which differences will ultimately survive this erosion, and which new differences will arise to take the place of obsolete ones as people on each side of the border strive to sustain linguistic symbols of their sense of community.

5.2. Canada within the dialect taxonomy of North American English

Some dialectologists, on the basis of lexical evidence, or selected phonological evidence, have classified Canada as an extension of the Inland North region of the United States, which is intuitively satisfying in a geographic sense. However, at a deeper, structural level, Canada differs from the Inland North in a crucial respect – the low-back merger – and this difference has produced an enormous phonetic divergence between Inland Northern and Canadian speech. Phonologically, Canada has more in common with the North Midland and Western regions of the United States than with the Inland North, probably because the genesis of Canadian English involved the same dialect-leveling among heterogeneous migrants and pioneers that made the low-back merger a general feature of the Western United States. This particularly applies to Ontario and western Canada, which together represent by far the largest portion of the Canadian English-speaking population. The speech of these regions can certainly be included with that of the American North Midland and West under one general type of English, at least at a broad level of analysis. As for eastern

Canada, while the Ottawa Valley, Montreal, the Eastern Townships, the Maritimes, and Cape Breton may all once have exhibited rich linguistic diversity, all of these regions (and even, to an extent, Newfoundland, especially since its confederation with Canada in 1949) now exhibit a rapidly advancing convergence with Standard Canadian English, at least among younger, middle-class speakers. They, too, can probably now be included under the same category as Ontario and the West.

It may be foolish to speculate on the future of Canadian English, given the uncertain outcome of the interplay of forces of global and local prestige that is always present in the evolution of languages, but the obvious importance of the increasing integration of the two English-speaking nations of North America cannot be overlooked. In an age of instant transmission of language across political borders, of frequent international travel and migration, and of ever-closer economic and cultural integration, Canadian English cannot help but come under greater assimilatory pressure than it has ever experienced in its history. Whether this pressure will overcome the obstacles to assimilation in the more resistant levels of grammar, particularly phonetics and phonology, remains to be seen. At present, there is no indication that Canadian English is about to disappear at these levels; on the contrary, it seems likely that, at a time when so many other differences have fallen prey to continental cultural convergence, the sound of Canadian English will be closely bound up with Canadians' sense of their national identity for many generations to come.

Exercises and study questions

1. Canada has enjoyed a longer and closer relationship with Great Britain than the United States. What effect has this had on Canadian English? Is Canadian English closer to British or to American English?

2. How important are regional dialect divisions in Canada, compared to those that exist in the United States or Britain? What explains this difference? To what extent are other former British dominions, like Australia and New Zealand, similar to Canada in this respect, and why?

3. How might the study of Canadian English shed light on the nature of the English spoken in the American colonies before the American Revolution?

4. What is the status of Canadian English with respect to the "low-back merger"? How does this status help us to characterize Canadian English with respect to other varieties?

5. Canadian English features a unique pattern in the phonological nativization of words of foreign origin spelled with the letter <a> as their main, stressed vowel. What is this pattern? What other words, beyond those mentioned in this chapter, are in this "foreign (a)" class, and what is the foreign (a) pattern in your dialect of English?

6. What is "Canadian Raising"? Is it unique to Canada?

7. What is the "Canadian Shift" and how is it related to the phonemic structure of Canadian English? Is there evidence of similar developments in other dialects that share the same phonemic structure?

Selected references

Please consult the General references for titles mentioned in the text but not included in the references below. For a full bibliography see the accompanying CD-ROM.

Avis, Walter S.
  1954–56 Speech differences along the Ontario-United States border. *Journal of the Canadian Linguistic Association* 1: 13–18, 1: 14–19 and 2: 41–59.
  1973   The English language in Canada. In: Thomas A. Sebeok (ed.), *Current Trends in Linguistics* 10: *Linguistics in North America*, 40–74. The Hague: Mouton.
Bailey, Richard W.
  1982   The English language in Canada. In: Bailey and Görlach (eds.), 137–176.
Bloomfield, Morton
  1948   Canadian English and its relation to eighteenth century American speech. *Journal of English and Germanic Philology* 47: 59–67.
Boberg, Charles
  2000   Geolinguistic diffusion and the U.S.-Canada border. *Language Variation and Change* 12: 1–24.
Chambers, J.K.
  1973   Canadian raising. *Canadian Journal of Linguistics* 18: 113–135.
  1979   Canadian English. In: J.K. Chambers (ed.), *The Languages of Canada*, 168–204. Montreal: Didier.
  1991   Canada. In: Cheshire (ed.), 89–107.
  1994   An introduction to dialect topography. *English World-Wide* 15: 35–53.
Clarke, Sandra, Ford Elms and Amani Youssef
  1995   The third dialect of English: Some Canadian evidence. *Language Variation and Change* 7: 209–228.
Gregg, Robert J.
  1957   Notes on the pronunciation of Canadian English as spoken in Vancouver, B.C. *Journal of the Canadian Linguistic Association* 3: 20–26.

Joos, Martin
   1942   A phonological dilemma in Canadian English. *Language* 18: 141–144.
Labov, William
   1991   The three dialects of English. In: Eckert (ed.), 1–44.
Scargill, Matthew H.
   1957   Sources of Canadian English. *Journal of English and Germanic Philology* 56: 610–614.
Scargill, Matthew H. and Henry J. Warkentyne
   1972   The Survey of Canadian English: A report. *English Quarterly* 5: 47–104.
Statistics Canada [Statistical Agency of the Government of Canada].
   2001   www.statcan.ca.

Newfoundland English: phonology

Sandra Clarke[*]

1.   Introduction

The vernacular speech of the North Atlantic island of Newfoundland has always been highly distinct from that of most of mainland North America. It does however share a number of structural characteristics with varieties spoken in the neighbouring Canadian Maritime provinces, as well as in other early-settled areas of the New World, including the Caribbean. The reasons for this distinctiveness can be traced to several sources – notably, the settlement history of the area, coupled with its relative geographical isolation at the eastern periphery of North America.

Along with its continental portion, Labrador, Newfoundland did not become a province of Canada until 1949; prior to that, as "Britain's oldest colony", the island constituted an independent British dominion. Newfoundland's association with Britain dates back to the 16th century. The island was officially claimed by the British crown in 1583, to ensure that British interests dominated in the European exploitation of the region's rich fisheries resources. Though it did not see its major influx of immigrants until the first decades of the 19th century, Newfoundland was one of the earliest British-settled areas of the New World, with continuous settlement from the beginning of the 17th century.

The European founder population of Newfoundland and coastal Labrador – henceforth referred to simply as Newfoundland – was quite distinct from that of much of mainland English-speaking Canada, the early population base of which consisted largely of British loyalists who migrated northward after the American War of Independence. Until the 20th century, settlers to Newfoundland were drawn almost exclusively from two principal, and highly circumscribed, geographical sources. These were the southwest (SW) counties of England, where the Dorset city of Poole served as the chief port of embarkation; and the southeast (SE) counties of Ireland, where the port of Waterford played a similar role. The extremely localized nature of its immigrant population sets Newfoundland apart from much of mainland North America.

The peripheral geographical location of the area has also proven a defining factor in the history and development of Newfoundland English (NfldE). Hand in hand with this go socioeconomic factors: the vagaries of the region's resource-based economy, in which the fishery has played a central role, resulted in lack of substantial in-migration after the mid-19th century. Throughout Newfoundland's history, many of the island's residents have been scattered in small rural coastal "outport" fishing communities, most of which were highly endocentric in that they displayed dense local networks, yet loose connections outside the local area. The overall population of the region has remained small: the province currently has a total of just over half a million residents, almost a third of whom reside in or near the capital city, St. John's. The population also remains remarkably homogeneous: over 90% of present-day residents were born within Newfoundland. From a linguistic perspective, these geographical, socioeconomic and demographic factors have had a conservative effect. Until fairly recently, NfldE was little influenced by the varieties spoken in mainland North America; rather, its dominant characteristic was retention of features which characterized its source varieties in SW England and SE Ireland (see Clarke 2004). Though many of these features are recessive today, they are still sufficiently strong to maintain the general distinctiveness of the Newfoundland accent.

Since World War II and union with Canada, Newfoundland's links with North America have expanded in all spheres: economic, social and cultural. NfldE has increasingly come under the influence of mainland North American models. While many present-day Newfoundlanders profess pride in their distinct ethnic and cultural identity, others – particularly younger and more educated residents of the province – view this heritage in anything but a positive light. Their negative feelings towards NfldE are compounded by the attitudes of mainland Canadians, who on the whole tend to disparage the province's distinctive dialects as symbolic of Newfoundland's "backwardness" and lack of economic prosperity. In spite of the economic opportunities offered by recent discoveries of offshore oil and gas, the almost total collapse of the cod fishery has resulted in increasing outmigration to the Canadian mainland, and the Newfoundland population is currently on the decline.

At present, there is a considerable range of dialect diversity within Newfoundland, which correlates with both social and regional factors, as well as speech register. At one extremity are upwardly mobile younger urban speakers, whose increasingly exocentric orientation is reflected in the fact that their accent is coming more and more to approximate standard mainland Canadian English (CanE). At the other are older, working-class and primarily rural speakers, whose more conservative phonological systems continue to display many traces of the regional British and Irish varieties brought to the province several centuries ago. Because of settlement patterns within Newfoundland, linguistic distinctions between the two principal founder groups – the SW English and the SE Irish – continue to be much in evidence. The Irish population is concentrated in the southeast corner of the island, in the southern part of the Avalon peninsula; the city of St. John's, situated towards the northern extremity of the Irish-settled Avalon, displays a number of characteristic southern Irish features, even in its more standard subvarieties. Outside the Avalon, settlement was overwhelmingly from SW England, with two notable exceptions – the southwest corner of the island, a mixed area of French, Scottish and Irish settlement; and the mainland portion of the province, Labrador, with its aboriginal substratum. Though both traditional "English" and "Irish" dialects of the province share certain conservative features (e.g. monophthongal pronunciations of the vowels of FACE and GOAT), they also maintain a number of inherited distinctions, including the articulation of /h/ and postvocalic /l/. Among younger rural speakers throughout the province, however, competition from more standard supralocal varieties is resulting in increasing loss of local variants, particularly in formal speech styles. A number of features that were the norm in rural fishing communities two or three generations ago are now highly recessive.

Though space does not permit full referencing for individual features, the following descriptions of the phonology of NfldE draw on a wide range of sources, among them Seary, Story and Kirwin (1968); Noseworthy (1971); Paddock (1981); Colbourne (1982); Story, Kirwin and Widdowson ([1982] 1990); Clarke (1991, 2004); Lanari (1994); and Halpert and Widdowson (1996). A number of observations also derive from transcriptions of recordings of conservative speakers held by the Memorial University Folklore and Language Archive (MUNFLA).

2.   Vowels

While the phonological inventory of standard NfldE displays the same number of phonemes as do standard North American varieties, their phonetic realization is by no means identical, particularly with respect to vowels. The NfldE low vowel associated with the LOT/CLOTH/THOUGHT classes is typically articulated in the low central area of vowel space, that is, as considerably more fronted than the usual mainland Canadian realizations of [ɑ] or [ɒ]. The low-mid /æ/ vowel, as in TRAP, is also usually more fronted in NfldE than in the Canadian norm; the same fronted /æ/ may occur in the START set. The phenomenon of "Canadian Raising - that is, the use of a mid rather than low vowel onset in the diphthongs /aɪ/ and /aɪ/ before a tautosyllabic voiceless obstruent – is often not in evidence among speakers of NfldE; this is particularly true for the MOUTH set. Rather, many Newfoundlanders use a somewhat raised mid-open vowel, in

the range of [ɐ/ə/ʌ], in all items of the PRICE/PRIZE and MOUTH/LOUD classes –
that is, irrespective of following linguistic environment. Many speakers, as
well, display a reduced system of vowel contrasts before /r/ in their casual
styles, the result of a tendency towards merger of the NEAR/SQUARE sets, as
well as of the NORTH/FORCE/CURE sets. Table 1 provides a summary of principal variants.

2.1.   Lax vowels

KIT
This vowel is typically realized in all varieties of NfldE as standard lax [ɪ].
More traditional or conservative vernacular speakers from all areas of the prov-

Table 1. Principal vowel variants in NfldE

KIT	ɪ > i ~ ɛ
DRESS	ɛ > ɪ > ẹ ~ æ̣
TRAP	æ̣ > æ
LOT	ạ ~ a > ɑ
STRUT	ʌ ~ ɔ̈
FOOT	ʊ > ụ
BATH	æ̣(ː) > æ > ẹɪ
CLOTH	ạ(ː) ~ a > ɑ > ɒ
NURSE	ɚ ~ ɝ ~ ɔ̈ɹ ~ ʌɹ
FLEECE	i > eː/ei > əɪ
FACE	ei > eː/ɛː > e(j)ə/ɛ(j)ə
PALM	æ(ː) ~ ɑ
THOUGHT	ạ(ː) ~ a > ɑ > ɒ
GOAT	oʊ > o(ː) > o⁽ʷ⁾ə > ɵʊ
GOOSE	u > ü > ɵwə
PRICE	ʌɪ ~ əɪ ~ ɐɪ ~ ɔ̈ɪ
CHOICE	ɔɪ > ʌɪ ~ ɐɪ ~ aɪ
MOUTH	ạʊ ~ ɐʊ ~ ʌʊ ~ ɛʊ ~ ɛü
NEAR	iɹ ~ iəɹ ~ ɪɹ > eɹ/ɛɹ

Table 1. (continued)   Principal vowel variants in NfldE

SQUARE	eɹ ~ ɛɹ > ɪɹ
START	æɹ > ɐɹ
NORTH	ɔɹ ~ oɹ > ɐɹ ~ aɹ
FORCE	oɹ ~ ɔɹ
CURE	uɹ ~ oɹ ~ ɔɹ
happY	i
lettER	ɚ ~ ɜˠ > ɔ̈ɹ ~ ʌɹ
horsES	ɪ ~ i̥ ~ ə
commA	ə

ince display a variable tendency towards tensing of the KIT vowel, though this is most noticeable on the Irish-settled Avalon peninsula. In areas of the province settled by the SW English, [ɪ] tensing appears to be phonologically conditioned among conservative rural speakers, occurring particularly before an alveopalatal fricative (e.g. *fish*) and, less frequently, an alveolar nasal, e.g. *in, wind*. Even among younger urban speakers, [ɪ] tensing frequently occurs in two morphemes: the *-ing* of words like *walking* or *going*, often pronounced [in]; and the possessive *his*, which often sounds identical to *he's*, and which may represent a reanalysis by analogy with the possessive marker *'s*.

In SW English-settled areas of the province, a more prevalent tendency among conservative speakers is the variable lowering of the KIT vowel to the range of [ɛ]. This tendency is phonologically conditioned, occurring in other than a following oral stop environment (most frequently before /l/, as in *children*, as well as anterior fricatives, e.g. *different, with*, and occasionally before /n/, as in *since*). Because for such speakers the DRESS vowel is variably raised to the [ɪ] range (see below), phonetic realizations of the KIT and DRESS sets may overlap to a considerable degree – though such tendencies as [ɪ] tensing do not generally affect items of the standard English DRESS set.

DRESS
For most speakers, the DRESS vowel is realized as standard lax low-mid [ɛ]. On the Irish Avalon, conservative rural speakers display variable and conditioned raising of this vowel to [ɪ] in the environment of a following stop or affricate, e.g. *pension, get, connected*. As noted above, the same phenomenon may be observed among conservative speakers in rural English-settled areas of the

province, where raising to [ɪ] occurs before a following non-velar stop or affri-cate, as in *head, hedge, engine, bench*. Before /l/ or a voiceless velar, however (e.g. *yellow, wreck, breakfast*), lowering to an [æ]-like articulation may occur in English-settled areas. In addition, [ɛ] before a voiced velar may be tensed and diphthongized in a stressed syllable, as in *keg* pronounced [kʰeig] (e.g. Noseworthy 1971).

A similar lowered and somewhat retracted pronunciation of [ɛ] for words in the DRESS set is beginning to make inroads, in a broad set of phonetic environments, in the speech of upwardly mobile younger urban Newfoundlanders. This reflects the influence of the innovative CanE tendency described as the "Canadian Shift" by Clarke, Elms and Youssef (1995), in which lax front vowels are lowered and retracted.

TRAP/BATH

The TRAP/BATH sets are pronounced identically in NfldE, though their /æ/ vowel may be lengthened before a voiceless fricative, as in BATH. For most residents of Newfoundland and Labrador, /æ/ is more raised and fronted than in StCanE. In certain lexical items (e.g. *catch*) the vowel may be raised to [ɛ]. In some Eng-lish-settled areas of the province, /æ/ tends to be raised and tensed to an [ɛɪ]-like realization before velars, as in *bag*, and more frequently, before alveolars and alveopalatals, particularly /n/, as in DANCE. This latter trend appears on the in-crease among younger residents of these areas, among them the young female speaker on the audio sample. At the same time, a recent innovation - apparent among upwardly mobile younger urban females, particularly in St. John's – is a lowering and retraction of the /æ/ vowel in the direction of [a], reflecting the influence of the Canadian Shift.

LOT/CLOTH/THOUGHT

For most Newfoundlanders, the vowels of the LOT/CLOTH/THOUGHT sets have fully merged, and are realized as unrounded [a], [a̠], or occasionally [a̤], well forward of the cardinal 5 position which characterizes StCanE. For some (par-ticularly older) speakers, the vowel of CLOTH/THOUGHT is distinguished from the LOT vowel via length; a very small minority retain a qualitative contrast, with a retracted unrounded [ɑ] or rounded [ɒ] for the CLOTH/THOUGHT sets. While some younger upwardly mobile speakers are tending to adopt more re-tracted CanE-like variants, the majority of the province's residents maintain a more traditional central to front low unrounded vowel for all three subsets.

STRUT
This vowel is typically realized as unrounded [ʌ], as in most North American varieties. However, its point of articulation is often more back than central. For many residents of the Irish Avalon, the vowel is usually accompanied by lip-rounding, and is best represented as [ɔ̈].

FOOT
The FOOT vowel is generally articulated as high back rounded lax [ʊ]. Occasionally, among conservative speakers on the Irish Avalon, the vowel is somewhat raised and tensed (cf. the similar tendency for the KIT vowel). As elsewhere in North America, more centralized variants also occur; but these are particularly evident among younger urban speakers, and in certain lexical items, e.g. *good*.

2.2.   Tense vowels

FLEECE
This vowel is typically realized in standard North American fashion, as tense and, when long, as slightly upglided. The conservative nature of traditional NfldE – whether of SW English or of Irish ancestry – is in evidence, however, in the form of a highly recessive FACE-like pronunciation in such -*ea*- words as *sea*, *heave* and *beat*. In standard varieties, such words (which in Middle English contained /ɛː/) underwent merger with the FLEECE set several centuries ago; in conservative NfldE, however, they maintained their historical mid vowel. Likewise, in highly conservative speech of the Irish Avalon, the FACE vowel has occasionally been noted in at least some FLEECE words deriving from Middle English /eː/, e.g. *seeing*, *sleepy*.

In a handful of English-settled rural areas of the province, both -*ee*- and -*ea*-words display variable centralization in conservative speech, so that *tea* may be articulated as [tʰəɪ].

FACE
In StNfldE, the usual realization is standard North American upglided [ei] or [eɪ]. Vernacular NfldE varieties, however, display a range of variants, including a lowered onset ([ɛɪ], [ɛ̝ɪ]). Older speakers – particularly on the Irish Avalon, but by no means only in this area – often exhibit the historically earlier non-upglided pronunciations, whether monophthongal [eː, ɛː] or, in closed syllables, inglided [e(j)ə, ɛ(j)ə]. Such realizations occur both for words which in Middle and Early Modern English contained a long monophthong (e.g. *made*) as well as those that contained an upglided diphthong (e.g. *maid*); however, these two

subsets continued to be distinguished by some conservative speakers in rural English-settled Newfoundland until fairly recently.

PALM

In vernacular NfldE varieties, most native lexical items incorporating the PALM vowel belong to the TRAP/BATH set; that is, they are articulated with [æ(ː)]. More educated speakers, however, tend to use the lower more retracted vowel of LOT/CLOTH/THOUGHT. They may even – as in the case of the speakers on the audio samples – utilize a more retracted [ɑ]-like sound in PALM words than they do in LOT etc.

GOAT

The usual realization in StNfldE is the standard North American upglided [oʊ] variant. As in the case of the FACE set, conservative older (and primarily rural) speakers throughout Newfoundland and Labrador often use non-upglided pronunciations. These may be monophthongal [o(ː), ǫ(ː)], or inglided [o⁽ʷ⁾ə] in checked syllables such as *boat*. For such speakers, non-upglided articulations appear to occur in the full range of GOAT words, that is, irrespective of whether their historical source was monophthongal (e.g. *no*) or upglided, e.g. *know*. A recent, though still minor, innovation is the adoption of "mainland-like" centralized [əʊ] or [ɵʊ] variants. This trend is being led by younger upwardly mobile urban speakers, particularly women.

GOOSE

In StNfldE this vowel is typically realized as high back rounded. Three different types of speakers, however, tend to use centralized variants; in two of these cases, centralization is an inherited or at least long-standing feature. The first involves certain English-settled areas of the province, which have preserved the tendency towards centralization of /u/ that characterized parts of West Country England. In some of these areas, centralized rounded [ü] appears to be on the increase (at least, apart from a pre-/l/ context), and is the usual variant today among younger females, including those on the audio samples. The second case is found on the Irish Avalon; here, though /u/ centralization occasionally occurs among older traditional speakers, it is by far most apparent before /l/. In Irish-settled communities, words like *school* may be pronounced with an ingliding diphthong the first element of which is centralized and lowered to the area of [ɵ], so that *school* may sound like [skɵwəl]. Finally, as for /o/, a minor tendency towards centralization of /u/ is evident in the speech of the chief urban centre of the province, St. John's. That this represents a recent innovation in the direction of perceived North American trends is suggested by its almost exclusive association with upwardly mobile younger females.

2.3. Diphthongs

PRICE, PRIZE

The diphthongs associated with these two lexical sets display a range of possible realizations in NfldE. Some speakers – among them urban residents of the Irish Avalon – tend to distinguish PRICE and PRIZE words via a non-low [ə] or [ʌ] onset in PRICE, but a low [ɑ] or [a] onset in PRIZE. That is, such speakers display the pattern commonly referred to as Canadian Raising. More typical among traditional speakers from all areas of the province, however, is the use of a low-mid to mid onset ([ɐ, ə, ʌ]) in all environments, not simply before voiceless obstruents as in PRICE. This pattern is in all likelihood inherited from both SW English and SE Irish source dialects.

For conservative speakers, particularly but by no means only on the Irish Avalon, the raised onset may also be retracted and rounded to an [ɔ̈]-like sound. Though this is most evident in post-labial position (e.g. *might, twice*), it is by no means restricted to this environment. Before sonorants (e.g. *time, fire, child*), glide-weakened pronunciations are not uncommon (as also for the MOUTH/LOUD sets).

CHOICE

Speakers of StNfldE distinguish the CHOICE set from the PRICE/PRIZE sets as do standard speakers elsewhere in North America, via the use of a rounded mid back [ɔ] or [o] onset in CHOICE words. More conservative (i.e. older, rural, working-class) NfldE speakers, however, exhibit a marked tendency to unround the nucleus of CHOICE, and to pronounce it as [ʌ, ə, ɐ], and even fully lowered [ɑ] or [a]. This leads to considerable overlapping of variants which characterize both the PRICE and CHOICE sets. In at least the casual style of some conservative speakers, total merger may occur; others appear to keep the two sets distinct via a greater degree of retraction and rounding for the PRICE set.

MOUTH, LOUD

Contrary to usage in the PRICE/PRIZE sets, the English of the capital, St. John's, does not traditionally display Canadian Raising in words containing /aʊ/. Rather, both the MOUTH and LOUD sets are usually articulated with similar low vowel nuclei, in the range of [a̠] or [a]. Conservative and rural speakers throughout the province, however, often exhibit (inherited) low-mid to mid onsets ([ɐ, ɜ, ə, ʌ]) in all positions. Such speakers also variably front the nucleus of /aʊ/ to a vowel approaching [ɛ] or, less frequently, [æ]. This fronting tendency – along with variable centralization of the glide, to an [ü]-like articulation – appears to be on the increase off the Irish Avalon; for example, it is a salient feature of the speech of younger middle-class women from English-settled areas, among them those on the audio samples. This inherited tendency may be enhanced by the /aʊ/ fronting tendency that is today obvious in innovative mainland Canadian speech, and that is also making inroads into the speech of some younger St. John's residents.

2.4. Vowels before /r/

NEAR, SQUARE

For many NfldE speakers, the vowels of these two sets are merged, with the merged vowel ranging from high or semi-high [i]/[ɪ] on the Irish Avalon, to a high-mid to mid vowel approximating cardinal vowels 2 or 3 elsewhere in the province. More educated speakers, however (including those on the audio samples), distinguish the two sets in the standard manner, though often the distinction appears more learned than inherited.

START

The low vowel in words like START – like the low vowels in non-pre-/r/ position (e.g. TRAP, LOT) – typically displays a considerably more fronted articulation in NfldE than that found in mainland Canadian varieties. For many speakers, representing the full social spectrum, the realization is [æɹ]. Some urban, younger and more educated Newfoundland residents, however, utilize a lower or more retracted vowel, in the region of [a], [a̠] or [ɐ].

NORTH, FORCE

These two sets are merged for most speakers of NfldE, with usual pronunciations of [oɹ] or [ɔɹ]. Older working-class (especially rural) speakers, however, display a variable tendency towards lowering, fronting and unrounding of the pre-/r/ vowel in words such as *morning*, *corner*, and *cork*, resulting in such highly stigmatized pronunciations as [ɐɹ] or [aɹ]. For such speakers, then, the range of articulation of the NORTH set may overlap with that of the START set in casual speech; the FORCE set, however, may remain distinct, in that it does not exhibit full lowering and unrounding (see, e.g., Colbourne 1982).

CURE

Many speakers of NfldE display, in casual styles at least, a merger of CURE items with those belonging to the NORTH/FORCE set: all (e.g. *tour*, *tore*) are articulated with [oɹ] or [ɔɹ]. More educated speakers may make the distinction in the standard manner, but – as in the case of /ir/ and /er/ – the /ur/-/or/

opposition tends to be a learned rather than a naturally acquired phenomenon in NfldE.

NURSE

Most speakers of NfldE realize stressed syllabic /r/ as in *nurse* or *fur* in the standard North American fashion, as [ɚ] or [ɜʳ]. Among more traditional speakers in Irish-settled areas, this vowel has a distinct quality which may derive from a greater degree of retroflexion than the norm, along with variable rounding and retraction, resulting in [ɔɹ] or [ʌɹ].

MARRY, MERRY, MARY

While the MERRY/MARY sets are merged for virtually all Newfoundlanders, many preserve the MARRY ([æɹ]) vs. MERRY/MARY ([eɹ] or [ɛɹ]) distinction. Younger, particularly urban, Newfoundlanders, however, are losing this contrast, since many are innovating in the general North American direction of raising of [æ] in MARRY words, e.g. *guarantee*. Some conservative and older speakers display a retracted [ɜʳ] or [ʌɹ]-like realization in the MERRY set (e.g. *berry*, *very*, *bury*); retraction to a [ɐ/ʌ]-like vowel may occur in the MARRY set, though much more rarely. However, centralization and retraction are increasingly recessive in NfldE.

2.5. Unstressed vowels

*happ*Y

As elsewhere in Canada, speakers of NfldE use a tense high [i] rather than lax [ɪ] in words containing a final unstressed high front vowel. Among conservative rural speakers in English-settled areas of the province, tense [i] was also a possible articulation of the word-final unstressed vowel in such lexical items as *follow* and *potato*. Today, however, this feature is highly recessive. Tense [i] is also found in traditional vernacular speech as an unstressed variant of the lexical items *my* and *by*, which in stressed position are realized in the standard fashion, as the diphthong [aɪ].

*lett*ER

The unstressed syllabic /r/ of the *lett*ER set has the same set of phonetic realizations as the stressed syllabic /r/ of the NURSE set. These include extra retroflexion, retraction and variable rounding in Irish-settled areas.

*hors*ES/*comm*A

In NfldE, the unstressed vowel of *hors*ES is generally higher and more fronted than the unstressed syllable-final vowel of *comm*A: as elsewhere in North America, the former is articulated in the range of [ɪ] or [ɨ], while realizations of the latter are more [ə]-like. As in many other varieties, this opposition distinguishes '*im* (= *him*) and '*em* (= *them*) in sequences like *Give 'im a book* and *Give 'em a book*. However, in many phonetic environments the two vowels may be pronounced identically, as in the unstressed syllables of *pig it* and *bigot*.

2.6.   Vowels: Lexical distribution

Several patterns of lexical distribution affecting the FOOT, STRUT and GOOSE sets differentiate NfldE, particularly its conservative and rural varieties, from StCanE, though these patterns are not unknown on the Canadian mainland. Firstly, the lexical incidence of the FOOT and STRUT classes in NfldE does not coincide with their lexical distribution in contemporary StE. A number of words nowadays articulated with [ʊ] belong in the STRUT set for conservative speakers of NfldE; these include *put, took* and *look*. Likewise, many speakers, primarily in English-settled areas of the province, display the use of the LOT rather than the STRUT vowel in *un*-sequences, e.g. *understand, undo, untie*. Finally, a small number of lexical items which are generally articulated with the high back tense vowel of GOOSE in contemporary standard varieties are often found with the high back lax vowel of FOOT in NfldE, particularly among older speakers. These tend to be restricted to environments involving a following nasal or a labio-dental fricative, notably *room, broom, groom, spoon, roof, hoof* (yet not *moon* or *proof*). Laxing also occurs sporadically in other environments, e.g. before /l/ in *foolish*.

3.   Consonants

TH

Throughout Newfoundland and Labrador, both /θ/ and /ð/ regularly occur in casual speech as the alveolar stops [t] and [d], or the affricates [tθ] and [dð]; in unstressed function words such as *the*, a stop realization for /ð/ is not uncommon even among middle-class urban speakers. In rural communities of the Irish-settled Avalon, dental and postdental variants, both stop and fricative, occur variably among traditional speakers, who may thereby maintain the phonemic contrast with alveolar /t/ and /d/. In rural areas of the province settled by the SW English, /θ/ and /ð/ in non-word-initial position are occasionally articulated as [f] and [v] e.g. in *bath, Matthew, breathe, father*. A highly stigmatized [s] articulation for non-initial /θ/ has also been noted in one such area; its voiced counterpart [z] does not occur, however. In two lexical items – *a'r* (= *either*, meaning *any*), *na'r* (= *neither*, meaning *none*) – medial /ð/ is deleted by traditional speakers (as occasionally in other such items, e.g. *whether*).

H

Vernacular varieties of NfldE of SW English origin are characterized by an /h/ patterning very different from the lexically-inherited pattern of standard English. In these varieties, /h/ is not a segmental phoneme but rather, displays a conditioned phonotactic distribution: [h] may be inserted before any syllable-initial vowel, the likelihood of insertion increasing when this vowel occurs in a stressed syllable, and when it is preceded by another vocalic segment. Thus each of the phonetic sequences [dæt'hɛɹ] and [dær'ɛɹ] may represent either *that hair* or *that air*. *H*-insertion in the latter type of sequence is highly stigmatized, however; possibly as a consequence, some speakers in English-settled areas exhibit a simple tendency towards syllable-onset *h*-deletion in all environments.

On the Irish Avalon, and in all standard varieties of NfldE, /h/ patterning is lexically determined, just as in standard English. The sole exception, in Irish-settled areas, is the pronunciation of the name of the letter *h* as *haitch*.

R

Rhoticity is the norm in NfldE. That said, a largely English-settled area in Conception Bay – located on the Avalon peninsula west of the capital, St. Johns – displays variable postvocalic /r/ deletion in syllable codas, e.g. *there, far, four*. This feature is locally stigmatized, yet continues to characterize the speech of some younger residents of the area, notably working-class males. It also occurs, though much less frequently, in rural communities within the greater St. John's metropolitan area. South of the capital, on the exclusively Irish-settled Avalon, traditional speakers in several rural communities likewise display a tendency towards *r*-deletion in syllable coda position. These are communities that in earlier times may have been characterized by a (highly marked) uvular pronunciation of *r* (cf. Hickey 2002: 296–297).

Elsewhere on the island and in Labrador, a number of traditional speakers from a range of communities display a variable tendency to postvocalic *r*-deletion in unstressed syllables (not only in *lettER*-words, but also in such cases as unstressed *there's*). For a small set of lexical items, an *r*-less pronunciation is common, as in the first syllable of *partridgeberry* (reanalysed by some as *patchyberry*). Conversely, some English-settled areas of the province display the now recessive feature of hyperrhoticity in the form of *r*-insertion in unstressed syllables following [ə] (as in *tuna, fellow, tomorrow*); *r*-insertion remains fairly common, however, in the stressed syllable of *Chicago* (and less so in *wash*).

L

In most urban NfldE, as well as in areas of the province settled by the south-west English, postvocalic /l/ is articulated as a "dark" or velar contoid, as is the norm elsewhere in North America. In some areas of English-settled Newfoundland, this dark /l/ is variably vocalized, or deleted. Deletion seems most frequent after low vowels (e.g. *fall*) and in consonant clusters (e.g. *myself*); occasionally, in clusters, /l/ is deleted outside of syllable-coda position, e.g. in the word *only*. In other environments (e.g. *coal, fell*), vocalization to a mid to high back rounded [o], [ʊ], or unrounded [ɤ] occurs variably. While deletion and vocalization appear primarily a rural phenomenon in Newfoundland, they are also observable among younger residents of the capital, St. John's. The traditional speech of St. John's and the Irish Avalon, however, is characterized by a "clear" or palatal articulation of postvocalic /l/, as are conservative varieties spoken on the southwest coast of the island, an area characterized by French, Scots and Irish settlement. Today, in all these areas, palatal variants are most associated with older speakers.

T

Posttonic intervocalic or pre-sonorant /t/ (as in *Betty* and *water*) is typically realized in NfldE as a flap, as in other North American varieties. In more careful styles, and particularly among older middle class speakers, it may be realized as a voiceless aspirated stop. On the Irish Avalon, the traditional variant (now associated more with older speakers, as well as female speech) is the alveolar slit fricative [t]; occasionally the realization is [h], as in *Saturday*. The slit fricative occurs most frequently, however, in word-final pre-pausal position, e.g. *hit, bet*.

As elsewhere in Canada, a glottal stop variant occurs before syllabic /n/ (e.g. *cotton*); in NfldE, however, a glottal realization is found variably before syllabic /l/, as in *bottle* (and much more rarely, syllabic /r/, as in *gutter*). Glottalization of /t/ may also occur in syllable onset position between sonorants (e.g. *partridge, mortal, country*), and in coda position in other than a pre-vocoid environment, e.g. *bootless, football*.

WH

In NfldE, there is an absence of contrast in pairs such as *which* and *witch*, both being pronounced with [w]. Voiceless [ʍ] is extremely rare; its occasional use appears to be in imitation of mainland North American models.

JU, HU

After coronal stops (e.g. *tune*, *new*), the usual variant is glideless [u], though glided [ju] also occurs, particularly in formal styles. In NfldE, /t/ and /d/ before historical /ju/ are often affricated in vernacular speech: thus *Tuesday* is often heard as [tʃuzdi], *due* as [dʒu] and *stupid* as [stʃupɨd]. In *hu-* sequences (e.g. *human*), most Newfoundlanders likewise display glide reduction, i.e. absence of voiceless aspirated [hj]; even well-educated speakers may exhibit no contrast in such pairs as *Hugh* and *you*.

S, SH, CH

In some parts of Newfoundland other than the Irish Avalon (especially the southwestern and western areas of the island), the alveolar fricative [s] is occasionally pronounced as alveopalatal [ʃ] in word-initial consonant clusters (as in *stutter* and *slap*). An unusual, and recessive, feature on parts of the southwest coast is the (variable) pronunciation of the voiceless alveopalatal fricative /tʃ/ as the corresponding alveopalatal fricative [ʃ], in word-initial position only; this results in such realizations as *shicken* for *chicken*.

Consonant sequences: Deletion and insertion

Vernacular NfldE exhibits extensive consonant cluster reduction. As in many other varieties, /t/ and /d/ deletion is frequent in syllable-coda position following a homorganic obstruent, nasal or liquid, e.g. *jus̲t̲, breakfa̲s̲t̲, wen̲t̲, groun̲d̲, wil̲d̲*. For some old-fashioned or "deep" vernacular speakers, this reduction applies not only in pre-consonant or pre-pause position, but also before vowels, suggesting absence of final stops in such clusters in underlying lexical entries, particularly when these are not subject to the effects of a following morpheme boundary. Single consonants in syllable-coda position are also subject to deletion in a number of (unstressed) words, notably *with, of, give*. (In a handful, however, /t/ may be added, as in *cliff* pronounced [klɪft] and *skiff*, [skɪft].) In syllable onsets following an obstruent, liquids may undergo deletion, particularly when the syllable is unstressed: thus *from* may be pronounced [fəm], and /l/ may be absent in the first syllable of the place-name *Placentia*.

Certain consonant sequences, on the contrary, tend to promote vowel epenthesis in conservative NfldE. These include non-homorganic syllable-coda clusters consisting of /l/ + non-coronal, as in *elm* pronounced *ellum* and *kelk* (a regional

English word meaning 'stone') pronounced [kʰɛlək] ('a stone anchor'). The syllable-final clusters *-sp*, *-st*, *-sk* may display epenthetic [ə] insertion before the noun plural marker in the speech of conservative rural Newfoundlanders, so that *desk* may be pronounced [dɛskəz] (with alternative realizations, through deletion/assimilation, of [dɛs(ː)əz] and even unmarked [dɛsː]). More rarely, epenthesis is found after /r/, as in the conservative Irish Avalon disyllabic pronunciation of *barm* ('yeast').

Consonant devoicing

In Irish-settled areas of Newfoundland, non-word-initial fricatives may be devoiced, as in *live*, *choose*, and *pleasure*. While the same tendency occurs in conservative speech throughout the province in some plural lexical items, including reflexives (e.g. *ourselfs*, *theirselfs*, *wifes*, *lifes*), these cases probably result from analogy with the singular rather than from an inherited phonological tendency, at least elsewhere than the Irish Avalon. Recessive devoicing is also found occasionally in fricative + oral stop sequences, as in *roused* pronounced with syllable-coda [st] and *shoved* with [ft]. Throughout the province, likewise, conservative speakers may exhibit variable post-sonorant /d/ devoicing (cf. Hickey 2002: 301) after /n/ and /l/, as in *hold* [(h)oːlt] (*got holt to 'em*) and *killed* [kʰɪlt].

Sibilant assimilation

Traditional speakers in English-settled areas of the province display assimilation of /z/ to /d/ before syllabic /n/. Just as in the southwest of England, however, this assimilation is restricted to contracted negatives of the verb *be*, i.e. (*it*) *isn't* > [(t)ɪdn̩], (*it*) *wasn't* >[(t)wʌdn̩]. A similar phenomenon occurs for the lexical items *seven* and *eleven*, which are variably pronounced with the sequence [bm̩].

Recessive consonant features

Varieties of NfldE with ancestry in southwest England display several consonant features which are today highly recessive. These include syllable-initial fricative voicing (e.g. *fan* pronounced *van*, *said* pronounced *zaid*); syllable initial glide insertion, e.g. (*h*)*ear* pronounced like *year*, *other* pronounced *yuther*; and variable deletion of syllable-initial /w/ (e.g. *wood* pronounced [ʊd]), yet its insertion before certain back vowels, e.g. *coil* pronounced [kwɔɪl]. Somewhat more frequent in such varieties is (inherited) metathesis in *s*+stop as well as *CrV* sequences, e.g. *wasp* pronounced *waps*, *children* pronounced *chil(d)ern*. In a few southern Labrador communities, syllable-initial /v/ (e.g. *vegetable*) is pronounced by older speakers as a bilabial [w].

4.   Prosodic features

Little research has been conducted into the prosodic aspects of NfldE. A popular observation, however, is that Newfoundlanders "talk fast", and many traditional and vernacular speakers exhibit a tendency towards allegro speech. This results in a high rate of application of such phonological processes as segment deletion and assimilation. For example, there is considerable elision of unstressed vowels: items like *electric*, *expect*, *according*, *away* are regularly articulated without initial vowel. Likewise, the (unstressed) vowel of *it* is often deleted before auxiliary and copula verbs, resulting in such old-fashioned realizations as *'twill* for *it will*, *'twas* for *it was*, and *'tis* rather than *it's*. Apheresis is also common in initial unstressed syllables; thus *before* is often pronounced as *'fore*, and *instead*, as *'stead*. In conservative NfldE, particularly in generations past, the vowel of the definite article *the* (in which *th-* was typically pronounced as a stop) was often elided before a vowel, resulting in such sequences as *d'en'* for *the end*. In addition, there is a rhythmic tendency towards open syllables, as in the pronunciation of *at all* as *a # tall*, with aspirated [t].

Intonation patterns associated with conservative and vernacular NfldE have yet to be described in any detail (yet see Paddock 1981). Distinctive "Irish" vs. "English" patterns appear to exist, both of which differ from those encountered in much of mainland Canada. As to stress, traditional speakers in Irish-settled areas of the province display a now recessive tendency towards Irish-like non-initial syllable stress in words like *inte*RESTed, *separ*ATE, and *appreci*ATE.

One distinctive feature of NfldE – a feature shared with varieties spoken in Canada's Maritime provinces, and to a much smaller degree parts of New England – is the use of the ingressively articulated discourse particles *yeah*, *mm* and *no*. Ingressives are more typical of women's than men's speech, and appear to be somewhat less frequent among younger generations. In contemporary NfldE, they are found among speakers of all social levels.

5.   Current issues

Though NfldE is relatively well described by comparison to CanE, much linguistic work remains to be done. Among the research needed is the investigation of vowel changes in contemporary varieties, and the degree to which these are influenced by ongoing change on the Canadian mainland. Further, the remarkably conservative nature of certain varieties of NfldE has much to offer from a sociohistorical perspective, in terms of insights into the structure of earlier vernacular regional varieties spoken in southwest Britain and southeastern Ireland – varieties that also played a major role in the early British colonization of America and the Caribbean.

*   I would very much like to thank my colleagues Robert Hollett and Philip Hiscock for the invaluable assistance that our joint work on the transcription of vernacular Newfoundland English has provided me, along with the Memorial University Folklore and Language Archive for allowing us access to its tape collection. I also extend sincere thanks to Harold Paddock for his many insights into Newfoundland English over the years. Both this chapter and the chapter on Newfoundland morphology and syntax would not have been possible without the data collected by a number of graduate and advanced undergraduate students in Linguistics at Memorial University. While I am enormously grateful to them all, I would like to thank in particular Catherine Lanari for allowing me access to her taped corpus of spoken Burin-area English.

Exercises and study questions

1. As noted, conservative speakers of NfldE pronounce not only unstressed *my* as *me*, but *by* as *be* [bi]. Historically (i.e. in terms of the Great Vowel Shift), these are conservative forms relative to their stressed counterparts *my* and *by*. Explain.

2. Pulmonic ingressive articulation (i.e., speech realized when inhaling rather than exhaling) is an uncommon feature in human language. Research this feature to determine what functions it serves in languages in which it has been documented. Can you find other varieties of English that use the ingressively-articulated particles *yeah*, *mm* and *no*?

3. What differences can you detect in the vowel realizations of speakers on the audio samples who represent areas of the island originally settled by the (southwest) English as opposed to the (southeast) Irish? Do these correspond to the differences outlined in this chapter?

4. As noted, in southern Labrador some conservative speakers use bilabial [w]-like pronunciations of initial /v/, as in *visit* or *vegetable*. Could this be an inherited feature, or must it have developed locally? In answering, check the *v-w* relationship in publications dealing with conservative 20th century regional dialects in the British Isles, as well as those dealing with earlier centuries.

5. Contrast the speech of the St. John's male on the audio sample (both word list and free speech segment) with the speech of the (younger) rural

Newfoundland female (word list and reading passage), who comes from a part of Newfoundland originally settled by immigrants from southwest England. Does he display any phonological features that, because of his age or his regional background, are either more "local-sounding" or more "Irish-like" than the corresponding features in the female's speech? Conversely, what features does the female display that are absent from the St. John's male's variety? (By way of example, examine the word list pronunciations of the vowels of *choice* and *beer*, and the *t* of *carter* and *daughter*.)

6. Contrast the same speakers in their pronunciations of the /aɪ/ and /aʊ/ diph-thongs (e.g. the words *price* and *prize* in the word list). Do any of these speakers display the feature known as "Canadian Raising"?

Selected references

Please consult the General references for titles mentioned in the text but not included in the references below. For a full bibliography see the accompanying CD-ROM.

Clarke, Sandra
    1991   Phonological variation and recent language change in St. John's English. In: Cheshire (ed.), 108–122.
    2004   The legacy of British and Irish English in Newfoundland. In: Hickey (ed.).
Clarke, Sandra, Ford Elms and Amani Youssef
    1995   The third dialect of English: Some Canadian evidence. *Language Variation and Change* 7: 209–228.
Colbourne, B. Wade
    1982   A sociolinguistic study of Long Island, Notre Dame Bay, Newfoundland. M.A. thesis, Department of Linguistics, Memorial University of Newfoundland.
Halpert, Herbert and J.D.A. Widdowson
    1996   *Folktales of Newfoundland*, Volumes I and II. (Publications of the American Folklore Society.) St. John's, Newfoundland: Breakwater.
Hickey, Raymond
    2002   The Atlantic edge: The relationship between Irish English and Newfoundland English. *English World-Wide* 23: 283–316.
Lanari, Catherine E. Penney
    1994   A sociolinguistic study of the Burin region of Newfoundland. M.A. thesis, Department of Linguistics, Memorial University of Newfoundland.
Noseworthy, Ronald G.
    1971   A dialect survey of Grand Bank, Newfoundland. M.A. thesis, Department of Linguistics, Memorial University of Newfoundland.

African American Vernacular English: phonology

Walter F. Edwards

1. Introduction

The variety of English known as AAVE (African-American Vernacular English) is spoken throughout the United States and in some parts of Canada (including Nova Scotia) primarily by African Americans. The variety is spoken most consistently by working-class African Americans, particularly in urban areas. The vast majority of middle class African Americans are bi-dialectal in AAVE and Standard American English (StAmE) and use AAVE in appropriate social contexts through a mechanism scholars have characterized as style-shifting (see Baugh 1983: 58). AAVE co-exists with the colloquial StAmE typically spoken by middle class African Americans and middle class whites; and with white vernacular American English typically spoken by working class whites, with both StAmE and white vernacular American English enjoying significantly more social prestige than AAVE. For this reason AAVE exhibits linguistic influences from both StAmE and white vernacular American English. Thus, in addition to the broad AAVE vernacular, the so-called *basilect,* we find StAmE and white vernacular American English-influenced varieties called the *mesolect* and the *acrolect* with the latter construct being very close to StAmE (Stewart 1968) and the former an intermediate variety. This chapter will describe the phonological characteristics of the broad AAVE vernacular in the United States, excluding the varieties of the Caribbean and the Gullah variety spoken in the coastal Carolina area (both of which, some argue, should also be included under the umbrella of AAVE).

Historically, AAVE has been thought to have derived from some combination of native African languages and historic dialects of English. Two competing theoretical positions on the provenance of AAVE currently hold sway in the literature. The African substratum position, sometimes called the creolist position (Rickford and Rickford 2000; Rickford 1999), proposes that AAVE is the descendant of the creole language synthesis smelted on southern plantations in ante-bellum America. From this perspective, when African slaves were brought to early America, directly or via the Caribbean, they arrived speaking a variety of African languages, probably including an English-based pidgin that was current on coastal West Africa during the slave-trading era. Slaves, it is assumed, had little or no exposure to the English of their owners; thus, they fashioned the original creole by combining the grammatical and phonological resources of their African languages with the English pidgin structures, which themselves were strongly influenced underlyingly by African linguistic habits. It is this early AAVE that has evolved to the present AAVE.

A second view, the English-origins position, held by Poplack (2000) and others, argues that when these languages came into contact, the slaves learned more or less the English varieties spoken by their white owners. Under this theory, the differences we now see between mainstream white AmE and AAVE are due to preserved features of preexisting nonstandard English variants. These theories have stimulated vigorous debate in recent years, regarding both the origins and the current structure of AAVE. However, the details of these arguments will not be discussed in depth here. What is generally agreed upon is that AAVE in the United States originated in the slave plantations of the antebellum South and shares a number of phonological and grammatical features with Southern dialects of American English. Whether the southern English absorbed these features from Early AAVE or vice versa is the subject of continuing research and debate. One notes, however, that southern vernacular English is most authentically spoken in areas where large plantations once flourished and which, subsequently, experienced some racial integration soon after the Civil War, when poor whites and ex-slaves became neighboring sharecroppers (Bailey 2001).

In the early parts of the 20th century, a "Great Migration" of African Americans and whites toward northern cities created new African American communities in many urban centers and brought AAVE to these cities. The isolation of AAVE on the basis of racial segregation, which continues up to today in many urban environments, divided working class inner-city African Americans from StAmE and white vernacular American English speaking whites in the big northern cities. It is this isolation that led to the preservation of AAVE and partially explains its apparent homogeneity, which would not otherwise be expected given the geographic distances between AAVE enclaves in northern cities such as Chicago, Cleveland and Philadelphia. Scholars such as Huang (2000) have suggested that the post-1960s desegregation is leading AAVE to become more similar to StAmE, while others (e.g., Labov 1994) see the two varieties becoming more distinct.

2.   Phonemic systems of AAVE

African-American Vernacular English differs from other English dialects in grammar and morphology (see Wolfram, this volume) as well as in phonology.

To some extent, phonological characteristics are intertwined with morphological ones, so we shall characterize AAVE through a "bottom-up" description, beginning with a phonemic inventory and individual phonotactic features and ending with a brief discussion of how these phonological characteristics influence the surface morphology of AAVE. We will refer to phonological characteristics in terms of a typological comparison with StAmE. This in no way implies that AAVE is a less legitimate, logical, or systematic language variety. Therefore, terms such as "consonant cluster simplification" or "deletion" of certain phonemes should be thought of as relative to the American idealized language type, rather than the simplification or deletion of sounds that should exist. The sound system of AAVE in many cases does not require the same sounds in the same contexts that StAmE does.

The basic phonemic span of AAVE is much the same as in other varieties in English. Table 1 charts the vowels of AAVE according to their place of articulation. Table 2 shows the consonants of AAVE listed according to their articulatory features.

Table 1.   Vowels of AAVE

	front	central	back
close	i	ɨ	u
	ɪ	ʊ	
	ɪɘ		
close mid	e	aʊ	o
	ə	ɔ	
open mid	ɛ	ʌ	
	aɪ		
	æ		
open		a	ɑ

Table 2.   Consonants of AAVE

	labial/labiodental	dental/alveolar	palatal	velar/glottal
stops	p b	t d		k g
fricatives	f v θ ð	s z		h
affricates		tʃ dʒ		
nasals	m	n		ŋ
liquids		l	r	
semivowels	w		j	

3.   Phonetic realizations

Many of the vowel and consonant phonemes in tables 1 and 2 have AAVE allophones that are different from StAmE and are either unique to AAVE or are shared by other non-standard American dialects. The Northern Cities Chain Shift is a phenomenon affecting the speech of white speakers in the northern United States. Its essential features are the tensing and raising of [æ] to [ɛ], the backing of [ɛ] to [ʌ], the lowering of [ɔ] to [a], and the fronting of [a] to [æ]. According to Labov (1994), AAVE speakers are not participating in this shift.

The vowel system of AAVE differs from other American English varieties in several ways, although it does share some of its features with Southern white varieties. In table 3 we display and comment on some of the more frequently noted AAVE variations from StAmE.

Table 3.   Phonetic realization of selected AAVE vowels

AAVE vowel	AAVE pattern	AAVE example	Comment
/ɪ/, /ɛ/	Merged before nasals	[pɪn] '*pen*', '*pin*'	Widespread in the South.
/ɪ/	Raised and diphthongized to [iɪ] in some words, including *kids, since, did*	[kiɪdz], [siɪns], [diɪd]	The tensing and raising of this lower high, lax vowel is consistent with the Southern Shift (Labov 1994). Interestingly, however, [ɪ] is lowered to [æ], contra the Southern Shift, in specific words including *thing* [θæŋ].
/ɛ/	Raised and diphthongized to [iɪ] in some words including *when, head*	[wiɪm], [hiɪd]	The tensing and raising of this lower high, lax vowel is consistent with the Southern Shift (Labov 1994).
/æ/	Raising and fronting of this sound towards [ɛ], especially before words with following nasals such as *Ann* and *bang*	[ɛn], [bɛŋ]	According to Labov (1994), this is not associated with the Northern Cities Chain Shift. Edwards and Diergard (2001) measured F1 and F2 acoustic values for the vowel in *Ann* as high and front as 458.5 and 2991.5 respectively for some AAVE speakers.
[e]	Laxing and lowering of this vowel to [ɛ] when it is followed by a nasal consonant or a heterosyllabic vowel, as in *same* or *saying*	[sɛm],[sɛɪn]	This habit does not seem general enough to be an expression of the Southern Shift.
[aɪ]	The glide reduction and monophthongization of this diphthong occurs especially before nasals, pauses and voiced obstruents. Words affected include *mine, hi, slide*.	[maːn], [haː], [slaːd]	This habit is extending to words in which [aɪ] is followed a voiceless obstruent. Thus [waːt] *white*.

Table 4 summarizes the realization of the AAVE vowels, based on Wells' system of lexical sets.

Table 4. Vowel pronunciations in AAVE based on Well's lexical set
StAmE equivalents taken from www.ic.arizona.edu/~anth383.lexicalsets.
html

	AAVE	AAVE	StAmE
PALM	/pæm/	/æ/	/ɑ/
TRAP	/træɛp/~/træɛ/	/æɛ/	/æ/
BATH	/bæɛθ/~/bæɛt/	/æɛ/	/æ/
MOUTH	/mæəθ/~/mæət/	/æə/	/aʊ/
SQUARE	/skwæə/~/skæə/	/æə/	/ɛr/, /ær/
LOT	/lɑt/, /lɑʔ/	/ɑ/	/ɑ/
CLOTH	/klɑθ/~,/klɑt/	/ɑ/	/ɔ/
START	/stɑːt/	/ɑː/	/ar/
PRICE	/prɑːs/	/ɑː/	/aɪ/
NEAR	/niɣ/, /nɪɻ/	/ɣ/, /ɻ/	/ɪr/
NURSE	/nɣs/, /nɻs/	/ɣ/, /ɻ/	/ɝ/
KIT	/kiət/ , /kiɪt/	/iə/,~/iɪ/	/ɪ/
DRESS	/drɛɪs/	/ɛɪ/	/ɛ/
FLEECE	/flɪɪs/	/ɪɪ/	/i/
FACE	/feɪs/, /feis/	/eɪ/	/eɪ/
STRUT	/stʌt/, /stʌʔ/	/ʌ/	/ʌ/
FOOT	/fʊt/, /fʊʔ/	/ʊ/	/ʊ/
CURE	/kʊə/	/ʊə/	/ʊr/
NORTH	/nɔəθ/, /nɔəf/	/ɔə/	/ɔː/
THOUGHT	/θɔʊt/, /θɔʊʔ/	/ɔʊ/	/ɔ/
FORCE	/fɔəs/	/ɔə/	/or/
GOAT	/got/, /goʔ/	/o/	/o/
GOOSE	/gus/	/u/	/u/
CHOICE	/tʃɔɪs/	/ɔɪ/	/ɔɪ/

The entries on Table 5 give examples of some distinctive AAVE consonantal allophones.

Table 5.   Phonetic realization of consonants of AAVE

AAVE consonants and clusters	Example	Variant pronunciation	Do AAVE and Southern white vernacular dialect share feature?	AAVE realizations
/t/,/d/in syllable codas	no*t*, ba*d*	Sounds sometimes realized as glottal stops; /d/ is frequently devoiced to /t/ or deleted in this environment	No	*not* [nɔʔ] *bad* [bæt] [bæʔ] *bid* [bɪt], [bɪ] *good* [gʊt], [gʊ]
/z/, /v/	*isn't, business, seven, eleven*	Sounds are fronted and stopped before nasals	Yes	*isn't* [ɪdnt] *business* [bɪdnɪs] *seven* [sebn]
/θ/,/ð/	*thing, those*	Word initially and word finally, these fricatives are frequently realized as stops, i.e. [t] and [d] respectively. Word-internally and word finally, the voiceless interdental fricative is sometimes realized as [f] and the voiced segment realized as [v]	Yes. Most frequent in AAVE	*thing* [tɪŋ] *those* [doz] *with* [wɪt] *tenth* [tɛnt] *bath* [bæf] *faith* [feɪf] *mother* [mʌvə], [mʌvɹ̩]
/r/	*floor, bird*	Frequently vocalized or deleted in post-vocalic, pre-consonantal and word final environments. The deletion or vocalization most often takes place after non-central vowels in unstressed positions; and least often after central vowels in stressed positions. The sound is often deleted between vowels also.	Yes. Most frequent in AAVE	*floor* [floə], [flo] *bird* [bɣd], [bɹ̩d] *record* [rekəd], [rekɣd], [rekɹ̩d] *Carol* [kaəl]
/l/	*help*	Frequently vocalized or deleted in post-vocalic, pre-consonantal and word final positions. When the sound is not realized as [l] it is more frequently vocalized than deleted. The sound is most frequently deleted before the mid front vowels [e] and [e].Vocalization of [l] as [w] most frequently occurs after back vowels. Deletion seldom occurs before high front vowels.	Yes. Most frequent in AAVE	*help* [hɛp] *bell* [bɛw] *roll* [ro] *school* [skuw] *feel* [fil], [fiw] *football* [fʊbɔw]

Table 5. (continued) Phonetic realization of consonants of AAVE

AAVE consonants and clusters	Example	Variant pronunciation	Do AAVE and Southern white vernacular dialect share feature?	AAVE realizations
/j/	*yet*	Following [u] this sound is sometimes deleted	No	*computer* [kəmputɪ] *beautiful* [butɪfl̩]
/n/	*man*	This sound and other nasals may be deleted when syllable final, with the nasality transferred to the preceding vowel. This process of deleting single consonants in syllable coda positions also affects other sounds in specific lexical items.	No	*man* [mæ̃n] *bang* [bæ̃]
/t/, /d/ and other consonants in word final clusters	*cold, left*	The second consonant in a cluster is frequently deleted when the two consonants share the same voicing feature. The deletion most frequently takes place when the cluster ends a monomorphemic word. The deletion occurs most frequently when the monomorphemic word is followed by a word that begins with an obstruent consonant, and occurs least often when a cluster ends a bimorphemic word and is followed by a word that begins with a vowel.	Yes. Most frequent in AAVE	*and* [æn] *left* [lɛf] *desk* [dɛs]
/s/+ stop	*ask, grasp*	In specific words the cluster metathesizes.	Yes	*ask* [æks] *grasp* [græps]
/k/, /t/ in *str* clusters	*street*	In some words the [t] is backed to [k].	No	*street* [skrit]

4. Stress, pitch, intonation and phonotactic patterns

In informal speech, AAVE speakers often move the stress to the first syllable of a word which in StAmE carries stress on some other syllable. This usually occurs in, but is not restricted to, bisyllabic words, the first syllable of which is open, as in *police* ['poˌlis], *Detroit* ['diˌtrɔɪt], and *Tennessee* ['tɛ ˌnə ˌsi]. In very informal speech, AAVE speakers use fore- stressing frequently. Thus, words like *define, produce, revise* and *detain* are often fore- stressed in the vernacular (Baugh 1983: 63). Intonational stress in sentences often carries meaning. For example, if [bɪn] is not stressed, it does not signify remote past as it does in sentences where it is stressed.

Studies to determine if the unique intonation contours occurring in AAVE are associated with specific sentence types have found that yes-no questions sometimes omit the final rise, often using a level or falling contour at the end of the question (Green 2002; Tarone 1972, 1973).

According to Tarone (1972, 1973), AAVE speakers frequently employ a wide pitch range, often using the falsetto register to signal various modalities, including anger, humor, or skepticism. However, this area is poorly studied, and has not been formally linked to pitch and tone patterns of West African languages (Green 2002).

Word-final clusters such as *sk* and *nd* are frequently produced as *s* and *n*. Thus, *mask* may be pronounced [mæs] and *land* may be pronounced [læn]. Two competing theories for the origin of this phenomenon exist. The first approach claims this occurs because of a robust deletion rule of consonant clusters. The Africanist approach claims the "missing" consonant to be nonexistent because West African languages do not have word-final clusters, and in certain environments (such as before a word-initial vowel) the final consonant is added to the following lexical item. Again, the details of these theories will not be debated here. It should be noted that this phenomenon occurs for many different clusters, including *ld, sp, kd, ft,* and so on (Green 2002).

5.   Phonology and grammar

Some of the phonological processes described above have consequences for the grammar of AAVE. The tendency of AAVE speakers to drop the final [t] or [d] in tautosyllabic two-member clusters with the same voicing specification leads to the loss on the surface of grammatical information. Thus the surface realization of [wɑk] "walk" for underlying [wɑkt] leaves the past morpheme unexpressed segmentally. However, that information is retrieved from the context by any addressee familiar with the AAVE dialect. Similarly, the word *tries* might be uttered as [traɪ] or [tra:] for [traɪz] by an AAVE speaker who naturally drops the final [z], even though that [z] carries the grammatical information that the subject of the sentence is singular. This grammatical fact is signaled elsewhere in the sentence or discourse and is automatically retrieved by an interlocutor who is familiar with AAVE. Thus, sentences such as "I see how *he try* to get a job" or "*He try* to get a trade" (third person), "Plus these kids, these orphanage *kid ...*" (plural), and "Every day ... I see my cousin, or go to *my uncle or somebody house*" (possessive), would be considered anomalous to a non-AAVE speaking listener although they are perfectly grammatical within AAVE.

6.   Discussion

As we see in tables 1-5, AAVE shares a basic sound system with most varieties of English. However, the rules for the combining of these sounds differ in notable ways. In fact, phonological markers of AAVE are noticeable features to the ears of those who speak other English varieties.

Historically, vowel systems of English have been known to systematically shift, with a whole chain of vowels moving uniformly in one direction or other in vowel space. Recent research by William Labov and his associates has shown that there are two major ongoing chain shifts affecting the vowels in American speech: the Southern Shift and the Northern Cities Chain Shift (Labov 1994). However this same research has proposed that African Americans are not participating in these chain shifts. This proposal is supported by several studies. For example, recent research conducted in Detroit by the author of this entry revealed that most AAVE speakers in the sample had vowel pronunciations quite different from what would be expected if they were participating in the Northern Cities Chain Shift. For instance, he observed [diɪd] for [dɪd], [gɪt] for [gɛt], [kiɪdz] for [kɪds], [wiɪm] for [wɪn] and [nɪks] for [nɛks]. These patterns indicate that the lax front vowels of the AAVE speakers in the sample were raised and tense, contrary to NCCS patterns that involve the lowering of [ɪ] and [ɛ].

Another interesting characteristic of the AAVE phonology is the nasalization of vowels in words such as [mãn] (for *man*). Nasal vowels in these environments are reminiscent of the fact that vowel nasality is phonemic in a number of African languages.

7.   Conclusion

The sound system of AAVE is similar to other English varieties in the United States. However, many of the phonemes of AAVE obey different phonetic rules than other American English systems. These differences are systematic and are part of the linguistic continuum that exists for each individual AAVE speaker, making many of these rules "optional" depending on sociolinguistic context. This entry summarized the basic phonological system of the variety and some of the better known phonetic principles that distinguish the AAVE variety from other dialects. Much work remains to be done on AAVE phonology, including work on prosody and intonation.

Exercises and study questions

1. Consider the word *twelve*, which has been documented as being pronounced as [krɛlv] by speakers of AAVE in Detroit. Why would this be?

2. How would you expect the word *tell* to be pronounced in AAVE, based on what you know about vowel raising and word-final /l/?

3. Consider the phrase *East Seven Mile* (the name of a major thoroughfare in Detroit). How would you expect this phrase to be pronounced in casual AAVE speech?

4. Compare the pronunciation features of African American English to those of Southern American English (as described, for instance, by Thomas in this volume). Which similarities do you find?

5. Listen to samples of performances by African American artists (e.g. in hip-hop) and try to identify features of African American pronunciation in their speech.

Selected references

Please consult the General references for titles mentioned in the text but not included in the references below. For a full bibliography see the accompanying CD-ROM.

Bailey, Guy
    2001   The relationship between African American and white vernaculars in the American South: A sociocultural history and some phonological evidence. In: Lanehart (ed.), 53–92.
Edwards, Walter and Nicola Diergardt
    2001   Detroit AAVE and the Northern Cities Chain Shift. Paper delivered at NWAVE conference at Michigan State University, 2001.
Green, Lisa
    2002   *African American English: A Linguistic Introduction.* Cambridge: Cambridge University Press.

Huang, Xiaozhao
    2000   *A Study of African-American Vernacular English in America's "Middletown": Evidence of linguistic convergence.* Lewiston, New York: Edwin Mellen Press.
Rickford, John and Russell Rickford
    2000   *Spoken Soul: The Story of Black English.* New York: Wiley.
Stewart, William
    1968   Continuity and change in American negro dialects. *The Florida FL Reporter 6;* reprinted in: Walt Wolfram and N. Clarke (eds.), *Black-White Speech Relationships*, 51–73. Washington: Center for Applied Linguistics.
Tarone, Elaine
    1972   Aspects of intonation in vernacular white and black English speech. Ph.D. dissertation, University of Washington.
    1973   Aspects of intonation in Black English. *American Speech* 48: 29–36.

Gullah: phonology[*]

Tracey L. Weldon

1. Introduction

Also known as Geechee or Sea Island Creole, Gullah is spoken primarily along the coasts of South Carolina and Georgia. Early descriptions of Gullah were linguistically unfounded accounts that attributed the distinctive features of the variety to laziness or physical limitations on the part of its speakers. However, dialectologists later debunked these myths by showing the systematic nature of the variety and arguing that Gullah was an English dialect whose distinctive features were retentions from earlier varieties of British English. Johnson (1930: 17), for example, noted that "[a]s the analysis proceeds it will become more and more apparent that practically every detail of the Gullah grammar and phonology is directly descended from the midland and southern English dialects". This theory was later challenged by Lorenzo Dow Turner's (1949) description of Africanisms in Gullah, which inspired some scholars to argue that the Gullah system, rather than descending from English dialects, was primarily an African variety (see, e.g., Van Sertima 1976).

A more widely accepted view, however, is that Gullah emerged through a process of language contact between African and English varieties spoken during the Atlantic slave-trading era. During this time, African slaves, speaking a variety of mutually non-intelligible languages, would have found an urgent need to communicate with one another and those that enslaved them. In response to this need, they are believed to have formed contact varieties which drew upon the English vocabulary of the British slave traders and plantation owners, while retaining phonological and grammatical features from their own West African languages.

There has been some debate over whether the process of creolization that eventually led to Gullah took place on the American plantations themselves, or whether the slaves arrived on these plantations already speaking a creole. Some have argued that Gullah, like other Atlantic creoles, may be traced back to a West African Pidgin English (WAfPE), which was transported by slaves to the North American plantations, where it was passed on to succeeding generations of slaves, eventually creolizing into Gullah (see, e.g., Stewart 1968). Another theory is that a putative Barbadian Creole spoken during the 17th century was the source of Gullah as well as Jamaican Creole and Sranan (e.g., Cassidy 1980). This theory was based on the observation that South Carolina, like Jamaica and Surinam, was initially colonized by Barbadian settlers. Yet another theory traces the period of creolization back to 16th-century Africa, where a Guinea Coast Creole English (GCCE), presumed to have been spoken along the Upper Guinea Coast of West Africa, is believed to have been the source of Gullah, as well as all of the Caribbean English Creoles (see, e.g., Hancock 1980).

An examination of the sociodemographic information available led Mufwene (1993) to argue that Gullah emerged in the Carolina colony between 1720 and 1750, i.e. 50 to 80 years after its initial settlement in 1670. This period in the Carolina region was marked by the growth of the rice plantation industry, institutionalized segregation, and an African majority – conditions that would have been conducive to the formation of a creole. Given this time frame, it is believed that three linguistic components – creole, English, and African – would have been most prominent in Gullah's development (see Hancock 1980). The extent to which already existing creoles influenced Gullah's development remains controversial. However, it may be assumed that some creole influence was present in its formation, introduced either by slaves brought over from the Caribbean or directly from Africa. The English that influenced Gullah's development was most likely spoken by Europeans as well as Africans who were present in the Charles Town colony during the early years of settlement (i.e., between 1670 and 1720) (see Mufwene 1993). And given the fact that the Charles Town colony was settled by Barbadian planters, who came primarily from the southwestern region of England, the most influential English dialects appear to have been those deriving from Southwest England (see, e.g., Niles 1980).

Theories regarding the African element in Gullah are somewhat more controversial. Several theories have derived from analyses of the data presented in Turner (1949). Some scholars have pointed to a significant amount of influence from the Kwa language family, spoken along parts of Southern Nigeria and the African Gold Coast (e.g., Cassidy 1980; Alleyne 1980). Others have pointed to the linguistic prominence of Kru and Mande languages, spoken along the coast of Senegambia, Sierra Leone, and Liberia (e.g., Hair 1965; Hancock 1980). According to Creel (1988: 29-30), most of the Africans brought into the South Carolina region came from trading stations in four areas of the Guinea Coast – Congo-Angola, Gambia, the Windward Coast (Sierra Leone and Liberia), and the Gold Coast (Republic of Ghana). It is likely, therefore, that at least four primary African language families contributed to Gullah's development, namely Bantu from the Congo-Angola region, Kru and Mande from Gambia and the Windward Coast, and Kwa from the Gold Coast.

Perhaps the most extensive research done to date on the phonology of Gullah is that presented in Turner ([1945] 1971), ([1949] 2002). The discussion below will, therefore, depend heavily on Turner's analyses, supplemented by the data that were elicited for the current project.

2.   Sound system

2.1.   Vowels

Table 1 summarizes some of the phonetic realizations of Gullah vowels. In each case, the first symbol or set of symbols represents the pronunciations provided by the speaker recorded for this project—an elderly African-American female basket maker from Mount Pleasant, South Carolina (see accompanying CD). Additional symbols summarize observations made by Turner (1971, 2002) with regard to these sounds. Since some changes are likely to have taken place in the Gullah sound system since Turner's fieldwork was conducted, any apparent differences in Turner's observations and those made with regard to the current data set are noted in the text. It should also be noted that none of these sounds have been acoustically measured.

Table 1.   Gullah vowels

KIT	ɪ̧ ~ ɨ	GOOSE	u
DRESS	ɛ̧ ~ ɛ	PRICE	ɐɪ ~ ɐɨ
TRAP	æ ~ a	CHOICE	ɔɪ ~ ɐɪ ~ ɐɨ
LOT	ɑ ~ ɒ	MOUTH	ɔʊ ~ ɐʊ
STRUT	ʌ	NEAR	ɪ ~ ɪə
FOOT	ʊ	SQUARE	ɛə
BATH	æ ~ a	START	a
CLOTH	o	NORTH	ɔ̂
NURSE	ɑ ~ ʌ	FORCE	o
FLEECE	i	CURE	jo
FACE	e	happY	i ~ ɨ
PALM	æ ~ a	lettER	з ~ з̄
THOUGHT	ɔ ~ ɒ	horsES	ɪ
GOAT	o	commA	ə ~ ə̄
GOAL	o ~ oɛ		

KIT

The speaker recorded for this project produces a fairly lowered variety of [ɪ] which approaches the positioning of [ɛ]. According to Turner, a more retracted, central vowel, which he describes by the symbol [ɪ], is also occasionally heard when there is an adjacent *k, g, l,* or *r* (1971: 125).

DRESS

As with [ɪ], the current speaker's [ɛ] is also quite lowered, approaching the positioning of [æ]. Turner (1971) describes a more cardinal pronunciation, but observes that a more open variety occasionally occurs before nasals (especially in Charleston, SC) and in all positions for one speaker from Harris Neck, Georgia (125).

TRAP

For the current speaker, [æ] is lowered to a position approaching [a]. According to Turner, [a] is practically cardinal in Gullah and is used instead of [æ] or [ɑ], which Turner describes as the General American (GA) pronunciation, henceforth referred to by the label Standard American English (StAmE). Given the current speaker's pronunciation, however, it appears that [æ] has since been added to the Gullah phonology, but in a more lowered position than that typically found in StAmE phonologies.

LOT

While the current speaker's vowel appears to be a low, back, unrounded [ɑ], Turner reports a more rounded [ɒ] for words such as *pot, body, dog,* and *wash.* He does, however, observe that there are varying degrees of lip-rounding for this sound (1971: 125–126; 2002: 18).

STRUT

Consistent with Turner's observations, the vowel in STRUT for the current speaker appears to be [ʌ]. Turner describes the tongue position for this vowel in Gullah as being "slightly lower than for Cardinal [ɔ] and somewhat more advanced" (1971: 126).

FOOT

Also consistent with Turner's observations, the current speaker's vowel in FOOT is [ʊ]. Turner describes the tongue position for this vowel in Gullah as "slightly higher than half-closed and … considerably advanced from the position required for [u]" (1971: 126).

BATH

As noted above for TRAP, the vowel in BATH for the current speaker appears to be a lowered [æ]. The vowel [a] is included in the table as well, however, in recognition of Turner's observations (see TRAP discussion above).

CLOTH

The speaker recorded for this project produces a very rounded [o] for this word. It is not entirely clear whether this represents a common pronunciation of this word in Gullah, or whether the speaker is mistaking this word for *clothe* or even *clothes*. As will be discussed in the section on consonants, the final fricative in this word is produced as [s] rather than [θ]. This might be an indication that this word was mistaken for *clothes* or it might represent a phonological process in Gullah by which voiceless interdental fricatives are replaced by voiceless alveolar fricatives. The latter theory is supported by the fact that the same replacements are made in BATH and, variably, in NORTH. Turner describes [o] in Gullah as "slightly above cardinal" and "never diphthongized". He also observes fully rounded lips for this sound in Gullah (1971: 126).

NURSE

The vowel produced by the current speaker for NURSE is the low back unrounded vowel [ɑ]. Turner reports use of [ʌ] in similar words such as *bird* and *earth* (2002: 20). Therefore, [ʌ] might represent an alternative pronunciation here.

FLEECE

As in StAmE, the vowel produced by the current speaker for this sound is [i]. Turner describes this sound in Gullah as "practically cardinal" (2002: 15).

FACE

The vowel in this word appears to be the pure vowel [e]. Turner describes this sound in Gullah as "slightly above cardinal" and "never diphthongized" (2002: 16; 1971: 125).

PALM

The speaker produces a lowered [æ] for this word. Turner, however, reports use of [a], noting that several of his speakers used a variety of [a] that was slightly above cardinal before and after plosives (1971: 125).

THOUGHT

For this word, the speaker produced the [ɔ] vowel. Turner describes words such as *brought* and *daughter* as having the lower vowel [ɒ], noting that "[ɔ] is seldom heard in Gullah" (2002: 18). However, the sound produced by the current speaker seems higher than [ɒ], suggesting that [ɔ] has perhaps since been added to the Gullah phonology.

GOAT

For this word, the vowel produced by the current speaker is the pure vowel [o]. See the discussion under CLOTH for Turner's observations regarding this sound in Gullah.

GOAL

Here the speaker appears to vary between the monophthong [o] and the diphthong [oɛ]. Turner observed very few diphthongs in Gullah at the time that he conducted his research. However, modern-day Gullah appears to exhibit quite a few diphthongs, as some of the examples to follow will show.

GOOSE

Consistent with Turner's observations, the vowel produced by the current speaker for this word is [u]. Turner describes this vowel as "practically cardinal", but notes that "an advanced variety occurs after alveolar consonants" (1971: 125–126).

PRICE

Another diphthong observed in Gullah is [ɐɪ], which is produced by the current speaker in the word PRICE. According to Turner, the nucleus of this diphthong is normally [ɒ]. However, he observes that it is advanced and raised to [ɐ] when it is followed by a voiceless consonant (as in PRICE) and often when it is preceded by what Turner calls a "fricative *r*" (2002: 21). Turner uses the term "fricative *r*" to refer to a "voiced post-alveolar fricative consonant" (2002: 28). It is not clear, however, that this is the sound preceding the diphthong in PRICE. With regard to the second member of this diphthong, Turner alternates between the symbols [ɪ] and the more retracted, central vowel [ɨ] (1971: 125–126; 2002: 21).

CHOICE

For CHOICE, the current speaker uses the diphthong [ɔɪ]. However, Turner observes use of the diphthongs [ɐɪ] and [ɐɨ] as options for similar words (1971: 125–126; 2002: 21). Turner cites words such as *boil, join,* and *boy,* which he describes as having the surface diphthong [aɪ], with the nucleus advancing from an underlying [ɒ]. It appears, however, that this group of words undergoes a nucleus shift to [ɐ] in pre-voiceless environments, comparable to that observed in words such as *die*, *mine*, and *side*.

MOUTH
For the current speaker, the diphthong in MOUTH appears to be [ɔʊ]. Turner, however, cites the diphthong as [ɒʊ], again with the nucleus advanced and raised to [ɐ] in pre-voiceless environments (1971: 125–126; 2002: 21). One might also note in the reading passage on the accompanying CD, that the speaker monophthongizes the vowel in *around*, transcribed as [əɹɔn]. So it appears that the production of this diphthong is variable.

NEAR
The speaker produces both the monophthong [ɪ] and the diphthong [ɪə] for NEAR.

SQUARE
The diphthong [ɛə] is used by the current speaker for SQUARE.

START
The speaker produces the low, front vowel [a] (with no apparent *r*-coloring) for START.

NORTH
For NORTH, the vowel [ɔ] is used by the current speaker, with *r*-coloring.

FORCE
For FORCE, the vowel [o] is used by the current speaker with no apparent *r*-coloring.

CURE
For CURE, the speaker produces [jo].

happY
The word happY ends in [i] for the current speaker. However, Turner observes "a shorter variety of the central vowel [ɨ]" occurring in the final open syllable of certain words in Gullah (1971: 125).

lettER

For the current speaker, the word lettER appears to end in the vowel [ɜ], with no *r*-coloring. Turner claims, however, that [ɜ] never occurs in his data. Instead, he observes two varieties of [ə] – "a short one with a tongue position somewhat higher than half-open" and "a fairly long one with a more retracted tongue position and approximately half-open but more advanced and higher than that required for [ʌ]" (1971: 126). According to Turner, the latter variety, [ɜ], occurs in final syllables, in words such as *daughter* and *Martha*. Turner's analysis is somewhat confusing here, however, since he claims that the longer variety [ɜ] is "used in the newer type of speech to replace [ʌ] by persons who try to distinguish stress" while the shorter variety [ɜ̆] "is always used in unstressed positions" (1971: 126). Presumably, the second syllable in words such as *Martha* and *daughter* is unstressed, but gets transcribed by Turner as [ɜ] rather than [ɜ̆] because of the word-final positioning of the vowel.

horsES

For the current speaker, the second vowel in horsES appears to be [ɪ].

commA

The second vowel in commA appears to be somewhat less open than that produced in *lettER* for the current speaker. It is, therefore, transcribed here as [ə]. See the discussion for lettER above, however, for Turner's observations regarding [ə] in Gullah.

In addition to the observations made above, one might note a few additional distinctive vowel patterns observed by Turner (1971: 124–125). Keep in mind, however, that these observations may not apply to all, or even any, current Gullah pronunciations, since several decades have passed since Turner conducted his fieldwork. According to Turner, the vowel [i] is found in words such as *hair*, *James*, *raisin* (first syllable), *give*, and *itch*. The vowel [ɪ] is found in *weave*, *deaf*, and *such*. The vowel [e] is found in words such as *air*, *clear*, and *egg*. The vowel [o] is reported for the word *oven* (first syllable) and [ʊ] for the words *coop*, *hoop*, and *room*. Turner also observes the vowel [ɛ] in words such as *make* and *shut*. Finally, there is a process of pre-stress syllable deletion that affects words such as *about*, which might be pronounced as *'bout*, and *away*, which might be pronounced as *'way* (see Klein and Harris 2000).

2.2. Consonants

A number of phonological processes affecting consonants may also be noted for Gullah.

Stops

In contrast to StAmE pronunciations, it has been observed that the voiceless stops [p], [t], and [k] in Gullah are generally unaspirated at the beginning of stressed syllables (Turner 1971, 2002; Mack 1984). According to Turner, these sounds are also occasionally produced as ejectives in this position. Turner notes that [p] is sometimes followed by slight aspiration "[b]efore long vowels in very emphatic speech" (1971: 127). He emphasizes, however, that variation among the aspirated, nonaspirated, and ejective variants of these three sounds is not phonemically distinctive in Gullah.

According to Turner (1971, 2002) the palatal stop [c] is used in Gullah where StAmE has [tʃ] in words such as *chew* and *March*. He notes that this stop is occasionally aspirated in emphatic speech. He also observes use of the palatal stop [ɟ] in words such as *Jack* and *pleasure*, where StAmE has [dʒ] and [ʒ], respectively. And he notes that [ɟ] is occasionally found where the sounds [z] or [ʃ] would be heard in StAmE.

Similar to speakers of many other varieties of English, Gullah speakers exhibit use of consonant cluster reduction, by which the word-final stop in a consonant cluster gets deleted. As an alternative strategy, consonant clusters are also occasionally separated by vowels in Gullah (Turner 1971: 130).

Finally, there are some additional alternations made by the current speaker for the stops [p] and [k] (see accompanying CD). In the reading list, the speaker pronounces the word *palm* as [sæm] and only after being questioned provides the alternative pronunciation of [pæm]. And in the reading passage, the speaker produces the word *cloak* variably as [klot] and [klok]. These pronunciations may represent some idiosyncratic tendencies on the part of this particular speaker or more productive processes in Gullah.

Nasals

Based on the narratives in the final chapter of Turner (1949), Klein and Harris (2000) discuss a process of nasal velarization in Gullah by which alveolar nasals [n] become velar [ŋ] following the diphthong [ʊ]. When this process occurs word-finally, as in *down* or *around*, Klein and Harris (2000: 4) call it assimilation "in the sense that the etymological alveolar nasal assimilates in velarity to the adjacent labio-velar off-glide of the diphthong". They observe, however, that a process of "dissimilatory blocking" of the velarization process takes place when another velar is found in the word. Thus, words such as *gown* or *ground* do not undergo the nasal velarization process. According to Klein and Harris, both processes are categorical in Turner's narrative data, although some variation is found elsewhere in Turner's text. Klein and Harris also note variable nasal velarization word-medially in words such as *pounding*. This process, however, appears to vary regionally. Klein and Harris give no indication of whether this process occurs in modern-day Gullah.

One other process involving nasals appears in the reading passage on the accompanying CD. Here one finds the absence of the nasal in the second syllable of the word *attempt*, which is pronounced [tɛp] by the current speaker. Again, given the limited data, it is not clear, at this stage, whether or not this represents a productive process in Gullah or something unique to the given speaker or given word.

Fricatives
Several processes have been noted with regard to fricatives in Gullah. According to Turner, the voiceless bilabial fricative [ɸ] is found in words such as *fall* and *staff*, where StAmE has [f]. And the voiced bilabial fricative appears in words such as *river*, *very*, *we*, and *while* where StAmE has either [v] or [w] (1971: 129; 2002: 241). Turner observes a process by which the alveolar fricative [s] is used instead of StAmE [ʃ] in words such as *shrimp* and *shrink* (1971: 129; 2002: 245–246). And he also observes word-initial intrusive [h] in words such as *umbrella*, *artichoke*, and *empty* (1971: 129).

Based on the current speaker's pronunciations, it appears that there is also a process by which word-initial [h] is deleted. Note in the reading list that the speaker pronounces *happy* as [api]. This speaker also variably pronounces *he* as [hi] and [i] in the reading passage. This latter pronunciation may be phonetically motivated (either by the same process affecting *happy* or by some more general fast-speech phenomenon) or morphologically motivated, given the fact that Gullah speakers often employ a gender-neutral pronoun [i] in place of *he*, *she*, or *it* (see, e.g., Nichols 1976).

Finally, it is observed by Turner that the interdental fricatives [ð] and [θ] are replaced by [d] and [t], respectively, in Gullah, in words such as *this*, *brother*, *month*, and *think* (1971: 128; 2002: 245). This process of fricative stopping is clearly still in effect in modern-day Gullah, as exhibited by the current speaker's pronunciations of words like *mouth*, *north*, *thought*, *the*, *than*, *then*, etc. For this speaker, however, an alternative substitution for [θ] appears to be the alveolar fricative [s]. This substitution is found in the speaker's pronunciations of the words *bath*, *cloth*, and, variably, *north*.

Approximants
With regard to approximants, it appears that the [j] sound was produced in words such as *duty* and *Tuesday* in Gullah at the time that Turner conducted his research, although Turner transcribes such words with the symbols [ɪu] (1971: 125). Thomas (this volume) reports that this pronunciation has been declin-

ing in the South since World War II, perhaps due in part to increased contact between Southerners and non-Southerners. It is possible, therefore, that this change has also affected Gullah pronunciations.

According to Turner, [l] is generally clear before vowels and consonants, as well as word-finally in Gullah. He also reports that [l] is used either instead of or interchangeably with [r] in words such as *Brewer, proud, fritter, Mary, bureau,* and *war*, especially in intervocalic positions. And he reports occasional use of [n] instead of [l] on Edisto Island, in words such as *lull* (1971: 126–129).

According to Turner, [r] never occurs finally or before consonants in his data, only before vowels. While modern-day Gullah appears to show some [r]-fullness, there is clearly still a preference for post-vocalic [r]-lessness in contemporary varieties. The speaker recorded for this project, in fact, provides numerous examples of [r]-lessness in words like *near, square, start, north, letter*, etc.

2.3.   Intonation

While not much has been done on intonation patterns in Gullah, some observations have been made. Turner (2002) offers several observations, many of which have been explored more recently in Bryan (2001). According to Turner, declarative sentences in Gullah often end in either a high, mid, or rising tone, as opposed to the falling tone typically found in StAmE varieties (2002: 249–250). According to Bryan, all three patterns appear to persist in modern-day Gullah. However, she observes that the rising tone pattern "seems to be the least affected by language contact" (2001: 3). Turner also observes many alternating tones throughout the course of a statement. For example, he notes use of level tones—mid, high, or low, use of low and mid or low and high tones, use of tones that fall from high to mid, and use of tones that rise from low or mid to high or from low to mid (2002: 250–252). Similarly Bryan observes that Gullah has many phrases that alternate high and low tones throughout the statement. She says this is particularly true of imperatives and pleas of desperation (2001: 4).

Finally, Turner observes that Gullah speakers tend to use a level tone "at the end of a question, whether or not *yes* or *no* is required for an answer" (2002: 253). This pattern, of course, contrasts with that found in StAmE, where a rising tone is used for *yes/no* questions and a falling tone is used otherwise. Bryan finds that, among the intonational patterns observed by Turner, this particular pattern has undergone the most change. She observes,

Younger speakers of Gullah (roughly from age 2–50) seem to almost always use a rising intonation for *yes/no* questions. When older Gullah speakers use the level tone for interrogatives, they sometimes preface the question with *yes* or *no*. For example, an elder would ask ... 'Yes, are you going to the farm tomorrow?' (2001: 5–6).

Bryan hypothesizes that this type of construction, by which *yes* or *no* prefaces the interrogative, was introduced by speakers who did not assimilate to the StAmE pattern, in order to clarify the intended *yes/no* interpretation (2001: 6).

3.   Conclusion

To the extent that the Gullah sound system has changed over the years, one factor that is likely to have contributed to these changes is the growth of the tourism industry. Following the end of the plantation era, the distinctiveness of Gullah was preserved for many years by the isolation of the Sea Islands. However, since the early 1900s, the building of bridges and subsequent growth of the tourism industry has resulted in a significant increase in mobility to and from the islands. In addition, negative stereotypes and misconceptions about the variety have discouraged some locals from speaking the variety in public for fear that they will be ridiculed by outsiders.

   Some believe that such factors have contributed to the merging of Gullah with mainland dialects. And many fear that this merging will eventually result in Gullah becoming extinct. However, Gullah still serves an important function among its speakers as a marker of culture, history, and identity. And even younger speakers, who are encouraged to speak dialects other than Gullah, seem to maintain some level of fluency in Gullah for purposes of in-group communication. This function alone may be enough to preserve the dialect for many years to come.

Speaker information (for lexical set and reading passage):
Name: Dorothy B.
Age: 60s (?)
Community: Mount Pleasant, South Carolina
National Ancestry: American
Year Interviewed: 2003

Gullah lexical set

KIT	ị	GOOSE	u
DRESS	ε̣	PRICE	ɐɪ
TRAP	æ̣	CHOICE	ɔɪ
LOT	ɑ	MOUTH	ɔʊ
STRUT	ʌ	NEAR	ɪ ~ ɪə
FOOT	ʊ	SQUARE	εə
BATH	æ̣	START	a
CLOTH	o	NORTH	ɔ˞
NURSE	ɑ	FORCE	o
FLEECE	i	CURE	jo
FACE	e	HAPPY	i
PALM	æ̣	LETTER	ɜ
THOUGHT	ɔ	HORSES	ɪ
GOAT	o	COMMA	ə
GOAL	o ~ oε		

Gullah reading passage

THE NORTH WIND AND THE SUN WERE DISPUTING
də nɔət wṇ an də sʌn wəɪ dɪspjurɪŋ

WHICH WAS THE STRONGER, WHEN A TRAVELER CAME
wịtʃ wʌz də stɪɔŋɡɜ wε̣n ə tɪævələ˞ kem
ALONG WRAPPED IN A WARM CLOAK. THEY AGREED
əlɔŋ ɪæpt ɪn ə wɔm klot de əgɪid
THAT THE ONE WHO FIRST SUCCEEDED IN MAKING THE
dæt də wʌn hu fɜs səksirəd ɪn mẹkiŋ də

TRAVELER TAKE HIS CLOAK OFF SHOULD BE
tɪævələ˞ tẹk ɪz klok ɔf ʃud bi

CONSIDERED STRONGER THAN THE OTHER. THEN THE
kənsɪɾə˞d stɪɔŋɡɜ dan də ʌðə dε̣n də

NORTH WIND BLEW AS HARD AS HE COULD, BUT THE
nɔət wn̩ blu az hæd æz hi kʊd bət də

MORE HE BLEW THE MORE CLOSELY DID THE
mo i blu də moə klosli dɪd də

TRAVELER FOLD HIS CLOAK AROUND HIM; AND AT
tɹævəlɜ foldɪd hɪz klok əɹon hɪm æn æt

LAST THE NORTH WIND GAVE UP THE ATTEMPT. THEN
læs də nɔət wn̩ gev ʌp də tɛp dɛn

THE SUN SHINED OUT WARMLY, AND IMMEDIATELY
də sʌn ʃɐɪn ɔʊt wɔmli an miɾiɪtli

THE TRAVELER TOOK OFF HIS CLOAK. AND SO THE
də tɹævələ tʊk ɔf hʌz klok an so də

NORTH WIND WAS OBLIGED TO CONFESS THAT THE
nɔət wn̩ (wʌz) (ə)blɐɪdʒ tu kənfɛs ðat ðə

SUN WAS THE STRONGER OF THE TWO.
sʌn wʌz də stɹɔŋgɜ əv ðə tu

* I would like to acknowledge Dorothy Brown and Margaret Bryant for their assistance in collecting the audio samples for this project, Eric Holt and Cherlon Ussery for their assistance with the transcriptions, and Michael Montgomery for his assistance in locating relevant written sources. I accept full responsibility for any errors.

Exercises and study questions

1. In the reading passage on the accompanying CD, the speaker pronounces *attempt* as [tɛp], *immediately* as [miɾiətli] and *obliged* as [blӓɪdʒ]. What phonological process is represented by all three words?

2. Also in the reading passage, the speaker variably pronounces *wind* as [wn̩], *and* as [ann] and *around* as [əɹon]. What phonological process is represented by these three words?

3. As noted in the text, the speaker on the audio sample variably substitutes [t] for [θ] in words such as *mouth*, *north*, and *thought*, [s] for [θ] in words such

as *bath*, *cloth*, and *north*, and [d] for [ð] in words such as *the, than, then*. Describe the substitution process in terms of voicing.

4. According to Turner, [r] never occurred word-finally or before consonants in his Gullah data, which was collected in the early 1900s. In the reading passage on the accompanying CD, the following words are candidates for [r]-lessness: *north, were, stronger, traveller, warm, first, considered, other, hard, more,* and *warmly*. What percentage of post-vocalic [r]-lessness is found in this modern-day sample? (Note: Some words occur more than once in the reading passage. Be sure to count all instances of each word).

5. To the extent that the modern-day sample exhibits more post-vocalic [r] than that observed by Turner (see exercise 4), what social factors might be responsible for this phenomenon?

Selected references

Please consult the General references for titles mentioned in the text but not included in the references below. For a full bibliography see the accompanying CD-ROM.

Bryan, Kisha C.
    2001   An intonational analysis of the Gullah dialect. Unpublished manuscript.
Cassidy, Frederick
    1980   The place of Gullah. *American Speech* 55: 3–16.
Creel, Margaret M.
    1988   *A Peculiar People: Slave Religion and Community-Culture Among the Gullahs*. New York: New York University Press.
Hair, Paul E. H.
    1965   Sierra Leone items in the Gullah dialect of American English. *Sierra Leone Language Review* 4: 79–84.
Hancock, Ian
    1980   Gullah and Barbadian: Origins and relationships. *American Speech* 55: 17–35.
Johnson, Guy
    1930   *Folk Culture on St. Helena Island, South Carolina*. Chapel Hill: University of North Carolina Press.
Klein, Thomas B. and Meta Y. Harris
    2000   Sound structure in Gullah: Evidence from the narratives in Turner's *Africanisms*. Unpublished manuscript.
Mack, Linda
    1984   A comparative analysis of linguistic stress patterns in Gullah (Sea Island Creole) and English speakers. M.A. thesis, University of Florida.

Mufwene, Salikoko
    1993   Gullah's development: Myths and sociohistorical facts. Revised version of a paper presented at the *Language in Society II Conference*. Auburn University. April, 1993.

Nichols, Patricia
    1976   Linguistic change in Gullah: Sex, age, and mobility. Ph.D. dissertation, Stanford University.

Niles, Norma
    1980   Provincial English dialects and Barbadian English. Ph.D. dissertation, University of Michigan.

Stewart, William
    1968   Continuity and change in American Negro dialects. *The Florida FL Reporter* 6, 1: 3–4, 14–16, 18.

Turner, Lorenzo D.
    1949   *Africanisms in the Gullah Dialect*. Chicago: University of Chicago Press. Republished in 2002 by University of South Carolina Press.
    1971   Notes on the sounds and vocabulary of Gullah. In: Williamson and Burke (eds.), 121–135.

Van Sertima, Ivan
    1976   My Gullah brother and I: Exploration into a community's language and myth through its oral tradition. In: Deborah S. Harrison and Tom Trabasso (eds.), *Black English: A Seminar*, 123–146. Hillsdale, NJ: Erlbaum.

Cajun Vernacular English: phonology[*]

Sylvie Dubois and Barbara M. Horvath

1. The Cajun speech community: an overview

Cajuns live all along the Gulf Coast from Texas to Mississippi but are primarily concentrated in the small rural towns of southern Louisiana. Lafayette is the metropolitan center of Cajun country. Cajuns are the descendants of Acadians from Nova Scotia, Canada, who fled to French Louisiana around 1765 when the British took control of their lands. In Louisiana they joined many other French dialect-speaking populations as well as other people who had a language other than French as their first language (Dubois 2003). Even after the Louisiana Purchase, when English became the *de facto* official language, the Cajuns living in rural communities continued to speak only French. The majority of the Cajuns were poor and had little education. They lived – as many continue to live today – in small towns in close-knit extended families. Whereas some of the people of French ancestry were held in high esteem in Louisiana, the same cannot be said for the Cajuns. They were often ridiculed and made the butt of jokes.

Although the state government mandated English as the sole language of education in 1929, English was not extensively used within the Cajun communities and in the family setting. Moreover, English was not well learned because many attended school irregularly or left school early. For quite a while English may have been the language of the classroom, but Cajun French was the language of the playground. It is this generation, people who are 60 years or older today, who are the original speakers of the dialect we have labelled Cajun Vernacular English (CajVE). Although language contact and language interference are clearly implicated in the origins of CajVE, we want to argue against the idea that CajVE is a variant of migrant English or foreigner English. We believe that the variable structure of CajVE is not Southern English and that these CajVE features are part of the vernacular of Cajuns. As Rubretch (1971) has mentioned for the nasalization process in CajVE, the phonological principles as well as the set of linguistic features we describe in CajVE represent a native development of English speech rather than a borrowing. CajVE is spoken fluently by Cajuns in their everyday lives within the community and often as the primary intergenerational language (Dubois and Horvath 2001).

World War II marks an important juncture for Cajuns; the military service introduced many of the men to American ways, particularly to American ways of speaking. Some of the men who were old enough to join the army were already bilingual or semi-bilingual because of a concerted effort on the part of the Louisiana state government to enforce the speaking of English. After WWII, the social changes that swept across the landscape came to have a profound effect on the Cajun way of life. The children of the original CajVE speakers, who had grown up speaking French within their families, began to learn English better than their parents, attended school more regularly and for longer, and became financially more secure because of the discovery of oil in the region and the introduction of large-scale agriculture, which brought economic opportunities not previously available. Many of this generation of speakers stopped using French with their own children, hoping to avoid the negative stereotypes associated with being Cajun in Louisiana. Cajuns increasingly adopted American cultural ways; even Cajun music, an important part of Cajun life, was rejected in favor of country and western music.

What stopped this cultural change from completely taking over is popularly called the Cajun Renaissance. Like many other ethnic groups, it is often the third generation in the language change/replacement process who feels the loss of culture the most. The old have not lost it, the middle-aged have consciously rejected it, and it is the young who suffer a sense of loss. Today, things Cajun have risen to an unprecedented status among Cajuns as well as outsiders. Cajun music, Cajun food, children's books about Cajun life, serious Cajun literature – all backed up by state government support for its formerly French-speaking citizens - are to be found everywhere. Tourists come from near and far to participate in Cajun festivities. Bilingualism, however, has suffered such a loss that it is only the ideologues who would suggest the possible survival of French as the primary language of everyday communication by Cajuns. The dilemma for Cajuns is that they no longer have the linguistic distinctiveness they once had; those who want to mark their Cajun identity linguistically have only English as a vehicle. The young, especially young men, have begun to use some aspects of the CajVE of their grandfathers, the variety of English that had been widely rejected by the middle-aged at the same time that they were rejecting French.

Not all people who identify as Cajuns speak CajVE and using the term "Cajun English" risks that interpretation. The term "ethnolect" is useful to identify a subtype of a vernacular such as CajVE, particularly because that term seems to describe a large number of locally based community dialects of English, widespread in the United States and elsewhere, which develop when a speech community collectively changes its language of everyday communication from French, Spanish, a Native American language, etc. to the politically dominant language, English in the case of the United States. Perhaps the key characteristic of an ethnolect is that "ethnicity" and the ethnic language are not given up concurrently so if ethnicity is to be marked linguistically, it can only be marked in the dominant language; this marking of ethnicity can become a source of language change in that language.

2.   Linguistic description of Cajun Vernacular English

CajVE has changed dramatically over three generations against a complex and changing social and linguistic background. Although some of the sociolinguistic variables that are characteristic of CajVE are also well-known variables in Southern American English (Rubrecht 1971; Scott 1992; Cox 1992; Eble 1993; Walton 1994; Cheramie 1999), we have argued that the origins of these sociolinguistic variables lie within the Cajun community and cannot be attributed solely to interference from French or to the spread of these features from the surrounding English dialects. CajVE represents an innovation from within the Cajun community so that some of the Cajun variants which began in the accented speech of the oldest of the speakers in our sample have either been passed on to the next generation of speakers or have been recycled as markers of social identity by the youngest speakers.

Further background information on the Cajun community is available in Dubois (1997b) and Dubois and Melancon (1997). Sociolinguistic descriptions of a number of phonological and morphological variables can be found in Dubois and Horvath (1998a, 1998b, 1999, 2001, 2002 and 2003). A description of the entire sample and data collection procedures are given in Dubois, Gautreaux, Melançon and Veler (1995) and Dubois (1997a).

2.1.   Core features of CajVE pronunciation

Two fundamental phonological principles are at the heart of CajVE. The first one is the deletion of final consonants. CajVE speakers do not pronounce final consonants and they also drop final consonant clusters [nd, st, lm]. Not only does this occur in bimorphemic words but there appears to be a very high rate of deletion in monomorphemes, in VC contexts as well as CC contexts. We have noted the deletion of final [t] *late, rent,* [d] *hand, food, wide,* [θ] *both,* [r] *together,* [l] *school,* and both final [r] and [k] in *New York* (the absence of the whole cluster). We also notice the variable absence of the final consonant [z] in *Larose* (town), final [ʋ] *twelve,* [s] *house, fence,* [n] *nine,* [m] *mom,* [f] *life* and even the absence of [ʃ] in *fish*. This phonological rule has an important morphosyntactical consequence: final consonants which happen to be morphological markers, e.g., final consonants representing *-ed* or *-s* (as reduced copula, possessive, plural or third sing person), will be deleted at the ends of words.

The second phonological principle is the reduction or absence of glides in the four long stressed vowels [i], [e], [o] and [u] in CajVE. The high front vowel [i] in such words as *me*, *street*, and *read*, the mid front vowel [e], as in *way*, *make* and *take*, the mid back vowel [o], in words such as *know*, *both*, and *over*, and the high back vowel [u], as in *food*, *school*, and *two*, are realized as monophthongs [iː, eː, oː, uː] respectively. Mid vowels [o, e] are monophthongized more frequently than high vowels [i, u]. The diphthongs [ai], [aʊ] and [ɔi] in words such as *fire*, *now*, and *oil* also loose their glide and become monophthongs [aː], [ɑː] and [ɔː]. This vocalic feature is very striking because Southerners produce considerable lengthening and gliding.

2.2.   CajVE vowels

Table 1 below summarizes the CajVE vocalic system. The phonetic inventory of CajVE is similar to Southern English (see Thomas, this volume). However, CajVE speakers do not prolong stressed vowels and diphthongs.

Table 1.   Representative vocalic forms of CajVE

KIT	ɪ, i	CURE	ʊə, uə
DRESS	ɛ, æ	FIRE	ai, ɑː
TRAP	æ	POWER	au, ɑː
LOT	ɑ, a	*happ*Y	ɪ, i
STRUT	ʌ	*lett*ER	ɚ, ə
FOOT	ʊ	*hors*ES	ɪ, ĩ
BATH	æ	*comm*A	ə
DANCE	æ, æ̃	HAND	æ, æ̃
CLOTH	a	PIN/PEN	ɪ, ĩ
NURSE	ʌɪ, ʌə	THINK, LENGTH	i, ĩ
FLEECE	iː	GOING	ɔi, ɔ
FACE	eː	GOAL	oː
PALM	ɑ	POOL	uː
THOUGHT	a	PULL	ʊ
GOAT	oː	FEEL	iː

Table 1. (continued)   Representative vocalic forms of CajVE

GOOSE	uː	FILL	ɪ
PRICE	ai, ɑː	FAIL	ei, eː
PRIZE	ai, ɑː	FELL	ɛ
CHOICE	ɔi, ɔː	MARRY	ɛ, æ
MOUTH, LOUD	au, aː	MERRY	ɛ
NEAR	iː	MARY	ɛ
SQUARE	ɛ, æ	MIRROR/NEARER	iː, ɪ
START	ɑ, a	TOMORROW	a, ɑ
NORTH	ɔɹ, ɔə	ORANGE	ɔɹ, ɑ
FORCE	ɔɹ, ɔə		

Glide absence in FLEECE, FACE, GOAT, GOOSE is typical of CajVE. Their nuclei do not fall or become fronted as in Southern English. The nuclei of KIT may rise but CajVE speakers lower the DRESS vowel in words such as *Texas*, *bed*, *red*, *better*, *well* and *egg* to [æ]. Consequently the words *bed* and *bad* sound the same, although the word *bed*, pronounced [bæ] has a shorter length than the word *bad* pronounced [bæː]. Although CajVE shows the PIN/PEN and THOUGHT/ LOT mergers, upgliding forms of THOUGHT, BATH and DANCE occur irregularly. By contrast, monophthongization of PRICE, PRIZE, CHOICE, FIRE, MOUTH, and POWER is prevalent. The non-rhotic aspect of CajVE can also be observed in NURSE, SQUARE, NORTH, FORCE (the last two are merged), CURE, and *lettER*. Like Southern English, the *happY* and *horsES* vowels are pronounced [ɪ], and *com- mA* as [ə]. Like the old white Southerners, CajVE speakers do not merge POOL/ PULL, FEEL/FILL, FAIL/FELL. However, the vowels in MARRY/MERRY/MARY are usually identical, but those in TOMORROW/ORANGE may be distinct.

CajVE provides an interesting case of shared phonetics with the dialects in its geographical region while maintaining a distinctive coherence as a separate dialect. The distinctiveness of CajVE is initially revealed quantitatively. Where comparisons can be made, the patterns of variability are not the same in terms of linguistic conditioning in each generation of speakers. Moreover, the actual rate of use of the features often far exceeds the results reported for Southern English varieties. When the scope of the variability is widened to include more data, i.e., the widespread deletion of all final consonants and the glide absence, it becomes clear that CajVE is qualitatively distinctive as well from Southern English, and especially American English.

2.3. The non-aspiration of [p', t', k] and [h'] dropping

CajVE speakers do not aspirate [p, t, k] in word-initial position preceding a stressed vowel or [r, l, w, j] (*plant, table,* and car). By not aspirating [p] in the word *pat,* it has the effect of sounding *bat* for American English speakers. The word *hair* pronounced without [h] is mistaken for *air.*

2.4. The replacement of interdental fricatives [θ, ð] by stops [t, d]

Interdental fricatives are highly marked sounds: they are rare in the languages of the world and learned late by children. The substitutions for interdental fricatives most frequently reported in the literature are the dental stops [t, d]. They are well known as variables throughout most of the United States, and maybe wherever English is spoken. As Rubrecht (1971:152) mentions, the paradigm "dis, dat, dese, dose" is well-known in Louisiana to describe how Cajuns talk. There is no lack of speculation about the sources of the substitutions but one fact is fairly clear, all of them are stigmatized.

2.5. Heavy nasalization

Despite its variable occurrence in English in general, vowel nasalization is also strongly associated with the Southern American English dialect. What seems to elicit negative comment from speakers of Southern English about CajVE is not so much the nasalization of the vowel but when the nasalization process spreads to adjacent sounds. "Heavy nasalization" in CajVE is likely to appear in monosyllabic words and can be characterized by a heavier than normal degree of nasalization, that is the nasalization spreads to the consonant before the vowel (e.g. where the [b] in a word like *Alabama* is nasalized). More front closed vowels are nasalized than back vowels.

2.6. The trilled -r and deletion of -l

CajVE is a non-rhotic variety. The sound /r/ is absent in stressed syllables (*letter*) and in syllable coda in word-final (*four*) and pre-consonantal (*hard*) positions. CajVE speakers use flap [ɹ] in word-initial consonant clusters [tr, dr, fr], as in *three* and *tree.* They also delete [l] in intervocalic and preconsonantal positions in words such as *celery, jewelry* and *help.*

3.   What is the social meaning of sounding Cajun?

The view from inside the Cajun community changes from one generation to the next. In order to explain why Cajun men and women have changed their ways of speaking over the three generations, we have to understand what kind of speech community we are dealing with: it is a subordinated cultural enclave which for several generations has been forced to change in the direction of the dominant culture. Massive language changes have taken place alongside massive social changes and the language change is an almost direct reflection of the sociohistory of this community. Language has played a central role in the relations between the Cajun enclave and the numerically and politically dominant English-speaking population in southwest Louisiana.

3.1.   The older generation

For hundreds of years, Cajuns were monolingual French speakers who lived in rural settlements where they were either the dominant group or the only group. It was some of our oldest speakers (the majority born before 1930) who first experienced the pressure to change their language at least to the extent of learning English. These first users of English were judged most harshly on their French and their English abilities. Men and women alike learned English as a second language but most would have had little use for it. All of them use a high rate of all of the CajVE features and there is no gender differentiation. The way they spoke English was unremarkable until the outside world began to impinge on the consciousness of the close-knit communities of southern Louisiana. Their variety of CajVE has little directly to do with the usual understanding of language change in progress except for two crucial facts: they, along with the generation earlier than theirs, begin the process of the creation of CajVE, and their ways of speaking provide the source for future change. The actual linguistic forms they use are relevant to what happens in the succeeding generations.

3.2.   The middle-aged generation

The industrialization process and the consequent process of language shift was in full swing with the middle-aged speakers in our sample (aged 40-59, the majority were born just before or during WWII). They were educated in English and reacted most vigorously to the denigration of both Cajun French and the Cajun way of speaking English. It is this generation that begins to use English extensively in the home in raising their children. When they were young, even the speakers who were raised bilingually started to speak English at home with their siblings. They were aware quite early of the stigma attached to both French and CajVE. Not only did they begin to sound like any other English speaker from south Louisiana, they also abandoned French. The dropping of many of the CajVE features is the attempt to attenuate the stigma of being Cajun for themselves and especially for their children. There are many pressures on this group of men and women to change in the direction of the dominant group. We find no gender distinction between middle-aged men and women but a rather uniform pattern of the adoption of an external norm for speaking English.

3.3. The younger generation

The late 1960s mark the beginning of the so-called Cajun Renaissance; in 1968 a series of laws were passed which were meant to encourage the use of French. The state was declared officially bilingual, French instruction in high schools was mandatory, there was to be television in French, and the state was to foster international relations with other francophone nations. By the 1990s Cajun culture had acquired a definite cachet. However, French was no longer considered necessary either for economic reasons or for symbolizing Cajunness (Dubois and Melançon 1997: 86).

Our youngest generation (born at the beginning of the 1970s) are most influenced by the Cajun Renaissance, are proud to be Cajuns and are able to profit most from the increasing status accorded to Cajun ancestry as well as the important economic benefits from the rapidly expanding tourist industry. However, if identity is to be signaled by language, then it is left to English to accomplish that because the majority of the young generation interact most of the time with outsiders as well as with their friends and immediate family members only in English. They use French only with some of their older extended family members. The public display of Cajun culture to outsiders – part of the tourist industry - reinforces the use of English as a carrier of Cajun identity. The Cajun Renaissance changed the meaning of sounding Cajun. In a rather sharp turnaround, things Cajun became interesting to insiders and outsiders alike, especially the food and music, and tourists wanted to visit, participate in Cajun life, and bring home souvenirs. Now it is good to sound Cajun.

There is an important gender differentiation in the usage of several CajVE features in the younger generation. Young men return to the CajVE forms used by their grandparents' generation, while young women generally use the standard variants introduced by the middle-aged speakers. We have called this change led by young men in the direction of the former stigmatized and stereo-typed CajVE variants "recycling".

The gendered pattern can be attributed to the fact that the Cajun Renaissance largely affects the sphere of traditional male activities such as boating, fishing and hunting, and the display of Cajun culture associated with tourism (e.g. few women participate in the traditional "courir du Mardi Gras" or take tourists on trips up the bayou). Music is traditionally an essential part of the Cajun male culture, although it is now in the hands of only the young men. Traditional Ca-jun music is coming back in favor, replacing the country-western style that the middle-aged generation preferred. Even Cajun cuisine is publicly displayed as part of the male domain. A higher percentage of Cajun men than women are involved in Cajun advocacy organizations or report listening to Cajun radio programs.

The symbols of traditional Cajun identity that are left to women are those associated with the family domain, including the raising of children and the pursuit of homecrafts. The shift from French to English which largely took place within the middle-aged generation means that young women no longer have any responsibility for passing on French to the children; their roles as Cajun torchbearers have been taken over by young men. Young women have not moved to recycle the CajVE features because they have fewer reasons than young men to associate themselves linguistically to the current understanding of a Cajun identity which is largely masculine.

4.   Conclusion

The birth of CajVE occurred less than a hundred years ago; in that time it de-veloped into a quite distinctive vernacular, came very close to dying and was reborn. In fact, without its rebirth in recent times, we may well have failed to notice the birth at all. We would have said it was just the way people who learn English as a second language speak. Like so many varieties of accented Eng-lish, it is not expected to be passed on to subsequent generations. The story of the fate of the languages of the Cajun people mirrors their history and the com-ings and goings of both Cajun French and Cajun English are intimately con-nected to the social and economic buffeting of the Cajun community since the 1920s. Capturing CajVE in speech and writing is part of the rebirth process.

*   This research project is supported by NSF (BCS-0091823).

Exercises and study questions

1. Describe the pattern of glide absence of FLEECE, FACE, GOAL and POOL on the audio sample with regard to the following phonetic contexts? Why is glide absence more frequent in FACE/GOAL than FLEECE/POOL?

2. In which words does the CajVE speaker lower the DRESS vowel? Does he raise it?

3. Dental stops substitutions for interdental fricatives in CajVE appear in different grammatical contexts. Which one seems to be the most favorable on the audio sample?

4. Explain the gender pattern for each generation of CajVE speakers.

5. What other minority groups in North American speak what is described as an ethnolect? Do African-Americans speak an ethnolect?

6. Why is it fashionable to sound Cajun now?

Selected references

Please consult the General references for titles mentioned in the text but not included in the references below. For a full bibliography see the accompanying CD-ROM.

Cheramie, Deany
    1999   Cajun Vernacular English and the influence of vernacular on student writing in South Louisiana. Ph.D. dissertation, University of Southwestern Louisiana.
Cox, Juanita
    1992   *A Study of the Linguistic Features of Cajun English*. ED 352 840, ERIC (Educational Resources Information Center. Microfiche collection. Clement C. Maxwell Library, Bridgewater State College, Bridgewater, Massachusetts.
Dubois, Sylvie
    1997a   Field method in Cajun communities in Louisiana. In: Albert Valdman (ed.), *French et Creole in Louisiana*, 47-70. New York/London: Plenum.
    1997b   Attitudes envers l'enseignement et l'apprentissage du français cadien en Louisiane. *Revue des sciences de l'éducation* 23, 3: 699–715.
    2003   Letter-writing in French Louisiana: Interpreting variable spelling conventions, 1685-1840. *Journal of Written Language and Literacy* 6, 1: 31–70.
Dubois, Sylvie, William Gautreaux, Megan Melançon and Tracy Veler
    1995   The quality of French spoken in Louisiana. *SECOL Review* 19: 16–39.

Dubois, Sylvie and Barbara Horvath
    1998a   From accent to marker in Cajun English: A study of dialect formation in progress. *English World-Wide* 19: 161-188.
    1998b   Let's tink about dat: Interdental fricatives in Cajun English. *Language Variation and Change* 10: 245–261.
    1999   When the music changes, you change too: Gender and language change in Cajun English. *Language Variation and Change* 11: 287–313.
    2001   Do Cajuns speak Southern English? Morphosyntactic evidence. *Working Papers in Linguistics* (Dept. of Linguistics, University of Pennsylvania) 7: 27–41.
    2002   Sounding Cajun: The rhetorical use of dialect in speech and in writing. *American Speech* 77: 264–287.
    2003   Verbal morphology in Cajun Vernacular English: A comparison with other varieties of Southern English. *Journal of English Linguistics* 31: 1–26.
Dubois, Sylvie and Megan Melancon
    1997   Cajun is dead—long live Cajun: Shifting from a linguistic to a cultural community. *Journal of Sociolinguistics* 1: 63–93.
Eble, Connie
    1993   Prolegomenon to the study of Cajun English. *SECOL Review* 17: 165–77.
Rubrecht, August
    1971   Regional phonological variants in Louisiana speech. Ph.D. dissertation, University of Florida.
Scott, Ann Marie (ed)
    1992   *Cajun Vernacular English: Informal English in French Louisiana.* Lafayette: University of Southwestern Louisiana Press.
Walton, Shana
    1994   Flat Speech and Cajun ethnic identity in Terrebonne Parish, Louisiana. Ph.D. Dissertation, Tulane University.

Chicano English: phonology

Otto Santa Ana and Robert Bayley

1.   Introduction

Chicano English displays a remarkable range of language contact phenomena. Speakers of this ethnic dialect enact their social practices with Chicano English, in conjunction with Chicano Spanish and in some cases other varieties of Spanish and English as well. In dynamic urban multicultural and binational settings, these social practices include surprisingly complex identities and roles (Mendoza-Denton 1997; Fought 2003). Sadly, the general public's awareness of Chicano English (ChcE) commonly involves stigma, a situation that has not changed in the last forty years. Many U.S. public school educators, in particular, falsely attribute to ChcE a general inadequacy for educational and wider social purposes (Valdés 1998; Valencia 2002). The hostility that ChcE arouses is consistent with the general public's disapproval of other U.S. ethnic dialects, such as African American Vernacular English (AAVE), whose communities seem to resist the national hegemony of English monolingualism and Standard English.

A commonplace often bandied about is that ChcE is merely "Spanish-accented English". Both lay people and linguists have this reaction, and the statement expresses some truth, as we will illustrate. However, in the context of some institutional settings, an insidious misunderstanding follows. The misconception is that ChcE is not a dialect, but simply the mispronounced English of Spanish speakers who are learning English as a second language. From this mistaken point of view it follows that if adults speak so-called Spanish-accented English, they are fossilized second language learners, while children demonstrate incomplete learning of English. This misconception has serious social consequences in U.S. schools, where an inordinate number of Chicano students do not advance scholastically. Since these schools are charged with teaching children standard English, educators often falsely conclude that Chicano student failure is a result of their inability to master the standard language.

Many teachers witness evidence each day in the classroom that sustains this falsehood. English-monolingual public school teachers come into contact with Mexican immigrant students, including new immigrant students who are learning English. Several articulatory mismatches strike native English-speaking teachers as discordant. But these classrooms are not linguistically homogeneous. At least three dimensions mark this diversity. Newly arrived immigrants and those who have been in public schools for several years mingle with U.S.-born Chicano students. Second, some of the U.S.-born students are monolingual while others are bilingual. Third, some Chicano students speak the English dialects of their Euro-American teachers, while others speak a native English dialect that both Chicano and Spanish-speaking immigrant children acquire in their home communities. This final variety is ChcE, which appears to maintain certain phonological features that are characteristic of Spanish native-speaker, English-as-a-second-language learner interlanguage, or in the current terminology of U.S. public schools, English language learner (ELL) speech. Speakers of ChcE express social solidarity in their native community dialect by way of these features.

Teachers and other observers, however, tend to conflate the heterogeneity. Upon hearing ChcE, some teachers presume it is learner speech. Accordingly, they are likely to believe that U.S.-born Chicanos also speak an incompletely-native, Spanish-accented English. These children's educational plight, they believe, can only be alleviated when they stop speaking Spanish, which is thought to interfere with their English, and learn English "well". This notion expands to the absurd to include children who speak no Spanish. How a language that children cannot speak can interfere with a language that they do speak is left unexplained. In this chapter, we attempt to dispel some of the common misconceptions surrounding ChcE by providing a description of ChcE phonology and its relationship to Spanish on the one hand and Euro-American varieties on the other.

2.   Vowels

When compared to English phonology, the Spanish vowel system does not distinguish between tense and lax peripheral vowels, nor does it employ distinctive sets of so-called long and short vowels, or a set of r-colored allophones of the long vowels. Finally, it does not have a set of diphthongs, in addition to a set of off-gliding vowels. Consequently, when an ELL initially reworks the five-monophthong Spanish vowel system, certain phonemic approximations and mergers tend to occur. For example, Santa Ana (1991: 154–160) spectrographically measured the naturally occurring speech of a seventeen-year old ELL male. His still developing English (his preferred language) was impressionistically marked with phonemic mergers, and the absence of off-glides, particularly in the high vowels, /i/ and /u/. The instrumental study provided evidence of two mergers, /i/ ~ /ɪ/ and /ɛ/ ~ /æ/.

The spectrographic analysis further indicated that he did not employ the English stressed vowel reduction system.

In striking contrast to this ELL, native speakers of ChcE share the catalog of vowel phonemes, as well as most of the associated surface phonological features, of their local U.S. English dialect (García 1984; Penfield and Ornstein-Galicia 1985; Galindo 1987; Santa Ana 1991; Veatch 1991; Mendoza-Denton 1997; Fought 1997, 2003; Thomas 2001). For example, Los Angeles ChcE shares with most other Euro-American dialects four historical or on-going vowel mergers, including the so-called 'short o' merger, which may be stated in terms of J.C. Wells (1982) lexeme sets (Veatch 1991: 184). In other AmE dialects, as in ChcE, the LOT class of lexemes merges with the THOUGHT, CLOTH and PALM lexeme sets. While the PALM or 'broad a' merged some time ago, Labov (1991) and others see the LOT or 'short o' and THOUGHT or 'long open o' to be a merger that is currently advancing. Second, ChcE also does not distinguish the BATH and TRAP lexeme sets. Third, Chicanos pronounce the familiar *merry*, *Mary*, and *marry* identically, that is, they share the merger of intervocalic non-high front vowels. Lastly, unlike some Southern U.S. English dialects, ChcE seems to have merged the NORTH and FORCE lexeme sets. The similarity of the ChcE inventory of vowel phonemes led Veatch to suggest that the ChcE system of stressed vowels may be the local Euro-American English system (1991: 188).

Nevertheless, ChcE elicits a quick and often negative judgment from local matrix dialect speakers. So the question remains what linguistic norms are flouted when Chicanos speak their home dialects. In an attempt to synthesize the work of our (above mentioned) colleagues, we suggest four characteristic differences:

I.   ChcE is more monophthongal, especially in monosyllabic words, than other AmE dialects.
II. ChcE is articulated with greater vowel space overlap of front vowels than other AmE dialects.
III. ChcE may have a different system of vowel reduction than other AmE dialects.
IV. ChcE has several linguistic variables (that is to say, variably-occurring ethnic dialect features, discourse markers and prosody contours) that signal Chicano community identities.

ChcE speakers use (IV), the ChcE-specific linguistic variables, in conjunction with other more widely-shared variables, such as (u-fronting) and negative concord, in complex ways to express their multifaceted identities, as shown by Fought (2003, chapters 5 and 6), who begins to tease out the simultaneous use of numbers of variables to express complex identities.

The ChcE-specific variables are local community variables, including Greater Los Angeles (ɛ), (ʃ/tʃ merger), and Texas (-ing), California (ɪ) and the Th-Pro discourse marker (Galindo 1987; García 1984; Mendoza-Denton 1997; Penfield and Ornstein 1985, chapter 3). We have yet to definitively locate a pan-ChcE linguistic variable, which in part is a consequence of the relative lack of sociolinguistic research on this dialect. Alternatively, it might be due to the separate beginnings of ChcE in different regions of the Midwest and Southwest (but cf. Bayley 1994 and Santa Ana 1996). However, the four characteristic phonological differences mentioned above characterize both bi- and monolingual ChcE speakers (Santa Ana 1991; Fought 2003).

Regarding (IV), we think that these ChcE identity markers are reflexes of Spanish-speaking ELL transfer features that were refashioned when local Chicano communities in distinct locales established themselves. For now, this hypothesis remains untested because no study has addressed the 20th century formation of ChcE dialects. Nor has anyone documented the creation of a new ChcE dialect. The new immigrant Mexican communities throughout the U.S. South and in northeastern cities, however, offer key sites to investigate on-going social processes that are possibly creating linguistic variables in new ChcE speech. For example, Spanish-speaking immigrants have only recently begun to work in agribusiness in large numbers in the U.S. South. At times they do not come from traditional sites of Mexican migration, bringing new Spanish dialects to the U.S. In addition to the interesting English that will develop, since their U.S. settings are new, Mexican Spanish may not hold sway over other Spanish dialects, as is the case in the Chicano urban centers established in the 20th century. These significant demographic changes portend significant sociolinguistic changes. Furthermore, the politics of immigration have changed (Finks 2003). All of these factors offer opportunities for innovative explorations of language contact.

2.1.   Monophthongs and diphthongs

ChcE tends to be monophthongal, particularly its high vowels, /i, u/ (Santa Ana 1991: 155). This contrasts with the typically diphthongal other AmE dialects. Santa Ana, whose work involved impressionistic transcription as well as spectrographic measurements of naturally occurring speech gathered in sociolinguistic interviews, noted more off-glides in ChcE mid vowel pronunciation. He sampled the speech of four U.S.-born Los Angeles residents who represented different generations of speakers, as well as a narrative of the previously-mentioned young male immigrant ELL.

Later studies have corroborated many of Santa Ana's findings. Fought (1997, 2003), for example, found that high vowels, /e, ʊ/, were articulated with fewer and shorter off-glides. According to Fought, Chicanos articulated /aɪ/ with no loss of glide, but seemed to employ a higher tongue-height (lower F1) nucleus. Fought also found that /aʊ/ is most often pronounced with the Euro-American off-glide, but older speakers articulated a glide-less [a], as in *counselor*. The monophthongal quality of ChcE vowels is most distinguished in exclamations, such as *Ah!*, *Oh!*, or in emphasized final syllables of vowel-final words, such as the underscored syllables in *"I do, too, live in East L.A.!"* ChcE speakers often pronounce sustained duration syllables with minimal off-gliding, no matter how long the segment is prolonged.

2.2.   Vowel distribution

The typical native Spanish-speaking ELL has difficulty distinguishing the so-called tense and lax vowel subsystems. In contrast, ChcE speakers resolve all such interlanguage mergers. They sustain the /i/ and /ɪ/ distinction. Still, some ChcE speakers pronounce the high vowel variably as from [ɪ] to [i], especially in the suffix, *-ing* (Fought 2003: 65).

Santa Ana's (1991) spectrographic study found the typical tense/lax front vowel distribution, in terms of F1/F2 parameters, among four native English-speaking Chicanos. Their front tense vowels had a dense narrow distribution in vowel space, while the corresponding distribution of their front lax /ɪ, ɛ/ vowels created a more diffuse, less peripheral cloud in vowel space.

The ChcE /æ/ patterns with low vowels, rather than front vowels, as is the case for other U.S. English dialects. Thus, /æ/ has greater F1 range than F2 (front/back). The distribution of this vowel creates a narrow cloud that is elongated along the height parameter. For this reason, ChcE appears to be participating in the General California English æ-raising process (Fought 2003, but cf. Veatch 1991). In addition, the ChcE articulation of the AmE low back vowel, /ɑ/, as in *mom* or *caught*, is often a Spanish [a], as in *talk*, *daughter* and *law* (Fought 2003).

A spectrographic study of four native speakers indicates that the nucleus of the high back vowel, /u/, is either fronted or fronting (Santa Ana 1991). The distribution cloud of /u/ extends across the upper top of the vowel space, from the back to an intermediate front of the /i/ cloud. There is little overlap with the front vowel distribution clouds; the /u/ distribution is higher than the mid-front vowel cloud.

While Santa Ana (1991) finds much less /ʊ/ fronting than u-fronting in the speech of the Los Angeles Chicano men he instrumentally plotted, Fought (2003) states that ChcE /ʊ/ is realized at times as a high rounded [ʉ], while at other times it is an unrounded fronted [ɨ], as in *look* or *looking*.

2.3.   Vowel centralization

Whereas unstressed vowels in most dialects of American English typically centralize to a schwa-mean, as in White Chicago English (Veatch 1991, chapter 7),
only some of ChcE unstressed vowels centralize (Santa Ana 1991). Their high
vowels, /i/ and /u/, do not reduce, while mid vowels reduce less frequently
than AmE mid vowels. As well, ChcE low vowels centralize (Santa Ana 1991).
On the basis of five speakers, Santa Ana found no language-internal or social
category explanation for their different centralization targets, and consequently
sought a dialect contact explanation. He hypothesized that the extent to which
ChcE-speakers accommodated to the general U.S. schwa-mean centralization
pattern corresponded to the amount of social contact and personal identification that an individual had with Euro-American dialect speakers (177).

In contrast, Veatch (1991: 200) instrumentally measured the ChcE vowel
centralization of a single individual. His measurements indicated that non-
stress articulation lowers ChcE /e, ɛ, æ/ and /ɥ/, that it backs /o, ʊ/, and finally,
that it has no effect on /i/. Veatch characterized ChcE vowel centralization as a
single process, namely all centralizing vowels shift to an [ɨ] vowel quality. In
this process, ChcE is similar to Alabama English in having an [ɨ] centralization
target (Veatch 1991, chapter 8). From the current authors' present perspective,
the issue of vowel centralization in ChcE has not been resolved.

2.4.   Linguistic variables

Mendoza-Denton (1997), building on the (-ing) studies of Galindo (1987), divided -*ing* into two variables: (ɪ) and Th-Pro. She conducted an ethnography in
a northern California high school, focusing on Chicana social groups. Among
other young women's groups, Mendoza-Denton worked closely with two rival
gangs. To become a gang member in this school, a girl must either identify as
a *sureña* or a *norteña*. These oppositional identities were expressed across the
full range of social symbols, from clothing and makeup to facial expression and
posture. One key feature of sureña identity is linguistic distancing from English,
which sureñas accomplish by eschewing English in favor of Spanish. Norteñas,
on the other hand, mark their identity via Spanish/English codeswitching and
use of English. While these groups of young women pull away from each other
via overt linguistic choices, at a more fundamental level they share identity
features that express antagonism toward Euro-American society.

Variable raising and lowering of (ɪ) is present of the speech of both norteñas and sureñas (Mendoza-Denton 1999). Chances are greatest that the vowel
will be lower before a nasal. An engma (which here corresponds to the U.S.

standard nasal in *-ing*) is less ethnically marked than an alveolar nasal (which corresponds to the substrate nasal consonant). The raising process occurs most prominently among gang members and gang-affiliated groups, and these young women raised (ɪ) most frequently with *-thing* words. Sureñas and norteñas both used increased frequencies of raised [iŋ] and especially [in] forms of (ɪ), to signal greater social distance from both Chicanas who identify with Euro-Americans, and from Euro-Americans. Chicana gang members also employ a meaningful lowering of /ɪ/. Hence they exploit iota, (ɪ), a front lax vowel with no Spanish correspondence, to express identity and ideology. Among Chicanos and Chicanas, in contrast, the closely-related tense vowel /i/ never lowers to [i] (Fought 2003: 65).

In northern California, *-thing* words such as *something, nothing*, and phrases such as *and everything*, may be characterized as Th-Pro, a gang discourse marker (Mendoza-Denton 1999). This is not *thing*, the pronoun, which is used to refer to noun antecedents. Rather Th-Pro serves to construct mutual understanding and reinforce solidarity between gang interlocutors. Consider the underscored discourse marker in: *"I was walking around the other day and José stopped to talk to me **and everything**."* Mendoza-Denton gives three reasons (1997: 139–141) why *"and everything"* is well suited to signal in-group referencing: 1) as an example of a clause-terminal discourse marker, it is stigmatized by middle-class speakers; 2) the underspecified semantics of *thing* allows it to be used widely across any number of inferences associated with in-group understandings; 3) the three phonemes in (-ing) are each subject to ELL transfer stigma, /θ/, /ɪ/, and /ŋ/, hence providing a full range of expression of in-group/out-group social positioning.

Mendoza-Denton has brought us full circle. We can imagine how an ELL rendering *something* as [santɪn] would trigger a White chauvinist's derisive remark, to the speaker's embarrassment. She has shown us that a mark of embarrassment has been subverted to become a marker of ethnic identification. Although (-ing) is currently an indicator (since it is not consciously recognized by these in-group speakers), it is associated with the stereotypical speech of ELLs. This overlap suggests that the classic empirical linguistic trinity of variables (indicator, marker, and stigmatized form) should be reconsidered. Mendoza-Denton has documented the rich heterogeneity of Chicanos, focusing on women's lives and language, and the tensions and conflicts within these communities. To further illustrate the complexity of identity matters in dialect contact settings, Fought (2003: 66) observed in West Los Angeles that Euro-Americans who live among Chicanos also use the raised [iŋ] and [in] forms of (-ing).

A major sound change in progress in California, /u/-fronting, has also been investigated in ChcE (Fought 1997, 2003). Fought also initiated studies of less well-known processes, (æ-backing) and (æ-raising). Not only did she account for system-internal factors, with sensitive ethnographic work across social classes, gender, age and employment groups of Chicanos in West Los Angeles, but she was able to characterize the social value articulated by (u-fronting) among these Chicanos and their Euro-American neighbors. At the risk of over-simplification, Fought ascertained that Chicanos associate this linguistic variable with Euro-American identity and hegemony. Accordingly, middle-class female ChcE speakers without gang affiliation fronted their /u/ to the greatest extent. Conversely, working-class or low-income earning Chicanos who are affiliates or members of gangs articulated /u/ in the most backed, least fronted vowel space. Other ChcE speakers having other mixes of these social factors have intermediate patterns of /u/-fronting. No single social category could account for indexical coding for assimilationist identity among the speakers who participated in Fought's study.

Furthermore, Fought demonstrated that Chicanos, as a linguistic minority community, do not necessarily have the same relationship that speakers of AAVE have with the matrix Euro-American local dialect. In 2001 William Labov stated, "no matter how frequently they are exposed to the local [Euro-American] vernacular, the new patterns of regional sound change do not surface in ... Black, Hispanic, or Native American ... speech" (cited in Fought 2003: 112). His statement was overly general, since Los Angeles Chicanos participated in u-fronting, as Veatch (1991) and Santa Ana (1991) noted in their separate instrumental studies. Moreover, Fought provided both a detailed description of the participation of the Chicano community in, and social meanings associated with, this Californian change in progress. Second, Fought made a crucial observation concerning language internal matters of sound change. Fronting of /u/ is not advancing in the expected "curvilinear pattern", namely where the most innovative, "most advanced vowel systems are found among younger speakers: young adults and youth in late adolescence", and that occupational groups with highest and lowest social status disfavor the changes in progress (Fought 2003: 125). Indeed, ChcE participation in (u-fronting) cuts across socioeconomic groups: "the group with the highest /u/-fronting includes women from both middle-class backgrounds, and very low socioeconomic backgrounds" (Fought 2003: 125).

3.   Consonants

ChcE has the same consonant phoneme inventory, and all the allophonic variants, of General Californian English (GCE). ChcE allo-consonantal variants occur in addition to GCE consonantal allophones, and these ChcE variants occur with greater or lesser frequency among different ChcE speakers (Fought 2003, section 3.3).

The ChcE alveolar stops often have an apico-dental point of articulation (which is the corresponding place of articulation in Spanish). Additionally, like some other English vernaculars, but not GCE, ChcE variably articulates its interdental fricatives as apico-dental stops. In her study of Los Angeles ChcE, Fought indicates that Euro-American participants did not use apico-dental stops, while even "very 'standard' sounding ChcE speakers who used few or none of the ChcE syntactic features" were heard to use apico-dental stops (2003: 68). Still, regarding the use and frequency of this substrate-based feature, Santa Ana's impressions corroborate Fought's claim that some Los Angeles ChcE speakers used the apico-dental stops "almost categorically" (2003: 68). It is often impossible to predict which ChcE speaker is bilingual and which is an English-speaking monolingual. This phonetic patterning again belies the commonplace view that ChcE pronunciation is merely a matter of Spanish-language transfer of ELLs.

Fought noted that for both GCE and ChcE, one variant of syllable-final voiceless stops is a glottalized form, which she describes as a tensing and closing of the vocal cords as the stop is closed orally. This is often called an unreleased stop. Fought remarks that the consonant pronunciation is often associated in ChcE with a preceding creaky voice vowel. A more pronounced version of this process that Fought observes is the complete substitution of the voiceless stop with a glottal stop. Finally, there is a rare ejective version in which the glottalized stop is pronounced with a sharp burst of aspiration.

The most studied consonantal process in ChcE is (-t, d), or final alveolar stop deletion (Santa Ana 1991, 1992, 1996; Bayley 1994, 1997; Fought 1997). By /-t, d/ deletion we mean the loss of final alveolar stops in the process of consonant cluster simplification, e.g. *last week* [læs wik]. There are other related simplification processes. One is assimilation of a consonant of the cluster, as in l-vocalization, e.g. *old* [od]. Another is the deletion of one of the consonants. There is also nasalization in English, in -nC clusters, e.g. *want*, [wãt], or in the context of a following unstressed vowel, a nasal flap. Then there is vowel epenthesis to create a syllable boundary between adjacent consonants to preserve the segments and eliminate the cluster. Finally, a process that is related to epenthesis is reassignment of the final consonant to a following vowel-initial syllable. Santa Ana (1991) stated that these ChcE forms also occur in other English dialects. However, Chicanos may reduce clusters to a greater extent than many other dialects.

A related process that calls for study is the deletion of single consonants in final or syllable-final position. We concur with Fought's impression that it occurs "more frequently than in any other English dialect", particularly among older speakers (Fought 2003: 69).

Santa Ana (1991, 1996) reviewed multivariate analyses of the patterns of the workhorse linguistic variable (-t, d) for several U.S. dialects (Standard American, several African American English studies, a vernacular Euro-American dialect, and Puerto Rican English) to determine the similarity of ChcE to other U.S. English dialects. He found the basic structure is shared across these dialects, but ChcE reanalysis has created a distinctive variable that reveals its Mexican Spanish substrate influence.

As a process operating in real time on the speech stream, many phonologists consider (-t, d) to be strictly a surface process, not a more foundational process (such as a Level-1 Process in models of Lexical Phonology). Santa Ana (1996) claimed otherwise, stating that the full range of conditioning effects on ChcE (-t, d) can be ordered in terms of the basic level concept of syllabification. He offered four generalizations. First, in ChcE, syllable stress is not a factor in deletion, which is a feature expected in stress-timed languages like English. Second, for both preceding environment and following environment, there is a correlation of the conditioning segment sonority to the frequency of deletion of the alveolar stop. An increase of the sonority of the preceding segment is correlated with increasing deletion. Conversely, a decrease of the sonority level of the following segment is correlated with an increase in deletion. Third, ChcE (-t, d) is correlated to [± coronal] place of articulation of the adjacent segment. Finally, regarding morphological categories, ChcE speakers attend to the regular past tense and past participle morphology of English, and tend to simplify alveolar stop clusters that carry this inflectional morphology at a very low rate. Santa Ana (1996) schematized ChcE (-t, d) as follows:

$$/\text{-t, d}/ \rightarrow \quad \underline{<\ \varnothing\ >} \quad / < [\text{sonority}_\alpha \text{ coronal}_\gamma] >$$
$$\text{morph}_\beta$$

The alveolar stop variably deletes as conditioned by three rank-ordered constraints: the major constraint, or α, the sonority of the environment; β, the grammatical category of the word containing the /-t, d/ segment; and γ, the coronal value of the environment. The conditioning constraints are placed in angle brackets to indicate their variable values. A feature of the analysis not displayed in this schema is the contrary directions of the effect that sonority has on the /-t, d/, namely that increasing sonority of the preceding coda increases deletion while decreasing sonority of the following onset increases deletion. Fought (2003: 72) suggests the surprising absence of the syllable-stress factor in ChcE (-t, d) may be due to the syllable timed quality of the dialect, to which we turn.

4.   Prosody

For some ChcE researchers and many lay people, prosody is the most salient feature of ChcE. For empirical linguists, it remains the most elusive. Some ChcE speakers readily employ strongly Spanish-like patterns at one moment, and utterly Germanic patterns at other times, while others exhibit a far more limited range at either end of the continuum. This aspect of phonology continues to bother ChcE researchers, and may need to wait for even greater ease-of-use advances in acoustic research technology. We want to reiterate that prosody is as mercurial in everyday speech, as it is prone to reification by the public.

Fought (2003) observes that the ChcE prosody system remains poorly understood. All we have are a few accumulated observations about word-stress patterns, intonation and syllabification. She centers her own review (2003: 70–80) on Santa Ana's comment that ChcE "has a syllable timed quality to it" (1991: 139). Both Fought and Santa Ana are quick to note that ChcE exhibits the features of English stress timing (namely, lengthening and peripheralization of stressed vowels), but a syllable-timed quality remains at the root of the ChcE dialect. Fought concludes that ChcE is "intermediate in some ways" to other strongly stress-timed English dialects and the syllable-timed Spanish language. We turn to our list of selected ChcE prosodic features.

4.1.   Word stress

Word stress differences in ChcE are idiosyncratic to the individual. These most often appear in compound words, such as *Thanksgíving Day* (unstressed *day*), *mòrning síckness, typewríter, shów up*, but also in polysyllabic words, as in *réalized, ássociate, téchnique*. Some time ago, Penfield (1984) suggested that ChcE compounds are stressed on the second word, rather than the first as they would be in most other English dialects. Of course, this does not capture the facts of the vast majority of ChcE word compounds that exhibit typical English stress patterns.

In phrasal stresses (across a breath group or some other set of words), Fought notes that main stress may occur at unexpected places. She offers (2003: 71) two sentences (main stress boldfaced) from a U.S.-born 16-year-old Chicano: *Some girls don't think what they're gonna **go** through. It's all right for her to talk to **her** homeboys, but it ain't all right for me to talk to **my** homegirls?* Fought states that this pattern would be only "marginally acceptable" to many speakers of other English dialects. She goes on to say it has many parallels to ELL stress patterning – again a substrate-influenced pattern. Fought points to potentially useful directions in ChcE prosody research, namely testing system-level hypotheses, and moving away from lists of word-stress anomalies, to characterizations of larger units of prosody.

4.2.   Intonation

Five major patterns occur variably in ChcE (Penfield 1984). First, there is the ChcE rising glide, which "can occur at almost any point in a contour" (Penfield and Ornstein 1985: 48), as in *rules* and *choking* in the following sentences:

(1)   Are there   r u l e s   for a   fair fight? #

(2)   He was   c h o k i n g   on it.#

The glide is accompanied by a lengthening of the affected syllables. Penfield and Ornstein indicate the distinctiveness of ChcE is that unstressed portions of multisyllabic words, e.g. *-ing*, are maintained at the higher pitch level (1985: 49). The equivalent pattern in AmE would be:

(3)   He was   c h o k   ing   on it. #

Penfield (1984) states that the rising glide is associated with emphasis on the specific word, and not the contrastive stress that would be the case in AmE. Penfield and Ornstein (1985) offer (4) as an example of the same word appearing twice in a sentence, once with the rising glide (marking emphasis), and the more general step-down pitch contour, which does not have this added meaning:

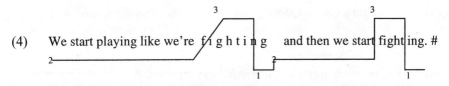

(4)   We start playing like we're f i g h t i n g   and then we start fight ing. #

A second aspect of this ChcE pattern is that, if the glide occurs on the last stressed syllable of the utterance, the pitch of glide can be maintained, whether or not the intent is emphatic or not. Neutral declarative utterances do not necessarily end with a falling step contour, as is the typical AmE pattern:

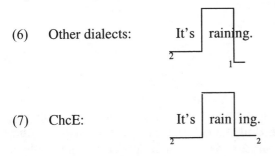

(5)   I want to be a w a k e . #

Example (5) is a contrastive use of the glide, spoken by a Chicana who narrated her conversation with her physician where she makes a "countercomment" (1984) stating that she did not want to be sedated when she delivered the baby. Penfield indicates that a syllable-final rising glide in AmE dialects tends to express doubt, surprise or questions. In ChcE, it does not necessarily convey such notions.

In a related final contour distinction, ChcE non-emphatic declarative utterances can end on middle pitch, rather than falling to low pitch in a step. This is the pattern that might briefly confuse speakers of other English dialects, who expect a more pronounced falling contour to signal the end of an utterance:

(6)   Other dialects: It's │ rain│ing.

(7)   ChcE: It's │ rain │ ing.

The third ChcE pattern concerns initial pitch position. A ChcE utterance can begin on a high pitch, which is mistakenly interpreted by speakers of other dialects as focus. This high pitch does not necessarily mark focus. In some cases, it apparently marks solidarity. At other times, its meaning is harder to pin down:

(8)   Other dialects: Query: Did **they** buy the house? #
                          Response: Yes. # **They** bought the house. #

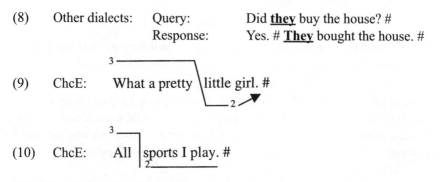

(9)   ChcE: What a pretty little girl. #

(10)   ChcE: All sports I play. #

This ChcE initial high pitch does not function to signal emphasis. Penfield and Ornstein suggest that it is this prosodic contour that gives AmE speakers the "folk conception that Chicanos are highly emotional or excited, since the use of a high pitch at pre-contour level—especially if it spanned over more than a word—would certainly convey such a meaning in Standard English" (1985: 50).

Four, ChcE has a distinctive gliding-final contour, that is, at the end of utterances/sentences. Compare the USEng step-like fall that marks its sentence-final contour. This ChcE terminal contour most often signals emphasis or affect. In contrast to the ChcE gliding contour, the Euro-American tune typically expresses emphasis with abrupt block-like steps of pitch:

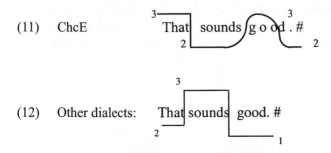

(11)   ChcE   That sounds good. #

(12)   Other dialects: That sounds good. #

This is the stereotypic pattern that Euro-American actors use when playing Mexican bandits or peasants in Hollywood Westerns. It is also the intonation of the Warner Bros. cartoon character, Speedy Gonzales. This is not a subtle caricature of a Mexican, no matter what its original intent. The mouse is outfitted with Mexican sombrero, and Mexican peasant clothing dating from no later than the 1920s, in contrast to the cartoon's origin in the 1950s. It offers a White American's derisive depiction of Spanish-accented English. It should be noted that ChcE speakers who use the rise/fall gliding final contour will also use the local matrix Euro-American English step-like final contour.

Five, rather than using the AmE yes/no question contour, which again is a block-like step that ends on a low pitch, ChcE speakers variably employ another gliding contour that does not end in a final low pitch:

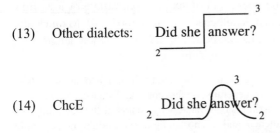

(13)   Other dialects: Did she answer?

(14)   ChcE   Did she answer?

Fought (2003: 75–76) continues that these terminal contours are distinct from the so-called U.S. American cross-dialect "uptalk" contour that is used in non-emphatic declaratives, in spite of the fact that both the ChcE contour and the uptalk contour do not end in a falling pitch. Santa Ana can confirm that in his current contact with Los Angeles ChcE speakers he can distinguish both declarative contours.

Intonational contours, arguably the most changeable and ephemeral elements of speech, are very readily reified. At this point it is useful to recall that these speech utterance patterns are rendered vexingly complex by individual language histories, speech event features such as topic, setting, and, among many other social factors, interlocutor. Add to this the complexity inherent in cultural features such as habituated verbal practice and, in contrast, mapping patterns of responses to novel interactional situations. Moreover, it is important to consider the open flexibility that individuals have in the moment of their speaking turn. In studies of naturally occurring prosody, we must add the issue of the observer's paradox, and the impossibility to replicate speech events—however closely one reproduces the setting. The traditional scientific response to such research circumstances, namely large-scale projects designed to wash out variation, are entirely inappropriate in these circumstances. This makes the goal of characterizing ChcE intonation in its dynamic contact setting a first-order methodological challenge.

Fought (2002: 72–76) provides a fascinating angle on some ChcE intonation patterns, drawing on Joseph Matluck's (1952) description of the Spanish language circumflex pattern of the Mexican *altiplano* (the high plateau formed between the eastern and western Sierra Madre mountain chains). To find the origin of the circumflex pattern, Matluck points to another substrate language: "The distinctive musical line in the unfolding of the phonetic group is probably the most striking trace that the Nahuatl language has left in the Spanish of the Valley [of Mexico

City] and the plateau: a kind of song with its curious final cadence, very similar to the melodic movement of Nahuatl itself". Fought continues to translate Matluck: "From the antepenultimate syllable to the penult there is a rise of about three semitones, and from there to the final a fall of six semitones more or less. Both the penult and the final syllables are lengthened" (Fought 2002: 74). Matluck also describes a working-class feature that can be found in ChcE, namely lengthening of stressed vowels at the start and the end of a phrase:

> Accented syllables in vernacular speech in the Valley tend to be much longer than those of the educated class and in Castilian generally; on the other hand, unaccented syllables are shortened. The overall impression is of syllabic lengthening at the beginning and especially at the end of the sentence, and of shortening in the middle. For example: *Don't be bad > Doont be baaad; I have to do it soon > III have to do it sooon* (quoted in Fought 2002: 75).

Fought states that not only is this pattern readily observed in the English ELLs, it is also heard in the speech of ChcE native speakers. Once again, the substrate Mexican Spanish influence has not disappeared in ChcE, it has been transformed into another feature of in-group solidarity.

4.3.   Syllabification

Two processes, both in need of more clarifying research, further contribute to the Spanish accent of ChcE, namely syllabic differences that involve changes of conversational tempo (Fought 2003). English has ambisyllabic consonants, namely an intervocalic consonant in which a syllable boundary can be placed. Spanish does not have ambisyllables. The result of ambisyllabification is that English sounds as if it has more closed syllables than a comparable stretch of Spanish speech does. Now for all languages, most of the dictionary entry consonants are pronounced in slow, enunciated speech. At more rapid tempos, consonant clusters are reduced, thus creating more open syllables. However, in English, more ambisyllables, such as flaps, are created as well. In ChcE, as the tempo increases, fewer ambisyllables are created because more single consonants, and even whole word-internal syllables are lost (Fought 2003). This follows the syllabification patterns of the ChcE substrate, altiplano Mexican Spanish. Mexican Spanish tends toward greater synocope (preserving final syllables while losing medials), in contrast to Caribbean Spanish dialects which tend toward greater apocope (loss of final syllables). Additionally, more ChcE syllable onsets are placed before intervocalic consonants rather than within them (Fought 2003). These processes contribute to the relatively larger open syllable count in ChcE. More empirical research will have to be undertaken to describe these processes with greater precision.

4.4. Suprasegmentals

While most of the features that we have presented in this chapter can be associated with the Mexican Spanish substrate, one feature of ChcE has its origins among Euro-American California English speakers. This is creaky voice, or laryngealization, a common phonation effect. In other dialects creaky voice is a paralinguistic marker that signals bored resignation. However, in her recent study, Fought offers tantalizing evidence that ChcE creaky voice, particular among Chicanas, must have other meanings as well (2003: 78).

Finally, Fought mentions the use of palato-alveolar or alveolar clicks in ChcE. Clicks in AmE are egressive airstream stops used as suprasegmentals to signal scolding, disapproval, and other kinds of censure. Fought provides provocative evidence that this paralinguistic marker is far more frequent and signals a wider variety of meanings in ChcE than it does in most other AmE dialects (2003: 79–80).

5. Conclusion

ChcE is a native variety of English that has been influenced by the Mexican Spanish substrate. Throughout this chapter we have indicated that the distinguishing features of ChcE are associated with the substrate, or the ELL interlanguage of Mexican Spanish-speaking immigrants. We believe its features originated as second language learning features that Euro-Americans made salient in the English/Spanish contact setting. The Chicano community somehow reworked some of these markers of stigma into the most distinctive elements of ChcE phonology, creating a set of linguistic variables and discourse markers (most of which still have yet to be documented) that affirm ethnic solidarity.

Further empirical dialect contact research in these communities can develop both linguistic and sociolinguistic understandings of dynamic language and dialect contact settings. Well-crafted research has the potential to develop a richer understanding of the complex interaction of the full complement of prosodic, syntactic, and phonological variables that express nuanced Chicana and Chicano identities. In the sociological sphere, it can render precise the human processes by which ethnic communities reformulate linguistic features of outgroup markers of stigma into in-group solidarity features.

Chicano communities show no sign of giving up these largely unconscious markers of identity, family, and neighborhood — even when Chicano youth shift from Spanish to English. This reveals a lasting sense of belonging to their community and culture, and a keen awareness of their circumstances in U.S. society. As Fought and Mendoza-Denton bring to light, Chicanos and Chicanas use the ChcE linguistic variables in their daily life to express a counterhegemonic stance toward a nation that still does not fully embrace all of its citizens.

Exercises and study questions

1. A common public misconception about Chicano English is that it is the consequence of incomplete learning of English by Spanish dominant immigrants. What so-called facts are employed to sustain this mistaken viewpoint? What evidence should be presented to demonstrate that ChcE is an ethnic dialect of English? What educational implications follow from both views regarding Chicano youth?

2. The Chicano English syntax exercise (2) provides the following excerpt from an interview with a 15 year old Chicana from Texas. What ChcE phonological features might occur in this excerpt? What ChcE discourse features can be noted?

   Ever since I've been here, you know, me and him, when I was with that other guy … you know, me and him would talk and everything, me and him got to know each other, and once I broke up with that other guy, me and him was still talking and everything and we just got together all of a sudden. And then, next day I flew to Dallas without letting him know … and, you know, he was in the penitentiary, just recently he got out you know, but, he don't do drugs or anything. He may drink a beer once in a while but he don't really get drunk.

3. A number of complex facts about vowel pronunciations in Chicano English are provided in sections 2.1 and 2.2 of this chapter. Make sure you understand all the articulatory and acoustic information provided there, including all technical terms. On the basis of this description, draw a vowel chart in which you contrast the vowels of Chicano English to those of Standard American English.

4. Summarize the facts provided on consonant cluster reduction in Chicano English in your own words; in particular, paraphrase the formula from section 3, "Consonants". Provide a list of five words in which consonant cluster reduction is likely to occur.

5. The chapter presents a number of sentences with intonation contours considered typical of Chicano English. Read these sentences out loudly, trying to reproduce the intonation exactly as symbolized. How do these intonation contours differ from the ones you would normally use yourself?

Selected references

Please consult the General references for titles mentioned in the text but not included in the references below. For a full bibliography see the accompanying CD-ROM.

Bayley, Robert
　1994　Consonant cluster reduction in Tejano English. *Language Variation and Change* 6: 303–326.
　1997　Variation in Tejano English: Evidence for variable lexical phonology. In: Bernstein, Nunnally and Sabino (eds.), 197–209.
Finks, Leon
　2003　*Work and Community in the Nuevo New South: The Maya of Morganton.* Chapel Hill, NC: University of North Carolina Press.
Fought, Carmen
　1997　The English and Spanish of young adult Chicanos. Ph.D. dissertation, Department of Linguistics, University of Pennsylvania.
　2002　Ethnicity. In: Chambers, Trudgill, and Schilling-Estes (eds.), 444–472.
　2003　*Chicano English in Context.* Houndmills/New York: Palgrave Macmillan.
Galindo, D. Leticia
　1987　Linguistic influence and variation on the English of Chicano adolescents in Austin, Texas. Ph.D. dissertation, Department of Linguistics, University of Texas, Austin.
García, Maryellen
　1984　Parameters of the East Los Angeles speech community. In: Jacob Ornstein-Galicia (ed.), *Form and Function in Chicano English,* 85–98. Rowley, MA: Newbury House.
Labov, William
　1991　The three dialects of English. In: Eckert (ed.), 1-44.
Matluck, Joseph
　1952　La pronunciación del español en el valle de México. *Nueva Revista de Filología Hispánica* 6, 2: 109-120.
Mendoza-Denton, Norma
　1997　Chicana/Mexicana identity of linguistic variation: An ethnographic and sociolinguistic study of gang affiliation in an urban high school. Ph.D. dissertation, Department of Linguistics, Stanford University.
　1999　Sociolinguistics and linguistic anthropology of U.S. Latinos. *Annual Review of Anthropology* 28: 375–395.

2002   Language and identity. In: Chambers, Trudgill, and Schilling-Estes (eds.), 475–499.

Penfield, Joyce
1984   Prosodic patterns: Some hypotheses and findings from fieldwork. In: Jacob Ornstein-Galicia (ed.), *Form and Function in Chicano English,* 71–82. Rowley, MA: Newbury House.

Penfield, Joyce and Jacob L. Ornstein-Galicia
1985   *Chicano English: An Ethnic Contact Dialect.* Amsterdam: John Benjamins.

Santa Ana, Otto
1991   Phonetic simplification processes in the English of the barrio: A cross-generational sociolinguistic study of the Chicanos of Los Angeles. Ph.D. dissertation, Department of Linguistics, University of Pennsylvania.
1992   Chicano English evidence for the exponential hypothesis: A variable rule pervades lexical phonology. *Language Variation and Change* 4: 275–288.
1996   Sonority and syllable structure in Chicano English. *Language Variation and Change* 8: 63–90.

Valdés, Guadalupe
1998   The world outside and inside schools: Language and immigrant children. *Educational Researcher* 27: 4–18.

Valencia, Richard R. (ed.)
2002   *Chicano School Failure and Success: Past, Present, and Future.* 2nd edition. London and New York: Routledge Falmer.

Veatch, Thomas
1991   English vowels: Their surface phonology and phonetic implementation in Vernacular Dialects. Ph.D. dissertation, University of Pennsylvania.

Bahamian English: phonology

Becky Childs and Walt Wolfram

1.   Introduction

The Commonwealth of The Bahamas (henceforth The Bahamas) represents a unique geographic, demographic, and linguistic situation among the islands of the Caribbean and North Atlantic. The Bahamas consist of more than 700 islands and over 5,000 square miles of land mass, ranging from Grand Bahama to the north, located 60 miles off of the Florida coast, to Inagua to the south, located approximately 50 miles from Cuba and Haiti. The 30 inhabited islands contain almost 300,000 permanent residents, two-thirds of whom now live in the urban area of Nassau. The map in Figure 1 outlines The Bahamas in relation to the United States, Cuba, and Haiti.

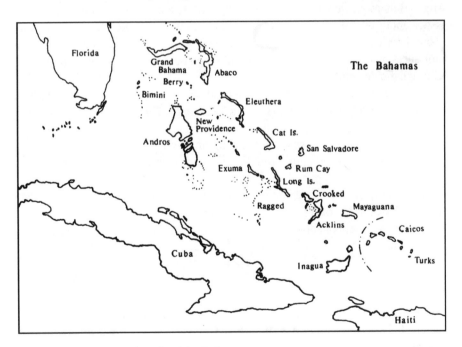

Figure 1.   Map of the islands of the Bahamas

Although The Bahamas are often associated with the Caribbean Islands, in many respects they are more closely linked to North America than to the islands bounded by the Greater and Lesser Antilles. Furthermore, they have an important sociohistorical and sociolinguistic affinity with the US. Many of the Afro-Bahamians, who comprise 85 percent of the population, came from the Gullah-speaking areas of South Carolina and Georgia and many of the original Anglo-Bahamian settlers were British loyalists from North America who came to The Bahamas from the US after the Revolutionary War. Furthermore, there is regular off-island travel to the US by many Bahamians.

There are a number of linguistic and sociolinguistic issues relating to this archipelago. One question concerns the significance of different founder English varieties that range from British and American English dialects to Gullah and other creoles in the African diaspora. Few Caribbean varieties have such a full range of potential English input dialects. Another matter is the past and present relationship between Afro-Bahamian and Anglo-Bahamian varieties. Although the black population has outnumbered the white population for several centuries, they have been socially and politically subordinate for the vast majority of that time. At the same time, there are a number of long-term mono-ethnic enclaves of Anglo-Bahamians in some of the outlying *cays* (pronounced as "keys"), raising issues about ethnolinguistic boundaries and accommodation. The demographic, sociohistorical, and sociolinguistic circumstances of the islands thus raise important questions about language norms and language ideology along with matters of linguistic description.

In this account, we describe the phonological traits of Bahamian English, including the relationship between enclave Anglo-Bahamian speech communities in outlying regions and the dominant population of Afro-Bahamians. Although some of these issues are just beginning to be addressed, current research suggests that bilateral ethnolinguistic convergence and divergence are exhibited in both salient and subtle ways. To situate the linguistic description of some of the diagnostic features of Bahamian phonology, we first offer a brief historical overview of The Bahamas, followed by a description of some of the major vocalic, consonantal, and prosodic traits typical of black and white Bahamian speech.

2.   Sociohistorical background

The Bahamas have experienced several different waves of migration that affected their demographic and social ecology. The first known inhabitants of The Bahamas were the Lucayan Indians who migrated to The Bahamas from South America as early as 600 CE and inhabited the islands until the Spanish invasion at the end of the fifteenth century. The Spanish conquest brought about the destruction of the indigenous population through disease and enslavement, although the Spaniards left after a brief occupation. Their lasting imprint was the name *Bahamas*, derived from the Spanish words *baja* and *mar,* meaning 'shallow sea'.

In 1648 the first English settlers to The Bahamas came from Bermuda and established a colony on the island of Eleuthera. The so-called Eleutheran Adventurers were looking for religious freedom and hoping to establish a republican government in The Bahamas. However, the settlers realized that limited natural resources of the island placed them in danger of starvation. Many of the settlers left the island and returned to Bermuda though the settlement remained intact. During this time, the first colony, New Providence Island, was established on the site that is now the home of the Bahamian capital city of Nassau. This settlement, established also by Bermudians, grew much more quickly than the earlier settlement of Eleuthera and by 1671 boasted a population of 913 people (Dodge 1995).

Though a proprietary government was adopted in 1670, it was unsuccessful and The Bahamas became a haven for pirates in the early 1700s. The geography of the islands was well situated for pirating hapless ships navigating the treacherous waters surrounding the islands. In 1718, the British sent Captain Woods Rogers to The Bahamas to drive the pirates from the islands and regain control for the British, and it was then turned into an official colony.

After the American Revolutionary War in the 1780s, many British loyalists fled the newly formed United States for both the major islands and the out islands of The Bahamas. Two-thirds of the loyalists came to The Bahamas via boats leaving from New York, the other third from boats leaving from St. Augustine, Florida, although they represented loyalists from throughout the US. One contingent, for example, came from the Carolinas, moving first to Florida and then departing after a brief stay there (Wolfram and Sellers 1998). Most wealthy loyalists returned to England within ten years, but those too poor to return stayed and relied on the resources of the land and the sea to maintain a subsistence living. Many loyalists also brought slaves with them from the US in hopes of setting up a plantation colony similar to that found in the American South, but the hope for cotton plantations died quickly as settlers realized that the thin Bahamian soil would not support the crop. Approximately 5,000 to 8,000 loyalists in all came to The Bahamas in the years following the American Revolutionary War, making them a significant early group in the establishment of The Bahamas (Dodge 1995).

With the passing of the Abolition of Slavery Act in Great Britain in 1833, the composition of the islands changed quickly. The population was growing rapidly and many Bahamians were again turning to the resources of the land and sea for their living. Various industries, for example, shipbuilding, sponging, fruit orchards, and sisal, have risen but none endured. Notwithstanding short-term economic surges, it was not until the 1950s that The Bahamas established long-term economic stability through the tourist industry. At the same time, politics was becoming an important part of Bahamian life, and by 1973 the Commonwealth of the Bahamas became independent and joined the Commonwealth of Nations even though it still retained Queen Elizabeth II as the head of state. Over the last three decades, Afro-Bahamians have gained control of civic life throughout the islands while Anglo-Bahamians have functioned on the periphery of mainstream modern Bahamian culture, living mostly on the outlying cays. Today The Bahamas are one of the world's most popular tourist destinations. Residents of the major islands now earn a living performing more contemporary jobs common to most large cities along with the service industry related to tourism, while residents of the out-islands have maintained more traditional jobs like fishing and boat building. The unique history, the demographics, and the past and present social dynamics of the islands have helped create and maintain distinct varieties of English.

3.   The phonology of Bahamian English

In this section, we describe some of the phonological features of Bahamian English. Although most Bahamians share some characteristic features, a number of structures are sensitive to ethnic, socioeconomic, and geographic factors. In addition, there is a basilectal-acrolectal continuum with respect to creole features that applies primarily to the Afro-Bahamian population; however, this dimension tends to be more relevant to the grammatical description of Bahamian English than to phonology. Our description is presented in terms of the major categories of vowels, consonants, and prosodic elements.

3.1.   Vowels

Many of the distinctive characteristics of the Caribbean Islands relate to the vowel system. In this respect, The Bahamas are no different. The constellation of vowel features unifies The Bahamas with Caribbean varieties of English but it also sets these islands apart in some significant respects, particularly in their affinity with some traits of Southern US English. In the following sections we consider some of these vowel characteristics, including the primary vowel system and diphthongs.

In table 1 we provide a summary of the vowels of Bahamian English in terms of the key words set forth in Wells (1982). Separate profiles are provided for Afro-Bahamian and Anglo-Bahamian speakers given the ethnolinguistic distinctions described in the preceding description.

Table 1.   Vowel sounds in Bahamian English

Key word	Anglo-Baha-mian	Afro-Baha-mian	Key word	Anglo-Baha-mian	Afro-Baha-mian	Key word	Anglo-Baha-mian	Afro-Baha-mian
KIT	ɪ	ɪ	FLEECE	i̠ ~ l̠i	i	NEAR	eə ~ iə	eə ~ iə
DRESS	ɛ	ɛ	FACE	ei	ɛi	SQUARE	eə	eə
TRAP	a~æ	a~æ	PALM	ɑ	ɑ	START	ɑː	ɑː
LOT	ɑ	ɑ	THOUGHT	ɔ	ɔ	NORTH	ɔɔ	ɔɔ
STRUT	ʌ̠	ʌ̠	GOAT	ɵu	ɵu	FORCE	oɔ	oɔ
FOOT	ʊ	ʊ	GOAL	ɵu	ou	CURE	uə	uə
BATH	a~æ	a~æ	GOOSE	ʉː	ʉː	happY	ɪ	ɪ
CLOTH	ɔ	ɔ	PRICE	ɑi	ai~ɑi	lettER	ə	ə
NURSE	ə~ɜ	ɜ~əi	PRIZE	ɑɪ ~ ai	aː	horsES	ə	ə
			CHOICE	oi	ɔi	commA	ə	ə
			MOUTH	aø~aɛ	aɔ~ɑɔ			

3.1.1. Front vowels

Wells (1982) notes that the Bahamian /æ/ of TRAP occupies a more central position of [a] rather than a front position, but his description needs to be qualified in order to take into account generational and ethnic differences. In acoustic measurements of Bahamian vowels by Thomas (2001) and Childs, Reaser and Wolfram (2003), the production of the vowel in TRAP by both black and white speakers is shown to remain low and somewhat retracted. However, among older Anglo-Bahamian speakers, the vowel is raised before *d* in words like *sad* or *plaid*, occupying a position closer to [ɪ]; this production is different from Afro-Bahamian speakers. The production of the vowel of TRAP by younger speakers in the white communities shows the vowel realized as [a] in all other environments. The lowered and backed *trap* production by the Afro-Bahamian speakers and the younger generation of Anglo-Bahamian residents is typical of many Caribbean varieties of English. The cross-generational analysis of different groups of Bahamians by Childs, Reaser and Wolfram (2003) indicates that Anglo-Bahamians are moving somewhat toward Afro-Bahamian norms.

Both Afro-Bahamians and Anglo-Bahamians produce the vowel of FACE as [ei] (Wells 1982; Childs, Reaser and Wolfram 2003). This phonetic production is typical of varieties of North American English in general and African American Vernacular English (AAVE) (Thomas 2001) but different from white Southern speech in the US and most Southern British English varieties, which have a lowered and centralized nucleus for /e/.

Thomas (2001: 106) reports that there is a merger of the vowels of NEAR and SQUARE in Bahamian English, making items like *fear* and *fair* or *ear* and *air* homophonous. In this respect, Bahamian English resembles the low country dialect of South Carolina, although a number of English dialects exist that exhibit this merger.

3.1.2. *Central vowels*

One of the diagnostic variants in The Bahamas is the mid-central vowel /ʌ/. Both Afro-Bahamians and Anglo-Bahamians have a backed variant for the vowel of *strut* that is somewhat rounded and produced close to the cardinal position of [ɔ] (Wells 1982; Childs, Reaser and Wolfram 2003). This variant has been well documented in Caribbean creole varieties such as Jamaican English (Wells 1982), but it is quite scattered in the United States, though it is found in the Low Country of South Carolina and Georgia (Thomas 2001). This production is, however, not found at all in British Cockney, the British dialect most often compared to Anglo-Bahamian English. The origin of this variant is difficult to determine given its rarity in some of the more obvious founder dialects of English in The Bahamas.

3.1.3. *Back vowels*

The back vowels of GOOSE and COAT indicate a distinct ethnic difference in their phonetic production. Anglo-Bahamians have fronted productions of GOOSE and COAT while they remain backed for Afro-Bahamians. The fronting of back vowels is a widespread feature of white Southern American English varieties, although it is an expanding trait of other North American varieties as well (Thomas 2001). Even though /u/ in Anglo-Bahamian speech is not as fronted as the variant in Southern American English [y], it may front to [ø]. The source of back vowel fronting in Bahamian white speech may be the result of contact with earlier or present-day Southern American English, but it may also be the result of an independent phonetic development, following the principles of vowel shifting set forth in Labov (1994). The lack of fronting for back vowels in Afro-Bahamian speech replicates the ethnic distribution found in

Southern speech in the US. For example, Gullah and general Southern AAVE do not exhibit back-vowel fronting (Thomas 2001), but white Southern speech does; this parallels the ethnolinguistic dichotomy in The Bahamas.

The fronted /o/ of GOAT found among Anglo-Bahamians does not have a lowered nucleus like that typically found in Southern American varieties. The /o/ is, instead, realized as [ɘu]. For Afro-Bahamian speech /o/ remains back and upgliding, similar to African American English [ou]. This production is more like American English and less like varieties of Caribbean English, which are known for producing /o/ as a monophthong (Wells 1982). This ethnic differentiation no doubt reflects the differing founder effects, the sociohistorical development of The Bahamas, and the persistent maintenance of ethnolinguistic boundaries.

Wells (1982) and Childs, Reaser and Wolfram (2003) report that the vowel of LOT is backed in both Anglo-Bahamian and Afro-Bahamian English; furthermore, the vowels of LOT and THOUGHT are not merged as is found in some varieties that have backed vowel in LOT (Thomas 2001). This pattern is quite different from the pattern throughout the rest of the Caribbean, which may exhibit a merger of LOT and TRAP. The pattern found in The Bahamas is much more similar to the pattern found in Southern white US speech, AAVE, and the Pamlico Sound area. Again, the presence of this variant in both black and white Bahamian speech provides important information about dialect accommodation in The Bahamas.

3.1.4. Diphthongs

The diphthong of words like PRICE and PRIZE shows quite a bit of variability ethnically and generationally in the Bahamas. Older Anglo-Bahamian speakers show a backed nucleus much like that of the Pamlico Sound area of coastal North Carolina, as well as a number of dialect areas in Southern England and in the Southern Hemisphere; they also have a fairly strong offglide. Younger speakers tend to show a less backed nucleus and a weakened glide preceding voiced consonants, not unlike that found in Southern American English varieties. Childs, Reaser and Wolfram (2003) show that Afro-Bahamians exhibit a pattern comparable to that found in African American English in the US, with a fully glided offglide for *price* (preceding voiceless consonants) and a drastically reduced glide for *prize* (preceding voiced consonants). There is also less of a tendency to back the nucleus of /ai/ among Afro-Bahamian speakers.

Some observers have mistakenly associated the diphthong of MOUTH in The Bahamas with Canadian raising. In Canadian raising the nucleus of the /au/ diphthong of MOUTH is raised before voiceless consonants so that *out* is realized as [ɜʉt]; however, this type of raising is not found in Anglo-Bahamian or Afro-Bahamian speech. Instead, in Anglo-Bahamian speech /au/ is front-glided and produced as [aɛ], while in Afro-Bahamian speech the diphthong is produced with a backing glide. Although the production of /au/ by the Afro-Bahamian population is fairly standard, the production of /au/ with a front glide by the Anglo-Bahamian population is a noteworthy departure from standard productions in The Bahamas and the US, though it is fairly typical of some coastal varieties on the Pamlico Sound area of North Carolina and the Chesapeake (Thomas 2001).

3.2.   Consonants

In this section, we consider some of the diagnostic characteristics of consonants; traits are discussed in terms of different processes affecting natural classes of sounds and phonotactics.

3.2.1.   Interdental fricatives

The stopping of voiced and voiceless interdental fricatives is one of the most stereotypical variables in English phonology, characterized by well-known icons such as *dis, dat,* and *dem* for *this, that,* and *them.* Studies of interdental fricatives in Bahamian varieties (Shilling 1978, 1980; Holm 1980; Wells 1982) show both similarities and differences with respect to the realization of the phonemes /θ/ and /ð/. Afro-Bahamians show a clear preference for stopping for both voiced and voiceless interdentals in all positions, as in *tank* for *thank, toot* for *tooth, dat* for *that,* and *smood* for *smooth.* Stopping of interdentals is, of course, the Caribbean creole model and the norm for the US creole Gullah. In syllable-coda position, there is little labialization of /θ/ as [f] and /ð/ as [v], respectively, (e.g. [tuf] for 'tooth' or [briv] for 'breathe') as found in AAVE. In most respects, then, Afro-Bahamians are more likely to follow the creole norm of stopping than the North American AAVE model, in which stopping is favored in syllable-onset position and mostly restricted to [d] for /ð/. However, the levels of stopping in Afro-Bahamian speech do not appear to be as high as they are in other Afro-Caribbean varieties. Anglo-Bahamian speech is much more inclined to follow the widespread English norm, with some stopping for the voiced interdental /ð/ and infrequent stopping of the voiceless phoneme /θ/.

The stopping of voiceless interdentals serves as an important ethnolinguistic divide between Afro-Bahamian and Anglo-Bahamian speech, and quantitative studies of interdental fricatives in The Bahamas have revealed the significance of this disparity. At the same time, these studies have indicated some unpredictable results. Although it is not surprising to see a preference for the stopped variants among Afro-Bahamians, studies of outlying black and white speech communities in Abaco show that Anglo-Bahamians are more likely than their black cohorts to delete or assimilate initial stops. That is, white speakers are more likely to produce *'at's all* for *that's all* or *an'nen* for *and then*, although it is not a particularly frequent phonetic production for either group.

3.2.2. w/v *alternation*

The alternation of /w/ and /v/ is a highly marked feature of Bahamian speech. While this feature is found in both black and white speech, it is especially prominent among Anglo-Bahamians. The historical background for this type of alternation, which can be found in scattered varieties of English throughout the world, suggests that *v*, or more phonetically specific, a labiodental approximant [ʋ], may replace [w], creating items such as *vatch* for *watch* or *vaste* for *waste*. A *w* or labial approximant may also replace *v*, yielding *wiolence* for *violence* or *wase* for *vase*. Childs, Reaser and Wolfram (2003) find that *w→v* tends to be much more frequent than the converse, and that Anglo-Bahamian communities tend to have more alternation in both directions than Afro-Bahamians. Wells (1982: 58) suggests that the pattern for this alternation among the white Bahamians is "the phonemic merger of standard /v/ and /w/ into a single phoneme with the allophones [w] and [v] in complementary distribution. The [w] allophone occurs in initial position … but the [v] allophone elsewhere." Although this pattern may be found in some white Bahamian communities, it does not appear to be representative of the majority of communities. Research on Abaco Island (Childs, Reaser and Wolfram 2003) in The Bahamas and with Bahamian transplants (the so-called Conchs) in the Florida Keys of the US (Huss and Werner 1940) indicates that the [v] allophone can and does occur more frequently in initial position, though it also occurs elsewhere. Most descriptions of Bahamian English (Shilling 1978, 1980; Holm 1980; Childs, Reaser and Wolfram 2003) agree that it is a relatively salient trait associated with Bahamian speech vis-à-vis English-based Caribbean creoles and North American and British English varieties of English.

There is some dispute as to the origin of this feature in Bahamian English. Holm (1980) suggests that the founder source for this phonological process appears to be African language contact, noting that Gullah and West African languages do not maintain a /w/-/v/ phonological contrast. For example, Gullah speakers use the approximant for both *v* and *w*. If this were the source of the alternation in Bahamian English, the use of this feature by the white population would have been the result of accommodation to the broader black Bahamian majority. An alternative explanation for this feature is the founder dialects of Anglo-Bahamians. Although *w/v* alternation is not a widespread feature of most contemporary British and American English varieties, it was fairly common in some earlier varieties of British English, including Cockney (Trudgill et al. 2003). Wolfram and Thomas (2002: 127) note that *w/v* alternation was also a characteristic of earlier Mid-Atlantic coastal speech in the US, so that it is possible that some loyalists from the Carolinas may have exhibited this trait.

One of the strongest arguments for a primary Anglo source for *w/v* alternation comes from the fact that this trait is more prominent in Anglo-Bahamian communities than in cohort Afro-Bahamian communities. Both earlier (Huss and Werner 1940) and more recent (Childs, Reaser and Wolfram 2003) studies of Bahamian speech observe that *w/v* alternation is more widespread in Anglo-Bahamian than in Afro-Bahamian English. The African- and British-based explanations are not, however, mutually exclusive and it is quite possible that Gullah influence, transfer effects from West African languages, and English founder dialects converged in the development and maintenance of this trait as a distinctive feature of Bahamian English.

3.2.3. *Syllable-onset* h *deletion*

The deletion of syllable-initial *h* in *harm* as *'arm* or *hope* as *'ope* is also a prominent feature of Bahamian speech showing regional, social, and ethnic variation in Bahamian English. Most studies (Wells 1982; Holm 1980; Childs, Reaser and Wolfram 2003) agree that it tends to be more prominent in the speech of Anglo-Bahamians than it is in Afro-Bahamian speech, and that it correlates with social status differences and regional location as well. However, the social and ethnic differences tend to be a matter of relative frequency rather than the categorical presence or absence of so-called *h*-dropping. Childs, Reaser and Wolfram's (2003) study of syllable onset *h* deletion on Abaco Island indicates that although both black and white Bahamian communities exhibit *h* deletion, members of the enclave Anglo-Bahamian communities drop *h* more frequently than their Afro-Bahamian cohorts, regardless of age. There are also linguistically based effects on the relative frequency of *h* deletion based on phonetic context: *h* deletion is most favored at the beginning of an utterance. It is also more favored when it follows a consonant rather than a vowel; that is, speakers are more likely to say *bees' 'ive* for *bees' hive* than *bee 'ive* for *bee hive*. The favoring effect in terms of the canonical shape of sequences is natural in terms of a universal preference for the preservation of CV sequences as opposed to VV sequences.

As with *w/v* alternation, British Cockney has sometimes been cited as a source of *h* deletion in Anglo-Bahamian English, although it is a relatively widespread and phonetically natural process that is found in many varieties of English (Trudgill 1999). The initial impetus for *h* dropping may have come from a British English founder effect but its maintenance certainly is reinforced by its apparent naturalness as a phonetic process.

3.2.4. h *insertion*

The insertion of syllable-onset *h* in items such as *heggs* for *eggs* or *hitch* for *itch* is also found in Bahamian English. As with the loss of syllable-initial *h*, it is more characteristic of Anglo-Bahamian than Afro-Bahamian speech (Shilling 1980; Childs, Reaser and Wolfram 2003). In fact, an empirically based comparison of isolated Afro-Bahamian and Anglo-Bahamian communities in Abaco (Childs, Reaser and Wolfram 2003) indicates that *h* insertion is rarely found among speakers in the black community though it is relatively common in the cohort white community. The insertion of *h* is sensitive to ethnic and status distinctions, but it is fairly widely distributed among white Bahamians in different locales, including a transplant community that settled in Florida Keys (Huss and Werner 1940). It is also sensitive to phonetic environment so that it is more likely to occur in intervocalic sequences such *my heldest* 'my eldest' than when it follows a consonant as *duck hegg'* 'duck egg', thus facilitating the retention of a natural CVC canonical sequence. It can be quite salient socially in some phonetic environments, such as utterance-initial position in a sentence like *Heggs are good* for 'Eggs are good'.

The phonological status of *h* insertion is elusive. At first glance, the occurrence of *h* insertion may seem like a type of hypercorrection related to the fact that variable *h* dropping as discussed above is a fairly prominent trait of Bahamian English. A number of cases of *h* insertion occur on items that have no historic *h* in English, for example, *hitch* for *itch* or even *hup* for *up*. This suggests that it may have arisen as a compensatory production by speakers unsure of the phonological status of initial *h* in words. However, it should be noted that hypercorrection tends to be related to social situations where speakers feel obliged to use more acrolectal forms, or situations calling for more "careful" speech (Labov 1966). Bahamians who insert *h* appear to do so in relatively casual conversations where there is no apparent obligation to speak "properly". Although some lexical items may be more prone to *h* insertion than others (e.g. *hage* for *age, honion* for *onion*), we have found no consistent pattern defined strictly on a lexical basis. Instead, *h* insertion simply seems to be a phonetic option for word-initial vowels that co-exists with syllable-onset *h* dropping. In most cases, *h* dropping is much more frequent than *h* insertion but they clearly co-exist as traits of Bahamian English, showing both socially constrained and individually based variation. The existence of both *h* dropping and *h* insertion can result in some potential confusion of lexical items such as *hear* and *ear* or *heel* and *eel*, but in most cases there is little perceptual misinterpretation in actual conversation.

3.2.5. *Consonant cluster reduction*

The reduction of stop-final syllable-coda consonant clusters such as *west* to *wes'*, *find* to *fin'*, and *act* to *ac'* is a well-known process affecting a wide variety of English dialects. Whereas all dialects of English reduce clusters pre-consonantly, as in *west side* to *wes' side* or *cold cuts* to *col' cuts*, in prevocalic position consonant cluster reduction (CCR) is quite sensitive to ethnic and language background. Wolfram, Childs and Torbert (2000) maintain, for example, that extensive prevocalic reduction can usually be traced to language contact situations involving transfer from a source language not having syllable-coda clusters. It is also a well-known feature of creolized varieties of English, including creole languages of the Caribbean (Holm 1988/89; Patrick 1996) and North America (e.g. Gullah), as well as ethnic varieties exhibiting such substrate influence. Both Holm (1980) and Schilling (1978, 1980) note extensive consonant cluster reduction as a characteristic of both black and white Bahamian English varieties.

The quantitative analysis of two outlying Bahamian communities in the Abaco region of The Bahamas, one exclusively Afro-Bahamian and one exclusively Anglo-Bahamian, suggests that there is an ethnolinguistic divide in the relative incidence of consonant cluster reduction. Afro-Bahamian communities tend to apply cluster reduction at much higher frequency levels than their Anglo-Bahamian cohorts. At the same time, Anglo residents in The Bahamas have higher levels of CCR than Anglo speakers in the US or in England. For example, Anglo-Bahamian speakers tend to reduce clusters more than vernacular-speaking white speakers in the Northern or Southern US, although their levels of reduction are not equal to those of their Afro-Bahamian cohorts (Wolfram and Schilling-Estes 1998). This pattern suggests that there has been some quantitatively based accommodation to the vernacular phonological norms of Black Bahamian speech by Anglo residents of The Bahamas.

As with other dialects of English where consonant cluster reduction applies, it can affect both monomorphemic (e.g. *guest* to *gues'*; *mist* to *mis'*) and bimorphemic clusters (*guessed* to *gues'* and *missed* to *mis'*), with CCR favored in monomorphemic clusters. For basilectal Afro-Bahamian speech, however, this pattern is confounded by the incidence of grammatically based unmarked tense (see Reaser and Torbert in this volume; Hackert 2004). That is, the lack of inflectional *-ed* suffixation may result from a grammatical difference in verb morphology as well as the phonological process of cluster reduction. The confluence of the grammatical process and the phonological process may thus have the effect of raising the overall incidence of past tense unmarking. It also makes it impossible to determine if a particular case of a past tense verb form (e.g. *missed* as *miss'*; *guessed* as *guess'*) results from the phonological or the grammatical process. This type of additive effect does not apply to Anglo-Bahamian speakers, who do not have grammatically based past tense unmarking and tend to have quite low levels of prevocalic CCR for bimorphemic clusters.

3.2.6. *Postvocalic* r

The pronunciation of postvocalic /r/ in *door*, *mother*, and *bird* is quite variable, although most speakers exhibit *r*-lessness to some degree (Wells 1982). The speech of both black and white speakers tends to be non-rhotic, aligning with many dialects of England and with American English in the earlier Plantation South. The use of postvocalic /r/ in The Bahamas shows a pattern similar to that found for African American Vernacular English (Fasold and Wolfram 1970). Vocalization occurs in a word-final position when followed by a consonant (e.g. *four cats*) or vowel (e.g. *four apples*), with a following consonant favoring postvocalic *r* loss over a following vowel. Stressed nuclear *r* in *bird* or *sir* is more likely to be rhotic, with some ethnic division; black Bahamians are more likely to vocalize stressed nuclear *r* than their white counterparts. Finally, there is some intra-word intervocalic *r* loss as in *ma'y* for *marry* or *Ca'ol* for *Carol*. These cases of intervocalic, intra-word absence are not consistent and appear to be lexically based. Hackert (2004) notes that even though most Bahamian varieties are non-rhotic, some speakers now perceive *r*-full pronunciations as standard because of the influence of the American media. It may well be that this influence will eventually lead to a more rhotic variety, if this trend has not started already among some younger speakers.

Afro-Bahamians also vocalize postvocalic *l* in items such as *steal* and *well*, as do AAVE speakers, but Anglo-Bahamians tend to use an alveolar or "light" *l* regardless of phonetic environment, setting them apart from varieties such as American English.

3.2.7.   Sibilants

In syllable-coda and intervocalic position, voiced sibilants may be devoiced in Anglo-Bahamian English. Thus, items like *buzz* and *booze* may be produced with a final [s] and *easy* and *lazy* may be produced with a voiceless sibilants, as *ea*[s]*y la*[s]*y*, respectively, and *measure* and *treasure* may be produced as *mea*[ʃ]*ure* and *tread*[ʃ]*ure*, respectively. Although many varieties of English have partial devoicing of obstruents in syllable-coda position, the final sibilant in Bahamian English may be fully voiceless. Furthermore, this devoicing even may apply to segments that are followed by a voiced segment, as in *hu*[s]*band* for *husband* and *bu*[s]*iness* for *business*. Although this pattern is quite prominent for Anglo speakers, it is not as extensive among Afro-Bahamians.

Older speakers in more remote areas of the islands may sometimes use [sr] for [θr] clusters, so that *three* and *through* may be pronounced as [sri] and [sru], respectively. However, this production is somewhat idiosyncratic; some speakers use it predominantly while others do not use it at all.

3.3.   Prosodic features

There have been few comprehensive studies of prosody in the Caribbean and North American islands and no detailed research on these features in Bahamian English. Wells (1982) describes the general prosodic characteristics of speech as sounding more syllable-timed than stress-timed. This applies to both Afro-Bahamian and Anglo-Bahamian speech, but it is also important to qualify this observation. Wells notes that the syllable–timing characteristics of Caribbean varieties, and more particularly, Bahamian English, are not like those of African second language learners and that syllable timing is not an absolute phenomenon. Bahamian English falls within a continuum of syllable timing in that it is more syllable-timed than British or American English varieties but not as consistent as varieties of English directly transferring syllable timing from a language with strict syllable timing, such as a native speaker of Spanish speaking heavily accented English.

One of the most recognizable features of Bahamian English is the relative lack of reduction of vowels in unstressed syllables as in most varieties of American English. This trait contributes to the perception of Bahamian English as being stress-timed rather than syllable- timed. Afro-Bahamian speech appears to be somewhat more syllable-timed than Anglo-Bahamian speech, though they share this trait to some extent.

There are also a couple of noteworthy characteristics of Bahamian English relating to sentence intonation. High rising terminal contours characterize

Bahamian English affirmative sentences. In this regard, they appear to align with varieties as disparate as Australian and New Zealand English, as well as younger speakers in some areas of the US, but this intonation pattern seems to be a longstanding characteristic of Bahamian English, as it is with Caribbean English elsewhere (Wells 1982: 580).

The intonational contours of Bahamian English tend to show a wider pitch range than varieties such as American English and British English, although it is difficult to measure these differences precisely. In addition, there also are some stress differences in the assignment of primary stress. For example, in some cases primary stress may occur on non-initial syllables rather than the first syllable, as in *Cherokée* for *Cherokee* or *moráy* for *moray*. Bahamian English still awaits extensive, detailed study of prosodic features, though it is clearly an essential part of the phonetic configuration of white and black Bahamian varieties.

3.4.   Conclusion

This description of Bahamian English illustrates the multi-faceted explanations necessary to understand the phonological structure of English in the Caribbean diaspora. Founder influences, language contact, ethnolinguistic accommodation, and independent innovation all seem to have played a role in the construction of Bahamian English. For example, we have seen that both British and American English varieties had some part in its formative development; furthermore, a consideration of both white and black founder effects must be considered in attributing sources of influence. In addition, we have seen that there is selective alignment with other varieties of English in the Caribbean diaspora. In understanding the development of Bahamian English, we need to consider both internal and external language contact situations, as we see manifestations of bilateral accommodation in the speech of Afro-Bahamians and Anglo-Bahamians along with influences from language varieties beyond The Bahamas. Some of this accommodation is salient but other types of accommodation can be quite subtle and must be ferreted out by examining quantitative details. The end product of differential influences and development in The Bahamas has resulted in the configuration of a unique constellation of structures that both unites and separates Bahamian English varieties from other varieties of English in the region and beyond.

Finally, we must recognize the significance of language variation under the rubric of "Bahamian English". Expanding research in different regions of The Bahamas that extend from the urban area of Nassau (Shilling 1978, 1980; Holm 1983; Hackert 2004) to the out islands of Abaco (Holm 1980; Childs,

Reaser and Wolfram 2003; Reaser 2002) suggests that there is a range of variation based on ethnicity, status, geography, and language contact. All of these parameters must be factored into an authentic description of Bahamian English that is consistent with the past and present sociohistorical development of this sprawling archipelago.

Exercises and study questions

1. In what ways do the islands of the Bahamas seem to be like other Caribbean islands with respect to language variation and in what ways do they seem to be more aligned with North American language varieties?

2. What are the prominent social and historical factors affecting the phonology of Bahamian English? How does it appear to be changing and why?

3. What are the primary factors accounting for the range of diversity among different speakers in the Bahamas? Based on your listening to the CD, how salient is the factor of ethnicity? Cite some differences in Afro-Bahamian and Anglo-Bahamian speakers based on your listening.

4. How is the production of word-initial /w/ in words like *watch* and *wait* and the production of /v/ in words like *vote* and *violence* distinct in Bahamian English? What might account for this production?

5. Listen to the production of word-initial interdental fricatives /ð/ (e.g., *the that, them*) and /θ/ (e.g. *think, thank through*) in the speech samples of Afro-Bahamian and Anglo-Bahamian speakers on the CD. How similar are they? Do they appear to match the Caribbean English norm of predominant stopping for these interdental fricatives?

6. Listen to the sample Afro-Caribbean and Anglo-Caribbean speakers on the CD with respect to their use of word-final consonant clusters and syllable-initial *h* deletion and insertion. In what ways do they differ and in what ways are they similar?

7. Listen to the production of the diphthong /ai/ for Afro-Bahamian and Anglo-Bahamian speakers on the CD. Describe the productions and note similarities and differences in the production of this diphthong.

Selected references

Please consult the General references for titles mentioned in the text but not included in the references below. For a full bibliography see the accompanying CD-ROM.

Childs, Becky, Jeffrey Reaser, and Walt Wolfram
  2003   Defining ethnic varieties in The Bahamas: Phonological accommodation in black and white enclave communities. In: Aceto and Williams (eds.), 19–59.
Dodge, Steve
  1995   *Abaco: A History of an Out Island and its Cays*. Decatur, IL: White Sound Press.
Fasold, Ralph W. and Walt Wolfram
  1970   Some linguistic features of Negro Dialect. In: Fasold and Shuy (eds.), 41–86.
Holm, John
  1980   African features in white Bahamian speech. *English World-Wide* 1: 45–65.
  1983   On the relationship of Gullah and Bahamian. *American Speech* 59: 303–318.
Huss, Veronica and Evelyn Werner
  1940   The Conchs of Riviera, Florida. *Southern Folklore Quarterly* 4: 141–51.
Patrick, Peter L.
  1996   The urbanization of Creole phonology: Variation and change in Jamaican. In: Guy, Rickford, Feagin and Schiffrin (eds.), 329–355.
Reaser, Jeffrey
  2002   Copula absence in Bahamian English: Evidence from ethnically contrastive enclaves in The Bahamas. In: *Proceedings of the 14th Biennial Conference of the Society for Caribbean Linguistics*.
Shilling, Alison
  1978   Some non-standard features of Bahamian dialect syntax. Ph.D. dissertation, University of Hawaii.
  1980   Bahamian English: A non-continuum? In: Day (ed.), 133–146.
Trudgill, Peter, Daniel Schreier, Daniel Long, and Jeff Williams
  2003   On the reversibility of mergers: /w/, /v/ and evidence from lesser-known Englishes. *Folia Linguistica Historica* 24: 23–45.
Wolfram, Walt, and Jason Sellers
  1998   The North Carolina connection in Cherokee Sound. *North Carolina Literary Review* 7: 86–87.
Wolfram, Walt, Becky Childs, and Benjamin Torbert
  2000   Tracing English dialect history through consonant cluster reduction: Comparative evidence from isolated dialects. *Southern Journal of Linguistics* 24: 17–40.

Jamaican Creole and Jamaican English: phonology

Hubert Devonish and Otelemate G. Harry

1. Introduction

1.1. The language situation

The popular perception within Jamaica of the Jamaican language situation is that it consists of two varieties. One is Jamaican Creole (JamC) popularly labelled 'Patwa' and the other Jamaican English (JamE). According to this view, the educated minority able to function in both varieties use the former in private, informal and predominantly oral interaction and the latter mainly in public, formal and written discourse. Viewed as a language situation with two varieties used in the complementary manner described, the Jamaican speech community is diglossic (Ferguson 1959), with JamC being the L variety and JamE the H.

For most speakers in Jamaica, formal education and writing are the main sources of knowledge of the idealised JamE variety labelled 'English'. On one hand, speakers, in their attempts to approximate the idealised norm of English, will, to varying degrees dependent in part on the extent of their formal education, fall short of their intended goal. On the other, speakers, in their approximations of JamC or Patwa, however, often fall short to varying degrees, mainly as a result of the intrusion of features which are associated with English. These linguistic features serve to distinguish between the Creole of educated bilinguals, on one hand, and uneducated near monolinguals on the other. As might be expected, the JamC speech of the former group tends to involve a greater degree of English interference than does the JamC of the latter.

1.2. History of the language varieties

Historically, JamC phonology represents the output of speakers of West African languages modifying the phonological shape of words coming into their speech from varieties of 17th century British English (Cassidy and Le Page [1967] 1980: xxxvii–lxiv). Items of English origin make up the vast majority of the lexicon of JamC. Whatever the historical origins of JamC, however, its phonological system is now the native phonological system of the vast majority of language users in Jamaica. Shared lexical cognates, coupled with the historical dominance of English, produces a linguistic ideology which considers JamC to be a form, albeit deviant, of English. JamE in contemporary Jamaica bears the main characteristics of standard varieties of English such as Standard British English, standard varieties used in the USA, Canada, etc. It, however, has features, particularly in its phonology, which mark it as peculiarly Jamaican. For us, JamE is the idealised form of English usage targeted by the educated population of Jamaica.

We propose that nearly all speakers of JamE, as the H language in the Jamaican diglossic situation, are native speakers of the L language, JamC. For them, JamE is a second language acquired mainly through formal education and writing, and is used for purposes of public and formal communication. JamC and JamE are, however, idealised forms of speech. Most actually occurring speech shows varying levels of interaction between each of these idealised systems. This interaction is systematic and rule governed. Against this background, speakers consider that the phonological relationship between the two varieties consists of correction rules applied to the phonological forms of JamC lexical items to produce their JamE equivalents.

Against this background, what we shall attempt here is to describe the phonology of the linguistic abstraction that is JamC and of the other that is JamE. We shall, in addition, attempt to provide evidence for the existence of JamC to JamE conversion rules and identify and describe how these operate. By way of evidence from the intermediate varieties, we shall seek to prove that JamC to JamE conversion rules lie at the core of the relationship between the phonologies of the two idealised language varieties. These rules operate, we shall demonstrate, within a context of the need to achieve a balance. This involves on one side the drive for the systematic convergence between the varieties to facilitate speakers shifting between them. On the other side is the need to maintain the separation between the two language varieties since, by remaining distinct, the varieties could carry out complementary social functions. We shall refer to this process as differential convergence.

1.3.   Theoretical framework

One of the characteristics of diglossia is the existence of linguistic convergence. In situations involving the functional separation of language varieties, speakers tend to modify their linguistic systems such that there is a level of one-to-one correspondence between elements of the coexisting systems (Gumperz and Wilson 1971: 154–166). Where some aspect of the linguistic system of one language variety is more complex than the other, there are consequences for trying to achieve this one-to-one correspondence.

Complexity may be defined in two ways. One system may make a greater number of distinctions than does another. Here, one consequence of convergence is that often the equivalent of a single form in a simple system may be two or more forms in a more complex system, one such form being common to both systems. Thus, in comparing the phonology of cognate lexical items of two language varieties, a form in the less complex system may be equivalent either to two or more cognate forms in a more complex one. The form in the more complex system will invariably predict its cognate in the less complex one, but not vice versa.

We make the following prediction about the relationship between phonological systems in the conditions of linguistic convergence which exist between JamC and JamE. If the simpler system, Variety A, has feature X and the more complex one, Variety B, has both the features X and Y, the initial hypothesis for speakers familiar with Variety A is that X in Variety A is equivalent to Y in Variety B. They thus convert all Xs to Ys in their effort to use Variety B. Later, with more exposure to B, speakers of A will learn that sometimes X in their native variety is equivalent to X in the target variety and only sometimes to Y. For speakers to know the difference requires lexical specification of individual items.

We make a second prediction about the relationship between the varieties in such conditions. Linguistic categories or variables often exist in pairs, e.g. the realisation of segments equivalent to JamE /θ/ versus the realisation of segments equivalent to JamE /ð/, or the realisation of segments equivalent to JamC /ia/ versus those equivalent to JamC /ua/. Let us take the case of pairs of related linguistic variables, Variables 1 and 2, which, in Variety A have reflexes T and X respectively, and in Variety B, U and Y. We predict that in actual everyday usage of Variety A, only one of the two Variety A reflexes, e.g. T, will be consistently used. The other, X, will be used varying with Y, the variant associated with Variety B. Along similar lines, in the case of Variety B, only one of the two Variety B reflexes, this time Y, will be used consistently. The other, U, will vary with T, the form associated with Variety A. This is demonstrated in the table below.

(1)	Idealised usage		Actual speech	
	Variable 1	Variable 2	Variable 1	Variable 2
Variety A	T	X	T	X~Y
Variety B	U	Y	T~U	Y

The relationship between JamC and JamE presented in (1) represents a classic example of differential convergence.

2. The vowel system

2.1. Jamaican Creole

2.1.1. The main vowels

JamC has twelve phonemic oral vowels. These are divided into five simple and seven complex vowels, as in (2) below:

(2)
	Simple			Complex		
i		u		ii		uu
e		o				
	a		ia, ai	aa	ua, au	

The relationship between the simple vowels and their longer equivalents is primarily one of length rather than that of height or tenseness (Cassidy and Le Page 1980: xlv). Following Cassidy and Le Page, we represent phonetically long vowels by a double vowel, e.g. /ii/, /aa/ and /uu/ rather than the /ː/ symbol. The aim here is to avoid obscuring the connection between these double-vowel nuclei and the other complex syllabic nuclei consisting of sequences of non-identical vowels.

Only two features, [back] and [high], are necessary to describe the vowel set. An analysis of the complex vowel set presented above shows that only the extreme vowels in the simple set, the high and the low, i.e. /i/, /a/ and /u/, combine to produce complex vowel phonemes. The combinations, as can be seen, are quite limited. The low vowel phoneme, /a/, neutral for the feature [back], combines either with itself in second position, or with a high counterpart, either the front vowel, /i/ or the back one, /u/. The high vowels either combine with themselves to produce long vowels, /ii/ and /uu/ respectively, or with the low vowel to produce the diphthongs /ia/ and /ua/. The system does not allow, within the same syllable nucleus, for the combination of vowels with different values for the feature, back, i.e. */ui/ or */iu/. Such sequences get realised by the first vowel functioning as a consonant, i.e. a semi-vowel.

The complex vowels, /ia/, /ua/ and /au/, are represented by Cassidy and Le Page (1980: xxxix) as /ie/, /uo/ and /ou/ respectively. However, they describe /ie/ as a diphthong covering the range between [iɛ] and [iɐ], /uo/, the range between [uo] and [ua], /ou/, the range between [ɵu] and [ɐu], and /ai/ the range between [ɐi] and [ɐɛ]. They also report that the simple vowel, /a/, covers the range between [a], [ɐ] and [ɑ]. We agree with their phonetic observations, but use these observations to arrive at quite different conclusions about the underlying phonemic representation of JamC diphthongs. Given that [a] and/or [ɐ] are the common denominators in all of the four diphthongs and that both of these are allophones of the simple vowel, /a/, we conclude that it is this same /a/ which appears underlyingly as the low vowel in all diphthongs.

(3) Phonetic realisations of JamC vowel phonemes

	Test words		Gloss/Lexical sets
/i/	[ɪ] ~ [i]	[fɪt] ~ [fit]	FIT
		[api]	*happ*Y
/e/	[ɛ]	[dʒɛs] ~ [dʒɹɛs]	DRESS
/a/	[a] ~ [ɐ]	[tʃɹap] ~ [tʃɐp]	TRAP
		[lat]	LOT
/o/	[ɵ] ~ [o]	[kʰɵp] ~ [kʰop]	CUP
		[lɛta]	*lett*ER
		[kama]	*comm*A
		[nors]	NURSE
/u/	[ʊ] ~ [u]	[fʊt] ~ [fut]	FOOT
/ii/	[iː]	[pʰiːs]	PIECE
/aa/	[aː]	[baːt]	BATH
		[kʰlaːt]	CLOTH
		[pʰaːm]	PALM
		[braːd]	BROAD
		(THOUGHT)	
		[naːt]	NORTH
		[tʰaːt] ~ [staːt]	START
/uu/	[uː]	[luːs]	LOOSE
/ia/	[iɛ] ~ [ie] ~ [ia]	[fiɛs] etc.	FACE
		[niɛr] etc.	NEAR
		[kwiɛr] ~ [skwiɛr] etc.	SQUARE
/ua/	[uo] ~ [ua]	[guot]	GOAT
		[fuos]	FORCE
/ai/	[ai]	[pʰrais]	PRICE
		[tʃais]	CHOICE
/au/	[aʊ] ~ [ɵʊ]	[maʊt] etc.	MOUTH

In our analysis, the phoneme /a/, when it shares a syllable nucleus with the high front vowel phoneme, /i/, is realised phonetically as the mid-front vowel, [ɛ]. This gives rise to the phonetic realisation, [iɛ], for the diphthong which we represent as /ia/. Along similar lines, /a/, when it shares a syllabic nucleus with the high back vowel /u/ is phonetically realised as the back vowel [o] in diphthongs /ua/ and /au/ producing the phonetic realisations [uo] and [ou].

2.1.2. Nasal vowels

As is normal in many language varieties, vowels in JamC are nasalized in the environment of nasal consonants. The examples below demonstrate this.

(4) a. /faam/   [fã:m]   'farm'
    b. /muun/   [mũ:n]   'moon'
    c. /wan/   [wãn]   'one, the indefinite article'
    d. /som/   [sõm]   'some'
    e. /im/   [ĩm]   'he, she, him, her'
    f. /dem/   [dɛ̃m]   'they, them, their'

There is a phonological rule which applies to monosyllabic grammatical morphemes ending in a nasal consonant. This vowel may be deleted leaving only the nasalisation on the vowel to signal its underlying presence. Note that, in the case of /wan/, which has both a lexical meaning 'one', and that of the indefinite article, it is only the latter, as shown in (5) a. below, which allows for the optional deletion of the final nasal.

(5) a. /wan/   [wã]   ~   [wãn]   'the indefinite article'
    b. /som/   [sõ]   ~   [sõm]   'some'
    c. /im/   [ĩ]   ~   [ĩm]   'he, she, him, her'
    d. /dem/   [dɛ̃]   ~   [dɛ̃m]   'they, them, their'

Distinct from nasal allophones of the vowel phonemes, there is a nasal vowel phoneme. This vowel is /ãã/ with the phonetic realisation of [ã:]. It appears in a small number of quite regularly used words. In the examples below, we see a case of a contrast in identical environments, involving the first pair, and, in the second pair, a contrast in analogous environments. These contrasts establish the phonemic status of /ãã/ in relation the phonetically closest vowel phoneme, /aa/, independent of suprasegmental features, which remain constant in each member of the pairs below.

(6) a. /waan/   [wã:n]   'warn'   b. /kaan/   [kã:n]   'corn'
       /wãã/   [wã:]   'want'   /kjãã/   [kjã:]   'can't'

JamC syllables with /ãã/ as their nucleus tend to have an equivalent syllable in JamE cognates consisting of the vowel /aa/ or /ɔɔ/ and a post-vocalic /nt/ cluster. Even though /nt/ exists in the vast majority of JamC items with English /nt/ cognates, e.g. /plaant/ 'plant', /aant/ 'haunt', etc., a small group of items such as /wãã/ 'want' and /kjãã/ 'can't' appear in JamC minus the word final /nt/ cluster of the English cognate. It is this fact which creates the lexical contrast.

2.1.3. Underspecified vowels

In words with an initial non-prominent syllable possessing a vowel in the environment /s/ _ Nasal Consonant, the vowel may predictably be either /i/ or /u/ depending on the phonological effects of the environment. In these words, the vowel is specified for the feature [high]. It is not, however, specified for the feature [back]. The reason is that the [back] feature, giving rise to /u/, in contrast to /i/, is predictable from the phonological environment. The [back] feature assigned to the vowel comes from the immediate environment. It may be assigned from the immediately following nasal when this is bilabial, i.e. /m/. The underspecified vowel derives its [back] feature here through the transfer of labiality, since back vowels in JamC are labial, i.e. produced with lip rounding. Otherwise, the back feature may be derived from the vowel of the immediately following syllable when such a vowel itself has the feature [back]. These items are all lexically specified as having an initial /sV/ sequence where V stands for the underspecified vowel, i.e. specified for [high] but not for [back] as demonstrated by the examples in the first two columns below.

(7) Underlying rep.	With back feature	Vowel devoicing (optional)	
/sV'maal/	[su'maːl]	[su̥'maːl]	'small'
/sV'mel/	[su'mɛl] ~ [si'mɛl]	[su̥'mɛl] ~ [si'mɛl]	'smell'
/sV'mit/	[si'mit]	[si̥'mit]	'Smith'
/sV'niak/	[si'niɛk]	[si̥'niɛk]	'snake'
/sV'nuar/	[su'nuor]	[su̥'nuor]	'snore'

Cassidy and Le Page (1980: lxii) note that the initial syllables in examples such as those above may be produced as a syllabic [s̩]. Meade (1995: 33) refers to Akers (1981) as making a similar observation. We would argue that this is a case of the underspecified vowel in the /sV/ sequence becoming optionally devoiced under the influence of the preceding voiceless fricative, producing phonetically [s] and a voiceless vowel, i.e. [si̥] or [su̥]. These forms are phonetically indistinguishable from the syllabic form, [s̩] proposed by Cassidy and Le Page. [si̥] and [su̥] are merely optional forms of [s̩] when the following consonant is a sonorant, as represented in the third column of the table. Where

the following consonant is a voiceless stop, as in /sVp/, /sVt/ and /sVk/, [si̥]
and [su̥] are the only possible manifestations of the underspecified vowel in an
entirely voiceless environment. In such sequences, the underspecified vowel is
obligatorily devoiced.

2.1.4. *Vowel variation*

There is variation between /au/ and /ua/ in the following items in JamC.

(8) a.   /bual/ ~ /baul/   'bowl (noun)'
    b.   /ual/ ~ /aul/   'old'
    c.   /kual/ ~ /kaul/   'cold'

This variation, however, seems restricted to these and perhaps one or two other
lexical items. For some speakers, in particular educated bilinguals, the choice
of the variant employing /au/ in these items is intended to signal an extreme or
intensive meaning, i.e. /aul/ 'extremely old', /kaul/ 'extremely cold'. This may
be a result of the fact that the /au/ version is an unusual reflex for JamE /oo/.
This deviation from the expected is interpreted to signal, at least for the bilinguals, a deeper and more extreme meaning than the regular JamC /ua/ reflex
would signal. In the case of the attributives meaning 'old' and 'cold', the /au/
alternant is only possible when the item is used as a predicator. When performing an adjective type function within a noun phrase, the /au/ alternant is not
possible in JamC. This is demonstrated in the following examples.

(9) a.   /di man ual ~ aul/   'the man is old'
    b.   /di plias kual ~ kaul/   'the place is cold'
    c.   /dis ual ~ *aul man a kil mi/ 'this old man is killing me'
    d.   /dis kual ~ *kaul plies a kil mi/ 'this cold place is killing me'

The awareness of the possibilities of alternation between /ua/ ~ /au/ is high
within the speech community, perhaps because of its lexical role. This is exploited for poetic effect by Bennett (1966: 126), in which she writes the JamC
item for 'roll', which is normally /rual/, as 'rowl', intending a pronunciation
/raul/, since it is used to rhyme in the poem with /faul/ 'fowl'. In addition, there
was the Dance Hall piece by Mr Vegas, 'Heads High', in which all the entire
rhyme scheme was based on the conversion of /ua/ into /au/, e.g. /nua/ 'no' to
/nau/, /shua/ 'show' to /shau/, etc. In JamC speech, the form /oo/ very often
varies with /ua/. The former is the equivalent vowel in JamE. The equivalent
JamE front vowel, /ee/, however, is not frequent as an intrusion into speech
which, otherwise, is consistently JamC in its features.

2.1.5. *Vowel assimilation across syllable boundary*

Sequences of /i/ across morpheme boundary produced in rapid speech usually participate in syllable amalgamation. When the two /i/ phonemes, as a result of syllable amalgamation across word boundary, appear in the same syllable, a long vowel, [iː] is produced, phonetically identical to the [iː] realisation of the vowel phoneme, /ii/. This supports our proposal to treat long vowels as being phonologically a sequence of two identical vowels. Examples are presented in (10) below.

(10) a. /si + it/   →   [siːt]
         see it   'See it'
     b. /im + a + luk + fi + it/ → [im a luk fiːt]
         he/she is look for it   'He/She is looking for it'

We have posited that the most complex syllable nucleus involves a VV sequence, i.e. either a long vowel or a diphthong. This is demonstrated by syllable amalgamation across morpheme boundaries involving V and VV sequences as in the example below. There, we see an underlying sequence of V+VV, i.e. /u + aa/, becoming C+VV, /w + aa/, with the C being the semi-vowel, /w/, carrying the feature [back] previously associated with the underlying /u/ vowel. A VVV syllable is avoided by the device or converting the vowel /u/ to the corresponding semi-vowel, /w/, i.e. making it function as a feature superimposed on a preceding consonant rather than a vowel.

(11)   /gu + aan/   →   [gʷaːn]
         go on   'Go on'

The rule which triggers syllable amalgamation across a morpheme boundary also applies to sequences of /u + i/. This demonstrates another aspect of our basic vowel analysis. We already noted that the sequence */ui/ is not possible within the same syllable nucleus. In the example below, when /u + i/ merge to produce a single syllable, adjustments there need to be made. In order to eliminate the tautosyllabic */ui/ sequence, the [back] feature borne by /u/ is shifted into a consonantal position in the onset, producing the semi-vowel /w/. This shift of the [back] feature to a consonant slot leaves the complex syllable nucleus with an unfilled vowel slot. This is filled by a spread of the values of the [back] and [high] features from the remaining vowel in the nucleus, producing a tautosyllabic [w + iː] sequence as in the examples below.

(12) a. /ju + neva + du + it/ →   [ju neva dʷiːt]
             you not do it   'You had not done it'
     b. /a + wa + du + im/   →   [a wa dʷiːm]
             is what do him   'What is the matter with him?'

This establishes what we have already proposed, that vowels with the features [high] and [back] cannot co-occur in the same syllable nucleus. Thus, the amalgamated syllable has been modified to accommodate the principle that high vowels occurring in the same syllable have to agree for the feature [back]. In our discussion of JamC syllable structure, we shall see that vocalic sequences [ui] and [iu] only occur provided the initial vowel in the sequence occupies a C-slot, i.e. functions as a semi-vowel.

Some syllables with the double vowel, /ii/, are the product of lexical specification with the vowel /ii/, e.g. an item like /tiit/ 'teeth', while others are derived from syllable amalgamation across word boundary, e.g. /siit/ < /si it/ 'see it' and /dwiit/ from /du it/ 'do'. Irrespective of their derivation, however, these double vowel sequences are treated within the phonological system of JamC as identical. This is demonstrated by the rhyme below. The nucleus /ii/ produced by lexical specification in /tiit/ participates in a rhyme with two syllables, /siit/ and /dwiit/, whose vowel /ii/ is the product of syllable amalgamation.

(13)	Skin ju tiit	'Show your teeth [smile]'
	An mek mi siit	'And make me see it'
	Mek mi nuo fram ju baan se	
	ju neva dwiit	'Let me know from the time you were born you have never done it.'
		(Mr Vegas, 'Heads High')

2.1.6. Distribution of vowels

There is a difference in the distribution of vowels across prominent as opposed to non-prominent syllables. In prominent syllables, any vowel can appear in word-final position. By contrast, in non-prominent open syllables, /ii/, /ia/, /uu/, /ua/ and /aa/ are blocked from occurring word finally. This reduces the range of vowel contrasts in such syllables to the three simple vowels, /i/, /a/ and /u/, and to the diphthongs /ai/ and /au/.

This distribution is well illustrated by the reduplicated items shown below. When the vowel in the non-final syllable is made up of complex nuclei, /ii/ or /uu/, the one in the final syllable will take the form of /i/ and /u/. Where the non-final syllable has either /ai/ or /au/ as its nucleus, these are maintained in the final syllable.

(14)	a.	/fii-fi/	'toy whistle'
	b.	/duu-du/	'faeces'
	c.	/pai-pai/	'pistol'
	d.	/pau-pau/	'nickname derived from the first syllable of "Powell"'

Where the complex vowel is /ia/ or /ua/, the reduced version is /e/ and /o/. With the simple version of the syllable appearing in second position in these reduplicated items, there is need to express on a single vowel segment both the feature High and the absence of High. This is done by way of the phonetically mid-vowels, /e/ and /o/, respectively. These are results which would be predicted from the analysis of the JamC phonological system, as seen in the examples below.

(15) a.   /sua-so/   'alone, by itself'
      b.   /tua-to/   'a kind of small cake'
      c.   /dua-do/   'dough, bread, dumpling'

2.2.   Jamaican English

2.2.1.   The main vowels

Below, we present our proposals for the vowel system of JamE.

(16)   Simple   Complex
        i   u   ii   uu
        e   o   ee   oo
                    ɔ   ɔɔ
        a   aa
                                                        ɔi
                                        ai   au

We propose here that JamE has 15 vowels. These are made up of six simple vowels. The three features necessary to describe these involve
(i)   high, covering /i/ and /u/,
(ii) back, covering /u/, /o/ and /ɔ/, and
(iii) low, covering /a/ and /ɔ/.
Redundantly, every vowel with the feature [back] also has the feature [labial].
    There are nine complex vowels in JamE, six of these being double vowels. Each simple vowel has a complex counterpart in the form of a long or double version of itself, i.e. /ii/, /ee/, /aa/, /ɔɔ/, /oo/ and /uu/. This introduces length or doubling as a feature which is characteristic of JamE complex nuclei. The remaining three complex vowels are diphthongs, rising from a low or lower-mid vowel to a high vowel. The first vowel element is always one of the two Low vowels, either /a/ or /ɔ/.

Wells (1973: 25) proposes that JamE has 16 vowels. His sixteenth vowel, /ɔɔ/, is treated by us as an allophone of /o/ when this vowel occurs before a tautosyllabic /r/.

(17) Phonetic realisations of JamE vowel phonemes

Test words

/i/	[ɪ]	[fɪt]	FIT
		[hapi]	*happ*Y
/e/	[ɛ]	[dʒɪɛs]	DRESS
/a/	[a] ~ [ɐ]	[tʃɹap]	TRAP
/ɔ/	[ɔ]	[lɔt]	LOT
/o/	[ɵ] ~ [o] ~ [ə:]	[kʰɵp] ~ [kʰop]	CUP
		[lɛto] ~ [lɛtə:ɹ]	*lett*ER
		[kʰɔmo]	*comm*A
		[nə:rs]	NURSE
/u/	[ʊ] ~ [u]	[fʊt] ~ [fut]	FOOT
/ii/	[i:]	[pʰi:s]	PIECE
/aa/	[a:]	[ba:θ]	BATH
		[pʰa:m]	PALM
		[sta:ɹt]	START
/ɔɔ/	[ɔ:]	[bɹɔ:d], [klɔ:θ]	BROAD, CLOTH
		[nɔ:ɹθ]	NORTH
		[brɔ:d]	BROAD
		[θɔ:t]	THOUGHT
/oo/	[o:]	[go:t]	GOAT
		[fo:ɹs]	FORCE
/uu/	[u:]	[lu:s]	LOOSE
/ee/	[e:]	[fe:s] etc.	FACE
		[ne:ɹ] etc.	NEAR
		[skwe:ɹ] etc.	SQUARE
/ai/	[ai]	[pʰɹais]	PRICE
/ɔi/	[ɔi]	[tʃɔis]	CHOICE
/au/	[aʊ] ~ [ɵʊ]	[maʊt] ~ [mɵʊθ]	MOUTH

The length feature implicit in our vowel inventory does not match the approach of Meade (2001: 42) to JamE vowels. He suggests that the main phonetic feature distinguishing between short vowels and long monophthongs was tenseness, with the short ones being lax and the long ones tense. This position, on the face of it, seems justified by the fact that, in JamE, much more so than in JamC, the non-low long vowels differ from their short equivalents not just in length but in height and tenseness. The long non-low vowels are always higher and tenser than their short equivalents. Whatever the merits of Meade's approach for JamE, there is contradicting evidence. This involves the relationship between the third pair of vowels, /a/ and /aa/, in which no height or tense differences are involved. Length is the sole distinguishing feature here. Thus, if one is seeking to find a feature which distinguishes all short vowels in JamE from all long monophthongs, then tenseness versus laxness would not do the job but length would. It is on these grounds that we single out length as the primary distinction between these pairs, with relative height and tenseness being secondary, predictable features of the distinction in the case of the non-low vowels. This approach is much more economical than that of Meade (2001: 42) which proposes that tenseness is the primary feature for the non-low pairs of vowels, and length the primary one for the low pair.

2.2.2. Nasal vowels

Vowels are phonetically nasalized in the environment of nasal consonants, for example,

(18) a. /fan/   [fãn]   'fan'
      b. /neːm/   [nẽː]   'name'
      c. /kɔin/   [kɔ̃ɪn]   'coin'.

JamE does not allow the variable deletion of a nasal consonant, leaving nasalisation of the preceding vowel as the only evidence of its presence underlyingly. Thus, JamE [sõm] 'some', unlike its JamC cognate, can never be realised as *[sõ] 'some'. In addition, the attested role of phonemic vowel nasalization JamC is absent in JamE. In JamC, there are items lexically specified to have a nasalized vowel with no following nasal consonant. In JamE, no such items exist. Below are the JamE cognates of the JamC items with lexically specified nasalized vowels. As can be seen, they both occur in JamE with an /nt/ sequence in the coda.

(19) a. /wɔɔnt/   [wɔ̃ːnt]   'want'
      b. /kjãant/ ~ /kãant/   [kjãːnt] ~ [kãːnt] 'can't'

2.2.3. Underspecified vowels

There are no underspecified vowels in the JamE of the type already noted for JamC. The result is that JamC words with such vowels have JamE cognates in which they are absent. This is demonstrated by the following examples.

(20) Jamaican Creole   Jamaican English
       /sV'maal/   [su maal] ~ [sumaal]   /smɔɔl/   [smɔːl]   'small'
       /sV'mel/   [su'mɛl] ~ /si'mɛl/   /smel/   [smɛl]   'smell'
       /sV'mit/   [si'mit]   /smiӨ/   [smɪθ]   'Smith'
       /sV'niak/   [si'niek]   /sneek/   [sneːk]   'snake'
       /sV'nuar/   [si'nuor]   /snoor/   [snoːr]   'snore'
       /sV'kuul/   [su'kuːl]   /skuul/   [skuːl]   'school'

Assuming as we do a derivation based on the JamC lexical form, there would also be the cases like JamC /tap/ 'stop', /tik/ 'stick', which would first have an initial /sV/ syllable produced as part of the process of conversion to English. Only then could the deletion of the underspecified V take place.

Our suggestion that at least some speakers do function from a JamC lexical input, applying conversion rules to these inputs, is supported by the example below involving two phonologically variant JamE forms for the word 'cement' and 'suppose'. The vowels /i/ and /u/ in the JamC items /siment/ and /supuoz/ have a distribution which is typical of the JamC underspecified V. There is evidence that at least some speakers apply, in the case of these items, the regular deletion of underspecified Vs to the first vowel in the JamC item. This can be seen in the second variant of each of these words presented below.

(21) Jamaican Creole   Jamaican English
       /sVment/ ~ {/siment/?}   /sment/ ~ /siment/   'cement'
       /sVpuaz/ ~ {/supuaz/?}   /spooz/ ~ /supooz/   'suppose'

Some speakers are aware of English norms in relation to the words 'cement' and 'suppose', in particular how the words are spelt in that language. This awareness is likely to cause them to treat the vowel of the first syllable in the presumed JamC inputs, /sVment/ and /sVpuaz/, as lexical exceptions. The JamC underspecified vowel, phonetically [i] or [u], should not be deleted to produce /sC/ consonant clusters in JamE. For speakers who do not have this as a lexically marked exception to their JamC to JamE conversion rule, the less socially acceptable JamE options, /sment/ and /spooz/, are produced. Speakers who do not apply the underspecified V deletion rule in these cases are likely in their JamC lexicon to have fully specified vowels for these items. This possibility is suggested by the question-marked JamC representations in the examples above.

2.2.4. Vowel variation

In JamE, the item /bool/ 'bowl', but not /oold/ 'old' and /koold/ 'cold' have the variant /au/ pronunciation we have already seen for the cognates in JamC.

The JamE variant form is /baul/. Irvine (2004) refers to a much revised school text in which 'bowl' is listed as having the same vowel as 'cow', 'towel', 'out', 'couch' and 'round'. She suggests that this pronunciation has been or is in the process of being normalized by this particular text. As Irvine notes, speakers who pronounced the noun 'bowl' as /baul/ distinguish it from the verb 'bowl' by pronouncing the latter /bool/.

The forms [uo] and [iɛ] are not part of the idealised phonological system of JamE. They nevertheless occur as variants respectively of the /oo/ and /ee/ variables. The idealised JamE variants are [oː] and [eː] respectively. The diph-thongal variants are clearly the result of diachronic and/or synchronic conver-gence with JamC. In this matching pair of back and front long vowel variables, the convergence with JamC is not exercised evenly. Irvine (2004) examines the formal JamE speech of a group of persons who, as a result of deliberate selection based on their speech to represent Jamaica in a promotional role, can be considered to represent models of idealised JamE speech. She finds that, for the back variable, there is 11% use of the [uo] variant, by comparison to 89% [oː]. However, the [iɛ] variant for the front variable appears 24% of the time as compared with 76% for [eː]. The JamC associated phone, [uo], is much less used and arguably a much more stigmatised JamC interference feature than is [iɛ]. By contrast, the frequency of the latter suggests that it is fairly well en-trenched as a variant JamE vowel form.

Significantly, the acceptability of the phone [iɛ] in JamE is concentrated in the environment before /r/, e.g. /beer/ > [biɛɹ] ~ [beːɹ] 'beer, bear', rather than elsewhere, e.g. /plee/ which would tend to have only [pleː] as its phonetic realisation (A. Irvine, p.c.). The differential convergence at work here may be focussed in and confined to a specific phonological environment.

2.2.5.   Vowel assimilation across syllables

This feature, as described for JamC, is absent from JamE. Sequences such as /duu it/ 'Do it', /sii it/ 'See it', /goo ɔːn/, 'Go on', etc. tend not to become monosyllabic in JamE. They retain their bisyllabic identity.

2.3.   From Jamaican Creole to Jamaican English: The vowel system

The only difference between the vowel inventories of the two language varieties involves the vowel /ɔ/ which exists in JamE but not in JamC. There is, therefore, for most vowels, a one-to-one relationship between JamC and JamE variants in cognate lexical items. However, there are three JamC vowels for which there are two possible JamE reflexes. These all involve the JamE vowel /ɔ/, once as a simple vowel and twice as part of the complex vowels, /ɔɔ/ and /ɔi/. Below are presented the vowel variants or reflexes across the two language varieties.

(22) Jamaican Creole   Jamaican English

/i/	=	/i/
/e/	=	/e/
/a/	=	/a/, /ɔ/
/o/	=	/o/
/u/	=	/u/
/ii/	=	/ii/
/ia/	=	/ee/
/aa/	=	/aa/, /ɔɔ/
/ua/	=	/oo/
/uu/	=	/uu/
/ai/	=	/ai/, /ɔi/
/au/	=	/au/

We argue that JamE phonological outputs are based on JamC lexical specifications modified by established conversion rules. These rules, we propose, are based on stereotypical notions of the difference between the phonetic outputs of lexical entries in JamC versus the phonetic outputs of their cognates in JamE. The level of success achieved by speakers operating these rules firstly depends on whether the correspondences between JamC and JamE are one-to-one or one-to-many. In the cases of JamC /ia/ > JamE /ee/ and JamC /ua/ > /oo/, we are dealing with one-to-one correspondences. The application of the conversion rule is, therefore, straightforward. The problem is less a linguistic one than a psychological one. With what consistency are speakers actually able to apply these conversion rules? Bilingual speakers will look for ways to keep the language varieties apart while minimising the effort they put into doing so, giving rise to what we have called differential convergence between the varieties. We have already seen the evidence which suggests that speakers, in their use of JamE, employ more consistently the JamE variant, [oo], in the /ua/ ~ /oo/ variable than they do the JamE variant, [iɛ] in the /ia/ > /ee/ one. Here, speakers economise on their efforts to keep JamC and JamE apart, by avoiding JamC features more consistently in the former variable than in the latter. As we have already seen, also, this economy of effort may be most active in the environment immediately preceding /r/.

Where two possible JamE reflexes exist for one JamC vowel, matters are more complex. Usually, one JamE reflex is identical phonetically to that in JamC. The other one, however, represents a phonetic form which does not exist in JamC. For any item, the JamE cognate might have a phonetic output identical to its JamC equivalent. On the other hand, the JamE cognate may take the phonetic form that does not exist in JamC. It is the second possibility which is most likely to attract the attention of a speaker relatively unfamiliar with JamE. This produces naïve conversions. Thus, in the variables involving JamE /a/ and /ɔ/ respectively, a naïve conversion would change all the JamC occurrences of /a/, /aa/ and /ai/ to JamE /ɔ/, /ɔɔ/ and /ɔi/. This approach presumes a one-to-one correspondence with JamC /a/ > JamE /ɔ/ and retains a feature characteristic of JamC:

(i)   the vowels of 'tap' and 'top' not distinguished, here realised as /tɔp/,

(ii) the vowels of 'mass' and 'moss' not distinguished, both realised as /mɔɔs/, and

(iii) the vowels of 'tile' and 'toil' not distinguished, both realised as /tɔil/.

This is typically discussed in the literature as hypercorrection and is one of the shibboleths of the speech community. It marks the speaker off as uneducated and unaware that the JamC > JamE conversion involves, based on lexical specification, either the form /a/, approximating phonetically to its JamC equivalent, or the form /ɔ/. For many speakers, the lexical marking is done using as a reference the way the words are spelt in English orthography.

3.   The consonant system

3.1.   Jamaican Creole

3.1.1. The consonants

There are 21 phonemic consonants in JamC. These include the semi-vowels, /w/ [w] and /j/ [j], which are the phonetic vowels [i] and [u] functioning as consonants due to distributional constraints.

The palatal stops /kj/ [c], /gj/ [ɟ] and /ny/ [ɲ] proposed by Cassidy and Le Page (1980) are not included in our inventory because we consider these phonetic palatals to be sequences of stops and the semi-vowels (cf. Devonish and Seiler 1991).

(23)   m   n   ɳ
       p   t   k   tʃ
       b   d   g   dʒ
       f   s   ʃ
       v   z
       r   l
       w   j   (h)

One feature little remarked on in the discussion of JamC consonant phonology over the years is the phonetics of the stop phonemes, /b/, /d/ and /g/. When these occur in the onset of a prominent syllable, they are phonetically realised as ingressive stops, [ɓ], [ɗ] and [ɠ]. In other environments, notably in the coda or in the onset of a non-prominent syllable, the egressive [b], [d] and [g] allophones are employed. The distribution of these stops parallels that of the aspirated and unaspirated allophones of the voiceless stops, /p/, /t/ and /k/, with the aspirated allophones, [pʰ], [tʰ] and [kʰ] occurring in the onset of prominent syllables, and the unaspirated ones, [p], [t] and [k], elsewhere.

Wells (1973: 12) suggests that /h/ occurs contrastively in the Western varieties of JamC, notably those of Manchester, St. Elizabeth and Westmoreland. This is supported by the intuitions of JamC speakers from the entire range of western parishes. For such speakers, /h/ would serve to distinguish between the following pairs.

(24) a.   /an/   'and'   /han/   'hand'
     b.   /iar/   'air'   /hiar/   'hair'

Such contrasts do not exist in the Eastern varieties of JamC, inclusive of that of Kingston. It is not, however, that the phone [h] does not exist in these varieties. Rather, it is employed for a different phonological function. Thus, the items above would, in the eastern varieties, be realised variably as [an] ~ [han] 'and, hand' and [iɛɹ] ~ [hiɛɹ] 'air, hair'. In items without a lexically specified onset consonant, [h] may variably appear as a marker of emphasis, as an '[h]emphatic' /h/. The phone [h], in the eastern varieties is simply marks off emphatic onset-less word initial syllables from their non-emphatic counterparts.

The consonant phoneme /ŋ/ has an unusual distribution in being the only one which is restricted to occurring in the coda.

3.1.2. Palatal and labial-velar consonants

The vowels /i/ and /u/ become the corresponding semi-vowels, /j/ and /w/, when they occupy a consonant position in the syllabic structure of lexical items. They occupy a position immediately preceding the vowel. Their presence in the onset, when preceded by velar and labial stops respectively, can produce phonetically palatal and labial-velar consonants whose role in the phonology of JamC has been the subject of some disagreement.

Cassidy and Le Page (1980: xxxix) treat [c] and [ɟ] as palatal consonant phonemes. By contrast, Devonish and Seiler (1991) treat them as consonant plus semi-vowel sequences, i.e. as combinations of /k/ or /g/ and /j/. We opt for the latter analysis. Were they underlyingly palatal stops, one would expect that they would also occur in the coda, as do all the other oral stop consonants. The consonant and semi-vowel is consistent with what we have noted about the structure of the onset, i.e. that the semi-vowel must immediately precede the vowel. Below are minimal pairs or near minimal pairs demonstrating the contrast between /kj/ and /gj/ on one hand, and /k/ and /g/ on the other.

(25) /kjuu/   'a quarter quart (of rum)'   /kuul/   'cool'
      /kjap/   'cap'   /kap/   'cop'
      /kjaaf/   'calf'   /kaaf/   'cough'
      /gjan /   'gang'   /gang/   'gong'
      /gjaad/   'guard'   /gaad/   'God'

Like the phonetic palatals, the labialized velars, [pʷ] and [bʷ], do not occur in syllable-final position and seem best dealt with as onset clusters consisting of stop consonant, /p/ or /b/, followed by the semi-vowel, /w/. The distribution is more restricted than the phonetic palatal stops, with [pʷ] and [bʷ] only normally occurring before the diphthong /ai/. Below are some minimal pairs illustrating the contrast between /pw/ and /bw/ on one hand, and /p/ and /b/ on the other.

(26) /bwai/   'boy'   /bai/   'buy'
      /pwail/   'spoil'   /pail/   'pile'
      /pwaint/ 'point'   /paint/   'pint'

3.1.3. Variation

Wells (1973: 11) does point to the historical basis for the variation between /b/ and /v/. It does seem that /v/ is a relatively recent entrant into the phoneme inventory of JamC, imported with modern loan words from JamE. The result is that some older JamC forms with /b/ have a reflex in JamE with /v/. These forms allow for /v/ ~ /b/ variation in modern JamC. However, more recent loans with a JamE /v/ reflex only allow for /v/ in JamC. Forms with /b/ in JamE do not vary in JamC, always retaining /b/.

(27) /beks/ ~ /veks/   'vexed'
      /neba/ ~ /neva/   'never'
      /vuot/   'vote'
      /van/   'van'
      /buat/   'boat'

3.1.4. Syllabic consonants

In JamC, consonants normally occur only at the margins of the syllable, i.e. in the onset or in the coda. However, there are two consonants which appear as syllabic nuclei. They are both required to be preceded by an oral consonant. Syllabic consonants produce an alternative syllable structure as presented below.

(28) (C) C [Syllabic Nasal/Lateral] (C)

In relation to the syllabic nasals, the phonemic distinction between the nasal stops /m/, /n/ and /ŋ/ in the onset and the coda is not maintained when nasals occur in the nucleus. There is simply a single syllabic nasal, /N̩/. This appears as the bilabial or the alveolar, depending on the place of articulation of the immediately preceding consonant. There seems to be a rule blocking the occurrence of a velar consonant before a syllabic nasal as can be seen by example c. below.

(29) Syllabic nasals
    a. /sompm̩/   'something'
    b. /miitn̩/   'meeting'
    c. */tuokn̩/ BUT /tuoken/   'token'

There seems to be an element of complementarity with the syllabic consonants. The other syllabic consonant, /l̩/, is restricted to occurring preceded by a velar consonant. Syllabic /l̩/ appears phonetically as a velarised or dark phone, [ɫ]. This has an impact on the selection of oral stops which may precede it. Oral alveolar and velar stops in syllable-initial position are normally contrastive. However, before a syllabic lateral, only velar consonants are allowed as in the examples below.

(30) a. /niigl̩/   [nĩːgl̩]   'needle'
      b. /bakl̩/   [bokl̩]   'bottle'
      c. /boŋgl̩/   [bõŋgl̩]   'bundle'

3.1.5. Constraints on the onset: /j/ and /w/

The composition of the onset may be constrained by the nature of the vowel(s) occupying the nucleus. We saw previously in the section on JamC vowels that vocalic sequences /ui/ and /iu/ do not occur. Put another way, however, phonetic [iu] and [ui] sequences are only possible provided the initial vowel in the sequence occupies a C-slot, i.e. functions as the semi-vowels /w/ and /j/

respectively. These produce the phoneme sequences /wi/ and /ju/. This is demonstrated in the following examples.

(31) a. /kjuu/   [kjuː]   'a quarter quart (of rum)'
     b. /mjuuzik/   [mjuːzik]   'music'
     c. /pjaa-pjaa/   [pjaːpjaː]   'weak'
     d. /kwiel/   [kwiɛl]   'to cause to wilt'
     e. /swimz/   [swimz]   'shrimp'

There is an uneasy relationship between /j/ and /w/ on one hand and their vocalic equivalents, /i/ and /u/, on the other. The occurrence of semi-vowels in
the onset is subject to a constraint which follows from their relationship with
vocalic segments. Underlyingly, syllable onsets tend not to consist of a semi-
vowel as the sole consonant, followed immediately by the vowel which is its
vocalic equivalent. This blocks underlying sequences such as */ji/ and */wu/.
Where [ji] and [wu] sequences do occur phonetically, it is in variation with a
form without the initial semi-vowel, e.g. [unu] ~ [wunu] 'you (plural)', [jimba]
~ [imba] 'a yam variety' (Cassidy and Le Page 1980: 225, 457).

   In JamC, the onset may have a maximum of two consonants. In such combinations, the first item is always an obstruent and the second an approximant.
Combinations with /w/ as the second consonant are /pw, bw, tw, dw, kw,
gw, sw/. Those involving /j/ include /pj, bj, tj, dj, kj, gj, fj, vj, sj, mj, nj/. Of
these, /tj/, /dj/ and /sj/ do not have transparent realisations at the surface level.
The matching phonetic forms, *[tj], *[dj] and *[sj] are blocked, in spite of a
contrary suggestion by Wells (1973: 21). They may be blocked because the
underlying phoneme sequences /tj/ /dj/ and /sj/ have their surface phonetic
manifestations merged by speakers with those of the affricate and fricative
consonant phonemes, /tʃ/, /dʒ/ and /ʃ/. Both sets of sequences become realised
phonetically as [tʃ], [dʒ] and [ʃ] respectively. The fact is, however, that the
consonants /tʃ/, /dʒ/ and /ʃ/ also occur in the coda, e.g. /matʃ/ 'match', /dʒodʒ/
'judge', /kjaʃ/ 'cash'. This establishes that [tʃ], [dʒ] and [ʃ] can and do represent the consonant phonemes /tʃ/, /dʒ/ and /ʃ/ rather than just underlying /tj/,
/dj/ and /sj/. We suggest nevertheless that in the onset, speakers do treat [tʃ],
[dʒ] and [ʃ] as representing a merger at the phonetic level between [tʃ], [dʒ]
and [ʃ], on one hand, and /tj/, /dj/ and /sj/ on the other.

   The only consonants occurring in the JamC onset which are blocked from
occurring before /j/ are /l/, /r/, /z/, /ʃ/, /tʃ/ and /dʒ/. Given the position of /l/
and /r/ in the sonority hierarchy, we may regard them as sonorant consonants
which, like /j/ and /w/, only occur in second position in the onset. An onset */zj/
cluster fails to occur because it cannot be phonetically reinterpreted. The expected form, */ʒ/, does not exist as a phoneme in JamC. The blocking of */ʃj/,

*/tʃj/ and */dʒj/ are, we would suggest, the result of the unacceptability of the alternative /sjj/, /tjj/ and /djj/ underlying representation. These would require a */jj/ sequence. The analysis is presented below.

(32)   /sj/   →   [ʃ]   ←   /ʃ/
        */zj/   →   *[ʒ]
        */ʃj/ = */sjj/
        */tʃ/ = */tjj/
        */dʒ/ = */djj/
        /tj/   →   [tʃ]   ←   /tʃ/
        /dj/   →   [dʒ]   ←   /dʒ/

The apparent occurrence of /dj/ on the surface as in /djam/ 'damn' really involves a disyllabic sequence /dijam/, with prominence on the second syllable.

3.1.6. Constraints on the onset: /r/ and /l/

The other approximants possible in second position in the onset are /r/ and /l/. When the obstruent consonant occupying initial position in such combinations is a stop, it may be either a voiced or a voiceless consonant. However, when it is a fricative, it must be [-voice] and [+anterior], i.e. it must be either /f/ or /s/. The allowed onset clusters involving initial stops are /pr/, /br/, /pl/, /bl/, /tʃr/, /dʒr/, /kr/, /gr/, /kl/, /l/. Those involving initial fricative consonants are /fr/, /fl/ and /sl/.

(33)   a.   /pria/   [prie]   'pray'
        b.   /briak/   [briek]   'brake'
        c.   /plia/   [plie]   'play'
        d.   /klaat/   [klaat]   'cloth'

Absent from the combinations listed above, though theoretically possible based on the cluster formation constraints mentioned, are /tr/, /dr/, /tl/, /dl/ and /sr/. This absence can be explained by a constraint which blocks onset clusters of consonants specified underlyingly for the features [anterior] and [coronal]. If, however, this constraint is interpreted to apply at the phonetic level instead, the way is open for the clusters involving initial phonetically alveopalatal affricates followed by [ɹ], i.e. [tʃɹ] and [dʒɹ], to be regarded by speakers as the surface output of underlying /tr/ and /dr/ clusters. This would produce a merger between the phonetic outputs of underlying /tr/ and /tʃr/, and /dr/ and /dʒr/. Members of each pair would be realised phonetically as [tʃɹ] and [dʒɹ] respectively.

We have already seen a fusing of /tj/ and /tʃ/ realised as [tʃ], and of /dj/ and /dʒ/, realised as [dʒ]. Where the phonetic realisations [tʃɹ] and [dʒɹ] are interpreted as involving the phonetic realisation of an underlyingly /tjr/ and /djr/, this would violate the constraint on there being no more than two consonants in the onset. This explains the fact, observed by Wells (1973: 10) that "/tr, dr/ are not altogether consistently contrastive with /tʃ/ and /dʒ/". This he illustrates with some examples, e.g. the variation between [tʃruu] ~ [tʃuu] 'true', the latter homophonous with [tʃuu] 'chew', and /dʒraa/ ~ /dʒaa/ 'draw', the latter homophonous with [dʒaa] 'jaw'. In each of the preceding pairs, the first form is based on an underlying /tr/ and /dr/ whereas the second is based on an adaptation of unacceptable underlying /tjr/ and /djr/ clusters.

3.1.7. Constraints on the coda: The distribution of /r/

In discussing the phonology of English-related language varieties, the issue of rhoticity is inevitably discussed. Post-vocalic syllable final /r/ occurs in items lexically specified to bear it. There is a constraint operating here, however. The immediately preceding segment in the nucleus in such cases has to be either /ia/, /ua/, /aa/ or /o/. (This distribution indicates that the preceding vowel segment must be /a/, whether this is linked to a V-slot as in the first three examples or to /o/, a vowel which we analyse elsewhere as consisting of a combination of the features associated with an /ia/ sequence, occupying, however, a single V slot.)

(34) a. /faar/   [faːɹ]   'far'
      b. /piar/   [piɛɹ]   'pear'
      c. /fuar/   [fuoɹ]   'four'
      d. /bor-bor/ [boɹboɹ]   'bur'

The phoneme /r/ is blocked from occurring after nuclei consisting of /a/, /ii/, /uu/, /ai/ and /au/. What these all lack, as opposed to /ia/, /ua/ and /o/ is the presence of an immediately preceding /a/, whether realised on the surface, as in the first three cases above, or underlyingly as in the last. JamC does not allow post-vocalic /r/ in the environment of a succeeding tautosyllabic consonant.

3.1.8. Constraints on the coda: The distribution of nasals

Nasal consonants may not appear in the coda when the nucleus consists of the diphthong /au/. The sequences so blocked are presented below.

(35) */aum/
      */aun/
      */auŋ/

It should be noted that this constraint is restricted to /au/ and does not apply to nuclei consisting of any of the other diphthongs, long vowels or short vowels in the language. The constraining effect which /au/ has on nasals in the coda has as its closest approximation the constraint already discussed involving /r/ in the coda. In the latter, however, the constraint operates with any vowel which does not have /a/ as the second element in the nucleus, either at the surface level or underlyingly. In the former case, by contrast, the constraint is restricted to a single diphthong, /au/. Of the three blocked combinations, it is /aun/ which assumes great sociolinguistic significance in the Jamaica language situation. This is because it is the one combination amongst those blocked by this constraint which occurs in JamE. All cognates which in JamE may appear with an /aun/ sequence are realised in JamC with /oŋ/.

Given the consistent pattern by which the more conservative varieties adapt JamE /aun/ patterns to /oŋ/ patterns, we may hypothesise that /ŋ/ is a velarised /n/, i.e. an /n/ with the velar feature of the vowel /u/ added to it. The source of the constraint on /aun/ in tautosyllabic sequences is, however, in a wider constraint which blocks /au/ from preceding any nasal, i.e. /m/, /n/ or /ŋ/.

3.1.9. Constraints on the coda: Consonant clusters

Like in onset clusters, a maximum of two consonants is allowed to occur in the coda. The coda clusters are much more robust than the onset clusters. Four types of bi-consonantal clusters are allowed in the coda.

Type 1: Nasal + voiceless stop cluster

Voiceless stops are allowed to precede nasals. Contrast between nasals is neutralized in this position. Only nasals having the same general place of articulation as the following stops are allowed to occur in this environment. Examples of Nasal + Stop clusters are given below.

(36) a. /tamp/ 'stamp'
       b. /sent/ 'cent'
       c. /tʃiŋk/ 'bedbug'
       d. /pintʃ/ 'pinch'

Type 2: Nasal + alveolar fricative

In this type, the alveolar fricatives follow the nasals. Unlike in type 1, in type 2, contrast between nasals is maintained in pre-alveolar fricative position. Examples are presented below.

(37)	a.	/glims/	'glimpse'
	b.	/mins/	'mince'
	c.	/spaanz/	'to span'
	d.	/aamz/	'alms-house'

Type 3: Voiceless stop + voiceless alveolar fricative

In type 3, where voiceless stops occur as the first consonant in the cluster, the following alveolar fricative must be voiceless. This is a case of voicing harmony, as the data illustrates.

(38)	a.	/mats/	'maths'
	b.	/saps/	'nerd'
	c.	/aaks/	'ask'

Type 4: Alveolar lateral + obstruents

The fourth type of coda cluster involves a lateral preceding obstruents, as shown below.

(39)	a.	/elp/	'help'
	b.	/saalt/	'salt'
	c.	/twelv/	'twelve'

3.1.10. The syllable structure: The vowel in the nucleus

It is against the phonotactic constraints already discussed that we are able to summarise the range of possible syllable structures in JamC. This may be summarised as follows:

(40)   (C)(C) V (V)(C)(C)

Some of the syllable types that can be derived from the structure above are exemplified in (41) below.

(41)	a.	/a/	[a]	V	'locational preposition'
	b.	/iat/	[iet]	VVC	'eight'
	c.	/ruas/	[ruos]	CVVC	'roast'
	d.	/pat/	[pat]	CVC	'pot'
	e.	/blua/	[bluo]	CCVV	'blow'
	f.	/plaant/	[plaːnt]	CCVVCC	'plant'

3.2.　Jamaican English

3.2.1.　The consonants

There are 24 consonants in the phonemic inventory of JamE, inclusive of the semi-vowels /w/ and /j/. The inventory below, adopted from Wells (1973: 26), shows the consonant phonemes of JamE.

(42)　Consonant phonemes of JamE

p	t	k	t
b	d	g	d
m	n	ŋ	
f	θ	s	ʃ
v	ð	z	ʒ
r	l		
w	j	h	

There are three consonant phonemes which exist in JamE but not in JamC. These are /θ/, /ð/ and /ʒ/. In JamE, by contrast with many varieties of JamC, /h/ is phonemic, appearing in this role in the same lexical items as it would in Standard British English.

3.2.2.　Palatals and labial velars

The distribution of palatals and labial velars in JamE is clearly influenced by the JamC-to-JamE conversion processes which many speakers carry out. One problem converting JamC lexical inputs into an acceptable JamE realisation is the fact that JamC /a/ may be realised as JamE /a/ or /ɔ/, depending on the lexical item. There is no way, taking the JamC phonological form, /pat/, of knowing whether the JamE form should be /pat/ 'pat' or /pɔt/ 'pot'. However, when JamC /a/ is part of a syllable with a palatal or labial velar stop onset, these invariably predict the correct JamE output.

Let us first take the palatals. In JamE, /kj/ and /ɡj/, phonetically palatal stops, [c] and [ɟ], have a distribution in which they vary with each other before /a/ and /aa/ but not in other environments. Thus, the item 'cap' has two realisations in JamE, /kap/ and /kjap/, whereas the items 'coo' /kuu/ and 'queue', /kjuu/ show a /k/ versus /kj/ phonemic contrast. The JamE /kap/ ~ /kjap/ 'cap' variation reflects the fact that /kj/ is part of the lexical specification of cognate items in JamC, serving to distinguish it from /kap/ 'cop'. With the JamE pronunciation of 'cop' being /kɔp/, the use of /kj/ in /kjap/ has no distinctive functional value.

It, however, represents a carry-over from JamC which, we argue, provides the lexical input that lies at the base of JamE phonetic output.

In the examples below, the item with /kj/ or /gj/ in the JamC item has /kj/ or /gj/ as variant forms in JamE, followed by /a/. The items which have /k/ or /g/ in the JamC item, require an invariant /k/ or /g/ in the JamE cognate and /ɔ/ as the following vowel. The weight of the phonemic distinction, transferred from the consonant in JamC to the vowel in JamE, is still expressed redundantly in the form of a residual /kj/ variant in JamE.

(43) Jamaican Creole   Jamaican English
      /kjap/   /kap/ ~ /kjap/   'cap'
      /kap/   /kɔp/   'cop'
      /kjaaf/   /kaaf/ ~ /kjaaf/   'calf'
      /kaaf/   /kɔɔf/   'cough'
      /gjaŋ/   /gaŋ/ ~ /gjaŋ/   'gang'
      /gaŋ/   /gɔŋ/   'gong'
      /gjaad/   /gaard/ ~ /gjaard/   'guard'
      /gaad/   /gɔɔd/   'God'

A very similar kind of situation applies with the labial velars, where again the presence of a semi-vowel linked feature predicts whether JamC /a/ is realised as JamE /a/ or /ɔ/. The difference is that there are environments in which palatals occur categorically, i.e. before vowels other than /a/ and /aa/. By contrast, labial velars only occur variably in JamE, before the diphthong /ɔi/. Its JamC reflex, /ai/, is the only environment in which they may occur in JamC. In JamE, it represents a redundant feature, the labialisation of /b/ in the environment of an /ai/ which has /ɔi/ as its JamE reflex. This represents independent support for the notion that the conversion process is from a JamC underlying input to JamE and not the other way around. Otherwise, we would have no way of understanding how a variable occurrence of /w/ in JamE can be converted into a categorical appearance of this form in the JamC cognates.

(44) Jamaican Creole   Jamaican English
      /bwai/   /bɔi/ ~ /bwɔi/   'boy'
      /bai/   /bai/   'buy'
      /pwail/   /spɔil/ ~ /spwɔil/   'spoil'
      /pail/   /pail/   'pile'

3.2.3. Variation

The pattern of differential use of variants across pairs of linguistically related variables exists in the area of consonants also. The voiceless dental fricative variant of the variable /ð/ ~ /d/, and the voiced dental fricative variant of the variable /θ/ ~ /d/, each idealised JamE fricative variant does not occur in JamE with the same frequency. As Irvine's (2004) table 2 intimates, model speakers of JamE produce a mere 48% of the JamE fricative variant, /ð/, and 52% of the JamC linked stop variant, /d/. The JamC linked variant is therefore very present in JamE and in fact occurs more frequently than the English variant. This is quite different with the parallel variable, /θ/ ~ /t/. Here, it is the JamE linked variant, [θ], which is in the ascendant, occurring in 88% of the occurrences of this variable.

3.2.4. Constraints on the onset: /j/ and /w/

The ambiguity in JamC in assigning [tʃ] and [dʒ] to either /tj/ and /dj/ or /tʃ/ and /dʒ/ manifests itself in the process of conversion into JamE. For some JamE speakers but not others, phonetic [tj] and [dj] clusters occur. For some of these speakers, these phonetic forms are the only ones allowed in certain environments. They also occur for such speakers in [tjuu] 'chew' and [djuːnjo] 'junior'. Such speakers, in these environments, have [tj] and [dj] allophones for the phonemes, /tʃ/ and /dʒ/. A second group would employ [tj] and [dj] respectively in items such as [tjuuzde] 'Tuesday' and [djuu] 'dew' whilst using the phones [tʃ] and [dʒ] for [tʃuu] 'chew' and [dʒuːnjo] 'junior'. Here, the [tj] and [dj] represent syllable initial phoneme sequences, /tj/ and /dj/ which contrast with [tʃ] and [dʒ] as phonetic manifestations of /tj/ and /dj/. Finally, there are speakers for whom [tj] and [dj] are not employed and for whom, in both sets of items, the only forms possible are [tʃ] and [dʒ]. The JamE system of such speakers is like that of JamC.

In the case of /w/ in the onset, /pw/ and /bw/ vary with /p/ and /b/ in 'oi' and 'oy' words, e.g. /spwɔil/ ~ /spɔil/ 'spoil', /bwɔi/ ~ /bɔi/ 'boy'. Even though the /pw/ and /bw/ clusters represent a carry-over from a JamC representation, the feature which is taken to diagnose use of JamE rather than JamC is /ɔi/. In this context, the JamC type /w/ occurs as a relatively unnoticed and redundant variant feature.

3.2.5. Constraints on the coda: The distribution of /r/

JamE is generally rhotic. This can be seen in the examples below.

(45) a.   /heer/   [heːɹ] ~ [hɛɹ]   'hair'
      b.   /boord/   [boːɹd] ~ [boːɹd]   'board/bored'
      c.   /sort/   [soːɹt] ~ [soːt]   'sort'

There is a degree of variability in the realisation of postvocalic /r/, usually in the environment of a following tautosyllabic consonant. As has been pointed out by Alison Irvine (p. c.), however, this inconsistency only occurs in relation to /r/ preceding another consonant in the coda, i.e. in relation to items b. and c. above but not a.

3.2.6. Constraints on the coda: The distribution of nasals

Idealised JamE has /aun/ [aun] as the phoneme sequence in the pronunciation of words such as 'brown', 'down' and 'town'. The JamC variant, [oŋŋ], is a highly stigmatised but frequently occurring variant in JamE. The stigma associated with [oŋŋ] is determined by the lexical item within which it appears. Thus, idealised JamE /dauntaun/ [dountoun] 'downtown' is very frequently produced as [donʈaun], i.e. with the [oŋ] variant on 'down' but not on 'town'.

(46) a.   /daun/   [doun] ~ [doŋ]   'down'
      b.   /taun/   [toun] ~ [toŋ]   'town'

3.2.7. Constraints on the coda: Consonant clusters

Consonant clusters follow a pattern in the coda characteristic of standard varieties of English around the world. Because more complex clusters are allowed in JamE than in JamC, some users of JamE are prone, beginning with a JamC lexical entry, to overgeneralise the conversion process as in the example below. This occurs with the creation of an /nd/ consonant cluster in the attempted JamE item below, based on the assumption that all rather then only some JamC /n/ codas had to be converted to JamE as /nd/.

(47) Jamaican Creole   Jamaican English
      lain   'line'   →   laind (the product of overgeneralising)   'line'

3.2.8. The syllable structure

The syllable structure for JamE is similar to that of other varieties of English. The structure is presented below.

(48) (C(C) (C)) V (V) ((C) (C) (C))

3.3. From Jamaican Creole to Jamaican English: The consonantal system

JamC has 21 consonants as compared with 24 for JamE. The difference in the consonant inventory of the two language varieties involves three JamE fricatives, /θ/, /ð/ and /ʒ/, which do not exist in JamC. Thus, the one-to-one relationship between JamC and JamE consonants breaks down on three occasions. These are presented below.

(49) Jamaican Creole   Jamaican English
      /t/   =   /θ/, /t/
      /d/   =   /ð/, /d/
      /dʒ/   =   /dʒ/, /ʒ/

These produce the following equivalences.

(50) Jamaican Creole   Jamaican English
      /taŋk/   'tank', 'thank'   vs. /θaŋk/   'thank'
                                        /taŋk/   'tank'
      /den/   'den', 'then'   vs. /ðen/   'then'
                                        /den/   'den'
      /medʒa/   'measure'   vs. /meʒo/   'measure'
      /edʒ/   'edge'   vs. /edʒ/   'edge'

In our discussion of variation, we already looked at the /θ/ ~ /t/ and /ð/ ~ /d/ variables. In relation to the /dʒ/ ~ /ʒ/ variation, Irvine, both with reference to her work as well as other material, concludes that [ʒomeko] 'Jamaica' and [ʒenorol] 'general', to be increasingly a feature of some formal speech. This might be perceived to be an overgeneralisation, i.e. JamC /dʒ/ → JamE /ʒ/ conversion even in words like 'Jamaica' and 'general' which, in JamC and most varieties of English, have /dʒ/. The form [ʒ] is often selected when the spelling of the word precludes a /dj/ interpretation possible in [soːldjo] 'soldier', for example.

4.   The prosodic system

4.1.   Jamaican Creole

Prosody is used to distinguish between two groups of words, both of which take prominence on the first syllable. In type I, the highest pitch occurs on the first syllable. In type II, the highest pitch is on the second syllable, with the first bearing falling pitch over its duration. The ability to bear type II prosody is lexically specified. Below is presented a pair of lexically contrastive items.

(51) Type I Only   Type I & II

     mada   'mother'   mada   'spiritualist'
     faada   'father'   faada   'priest'

Even where no minimal pairs exist, bisyllabic items with prominence on the first syllable have to be lexically specified for the ability to take type II prosody. Below is a sample.

(52) Type I Only   Type I & II
     ieti   'eighty'   biebi   'baby'
     foni   'funny'   moni   'money'
     daata   'daughter'   waata   'water'
     pwaizn   'poison'   laisn   'licence'

4.2.   Jamaican English

The patterns discussed for JamC are maintained for JamE bisyllabic items with prominence on the first syllable.

(53) Type I Only   Type I & II
     /moðo/ ~ /mɔðo/   'mother'   /moðo/ ~ /mɔðo/   'spiritualist'
     /faaðo/   'father'   /faaðo/   'priest'
     /eeti/   'eighty'   /beebi/   'baby'
     foni/   'funny'   /moni/   'money'
     dɔɔto/   'daughter'   /wɔɔto/   'water'
     pɔizn/ ~ /pwɔizn/   'poison'   /laisns/   'licence'

4.3.   From Jamaican Creole to Jamaican English: Prosody

If we presume that the major model for JamE is written English supported by written normative works such as dictionaries, we can make some reasonable extrapolations about the process by which JamC input becomes JamE output at the prosodic level. Cues from the English writing system, coupled with reference to dictionaries, gives an indication of the location of word stress. In the JamC cases and their JamE equivalents, type I only and type I & II items both bear prominence or word stress on the first syllable. They are, however, over-differentiated in relation to such a model by having two lexically specified prosodic classes amongst such words. Where JamC is over-differentiated in relation to the written English model but does not clash with that model, JamC features are simply transferred to JamE, unnoticed.

5.   Interdependent but autonomous: Theorising phonological interaction in the Jamaica continuum/diglossic situation

There is no way in which the assumption of underlying English phonology for JamC, by way of simplification and deletion rules, could account for the inter-mediate and even variant JamE forms. The frequent areas of overgeneralisation in every aspect of the segmental phonological system discussed here suggests that JamE, for many speakers, is based on a JamC lexical input. A proposal for deletion rules, working from either JamE or from 17th century British English, would not produce the overgeneralisations discussed. Rules of elaboration, in-volving the lexical marking of some items to receive this elaboration, are a crucial part of the link between the phonological systems of JamC and JamE. It is the absence of lexical marking that produces the initial overgeneralisations.

Simultaneously, in the area of the prosodic system, we have seen what hap-pens in the process of conversion from complex to simple. Since written English largely provided the model for the development of JamE, the fact that Standard British English and other metropolitan varieties of English were simple in this area had no impact on the conversion process. In fact, the greater complexity of JamE, relative to its external models, has gone unnoticed by speakers of JamE themselves. This fact underlines the largely written character of the model on which JamE has been built. It also supports the notion that much of the special lexical marking for conversion from JamC to JamE comes from cues given by the spellings of words in conventional English orthography.

The jury is out on whether a complex aspect of the phonology of a natively used variety can be suppressed in the acquisition of a non-native variety which is less complex. We would theorise that this would not occur unless strong social stigma were associated with this more complex set of features. Since, in the Jamaica situation, all the users of the potentially less complex system are also native users of the more complex one, the likelihood is that the greater complexity would go unnoticed, which is what we suggest happens with the complex JamC prosodic system in JamE. In addition, the distinction has some functional load. Thus, failure to carry it over into JamE would leave a communicative gap which would be noticed by speakers since they regard JamC and JamE as varieties of the same language.

The fact that, in pairs of related phonological variables, one variant would have a high frequency of occurrence in the variety to which it does not ideally belong, and that another would not, suggests that we are dealing with two language varieties which interact with each other, sharing on a variable basis some features of the other, but reserving other features for its own exclusive use. We have a pair of phonological systems that converge with each other but that are, in a systematic manner, nevertheless kept apart by their users.

Exercises and study questions

For technical reasons, the audio file from Jamaican Creole referred to here (a reading passage) is not available on the CD-ROM. It can be obtained from the publisher's website.

1. Jamaican Creole phonology historically derives forms from speakers of West African languages and forms from speakers of 17th century British English varieties. Listening to the recorded speech sample of Jamaican Creole, identify salient phonological features which Jamaican Creole speakers have in common with contemporary West African languages and contemporary forms of British English.

2. Given the analysis presented in the study, do you think that Jamaican Creole is a variant of Jamaican English? Identify salient phonological features which support your position.

3. Jamaican English shares phonological features with other Caribbean varieties of English. Identify some phonological features Jamaicans have in common with other Caribbean English speakers. Identify features which are unique to Jamaican English.

4. Compare the treatment of vowel assimilation across syllable boundaries in Jamaican Creole and Jamaican English. Construct a set of phonological structures which illustrates the application of conversion rules in the Jamaican speech continuum.

5. Given the Jamaican Creole phrase, [tin tik] 'thin stick', produce the possible versions of this phrase that can occur in the Jamaican speech continuum. Identify and explain any implicational relationship between the presence and absence of st-cluster and [T] at each point in the continuum.

6. Listen to the Jamaican Creole speech sample and identify phonological features which are similar to other Caribbean Creoles and Creoles spoken in West Africa. Identify features unique to Jamaican Creole.

7. The common assumption is that [h]-insertion/[h]-deletion in Jamaican Creole items occurs as a result of an overgeneralization of conversion rules from Jamaican English. Can you find some other evidence within the Jamaican Creole phonology for the presence of these processes?

Selected references

Please consult the General references for titles mentioned in the text but not included in the references below. For a full bibliography see the accompanying CD-ROM.

Akers, Glen A.
    1981   *Phonological Variation in the Jamaican Continuum.* Ann Arbor, MI: Karoma.
Bennett, Louise
    1966   *Jamaica Labrish.* Kingston: Sangster Bookstores.
Cassidy, Frederic G. and Robert B. Le Page
    [1967] 1980   *Dictionary of Jamaican Creole.* Cambridge: Cambridge University Press.
Devonish, Hubert and Walter Seiler
    1991   *A Reanalysis of the Phonological System of Jamaican Creole.* Society for Caribbean Linguistics Occasional Papers 24.
Ferguson, Charles
    1959   Diglossia. In: Pier Giglioli (ed.), *Language in Social Context*, 232–251. Harmondsworth: Penguin.
Gumperz, John J. and Robert Wilson
    1971   Convergence and creolization. In: Hymes (ed.), 151–167.
Irvine, Alison
    2004   A good command of the English language: Phonological variation in the Jamaican acrolect. *Journal of Pidgin and Creole Linguistics* 19: 41–76.
Meade, Rocky R.
    1995   An analysis of Jamaican /s/-stop cluster reduction within Optimality Theory. *UWILING*: Working Papers in Linguistics: 1, 30–42.
    1996   On the phonology and orthography of Jamaican Creole. *Journal of Pidgin and Creole Languages* 11: 335–341.
    2001   *Acquisition of Jamaican Phonology.* The Netherlands: Holland Institute of Linguistics.
Wells, John C.
    1973   *Jamaican Pronunciation in London.* Oxford: Basil Blackwell.

Eastern Caribbean English-derived language varieties: phonology

Michael Aceto

1. Introduction

As a geographical region, the Eastern Caribbean has been left virtually un-tapped as a source of fieldwork data in creole studies and English dialectology. Of course, there are individual pieces of research derived from some islands of the Eastern Caribbean, and at least two geographical exceptions to these gen-eralizations are Barbados, Guyana, and perhaps Trinidad. Barbados has been central to previous discussions and debates in trying to determine its possible role in the diffusion of shared features heard throughout the Anglophone Carib-bean as well as in answering questions related to the concept of "decreolization" as to whether Barbados once contained significant communities of speakers of a "deeper" Creole than typically seems to be spoken today (Cassidy 1980; Han-cock 1980; Rickford 1992; Van Herk 2003). Trinidad has received significant attention from Winer (1993). These cases aside, the Eastern Caribbean is still largely absent from contemporary research and fieldwork in creolistics. For ex-ample, Neumann-Holzschuh and Schneider (2000), one of the most recent ad-ditions to the excellent Creole Language Library series published by Benjamins, contains few references to the Anglophone Eastern Caribbean. For reasons dis-cussed in Aceto (2002a) and Aceto and Williams (2003), the "action" in creole studies is not centered in the Eastern Caribbean, except perhaps as represented by Guyana in South America. Researchers have largely ignored the approxi-mately one dozen other Anglophone islands in the Eastern Caribbean chain.

Aceto (2002a) designates specific islands of the Eastern Caribbean (among other areas of the Americas as well) as sites for future research by compiling the relatively few bibliographic references that have been published on Anglo-phone Caribbean varieties other than Jamaican and Guyanese and by indicat-ing which specific islands or areas have received little or no attention from linguists. Some of the goals that prompted Aceto (2002a) have been rectified to some degree by Aceto and Williams (2003). Nonetheless, even after the publication of Aceto and Williams (2003), most of the Eastern Caribbean is still wide open for researchers interested in pursuing future fieldwork in Anglo-phone West Indian locations for which we have relatively little data.

Phonology as a general linguistic-based topic has not received the same attention from researchers that Creole language syntax has. Perhaps this observation relates to the fact that syntax is often tied directly to cognitive science (which has influenced the field of linguistics enormously) as well as the popularity of substrate arguments in discussing creole language genesis. Perhaps it is because of the highly variable nature of sound segments, especially vowels. Whatever the reason, in-depth phonological treatments of any specific Creole language have been few and far between. For evidence of this descriptive statement, simply examine the titles in the Creole Language Library. Though individual articles on Creole phonology appear in edited collections, not a single volume examines Creole phonology in depth while several volumes concentrate largely if not exclusively on syntactic data.

Map 1.   (Courtesy of http://www.lib.utexas.edu/maps/americas/caribbean.gif)

This chapter is largely based on Holm (1989), Volume 3 of Wells (1982), Aceto and Williams (2003), various specific articles referenced below, and the author's own notes from fieldwork whose results have not yet appeared in published articles. Map 1 shows the location of the islands discussed in the paper.

2.   Some general phonological features of Eastern Caribbean English-derived languages

2.1.   Introduction

It is worth remembering that the varieties of English that Africans in the Western Hemisphere originally heard were regional, social, and ethnic (e.g. Irish and Scottish) dialects of British English as spoken in the 17-19th centuries. As Africans and African-descended peoples began to acquire English forms, initially as a second language, they would have heard varieties of English spoken by Europeans and whatever earlier restructured forms they might have heard on the West African coast or perhaps at slave entrepots in the Caribbean such as St. Eustatius or St. Kitts (see Baker and Bruyn 1998 for references to a scenario in which St. Kitts may have influenced emerging Englishes on other islands). Later, as local varieties began to emerge in the decades to follow, slaves would have acquired local varieties as first-languages or as native speaker varieties as spoken in the relevant communities by peoples of both African and European descent. Thus, from a diachronic perspective, English-derived Caribbean varieties in general are more British-oriented in their phonology, though in the last century American and Canadian influence can be expected and documented (e.g. see Van Herk 2003).

There appear to be some satisfactory reasons for linguistically dividing the region of the Caribbean into geographical-designated Western and Eastern varieties on the basis of comparative phonology and syntax (see Holm 1989: 445; Volume 3 of Wells 1982; 1987). However, the grounds for this division are largely abstract and impressionistic since it is my experience, having done fieldwork in both general locations, that there are few specific features that one may absolutely find in one region that cannot be found in the other. In general, creolists are often comfortable with the highly questionable assumption that earlier varieties of creole languages were monolithic and contemporary synchronic variation is a more recent (i.e. post-emancipation) phenomenon. Whether these overlapping patterns represent parallel historical developments or are due to intra-Caribbean migration, especially in the post-emancipation period, is open to debate. Aceto and Williams (2003) focused on the Eastern Caribbean simply because the locations that comprise this chain of islands have rarely if ever been documented via fieldwork. However, as has been made clear in dialect studies over the last 50 years, it is not any specific feature that is diagnostic of a dialect (whether it be a regional, ethnic, or social one), but the bundle of features that is associated with a particular designation. And it is on these grounds that one may find some validity in the motivation for separating Caribbean Englishes into Western and Eastern varieties. However, due to the lack of research in the Eastern Caribbean, no table of "typical" Anglophone Eastern Caribbean speakers and their sound segments can be considered to be accurate and inclusive at this point in time. Many of the islands of the region have never been documented via linguistic fieldwork.

In this chapter, I discuss some phonetic/phonological features found in the general Eastern Caribbean (while making reference to features believed to be representative of the Western Caribbean as well), and then discuss specific islands and their English-derived varieties. It should be acknowledged that we do not have much research on many of these varieties, at least when compared to the impressive amount of research carried out on, say, Jamaica and the Surinamese Creole languages. The Surinamese Creoles are ignored in this discussion. However, though not specifically considered in this section, the geographically proximate English-derived languages spoken in the Bahamas (which is often geographically linked with North American varieties of English such as Turks and Caicos and Gullah rather than the Eastern Caribbean, though included in Aceto and Williams (2003) because of its general proximity), Trinidad, Barbados, and Guyana are referenced occasionally for comparative purposes since their creole language varieties manifest some phonological similarities with the Anglophone Eastern Caribbean chain in general.

2.2. Vowels

2.2.1. *Long vowels*

In words of the FACE and GOAT/GOAL sets, the off glides [ei] and [ou] of standard varieties of English are often not found in the Eastern Caribbean where these sounds most often correspond to [eː] and [oː]. However, recent work by Childs, Reaser and Wolfram (2003) suggests that in some Bahamian communities the sound [ei] can be heard. In many Western Caribbean varieties these same sounds correspond to those with on-glides, e.g. /ie/ and /uo/ as in [fies] *face* and [guot] *goat*. These same vowels can be realized as diphthongs with variants such as [iɛ] and [uɔ]. In the Leeward Islands, specifically Montserrat (see Volume 3 of Wells 1982: 587), words that historically had long vowels are shortened and they have no off-glides (e.g. [eʲ]) as they do in metropolitan varieties, e.g. /ki/ *key* and /de/ *day*.

2.2.2. Unreduced vowels

Many other varieties in the Eastern Caribbean (except for Bajan), especially the deeper or so-called basilectal ones, have no mid-central vowels, i.e. /ə/ or /ʌ/. Even in positions not associated with word-final or post-vocalic /r/, West Indian varieties of English often display a preference for unreduced vowels, e.g. [abɪlɪtɪ] *ability*, [tawɪl] *towel*, where other dialects of English often display schwa [ə] in the third and second vowel positions respectively.

2.2.3. Other vowels

The low front vowel /æ/ found in many metropolitan varieties of English in words such as TRAP is often realized further back in the mouth as [a]. The /ʌ/ of words like STRUT in metropolitan varieties is backed and close to [ɔ]. However, some varieties of English in the Turks and Caicos Islands (as well as in Bermuda) reveal the presence of [æ].

Eastern Caribbean English-derived varieties often maintain the difference between sounds in words in metropolitan dialects like the /ɔ:/ in *jaw* and the /a:/ in *jar* (which often has an r-less pronunciation in many varieties but not all, e.g. Bajan). Both sounds have typically merged into /a:/ in the Western group.

2.3.   Consonants

2.3.1. Rhoticity

Except for varieties of English in Barbados, post-vocalic /r/ is often not heard in the Eastern Caribbean. Bajan English is recognized by its full rhotic nature at all levels of society. Van Herk (2003:260) states that Bajan is "if anything, more rhotic than North American [Standard English]." This is not the case in other areas in which full r-lessness after vowels (e.g. in Trinidad and the Bahamas) and the variable nature of [r] across a geographical space (e.g. in Guyana) are salient dialect features. In non-rhotic dialects, additional phonemes such as /ea/ (e.g. /nea/ *near*) and /oa/ (e.g. /foa/ *four*) are often created by absence of /r/ after vowels.

One correlate associated with non-rhoticity in general West Indian English varieties is the avoidance of central [ə]-like vowels in favor of unreduced vowels or a vowel identical or similar to [a] in word-final cases, e.g. /lɛta/ *letter*. Wells (Volume 3, 1982: 571) believes this vowel to be the same as found in words such as /an(d)/ *and* and /at/ *at*. He adds that "it is very hard to find a satisfactory criterion for determining whether or not a phonemic opposition really exists between /a/ and a putative /ə/, but the existence of such a phoneme is something of a hallmark of educated speech". However, middle-class and educated West Indians often use the unreduced vowels (i.e. they avoid [ə]) as well.

2.3.2. /v/-/w/ merger

The contrast between /v/ and /w/ is often neutralized or merged in the Eastern Caribbean. That is, many dialects of Caribbean English (e.g. Bahamian, Bermudan, and Vincentian) may alternate [w], [β] (the voiced bilabial fricative), or [ʋ] (the voiced labiodental approximant) for words which in metropolitan varieties begin with [v], e.g. *village* [wɪlɪdʒ]. This feature may be related to component dialect varieties of English heard in the Caribbean in the 18ᵗʰ century which contain this same alternation (e.g. Cockney) or possibly to African languages that lacked the /v/ segment. Some Anglophone Caribbean communities may reveal /b/ where metropolitan Anglophone varieties display /v/, e.g. *vex* "angry" [bɛks], *river* [rɪba], and *love* [lʌb].

2.3.3. Word-initial /h/

In the Leewards (Antigua, St. Kitts, Nevis, Montserrat, Anguilla, Barbuda), unlike in Jamaican and other Western Caribbean varieties, /h/ is most often *not* dropped from the beginnings of most words. So-called "*h*-dropping" or word-initial "*h*-deletion" is common in Jamaica and in the Bahamas as well. *H*-dropping also occurs in other dialects of English; often British Cockney is cited as the source of *h*-dropping in English-derived Caribbean varieties. In dialects with this feature, which is generally not found in the Eastern Caribbean, pairs such as *hair* and *air* are homophonous (both are sometimes [ɪɛr]).

2.3.4. Nasals

Syllable- or word-final alveolar nasals following /ʌ/ are often velarized or become /ŋ/, e.g. /dʌŋ/ *down*, which often creates new homonyms (e.g. in this case with *dung*). A variant of this type of pronunciation, although likely archaic, is where the preceding vowel becomes nasalized instead of displaying a consonantal segment, e.g. [dɔ̃].

2.3.5. Th-stopping

The neutralization of /ð/ and /θ/ as /d/ and /t/, e.g. /tɪŋ/ *thing* and /fada/ *father*, is a common feature of many dialects of Caribbean English as well as in regional, ethnic, and social dialects spoken in North America and Great Britain (which often display reflexes different from those in the Caribbean). This process creates new homonyms in the specific dialects in question. Some of the many examples are: *thin-tin* [tɪn], *faith-fate* [fet], *though-dough* [do], *breathe-breed* [brid].

Neutralization appears to operate particularly readily in the environment preceding an /r/ in an onset consonant cluster: *three-tree* [triː], *through-tru* [truː], though often these segments are realized as palatalized allophones [tʃruː] or [tʃriː]. Sometimes interdental fricatives in metropolitan varieties do not correspond with a stop consonant in Caribbean Englishes. In Kokoy, a variety of Creole English spoken in Dominica, where /θ/ occurs in onset consonant clusters in metropolitan varieties with /r/, the output often becomes [f], e.g. *three* [fri], *through* [fru].

Many so-called acrolectal speakers of many varieties of Caribbean Englishes realize interdental fricatives as similarly articulated in metropolitan varieties. In St. Eustatius, many speakers, at all levels of society, display interdental segments, while the stop correspondences are still the preference for most speakers. Cutler (2003) makes a similar observation about this feature in the English of Gran Turk Island as does Williams (2003) about some varieties of English spoken in Anguilla.

2.3.6.   Consonant cluster reduction

As is typical in many dialects of English around the world, the word-final /t/ segment in consonant clusters preceded by an obstruent is often not realized, e.g. /-ft, -st, -kt/. For example, words such as *left*, *nest* and *act* are realized as /lɛf/, /nɛs/, and /ak/. Consonant clusters in codas in which /d/ is in the final position are also often not realized in many English-derived West Indian creoles, e.g. /sɛn/ *send* or /bɪl/ *build*.

The reduction of consonant clusters in codas also affects the realization of past tense allomorphs as heard in metropolitan varieties of English as in *pushed* /puʃt/, *stopped* /stapt/ and *staged* /stedʒd/. The past tense allomorphs /-d/, /-t/ and /-ɪd/ are generally absent in Creole varieties of English, but it is difficult to be certain if they always were. However, they are part of the metropolitan speech varieties spoken in many Anglophone Caribbeans locations today.

Word-final clusters of a nasal and a voiceless consonant are heard in West Indian varieties of English, e.g. [lamp] *lamp*, [tɛnt] *tent*, *tenth* (see description above regarding th-stopping), and [baŋk] *bank*. Clusters in codas are also found in combination with liquids (in combination with [l] and [r], if it is a rhotic dialect such as Bajan), e.g. [mɪlk] *milk*, [ʃɛlf] *shelf*, [part] *part*, and [hard]

hard. Other consonant cluster combinations occur freely such as /ks/, e.g. [aks] *ask*, [baks] *box*, [sɪks] *six*. In some deep Creole varieties, consonant clusters in onsets or word-initially are dispreferred, e.g. [taːt] *start*, [tan] *stand*, [tap] *stop*.

2.4. Stress, tone, prosody, and suprasegmentals

There are many words in West Indian varieties of English that receive final stress as opposed to initial stress found in metropolitan varieties of English (an apostrophe before the syllable in question indicates final stress), e.g. *rea'lize*, *cele'brate*, *ki'tchen*. Sutcliffe (2003: 265) adopts the approach of Carter (1987) in her analysis of Guyanese and Jamaican Creole suprasegmentals and of Devonish (1989) in his study of Guyanese suprasegmentals. Sutcliffe defines *suprasegmentals* "as pitch patterns mapped onto syllables or phrases, creating intonation and tonal patterns". He shows that English-derived Caribbean Creoles can be analyzed as having tonal systems, even if somewhat evolved in the direction of metropolitan English varieties that do not display tonal systems. By "tonal systems" Sutcliffe means those that organize the melodic pitch used by speakers into two or more pitch phonemes or tones (contrasting high and low in the case of two-tone systems). Sutcliffe focuses on Bajan, Trinidadian and Guyanese suprasegmental systems within the wider context of the Anglophone Caribbean. Sutcliffe views lexical tone, in the sense of distinguishing one word from another, as particularly developed in the Eastern Caribbean, compared with restructured English-derived varieties in the Western Caribbean and North America.

Sutcliffe suggests that basic features of the suprasegmental system indicate a link between Bajan and Guyanese in the Eastern Caribbean. Both languages display lexical minimal pairs in common, mostly disyllables, which are differentiated by pitch patterns alone: *síster* (with the pitch pattern / – _ /) "female sibling", *sistér* (with the pitch pattern / _ – /) "a nun or sister in the religious sense"; *wórker* (with pitch pattern / – _ /) "one who works," *workér* (with the pitch pattern / _ – /) "seamstress or needlewoman" (Sutcliffe 1982: 111). This feature has not been attested for other Caribbean creoles. Sutcliffe (2003) provides data derived from Roberts (1988: 94) for Bajan: múhda "mother, i.e. female parent", mùhdá "female head of a religious order or organization"; fáada "father, male parent", faadá "priest"; brúhda "male sibling", brùhdá "male member of a religious order"; fárma "one who farms", fàrmá (Fàrmér) surname; béeka "one who bakes", bèeká (Bàkér) surname. Sutcliffe (2003) also presents Guyanese data derived from Devonish (1989): práblem "problem", pràblém "a mathematics problem"; sìngín "singing practice", síngin "singing" (verb); wàshá "washing machine", wáshà "one who washes"; rìidá "reader (text book)", ríida "someone who reads." Sutcliffe (2003) also discusses such suprasegmental features as lexical tone, downstepping, final cadence, final rise, high rise intonation, emphasis, and focus marking.

3.   Features of specific Eastern Caribbean Islands

3.1.   Turks and Caicos Islands

The following information is from Cutler (2003). The Turks and Caicos Islands (TCI) are a British dependency comprised of eight major islands and more than forty islets and cays forming the southeastern end of the Bahamas archipelago. The Turks Islands are Grand Turk (the capital) and Salt Cay. The Caicos Islands are West Caicos, Providenciales, North Caicos, Middle Caicos, East Caicos, and South Caicos. The population of the TCI in 2000 was 17,502 (U.S. Census Bureau). The official language of the TCI is English. Most of the population is concentrated on Providenciales (Provo) and Grand Turk. Approximately 90% of the population throughout the islands is black. The TCI have been under political and cultural influence from the United States during the 20th century (e.g. Grand Turk was home to two U.S. military bases from World War II until 1983). In the mid 1960s, when the salt industry closed, many Turks and Caicos Islanders sought employment in the Bahamas and the United States.

The islands of the Bahamas and the Turks and Caicos were originally inhabited by Lucayan Indians. The Spanish deported the Lucayans to work in silver mines on Hispaniola in the early 16th century. The islands remained uninhabited until the late 1600s when Bermudian traders began sailing there to gather salt, which was exported to British colonies in North America. In 1676, Bermudians established the first settlement on Grand Turk. In 1799 the islands were placed under the jurisdiction of the Bahamas. Subsequently, the islands were annexed to Jamaica as one of its dependencies in 1873. When Jamaica gained its independence in 1962, people in the TCI voted to remain a colony and were placed once again under the governance of the Bahamas. When the Bahamas gained its independence in 1972, the TCI received its own governor. Today, the TCI is one of twelve so-called "Dependent Territories" with British colonial status.

The Caicos Islands remained uninhabited from the 16th century until the arrival of the Loyalist refugees, mainly from the southern American colonies, in the 1780s following the American Revolutionary War. Many of the slaves brought to the Caicos Islands from Georgia and South Carolina may have spoken a creole language, either a Caribbean Creole or an early form of Gullah, an English Creole that had been established in coastal areas of South Carolina and Georgia between 1720 and 1750, or had some familiarity with the variety of English emerging in that region. Most of the Loyalists who had previously arrived in the Caicos Islands abandoned their plantations and departed for other destinations in the British West Indies by 1820 after cotton crops began to fail. In many cases, they left their slaves behind. Over the course of the 19th century and well into the 20th century, the remaining inhabitants in the Caicos Islands (virtually all descendants of American-born slaves) lived in relative isolation. The Caicos Islanders represent one of the few remaining unstudied "enclave" speech communities of persons descended from American-born slaves living outside the USA. The population of the Caicos Islands dropped to a low of 2,995 in 1970; it began increasing slowly over the next two decades to its present level of about 11,000 people.

Cutler (2003) presents an overview of the variety of English spoken on Grand Turk, which is part of the Turks and Caicos Islands in the British West Indies. No prior linguistic research has been carried out in the Turks and Caicos Islands (see Aceto 2002a). Sometimes the Turks and Caicos islands are seen as part of the chain of islands associated with the Bahamas and thus considered part of the category designated as North American varieties of (restructured) English. Again, Aceto and Williams (2003) have included these islands in their presentation of Eastern Caribbean varieties because of their general proximity. Cutler concludes that Turks Island English is an intermediate variety that may have more in common with African American Vernacular English, Gullah, and Bermudan English than other West Indian varieties of English to the south.

Regarding the phonology of Grand Turk, Cutler (2003) sees parallels between its system and that also heard in Bermudan English: the alternation of /æ/ and /ɛ/, e.g. *hat* [hɛt], *ten* [tæn], and the interchange of /w/ and /v/, as discussed above. Whites in Bermuda pronounce *grass* [græs], but blacks favor the vowel [a]. Cutler states that Turks Islanders were similar in this regard in that they did use /æ/ in words where many other West Indians would use /a/. Perhaps this feature is due to influence from North American varieties of English. Further features of the English spoken on Grand Turk as listed by Cutler are: speakers have little or no monophthongization of diphthongs such as [aɪ]; they do not centralize the diphthong in words like *oil* to [aɪ] as is common in other parts of the West Indies like Jamaica; unlike other Caribbean varieties of English, speakers do not palatalize velar stops; and speakers do not have "h"-dropping or insertion as is common in varieties of Jamaican and Bahamian

Cutler lists the following features of the vowel system of Grand Turk English. Words like *if* often sound like [ɛf]. The mid front vowel /ɛ/ in words like *rest* and *Betty* is lowered to [æ] i.e., [ræst] and [bærɪ]. The second vowel in *again* is closer to [e] than [ɛ], i.e., [əˈgen]. The vowel in *company* and *nothing* is closest to the low front vowel [a], i.e., ['kampəni] and ['naʔtən]. The vowel in *up* is close to [ɔ]. Low mid back rounded vowels are slightly diphthongized before nasals as in *gone* [gɔan] and *haunted* ['hɔanɛd]. The vowel in *could* is closer to a rounded one like [u]. Speakers in Grand Turk reveal the widespread use of [æ] in *back* and *man* where many other Caribbean varieties use [a] or [aː]. However, there is considerable variation among speakers: Some use [æ] in *master* but [a] in *after* and *can't*. The diphthong in words like *go* and *boat* is fronted, sounding closer to [öu]. The diphthong in *about* is closer to [ou].

English on Turks Island has no rhotic vowels. Words like *birth* are pronounced [baf] or [bʌf]. This feature contrasts with Bahamian English and Gullah, both of which have the diphthong [ʌɪ] in words like *first* and *skirt*. In fact, Turks Islanders identified the [ʌɪ] diphthong as a feature of Bahamian English.

Cutler also describes the consonants of Grand Turk English. The definite article *the* is categorically pronounced [di], but some speakers vary between stops and interdental fricatives for other words. The same description applies to St. Eustatius Creole English as well (Aceto 2006). Voiceless initial dental fricatives are variably realized as affricates. The Turks Island pronunciation of *thief* does not involve a full stop as it does in Jamaica and other parts of the Caribbean (i.e. ([tif]). Instead Turks Islanders say [tθif]. Medial dental fricatives are realized as labiodental fricatives, i.e., birthday [bʌfdeɪ], as they often are in African American Vernacular English. The so-called *–ing* suffix is most commonly realized as [ɪn], e.g. [sɪŋɪn] as is common in many English vernaculars in the Caribbean as well as in North America and Great Britain. In some words, the nasal is syllabified, e.g. *meeting* [miʔtn̩]. Initial /v/ and /w/ merge into a voiced bilabial approximant, e.g. *well* [βɛl], *vex* [βɛks] (see discussion above). Syllable final /t/ and /k/ are preceded by or replaced by glottal stops, e.g. *that* [dæʔt]. Other speakers do not have complete closure on final stops. Turks Islanders variably apply flapping to medial alveolar stops, e.g. *Betty* [bæɾɪ].

Cutler presents some discussion of syllable structure in Turks Island English as well. Consonant clusters are reduced in morpheme final consonant clusters of the same voicing, e.g. *last* [las], *stricter* [strɪkə]. Medial consonants are elided in specific words, e.g. *little* [lɪl]. Turks Island English is non-rhotic (see discussion above), e.g. *Turks Island* [taksailən]. In some cases, vowels that may have been combined with [r] historically are slightly diphthongized, e.g. *Lord's* [lɔadz].

3.2.   Virgin Islands

The US Virgin Islands are comprised of St. Thomas, St. Croix, and St. John; The British Virgin Islands are Tortola, Virgin Gorda, Anegada, and Jost Van

Dyke. The following sociohistorical information is from Holm (1989: 455). The Dutch occupied Tortola in 1648; the British claimed it in 1672. English varieties have been spoken on the British Vrigin Islands beginning with this contact. In 1672, the Danes occupied St. Thomas but allowed Dutch and British colonists to settle there as well. The Dutch comprised nearly half of the European-derived population of St. Thomas, and among the majority African and African-descended population, a Dutch-derived creole began to emerge as did an English-derived creole as well. St. John was settled from St. Thomas; St. Croix was purchased by the Danes from the French in 1733. Danish seems to have been reserved for administration and within Danish social groups; English varieties, both creolized and otherwise, began displacing the Dutch-derived creole as more English-speaking settlers arrived. After abolition in 1848, as ex-slaves moved from plantations (which were centers for Dutch Creole speakers) to the towns, the influence of English language varieties became even stronger on these islands. Danish schools adopted English as the language of instruction in the 19ᵗʰ century. In 1917, the USA purchased St. Croix from Denmark. Dutch Creole is believed to be extinct on these islands.

St. Thomas and St. John lack the off-glide found in tense vowels of metropolitan varieties, e.g. /eː/ and /oː/ as in /feːs/ *face* and /boːt / *boat* respectively (Holm 1989: 456). These two islands of the American Virgin Islands chain also display the alternation and merger of /w/ and /v/. St. Croix (the remaining island of the American Virgin Islands) and the chain in the British Virgin Islands (i.e. Tortola, Virgin Gorda, Anegada) may also contain this feature, but there has been little linguistic research in general on these islands (see Aceto 2002a; see Sabino, Diamond and Cockcroft 2003 for a treatment of plural marking in some of these same neglected locations). St. Thomas and St. John also reveal the use of /ɛː/ in words like *fierce* and *bare*. Holm (1989: 456) believes this last feature may represent a local innovation.

3.3. St. Eustatius

St. Eustatius is part of the Dutch Windward Islands, which also comprise Saba and St. Martin. English-derived vernaculars are spoken on all three islands (except for the French side of St. Martin). St. Eustatius has played a central though often unrecognized role in the European colonization and settlement of the West Indies. Le Page (1960: 30) states that "the Dutch islands of Curaçao and St. Eustatius became great slave depots for the Caribbean in the seventeenth century, supplying all other colonies there, including Jamaica, either legally or illegally." In the 17ᵗʰ century, St. Eustatius was sought after by various European colonial interests due to its central location and proximity to other islands in the Eastern Caribbean. Williams (1983: 97) writes, "St. Eustatius was highly prized by the Dutch due to its proximity to St. Kitts and other British possessions." Both French and English settlers began to arrive in 1625, and again in 1629, but soon left in both instances due to the lack of fresh water. In 1636, the Dutch established themselves on Statia. At first tobacco, coffee, and cotton were the dominant crops (with some salt gathering). These activities were later replaced, albeit limitedly, by sugar production. Amerindian slaves mostly from Guiana were shipped to work on the island, but they were soon replaced with African slaves by the middle of the 17th century. The island is relatively small and its drought-ridden climate eventually made it largely unsuitable for use as a significant plantation colony.

French, Spanish and English colonists were already buying slaves at Statia by 1675 (Hartog 1976: 49). Keur and Keur (1960: 39) state, "[t]he main traffic was with St. Kitts, Barbados and St. Thomas." In 1679, one transport of African 200-250 slaves went directly to St. Eustatius. Until this event, slaves were generally supplied from Curaçao, the center of the Dutch West India Company slave trade during this period. In 1665, Statia contained 330 Europeans, including children, and somewhere between 800-1000 slaves.

By 1689, Attema (1976: 16) states, "besides Dutch, there were also English, French, Germans, Scots, Irish and Koerlanders" living on the island. Hartog (1976: 29) suggests that Statia was always multilingual from it earliest colonialization, and that, because it was situated among other islands in the Caribbean being colonized by the British, "English soon became the common language of trade". He explicitly states that "the Dutch customarily adopted the language of the colonized people, whereby Dutch remained as a sort of ruling language for the upper-ten. So the settlers on Curaçao began to speak Papiamento and those on St. Eustatius, Saba and St. Maarten spoke English." Keur and Keur (1960: 43) report that "the Dutch language was gradually replaced by English, and by 1780 St. Eustatius had adopted and [sic] English pattern of life. The churches asked for bilingual preachers from the homeland. Continued relations with the USA after 1780 kept the English language alive on the islands [i.e. both St. Maarten and St. Eustatius] to the present day".

In the 18th century, Statia briefly found its niche in the West Indian economy as first a central slave trading depot in the 1720s, and later in the 1770s, when it became known as the shopping center of the West Indies where all manner of material goods (as well as slaves) could be purchased and exported. Statia emerged as a local slave-trading center by about 1721, just as Curaçao was losing this distinction. The St. Eustatius slave trade reached its peak in 1726 and then seemed to end abruptly by 1729. From this brief peak in Statian slave-trading, the island fell into a lull in general trade until the 1750s-1770s when it earned the names associated with great commerce listed below (e.g. Golden Rock, etc.), without ever reasserting its dominance in the slave trade again.

In 1757, the slave markets in Suriname and Curaçao had reassumed their prominent roles in the distribution of slaves for the Dutch West Indies, while the free trading policy caused St. Eustatius (also known during this period as Money Mountain, Golden Rock, Diamond Rock, Emporium of the Caribbean) to become the commercial center of the Caribbean (Keur and Keur 1960: 40), especially regarding the sale and movement of sugar. Colonists, settlers, and ships of many origins navigating the Americas docked at St. Eustatius to purchase goods and still, to a limited extent, slaves. Ships originating from the so-called 13 colonies in what would eventually become the USA used the facilities on Statia in order to purchase goods and arms in fighting the subsequent American War of Independence. In 1774, as many as 20 American ships at a time could be found in Statia's harbor. Thus, contact with varieties of English was intense on St. Eustatius during the latter half of the 18th century. Regarding the island's role as a meeting place of goods and people during this era, Hartog (1976: 40) states, the number of ships annually anchored at Statia were between 1,800 and 2,700, with its peak reached in 1779 with 3,551 ships. In 1781 the British Navy, under the command of Admiral George Rodney, attacked the island, looted its warehouses, confiscated millions of dollars in goods, and expelled many of its merchants (especially Jews).

In the years following the attack on Statia by Rodney and the British Navy, the free trade in slaves was forbidden in 1784. The Netherlands abolished the slave trade in 1814 and the importation of slaves from Africa to its islands in the Caribbean in 1821 (Attema 1976: 30). The French controlled the island again from 1795 to 1801. The English took over again for one year in 1801. The territory did not return to Dutch control until 1816.

From the population peak of 8,124 persons in 1790, the number of Statia's residents began to dwindle. The population of Statia has stabilized at approximately 2,000 persons today.

Preliminary data from St. Eustatius (Aceto 2006) reveals a high incidence of interdental fricatives. Th-stopping is the general norm in the Caribbean, including in Statia, but the fricatives [θ] and [ð] are also heard to a significant degree in naturally occurring speech in informal contexts (i.e. playing poker or dominos, drinking in a bar). The social correlates for the distribution of interdental fricatives versus alveolar stops in this location have yet to be determined. Furthermore, Statian Creole English is primarily non-rhotic, though [r] is variably pronounced by speakers in some contexts.

3.4.   Anguilla

The following information is from Williams (2003). The English undertook the first permanent European settlement on the island in 1650. The sugar industry on Anguilla suffered throughout the 17th and 18th centuries due to drought and a lack of investment capital by local planters. Anguillian settlers owned small plots of land, and typically only a few slaves worked with them and their family members in the fields. Slavery did not become fully established on Anguilla until late in the 18th century, and even then, the ratio of slaves to whites and free coloreds never matched the proportions found in other Caribbean plantation economies. The 1750 population information for Anguilla shows 350 whites, 38 free coloreds, and 1,962 blacks. The census of 1830 reveals the following demographics: 200 whites, 399 free coloreds, and 2,600 blacks. The 1830s on Anguilla saw a period of prolonged droughts that destroyed food crops, animals, and caused human famine.

After emancipation in 1838, a number of white colonists left the island to settle in North America and other parts of the Caribbean. The general distressed conditions of Anguillian life prompted some Anguillians to work as indentured laborers on the sugar plantations in St. Croix during the 1870s. The 1880 census of the island shows 202 whites and 3,017 free coloreds and blacks. The end of the 19th century brought Anguilla a devastating drought and corresponding famine.

Until recently Anguilla was relatively isolated from other islands of the area. Phone service was not available on the island until the 1960s. Electricity was not brought to the far eastern end of the island, to the villages of Island Harbour, East End, and Mount Fortune until the 1980s. The most recent census of May 2001 reveals a population of 11,300 for Anguilla.

Williams (2003) is the only source for linguistic features in Anguilla. His research focuses on the Webster dialect of Island Harbour, a white enclave dialect of English in the Eastern Caribbean. Non-Afro-American Anglo-Caribbean varieties, i.e. those English varieties spoken among the descendants of Irish, Scots, and English settlers, have largely been ignored within research paradigms except for the work of Williams (1985, 1987). These English-derived language varieties spoken largely by Euro-Caribbeans on the Bahamas, Saba, St. Barts, Bequia, the Cayman Islands, Barbados, and Anguilla may shed light on the Anglophone component heard by Africans and Afro-Caribbeans working alongside many of these European immigrants. Historically, these white indentured servants were often treated socially no differently than African slaves; some of them even joined African-derived Maroon communities. Williams (1987, 1988) uses the term Anglo-Caribbean English to designate the variety spoken by these speech communities.

Williams' research reveals some phonological features that are clearly derived from Scots or Scottish English sources. Unlike other dialects of English spoken in West Indian white enclave communities such as Cherokee Sound in the Bahamas, the Webster variety does not exhibit a significant degree of *h-* dropping. Williams correlates this pattern with the fact that there is no *h-*dropping in Scotland (Volume 1 of Wells 1982: 412). (However, the absence of h-dropping is a regional feature of the Eastern Caribbean in general.) Another feature associated with the Scottish component of this variety is that lexical items with vowels similar to *mouth* in metropolitan varieties are typically realized with the Scots pronunciation /u/.

The Webster dialect is primarily non-rhotic, although [r] is variably pronounced in some contexts by some speakers, e.g. [gʸanʔfaðər] *grandfather*, [wamz] *worms*. The Webster dialect exhibits the /w/ and /v/ alternation (typically with the intermediate value of [β]) that is found in many of the English-derived languages of the Eastern Caribbean and beyond (see discussion above). The Webster dialect differs in this regard from the Bahamian white dialect of Cherokee Sound where only the use of *v* in place of *w* was recorded by Childs, Reaser, and Wolfram (2003).

Th-stopping is a feature of the Webster dialect and other dialects of Anguilla, e.g. [diz] *these*, [doz] *those*, yet there are instances of interdental fricatives, e.g. [gʸanʔfaðər] *grandfather*. There is a degree of variation in the replacement of the fricatives with the corresponding stops, especially in careful speech. Williams (2003) states, "[c]ontext and the effect of vernacular language loyalty are the factors that affect whether pronunciation /θ/ and /ð/ will occur". Similar factors are discussed in Aceto (2006) for the St. Eustatius speech community and in Cutler (2003) for Turks Island English.

The Webster dialect also exhibits a slight degree of palatalization of velar stops before non-back vowels, e.g. [gʸɪlz] *girls*, [kʸarɪdʒ] *carriage* but [golʔ] *gold*, [kolor] *color*. Other features include the intervocalic voicing of /f/, e.g. [nevuz] *nephews*, and the lenition of word-final /t/ and /d/ when preceded by another consonant, e.g. [golʔ] *gold*, [ainʔ] *ain't*.

3.5.   Montserrat

Part of the local folk history in Montserrat is that Irish or Irish English has influenced the variety of English that emerged there. However, in Volume 3 Wells (1982: 586, 1983) reports there is no linguistic justification for this claim, even though Irish Catholics from nearby St. Kitts did settle the island in the early 17th century and several place names and surnames reflect Irish influence.

Montserrat English reveals short vowels in open syllables in segments that were long historically, e.g. *tea* [ti], *play* [ple], *straw* [stra]. However, in closed syllables there appears to be a contrast between long and short vowels, e.g. *beat* [biːt] vs. *bit* [bit], *pool* [puːl] vs. *pull* [pul]. In Volume 3, Wells (1982: 586) insists that this is not a difference in vowel quality but in length as presented above (however, two allophones of /o/ do reveal differences in quality, e.g. *show* [ʃo] and *cut* [kɔt]). This issue of short vowels in open syllables in Montserrat English means that the short vowels of words like *tea* are linked phonemically with the /i/ of *bit* rather than the [iː] of *beat*. Likewise, the [u] of *two* is linked with /u/ of *put* rather than the /uː/ of *boot*. Furthermore, in closed syllables, Montserratians often reveal diphthongs for mid vowels reminiscent of those heard in Western Caribbean varieties like Jamaican, e.g. *boat* [buot] and *bait* [biet], but these diphthongs are not found in open syllables, e.g. *bay* [be], *show* [ʃo].

Montserrat English is non-rhotic. Consequently, long vowels are found in open syllables (as well as closed ones) where historical /r/ was once present, e.g. *star* [staː], *war* [waː], *start* [staːt], *farm* [faːm]. Other words with long vowels that revealed /r/ historically resulted in the emergence of new diphthongs, e.g. *near* [nia] and *four* [fuo].

3.6.   Barbuda

The following information is from Aceto (2002b). Barbuda lies 28 miles north of Antigua. As is common in the Leeward Islands, droughts are often prolonged. Amerindian sites on the island indicate that Arawaks lived on Barbuda until the 13th century. Carib Amerindians visited the island occasionally from (what would eventually be called) Dominica from the 13th century to the early European period. The first group of European colonists arrived from nearby St. Kitts in 1628; due to Carib attacks and poor soil, this first effort was soon abandoned. In 1632, colonists, again from St. Kitts, made another attempt to settle Barbuda; however, they were driven away again by Caribs. In 1681, Caribs from St. Vincent and Dominica raided a settlement of 20 Europeans on Barbuda in several hundred canoes, killing eight of the settlers.

In 1668, James Winthorpe leased Barbuda and began the first period of private "ownership" of Barbuda by English speakers from Europe. Winthorpe eventually relinquished his lease, and in 1685 Christopher and John Codrington leased the island for the next 200 years. Thus, Barbuda became the private property of the Codrington family, who first settled in Barbados but were often absentee owners living in Somerset, England. The Codringtons' goal was to use Barbuda as a means to create supplies for their plantations on nearby Antigua. Barbuda was not a "true colony" since it was the private property of the Codringtons. The presence of Europeans on the island during the colonial period varied from a single Anglophone to perhaps as high as three or four. Slaves lived virtually on their own except for a solitary (and often absent) Codrington manager and one or two overseers.

The population of Barbuda has never been large. Even today it is only about 1,500 persons. In 1715, there were 118 persons on the island; in 1804, 314; and in 1832, 492.

Barbudan Creole English (BCE) exhibits many of the same sound segments typical in the Anglophone Eastern Caribbean. However, there are contraction processes and reciprocal phonetic effects similar to vowel harmony rules that, to my knowledge, have not been described in the creolistics literature. That is, discrete grammatical markers may appear to be reduced or even disappear on the surface of some utterances. Some examples of the vowel harmony-like effects (in bold) are: [**ya ga** du dat tumaro] "Are you going to do that tomorrow?" and [**mo go** du dat tumaro] "I'm going to do that tomorrow." In isolation, the future marker is [go] and the first person singular pronoun is [mi]. Examples of contraction processes at play are (note that the forms within parentheses are a transitional stage assumed by this researcher; contracted forms are in bold): [ʃi a go siŋ (ʃi a ga siŋ) ~ ʃi **gaa** siŋ] "She is going to sing" (the [a] of the future tense marker *a go* influences the quality of the vowel in *go*) and [(mi go biit yu) ~ mo go biit yu ~ **moo** biit yu] "I'm going to hit you" (the [o] in *go* influences the quality of the earlier vowel in the pronoun *mi*).

Some of the more robust contraction processes involve the co-occurrence of bilabial nasals when past tense utterances are spoken in the first person singular. That is, when the first person pronoun *mi* is immediately followed by [mɪn], the past tense marker, the pronoun *mi* is often submerged or contracted within the past tense form: [**mɪn** de krai haad ~ mi mɪn de krai haad] "I cried hard" and [**mɪn** da taak ~ mi mɪn **da** (~ de + a) taak] "I was talking."

3.7.   Windward Islands (Dominica, St. Lucia, St. Vincent and the Grenadines, Carriacou, and Grenada)

Though English restructured varieties are common on these islands today, they all share a joint Francophone/Anglophone history. That is, before the 19th century these islands were all once controlled by the French, and consequently, in most locations, there are speakers of earlier French-derived creoles that predate the emergence of later English-derived restructured varieties. Dominica has two English-derived creoles that emerged in the 19th and 20th centuries: one is an intermediate variety that emerged locally and the other is a deep creole called Kokoy that is related to immigrants from Antigua and Montserrat who arrived to work on fruit plantations in the post-emancipation setting. Carriacou Creole English emerged largely in the late 18th and 19th centuries, according to Kephart (2003). St. Lucian Vernacular English, which Garrett (2003) insists is *not* a creole, emerged in the late 19th and 20th centuries in largely educational institutional contexts. There is not much linguistic information on English-derived varieties spoken on St. Vincent and the Grenadines as well as on Grenada, but these areas seem to be largely Anglophone today. Francophone varieties that were once spoken widely on these islands appear to be disappearing.

In regards to phonology, none of the Anglophone Windward islands have been linguistically documented to any significant degree. In Dominica, Kokoy speakers exhibit voiceless labio-dental fricatives, i.e. [f], in onsets that correspond to voiceless interdental fricatives in metropolitan varieties, i.e. /θ/ and /t/ in other Caribbean Englishes. For example, the words *three* and *thing* are often realized as /friː/ and /fɪŋ/ respectively in this Creole language variety. St. Vincent and Grenada lack a contrast between *by* and *boy*. Both locations lack /ə/, /ʌ/, and the post-vocalic /r/ found in Bajan.

Kephart (2003) offers a brief presentation of Carriacou phonology. Carriacou Creole English has a basic seven-vowel system, which marks it as quite different from other creoles, especially Jamaican. To find a similar system in the Caribbean we have to go to Dominica, which also contains an earlier variety of Creole French similar to that found in Carriacou. Kephart believes that, among the Atlantic English-derived Creoles, the Suriname creoles probably come closest to the Carriacou Creole English system. In both systems, the only tense/lax contrast is in the mid vowels. Another phonological feature that distinguishes this variety of Creole English is the presence of nasal vowels. These vowels occur in words that Carriacou Creole English shares with Carriacou Creole French, e.g. [sukuyã] *vampire*, [tetshẽ] *boa constrictor*, [kɔ̃koʃã] *biased*, [gwãgozhei] *brown pelican*. Kephart insists that speakers pronounce these words with the nasalization intact; that is, these nasalized vowels do not correspond to a vowel plus nasal consonant, even in word-final position.

4.   Conclusion

There are many polemical topics of great interest to creole studies (e.g. the nature of the creole continuum, the possible effects of decreolization, possible loci of creole genesis and language diffusion, the structural features and historical processes shared by the group of languages called creoles by linguists, et al.) and most conclusions based upon English-derived data are largely drawn from

Jamaican, Guyanese, and, most often, one of the several English-derived creoles of Suriname. This reductionist attitude is insufficient since the sociolinguistic profiles of many of the locations in the Anglophone Eastern Caribbean have never even been documented. Once we have documented the languages spoken in these neglected locales, only then, will researchers be able to accurately and precisely discuss – with an extensive set of attested data in hand – how these varieties fit into a larger linguistic and sociohistorical view of English-derived language genesis in the Caribbean and the Atlantic region in general.

Exercises and study questions

1. Is the Anglophone Eastern Caribbean a rhotic area? Are there are any exceptions to your characterization?

2. What is the status of reduced vowels like schwa in the Eastern Caribbean? Do they typically occur, and, if so, in the speech of what kind of speaker?

3. Explain the /v/ and /w/ merger in the Eastern Caribbean. Which segments typically correspond to /v/ in these other dialects and/or creole varieties of English?

4. Explain what *th*-stopping is. Which segments generally correspond to /ð/ and /θ/ in which locations in the Eastern Caribbean? Which locations display /ð/ and /θ/ regularly in some portions of the population?

5. Explain what *h*-dropping is. Which dialect of British English is generally cited in order to explain the *absence* of *h*-dropping in Anguilla and the Eastern Caribbean in general?

6. How are historic long vowels represented in Montserrat Creole English? How is this pattern different from other areas of the Eastern Caribbean?

7. How was the sociohistorical context of English creole language emergence in Barbuda different from other areas of the Eastern Caribbean?

Selected references

Please consult the General references for titles mentioned in the text but not included in the references below. For a full bibliography see the accompanying CD-ROM.

Aceto, Michael
  2002a   Going back to the beginning: Describing the (nearly) undocumented
           Anglophone creoles of the Caribbean. In: Glenn G. Gilbert (ed.), *Pidgin
           and Creole Linguistics in the 21st Century*, 93–118. New York: Peter
           Lang.
  2002b   Barbudan Creole English: Its history and some grammatical features.
           English World-Wide 23: 223–250.
  2006   Station Creole English: An English-derived Language emerges in the
           Dutch Antilles. *World Englishes* 25: 411–435.
Attema, Y.
  1976   *St. Eustatius: A Short History of the Island and Its Monuments*. De Walburg
           Pers Zutphen Holland.
Baker Philip and Adrienne Bruyn (eds),
  1998   *St. Kitts and the Atlantic Creoles: The Texts of Samual Augustus Mathews
           in Perspective*. (Westminster Creolistics Series 4). London: University of
           Westminster Press.
Carter, Hazel
  1987   Suprasegmentals in Guyanese: Some African comparisons. In: Gilbert
           (ed.), 213–263.
Cassidy, Frederic G.
  1980   The place of Gullah. *American Speech* 55: 3–15.
Childs, Becky, Jeffrey Reaser and Walt Wolfram
  2003   Defining ethnic varieties in the Bahamas: Phonological accommodation
           in black and white enclave communities. In: Aceto and Williams (eds.),
           1–28.
Cutler, Cecilia
  2003   English in the Turks and Caicos Islands: A look at Grand Turk. In: Aceto
           and Williams (eds.), 51–80.
Garrett, Paul B.
  2003   An "English Creole" that isn't: on the sociohistorical origins and linguis-
           tic classification of the vernacular English in St. Lucia. In: Aceto and
           Wiliams (eds.), 155–210.
Hancock, Ian
  1980   Gullah and Barbadian: Origins and relationships. *American Speech* 55:
           17–35.
Hartog, J.
  1976   *History of St. Eustatius*. Aruba: De Wit.
Kephart, Ronald
  2003   Creole English on Carriacou: A sketch and some implications. In: Aceto
           and Williams (eds.), 227–240.
Keur, John Y and Dorothy L. Keur
  1960   *Windward Children: A Study in the Human Ecology of the Three Dutch
           Windward Islands in the Caribbean*. Assen: Royal Vangorcum.
Le Page, Robert B
  1960   An historical introduction to Jamaican Creole. In: Robert B. Le Page and
           David DeCamp (eds.), *Jamaican Creole*, 3–124. New York: Macmillan.

Rickford, John R.
1992   The creole residue in Barbados. In: Joan H. Hall, Nick Doane and Dick Ringler (eds), *Old English and New: Studies in Language and Linguistics in Honor of Frederic G. Cassidy*, 183-201 New York: Garland Publishing.

Sabino, Diamond and Cockcroft
2003   Language variety in the Virgin Islands: Plural markings. In: Aceto and Williams (eds.), 81–94.

Sutcliffe, David
1982   *British Black English.* Oxford: Basil Blackwell.
1987   Phonological relationships in Caribbean and West African English. *English World-Wide* 8: 61–68.
2003   Eastern Caribbean suprasegmental systems: A comparative view, with particular reference to Barbadian, Trinidadian, and Guyanese. In: Aceto and Williams (eds.), 265–296.

Van Herk, Gerard
2003   Barbadian lects: Beyond meso. In: Aceto and Williams (eds.), 241–264.

Williams, Jeffrey P.
1983   Dutch and English creole on the windward Netherlands Antilles: An historical perspective. *Amsterdam Creole Studies* 5: 93–111.
1985   Preliminaries to the study of the dialects of white West Indian English. *Nieuwe West-Indische Gids* 59: 27–44.
1987   Anglo-Caribbean English: A study of its sociolinguistic history and the development of its aspectual markers. Unpublished Ph.D. dissertation, The University of Texas at Austin.
1988   The development of aspectual markers in Anglo-Caribbean English. *Journal of Pidgin and Creole Languages* 3: 245–263.
2003   The establishment and perpetuation of anglophone white enclave communities in the Eastern Caribbean: The case of Island Harbor, Anguilla. In: Aceto and Williams (eds.), 95–119.

Bajan: phonology

Renée Blake

1.   Introduction

Barbados is a contemporary nation-state that won its independence from Britain in 1966. This island, the most easterly of the Caribbean countries, is 21 miles long by 14 miles wide and has an approximate population of a quarter million people. It is a densely populated country, with more than 1 500 persons per square mile in urban areas; and much less in the rural areas where the land is appropriated for tillage. Geopolitically, the island is divided into eleven parishes, with the capital, Bridgetown, located in the southwest parish of St. Michael. The remaining parishes are divided into subsidiary centers in terms of region (e.g., southern, etc.). The eastern side of the island has been relegated to national historical landmark status, thereby prohibiting industrial development and limiting tourism.

While the official language of this country is English, the population also speaks an English-related Creole, Bajan, arising out of a particular language contact situation, slavery and bond servitude, under British colonization. As opposed to "Barbadian English" or "Barbadian Creole (English)", the name Bajan (also Barbadian or Badian) for the vernacular language of Barbados is derived from the island name and does not carry the potential charge that suggests a position on the origins of the language, as discussed below. Although Barbados was an entrepôt for slaves (serving as the springboard for settlements elsewhere in the Caribbean), Bajan is unique amongst languages in the Anglophone Caribbean territories, i.e., from Jamaica to Guyana, because its creole affiliations have been questioned (as is the case for African American English). This is largely due to the nature of the island's historical links to Britain and its demographics during the early colonial period. Almost twice as long a term as its sister territories in the Atlantic, Barbados experienced an uninterrupted colonization period of more than three hundred years by English-speaking rulers, lending to the cognomen "Little England". Moreover, in the first quarter century of colonization, whites outnumbered blacks, further lending to its image.

2.   Historical background

Archeological records indicate that prior to the appearance of the English in Barbados, the island had been inhabited by Arawak or Taino Indians, since sometime between 200 and 400 BC, sailing from what is now known as Venezuela. However, it is believed that these tribes no longer inhabited the island by the time of the first British arrival in 1625 under the authority of King James I. Under British rule, two racial groups, whites and blacks, populated the island, with their proportion changing over time according to the needs of the plantation system. For instance, during the early colonial period (1627–1660), the island consisted of small farms on which tobacco, cotton, ginger and indigo were cultivated, necessitating servants but few slaves. As a result, African slaves were outnumbered by whites, comprised of planters and a large prisoner of war and bondservant population from Ireland and later Scotland who performed servile and agricultural work under several years of indentureship.

Within a quarter of a century of colonization, planters found it more lucrative to cultivate sugar, which required large amounts of manpower. Thus, accompanying the "sugar revolution" was a dramatic increase in the importation of African slaves originating from present-day Ghana, Togo, Dahomey, and western Nigeria. This increase of Africans in Barbados resulted in a reverse shift in the population, such that between 1667 and 1670 blacks outnumbered whites two to one. This process continued until the 1800s at which point blacks would henceforth represent the overwhelming majority of the island's population. Emancipation of slaves was finalized in 1838. Due to a large African slave population, Barbados, unlike many of the other Caribbean islands, did not lack manpower, hence the low percentage of other ethnic minorities (e.g., East Indians, Chinese) comprising the island's population. In terms of the nation's economy, since the mid-17th century the vast majority of Barbados' landmass has been under sugar cane. However, in recent times, the massive growth in tourism as its major income-generating activity has caused a shift in the country's economy. As a result, recently, there has been a shortage of agricultural manpower leading to recruitment of temporary labor from neighboring islands.

3.   Research background

Researchers have almost exclusively examined the morphosyntactic structure of Bajan in their quest to discover the linguistic origins of the language. Since the 1980s, linguistic research on the Bajan language has focused on the extent to which the language was influenced by the provincial dialects of England and the West African languages spoken by the slave populations. Debates ensued regarding the genesis of Bajan in terms of whether it should be considered a dialect of English or a Creole (similar to other Caribbean Creoles) with linguistic links to West Africa (cf. Hancock 1980; Cassidy 1986; Fields 1995; Rickford and Handler 1994). In the end, historical and synchronic studies of its grammatical structure suggest that Bajan has shown a wide range of linguistic variation throughout its history, with great co-occurrence of features attributable to superstrate (British dialects spoken in Ireland and southwest England), as well as substrate (African) influences (cf. Winford 2000).

The work of Fields (1995) reveals linguistic residues (e.g., invariant word order for questions, absence of number distinction in nouns, invariant pronoun usage) of a pidgin stage for Bajan that appears at least since the 18th century. Fields argues that the social history and demographics of Barbados in the 18th century provided an environment conducive to the formation of a creole from an earlier formed pidgin. Firstly, there was a dominant white planter group and a subordinate slave group with little social interaction between the two. Secondly, there was a period in which blacks vastly outnumbered whites. And thirdly, there was at some point a steady influx of new African slaves onto the island. Due to its extensive contact with English, Bajan has decreolized. One may argue that the language has decreolized to the extent that the range between its most creolized forms and Standard English is the smallest for the Anglophone Creoles spoken in the Caribbean.

4.   Bajan

4.1.   Survey

Bajan, then, a member of the Caribbean English Creole (CEC) family, shares a number of distinctive linguistic features at the level of phonology, grammar and lexicon with its sister territories. Nonetheless, it has several marked phonological features that lend to the distinctive Bajan 'accent'. Very often speakers of other CECs stereotype Bajan speakers by their r-fullness, their seemingly ubiquitous use of glottal stops and the quality of the first vowel of PRICE/PRIZE. Unlike the other CECs, Bajan is fully rhotic, with [r] rarely deleted among all levels of society. Moreover, within the Caribbean, glottalizing of the voiceless obstruents [p, t, k] in syllable-final position is specific to Bajan; an example is *departments* pronounced [dɪˈpaːɹʔmənʔs]. Also distinctive to Bajan is the phonetic quality of the first element of the diphthong that is pronounced as [ai] in the other CECs. Typically, the nucleus of PRICE/PRIZE backs and heightens to [ʌɪ]. The last two features, specifically, often cause non-native Bajan speakers to conjecture that Barbadians are speaking some form of dialect reminiscent of the west of England, or an Irish English brogue.

4.2. Phonological system

Although Bajan is most distinguished by its phonology, there has been little research on its phonological system, most likely due to the nature of the inquiries surrounding the linguistic origins of the language. Most notably, Wells (1982) provides an essential phonological inventory of Bajan, and Haynes (1973) correlates the degree of use of several stigmatized phonological features with individuals' ethnic identity, education and geographical location on the island. Researchers and locals note that language varies by parish, but this is largely impressionistic. Generally, there is agreement that the speech of the most northern parish, St. Lucy, and most eastern parish, St. Philip, (both of which may also be considered rural) are most distinct from the rest of the island. In her research, Haynes' found a distinct intonation in the northeastern parish of St. Andrew, also referred to as the Scotland District, physically demarcated from the rest of the flat island by its "hilly" character. That dialect differences exist can be attributed to degree of proximity to urban centers, and the ramifications stemming from this (e.g., education, industry).

The phonological inventory of Bajan has much in common with the other CECs. Together it stands in contrast to other varieties of English, particularly in terms of vowel quality (primarily with respect to its diphthongs) and prosody. Unlike RP and General American, the mid [eː] and low [oː] vowels in FACE and GOAT generally have not undergone Long Mid Diphthonging in the Caribbean English Creoles. Whereas in RP and General American, the long vowels have diphthongal allophones, in the CECs, the long vowels tend to remain pure. The CECs also tend to have unreduced vowels in unstressed syllables instead of the reduced [ə] typifying other varieties of English. This contributes to the perception of these creoles as syllable-timed, as opposed to stress-timed languages, and conveys a rhythmic quality. Finally, the intonation of the CECs tends to utilize a broad pitch range. For example, more than other varieties of English, these languages employ rising intonation at the end of clauses to indicate a question. Table 1 summarizes the distinctive vowel realization of Bajan.

Table 1.   Bajan vowel realizations

KIT	ɪ	FLEECE	iː
DRESS	ɛ	FACE	eː ~ ei / ɛː ~ iɛ
TRAP	a	PALM	aː
LOT	ɑ ~ ɒ	THOUGHT	ɑː ~ ɒː
STRUT	ʌ	GOAT	oː > oə
FOOT	ʊ	GOOSE	uː
BATH	aː	PRICE	ʌɪ
CLOTH	ɒː	CHOICE	ʌɪ / ɔɪ
NURSE	ɤ	MOUTH	ʌu ~ ʌʊ
NEAR	eːr	CURE	oːr
SQUARE	eːr	happY	iː
START	aːr	lettER	ɤ
NORTH	ɑːr / ɒːr	horsES	ɪ
FORCE	oːr	commA	ə

4.3.   Vowels

Unlike what is found for some popular CEC speech, TRAP and LOT are not merged in Bajan. However, the vowels of LOT, CLOTH and THOUGHT are generally merged like in many rhotic accents. While CLOTH always appears to be rounded, this feature is variably manifested as unrounded for LOT and THOUGHT. Realization of FACE may vary by region and education/class. In the speech of urban and more educated speakers of Bajan, FACE is generally realized as monophthongal [eː], although it appears that, more recently, Long Mid Diphthonging has become productive in the language, adding a closing offglide to the long mid vowel [ei]. FACE is manifested in rural and uneducated speech with the more open and lower monophthongal variant [ɛ]. While Wells (1982: 584) notes that the alternating variant may be the centering diphthong [eə], I suggest that it is rather the opening diphthong [ɪɛ], common in popular CEC speech. GOAT, on the other hand, while traditionally monophthongal in Bajan, appears to be moving towards the centring diphthong [oə]. Like STRUT, the first element of the PRICE diphthong is generally half-open and unrounded [ʌ] (although Wells provides a broader range between [ʌ] and [ə]). Highly educated speakers may have the more fronted open [a] as the first element of this diphthong. CHOICE is variably manifested as [ʌɪ] and [oi], the latter viewed as markedly Bajan for this lexical class by neighboring CEC speakers. The first element of the MOUTH diphthong appears to be slightly more rounded than [ʌ], although not to the extent of [ɔ]. START, BATH and PALM are in the same phonetic class, realized as the relatively front unrounded [a]. In other rhotic environments, NEAR and SQUARE are merged, and NORTH and FORCE are phonemically distinct, although FORCE and CURE are manifested as the pure variant of GOAT.

5.   Current issues

Today in Barbados, one still finds remnants of class and race stratification delineating the vestigial struggles of the colonial era. While black Barbadians have made social and economic strides, largely controlling the local political sector in the upper and middle classes, whites have near monopoly in the larger commercial sectors. Along these lines, class differences within the racial strata of the island are also evident. Within the scholarly literature on Barbados and other Anglophone islands, poor whites, although relatively small in number, are historically and socially placed in the national sphere, albeit as a mythical or oftentimes autonomous entity. Despite the social existing partitions, researchers note that Barbadian identity is tied to a strong sense of and commitment to a national identity and shared culture. Such portrayals are evident in the unofficial national slogan, "All O' We Is One" [All of us are one]. However, the Bajan language, despite being viewed as the local national language, has been ideologically linked to the island's black population. Blake's (1997) research on a racially-mixed poor community in Barbados shows its black and white populations to speak the local vernacular in a typically creole manner, particularly regarding morphosyntactic features, with whites at times displaying even more creole-like behavior. The linguistic similarities of these two groups may be crucially linked to their socioeconomic status on the island, which can be located in the political economy.

Clearly, diachronic and synchronic studies of all aspects of the Bajan language are wanting. Rich areas for linguistic inquiry include internal and regional variation, contact-induced change, race relations, as well as changes due to the current social and political economy of the island. While the Bajan language has been adequately examined in terms of genesis arguments, it remains an area for research in terms of broader issues arising in creole studies and sociolinguistics.

Exercises and study questions

1. Listen to the words under "The Lexical Set" on the accompanying CD. Transcribe the words as accurately as possible and describe the articulatory processes in phonetic terms. Pay particular attention to DRESS, TRAP, CLOTH, FACE, GOAT, PRICE, MOUTH, SQUARE and HAPPY. What is noteworthy about these pronunciations?

2. Which metalinguistic statements does the speaker of the free passage on the CD make? Compare these to what the article says.

3. Is Bajan a "deep" creole? Consult the references quoted in section 3 of the article for conflicting views on the origin and nature of the variety; summarize these in your own words.

4. Which diphthongs does Bajan share with other Caribbean Creoles but not with British or American English?

5. Compare Bajan with neighboring varieties with respect to rhoticity. Is it special? Attempt a historical explanation for what you find.

6. Compare the vowel realizations of Bajan to those of Jamaican English and Bahamian English. Which features are shared? How could you possibly tell a Bajan from one of their Caribbean neighbors?

Selected references

Please consult the General references for titles mentioned in the text but not included in the references below. For a full bibliography see the accompanying CD-ROM.

Blake, Renée
    1997   All O' We Is One?: Race, class and language in a Barbados community. Ph.D. dissertation, Stanford University.
Cassidy, Frederic G.
    1986   Barbadian Creole — possibility and probability. *American Speech* 61: 195–205.
Fields, Linda
    1995   Early Bajan: Creole or non-creole? In: Jacques Arends (ed.), *The Early Stages of Creolization*, 89–112. Amsterdam/Philadelphia: Benjamins.

Hancock, Ian
  1980   Gullah and Barbadian — origins and relationships. *American Speech* 55:
            17–35.
Haynes, Lilith
  1973   Language in Barbados and Guyana: attitudes, behaviors and comparisons.
            Ph.D. dissertation, Stanford University.
Rickford, John and Jerome Handler
  1994   Textual evidence on the nature of early Barbadian speech, 1676–1835.
            Journal of Pidgin and Creole Languages 9: 221–255.
Roberts, Peter
  1988   *West Indians and Their Language*. Cambridge: Cambridge University
            Press.
Wells, John C.
  1982   *Accents of English*. Cambridge: Cambridge University Press.
Winford, Donald
  2000   'Intermediate' creoles and degrees of change in creole formation: The case
            of Bajan. In: Neumann-Holzschuh and Schneider (eds.), 215–246.

The creoles of Trinidad and Tobago: phonology

Valerie Youssef and Winford James

1. Sociohistorical background

1.1. Introduction

The histories of the islands of Trinidad and Tobago (see Map 1) are divergent, and although the two have comprised a single political entity since 1889, they must be considered as separate entities for the purposes of describing both their histories and the distinct linguistic elements in their language varieties. This need has been under-stated in the literature on Trinidad and Tobago, since the two islands have hardly been treated differentially in any detail in survey texts (e.g., Holm 1989/90; Winford 1993).

Solomon (1993: 2) mentions a paucity of information available on Tobago, but there has been work (e.g. James 1974; Minderhout 1979; Southers 1977) which has simply drawn less attention to itself because of the political ascendancy of the larger island. It is hoped that a new publication on Tobagonian will redress the balance (James and Youssef 2002), since the basilectal variety peculiar to Tobago alone merits attention in its own right, and the interplay among varieties in the island is also unique. For phonology, this is undisputably the most comprehensive source. The best sources on the phonology of Trinidad are Winford (1972, 1978), Winer (1993) and Solomon (1993).

Broadly it can be said that the history of conquest, exploitation and migration was different for Trinidad and Tobago, notwithstanding their common Amerindian indigenous base and initial Spanish incursions. Both were claimed by Columbus in 1498, but Tobago was sighted and not invaded at this time. However, Trinidad remained officially Spanish until 1797, with a strong French presence up to the late-eighteenth century, while Tobago was continuously squabbled over until 1763, but with no lasting linguistic impact either from Spanish or French. The difference was one of skirmishes in Tobago versus long-lasting settlement in Trinidad, with the latter having more far-reaching linguistic results on the lexicon.

With regard to the history and development of Caribbean creole languages generally, there is likely to have been a spectrum of language varieties from the outset. A full language continuum ranging from the basilectal creole to the standard is likely to have developed in early slave societies according to the extent

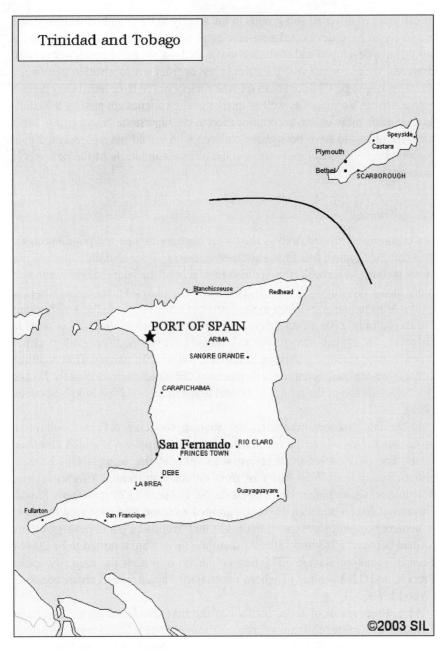

Map 1.   Trinidad and Tobago

of exposure of different sub-groups in the society to the Standard. House slaves are likely to have developed near-acrolectal varieties, whereas the field slaves would have developed and continued to use the basilect. Field slaves were cut off from real social contact with the ruling class or from any motivation to move towards its language. Children born into the society would have heard their parents' native African languages as well as interlanguage varieties adopted by the adults as they made more or less accommodation to the superstrate languages. In some measure, it would have been these children who would have augmented their parents' language creation, becoming the ultimate architects of the new creole language.

1.2.   Trinidad

If we examine Trinidad first, as the larger territory in size and population, we find that the Spanish had little sustained interest in it since it did not yield precious metals. As a result, the Spanish residents of the island never numbered more than a few hundred, though these did succeed in severely decimating the native Amerindian population in the course of time. By 1765, the Amerindians numbered only 2503 of an original 30-40000 (Brereton 1981). It is notable, however, that a great many towns in Trinidad have retained Amerindian names down to the present e.g. Arima, Tunapuna, Arouca, Tacarigua. This is unlike Tobago, whose main retention is the name of the island itself, originally Tavaco (for full coverage of the ranges of lexical items in Trinidad see Baksh-Soodeen 1995).

In the late eighteenth century, the Spanish encouraged French migration to Trinidad. This allowed those fleeing the political upheaval which climaxed in the French Revolution to set up sugar plantations, using slaves brought either directly from West Africa or from French Caribbean territories such as Martinique, Guadeloupe, Haiti, Grenada, St. Lucia and Cayenne (now French Guyana). Chacon, the then governor, granted a second Cedula giving free land to settlers bringing slaves with the result that Trinidad's population was transformed between 1783 and 1803. At that time there were reported to be 20,464 'French'-speaking slaves, 5275 free coloureds of whom the majority spoke French, and 2261 whites of whom the majority again were French speaking (Wood 1968: 33).

As a direct result of these incursions the first Creole language spoken in Trinidad was a French-lexicon creole (Thomas 1869). That language, which we see recorded by Wood as French, was undoubtedly a French-lexicon creole, for the slaves at least, and most probably for the plantation owners at that time. This language survived intact throughout the nineteenth century, notwithstanding the establishment of a strong British rule during that period. The first attestations of an English creole are found recorded for 1838 in the diaries of a Mrs. Carmichael (quoted in Winer 1984) and by others. They reported on some of the slaves knowing two creole varieties, French- and English-lexicon, and feigning ignorance of the latter for reasons of excluding the British master class from their conversation.

Trinidad is sometimes held not to have had a basilectal English-Creole variety, but the Spectator texts found by Winer and Gilbert (1987) show that she did have a basilect in the 1860's. It appears that the island experienced a gradual shift in language use from a French-lexicon basilect to an English-lexicon mesolect under the steadily encroaching influence of English varieties. Villages such as Paramin, Blanchisseuse and La Fillette on the north coast, and Carenage in the west, retain elderly native French Creole speakers down to the present time.

Solomon (1993) makes a strong case for a language crossover element in the evolution of the creole languages, noting the lack of syllable final -*r* in words such as *car* and *cart* as being a direct effect of this. He argues that this feature distinguishes Caribbean islands with a French background e.g. Grenada, St. Lucia, Dominica, from those with an English background like Barbados, Guyana and Jamaica with a history of colonization by r-pronouncing British varieties including the south-west of England and Ireland. However, basilectal Tobagonian exhibits lack of syllable-final [-r] also as well as some Jamaican varieties with no French influence.

Trinidad had to look outside for the support of its agrarian economy. From 1845 until 1917 there was continuous Indian migration to Trinidad as the British government encouraged labourers to come mainly from Uttar Pradesh in Northern India to populate the plantations that the African population had abandoned following emancipation. They brought a number of languages including Bhojpuri and Tamil, but the one which won out and became a lingua franca was Bhojpuri, a language related to, but not a dialect of, Hindi. Moving to the rural areas of central Trinidad, the Indian population retained Bhojpuri for some time with French Creole as their first Trinidadian language. Historically it has been difficult to disambiguate some of the lexicon between these two languages. Winford (1972; 1978) found the speech of rural Trinidadians to be the most conservative phonologically, and this is discussed further in Section 2.2. below. Solomon (1993: 166) has also noted the fact that syllable-final [-r] is pronounced in words and names of Indic and Arabic origin as distinct from those of European origin.

There was a Spanish presence in the nineteenth century through a group of 4000 Spanish-Amerindian persons who came mainly from Venezuela and settled in the foothills of the Northern Range to cultivate cocoa. These were the ancestors of the few remaining Spanish speakers in Trinidad today.

Also contributing to the multiracial and cultural environment of the time were 1298 Madeirans who arrived in 1846 and approximately 2400 Chinese who arrived between 1853 and 1886. Between 1841 and 1861 a large number of African ex-slaves, including 6500 from St Helena and Sierra Leone, came into Trinidad; these Alleyne (1980: 211) considers to have had a direct influence on the emerging English-lexicon creole of Trinidad. There were others who spoke Yoruba, Ibo, Congo and Manding. In addition, there were many who migrated from other parts of the Caribbean, including 14,000 Barbadians. These migrant Caribbean people introduced a number of creole varieties to Trinidad and were particularly important in the transition of Trinidad from French-lexicon to English-lexicon Creole earlier alluded to.

1.3.   Tobago

Tobago was nominally Spanish from 1498 until the first British settlers arrived in 1625 but, as with Trinidad, the Spanish had little real interest in the territory. The Dutch landed settlers in 1628, but a Spanish and Amerindian force from Trinidad invaded and retook Tobago. The British landed again in 1639 and again the Amerindians fought them off. By 1674, when Tobago was ceded to the Dutch, the island had changed hands more than a dozen times. European policy at that time was that the island should be sufficiently desecrated as to hinder all development, so intense was the competition over it. The island was granted a neutral status from 1684-1763, which was virtually ignored. None of the European forces, save the British, stayed sufficiently long to impact the language situation.

With regard to the ethnic origins of the Africans of Tobago and their languages, the records are few. Elder (1988:16, 19) states that Congoes lived in the Tobagonian villages of Culloden Moor, Belle Garden, Pembroke and Charlotteville, as reported in 'oral accounts of living informants'. Ibos are also mentioned in government records, and a Moravian minister apparently reported to the pioneering creolist Hugo Schuchardt in the 1880s that most Negroes at that time were Cramanti, with a few Ibos (Winer and Gilbert 1987).

Tobago was ceded to the British by the French in 1763, and from that year, the British proceeded to purposefully build a colony. Planters, mostly of Scottish origin, sailed from Barbados, Grenada, and other already colonised islands, as well as from Britain itself, with their slaves, to carve up the island into parishes and plantations as part of Britain's great sugar enterprise. The colony started out as part of the Grenada government. Except for a very brief 12-year discontinuous French interregnum (1781-1793; 1802-3), the British formally governed Tobago until 1962, when the country of Trinidad and Tobago became independent. Tobago became a formal part of Trinidad and Tobago, as a ward of the colony, from 1899.

Although slavery was abolished in 1838, the plantation continued to be the focal point of Tobagonian life to a much greater extent than in neighbouring Trinidad. The Tobagonian planters passed a number of laws after Emancipation in 1838 to keep the ex-slaves tied to the land by a metayage (share-cropping) system; this served to preserve the sugar estates initially but brought competition between the sugar work of the estates and the metayers' trend towards developing other crops for internal trade. Sugar and cotton production gradually gave way to the production of cocoa, coconuts, hides, animals, vegetables and fruits. Skilled tradespeople, artisans, shopkeepers and seamstresses came to proliferate, and moved away from plantation work, with the result that the sugar economy collapsed in the 1880's despite the planters importing labour from other islands for their estates. Nonetheless, the island of Tobago remained village-based in a way that Trinidad did not.

The continuation of such a social and economic state meant that the English lexicon Creole, which had undergone no noticeable effect from the brief French incursions to the island, remained intact.

1.4.   Twentieth century developments

One further fact that distinguished Trinidad from Tobago linguistically, apart from ethno-historical difference, was the faster spread of education through urbanization in the former. Both islands witnessed the spread of primary education through Canadian missionaries from 1868 since they focussed on rural areas in both territories initially. In the long term, rural areas in Tobago remained more resistant to education because of the need for children to be employed in estate work, such that there was an earlier trend towards Standard English in the urban rather than rural environments. More schools were built in Trinidad than in Tobago as part of a government policy which underdeveloped the smaller island in relation to the larger. It is true, however, that, from the 1960s, parents in Tobago insisted that their children go to school at all cost. Prime Minister Eric Williams, who came to power in 1956, decreed that "the future of the children" lay "in their schoolbags" and this focus determined a shift from the land by the new generation. Unfortunately there was not the level of infrastructural and economic development to provide employment for these newly educated youngsters in Tobago, however.

Today the two islands share a mesolectal English-lexicon creole, which is alike in most particulars. Since the Creole was officially recognized as a language variety in its own right from 1975, it has been more used by teachers in schools, and contexts for monolingual Standard production are declining. The mesolect has become increasingly shared because of continuous movement between Tobago and Trinidad, the upsurge in education across the board, and especially because of Tobagonian migration to Trinidad as the territory offering greater opportunities for training, employment and other benefits.

A common factor in both territories are both North American and Jamaican influences, which manifest particularly among radio announcers and teenagers. Solomon (1993: 167-8) comments that, like most imitations, the changes towards American English in phonology are not consistently maintained, and this is also true for Jamaican.

Increased status for the creole and an identification with it as the language of the territory have made for greater use of it in public contexts, such as parliament; motivation towards a pure Standard is disappearing since most people balance out their use of standard and creole in relation to the demands of each situation. If StE is the language of power, TrnC is the language of solidarity, and appropriate language use necessarily entails balancing the two varieties.

In a study focussed on the village of Bethel in Tobago, Youssef (2001) found that the oldest and least educated informants still spoke largely the basilect, with shifts to the lower mesolect in public contexts. Retired professionals spoke both the acrolect and the basilect and had negative views of the mesolect as a mixed unstable variety. Young people, in contrast, spoke more mesolect, although they commanded the basilect; some disdained the acrolect, and all showed a measure of identification with the mesolect and specific features within it particularly characterized that group. These kinds of complex interaction demand further investigation.

2.   Phonological description

2.1.   Introduction

Firstly, we must acknowledge considerable phonological variability in both islands and a situation of ongoing flux in the language varieties caused by internal and external influences upon them alluded to in the previous section. It is unclear whether the language varieties are achieving a measure of overall stability in relation to one another or whether there is a steady process of decreolization brought about by the overarching effect of English in education.

In public contexts too, the upper mesolect is merging to some extent with the Standard in general usage with the result that many educators are not entirely clear on their separate and distinct features. So where we might still expect to hear Standard English, as for example in church or school, a pseudo-acrolect is emerging within which both grammatical and phonological features often show variability (cf. Youssef, James and Ferreira 2001). Some speakers, constrained towards Standard, but limited in its grammar, imitate a pseudo Standard 'accent' with which they are not very familiar, and a great deal of variation results.

It is worth noting again that we may link Trinidad and Tobago more readily at the acrolectal and mesolectal levels but, beyond this, need to consider the Tobagonian basilect separately.

2.2. Trinidad and Tobago: Acrolect and mesolect

2.2.1. Vowels

There has been little careful sociolinguistic study of the distribution of vowel sounds according to features such as age, class, ethnicity and geography, but a notable exception is Winford (1972, 1978). He was able to posit a system of vowel change in progress in Trinidad, with the number of vowels in the system very reduced for older rural Indians and their descendants but gradually broadening towards the norms at the acrolectal end of the scale. He studied the variables (ɜː) as in *work* (ʌ) as in *hut*, (ɔ) as in *hot* and (ə) as in the unstressed syllable in *father* and found considerably more variation among the rural community than the urban. Urban informants used the prestige variants, corresponding with those documented in table 1 below, more than any other, but the rural informants showed more variability with 'significant patterns of age and ethnic differentiation' (1978: 285). Younger rural speakers evidenced more use of the urban patterns than did older, while the older rural speakers used the more stigmatized variants. The oldest rural Indians of the lowest status group, whose first language was Bhojpuri, used highly stigmatized variants absent from the urban varieties. Most evidenced was a generalized [a] for the variables above, and here we notice an interesting correlation with the Tobagonian basilect. Winford hypothesized that they had reduced the range of vowels available in the StE system considerably at the time of first contact and that these were now in process of re-establishment. As the reader will observe in the discussion below, however, a considerable measure of vowel mergence does exist and persist across the more normative variety.

With such a measure of variation in mind we can proceed to table 1 below, which sets out Wells' list of 28 items with most typical norms represented. Where there are significant differences from other national varieties these are bolded, and where there is a range of variation about the norm this too is specified. Overall it will be noted that there is a tendency to produce as monophthongs what in other national varieties are diphthongs. Four items are added finally from the extended Foulkes/Docherty listing and one other, BARE:

Table 1.   Vowels of decreolized varieties

KIT	[ɪ] > [i]	CLOTH	[ɔ>ɔː]	GOOSE	[uː]
DRESS	[ɛ]	NURSE	[ɜː>ɔ]	PRICE	[aɪ]
TRAP	[a> æ]	FLEECE	[iː]	CHOICE	[ɔɪ]
LOT	[ɔ>ʌ>ɒ]	FACE	[eː]	MOUTH	[ɔu]
STRUT	[ʌ>ɔː>ɒ]	PALM	[aː]	NEAR	['ɛː]
FOOT	[ʊ]	THOUGHT	[ɔː>ɒ]	SQUARE	[ɛː>'ɛː]
BATH	[aː]	GOAT	[oː]	START	[aː]
NORTH	[ɔː]	FORCE	[ɔː]	CURE	[juɜ]
HAPP<u>Y</u>	[ɪ> i]	LETTER	[ə>ʌ]	HORSES	[ɪ]
COMM<u>A</u>	[a>ə>ʌ]	FIRE	[aiə]	BEER	['ɛː>iɛ]
EIGHT	[eː]	MET<u>ER</u>	[ə>ʌ]	BARE	['ɛː>iɛ]

Most of these features of the vowel system of the normative national Trinidadian and Tobagonian variety are adapted from a chart compiled by Ferreira for Youssef, James and Ferreira (2001) which was verified and extended for this paper. In putting it together she drew upon her own native speaker competence as well as on that of Solomon (1993) and on the work of Allsopp (1996). Ferreira isolated 22 phonemes in comparison to 17 isolated by Winford (1978).

Vowel length is one of the most variant features in Trinidadian and Tobagonian speech. The most striking difference with other StE varieties is the low incidence of [æ]. Often it is lost in one place so that, for example, [a] and [æ] may merge rendering *heart* and *hat* the same, and then length may be reintroduced elsewhere, e.g in a word like *salad*, pronounced /sæˈlaːd/ with stress on the final syllable. (In the Tobagonian basilect, however, *heart* and *hat* are distinguished by vowel length and *salad* has two short vowels.)

There is a tendency towards neutralization of complex vowel sounds particularly in combination with [ə] and occurring word finally. These produce homophones that are distinguishable by context and include *beer* and *bear, peer* and *pear* and similar combinations. Solomon (1993: 15-16) has observed that acrolectal speakers may have either [i] or [ɛ] before [ə] but not both and suggests that education may be a critical factor with women outstripping men in production of [ɛə] particularly on the Trinidad radio. He believes that this variant correlates with a higher level of education and is more prestigious, but admits to a general increase in the use of [iə] in the media for both sexes. In the mesolect and increasingly in the acrolect [eː] is produced.

In the Trinidadian mesolect it is generally recognized that the vowel sounds in *cut, cot, caught* and *curt* may not be distinguished with the sounds /ʌ/, /ɒ/, /ɔ/, and /ɜ/ rendered as the single back open rounded vowel /ɒ/. Other neutralizations in the same vowel group produce the following:

- [ɒ] and [ʌ] in StE as in *body* and *buddy* merge in [ʌ], rendering these items as well as others like *golf* and *gulf* homophonous.
  Sometimes, however, there may be a lengthening resulting in the following merger of [ɒ] and [ɔ]; *body* and *bawdy* become neutralized, *long* becomes "*lorng*".
- [ɜ] and [ʌ] merge so that *bird* and *bud* are homophonous.

The major other neutralizations, which do not hold for all speakers, are as follows:

- [ɑ] and [a] in SE as in *ask* and *axe* (where metathesis can also occur) merge in [a];
- the vowels in *harm* and *ham*, become homophonous with the use of [a].
- the vowels in *bit* and *beat* become homophonous with the use of [iː].

Warner (1967) associated these last two mergers with French Creole, Spanish or Bhojpuri influence, but today they are more generalized allophonic variants, as real contact with these disappearing languages rapidly diminishes.

Other characteristic vowel sounds occur in words like *down* and *sound* which are rendered [dɒŋ] and [sɒŋ] respectively. Most usually the vowel is nasalized.

2.1.3. The consonants

The consonants show much less variation than the vowels, being mostly shared between Creole and English. As with other Caribbean Creoles, in both Trinidad and Tobago there is the shift to representation of [θ] as [t] and [ð] as [d] across the board, and these features are ceasing to be stigmatized even in pseudo-acrolectal speech. In Winford's study in the 1970's he found variation in the alternation among these variables in predictable patterns according to class and style, but in 2002 [t] and [d] as norms are a recognized and accepted part of pseudo-acrolectal speech with these variants having become markers with no censure attached to their use.

Final consonant clusters which exhibit the same voicing quality are reduced in all Caribbean creole varieties and Trinidad and Tobago are no exception. This is particularly the case with final /-t/ or /-d/ (although not [-nt]), and unusual with /-s/ or /-z/. As Labov (1972a) has pointed out for African American and Winford (1972) for Trinidadian, items that omit these behave differently according to their grammatical status, however, and are more likely to be retained when they represent a grammatical meaning, e.g. *passed* as opposed to *past*. From Winford's (1972) data he was able to order such clusters according to frequency, showing some phonological constraint, but also, for speakers in the middle class, grammatical constraint. A variable which shows little social or stylistic stability is final *-ng*, which is realized word-finally as either [n] or [ŋ].

The consonantal features outlined thus far are becoming increasingly consistent in usage across the social and stylistic board.

Less frequent are the variation between [v] and [b] as in [bɛri] for *very*, and the palatalization involved in the production of [tʃ] for [tr] as in [tʃri] for *tree*. Metathesis commonly occurs in voiceless clusters like *ask* which is rendered [aks], and *crisp* realized as [kips]. For older Indian speakers there is aspiration on voiced stops, as in [bʰɑji], *bhaji,* a leafy spinach, cited by Winer (1993: 17) from Mohan and Zador (1986). These sound types have all become stereotypes associated with rural and Indian speech. The variation on /r/, as for example when it is rendered [w], is derived from French Creole and the retroflex flap [ɽ] from Bhojpuri.

Trinidad is distinguished for its non-rhoticity, in this contrasting with neighbouring Barbados and Guyana, as well as Jamaica. Wells (1982: 578) has noted that metropolitan English had become non-rhotic at the time when English was established in Trinidad but this connection remains speculative. It is also distinguished by the palatalization of velar consonants /k/ and /g/ so that [kjã] represents *can't* and [gjɑːdɛn] represents *garden*. In this feature there is no clear style or social differentiation (Solomon 1993: 181). But it is found more in rural Indianrather than rural African speakers, with less clear-cut distinctions in urban areas (Winford 1972; Solomon 1993). Solomon suggests that it is word particular, being obligatory in *can't,* and rare in words like *calypso* and *ganja*.

2.3.   Tobagonian basilect

2.3.1.   Vowels

A number of vowel sounds are particular to Tobagonian and occur mostly in the basilect in the shortest words and in function words. Where the basilect and the mesolect share a pronunciation it is usually on distinctive content words.

The table of words equivalent to table 1, which displays acrolectal and mesolectal vowels, is presented below in table 2 but it should be noted that the basilect variants are not consistently produced in the reading of a Standard English text or word list. The variety in question is not used for reading purposes and informants necessarily shift varieties in reading.

Table 2.   Vowels of the basilect

KIT	[ɪ]	CLOTH	[ɑ:]	GOOSE	[u:]
DRESS	[ɛ]	NURSE	[ɔ:]	PRICE	[aɪ]
TRAP	**[a]**	FLEECE	[i:]	CHOICE	[ai]
LOT	[ɑ]	FACE	[e]	MOUTH	[ɔu]
STRUT	[ɔ]	PALM	[ɑ:]	NEAR	**[er]**
FOOT	[ʊ]	THOUGHT	NA	SQUARE	**[er]**
BATH	[ɑ:]	GOAT	[o]	START	**[a**:]
NORTH	[ɑ:]	FORCE	[o]	CURE	[jɔ:]
HAPPY	**[ɪ]**	LETTER	**[a]**	HORSES	[ɪ]
COMMA	**[a]**	FIRE	[aiə]	BEER	**[er]**
EIGHT	**[e]**	METER	[ɑ]	BARE	**[er]**

Major vowel oppositions according to variety and territory include the following:

Tobago's basilect retains [a:] for Trinidad's [ɔ>ɔ:] *cloth, lot, north.*

Also characteristic are [o], e.g. *force*, for Trinidad's [ɔ:] and [ai] e.g *choice* for Trinidad's [ɔɪ].

Among consonants the occurrence of [ʔ] word-initially for general English [h] is prevalent.

[a] is the most frequently occurring Tobagonian vowel. It is used in a vast number of words where the vowel sounds [æ], [ə], and [ɒ] would be used in British English.

Table 3 below, adapted from Youssef and James 2002, gives examples of words it is used in as compared to corresponding words in Standard English.

Table 3.   Tobagonian [a] on English words

Monosyllabic æ words	Stressed syllable æ of non-monosyllabic words	Monosyllabic ɔ- words	ə in non-monosyllabic words	Stressed syllable ɔ- in non-monosyllabic words
hat, cat, back	DA.ddy, HA.ppy, PAM.per	flop, long, knock (> flap, lang, knack)	CO.llapse, wa.TER, to.LE.rant (> CA.llapse, war.TA,)	BO.dy, FO.llow, CON.fi.dent (> BA.dy, FA.llow, KAN.fident).

(Relevant syllables in non-monosyllabic words capitalised)

In the first two categories of words, [a] is general Tobagonian but for the third it is purely basilectal; [a] gives way to [ɐ] in both mesolectal and acrolectal usage (though, for [ə] words, it may be retained). [a] is an unrounded sound while its mesolectal counterpart is rounded [ɐ]. Apparently because of this varietal distinction, [a] is, to an extent, socially stigmatised.

There are two diphthongs that occur particularly in certain word types in basilectal speech; these are [ai] (e.g. *bwai>* 'boy', *spwail>* 'spoil'), and their counterparts in mesolectal speech are respectively [oi] and [ai]. [ei] is associated particularly with the towns of Charlotteville and Speyside in the eastern part of Tobago and with Bethel and Plymouth in the west.

There are two single vowels in all varieties that seem to be reduced monophthongal versions of English diphthongs: [e:]/[e] (<[ei]), and [o:] (<[əu]). BrE /æ/ is lowered to /a/.

The single vowel [e:] in function words in basilectal speech seems to be a reduction of both of the diphthongs [iə] and [eə], while [(y)i] is its mesolectal and acrolectal counterpart which is shared with Trinidad.

[o] represents a reduction of the diphthong [ow] in basilectal, but not mesolectal or acrolectal, speech. As example we find *ho >* 'how'.

Because Tobagonian speech involves an interaction of three varieties which share the same general lexicon, it is impossible to totally separate basilect or mesolect, and so it would be difficult to specify all the vowels that occur in basilectal speech.

The short vowels that occur most in function words in basilectal speech are the nasal vowels (ĩ, ũ, õ and ã) and oral [a]. The long vowels that occur most in basilectal speech are nasal [ã:] and oral [a:], [õ:], and [ẽ:]. Examples of all these sounds are given in the following:

[ĩ]e.g *di* (remote past marker, reduced form of *did* e.g. *he di go*)
[ã] e.g. *an* (shortened form of *and*)
[ũ] e.g. *kũ* (reduced form of *couldn't*)
[õ] e.g. [dõ] (a reduced form of *don't*)
[ã:] e.g. [wã:] (a reduced form of *wan* '*one*')

A striking feature of fast basilectal speech is the lengthening of the single vowels [a], [o], and [i] in association with pronoun subjects or the negator *no*; these are full words that end in a short vowel, which is then incorporated in the lengthened vowel. These vowels at the same time represent words. /a/ is both a copula and an imperfective marker; /o/is a future marker that has lost its onset *g (go > o*); and /i/ is the remote past marker that has lost both its onset /b-/ and its coda /-n/ (*bin > i*).

2.3.4.   Consonants

The most distinctive Tobagonian consonant sound is /ʔ/. It may be heard in the pronunciation of words like [ʔows] 'house', [ʔow] 'how', and [sooʔm] 'something'. In addition, the word-initial consonants [h], [b], [d], [g] and [y] are most usually dropped in basilectal Tobagonian speech. In the speech of some speakers, the *h-* is absent from all English words containing it—a phenomenon that is not unusual in speakers of a range of non-standard English dialects across the world. Examples of content words with this form are: *home* > *ome, house* > *ouse, hot* > *at, hat* > *at, hit* > *it, hoe* > *oe, hand* > *an(d)*. The *h-* is absent from monosyllabic words, and the stressed syllable of non-monosyllabic words such as *appy*. For function words we find the unstressed-stressed pronoun pair *hi-hii* > *i* 'he/his' and *ii* 'he/him/his', and *huu* > *uu* 'who', which may occur as an interrogative pronoun, relative pronoun, or clause intensifier.

Syllable structure differs in Tobagonian from both Trinidadian and StE in that, word initially, there is only a single sound produced rather than a cluster; hence we find: [fr-]> [f-]. In adult speech, this feature is limited to *from* > *fom/fam*, which is the only function word in English that starts with the cluster [fr-].

Whereas /s/ can be the first of up to three consonants at the onset of a word in English, in basilectal Tobagonian speech it may be dropped, for example, from words like *skin*, s*queeze*, *smell*, *spit*, and *start* (> *kin*, *kweeze*, *mell*, *pit*, and *tart*). [s-] is not dropped when it combines with the liquids and semi-vowels [r], [l], [w], and [y].

In even the most acrolectal speech in Tobagonian (but not in Trinidadian), the single-initial consonants *b* and *p* are lengthened by the addition of bilabial [w] to become [bw-] and [pw-] before the diphthong [oi] in a small group of words that include *boy* > *bwoi, boil* > *bwoil, boycott* > *bwoicott, spoil* > *spwoil*, and *poison* > *pwoison*.

The shift from [v] to [b] recorded variably for Trinidadian also occurs in basilectal Tobagonian. It is found in words like the following: *crave* > *crabe*, *love* > *lob, governor* > *gobna*, and *heavy* > *(h)eaby*. As the list suggests, it occurs wherever the [v] may occur in a word. The shift does not seem to be motivated by any special phonological conditioning. When a fricative gives way to a plosive there is a change in lip movement which historically was important for registering negative emotions visibly.

The cluster [-lf] is reduced to [-f] in the grammatical word *self* as the latter compounds with pronouns, *even*, and adverbs of place and time.

Basilectal Tobagonian speech also evidences the dropping of final single-consonants especially the nasal ones, from grammatical words.

In the second syllable of words, and intervocalically, [t] is replaced by [k] and [d] by [g]. The effects are seen in the following words: *little > likku, bottle > bokku, riddle > riggu, middle > miggu, handle > ha[ŋ]gu, gentlemen > jenku-men*. Voiceless [t] becomes voiceless [k], and voiced [d] becomes voiced [g]. The movement from front to back consonants seems motivated by the back vowel [-u], with which syllabic [l] is produced. This change may also be heard in some mesolectal Trinidadian speech.

2.4.   Suprasegmental features

The most common lay reaction to Trinidadian speech world-wide is that it is 'sing-song'. Associations have been made very broadly to Welsh as well as to African tone languages (e.g. Carter 1979) and, for Trinidad specifically, some speakers' intonation patterns have also been linked with Spanish, French creole, and Bhojpuri. The current and overall reality is a prosody which has been adapted through all these influences, and which is, at this point in time, peculiarly 'Creole'.

Trinidadian and Tobagonian also exhibits a peculiar intonational characteristic in mesolectal speech of a rising intonation at the end of an utterance as if the speaker is in doubt or questioning (cf. Allsopp 1972). It may be that the speaker is seeking a responsiveness in the hearer as he/she does when using the very popular local tag *Right?*

Solomon (1993: 34) identifies pitch as the critical prosodic feature rather than stress although he admits it is difficult to abstract pitch from tone. Winer (1993: 19-20) also notes 'a higher and wider' pitch range than in StE and 'less degree of fall at sentence end'. The features of pitch and stress are confounded between English and Trinidadian speakers, the former hearing Trinidad pitch as stress. Solomon (1993: 34) equates the system with the Guyanese one as described by Allsopp (1972). The result is that disyllable words are most often either high-low or low-high, the latter being the more common and older pattern; in trisyllable words it is common to find a low-low-high or high-high-low pattern. Solomon has described longer items, as characteristically either low-low-high-high or, when they break into two, as low-high-high, low-high. All this can often result in a change of the characteristic English pattern such that unstressed syllables in that variety often come to carry high pitch in Trinidadian. The most common patterns in Trinidadian overall are low-high, low-low high and low-high high, and this creates some contrasting patterns with many varieties of Standard English, e.g (Capitals indicate stress, apostrophes denote pitch) *COCKroa'ch, MAChine; TRInida'd; CARpe'nte'r*. Interesting contrasts may be observed between *'opponent* and *cha'racter, 'component* and *com'merce*. These features of the language can cause difficulty in comprehension for speakers of other varieties and the inconsistencies are very challenging for learners of the Trinidadian variety.

James (2003) analyses the role of tone in the organisation of grammatical morphemes in a number of the subsystems of TobC. Among his findings about tone are that:

a)   In TobC tone is morphemic in the case of the homophones *kyã* 'can' *vs. kyã* 'can't');

b)   In TobC tone distinguishes emphatic from non-emphatic meanings in the homophones *dèm* vs. *dém*;

c)   In TobC tone typically combines with rhyme length to distinguish the members of emphatic-nonemphatic pairs—high tone with long-vowel and vowel-consonant sequences, and low tone with single vowels (e.g., *shíí* vs. *shì* and *dém* vs *dè*);

d)   In TobC tone is differentially associated with certain grammatical (sub)categories, with low tone associating with the definite article *dì*, the singularising article *wàà*, certain preverbal articles (e.g., imperfective *à* and future *gò*), the third person singular general object pronouns *àm / òm*, certain prepositions (e.g., *à* and *pàn*), and infinitival/possessive *fù*; and high tone associating with negators (e.g., *nó* and *é*), emphasiser *dúú*, interrogative / relative *wé*, demonstrative *dà(t)*, certain prepositions (e.g., *tón* 'according to', *gí* 'to/for'), intensifier *húú*, reportive *sé*, and certain preverbal particles (e.g., completive *dón* and passive *gé*); and

e)   In TobC tone is variable on suffixes (e.g., *sèf, séf*) and the morpheme *wan*, among other morphemes, depending on where they occur in the syntax.

All in all, prosody contrasts markedly with other English varieties; the tendency to shared tonal and intonation patterns across Caribbean Creoles undoubtedly links back to the sharing of a common African tonal base despite the fact that no direct and precise links now survive.

3.   Conclusions

Separate recordings are included with this chapter for both Trinidadian and Tobagonian to highlight their most characteristic similarities and differences, which, as illustrated throughout the chapter, appear mainly in basilectal features which distinguish Tobagonian from Trinidadian speech overall. As travel between the two islands becomes increasingly frequent, and as young people in particular look to Trinidad for employment and advancement, the differences may slowly break down at every level. The mesolect is becoming increasingly widespread in usage right across the twin-island territory.

Thus far language change is indicated. But there remains a distinct nationalism rooted in Tobago, as well as an essentially rural lifestyle, which ensures the continued vitality of the basilectal variety. As noted earlier, Youssef (2001), in a small-scale study in the village of Bethel, indicates that there remains a common level of basilectal usage for both old and young at home, but that the young favour the mesolect over the acrolect as a badge of modern identity in the wider world. The continuing use of the basilect as a home variety, and the relative weight of the mesolect in wider contexts, suggests that the continuous change from basilect to acrolect, considered to characterize a continuum situation, is not going through and that the situation may become relatively stable, with each variety having its own contexts for usage in the society at large.

Exercises and study questions

For technical reasons, the audio files from Trinidad and Tobago referred to here (two interviews and two reading passages) are not available on the CD-ROM. They can be obtained from the publisher's website.

1. Identify the most salient features of history and geography in Trinidad and Tobago which have determined their persisting with separate varieties of language at the most creole level.

2. In listening to the reading passage in Trinidadian and Tobagonian, identify three features of the vowel system which distinguish it from Standard varieties such as British or American.

3. In listening to the basilectal Tobagonian recording, identify three distinguishing vowel features in this variety which separate it from Trinidadian.

4. What consonantal features can you identify as markers in this variety?

5. What consonantal features are more likely to be indicators in the two varieties? Give reasons for your answer.

6. Are there any features of Trinidadian vowel development which show some similarity with the Tobagonian basilect today?

7. Identify three phonological features characteristic of all Caribbean creole varieties.

8. Identify three distinguishing features of Tobagonian consonants occurring word-initially.

9. From the conversational recordings identify two major differences in vowel production among the family members.

10. Are there any features of the mesolectal variety used by mother and son which distinguish them as Tobagonian and not Trinidadian? If so, list the features.

Selected references

Please consult the General references for titles mentioned in the text but not included in the references below. For a full bibliography see the accompanying CD-ROM.

Allsopp, Richard
    1972   Some suprasegmental features of Caribbean English. Paper presented at the conference on creole languages and educational development, UWI, St. Augustine, 1972.
Baksh-Soodeen, Rawwida
    1995   A historical perspective on the lexicon of Trinidadian English. Ph.D. dissertation, The University of the West Indies, St. Augustine.
Brereton, Bridget
    1981   *A History of Modern Trinidad*. London: Heinemann
Carter, Hazel
    1979   Evidence for the survival of African prosodies in West African Creoles. Society for Caribbean Linguistics Occasional Paper 13.
Elder, John D.
    1988   *African Survivals in Trinidad and Tobago*. London: Paria Press.
James, Winford
    1974   Some similarities between Jamaican Creole and the dialect of Tobago. Caribbean Studies thesis, University of the West Indies, St. Augustine.
    2003   The role of tone and rhyme structure in the organisation of grammatical morphemes in Tobagonian. In: Plag (ed.), 165-192.
James, Winford and Valerie Youssef
    2002   *The Languages of Tobago*. Trinidad and Tobago: School of Continuing Studies, University of the West Indies, St. Augustine.

Minderhout, David
    1973   A sociolinguistic description of Tobagonian English. Ph.D. dissertation, Georgetown University, USA.
Mohan, Peggy and Paul Zador
    1986   Discontinuity in a life cycle: The death of Trinidad Bhojpuri. *Language* 62: 291–320.
Solomon, Denis
    1993   *The Speech of Trinidad - A Reference Grammar.* Trinidad: School of Continuing Studies, The University of the West Indies.
Southers, Donna
    1977   A transformational analysis of Tobagonina English Creole. Ph.D. dissertation, University of North Carolina at Chapel Hill, USA.
Thomas, J. J.
    1869   *The Theory and Practice of Creole Grammar.* (1964 reprint London: New Beacon Books).
Warner, Maureen
    1967   Language in Trinidad with special reference to English. Ph.D. dissertation, University of York, UK.
Winer, Lise
    1984   Early Trinidadian Creole: The Spectator texts. *English World-Wide* 5: 181–210.
Winer, Lise and Glen Gilbert
    1987   A 19th century report on the Creole English of Tobago: The Uh-Schuchardt correspondence. *English World-Wide* 8: 235–262.
Winford, Donald
    1972   A sociolinguistic description of two communities in Trinidad. Ph.D. dissertation, University of York: UK.
    1978   Phonological hypercorrection in the process of decreolization – the case of Trinidadian English. *Journal of Linguistics* 14: 129–375.
Wood, Donald
    1968   *Trinidad in Transition.* London: Oxford University Press.
Youssef, Valerie
    1996   The competence underlying code-mixing in Trinidad and Tobago. *Journal of Pidgin and Creole Languages* 11: 1–22.
    2001   Age-grading in the anglophone creole of Tobago. *World Englishes* 20: 29–46.
Youssef, Valerie, Winford James and Jo-Anne S. Ferreira
    2001   Is there a Trinidad and Tobago Standard English? Paper presented at a Workshop on English Language Teaching, UWI, St. Augustine, Trinidad and Tobago, April 2001.

Suriname creoles: phonology

Norval Smith and Vinije Haabo

1.   Introduction

The question of the origins of the English-lexifier creole languages spoken in Suriname, and also French Guyana, by several hundred thousand people is a controversial one. By origins we mean *linguistic origins* rather than population origins, although we have of course to take into account the influences of the languages spoken by the earliest African populations.

  In the case of creole languages it is also controversial whether one can speak of a break in continuity or not. Did creole languages develop in a special fashion, or were normal processes of language change involved? With the Surinamese creole languages in mind, it appears patently ridiculous to envisage any direct continuity in the sense of normal complete language transmission between the kinds of (sub)standard English reflected in the segmental phonologies of Surinamese creole words and the Surinamese creoles themselves. Smith (1987) claims that there is a regular relationship between the forms of lexical items in the Surinamese creoles and the *incidence of phonemes* in the various forms of English – standard and substandard – spoken in mid-17th century London. However, this is not the same as claiming that normal intergenerational language transfer took place. No kind of popular or colonial English is known which could fulfill the role of *overall* direct precursor to these languages. In regard to syntax, morphology, lexical semantics and even phonotactics all known varieties of popular/colonial English are far removed from the Surinamese creoles. The records of Sranan now go back to 1707 (Van den Berg 2000), a mere two generations after the settlement of Suriname by the English in 1651, and only three generations after the founding of the first Caribbean English colonies of St. Kitts and Barbados. The Sranan of the early 18th century is not however radically different from present-day Sranan in respect of its distance from the standard Englishes of England and the United States.

  Smith (2001) assumes the creation of a Proto-Caribbean Plantation Pidgin in the English colonies in the Caribbean in the first generation of slavery – roughly between 1625 and 1650. One reason for this is the existence of a common core of loans from a disparate selection of African languages, referred to by

Smith (1987) as Ingredient X. Together with English vocabulary displaying common deviations from the regular Standard English developments in semantics and phonology, reconstituted function-words, and innovative syntactic constructions, these are shared by a considerable number of circum-Caribbean creole languages, such as St Kitts Creole, Jamaican Creole, Guyanese, Krio, Providencia Creole, Miskito Coast Creole, the Surinamese creoles and others. The conclusion seems to be warranted that there was some common linguistic stage showing a degree of stability underlying these creoles. The fact that some function-words and syntactic constructions are shared would also seem to rule out a pidgin of the most primitive type, a jargon pidgin.

This stable pidgin must have come into existence during this first generation of English plantation-holding in the Caribbean. This is guaranteed by the fact that Suriname was settled in 1651, and that the English colonial presence lasted only until 1667. The vast majority of the English population had left by 1675, so that all the ingredients of Sranan must have been in place before then.

This is not to deny that there are clear differences in type between the various English-lexifier creoles spoken in the Caribbean area. These are particularly observable in the typology of the vowel systems.

1.1.   The Suriname creole languages

Let us now turn to a consideration of the phonologies of the three Surinamese creole languages we will deal with here. The first is Sranan, the former language of the coastal plantations, and of the capital, Paramaribo. The second is Ndyuka, which we may take to be descended from an 18th century plantation variety of Sranan. The speakers of Ndyuka descend from maroons (escapees) from the coastal plantations. The third language is Saramaccan, which has a more complex history. This is also a maroon language, but one spoken largely by the descendants of slaves who escaped from the Jewish-owned plantations on the middle Suriname River. In the late 17th and early 18th century there was a concentration of Jewish-owned plantations in this area, with as its mini-capital the settlement of Joden-Savannah ('Jews' Savanna').

The origin of this Jewish population is the subject of controversy (cf. Arends 1999; Smith 1999a), but we will adhere here to the scenario sketched by Smith that the Jews hailed indirectly from Brazil, and that they brought Portuguese-speaking slaves with them, who influenced the local Sranan to the extent that some 300 English-derived forms were replaced by Portuguese Creole forms, giving rise to a new creole language that was to some extent mixed in vocabulary. This was the precursor of Saramaccan.

There are other creole languages/dialects spoken in Suriname, but these do not differ to any large degree from the three we will be dealing with. Closely related to Ndyuka are Aluku, Paramaccan and Kwinti, while Matawai resembles Saramaccan. For more on these see Smith (2002) and other articles in Carlin and Arends (2002).

1.2.   Methodological preliminaries

We exclude from consideration here any word whose source is not clearly English. As the Netherlands was the colonial power for over 300 years there are a number of forms whose origin could be either Dutch or English. We will not go into any detail on why we consider a particular form to be of English origin. Some aspects of this methodological problem are discussed in Smith (1987).

2.   Phonological systems of the Suriname creoles

We will deal with the vowel systems, consonant systems and tone systems in that order. Two of the three languages are lexical tone languages and we will give a very brief characterization of this aspect here.

All three languages are in a sense unusual—for varieties of English—in that they have official or semi-official writing-systems, which are very close to being phonemic. As these are already very familiar to linguists who work on these languages, we will make use of them here, with slight modifications where they deviate significantly from the IPA, such as in the use of *y* for /j/, or where they fall short. This we will take account of. We provide a description of the IPA values of the principal allophones.

One major difference from most other varieties of "English" is the large-scale occurrence of anaptyctic (epithetic) vowels. For instance *foot* appears as /fútu/ in all three languages. The first /u/ here we will refer to as the *organic* vowel, and the second as *anaptyctic*.

2.1.   Vowel systems

Sranan and Ndyuka have a five-vowel system: /i, e, a, o, u/, and Saramaccan has a seven-vowel system: /i, e, ɛ, a, ɔ, o, u/. In Saramaccan there is an additional vowel harmony restriction forbidding contiguous sequences of low-mid and high-mid vowels. A further restriction affects the incidence of vowels in Saramaccan insofar as /..é.e#, ..ó.e#/ sequences seem only to occur

in more recent forms. Older English-derived forms seem to have /..ɛ́.ɛ#, ..ɔ́.
ɛ#/ instead.

The approximate phonetic qualities of the vowels are as follows:

(1) a.   Sranan: /i/   [i]
                       /e/   [ɛ ~ ɪ]
                       /a/   [a̰ ~ ɑ]
                       /o/   [ɔ ~ ʊ]
                       /u/   [u]

    b.   Ndyuka: /i/   [i]
                       /e/   [ɛ ~ e]
                       /a/   [ä]
                       /o/   [o]
                       /u/   [u]

    c.   Saramaccan: /i/   [i]
                       /e/   [e]
                       /ɛ/   [ɛ]
                       /a/   [a]
                       /ɔ/   [ɔ]
                       /o/   [o]
                       /u/   [u]

Note that tenseness and laxness play no role in these vowel systems. /e/ and /o/
in Sranan, and /ɛ/ and /ɔ/ in Saramaccan would appear to be [–ATR], the other
vowels being [+ATR].

Long vowels occur in all systems, although only marginally in Sranan. In
Sranan stressed vowels preceding /r/ are lengthened considerably, and those
following consonant-/r/ clusters are lengthened to a lesser degree.

2.2.   Consonant systems

(2) a.   Sranan: p   t   tj   k
                   b   d   dj   g
                   f   s   sj   h
                   m   n   nj   ŋ
                         l~r
                   w   j

b.	Ndyuka:	p	t	tj	k	kp~kw
		b	d	dj	g	gb~gw
		f	s		h	
		v	z			
		m	n	nj		
			l			
		w		j		

c.	Saramaccan:	p	t	tj	k	kp	(kw)
		b	d	dj	g	gb	(gw)
		f	s		h		
		v	z				
		mb	nd	ndj	ŋg		
		m	n	nj			
		ɓ	ɗ				
			l				
		w		j			

The phonetic values of /tj, dj, sj, nj/ are [tʃ, dʒ, ʃ, ɲ]. The distinction between /kp/ and /kw/ is only made in some forms of Saramaccan. Other forms have /kp ~ kw/, and the concomitant /gb ~ gw/ indifferently.

2.3.   Tone systems

The two tone languages, Ndyuka and Saramaccan, have high tones H (marked by acute accents) opposed to low tones L (unmarked). Saramaccan also has changeable tones, which must be regarded as underlyingly unspecified ∅. These occur in words of European origin, and represent generally the old unaccented vowels in those words, as well as some epenthetic and all anaptyctic vowels. These are subject to raising under a combination of phonological and syntactic conditions. Unmarked vowels in words of African origin are lexically low.

Examples of tone contrasts would be the following:

(3) ɓɛ	L	'red'
ɓéɛ	H∅	'belly'
ɓɛɛ	LL	'fiery red'
ɓɛ́ɛ	∅H∅	'bread'
ɗɛ́	H	'they'
ɗɛ́ɛ́	HH	'the' (plural)

3.   Detailed phonological descriptions

3.1.   Vowel systems

Each vowel described will be introduced in terms of Wells sets, with the addition of only a few supplementary keywords. The total list of keywords used to define vowel-sets is as follows:

(4)   KIT   DRESS   TRAP   LOT   STRUT   FOOT
      BATH   CLOTH   NURSE   FLEECE   ACE   PALM
      THOUGHT   GOAT   GOOSE   PRICE   CHOICE   MOUTH
      NEAR   SQUARE   START   FORCE   NORTH   CURE
      FIRE   POWER   happY   horsES   lettER   commA
      rottEN

3.1.1.   *KIT*

The KIT set of words with Middle English (henceforth ME) /ɪ/ are represented in Suriname creoles by words derived from Early Modern English *ship*, *bit*, *dig*, *skin*, *drink*, *dinner*, *sieve*, *busy*, and so on. In the rest of this article we will simply describe these for convenience as English words, whether the meaning has undergone a change or not. The normal realization of these words in the Suriname creoles is [i], a short high front vowel.

Table 1.   The KIT set

English	Sranan	Ndyuka	Saramaccan
fit	fíti	fíti	fíti
bitter	bíta	bíta	ɓíta
skin	skin	sikín	siŋkíi
drink	dríɲi	diíŋgi	diíŋgi
finger	fíɲa	fíŋga	fíŋga
bit	-	-	aɓíti
live	líbi	líbi	líɓí

A number of words that belong to this incidence set in RP and AmE have different realizations in the Suriname creoles.

Table 2.   KIT words with deviant vowels

English	Sranan	Ndyuka	Saramaccan
whip	(wípi)	(wípi)	húpi, úpi
if	éfu,éfi	éfu	ée
him	en	én	(h)én
mix	móksi	mókisi	mɔkísi

Whip has a form in Sranan and Ndyuka concomitant with a derivation from a form [wɪp]. Saramaccan, however, might be based on a form [hwɪp], to judge by the optional /h/. The /u/ vowel appears in a number of other forms where it must also stand for earlier /wi/.

If has a lower vowel in other Caribbean creoles as well. Compare Krio /ɛf/, Jamaican /ef, efn/, Miskito Coast Creole /ef/ etc.

Mix must derive from an unrecorded EModE form /*mʌks/. In ME we do have a rounding of /ɪ/ to /ʊ/ after /w/, and in isolated words after /b/ as well as before /m/ (Dobson 1957). A possible parallel for this form is found in Cameroonian Pidgin /bɔks/.

3.1.2.   DRESS

DRESS words with ME /ĕ/, and to some extent /ɛː/, are represented in Suriname creoles by English words like *neck, bed, egg, bread, dead, head, any, bury, ready*, etc. The /ɛː/ words are generally spelt *ea*. The normal representation of these differs in the various languages, although the phonemic symbol /e/ is traditionally used in all of them. In Sranan /e/ is usually [ɛ ~ ɪ] for instance. In Ndyuka /e/ is normally [e ~ ɛ], and in Saramaccan /e, ɛ/ are usually [e, ɛ] respectively. /ɛ/ is employed largely in Saramaccan in these words in combination with an anaptyctic vowel /-ɛ/.

Table 3.   The DRESS set

English	Sranan	Ndyuka	Saramaccan
bed	bédi	bédi	ɓédi
bread	bréde	beéle	ɓɛɛ́ɛ
dead	déde	déde	déɗɛ

Table 3. (continued)   The DRESS set

English	Sranan	Ndyuka	Saramaccan
yesterday	ésrede, ésde	ésíde	ésiɗe
gentle	géndri, djéndri	djéndée	djéndɛ
beg	bégi	bégi	bégi
remember	mémre	mémbée	mémbɛ
wench	wéŋke, wéntje	-	wéndjɛ

A number of words that belong to this incidence set in RP and AmE have different realizations in the Suriname creoles.

Table 4.   DRESS words with deviant realizations

English	Sranan	Ndyuka	Saramaccan
heavy	(ébi)	(ébi), íbi	(héɓi)
every	íbri	íbíi	(h)íbi
any-	íniwan	íni	(h)íniwán
egg(s)	(éksi)	ígi	-

Smith (1987) states: "According to Dobson (1957) raising of /e/ to /i/ is a fairly common process in the fifteenth or sixteenth century in the South-east. In the seventeenth century ships' logs we find frequent examples of this raising, e.g. *chists* 'chests'. Matthews (1938) provides many examples from Cockney including *chistes* (1553)."

3.1.3.   TRAP

TRAP words with ME /ă/ are represented in Suriname creoles by English words like *cat*, *back*, *have*, *ants*, *thank*, *arrow*, etc. The normal realization of these words in the Suriname creoles is as a short low centralized vowel.

The anaptyctic vowel here seems to be normally sensitive to the nature of the final consonant:

(5)   Organic   Anaptyctic
    aP   u
    aT   i
    aK   a

Table 5.   The TRAP set

English	Sranan	Ndyuka	Saramaccan
fat	fátu	fátu	fátu
back	báka	báka	ɓáka
ask	áksi	ákísi	(h)ákísi
cabbage	kábisi	tjábísi	tjábísi
carry	tjá(ri)	tjái	tjá
garden	djári	djáli	djái
candle	kándra	kándáa	kánda
ashes	asísi	asísi	-

The metathesis of /sk/ removes *ask* from the ambit of the BATH words. *Cabbage* was also earlier /tjábisi/ in Sranan.

A number of words that belong to this incidence set in RP and AmE have different realizations in the Suriname creoles.

Table 6.   TRAP words with deviant realizations

English	Sranan	Ndyuka	Saramaccan
catch	kísi	kísi	kísi
hang	(áŋa), *hengi* (1783)	éŋge	héŋgi

Catch is widely realized with a mid vowel in other creoles, as well as in many English and American dialects: Jamaican /k(j)etʃ/, Guyanese /ketʃ/, etc. Further, a form [kɪtʃ] is found in a number of places in S. and E. England.

The raising of the vowel of *hang* is present in the modern dialects around London, and had taken place by the seventeenth century in Cockney (Matthews 1938).

3.1.4. *LOT*

LOT words with ME /ŏ/ are represented in Suriname creoles by English words like *stop*, *pot*, *box*, *wasp*, *watch*, *dog*, etc. The normal realization of these words in the Suriname Creoles is [ä], a short low retracted front vowel.

Table 7.   The LOT set

English	Sranan	Ndyuka	Saramaccan
dog	dágu	dágu	dágu
hog	águ	águ	hágu
god	gádo	gádu	gáɗu
wasp	waswási	wasiwási	wasiwási
yonder	jána	ánda	-
strong	tráŋa	taáŋga	taáŋga
stop	tápu	tápu	-
bottle	bátra	bátáa	ɓáta

3.1.5. *STRUT*

STRUT words with ME /ŭ/ which developed to EModE /ʌ/ are represented in Suriname creoles by English words like *cut*, *jug*, *run*, *love*, *rub*, *money*, *enough*, *country*, etc. The main realization of this set of words is with /o, ɔ/.

It is fairly clear that there must have been a Proto-Suriname-Creole vowel phoneme /*ʌ/ which could be responsible for these /o, ɔ/-reflexes. We claim this because of the usual distribution of the anaptyctic vowels, which is different from other items with mid rounded organic vowels:

(6)   Organic   Anaptyctic
      oP   u
      oT   i
      oK   o

Table 8. The STRUT set

English	Sranan	Ndyuka	Saramaccan
cut	kóti	kóti	kóti
gutter	gótro	gótóo	(ŋ)gɔ́tɔ
jug	djógo	djógo	djógu
ugly	ógri	ógíi	(w/h)ógi
rub	lóbi	lóbi	loɓi
bubby	bóbi	bóbi	ɓóɓi
enough	nófo	nófo	-
gun	gon	góni	góni

A minority of words that belong to this incidence set in RP and AmE have the phoneme /a/ in the Suriname creoles.

Table 9. STRUT words with /a/

English	Sranan	Ndyuka	Saramaccan
suppertime	sapatén	sapaten	sápate(n)
brother	bráda, brára	baála	ɓaáa
tother	tra	taá	-
one	wan	wán	wán
sun	(son)	sán	(sónu)
hungry	áŋri	aŋgíi	háŋgi
someone	(s(ú)ma)	samá	-
something	san(í)	sán(i)	(son(d)í)

The causation of this /a/-variant is not obvious. Possibly this is supportive of the hypothetical Proto-Suriname-Creole vowel phoneme /*ʌ/ referred to above.

Another group of deviant items in the Suriname creoles go together with the FOOT set of words and will be dealt with there.

3.1.6. *FOOT*

FOOT words with ME /ŭ/ preserved in EModE are represented in Suriname creoles by English words like *bush, full, cushion, look, cook, wood, woman*, etc. The normal realization of these *u-* words in the Suriname creoles is [u], a short high back rounded vowel. The split between the STRUT set and the FOOT set is at least partially phonologically conditioned in EModE, the latter class having a concentration of items with initial labials and, to a lesser extent, with postvocalic /k/.

Table 10.   The FOOT set

English	Sranan	Ndyuka	Saramaccan
foot	fútu	fútu	fútu
book	búku	búku	ɓúku
hook	úku	(h)úku	húku
look	lúku	lúku	lúku
crooked	krúktu	kúkútu	kuukútu, kúkútu
wood	údu	údu	(h)úɗu
full	fúru	fúu	fúu
pull	púru	púu	púu
cushion	kúnsu	kúnsu	kúnsu

The odd word that belongs to this incidence set in RP and AmE has the phoneme /o/ in the Suriname creoles. However, as we will shortly see, the exceptions in the other direction are more numerous.

Table 11.   FOOT words with /o/

English	Sranan	Ndyuka	Saramaccan
put	póti	póti	-

The fact that a number of words where Standard English has /ʌ/ have /u/ in the Suriname creoles has to be seen in connection with the fact that the change in Standard English (of London) is first evidenced around 1640 (Dobson 1957).

It was just after this that Suriname was colonized. The following words have unexpected /u/.

Table 12. Words with unexpected /u/

English	Sranan	Ndyuka	Saramaccan
must	músu	músu	músu
too much	(túmsi)	(túmísi)	túmúsi
thrust	trúsu	(toósi)	tuúsi
drunk	drúŋu	duúŋgu	(dɔɔ́ŋgɔ)
sunk	súŋu	súŋgu	-
blood	brúdu	buúlu	ɓuúu
flood	frúdu	fuúlu	(foóo, foóu)
just now	(djónsro)	(djónso)	djúnsu

Note that four of the words exhibit variation between /u/ and /o, ɔ/ among the languages, suggesting the presence of variable pronunciations in the seventeenth century.

3.1.7. *BATH*

There is no sign of a separate BATH set as distinct from the TRAP set. This is not unexpected given that the TRAP-BATH split only occurred in the eighteenth century (Wells 1982: 134). Examples of BATH words in the Suriname creoles are:

Table 13. The BATH set

English	Sranan	Ndyuka	Saramaccan
paths	pási	pási	pási
fasten	fási	fási	-
master	másra	másáa	mása
nasty	nási	-	nási
half	áfu	áfu	háfu
laugh	láfu	láfu	láfu

3.1.8. *CLOTH*

There is no sign of a separate CLOTH set as distinct from the LOT set. Once again this is not so surprising given that the LOT-CLOTH split occurred in the seventeenth century. Examples of CLOTH words in the Suriname creoles are:

Table 14. The CLOTH set

English	Sranan	Ndyuka	Saramaccan
cross (v.)	krási	kaási	-
lost	lási	lási	lási
softly	sáafri	sáfili, saáfi	sáápi
soft	sáfu	sáfu	-

3.1.9. *NURSE*

With NURSE words, as with the other /r/-sets, we have clearly to take account of /r/-less as well as /r/-ful dialects. Where /r/ is preconsonantal, we cannot distinguish with complete confidence between an early /r/-deletion, mainly affecting sibilants but also to a lesser extent other coronals, which had taken place before the sixteenth century (Wells 1982: 222), and the later general 18th century loss of /r/ in word-final and preconsonantal environments. The fact remains that pre-consonantal loss is only evidenced before coronal sounds.

Firstly, /r/-less forms:

Table 15. /r/-less NURSE words

English	Sranan	Ndyuka	Saramaccan
hurt	áti	áti	(h)áti
curse	kósi	kósi	kósi
first	fósi	fósi	fósu
dirt	dóti	dóti	dóti
curtsey	kósi	-	-

The same vaccilation between /o/ and /a/ as in the STRUT set appears here.
And secondly, /r/-full forms:

Table 16.   /r/-full NURSE words

English	Sranan	Ndyuka	Saramaccan
burn	bron	boón	boónu
turn	tron	toón	toón
work	wróko	woóko	woóko

3.1.10. *FLEECE*

The FLEECE set of words, corresponding to ME /eː/ and /ɛː/, is represented in Suriname creoles by the English words *meet, teeth, speak, leave, sweet, feel, believe, field*, and so on. The normal realization of these words in the Suriname creoles is [i], a short high front vowel. In other words this set has fallen together with the KIT set.

Table 17.   The FLEECE set

English	Sranan	Ndyuka	Saramaccan
meet	míti	míti	míti
speak	píki	píki	píki
creek	kríki	kiíki	kiíki
week	wíki	wíki	wíki
sleep	sríbi	siíbi	-
heap	ípi	(h)ípi	(h)ípi
seed	síri	síi	síi
greedy	grídi	giíli	giíi

A feature of the Suriname creoles is the membership of an unexpectedly large number of ME /ɛː/ words in the FACE set. We will give these in the next section.

3.1.11. FACE

The FACE set words, corresponding to ME /ai/, /aː/, and to a certain extent /ɛː/, is represented in Suriname creoles by words derived from Early Modern English. When followed by a consonant this set is indistinguishable from the DRESS set.

Table 18.   The FACE set

English	Sranan	Ndyuka	Saramaccan
make	méki	méke	mbéi
take	téki	téke	téi
shake	séki	séke	séki
snake	snéki	sinéki	sindéki
afraid	fréde	feéle	fɛέɛ
eight	ájti	áiti(n)	áiti
payment	pájman	-	paimá

When this vowel occurs word-finally it is often diphthongized. The occurrence of a semi-vowel in Sranan or a diphthongal element in Ndyuka is unforecastable. Very exceptionally, we also see two words in the above table whose forms seem to preserve diphthongs word-internally.

Table 19.   The FACE set in word-final position

English	Sranan	Ndyuka	Saramaccan
day	dej	déi	-
today	tidé	tidé	tidé
play	prej	peé	pɛέ
pay	paj	pái	-
clay	klej (obs.)	keléi (< Sranan)	-

Words that normally belong to the FLEECE set include:

Table 20.   FLEECE at FACE value

English	Sranan	Ndyuka	Saramaccan
meat	méti	méti	mbéti
peas(e)	pési	pési	pési
beam	-	-	ɓén
dream	dren	deén	-

Some words that should normally belong to the FACE set in fact belong to the FLEECE set.

Table 21.   FACE at FLEECE value

English	Sranan	Ndyuka	Saramaccan
grate	gríti	giíti	-
wake	wíki	(wéki)	(wéki)

3.1.12. PALM

There are no items belonging to the PALM set in the Suriname creoles.

3.1.13. THOUGHT

In EModE /au/ gave [ɒː] by the mid-seventeenth century, by which time the LOT-words had [ɒ]. The neutralization of length in Suriname would nullify this distinction. So this set falls together with the LOT set as /a/ in Suriname. Examples of THOUGHT words in the Suriname creoles are the following;

Table 22.   The THOUGHT set

English	Sranan	Ndyuka	Saramaccan
saw	sa	sá	sán
talk	táki	táki	táki
walk	wáka	wáka	wáka
bawl	bári	báli	ɓái
call	kári	kái	kái
haul	ári	(h)áli	hái

The nasal vowel in /sán/ probably reflects the influence of Gun /sán/ 'to cut'.

3.1.14. GOAT

The GOAT set of words, corresponding to ME /ɔː/ and /ou/, is represented in
Suriname creoles by the English words *grow, blow, bow, hold, broke, smoke,
soap, clothes*, and so on. The normal realization of these words in the Suriname
creoles is [o/ɔ], a short round mid back vowel. When word-final, a diphthongal
realization /ow/ is also possible.

Table 23.   The GOAT set

English	Sranan	Ndyuka	Saramaccan
bow	bo	bó	ɓɔ́
blow	bro	boó	ɓɔɔ́
go	go	gó	gó
grow	gro	goó	gɔɔ́
tow	tow	tóu	-
broke	bróko	boóko	ɓoóko
locust tree	lóksi	lókísi	lókísi
soap	sópo	sópu	sópu
toad	tódo	tódo	tɔ́ɗɔ
clothes	krósi	koósi	koósu

Occasionally a vowel /u/ appears in Saramaccan.

Table 24.   GOAT words with exceptional realizations

English	Sranan	Ndyuka	Saramaccan
nose	(nóso)	(nósu)	núsu
smoke	(smóko)	(somóko)	sumúku

Dobson (1957: 674) does mention an occasional raising in ME of /ɔː/ to /oː/
which would give /uː/ in EModE: "The raising is not characteristic of Standard
English but seems to have been common in Northern and Eastern dialects; but
it made its way early into London English, in which it was found chiefly in
vulgar but occasionally in educated speech."

Confusingly, in eighteenth century Saramaccan (Schumann 1778) we find *smoko* but *nusso*.

Unusually, for *over* we have a reflex of the stressed vowel in /a/.

Table 25.   Over

English	Sranan	Ndyuka	Saramaccan
over	ábra	ábáa	á6a

This presumably goes back to the form /ɔvər/ recorded by orthoepists (Dobson 1957: 482) in the sixteenth and seventeenth centuries. This would naturally give /a/.

The words *old* and *cold* display deviant reflexes in the Suriname creoles, even when compared with words like *hold*. The reflex is the same as in *fowl*.

Table 26.   GOAT words with deviant reflexes before liquids

English	Sranan	Ndyuka	Saramaccan
old	**ówru**	ólo, háu (< Dutch?)	**awoo**
cold	**kówru**	kóo	-
hold	óri	(h)óli	hói
fowl	**fówru**	fóo	**fóu**, fóo

Older recordings such as Van Dyk (ca. 1765) reveal that words like *old* were originally trisyllabic – *ouwere* for [ówuru]. Dobson (1957: 691) infers from the EModE evidence that /ɔ:/ sometimes became /u:/ before /l/, with a subsequent diphthongization to /ʌu/ (> /au/), i.e. it joined the MOUTH set. Wells (1982: 312) sees rather an allophonic development before /l/ of London /ʌu/ (=EModE /o:/, the GOAT set), to [ɒu ~ ɔu ~ aɤ], etc. This has subsequently been involved in a phonemic split. We will not dwell further on this.

3.1.15. *GOOSE*

The GOOSE set of words, corresponding to ME /o:/, is represented in Suriname creoles by the English words *shoot, spook, loose, spoon, fool, too, lose, do, two*, and so on. The normal realization of these words in the Suriname creoles is [u], a short high back round vowel. Because of the lack of a length distinction this means that there is no contrast with the FOOT set.

Table 27.   The GOOSE set

English	Sranan	Ndyuka	Saramaccan
do	du	dú	dú
too	tu	tú	tu
two	tu	tú	tú
true	tru	tuú	tuú
shoot	sútu	sútu	súti
play fool	prejfúru	-	peevú
loose	lúsu	-	lúsu
spoon	spun	supún	-
root	lútu	lútu	lútu

The following derive from original /eu, iu/.

Table 28.   GOOSE words with original /eu, iu/

English	Sranan	Ndyuka	Saramaccan
Jew	dju	djú	djú
new	njun	njún	njún
usen (=used) to	njúsu	-	(n)jú(n)su

3.1.16. PRICE

The PRICE set of words, corresponding to ME /iː/, is represented in Suriname creoles by the English words *eye, cry, fly, tie, fight, night, white, ripe, wife, knife, time, find,* and so on. The normal realization of these words in the Suriname creoles is [e], a short mid front vowel. This set falls together with the FACE and DRESS sets.

Table 29. The PRICE set

English	Sranan	Ndyuka	Saramaccan
fight	féti	féti	féti
night	néti	néti	ndéti
right	léti	léti	léti
white	wéti	wéti	wéti
ripe	lépi	lépi	lépi
knife	néfi	néfi	-ndéfi
time	ten	tén	té(n)
find	féni	fénde	fén(d)i

When the vowel is word-final we find variation between /e, ej, aj/ as in the FACE set.

Table 30. The PRICE set word-finally

English	Sranan	Ndyuka	Saramaccan
buy	baj	bái	ɓái
cry	krej	keé	kɛɛ́
dry	drej	deé	dɛɛ́
high	ej	éi	héi
tie	taj	téi	tái

3.1.17. *CHOICE*

The CHOICE set of words, corresponding to ME /ɔi, ʊi /, is represented in Suriname creoles by words derived from EModE *boy*, *boil* (n.), *boil* (v.), and *spoil*. According to Dobson (1957) the /ɔi/ found in modern Standard English is derived from one ME variant, alternating in many words with /ʊi/ which later became /ai/ (< /əi/) in advanced pronunciation in EModE.

Table 31.   The CHOICE set

English	Sranan	Ndyuka	Saramaccan
boy	boj	bói	-
boil (v.)	bóri	bóli	ɓói
boil (n.)	-	-	ɓói
spoil	póri	póli	pói

The forms for *boy* are not (necessarily) problematic, but those for the other three words are. The reason is the unusual combination of organic and anaptyctic vowels here. Usually, features of the organic vowel are repeated in the anaptyctic vowel:

(7)   <u>Organic</u>   <u>Anaptyctic</u>
       i   i
       e   e, i
       ɛ   ɛ
       ɔ   ɔ
       o   o, u
       u   u

or, as in the case of low vowels, the final consonant plays a role:

(8)   <u>Organic</u>   <u>Anaptyctic</u>
       aP (a<*a,ɔ)   u
       aT   i
       aK   a
       oP (o < *ʌ)   u
       oT   i
       oK   o

Here, however, the diphthong /ɔi/ gives us /o-i/. The other two diphthongs in English /ai/ and /au/ result in /e-i, e-e/ (see PRICE set) and /o-u, o-o/ (see MOUTH set) respectively. In other words diphthongs are generally compressed to single vowels, of forecastable quality. /e/ reflects the features of both /a/ and /i – low] and [front], and /o/ the features of both /a/ and /u – low] and [round]. But, the /o/ in /bóri/ does not reflect both the features of /ɔ/ and the features of /i/. We must look further.

Let us start from the anaptyctic vowel /-i/. This implies in general a front organic vowel. We ignore the fact that coronal consonants following organic historic low vowels trigger anaptyctic /-i/ because we expect the three English diphthongs to be treated in a parallel fashion. As Smith (1987: 432) observes "The only case that would fit the occurring patterns would be a model involving the EModE vowel /ʌ/ followed by an alveolar". Why /ɔi/ should result in /ʌ/ is not at all clear. It is of course the case that the CHOICE set has fallen together with the STRUT set.

Rounded vowels do have another source in the Suriname creoles than English back or round vowels. We find not infrequent cases of the following (unsystematic) changes:

(9)   *wi   >   u
      *we   >   o
      *wa   >   o

Further, in these cases the comparison drawn with Krio and Jamaican by Smith (1987) is illuminating:

Table 32.   CHOICE words in Jamaican, Krio, and Suriname

English	Jamaican	Krio	Suriname creoles
boy	bwaj	boj	boj
boil (v.)	bwajl	bwɛl	*bóli
spoil	pwajl	pwɛl	*póli

If the diphthongs in the cases with codas were preceded historically by a situation like that in Krio, then the anaptyctic front vowels can be explained. This is then due to the organic front vowel present. Note that Krio, like the Suriname creoles, systematically compresses pre-coda diphthongs /ai, au/ into single vowels. We could then imagine a derivational path as follows:

(10)   *boy*   (bwai)   >   boi
       boil   bwail   >   *bwel   >   *bwéli   >   bóli
       spoil   pwail   >   *pwel   >   *pwéli   >   póli

Where does this vocalic structure /wai/ come from? Presumably from EModE /ʊi/. On the evidence of Wright (1905) [wai] and [wəi] only occur after labials.

Dobson (1957: 825) compares the retention of /ʊi/ here to the parallel tendency to retain /ʊ/ after labials. The intermediate stages he posits are of lesser interest so we will ignore Dobson's further discussion here.

3.1.18. MOUTH

The MOUTH set of words, corresponding to ME /uː/, is represented in Suriname creoles by the English words *proud, house, louse, mouth, cow* and so on. The normal realization of these words in the Suriname creoles is [o], a short high back round vowel. This set falls together with the GOAT set. There is only one vowel-final case, varying between /ow/ in Sranan and /au/ in Ndyuka.

Table 33.   The MOUTH set

English	Sranan	Ndyuka	Saramaccan
proud	pródo	poólo	poólo
louse	lóso	lósu	lósu
house	óso	ósu	(w)ósu
cow	kow	káu	káu
ground	gron	goón	goón, goún

3.1.19. NEAR

The NEAR set of words, corresponding to ME /eː/ and /ɛː/ before /r/, is represented in the Suriname creoles by words like *deer, here, overseer, beard*.

Table 34.   The NEAR set

English	Sranan	Ndyuka	Saramaccan
deer	día	dí(j)a	-
here	dja (older *día, hía*)	já	-
overseer	basjá	basía	ɓasi(j)á
beard	-	-	ɓí(j)a

3.1.20. *SQUARE*

The SQUARE set of words, corresponding to ME /ɛː/ and /aː/ before /r/, is represented in the Suriname creoles by such words as *square, care, wear, swear, there*. Unlike in the case of the front high vowel we clearly have two different developments with regard to /r/. In some cases it is retained, and in others it is not.

Hare shows a peculiar vowel development, which we will discuss together with *shear* immediately below.

Table 35. /r/-less SQUARE words

English	Sranan	Ndyuka	Saramaccan
there	de	dé	dɛ́
care	ke	-	-
hare	ej	hé	-

Table 36. /r/-full SQUARE words

English	Sranan	Ndyuka	Saramaccan
square	kwéri	kwéli	kwéi
wear	wéri	wéi	-

Just as with the FLEECE set of words, there are also words with ME /ɛː/ that in Standard English are in the NEAR class but show a different development in the Suriname creoles.

Table 37. /r/-less SQUARE words with NEAR set vowels

English	Sranan	Ndyuka	Saramaccan
ears	jési	jési	jési
shear (share)	siséj, seséj	seséi	seséi

Table 38. /r/-full SQUARE words with NEAR set vowels

English	Sranan	Ndyuka	Saramaccan
hear	jére	jée	jéi
weary	wéri	wéli	wéi

Shear and *hare* show the same development in the vowel, neither a lowering diphthong nor a monophthong as might be expected, but a raising diphthong. What is the source of this? Smith (1987: 335–336) provides a long technical discussion, the conclusion of which is that we may be able to see a distinction between disyllabic and monosyllabic /r/-less vowel reflexes here.

(11)

		Model	Suriname
disyllabic		aiə	ája
		auə/ uə	ówa
		iːə	í(j)a
		uːə	úwa
monosyllabic		ɛə	e/ɛ
		ɔə	o/ɔ
		ɛˈə	ej

Similar reflexes such as [ɛɪə] are actually encountered in words like *hair* in Southern England, and something similar is recorded for Cockney.

3.1.21. START

The START set of words, corresponding mostly to ME /a/ before /r/, is represented in the Suriname creoles by such words as *arse, garden, far, tar, yard, sharp*, and *shark*. Here /r/ is mostly retained. We have one case of early loss (*heart*) and one case (*arse*) where metathesis uniquely occurs in a vowel-initial word. Note however that this is parallelled by Jamaican /raas/ and similar forms in other Caribbean creoles.

Table 39.   /r/-less START words

English	Sranan	Ndyuka	Saramaccan
heart	áti	áti	(h)áti
arse	lási	lási	–

Table 40.   /r/-full START words

English	Sranan	Ndyuka	Saramaccan
bargain	bárki	-	
garden	djári	djáli	djái
"parmacety" (spermacety)	pramaséti	-	-
crowbar	krubári	-	ku(lu)báli (< Sranan)
far	fára	fáa	-
star	stári	sitáli	-
tar	tára	táa	táa, tála
yard	jári		-
sharp	srápu	saápu	saápu
hark	árki	álíki	(h)aíka
shark	sárki	sáliki	-

3.1.22. FORCE

In FORCE words we see three developments: the reflex of possible early pre-consonantal loss in *fort*, final loss in *four* and *before*, and preservation in *more*, *sore*, *door* etc.

Table 41.   /r/-less FORCE words

English	Sranan	Ndyuka	Saramaccan
before	bifó(si)	bifó	ɓifɔ́
four	fo	fó	fɔ́
poor thing	póoti	poóti	pootíma
gourd	gódo	góo, gódu	gólu
fort	fóto	fóto	fóto

Table 42.   /r/-full FORCE words

English	Sranan	Ndyuka	Saramaccan
more	móro	móo	mɔ́ɔ
sore	sóro	sóo	-
door	dóro	fóo	dɔ́ɔ
shore	ʃóro	sóo	-
story	tóri	tóli	-

3.1.23. NORTH

As we can see the contrast between FORCE words and NORTH words – derived from ME /ŏ/ before /r/ – is maintained. Once again we have the two options with ME short vowels preceding /r/ of possible early pre-consonantal loss and maintenance of /r/.

Table 43.   /r/-less NORTH words

English	Sranan	Ndyuka	Saramaccan
short	ʃátu	sátu	sáti
mortar	máta	máta	máta
horse	ási	ási	hási

Table 44.   /r/-full NORTH words

English	Sranan	Ndyuka	Saramaccan
corn	káru	kálu	kálu
man o'war	manwári	-	-

3.1.24. CURE

There is only one clear case of /uː/ preceding /r/. And this is a non-standard case of a word which would more normally belong to the FORCE set.

There are also two possible cases of retention of ME /uː/, i.e. non-shifting of this to a diphthongal reflex. However, as the developments are not clear, and also involve forms which do show a development to a diphthong, we will deal with these cases when we discuss the POWER set.

Table 45.   The CURE set

English	Sranan	Ndyuka	Saramaccan
court	krútu	kuútu	kuútu

For an opposite case compare Table 11 above.

3.1.25. FIRE

The FIRE set of words is very small, but does show two interesting forms (deriving from ME /iː/ before /r/). The one is an example of /r/-loss finally, while the other must derive, because of the double vowel in Ndyuka, from an intermediate structure like /*ájeren/. Something resembling the r-full standard pronunciation variant /aiərn/ must lie behind this form. As far as the /e/-colour of the vowels is concerned, we may see a parallel in the non-rhotic Krio /ajɛn/.

Table 46.   /r/-full FIRE words

English	Sranan	Ndyuka	Saramaccan
fire	fája	fája	fája

Table 47.   /r/-less FIRE words

English	Sranan	Ndyuka	Saramaccan
iron	-	ájee	-

3.1.26. POWER

We have few examples of the POWER set. We assume the /ow/ alternants represent the shifted reflex of ME /uː/. The /u(w)/ variants are either non-shifted high vowel reflexes, or later assimilations of /ow/ to /uw/.

Table 48. The POWER set

English	Sranan	Ndyuka	Saramaccan
flour	frowa, frúwa	foówa	-
sour	s(u)wa	sú(w)a	sówa

3.1.27. *happY*

The happY set has two main reflexes. After mid vowels we get frequent assimilation to /e, ɛ/, and in other cases we get /i/. Words illustrating this set include *ready*, *heavy*, *busy*, *bury*, *sorry*, *money*, *curtsey*.

Table 49. The happY set

English	Sranan	Ndyuka	Saramaccan
greedy	grídi	giíli	giíi
already	aréde	-	-
hungry	áŋri	áŋgíi	háŋgi
every	íbri	íbíi	(h)íbi
country	kóndre	kóndée	kɔ́ndɛ
ugly	ógri	ógíi	(w/h)ógi
belly	bére	bée	ɓéɛ

3.1.28. *horsES*

This set was added to cover the vowel used in the plural forms of nouns, etc. However, as plurals, etc. are not formed in this way in the Suriname creoles the only cases of such a vowel found are two cases of obsolete lexicalized plurals of nouns ending in sibilants: *ashes*, *peases*. This second form is a plural of *pease*. The form *peas(e)* 'pea' also exists in the modern languages, but with a different development of the vowel: /pési/.

Table 50.   The horsES set

English	Sranan	Ndyuka	Saramaccan
peases (sic)	*pisis* (?) (1783)	-	*pisis* (1778)
ashes	ásisi	ásísi	-

3.1.29. lettER

This set also involves an /r/-final variant and an /r/-less one in Sranan. There does not seem to be any conditioning involved. The /r/-less variant replaces /-ər/ with /-a/. The /r/-full variant has a final vowel that echoes the previous vowel. Words illustrating this set include: *river, bitter* and *gutter*.

It is clear from older forms that the original starting-point for a word like /másra/ was a form like /*másara/. To reach the modern forms we had syncope in Sranan, /r/ > /l/, followed by liquid-loss in Ndyuka, and probably a further reduction of final /v́v/ to /v/ in Saramaccan, which maintains the distinction between the two sets.

Table 51.   /r/-less lettER words

English	Sranan	Ndyuka	Saramaccan
river	líba	líba	-
bitter	bíta	bíta	ɓíta
finger	fíŋa	fíŋga	fíŋga
sister	sísa	sísa	sísa
brother	bráda, brára	baála	ɓaáa

Table 52.   /r/-full lettER words

English	Sranan	Ndyuka	Saramaccan
remember	mémre	mémbée	mémbɛ
master	másra	másáa	mása
gutter	gótro	gótóo	ŋgɔ́tɔ
cover	kíbri	kíbíi	-
over	ábra	abáa	áɓa

3.1.30. commA

The commA set in the Suriname creoles largely comprises words ending in
-*o*(*w*) in Standard English. In substandard accents this frequently becomes /-ə/.

Table 53.   The commA set

English	Sranan	Ndyuka	Saramaccan
narrow	nára	-	-
yellow-	jara-	jaa-	-
tomorrow	tamára	tamáa	-
mosquito	maskíta	makisíta	-

3.1.31. rottEN

The rottEN set has two types of reflex in the Suriname creoles. One set has
the reflex /-i(n)/. This is shared by other creoles in the Atlantic area like Krio,
which is fairly similar to the Suriname creoles in various respects.

Table 54.   rottEN words in /-in/

English	Sranan	Ndyuka	Saramaccan
bargain	bárki	-	-
rotten	ratín	-	-
fashion	fási	fási	fási
fasten	fási	fási	-
garden	djári	djáli	djái

The other involves a repetition of the main vowel of the preceding syllable.

Table 55.   rottEN words with echo vowels

English	Sranan	Ndyuka	Saramaccan
open	ópo	óbo	-
cotton-	kánkan- (*kattan-* 1783)	-	kankan- (*kattan-* 1783)
"usen" (used)	júnsu	-	júnsu
cushion	kúnsu	kúnsu	kúnsu
payment	pajmán		paimá

The two above reflexes also occur with *-ing* items.

Table 56.   *-ing* words

English	Sranan	Ndyuka	Saramaccan
pudding	*pudun* (1856)	-	-
herring	elén	-	-
cunning	kóni	kóni	kɔ́ni
dumpling	adómpri	dómíi	-

3.1.32. Neutralizations of the Wells sets

The following are the neutralizations of the Wells stressed vowel sets observed in the Suriname creoles:

(12)   KIT = FLEECE
        DRESS = FACE = SQUARE = PRICE
        TRAP = LOT = BATH = CLOTH = THOUGHT = START = NORTH
        STRUT = NURSE = CHOICE
        GOAT = FORCE = MOUTH
        FOOT = GOOSE = CURE

3.2.   Consonantal specifics

We will restrict ourselves to mentioning the most significant deviations from Standard English consonantal values.

3.2.1. Reflections of non-standard consonantism

3.2.1.1. Palatalization of velars before /a/

The pronunciation of /#k, #g/ as [kj, gj] before /a/ had a brief vogue in standard forms of English in the seventeenth century. It still occurs in a recessive form in scattered dialects in England, and is also frequent in English-lexifier creoles in the Caribbean. As far as London English is concerned, the *Survey of English Dialects* recorded it for Cockney in Hackney, E. London in the word *cabbage*: [kʲæbɪdʒ].

Table 57.   Palatalization of velars before /a/

English	Sranan	Ndyuka	Saramaccan
cat	-	káti	-tjáti
cabbage	kábisi (earlier *kjábbisi*, *tjábbisi*)	tjábísi	tjábísi
carry	**tjá(ri)**	**tjái**	**tjá**
cast-net	**tjasnéti**	-	-
candle	kándra	kándáa	kánda
garden	**djári**	**djáli**	**djái**
braggard	**bradjári**	-	-

The further change of /kja, gja/ to /tʃa, dʒa/ can be associated with a change in the substrate. See section 3.2.2.6. below.

3.2.1.2. Preservation, loss, and insertion of /h/

In modern Sranan [h] at the beginning of words is a mark of emphasis. However up till the 19th century /h/ was a phoneme of Sranan. It also occurs optionally in Ndyuka and Saramaccan at the present. There is a set of words in the Suriname creoles that may begin (or in the case of Sranan, began) with /h/, and another set that always begins with a vowel. These do not however agree with the corresponding sets in English.

Table 58.   Preservation, loss, and insertion of /h/

English	Sranan	Sranan 1855	Ndyuka	Saramaccan
hunt	ónti	hónti	(h)ónti	(h)ɔ́ndi
heap	ípi	hípi	(h)ípi	(h)ípi
eight	ájti	aíti	aíti(n)	áíti
axe	áksi	áksi	akísi	-
Indian	íɲi	iéngi	íŋgíi	íŋgi
ask	áksi	(h)áksi	ákísi	(h)ákísi
ugly	ógri	(h)ógri	ógíi	(h)ógi

The answer to the question how this state of affairs could come about must lie in the presence of a mixture of /h/-less and /h/-full dialects. Cockney, for example, is like most Southern and Midland dialects in not having initial /h/. However, Cockney is famous for optionally inserting an [h] before vowel-initial words.

The statistical connection between /h/-initial words in Standard English and those in the Suriname creoles must be explained by a basic Standard English heritage. On the other hand, the occurrence of /h/ in non-/h/-inital words must reflect the influence of a Cockney-like dialect. There are no /h/-words in Standard English that lack an /h/ completely in all Suriname creoles, a fact which argues for a greater degree of standard than sub-standard influence.

3.2.2.   Substrate features of African origin

3.2.2.1.   Implosives

A feature of Saramaccan that escaped notice until quite recently was the fact that it distinguished plain voiced /b, d/ phonemes from implosive voiced /ɓ, ɗ/. This was first described in Haabo (2000), and is clearly an African feature. The distribution of plain and implosive stops over the sets of words of different origins is interesting, but has yet to be fully explained. Some examples follow:

Table 59.   Examples of implosive voiced stops

English	Saramaccan
bottle	ɓáta
heavy	héɓi
dead	ɗédɛ
toad	tɔ́ɗɔ

Table 60.   Examples of plain voiced stops

English	Saramaccan
cabbage	tjábísi
every	(h)íbi
burn	boónu
paddle	páda
drum	dóun
doctor	dáta
devil	didíɓi

English-derived items with plain /b/ are very rare. Voiced stops in nasal clusters are however always plain. This also applies in Ndyuka where voiced stops /b, d/ are otherwise normally pronounced as implosives [ɓ, ɗ]. There is no phonemic contrast in Ndyuka, however.

3.2.2.2. Tones

Ndyuka and Saramaccan (but not present-day Sranan) are clear tone languages. In words of English origin the English stress accent virtually always corresponds to a high tone. Many examples have already been given in the text so we will not give any more here.

3.2.2.3. Final nasals

The subject of the developments undergone by the word-final nasals in the Suriname creoles is a complex one. We will merely mention here that all three languages allow for a final /VN/ combination to be pronounced as a nasalized vowel, as in one of the substrate groups – the Gbe languages. However, from a phonological point of view there is a lot to be said for analysing these as underlying sequences in all three languages.

In Sranan in particular the more normal pronunciation is with a vowel (nasalized or not) followed by a velar nasal [ŋ].

3.2.2.4. Initial sibilant clusters

The treatment of initial sibilant clusters by which the sibilant is lost is another probable substrate effect, and one that appears in other creoles too. It is also one that does not operate in new or nineteenth-century loans. As such it may provide clues as to the relative age of an element. In general, nearly all English words of this kind appearing in the Suriname creoles lose the initial sibilant.

Saramaccan has very few such sibilants preserved, while Ndyuka has more, and Sranan has most of all. Words only occurring in Sranan are under suspicion of being late loans.

Table 61. Initial loss of sibilant from cluster

English	Sranan	Ndyuka	Saramaccan
square	kwéri	kwéli	kwéi
squeeze	kwínsi	kwínsi	kwínji
scrape	krébi	keébi	-
skin	skin	sikín	sinkíi
squall	skwála	-	-
speak	píki	píki	píki
spoil	póri	póli	pói
spit	spíti	-	-
spoon	spun	supún	-
stop	tápu	tápu	-
stand	tan	tán	tán
stink	tíŋi	tíŋgi	tíŋgi
star	stári	sitáli	-
stewpan	stjupan	-	-

3.2.2.5. Final consonants—vowel anaptyxis

We have discussed this undoubted substrate feature—in neither the Gbe languages nor in Kikoongo are final consonants permitted—in the course of our treatment of the various vowel sets.

3.2.2.6. Palatalization of velars

The velar phonemes have optional palatal/palato-alveolar realizations /tj, dj, nj/ in the Suriname creoles before front vowels. We associate this with a change of /*ki, kj/ to /tʃi, tʃ/ in Gbe languages,

Table 62.   Palatalizaton of velars

English	Sranan
skin	[skiŋ ~ stʃiŋ]
catch	[kísi ~ tʃísi]
give	[gi ~ dʒi]
shark	[sá˙rki ~ sɑˈrtʃi]
beg	[bígi ~ bídʒi]
drink	[dríŋi ~ dríɲi]

It is not strictly possible to refer to these as allophones, because of the existence of phonemic contrasts with non-front vowels.

3.2.2.7. Palatalization of /s/ before /i/ and /w, j/

Sranan and Ndyuka exhibit another optional palatalization, this time of /s/ to /ʃ/ before /i/ or /w/. Also /s/ and /j/ combine in onset to give /ʃ/ in Ndyuka. This also appears to operate in Sranan across word boundaries: *fos(i) júru* > [fɔʃjúru] 'first hour'. We interpret the alternate forms provided by Focke (1855) as indicating the options /sj/ (*si*) and /ʃ/ (*sj*) for the onset position as well in 19th century Sranan. Although /s/ is palatalized preceding /i, j/ in some Gbe lects, we are less certain that this change is due to substrate effects.

Table 63. /ʃ/ in Sranan and Ndyuka

English	Sranan	Sranan 1855	Ndyuka	Saramaccan
swim	swen, ʃwen	-	suwén	(sún)
sweet	swíti, ʃwíti	-	swíti, ʃwíti	(súti)
see	si, ʃi	-	sí, ʃí	(sí)
sleep	sríbi	-	siíbi, ʃiíbi	-
short	ʃátu	*siättoe, sjátoe*	sátu	(sáti)
shore	ʃóro	*sjóro*	sóo	-
shame	ʃen	*siëm̂, sjem̂*	sjen, ʃen	(sén)

3.2.3. Innovations

3.2.3.1. /v/ > /b/

Most words of English origin in the Suriname creoles which had a /v/-sound replace this with a stop. This change is probably rather an innovation of the pidgin precursor of the Suriname creoles, since items from Gbe languages and Kikoongo which contained a /v/-sound retain this in Ndyuka and Saramaccan, and have altered this to /f/ in modern Sranan. This last appears to be a nineteenth century change, however.

The same change is recessive in other English-lexifier creoles of the Atlantic region.

Table 64. /v/ > /b/

English	Sranan	Ndyuka	Saramaccan
heavy	(ébi)	(ébi), íbi	(hé6i)
every	íbri	íbíi	(h)íbi
over	ábra	ábáa	á6a
river	líba	líba	-
love	lóbi	lóbi	ló6i

3.2.3.2. /θ/ > /t, f/

The Suriname creoles display both of the most frequent replacement sounds for /θ/ in English. However, the distribution is unusual. English syllable-initial /θ/ goes to /t/, and English syllable-final /θ/ to /f/. Note that due to anaptyxis all the realizations are syllabe-initial in the Suriname creoles.

Table 65.   /θ/ > /t, f/

English	Sranan	Ndyuka	Saramaccan
think	-	-	*tíŋga* (1778) > níŋga
throw away	trowé	towé	túɛ
thrust	trúsu	toósi	tuúsi
nothing	nóti		-nóti
poor thing	póoti	poóti	pootí-
teeth	tífi	tífi	-
mouth	mófo	mófu	-
broth	brafú	baafú	baafu

3.2.3.3. /ð/ > /d, r/

There are not very many examples of items with English /ð/. In a number of them a development to /d/ is observable. The item *t'other* shows a development /ð/ to /r/. However this is parallelled in this word by forms in other creoles such as Jamaican /tára/ and Gullah /tʌ́rə/. Finally, the developments in Nduka (and Saramaccan) in *brother* are a purely internal affair of the Suriname creoles, which we will briefly discuss below.

Table 66.   /ð/ > /d, r/

English	Sranan	Ndyuka	Saramaccan
this	dísi	dísi	dísí
there	de	de	dɛ́
them	den	den	dɛ́
feather	féda	-	-

Table 66. (continued) /ð/ > /d, r/

English	Sranan	Ndyuka	Saramaccan
together	tigédre	-	-
t'other	tra (older *tára*)	taá	-
brother	bráda	baála	ɓaáa

3.2.3.4. Liquids

In general there are three Suriname-internal developments concerning liquids.

Firstly, a tendency to neutralize the distinction between /l/ and /r/. In Ndyuka and Saramaccan the result is always /l/. In Sranan we see a more complex near-neutralization. "Near-neutralization", because the process is not totally complete. Word-internally liquids go to [r], and initially to [l]. The first liquid also goes to /l/ if pre-stress, even if a vowel precedes.

Secondly, a tendency to lose word-internal liquids altogether in Ndyuka and Saramaccan. In Ndyuka intervocalic liquids tend to be preserved only if the surrounding vowels are different; they are lost if the vowels are identical. Word-internal liquids are virtually always lost in Saramaccan, except in recent loanwords. Clusters were epenthesized away, followed by loss of the liquid in Ndyuka and Saramaccan.

Table 67. The treatment of liquids

English	Sranan	Ndyuka	Saramaccan
love	lóbi	lóbi	lóɓi
rub	lóbi	lóbi	lóɓi
rain	alén	alén	-
cully	kóri	kóli	kɔ́i
bury	béri	béli	ɓéi
belly	bére	bée	ɓéɛ
tomorrow	tamára	tamáa	-
clothes	krósi	koósi	koósu
scratch	krási	kaási	kaási
middle	míndri	míndíi	míndi
remember	mémre	mémbée	mémbɛ

The third tendency is one of liquefaction of word-internal /d/'s following earlier liquids. This is nowadays restricted to Ndyuka and Saramaccan, although in older Sranan recordings it makes a sporadic appearance. As we can see, subsequent /l/-loss has virtually removed the resultant liquid in Saramaccan.

Table 68.   The liquefaction of /d/

English	Sranan	Ndyuka	Saramaccan
greedy	grídi	giíli	giíi
afraid	fréde	feéle	fɛɛ́ɛ
proud	pródo	poólo	(poólo)
brother	bráda	baála	ɓaáa
broad	brádi	baála	ɓaái
blood	brúdu	buúlu	ɓuúu
flood	frúdu	(fuúdu)	foóo, foóu

4.   Conclusion

The Saramaccan form /ɓaái/ 'broad' just quoted illustrates by itself how far removed phonologically the Suriname creoles are from the – standard and substandard – London English on which they are ultimately based. This form begins with an African substrate-derived implosive stop. Then we have a vowel that is in origin an epenthetic vowel whose function was to break up the original liquid cluster. The liquid itself has been lost although it was still present in the 18th century. Then we have a vowel from the LOT set, but bearing a high tone. The original final /d/ was first subject to liquefaction, and then lost. Finally we have an anaptyctic vowel /-i/, whose original function was to prevent the occurrence of final consonants. The only segments corresponding directly to the original structure are the /ɓ/ and the /á/, and even they are very un-English!

Exercises and study questions

1. Can we assume that normal intergenerational transfer took place in the passage from EModE to the Surinam creole languages?

2. What is Ingredient X?

3. Are any of the Surinam creole languages tone languages or not?

4. The form derived from EModE *catch* in the Surinam creoles is /kísi/ in all three creoles treated here. Can we associate this with similar developments in other forms of English?

5. What could the explanation be for the fact that in the Surinam creoles a significant number of words that normally belong to the STRUT set belong to the FOOT set?

6. What can we conclude from the fact that the form of the words *old* and *cold* in Sranan – /ówru, kówru/ rhyme with the form of the word *fowl*?

7. What is the problem with the anaptyctic vowels in the Surinam creole forms of words like *boil, spoil*? And what historical phonological conclusions can we draw from this?

8. Can you mention any African phonological features present in the Surinam creoles?

Selected references

Please consult the General references for titles mentioned in the text but not included in the references below. For a full bibliography see the accompanying CD-ROM.

Arends, Jacques
    1999   The origin of the Portuguese element in the Surinam creoles. In: Huber and Parkvall (eds.), 195–208.
Carlin, Eithne and Jacques Arends (eds.)
    2002   *Atlas of the Languages of Suriname*. Leiden: KITLV Press.
Dobson, Eric J.
    1957   *English Pronunciation, 1500–1700*. Oxford: Oxford University Press.
Focke, H.C
    1855   *Neger-Engelsch Woordenboek*. Leiden: P.H. van den Heuvell.
Haabo, Vinije
    2000   Fonologie van het Saramaccaans. Unpublished manuscript, University of Leiden.

Matthews, W.
1935   Sailors' pronunciation in the second half of the seventeenth century. *Anglia*
          59: 192–251.
Schumann, C.L.
1778   Saramaccan Deutsches Wörter-Buch. [MS., Moravian Brethren, Bam-
          bey, Surinam. Republished in Hugo Schuchardt, *Die Sprache der Sara-
          makkaneger in Surinam* (= *Verhandelingen der Koninklijke Akademie van
          Wetenschappen te Amsterdam, Afdeling Letterkunde* Nieuwe Reeks XIV,
          6). Amsterdam: Johannes Müller.]
Smith, Norval S.H.
1987   The genesis of the creole languages of Surinam. D.Litt. thesis, University
          of Amsterdam.
1999a   Pernambuco to Surinam 1654–1665. The Jewish slave controversy. In:
          Huber and Parkvall (eds.), 251–298.
1999b   The vowel system of 18th-century St Kitts Creole: Evidence for the his-
          tory of the English creoles? In: Baker and Bruyn (eds.), 145–172.
2001   Reconstructing Proto-Caribbean Pidgin English. Paper given at the
          Pidginfest, University of Westminster, April 2001.
2002   The history of the Surinamese creoles II: Origin and differentiation. In:
          Carlin and Arends (eds.), 131–151.
Van den Berg, Margot
2000   "Mi no sal tron tongo". Early Sranan in court records 1667–1767. MA
          thesis, University of Nijmegen.
Van Dyk, P.
ca. 1765 *Nieuwe en nooit bevoorens geziene Onderwyzinge in het Bastert Engels,
          of Neeger Engels, zoo als het zelve in de Hollandsze Colonien gebruikt
          word (...).* Amsterdam: Jacobus van Egmont. [Republished with an Eng-
          lish translation in Jacques Arends and Matthias Perl (eds.), 1995. *Early
          Suriname Creole Texts: A Collection of 18th-century Sranan and Sara-
          maccan Documents* (= *Bibliotheca Ibero-Americana* 49). Frankfurt am
          Main/Madrid: Vervuert Verlag/Iberoamericana, 93–242.]

Synopsis: phonological variation in the Americas and the Caribbean

Edgar W. Schneider

1.   Introduction

This chapter attempts to survey and systematize the phonetic and phonological variability that can be observed in North America and the Caribbean. No fundamental distinction is drawn between dialectal and creole varieties beforehand – such a division has been questioned in recent research, and it would seem to be even less called for on the level of phonetics and phonology than on the level of morphosyntax, where, based on earlier research, the presupposition of existing differences seems more justified. In categorizing the wide range of possible pronunciation phenomena, I start out from the listing of feature categories as suggested originally to future contributors, and I adopt a categorization scheme based upon traditional articulatory classifications. Basically, I distinguish between vowels, consonants, and prosodic features. Given that most of the variability to be observed concerns vowels, this broad category needs to be further subdivided, although any such categorization on the basis of observed variation turns out to be problematic: Given that processes of diphthongization/monophthongization, lengthening/shortening (or blurring of quantity distinctions), fronting/backing, and raising/lowering are almost ubiquitous, any categorization is bound to leak. Hence, for purely practical reasons, to enable comparisons on a global scale in the present context, I employ an RP-based scheme of vowel types, distinguishing between "short" vowels (which can also be called "checked", many of which are also "lax"), "long" (or free, frequently described as tense) vowels, diphthongs, and unstressed vowels. As a general reference system in this project context, it was decided (and authors were instructed) to employ Wells' (1982) system of "lexical sets", meant to identify vowel types in specific contexts without having to go into the knotty issue of whether or not these are phonemic in any given variety. I am grateful to the contributors to this volume for having accepted this procedure despite the fact that in the American academic context this system is less widely accepted (and perhaps more difficult to accommodate) than in a British-based perspective. It should also be noted that this system was not imposed slavishly. Contributors were advised and authorized to adopt and expand it when this was felt to be necessary for a reliable coverage of their respective variety, i.e. either to use some of the items which Wells suggests in a "reserve list" or to replace target words by others of their own choice. This was felt to be necessary especially in the cases of creole varieties, where some of Wells' key words are not lexicalized (but the respective vowel can be identified using an alternative lexical item) or where the phonological system of sounds, in the perspective of the English superstrate input, has been restructured substantially.

The following discussion starts out from authors' responses to a feature list of possible phonetic processes that I devised and that was provided to the contributors as a stimulus for these categorizations; this feature list underlies the interactive phonological maps on the accompanying CD-ROM. Further details and comparative statements are then based upon the articles in this volume. By necessity, a survey of the present kind needs to ignore many aspects and to abstract from idiosyncrasies to reach a more global picture. Readers interested in phonetic details and distributional specifics are warned to be cautious, to take the statements below with a grain of salt, and to check the original sources for more accurate and locally relevant information.

2.   "Short" vowels

2.1.   KIT

Throughout North America and the Caribbean the KIT vowel is a "canonical" high front short [ɪ], with relatively little variability. Most notably, in Southern dialect (and, consequently, to some extent in AAVE) this vowel can be "drawled" by adding a centralizing offglide, but in the new urban South the drawl, also with this vowel, is regarded as recessive. Raising and fronting to [i] occurs in SurCs, JamE and, conditionally, in NfldE and some contact varieties (CajE, ChcE, JamC, and T&TC [henceforth, this abbreviation is taken to refer to the entire continuum of Trinidad, usually including the mesolectal and acrolectal forms of Tobago but set off against basilectal TobC]); this tensing is also a part of the "Southern Shift". Centralizing to [ə] is not the norm anywhere but may occur in the dialects of Philadelphia (henceforth abbreviated as PhilE), the inland North (henceforth InlNE), the South (henceforth SAmE), in JamE, and in T&TC and TobC. Centralization of KIT is spreading as an element of the "Northern Cities Shift". Lowering of this vowel to [ɛ] seems to be a recent innovation of California speech and of young Canadians.

2.2. DRESS

Equally generally, the DRESS vowel is a half-open short [ɛ]. Again, offgliding is characteristically and exclusively southern, normally centralizing to [ə] but possibly also raising to [ɪ]. In InlNE, CanE, AAVE and T&TC the vowel may be backed, and in California and among young Canadians the vowel may be lowered to [æ].

2.3. TRAP

The TRAP vowel serves to globally distinguish North American dialects, where it is realized as a slightly raised front [æ], from Caribbean varieties, which have a low front [a] (except for the Turks and Caicos Islands, apparently). Further raising to mid-front positions (an element of the "Northern Cities Shift") may be observed in some dialects of southern and eastern North America (SAmE, PhilE, InlNE, New York City [henceforth NYCE], younger speakers of New England dialect [henceforth NEngE], NfldE, BahE, and ChcE). In contrast, lowering to [a] and also backing appears in California and also, as the most salient element of a chain shift labeled "Canadian Shift", among young Ontario speakers. This vowel is more prone to diphthongization with a centralizing offglide, normal in SAmE (though, again, recessive in urban environments) and AAVE and possible in a wider range of mostly mainland dialects (PhilE, InlNE, NYCE, NEngE, NfldE, and ChcE, as well as T&TC).

2.4. STRUT

Realizations of the STRUT vowel are highly variable. In North American dialects (but also Baj), it is typically a relatively back, unrounded and slightly raised [ʌ] (exclusively in NEngE, CanE and CajE) or a more central [ɐ] or [ə] (predominantly in SAmE). A backed realization of this vowel, roughly as [ɔ], characterizes the Caribbean (SurC, JamE/C, TobC, BahE, Eastern Caribbean islands, also T&TC) and Gullah and can also be found in NEngE and, as part of the "Northern Cities Shift", InlNE. Except for traces in ChcE and possibly as a recent innovation in PhilE, raising of this vowel to [ʊ] (or [u] in PhilE) is not normally heard in America. A rounded realization, [ɔ̈], is a regional variant within NfldE.

2.5. LOT, CLOTH

AmE LOT is typically a low back unrounded vowel, [ɑ], though rounded [ɒ] may come up in the West and Midwest (henceforth WMwE), in NEngE and CanE, as well as, in the Caribbean, in JamE, Baj and T&TC. On the other hand,

Caribbean creoles (e.g. JamC, TobC, SurCs) more typically realize this vowel as a front unrounded [a], a pronunciation which also characterizes AAVE, ChcE and NfldE and which can at times also be observed in InlNE and CajE. Offglides with this vowel are reported as normal in Gullah and possible in NYCE and CanE. The vowel of CLOTH, on the other hand, is more commonly rounded than unrounded (the latter variant characterizes NEngE, AAVE, ChcE, parts of the Midwest and TobC). In this case, [a] is found in CajE and NfldE, with restrictions also in ChcE.

2.6.   FOOT

The FOOT vowel shows little variation: the canonical realization as a relatively high and back [ʊ] predominates everywhere. Possible variants are a tensed [u] in NfldE, ChcE, JamE/C and SurC, or a lowered type, close to [ʌ], in NfldE, ChcE, and T&TC/TobC. In SAmE, mostly in urban contexts, this vowel may be fronted (as part of the "Southern Shift") to [ɵ ˜ ʏ].

3.   "Long" vowels

3.1.   FLEECE

The FLEECE vowel is commonly realized as a relatively high and front, long [iː] everywhere, but in addition to this there are a number of regional alternatives. These include the possibility of shortening it (in NfldE, AAVE, ChcE, BahE, T&TC, TobC and SurC), but more commonly some sort of gliding movement results in diphthongized types. Ingliding, i.e. [iə], occurs in WMwE, NYCE, NfldE, AAVE and T&TC. Alternatively, upglides can be observed, either with high onsets and relatively short gliding movements, [ɪi], in CanE and NfldE, or with longer glides after mid-front or central onsets, i.e. [əɪ/ei], in NfldE or TobC.

3.2.   BATH

In almost all North American dialects the BATH class is realized as a half-open front [æ] sound. A low [a] counts as a Boston accent shibboleth and tends to be associated with NEngE in general, although it is only one of the variants found in the region and felt to be increasingly conservative; it also predominates in T&TC, Baj, TobC (together with other realizations), and SurC. CanE and BahE have both types variably. A low back [ɑ] is possible in T&TC and some regions of New England. Raising of this vowel, together with TRAP, constitutes an element of the Northern Cities Shift, supposedly an early stage of this chain shift which may have spread from northwestern New England to cities of the Inland North. Lengthening of this vowel is generally found in TobC, JamC/E, Baj, and AAVE, and possible in PhilE, NYCE, NfldE, and T&TC. Variants with an off-glide, e.g. [æə/æɪ/ɛə], characterize SAmE (less so in younger, urban speech), AAVE, and TobC, and may be observed in InlNE, PhilE, NYCE, and NEngE.

3.3.   PALM, START

The vowel of PALM and START is a low back [ɑ] in practically all North American dialects. A low front [a] in these lexical types is reported as the main variant in Jam (C and E), T&T (in all lects), Baj, SurC, ChcE and Gullah (primarily in START), and NEngE in PALM, variably also for NEngE in START, InlNE and NfldE in both types, CanE in PALM, and CajE in START. An offglide in PALM, e.g. [ɑə/ɒə], is possible in NYCE, CanE and AAVE; in START, this is common in PhilE and NYCE and possible in the South. Fronting and raising to a realization close to [æ] may occur in NfldE.

3.4.   GOOSE

The main pronunciation of GOOSE, a high, back and long vowel [uː], predominates in the entire Caribbean (with quantity playing no role in SurCs) and in western and northern dialects of AmE (including the urban staging cities of NYC and Philadelphia) but not in Canada, New England and the South. CanE and SAmE have both fronted (e.g. [ʉ(ː)]) and diphthongal (e.g. [ʊu/ɪu/ə(ː)ʉ]) variants; in NEngE the latter predominate. Both types of variants can be found under certain conditions in PhilE, InlNE, WMwE (with fronting being regularly used there), and NYCE. NfldE has all three variants. With limitations, fronting can be observed in BahE, and diphthongization in ChcE. The fronting of this vowel in the South is a crucial element of the so-called "Southern Shift".

3.5.   THOUGHT, NORTH, FORCE

For THOUGHT, the main variant is a back, half-open and rounded vowel, [ɔ(ː)], but there are some varieties in which a low variant [ɑː] occurs normally (CanE, NfldE, NEngE, JamC, Baj), with the other one being a possible variant in a number of instances; the West and Midwest (and also the inland North, where the higher type is preferred) have both pronunciations. Off-gliding, possibly in combination with raising of the onset, is also an option with this vowel, resulting in variants such as [ɔə/ʊə] – regularly in SAmE, conditionally in PhilE, NYCE (where raised monophthongs may also be heard), and AAVE. In many regions of North America, in particular in the West, this vowel has merged with the LOT class (see below, section 6.).

NORTH is typically realized as a half-open monophthong [ɔ:] in the Caribbean, in SAmE, NEngE, NfldE, Gullah and CajE. The South and CanE have a half-closed [o:] vowel as an equally strong option, a variant which predominates in WMwE, InlNE, PhilE, NYCE, AAVE, and ChcE. Lowering to [ɒ] is a conditional option in WMwE, NfldE, and T&T (all lects). A diphthongal pronunciation of this vowel, as [ɒə/oa], is characteristic of NYCE and possible in NEngE, SAmE, NfldE, and ChcE.

Realizations of FORCE vary between a half closed [o:], used widely in North America and the Caribbean, and a more open [ɔ:], which is strongest in NEngE, NfldE, CajE, and T&TCs, but also used quite widely. Ingliding diphthongal realizations, e.g. [ɔə/oə/ao], are given for NYCE, AAVE and JamC, as well as, variably, for SAmE, NEngE, CanE, CajE, and ChcE. An upglide, e.g. [ou], is typical of SAmE and possible in AAVE and NEngE.

The SurCs have a low short [a] in these words, homophonous with LOT.

3.6.   NURSE

NURSE is a central vowel, [ɜ:/ɚ], in all North American dialects; CajE has [ʌ]. The Caribbean displays more variability with this vowel. JamE has mid front [ɛ/e]; JamC, the SurCs (where [a] is also possible) and TobC prefer a backed variant [o/ɔ], which is also possible in T&TC, BahE, and NfldE. For Baj, a half-closed back unrounded vowel [ɤ] is cited. The mid-front variant can also be observed in TobC, BahE, and AAVE, a raised one in InlNE and TobC. Diphthongal realizations such as [əɪ/ɔɪ] occur in NYCE (stereotypically associated with the city dialect but stigmatized nowadays) and SAmE.

4.   Diphthongs

4.1.   FACE

The FACE vowel serves to set North American pronunciation types off from Caribbean ones quite clearly. A canonical variant, an upgliding diphthong with a half-close onset, [eɪ], is the main form of all North American dialects except for CajE (which has a monophthong) and SAmE, where a diphthong with a front but lower onset, [ɛɪ/æɪ], is cited as even more characteristic, as part of the "Southern Shift" (the low-onset variant may also occur in CanE, AAVE, and ChcE). SAmE may also have variants with a low-back ([aɪ/ʌɪ]) or central ([əɪ]) onset. The highly conspicuous main Caribbean variant of this vowel type is a long half-close monophthong [eː], the characteristic pronunciation of JamE, Baj, the T&TCs, and also Gullah, found also, as a variant, in AAVE, NfldE, the Upper Midwest, InlNE and ChcE. The prototypical basilectal pronunciation, however, the main variant of JamC (and a possibility in Baj, SAmE and NfldE) is an ingliding diphthong, [ɪə] or [ɪɛ]. SurCs have a short vowel, homophonous with DRESS, except in word-final position, where the diphthong can occur.

4.2.   PRICE

For the PRICE vowel, the long upgliding diphthong [aɪ] associated with StE is found everywhere (with the exception of SurC), and in almost all varieties it is the main variant. The only dialect in which monophthongization, yielding [aː], predominates in all phonetic environments is CajE. Elsewhere this is a phonetically conditioned option: In SAmE, monophthongization is universal before voiced consonants and possible in other environments; the former, favorable context promotes it also generally in BahE and sometimes in NfldE. Two more variants are restricted options in some regions: a type with a raised or central onset, [əɪ/ɜɪ], in WMwE, InlNE, PhilE, SAmE, NEngE, CanE (before voiceless consonants, a pattern known as "Canadian Raising"), NfldE, AAVE, and T&TCs; and the backed [ɔɪ/ɒɪ] (which work by Wolfram and associates has made widely known as the *hoi toiders'* pronunciation of North Carolina), an option of SAmE, NYCE (spreading) and NfldE. Baj has a slightly backed and raised [ʌɪ] diphthong in these words, which is distinctive within the Caribbean. SurCs have the short DRESS vowels in these words, and occasionally, word-finally, the [eɪ] diphthong.

4.3   CHOICE

The pronunciation of the CHOICE vowel is [ɔɪ] almost everywhere. JamC prefers [ɒɪ] with a low onset, and NfldE, BahE and T&TC allow a central onset, i.e. [əɪ/əi]. In conservative varieties of SAmE two distinctive variants may occur, namely triphthongization (resulting in, e.g., [ɔɔɪ]) and glide reduction (to forms like [ɔə] or, especially before /l/, [o]).

4.4.   MOUTH

Most North American dialects (though not CanE and AAVE, and not generally SAmE) have a low to high-back glide [aʊ/ɑʊ] in these words. The T&TCs, Baj, Gullah and ChcE have a main variant with a raised and backed onset, e.g.

[ʌu/ɔʊ], which is also possible in CanE, NfldE, and JamC/JamE. The process of so-called "Canadian Raising" (also with PRICE, though perceived more stereotypically in MOUTH words) implies that the onset is raised to schwa only before voiceless consonants; in addition to CanE and NfldE, this occurs in InlNE and WMwE, SAmE and BahE dialects. In NEngE, also NfldE, T&TC, and AAVE raising to [əʊ] can be observed without such phonetic conditioning. A pronunciation with a fronted onset is the main realization of this vowel in rural SAmE (less so, and recessive, in urban SAmE), AAVE, and BahE, and an alternative possibility in WMwE, PhilE, NYCE, and NfldE. Older Southerners may have a "drawled" triphthongal realization, [æɛɒ]. Monophthongizations of this vowel are quite rare, but a low monophthong [aː] uniquely characterizes the speech of Pittsburgh and some of western Pennsylvania and can also be found in CajE, and a raised back variant, e.g. [ɔː], occurs in TobC and, without quantity distinctions, SurC.

4.5.   GOAT

It is interesting to see that the FACE and GOAT vowels are not only phonetically related as something like mirror images of each other in the front and back areas of the vocalic space, as glides from a mid onset to a high position, front and back respectively, but they also share a number of regional distribution patterns of their main, mutually corresponding, phonetic variants. In GOAT, again, the main Caribbean realization (of JamE, the T&TCs, SurCs, Baj, and Gullah), shared by CajE and ChcE, is a half-close (this time back) monophthong, [oː], but JamC prefers an ingliding type, e.g. [ʊə], which is also possible in Baj as [oə]. (With restrictions, the monophthong is also possible in the Upper Midwest, InlNE, NEngE, NfldE and AAVE, the ingliding version in SAmE and NfldE). AmE and most of its dialectal variants (except for NEngE, and not generally SAmE) are characterized by a pronunciation with a back and rounded onset, e.g. [oʊ/ou] (in SurCs this may occur word-finally only). The pronunciation typically associated with BrE, [əʊ] with a central onset, predominates in varieties where relatively closer cultural and historical ties with southern British influences are attested, viz. SAmE, NEngE and BahE, and it may also come up in WMwE, PhilE and NfldE. In the "Southern Shift" this vowel may be fronted and also lowered to [ɜʉ] or [æʉ]. Fronting occurs in PhilE as well.

4.6.   NEAR

In North American dialects of English, the NEAR vowel typically starts at the high front but non-peripheral position of KIT. In some rhotic dialects this [ɪr] type may be the only realization before /r/ (predominantly in WMwE and In-lNE, also JamE); in others a diphthongal realization gliding to schwa, [ɪə(r)], is common (PhilE, NYCE, NfldE, Gullah, ChcE), or the onset of the diphthong may be tensed to [i] (NEngE, CajE). Some varieties, like SAmE, AAVE, and CanE, have all of these realizations, with internally differentiating factors, and in most of the others the alternative pronunciations are also possible in addition to the main variant. Conservative American dialects, notably SAmE and NfldE, as well as Caribbean creoles, have lowered onsets, i.e. realizations with [e] or even [ɛ] (before schwa or /r/ or even as monophthongs), and in "deep" basilects like JamC and the SurCs a long gliding movement from a high front to a low position, [ia], is found.

4.7.   SQUARE

Similarly, the SQUARE vowel is either a half-open, usually lengthened monophthongal [ɛː] (WMwE, InlNE, SAmE, NEngE, CajE, ChcE, T&TC) or a diphthong with this onset and a schwa (PhilE, NYCE, CanE, Gullah), or any of these or a set of less widely used alternative pronunciations, e.g. raised [eə] (NEngE, SAmE, NfldE) and [ɪə] (NfldE, T&TCs), lowered [æə] (SAmE, CajE, BahE), or [ɪɛ] (JamC). The monophthongal type may also be realized as a half-close vowel [eː], mostly in the Caribbean (T&TCs, JamE, Baj, without lengthening also in SurC) but also in SAmE and, less commonly, NfldE.

4.8.   CURE

The CURE vowel, before schwa or /r/, typically is [ʊ] or alternatively, predominating in SAmE, T&TCs, BahE and AAVE, a raised and tensed [u]. Lowering to [o/ɔ] is strong in NfldE, Gullah and Baj and possible in SAmE, TobC, JamE and JamC; other variants, like [oʊ] in SAmE or NfldE and [ua/oa] in ChcE, are restricted.

5.   **Weak vowels**

5.1.   happY

Both North American and Caribbean varieties realize this unstressed vowel primarily as a relatively high front [i] type; the more central [ɪ] is a variant in some places (SAmE, BahE) and reported to be the primary type only in the T&TCs and CajE. ChcE may also have a schwa. SurCs have [e] after mid vowels, otherwise [i].

5.2.   lettER

A relatively open [a] realization of the word-final unstressed vowel marks JamC, SurC and TobC, and Eastern Caribbean island varieties, and is possible in NEngE, NfldE, T&TC, AAVE, and ChcE, but in most cases the expected schwa realization (with constriction in rhotic dialects) is to be found. For Baj a relatively high and back [ɤ] is reported.

5.3.   horsES

Both a central [ə] and a high front [ɪ] are widely observed as the realizations of the regular plural suffix. The former is reported to be exclusive to CanE and BahE, the latter to TobC, Baj and SurC (to the extent that these creoles have traces of this suffix); SAmE, NEngE and NfldE have both variants quite regularly, and in all other dialects [ɪ] is normal but schwa is also possible under specific circumstances.

5.4.   commA

JamC, SurC and the T&TCs have a full open vowel, [a], in this lexical set, but most dialects have a schwa; some (CanE, also AAVE and ChcE) allow both.

6.   Vowel distribution

Vocalic mergers affect the set of sounds available in any given dialect, but full phonological analyses of dialects are usually missing, perhaps as a result of the variability observed and the difficulties involved in any categorization. Thus, pointing out distributional facts, like the homophonies between certain vowels, will bring us closer to a systemic perspective.

A number of mergers affect what may be regarded as corresponding pairs of tense and lax vowels. KIT and FLEECE are mostly kept distinct (except in SurC) but may collapse in WMwE, CajE, JamE, and the T&TCs, and before laterals also in innovative urban varieties of SAmE. Similarly, homophony of FOOT and GOOSE is extremely rare, found occasionally in WMwE and TobC and regularly in SurC only; before laterals this merger is spreading in urban SAmE, however. The merger of LOT and THOUGHT, on the other hand, has been widely observed to be spreading in North American English; it is reported for WMwE, CanE, NfldE, CajE and ChcE and occurs conditionally also in NEngE, SAmE, AAVE, and T&TCs. The SurCs also have the merger of these vowels, but their phonetic realization is quite different, a low front [a]. The speech of St. Louis exhibits a characteristically local merger, of the NORTH and START vowels.

TRAP and BATH are pronounced identically practically everywhere with the exception of Jamaica and, with restrictions, T&TCs. TRAP and DRESS may merge before a lateral consonant in NfldE, BahE, and CajE. The so-called *pin/ pen*-merger, i.e. homophony of KIT and DRESS before nasals, is a hallmark of SAmE, including CajE, and a conditioned possibility in WMwE, ChcE, InlNE, NfldE, and BahE; however, it is said to be recessive in urban centers of SAmE today. DRESS and FACE are distinct, except possibly for parts of WMwE (and SurC). Mergers of mid-front vowels before /r/ have been widely observed in North American English and frequently discussed in the dialectological literature; to some extent they seem to be lexically conditioned. *Mary* and *merry* are homophonous in WMwE, InlNE, CanE, SAmE (where the two words were kept distinct until late into the nineteenth century), NfldE, Gullah, AAVE, CajE, and ChcE, possibly so also in NYCE, NEngE, BahE and the T&TCs. The homophony of these vowels also includes *marry* in WMwE, InlNE, SAmE (a recent extension of the previous merger, spreading from urban contexts), AAVE, and ChcE, and potentially a few other dialects as well.

LOT and STRUT are pronounced identically in JamE and possibly the T&TCs but not elsewhere. NEAR and SQUARE fall together in much of the Caribbean (JamE/C, T&TCs), and, with restrictions, SAmE and NfldE.

Vowel nasalization before nasal consonants is the norm almost everywhere. Mutual assimilation phenomena between vowels in the same words occur regularly in Saramaccan, JamC and ChcE, and are possible in SAmE, NfldE and T&TCs. Spelling pronunciation of weak vowels is common in JamC and possible in other Caribbean varieties (T&TCs, BahE) and AAVE.

7.   Consonants

7.1.   Stops: P/T/K, B/D/G

Word-initial voiceless stops are aspirated in American and Caribbean varieties, with few exceptions: a lack or weakening of this aspiration is the norm in CajE and Gullah, and possible in JamE/C. All North American dialects, including BahE but not the Caribbean varieties, regularly allow the lenisation (flapping, voicing) of intervocalic /t/ (so that *writer* sounds like *rider*); CajE is the only dialect in which this is found only under specific circumstances. The realization of /t/ as a glottal stop word-finally or intervocalically is regularly found only in AAVE and, in the Caribbean, in Baj; in SAmE, NEngE, NfldE and BahE this is a possible variant. The palatalization of word-initial velar stops (so that *can't* and *garden* are pronounced with /kj/ and /gj/, respectively) marks Caribbean creoles (JamC, T&TC, TobC, SurC – where [tj/tʃ/dj/dʒ] are also found in such words). The same applies to the pronunciation of words with an initial *b-* with *bw-* (e.g. *bwoy* 'boy'), documented for the same varieties and, marginally, also for NfldE. Saramaccan is noteworthy for the existence of implosive voiced stops, /ɓ, ɗ/. In Saramaccan and Ndyuka word-internal /d/ may be replaced by a lateral /l/.

7.2.   Fricatives: TH, F/V, S/Z, H/CH, etc.

Voicing of word-initial /s/ and /f/, yielding /z-/ and /v-/, respectively, is rare in America; it is reported regularly for BahE only and as a highly recessive feature for NfldE. A stop realization of a word-initial voiced dental fricative, e.g. *dis* for 'this', is normal in Caribbean creoles, BahE, Gullah, AAVE, and CajE, and possible in all North American dialects except for CanE (it occurs in NfldE, however). With voiceless dental fricatives (e.g. *ting* for 'thing'), the same process occurs in roughly the same distribution, though not quite as widely: in comparison with the previous feature, it is reported as conditional rather than universal in BahE and AAVE, and as not occurring at all in WMwE, InlNE, and SAmE. Realizations of word-initial dental fricatives as affricates are less common, and also more widely in use with voiced rather than voiceless variants. In the former case, i.e. [dð-] for [ð-], we find the feature reported as in regular use for AAVE only, and as used occasionally in WMwE, InlNE, PhilE, NYCE, SAmE, NfldE, CajE, and T&TCs; in the latter, i.e. [tθ-] for [θ-], in comparison with the previous list the feature is not mentioned for WMwE, InlNE, SAmE and AAVE. In intervocalic position, the voiced dental fricative may be labialized (so that, for instance, *brother* is pronounced with a central [-v-] consonant) in a few dialects, but this is a relatively exceptional process, reported as a possible variant for CajE, NfldE and BahE only. Similarly, an intervocalic labial consonant –*v*– may be rendered as a voiced bilabial stop –*b*– (so that *river*, *never* become *riba*, *neba*); this occurs regularly in TobC, SurC and BahE and with restrictions in JamC, T&TC, ChcE, and SAmE. Word-finally, the devoicing of obstruents (e.g. of a plural –*s* after a voiced sound) is a stereotypical feature of Chicago working-class speech.

The only American variety in which a voiceless velar fricative [χ/x] occurs at least conditionally is ChcE. Word-initial *h*-deletion, e.g. *'eart* for 'heart', is common in much of the Caribbean (JamC, TobC, SurC, BahE; but not in the Leeward Islands) and in CajE, and possible in a few other related dialects (Gullah, AAVE, T&TC), among Franco-Americans in New England, and in NfldE. The distribution of the converse feature, word-initial *h*-insertion, e.g.

haxe for 'axe', is similar: regular in JamC, Gullah, and BahE; possible in the T&TCs and NfldE. In word-initial /hj-/ clusters, i.e. in words like *human* or *huge*, the initial *h-* is omitted regularly in NfldE, among young urban speakers in SAmE, in NYCE, and CajE, and under specific conditions in PhilE, rural SAmE, ChcE, BahE, and JamC.

7.3.   Semi-vowels: W/WH, J

In words beginning with *wh-*, some American dialects have retained a historically older consonant cluster with an initial velar fricative [x] before the approximant [w], so that, unlike many mainstream varieties of English, *which* is not homophonous with *witch*; this occurs in WMwE, InlNE, CanE, conservative NEngE, SAmE (though no longer among young urban speakers), ChcE, and JamC. The approximant [w] itself may be substituted by a labiodental voiced fricative [v] – regularly in TobC, possibly in T&TC, BahE, NfldE and CajE; both sounds are reported to have merged in several Eastern Caribbean islands as well.

So-called "jod-dropping", the omission of /j/ after alveolars and before [uː] in words such as *tune* or *news*, is widely considered a characteristic feature of AmE as against BrE/RP, although within North America some dialects have retained the historical pronunciation with /j/. In our data, the feature of "jod-dropping" is reported as occurring normally in WMwE, InlNE, PhilE, NYCE, NEngE, and BahE, and as occurring in certain environments in SAmE (notably in new urban dialects), CanE, NfldE and ChcE.

7.4.   Sonorants: N, L, R

Little variation is found concerning nasals in America. The realization of velar nasals with a velar stop following, i.e. of words spelled with <-*ng*-> as [ŋg], is reported to occur normally in AAVE and ChcE and sometimes in NYCE (stereotypically associated with the city accent) and some Caribbean varieties (T&TCs, JamC/E). The velarization of word-final alveolar nasals, i.e. the pronunciation of words like *down* with a final [-ŋ], is characteristic of Caribbean (and related) creoles , i.e. JamC, T&TC, TobC, Eastern islands, Sranan, Gullah, and possible also in ChcE.

Post-vocalic /l/ may be vocalized commonly in SAmE (both rural and urban), NEngE, PhilE and JamC and in some contexts in WMwE, InlNE, NYCE, NfldE, AAVE, ChcE, BahE, TobC and JamE. A tendency to confuse or neutralize /l/ and /r/ is documented as occurring regularly in SurC and Gullah and possibly in T&TC and NfldE, but in general this is not common in AmE.

On the other hand, rhoticity and possible phonetic realizations of /r/ are an important issue in American and Caribbean types of English. Generally, StA-mE is considered to be fully rhotic; more specifically, this applies to WMwE, InlNE, PhilE, CanE, most of NfldE and ChcE, and also, as a consequence of recent changes, urban SAmE, whereas NYCE, rural SAmE, NEngE, a small part of NfldE, AAVE, BahE and JamE/C are variably rhotic. Baj is the only Caribbean variety which is described as consistently rhotic. This leaves Gullah and CajE in North America and the Eastern islands dialects as well as T&TCs in the Caribbean as non-rhotic varieties. Phonetically, postvocalic /r/ tends to be realized as velar retroflex constriction in AmE, less commonly also as an alveolar flap (in CajE, JamE/C, and possibly ChcE), not at all as an apical trill and highly exceptionally (possibly in T&TC) as a uvular sound. An intrusive r, e.g. *idea*-[r]-*is*, may be heard in NYCE, NEngE, SAmE, NfldE, JamE/C, and the T&TCs.

7.5.   Consonant deletion

The reduction of word-final consonant clusters occurs very widely: regularly and without functional constraints in Caribbean and creole-related varieties (Eastern islands, T&TC, TobC, JamC, SurC, BahE, Gullah); generally with monomorphemic clusters (e.g. *desk* > *des'*) but variably and less frequently with bimorphemic ones (e.g. *helped* > *help'*) in NfldE and AAVE, and variably irrespective of the functional load of the final sound in WMwE, InlNE, PhilE, NYCE, NEngE, SAmE, and ChcE. Word-final single consonants (e.g. *cut* > *cu'*) are omitted much less widely: generally in CajE only, variably in NfldE and contact dialects, notably AAVE, ChcE, BahE, and the T&TCs. Word-final single nasals may be deleted in JamC, rendering the preceding vowels nasalized. The simplification of word-initial consonant clusters (in words such as *splash* or *square*) is not typical of American varieties; it is attested as occurring variably in SAmE, NfldE, T&TCs, SurCs, and JamC.

8.   Prosodic features

Unstressed word-initial syllables may be omitted, so that *about* and *except* result in *'bout* and *'cept*, respectively. This is common in the T&TCs, Gullah, AAVE, and NfldE, and occurs variably in JamC, BahE, ChcE, CajE, WMwE, NEngE, SAmE, and CanE. The shifting of stress from the first to a later syllable, as in *indi'cate* or *holi'day*, is reported as occurring not infrequently in T&TC and TobC and sometimes in JamE/C, CajE, ChcE, NEngE, and NfldE. In general, a tendency toward a relatively syllable-timed rather than a stress-timed rhythm is reported for Caribbean creoles and varieties quite strongly (TobC, T&TC, Baj, JamC, BahE), and also variably for ChcE, but not at all for all other North American dialects. In comparison with British-based varieties, AmE is stated to preserve secondary stress more strongly, a process which tends to result in less vowel reduction and a characteristically different stress pattern.

Distinctive, perhaps idiosyncratic intonation contours appear to characterize a number of varieties, although relatively little attention has been paid to such questions in sociolinguistic research. For some pertinent observations, see the papers on NfldE, AAVE, ChcE and T&TCs.

High-rising terminal contours, i.e. a rise of intonation at the end of statements, (sometimes called "HRT" or also "American question intonation") are said to occur variably in all American and Caribbean varieties under consideration, with the sole exceptions of CajE and TobC. Tone distinctions are restricted to creoles; they are reported as characteristic of TobC and T&TC and possible in JamC. Saramaccan and Ndyuka are tone languages.

Exercises and study questions

1. Draw a chart in which you compare the realizations of the vowels of Gullah with those in African American English, Standard American English, Bahamian English, and Jamaican Creole. Discuss similarities and differences.

2. Draw a map of the rhotic and non-rhotic areas in North America and the Caribbean. Where do you find clear preferences for either pattern, where do you find variability? Explain your findings historically.

3. Provide a survey of the varying pronunciations of the grapheme <th> in North America and the Caribbean. (Do not forget to consider both function words and major grammatical word classes, as well as word-initial, word-central and word-final occurrences!)

4. Make a list of phonetically corresponding vowels in the front and back areas of the vowel trapezium (e.g. KIT and FOOT, FACE and GOAT, respectively) and check on the interactive maps on the CD which types of features (e.g. raised, glided, monophthongized variants) provide similar regional patterns of distribution for any pair in the Americas and the Caribbean.

5. The semi-vowel /j/ shows variable occurrences after word-initial stops in both North America and the Caribbean (e.g. in words like *new* or *garden*).

Describe these processes regionally and phonotactically (where, and after which classes of stops, is /j/ pronounced or not?). How are these processes commonly labeled?

6. Listen to the recordings of "The North Wind and the Sun" from Barbados, Jamaica, New England and the rural South on the CD. Which pronunciations from each of these samples do you find most distinctive or interesting (compared to, for instance, your own accent or your notion of "Standard English")? Describe these pronunciations phonetically, using appropriate articulatory terminology. Transcribe select portions of these recordings phonetically. Pick five words from the text and compare their different realizations across the four varieties under comparison.

7. Listen to the 76-year-old speaker of Appalachian English and to the female Anglo-Bahamian speaker on the CD. Record, discuss and compare noteworthy occurrences of monophthongization and diphthongization which you hear in their speech.

8. Listen to the free passage audio samples from North America and the Caribbean on the CD and record and transcribe occurrences of numerals (e.g. three, five, thousand) and ordinals (e.g. first, third) in these conversations. Explain the variability that you find. Compare different varieties for occurrences of the same words.

Morphology and Syntax

Colloquial American English: grammatical features

Thomas E. Murray and Beth Lee Simon

1. Introduction

Conventional wisdom has long dictated that, excluding the dialects used in New England, the South, and such northern cities as New York and Chicago, and aside from many ethnic-based vernaculars (Chicano English, Pennsylvania Dutch, and the like), nothing very interesting occurs in the grammar of American English. From the early twentieth century well into the 1950s, some linguists even used "General American" to describe what they perceived as a monolithic variety of the language (grammar included) that extended westward from Pennsylvania and included nearly everything north of the Ohio River and west of the Mississippi. Now, half a century later, the grammar of the North, Midwest, and West has still received remarkably little attention. And the same attitude of uninterest appears in the opinions of laypeople, who, like the Ohioan interviewed in the educational video *American Tongues*, believe that these dialects come "right out of the dictionary".

Such perceptions dictate the reality of many Americans, and are difficult to dismiss. Yet much empirical evidence suggests that the grammar of the North, Midwest, and West is not "right out of the dictionary". In fact, we will document that the morphological and syntactic constructions of these regions render the English used there as distinctive as that occurring anywhere in the United States.

Broadly speaking, these constructions fall into two categories: those that are socially and stylistically diagnostic but have no regional affiliation, and those that are regionally restricted but (within those regions) usually not diagnostic socially or stylistically. Features in the first category are typically recognized as vernacular, so draw the attention of English teachers, prescriptive dictionary editors, and other language watchers concerned about the health and vitality of the language. Features in the second category, however, may either occur so transparently that they go unnoticed until attention is drawn to them, or be widely recognized as dialectal stereotypes (in the latter case, they may then either be consciously avoided or used proudly as sources of identity).

Below we present all the features in each category, sub-grouping them by form or function and, for the regionalisms, discussing their areal distributions.

We have drawn especially heavily from the inventories given in Wolfram and Schilling-Estes (1998: 331–344) and Christian, Wolfram, and Dube (1988), from the *Dictionary of American Regional English* (Cassidy 1985–2002; Cassidy 1991, 1996), and from Randolph and Wilson (1953) and Mencken (1963), though all the sample sentences are taken from the vast corpus of our own research done between 1982 and 2002.

Several brief notes are necessary before we proceed to the features themselves. First, though we do characterize each feature socioeconomically or contextually or geographically, none is used by all or only the speakers in those classes or contexts or regions, just as no feature occurs categorically in the speech of any individual who actually uses it. Moreover, unlike is often true of differences in pronunciation and vocabulary, most features we discuss here are not usually responsible for lapses in communication: the grammars of *The car needs washed* and *He don't want no more*, for example, are unlikely to be misinterpreted anywhere.

We should be clear about our mission, too, which is entirely descriptive. Though most of the features we discuss here result from rule extension or analogy, we will not try to account more specifically for why the various dialects and their features occur as they do. The historical, social, and other causes we would adduce have been explained by Wolfram and Schilling-Estes (1998: 24–55), and we can do little to improve on that discussion.

Another notable detail of our presentation is that we use nonstandard orthography to capture the phonological flavor of the examples we cite. We discovered early on that divorcing grammar from pronunciation produced sample sentences which sounded awkward or unnatural at best. Co-occurrence rules simply prohibit *going to* from being juxtaposed with *ain't never* in a sentence like **He ain't never going to understand that*. A more natural rendering would entail the reduction of *going to,* as in *He ain't never gonna understand that,* and that is how we present it here.

Finally, though we characterize the features below as "colloquial" or "vernacular", and compare them to "standard" English, of course such labels are social rather than linguistic judgments: matters of right and wrong in language are decided not by the structure of the language, but by the sociocultural biases of the people who speak it. Indeed, many features we discuss here had a long tradition of acceptance in the history of English (Chaucer and Shakespeare, for example, often used multiple negation), continue to occur in the standard forms of other languages, and may one day be accepted in the United States on a wider scale than they are currently.

2. Non-regional, socially/stylistically diagnostic features

These features do not link speakers to a given region, but occur more often as one descends the socioeconomic scale and the scale of contextual formality. We discuss as many features as possible in the space allotted, but cannot be comprehensive: we favor systemic patterns over individual usages (though we discuss a fair number of the latter as well), and generally restrict ourselves to grammar *per se* rather than matters of style/usage, or features so common that they occur throughout the language.

2.1. The verb phrase

2.1.1. Irregular verbs

Atwood (1953: 43) noted long ago that "[t]he most striking characteristic of [vernacular verb usage in the eastern United States] is the leveling of the preterite and the past participle forms [of irregular verbs]". Subsequent research has confirmed that this is true in the North, Midwest, and West as well. Moreover, again after Atwood (1953: 44), "the standard preterite and past participle forms are [not] habitually reversed"; instead, speakers "waver between two forms, either of which may serve as preterite or as past participle". The bare root of a verb may also serve as the simple past; thus irregular verbs typically occur in the three categories listed here (see Mencken 1963: 527–528 for more examples of specific verbs).

2.1.1.1. Simple past used as participle

(1)   a. Me and Bob have *swam* in that pond lotsa times.
       b. She'd *sang* that song her whole life, and then up and forgot the words.

2.1.1.2. Participle used as simple past

(2)   a. I *seen* somethin' real strange up in them hills last night.
       b. Everybody knows he *done* it, but ain't nobody gonna tell.

2.1.1.3. Bare root used as simple past

(3)   a. He *swim* in that river just about every day of his life.
       b. Why, he *give* Junior here more for it used than he [Junior] paid for it new.

Additionally, a fourth classification includes usages that may fall either into category 2.1.1.2. or 2.1.1.3. above.

2.1.1.4. *Bare root/participle used as simple past*

(4)   a. He *come* in about fifteen minutes late, like usual.
        b. We *run* over that hill faster'n you could blink.

2.1.2. *Subject-verb concord*

Nonstandard agreement patterns are frequent; those involving *be, do,* and *have* are most prominent, though nonstandard agreement can occur with any verb.

2.1.2.1. *Plural subject + singular* be

(5)   a. Them kittens *is* really startin' to aggravate me.
        b. They *was* there all night, spent the whole night there.

2.1.2.2. *Singular subject + plural, present tense* do *+ contracted* not

(6)   a. Well, it sure *don't* help things none when we get hail like that.
        b. That meatloaf *don't* look too healthy.

2.1.2.3. *Plural subject + singular, present tense* have

(7)   a. The cars on that lot across the street there *has* just got to go.
        b. I think John and Melody there *has* the right idea.

2.1.2.4. *Plural subject + singular, present tense [other verb]*

(8)   a. So me and Billy *takes* this cow over to the barn…
        b. Them city people *eats* out a lot more'n we do.

2.1.3. *Inversion of auxiliary verb and subject in indirect questions*

Once believed to be a characteristic of only African American Vernacular English (AAVE), this has since been shown to occur throughout the United States. In embedded questions the expected word order of subject + auxiliary verb + main verb is permutated to parallel that of main-clause interrogatives: auxiliary verb + subject + main verb.

(9) a. He asked *could he get there* about fifteen minutes late.
     b. Susan wants to know *should she bring* a casserole.

2.1.4. Historical present

This occurs when the speaker becomes especially involved in the retelling of a past incident. In every instance there is a shift, often mid-sentence, from the past or past progressive to the present tense, which signals the beginning of the event serving as the story's focus.

(10) a. So I walked in the classroom, and the professor *comes up* to me and *says*, "Well, you're late again".
      b. Heather was just sitting there, minding her own business, and suddenly the whole desk just *collapses*.

2.1.5. Multiple negation

The first category of multiple negation listed below is especially prominent. (Note: we use "multiple negation" rather than "double negatives" since sentences may contain more than two negative markers.)

2.1.5.1. Negative marking on auxiliary verb and on indefinite(s) following the main verb

(11) a. He *didn't* do *nothin'* all day.
      b. *Don't* be sittin' there tellin' me *no* lies or *nothin'*.

2.1.5.2. Negative marking on auxiliary verb and on indefinite preceding the verb phrase

(12) a. *Nobody won't* show up late when he coaches.
      b. *Nothing can't* stop him now!

2.1.6. Ain't

Though *ain't* is becoming increasingly accepted, it still is widely stigmatized. Both categories of usage are extremely common.

2.1.6.1. *As a substitute for* be + not

(13)   a. You know they *ain't* gonna be here on time.
       b. Well, *ain't* you the lucky one.

2.1.6.2. *As a substitute for* have + not

(14)   a. We *ain't* gone to that church for a long time.
       b. *Ain't* she been to the doctor yet?

2.2.   Adverbs and adjectives

2.2.1. *Comparatives and superlatives*

Standard English forms most comparatives and superlatives thus: one-syllable adjectives and adverbs take *-er* and *-est*; those of two or more syllables take *more* and *most*. As was true in Elizabethan English, however, and has long occurred in Appalachian English (AppE) and Ozarkian English (OzE), it is becoming more common in vernacular varieties for nearly any adverb or adjective to be made comparative or superlative by adding either the suffix or *more/most*, respectively, or even by adding *-er* and *more* or *-est* and *most* together, to form a pleonastic construction (which functions pragmatically to indicate force or significance). In a third category of usage, participles used attributively compare like other adjectives.

2.2.1.1. *Freedom of occurrence of* -er/more *and* -est/most

(15)   a. That's just one of the *most pretty* sunsets I believe I've ever seen.
       b. You can get a little *more close* than that.
       c. Why, he's the *regularest* kinda guy I know.
       d. It was the *awfulest* lookin' sewin' job I ever seen, let me tell you.

2.2.1.2. *Co-occurrence of* -er/more *and* -est/most

(16)   a. Ain't nobody around here *more cheaper'n* old Bill.
       b. That was the *bestest* chocolate gravy I've ever ate.

2.2.1.3. Attributive particles compare like other adjectives

(17)   a. Oh, she's just about the *lovin'est* [= 'most loving'] one of the bunch.

         b. That man is the *shootin'est* [= 'prone to shoot a gun'] fool I know.

2.2.2 Absence of adverbial -ly

Historical *-ly* adverbs are often used without the *-ly* (see Mencken 1963: 562–564).

(18)   a. This pie of Grandma's is *awful* good.

         b. He treated her *wrong* right from the start.

2.2.3. Good and + [descriptive adjective]

This is a particularly prolific combining form.

(19)   a. If you don't get out of that draft, you're gonna get *good and sick.*

         b. I'm sure by now everybody's *good and hungry.*

2.2.4. Hopefully as a sentential adverb

Though old in the history of the language (Shapiro 1998), *hopefully* as a sentence modifier has been occurring more frequently since the 1960s.

(20)   a. *Hopefully,* I'll pass the next test.

         b. No, *hopefully* Charlie won't wait till Christmas to pop the question.

2.3.   Nominals

2.3.1. Addition of inflectional morphemes to phrases

The two inflectional morphemes affecting nouns, {plural} and {possessive}, can be attached to phrases rather than the principal nouns in those phrases, forming "group plurals" and "group genitives" (both of which are old in the history of the language).

2.3.1.1. Group plurals

(21)   a. That President had two *Secretary of States.*

         b. All three *sister-in-laws* wound up going to medical school.

2.3.1.2. Group genitives

(22)   a. That's the *guy who won the gold medal's* girlfriend.
         b. No, I meant the *lawyer in that office's* secretary.

2.3.2. Personal pronouns

Several categories of personal pronoun variation occur (Mencken 1963: 543–
557); the fourth listed below has regional variants such as *you'uns*, *y'all*, and
youse. Pronominal apposition, involving the use of a redundant subject pronoun, was once identified with AAVE, but now is known to occur throughout
the language.

2.3.2.1. Regularization of third-person reflexives

(23)   a. He always did think he could do just about everything all by
             hisself.
         b. And then they went and locked *theirselves* out of the trailer.

2.3.2.2. Extension of object forms to demonstratives

(24)   a. *Them* roosters across the road there has just got to go.
         b. Just hand me *them* pliers there, will ya?

2.3.2.3. Extension of object forms to coordinate subjects

(25)   a. When are *Julie and them* gonna go pick her up?
         b. Yeah, *me and Jodie* broke up last October.

2.3.2.4. Adoption of *you guys* as second-person personal pronoun

(26)   a. When did *you guys* get outa class?
         b. [Are] *you guys* gonna go over to Michael's house?

2.3.2.5. Pronominal apposition

(27)   a. Yeah, my brother, *he* dropped outa school again.
         b. Ted's cousin, *he* really messed up bad this time.

2.3.3. Relative pronouns

Each category below involves the use of specific pronouns in nonstandard contexts. The second, also frequent in southern varieties of American English, is particularly stigmatized.

2.3.3.1. That *for* who(m)

(28)   a. He's the professor *that* I told you about.
       b. Isn't Steve the one *that* took first place?

2.3.3.2. What for *[relative pronoun]*

(29)   a. That dog there's the one *what* wet on the carpet.
       b. The bulletin board *what's* on that wall is yours.

2.3.3.3. Which *for the coordinate conjunction* and

(30)   a. He told me I could jog after seven days, *which* he knows I don't like to run.
       b. Carla bought Ted that sweater, *which* she knows he's allergic to wool.

3.   Socially/stylistically non-diagnostic, regional features

These are regionally restricted non-diagnostic features. Again, since many involve specific lexical items, we cannot be comprehensive. Since we divide the discussions below according to dialect area, we have included a map with those areas clearly labeled (see Map 1). The major east-west boundaries and the regions they delimit are from those suggested by Raven McDavid (1958: 580, following Kurath 1949) as they have been revised and expanded by additional research; the Ozarkian borders are taken from Christian, Wolfram, and Dube (1988: 25, fig. 2.4). We do not delimit the West since, though its lexicon and phonology are distinctive (Carver 1987; Labov, Ash and Boberg 2006), its grammar is not.

3.1.   Inland northern

The grammar of this area is defined more by negative evidence than positive, so we record very few features here.

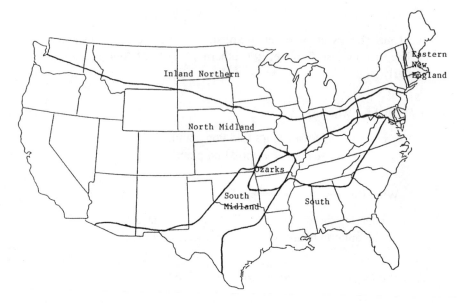

Map 1.   Dialect areas of the USA

3.1.1. Dove *as simple past of* dive

This is an innovation counter to the general analogical trend of strong verbs >
weak verbs.

(31)   a. The boy *dove* off the platform and into the lake.
        b. The plane *dove* and then went into a spiral.

3.1.2. Sick to the stomach

Once restricted to just the Inland North, this is now leeching into the Midlands.

(32)   a. The little girl felt sick *to* her stomach.
        b. Is he sick *to* his stomach, too?

3.2.   Midland

The language used in the North Midland and especially the South Midland
shares features with that used in the Inland North and South, respectively – so

many that some believe the division to be primary rather than secondary (Carver 1987). That debate does not bear on our discussion here; we use Kurath's terminology only for the sake of historical consistency.

3.2.1. *Positive* anymore

Formerly regarded as having negative/interrogative bias, *anymore* now occurs with increasing frequency in positive, non-interrogative sentences (Murray 1993), with the approximate meaning of 'nowadays'. This usage was restricted to western Pennsylvania, Appalachia, and the Ozarks as recently as the early twentieth century, but now occurs extensively throughout the Midlands and is leeching strongly into the Inland North. The *anymore* can occur before or after the phrase it modifies, and occasionally even stands alone.

(33)   a.   Sam didn't useta eat red meat, but he sure does *anymore.*
      b.   *Anymore* them crows just come and eat all the corn.
      c.   [Do you use disposable diapers?] *Anymore.*

3.2.2.   *[Verb of volition]* + *V*-en

Like + V-*en* occurs largely east of the Mississippi; *need/want* + V-*en* are leeching into the Inland North (Murray, Frazer, and Simon 1996; Murray and Simon 1999, 2002).

3.2.2.1. Need + *V*-en

(34)   a.   Those shirts still *need ironed.*
      b.   The car in the driveway *needs washed.*

3.2.2.2. Want + *V*-en

(35)   a.   That cat there sure does look like she *wants petted.*
      b.   Is the baby crying because she *wants picked up?*

3.2.2.3. Like + *V*-en

(36)   a.   The baby *likes cuddled.*
      b.   Be sure to let us know if you'd *like picked up* from the airport.

3.2.3. Quarter till *(the hour)*

This is also common throughout much of the South.

(37)   a. He said he'd meet us there at quarter *till* five.
        b. We'll need to leave at quarter *till* if we don't want to be late.

3.2.4. All the + *[singular count noun] or* one *'the only'*

Both categories are especially common in the South Midlands, and also occur in AppE.

(38)   a. That's *all the coat* (= the only coat) he has.
        b. Is this *all the one* (= the only one) you have?

3.2.5. All the + *[adjective/adverb of positive degree]*

This is especially common in the South Midlands and South (cf. the feature just below).

(39)   a. That's *all the fast* it can fly.
        b. That's *all the far* she can throw it.

3.2.6. All the + *[adjective/adverb of comparative degree]*

This occurs throughout the North Midlands and Inland North (cf. the feature just above).

(40)   a. That's *all the faster* he can run.
        b. Is that *all the farther* you're willing to go on that topic?

3.2.7. Want + *[preposition]*

In these elliptical constructions, the missing infinitive is understood.

(41)   a. Does the dog *want in/out?*
        b. Do you *want on/off* that list of names?
        c. The baby *wants up/down.*

3.2.8. Wait on *'wait for'*

This occurs throughout the Midlands, and is leeching strongly into the Inland North.

(42)   a. We're not going to *wait* on you all day.
        b. She's been *waiting* on that bus nearly half an hour.

3.2.9. *[Interrogative pronoun]* + all

Who and *what* are common. This occurs especially in the South Midlands.

(43)   a. *Who all* did you say was gonna be there?
        b. *What all* do you want me to get out for lunch?

3.2.10. *Second-person plural personal pronoun* you'uns

This occurs frequently in western Pennsylvania and the South Midlands.

(44)   a. If *you'uns'd* just apply yourselves a little more, you'd do so much better.
        b. Do *you'uns* want to come with us?

3.2.11. One + *[noun]*

The *one* of this phrase is redundant when the following noun is singular, and does not limit the number of things specified when the noun is plural.

(45)   a. I wouldn't mind having that *one dog* in the back.
        b. Remember those *one kids* we saw last week?

3.2.12. Whenever *'at the time that'; 'as soon as'*

This occurs in the eastern South Midlands, especially AppE. It may cause misunderstandings, since *whenever* can also connote indifference (Montgomery and Kirk 2001).

(46)   a. *Whenever* I first heard the news, I about fell over.
        b. The plumber said he'd be here *whenever* he got the chance.

3.2.13. *Compound modals*

Common throughout the South and South Midlands, this involves the clustering of modals such as *might* and *could*. (Note: we use "compound modals" rather than "double modals" because more than two occasionally occur together.) Semantically, compound modals tend to lessen the force of attitude/obligation expressed by single modals, so *might oughta* would be understood as less forceful than either *might* or *oughta* alone.

(47)   a.   You *might oughta* go to that meeting and express your opinion.
       b.   You *might could* get a second job.

3.2.14. Come/go with

These elliptical constructions, though found throughout the North Midland region, occur especially often in areas with historically dense concentrations of German settlers. They are frequently interchangeable structurally.

(48)   a.   We're gonna go to the store now. You wanna *come/go with?*
       b.   Dustin's coming over at 4:00 o'clock, and Michaela wants to *come with.*
       c.   Honey, Johanna has to leave now. Do you want to *go with?*

3.2.15. Wakened *(as the past participle of* wake*)*

This is restricted largely to the North Midlands, and may be dwindling in frequency, being supplanted by the more widespread *awakened* (or, occasionally, *woke*).

(49)   a.   Sylvia has *awakened* late every day this week.
       b.   When Jim *awakened*, Cathy was already in the kitchen eating breakfast.

3.3.   Ozarkian English

The Ozarks encompass northwestern Arkansas, most of southern Missouri, as well as small pieces of northeastern Oklahoma and southeastern Kansas. As such, they are Midland, with the Missouri Ozarks bisected by the North Midland-South Midland boundary. OzE is South Midland in nature, yet is different enough to justify separate consideration here. Indeed, the rugged hills of the Ozarks, combined with many of the original settlers being transplants from Appalachia, created a dialectal island that tourists and back-to-the-landers began to penetrate in earnest only in the second half of the twentieth century. Predictably, OzE shares much in common with AppE (Christian, Wolfram, and Dube 1988).

3.3.1. The verb phrase

3.3.1.1. Verb forms

Regular and irregular verbs may take on irregular forms in the present, simple past, and participle. Those in the present tense are restricted to forms with *-en(ed)* and first person *wished* 'wish that'.

3.3.1.1.1. Simple past forms (those with –en[ed] are especially numerous)

(50)   a.   He *div* into that pond, went all the way to the bottom.
      b.   That bear *riz* up on his hind legs, musta stood eight foot tall.
      c.   He said he *boughtened* himself a new truck.

3.3.1.1.2. Participle forms (those with be- or -en[ed] are especially numerous)

(51)   a.   She's *het* up the coffee; go get you a cup.
      b.   They've cried and *holden* auctions there for years.
      c.   He got all drunk and *benastied* [= 'soiled', as with vomit] hisself.

3.3.1.1.3. Present forms with -en(ed)

(52)   a.   Just wait'll things *quieten* down some.
      b.   Them chickens there *belongen* to ole Joe across the way.

3.3.1.1.4. Present tense, first person wished 'wish that'

(53)   a.   I don't like it here. I *wished* I hadn't never come.
      b.   I *wished* you'd just get on with it.

3.3.1.2. A-prefixing

An *a-* may occur on *-ing* forms that function as verbs or adverbs (but never on forms that function as nouns or adjectives). This *a-* occurs only on words in which the first syllable is accented, and most typically on words beginning with a consonant sound. Pragmatically, the *a-* may be used to indicate intensity. The feature is also ubiquitous in AppE and may occur in other (usually rural) Southern/South Midland locations.

(54)   a. He come *a-runnin'* around that corner, *a-hollerin'*, makin' more
            noise'n a herd o' turtles.
        b. They wasn't *a-doin'* nothin' wrong.

3.3.1.3. Subordinate hope how 'hope'

The syntax of the clauses containing this seems generally to be [adjective of
measurement] + [subject] + [predicate].

(55)   a. I just *hope how* long the frost holds off.
        b. I *hope how* soon you'll come back and visit some more.

3.3.1.4. Completive done

This auxiliary *done* in a verb phrase may aspectually mark a completed action or event, and may also designate intensity. It also occurs in AAVE and in
southern vernacular dialects.

(56)   a. He *done* asked her to marry him.
        b. I *done* told you to take your shoes off before walkin' on that carpet.

3.3.1.5. Multiple modals with useta

This feature, discussed earlier, occurs in OzE with *useta* as the first element. It
also occurs, less frequently, throughout the Inland North and Midlands.

(57)   a. You *useta couldn't* get by with that in school.
        b. It *useta didn't* matter whether you walked in late or not.

3.3.1.6. Liketa *and* supposeta

These mark speakers' perceptions of events that were on the verge of happen-
ing. *Liketa*, a "counterfactual", is used to indicate that an incident almost but
did not quite occur, and may suggest that the proposition carries an exaggerated connotation. *Supposeta*, often substituting for *supposed to have*, occurs
less frequently and conveys weaker pragmatic assumptions about the event on
the part of the speaker. Both features also occur in AppE.

(58) a. The wind blowed so hard it *liketa* knocked every apple off that tree.
b. That movie *liketa* scared me half to death.
c. She *supposeta* wasn't gonna go to the dance.
d. I heard tell, Billy was *supposeta* eaten darn near the whole pie.

3.3.1.7. Co-occurrence relationships and functional or semantic shifts

All these occur at least sporadically in AppE as well; most can also be heard, if infrequently, throughout the Midlands.

3.3.1.7.1. Shifts in verbal transitivity

(59) a. He *complained* me off and on for weeks after that happened.
b. Go outside and *holler him* over, will ya?

3.3.1.7.2. Functional shifts resulting in new verb forms

(60) a. Come fall he plans to *veal up* that calf in the field.
b. The folks on that side of the hill don't *neighbor* [= 'socialize'] with us much.

3.3.1.7.3. Other complement structures co-occurring with particular verbs

(61) a. Now, don't you start to *messing around* with that one.
b. Once he *gets to movin'*, the other team'll never be able to stop him.

3.3.1.7.4. Main clause have + infinite complements

(62) a. I'll just *have* her to *put* dinner on the table early, then.
b. He *had* three of his best fightin' cocks to *die* on him last month.

3.3.1.7.5. Initial for to in infinitive complements

(63) a. He come early *for* to get a hot cuppa coffee.
b. Mavis there believes it's awful *for to* serve leftovers.

3.3.1.7.6. Verb + particle constructions (after is especially common)

(64) a. Well, *get on outa* the way then.
b. It'll be good music, easy to *dance after.*

3.3.1.7.7. Semantic shifts

(65) a. *He took sick last Tuesday.*
   b. *Are you aimin' to get that roof finished 'fore sundown?*

3.3.1.8. Verb coinages with -(i)fy

The final *-y* here is diphthongal.

(66) a. Don't you *argufy* with me, young man.
   b. If I'd known he was gonna *speechify* so, I wouldn'ta asked the
       question.

3.3.1.9. Multiple negation

This occurs throughout most southern vernaculars and AAVE; the first category
is especially common. Pragmatically, multiple negation generally signals force
or intensity.

3.3.1.9.1. Inversion of the negative auxiliary verb and the pre-verbal
indefinite

(67) a. *Ain't nobody* gonna show up dressed as pretty as you.
   b. *Didn't nothing* that boy ever done turn out right.

3.3.1.9.2. Multiple negative marking in different clauses

(68) a. Well, Bill *wasn't* sure if maybe *nobody'd* come.
   b. There *ain't* much *won't* happen here on a Friday night.

3.3.2.   Adverbs and adjectives

3.3.2.1. Adverb placement

Temporal adverbials, especially those related to frequency of occurrence, may
be moved into the verb phrase. This also occurs in AppE and other southern
rural dialects.

(69) a. Oh, he's *all the time* goin' back up into them woods by hisself.
   b. So why don't you *once in a while* come over and see us at the
       church?

3.3.2.2. *Morphemic inversion in compounds containing* ever

This also occurs in AppE.

(70)   a. You can just put that in there *everwhich* way it goes.
         b. He's been like that *since ever* he was little.

3.3.2.3. *Intensifying adverbs*

Some adverbs, especially *plumb* and *right*, may be used as intensifiers – *plumb* in terms of totality, *right* (often with *smart*) in terms of degree (analogous to *completely* and *very*, respectively, in Standard English). This feature is also found in other rural dialects of the South, and is leeching into the Midlands.

(71)   a. I looked in the basement, but we're *plumb* out of canned tomatoes.
         b. That's a *right smart* lookin' tie.

3.3.2.4. *Adverbial* but *'only; merely'*

This has negative bias, and occurs in the restrictive sense of 'only' or 'merely'.

(72)   a. Why, he couldn't eat *but* one of 'em.
         b. She's not *but* 14 years old, and you've already got her married!

3.3.2.5. *Absence of adverbial* -ly

Many adverbs with *-ly* in Standard English occur without the suffix in OzE.

(73)   a. I believe he's from Oklahoma *original.*
         b. Ole Doc Martin'll do it *painless,* don't you worry.

3.3.2.6. *Adjectival coinages*

The first category involves adding *-(e)y* to a noun, verb, or adjective, often resulting in a new word. In the second category are adjectives formed by adding *-(i)fied* to existing adjectives (*-[i]fy* is the same suffix discussed earlier in the creation of new verbs). The third category consists of compound adjectives that result from combining a nominal and a participle.

3.3.2.6.1. *With -(e)y*

(74)   a. That road there is *ledgey* [= 'full of ledges, or uneven spots'], so be careful.

b. Oh, she's a *visity* [= 'sociable'; 'prone to go visiting'] one.

3.3.2.6.2. *With -(i)fied*

(75)   a. That girl there's all *airified* [= 'conceited'; < 'one who puts on airs'].

b. Why, once she's *prettified* up some, all the boys'll be askin' her out.

3.3.2.6.3. *Compound adjectives*

(76)   a. He got hisself *polecat-stunk* yesterday.

b. That girl who was *car-hit* last week near died.

3.3.3. *Nominals*

3.3.3.1. *Plurals*

Both categories also occur in AppE, and the second, especially, has leeched well into the North Midlands.

3.3.3.1.1. *Absence of plural morpheme when the noun refers to weights/ measures (including measurements of time) and is preceded by a quantifier*

(77)   a. We walk every mornin', about two *mile* right down that road and back.

b. Millie was born 93 *year* ago, and she been kickin' and screamin' ever since.

3.3.3.1.2. *Regularization of irregular plurals, especially those unmarked in Standard English*

(78)   a. He got seven *deers* this year, kept us all in meat the whole winter.

b. There ain't no place for *sheeps* to graze, too many rocks and such.

3.3.3.2. Coinages

3.3.3.2.1. From adjectives

(79)   a. The people in that church is all *hatefuls,* pure and simple.
        b. If they come over here lookin' for trouble, they'll sure get a *lavish* of it.

3.3.3.2.2. From other nouns, by adding agentive -er

(80)   a. The *meetin'ers* [= 'churchgoers'] always get out about noontime.
        b. She's a good little *musicker* [= 'musician'], she is.

3.3.3.2.3. From other nouns, by adding -ment

(81)   a. Oh, the baby threw up her *nursement* [= 'milk that the baby nursed'].
        b. You go put all your *playments* [= 'toys', or things played with] away now.

3.3.3.3. Pronouns

The third category is also widespread, especially in southern vernaculars. Personal datives result from the use of two personal pronouns in the same clause, the second being an object pronoun (if it is third person and reflexive, that object pronoun may be regularized). The resultant meaning is benefactive, similar to Standard English *for* + [reflexive].

3.3.3.3.1. Compound forms with here or there

(82)   a. *This here* barn is over a hundred years old.
        b. Then he started storyin' again, tellin' about *them there* flyin' saucers he seen.

3.3.3.3.2. Absolute possessives with -n

(83)   a. That there's *hisn* applepicker.
        b. Why don't you come over to *ourn* orchard and take a few bushels?

3.3.3.3.3. Personal datives

(84) a. I got to go get *me* a new truck.
   b. Annie sewed *herself* a new dress, looked right pretty.

3.3.3.3.4. Existential they/it

These occur frequently with contracted *is*. *They* is also found in other southern vernaculars; *it* has leeched throughout the Midlands.

(85) a. *They's* a den of snakes under that there slab of concrete.
   b. *It* ain't no rhyme or reason, boy, it's just the way it is.

3.3.4. Prepositions

At least the first two categories exist in AppE as well; the first is also leeching northward.

3.3.4.1. Selection of a preposition (usually of) serving as the axis of the phrase

(86) a. We like to set on the porch *of* an evening and just enjoy the quiet.
   b. She come over about 8:00 *of* the mornin' and give us the news.

3.3.4.2. Absence of a preposition

(87) a. Let's go over *[to]* the church a little early.
   b. He woulda been 76 *[on]* his next birthday.

3.3.4.3. Substitution of to for at

(88) a. Sorry, there's no one *to* [= 'at'] home.
   b. They all jumped him *to* once.

3.3.5.   Conjunctions

3.3.5.1. Pleonastic constructions

The first also appears in southern vernaculars like AppE. *Like as if* occurs especially in constructions reflecting great emotion; *but though* may carry no special pragmatic force.

3.3.5.1.1. Like as if

(89) a. You're talkin' at 'im *like* as *if* he's just a boy when he's near
19 year old!
b. Don't treat me *like as if* I'm some damn cripple!

3.3.5.1.2. But though

(90) a. He don't really want to go, *but though* he will.
b. I can't hardly ride that horse no more, *but though* I will.

3.3.6. Miscellaneous

This characteristic crosses many categories of traditional grammar.

3.3.6.1. Expansive a-

Several *a*-usages occur besides the *a*-prefixing discussed earlier. The second
appears to be leeching farther northward into the Midlands; the third may be
obsolescing.

3.3.6.1.1. Corresponding to a preposition in Standard English

(91) a. We seen a skunk right there *a*-back the barn.
b. Just keep goin' right on *a*-down that road till it forks, and you'll
see it.

*3.3.6.1.2. As part of an alternate representation of a lexical item (usually a
restricted set of adverbs or nouns)*

(92) a. You go *a*-way back up there, you'll find some [moonshine] stills,
guarantee.
b. They talk a good line, but not *a*-one of 'em shoots better than Joe
here.

3.3.6.1.3. With forms other than -ing *participles*

(93) a. He just up and *a*-quit, no explanation or nothin'.
b. He hadn't *a*-run that far in years.

4.   Final remarks

The picture we have painted here is a synchronic one, and therefore temporary. For sociocultural, sociohistorical, and linguistic reasons, American English will continue to evolve in ways that reflect the changing needs and priorities of its users. To conclude our essay, we anticipate the future state of the variation we have considered. We can offer only intelligent guesses, but linguistic history suggests that very few surprises are on the horizon.

We can be relatively sure, for example, that regardless of what specific changes occur, the dialects discussed here will continue to remain distinct. The common lay assumption is that the increasing social/geographic mobility of the American people, coupled with their great reliance on the media for information and entertainment and their general tendency toward cultural homogenization, will eventually cause the dialects in the United States to level out. But most linguists agree that, however much the varieties of American English change and simplify, the people who use them are too diverse ever to converge their linguistic choices into a single way of speaking. Social class, gender, age, ethnicity, group and personal identity, and other factors are reflected in the language Americans use, and probably always will be.

We can also be relatively sure that the dialects of the North, West, and Midwest will retain some of their nonstandard characteristics. For example, analogy and rule extension have regularized some part-of-speech paradigms in the dialects we discussed: the third person, singular, present tense morpheme is often deleted (*It don't matter*), and the plural morpheme may not be applied to measurement nouns (*We walked two mile down that road*). Now, sentences in which the vernacular elements of these regularized paradigms occur have the same meaning as, and are less redundant than, those found in Standard English (the *it* of *It don't matter* signals third person and singular, and the *two* of *We walked two mile down that road* indicates plurality), and, given that languages tend to evolve toward structural simplicity, it is unlikely those redundant elements will be reinstated.

When simplicity conflicts with the retention of meaning, however, speakers will preserve the meaning – that is, will adhere to the "transparency principle" (Wolfram and Schilling-Estes 1998: 43–44). While the negation in *It don't matter* is structurally simpler than that in *It don't matter none*, for example, the transparency principle will prevent the loss of *none* from the second sentence since multiple negation signals a pragmatic force or emphasis not present in single negation. In short, *It don't matter* and *It don't matter none* have slightly different meanings, and the transparency principle will preserve that difference (that is, to the degree to which it is valued by speakers who use multiple negation).

We also know that people's opinions about the standardness of individual features will change. We have already said that many of the forms discussed above are spreading socially and/or geographically; we note here that such spreading often occurs in the face of loud objections by language purists. Eventually these objections will probably cease, some of the forms now objected to will come to be accepted, and new disapproval will rise against a different set of shibboleths. Adverbial *sure* (as in *John sure does like chocolate cake*), participial *proven* (as opposed to *proved*), conjunctive *like* (as in *He went through that store like he'd won a million dollars*) nominative *me* (as in *Danny's four years older than me*), and a host of other constructions were once nonstandard, but are now widely judged respectable if not altogether cultured.

Will all the features currently labeled "vernacular" ultimately be accepted and used by speakers of Standard English? Of course not. And herein lies another certainty about the future of the dialects we have examined here – one that may, indeed, determine their development more than any other: people will always judge the quality of those dialects, and of those dialects' features, by those who use them, and people judged less desirable overall will continue using dialects that mirror that lack of desirability. As we mentioned in our introduction, correctness in language is social, not linguistic.

Exercises and study questions

1. We noted that while each of the features we discuss in this essay can be characterized socioeconomically, contextually or geographically, "none is used by all or only the speakers in those classes or contexts or regions, just as no feature occurs categorically in the speech of any individual who actually uses it". Does your own grammar, or the grammar of people you know, reflect this observation? For example, do you live in one of the geographic regions discussed here, yet find yourself unfamiliar with one or more of the features ascribed to the region's dialect? Or do you know people who live outside the region, yet use one or more features associated with it? What do such observations imply about the concept of "dialect"? How many linguistic features do you believe two speakers must have not in common before those speakers can be said to speak two distinct dialects?

2. Our concluding comment in this essay reiterates a point we made earlier – correctness in language is social, not linguistic – and suggests that when social attitudes toward one or another grammatical feature change, that feature will become more or less acceptable in society at large. What implica-

tions do such truisms have for English teachers, most of whom believe one of their primary responsibilities is to enforce certain irrefutable notions of correctness in the language?

3. Which of the dialects discussed in this essay, if any, would you associate with the form of the language often referred to as Standard English? Why? Do people who use other dialects, then, speak *non*standard forms of the language? Is it possible that more than one standard exists in the United States, defined perhaps by geographic region, social class, age, ethnicity, context, and other factors? (Consider the diverse dialects used by those who have served as President of the United States in recent decades. If there were only one standard in this country, wouldn't the country's leader be expected to use it?)

4. Grammatical dialect differences often do not catch our attention unless they are responsible for lapses in communication, yet we can often notice them if we concentrate specifically on the form or structure of the language being used (as opposed to just the message that the language contains). Begin paying particular attention to the language that you use and that is used around you on a daily basis. Which features do you notice that you hadn't noticed before? Do you especially notice any features of your own language that you didn't know were there? Are you surprised that one or more features you notice in your own language are considered nonstandard outside the geographic region in which you live?

5. If you have lived in more than one of the dialect areas discussed here, has it been relatively easy or difficult for you to "pick up" the dialect of the new area(s) to which you have moved? Most people who have an easy time adapting to new dialects learn the lexicon of those dialects first, then the grammars, and finally the pronunciations. Why should this pattern of acquisition be typical?

Selected references

Please consult the General references for titles mentioned in the text but not included in the references below. For a full bibliography see the accompanying CD-ROM.

McDavid, Raven I.
  1958   The dialects of American English. In: W. Nelson Francis (ed.), *The Structure of American English*, 480–543 (maps 579–585). New York: Ronald.

Montgomery, Michael B. and John M. Kirk.
2001   'My mother, whenever she passed away, she had pneumonia': The history and functions of *whenever*. *Journal of English Linguistics* 29: 234–249.

Murray, Thomas E.
1993   Positive *anymore* in the Midwest. In: Timothy C. Frazer (ed.), *"Heartland" English: Variation and Transition in the American Midwest*, 173–186. Tuscaloosa: University of Alabama Press.

Murray, Thomas E., Timothy C. Frazer and Beth Lee Simon.
1996   *Need* + past participle in American English. *American Speech* 71: 255–271.

Murray, Thomas E. and Beth Lee Simon.
1999   *Want* + past participle in American English. *American Speech* 74: 140–164.

2002   At the intersection of regional and social dialects: The case of *like* + past participle in American English. *American Speech* 77: 32–69.

Randolph, Vance and George P. Wilson.
1953   *Down in the Holler: A Gallery of Ozark Folk Speech*. Norman: University of Oklahoma Press.

Shapiro, Fred R.
1998   A study in computer-assisted lexicology: Evidence on the emergence of *hopefully* as a sentence adverb from the JSTOR journal archive and other electronic resources. *American Speech* 73: 279–296.

Appalachian English: morphology and syntax

Michael B. Montgomery

1. Introduction

Appalachia is a large, mainly mountainous region of the eastern United States that is variously defined. Its core territory encompasses seven states (or parts thereof) from West Virginia and Ohio to Georgia, but the definition formulated by the Appalachian Regional Commission, a federal agency, is the broadest (from central New York southwest to northeastern Mississippi, with a population of 23 million) and is the only one having semi-official status. Settlement of Appalachia by Europeans began in the 1730s, mainly with Scotch-Irish and Germans moving southwestward from Pennsylvania and by English from eastern Virginia and the Carolinas, with smaller numbers of Welsh, French, and other nationalities. With the well-known exception of the Cumberland Gap linking northeastern Tennessee to southeastern Kentucky, the path of settlement usually followed river valleys and led to market towns such as Roanoke, Virginia (1740), and Knoxville, Tennessee (1786). Only later did people begin to move into higher elevations and establish the traditional culture now commonly associated with the region. Today the population of Appalachia is more than twice as rural as the country at large.

More has been written about the English spoken in Appalachia than about any other American region, with the possible exception of the Deep South (for a comprehensive listing, see McMillan and Montgomery 1988). Since the 1880s commentators have stressed its conservatism above all other qualities and claimed that it was "Elizabethan" (Montgomery 1998), preserving early stages of development superseded elsewhere (*afeard* 'afraid', *holp* 'helped', etc.); for the development of research paradigms in the field, see Montgomery (2004) and Wolfram (1977). Until recently travel in or across the largely mountainous region has often been difficult (peaks range to more than 6600 feet high), and many smaller communities have been physically remote from centers of population. For these reasons, commentators have characterized the entire region as "isolated", a quality that is, however, as much socio-psychological (having to do with adherence to a rural folk culture, cultural solidarity, and so on) as geographical, and one that has been greatly overstated (Montgomery 2000).

Three historical characteristics of English in Appalachia other than its conservatism are noteworthy. First, its ancestry from the British Isles is quite mixed, and it has few borrowings from other languages. Its distinctive grammar is sometimes traceable to southern England (*a-* as a prefix on verb present participles, as *a-goin'*; *-n* on possessive pronouns, as *hern*, *yourn*), but is more often Scotch-Irish, deriving from Scotland and northern England through the Irish province of Ulster (*you'uns* 'you (plural)', *whenever* in reference to a single event, as *I was just eight whenever she died*). In contrast, the phonology of its vowel system and individual words comes, except for a few minor details, from Southern England. Appalachian vocabulary comes predominantly from England in general, to a lesser extent northern England (*galluses* 'suspenders'), western England (*counterpane* 'bedspread'), Scotland (*residenter* 'resident, old-timer'), and Ulster (*airish* 'chilly, cool'); see Schneider (1994).

Second, Appalachian speech is far more accurately described as "colonial American" than "Elizabethan", because it shares many more forms with the 18th-century (*obleege* 'oblige', *jine* 'join') than with Shakespeare's English. Third, it is as innovative as it is conservative. This is true for grammar (as in the reversal of elements in *wh-* compounds, producing *everwhat* 'whatever,' *everwho* 'whoever,' etc.), phonology (merger of vowels in *pen/pin* and so on), and especially vocabulary (*hippoes* 'an imaginary or pretended ailment,' from *hypochondria*; *man-power* 'to move by brute effort'). Of the vocabulary, pronunciations, and grammatical patterns found mainly in Appalachia and not shared by the U.S. in general, only about twenty percent can be traced to the British Isles.

Because of its varied history, its large expanse, and its loose borders, Appalachia represents neither a distinct nor a unified speech region. Settlement by different groups or different proportions of groups, along with subsequent innovations, produced several sub-regional varieties, but much less so in grammar than in vocabulary. This chapter surveys the traditional morphology and syntax of only one part of southern Appalachia, the mountains along the Tennessee/ North Carolina border. It is based on a longer sketch in Montgomery and Hall (2004), in which each example cited here can be found, with its source identified. Most are authentic utterances from recorded interviews conducted either by Joseph S. Hall in 1939 or by personnel of Great Smoky Mountains National Park in the 1960s/70s. (For an account of selected grammatical patterns in the central Appalachian state of West Virginia, see Wolfram and Christian 1976).

2.   Verbal morphology

In Appalachian English (AppE), inflections to mark agreement and tense are usually the same in form as in general American usage, but are often found in different contexts and follow different rules.

2.1.   Concord

Verbs in the third singular conform to general usage in nearly all regards. *It seems* may appear as *seem*, with the pronoun omitted (***seem** like I've heard it*), and *don't* may occur in the third singular (*she **don't** care*). Verbs ending in *-st* may take a syllabic suffix (parallel to nouns, as in section 9.4.).

(1)   a. *That water freezes on the bark and **bustes** [i.e. bursts] it.*
       b. *It **disgustes** me now to drive down through this cove.*

The principal difference in subject-verb concord between AppE and general usage lies in third-person plural contexts. In these, *-s* may occur on verbs having any type of subject other than an adjacent personal pronoun as their subject (as *people knows*, *some goes*, etc.). Except when expressing the historical present, *-s* is extremely rare when the subject is *they*. This pattern follows a rule that can be traced to fourteenth-century Scotland and operates also for the verbs *be* and *have*.

(2)   a. *This comes from people who **teaches** biology.*
       b. *Some **tells** you one dog's best.*
       c. *That's the way cattle **feeds**. They feed together.*

The pattern involving verbs with a non-adjacent personal-pronoun subject is found in old letters from the region, but apparently did not survive the nineteenth century:

(3)   a. *We have some sickness in camp of mumps and **has** had some of fever.*   (1862 letter)
       b. *I am now Volenteard to gow to texcas against the mexicans and **Expecks** to start the last of September or the first of October.*
                                                                           (1836 letter)

For uses of the suffix *-s* to express habitual aspect and the historical present, see sections 6.4. and 6.5.

2.2.   Principal parts

As with the agreement and plural suffixes (sections 2.1. and 10.4.), a syllabic variant of the tense suffix may be added to verbs ending in -*st*.

(4)   *It never **costed** me one red [cent].*

AppE exhibits much variation in the principal parts of verbs. Verbs regular in general usage may be irregular in the mountains, and vice versa. More often verbs are irregular in both varieties but differ in their past-tense or past-participle forms. The list below identifies common verbs whose principal parts vary.

Verb	Past-tense form(s)	Past-participle form(s)
ask	ask, ast, ax	ask, ast, ax
become	became, become	become
begin	began, begin, begun	begin, begun
bite	bit	bit, bitten
blow	blew, blowed, blown	blowed, blown
break	broke	broke, broken
bring	brought, brung	brought, brung
buy	bought	bought, boughten, boughtened
catch	catched, caught, cotch, cotched	caught, catched, cotch, cotched
climb	clim, climbed, clome, clum	clim, climbed, clum
come	came, come	came, come
creep	crept, crope	crept, crope
dive	div, dived, dove	div, dived, dove
do	did, done	did, done
drag	dragged, drug	dragged, drug
draw	drawed, drew	drawed, drawn
drink	drank, drink, drinked, drunk	drank, drunk
drive	driv, drived, drove, druv	driv, driven, drove, druv
drown	drowned, drownded	drowned, drownded
eat	ate, eat	eat, eaten
fall	fell	fallen, fell
fight	fit, fought	fit, fought
forget	forgot	forgot, forgotten
forgive	forgave, forgive	forgave, forgive, forgiven
freeze	friz, froze	friz, froze, frozen

get	got	got, gotten
give	gave, gin, give	gave, gin, give, given
go	went	gone, went
grow	grew, growed	grew, growed, grown
hear	heard, heared, hearn	heard, heared, hearn
heat	heated, het	heated, het
help	helped, hept, holp, holped	helped, holp, holped
hold	held, helt	held, helt
kill	killed, kilt	killed, kilt
know	knew, knowed	knowed, known
lean	leaned, lent	leaned, lent
learn	learned, learnt	learned, learn
reach	reached, retch, retched	reached, retch, retched
ride	rid, rode	rid, ridden, rode
ring	rang, rung	rang, rung
rise	riz, rose	risen, riz, rose
run	ran, run	ran, run
see	saw, see, seed, seen	saw, see, seed, seen
set	set, sot	set, sot
shake	shook, shuck	shaken, shook, shuck
sing	sang, sung	sung
sit	sat, sit, sot	sat, sit, sot
skin	skinned, skint, skun, skunt	skinned, skint, skun, skunt
speak	spoke	spoke, spoken
spring	sprang, sprung	sprung
strike	strook, struck	strook, struck
swear	swore	swore, sworn
swell	swelled, swole	swelled, swole, swolen
take	taked, taken, took, tuck	taken, took, tuck
teach	taught, teached	taught, teached
tear	tore	tore, torn
tell	told	tell, told
throw	threw, throwed	threw, throwed, thrown
wear	wore	wore, worn
weave	wove	wove, woven
write	writ, wrote	writ, written, wrote

3.   *Be*

3.1.   Present tense forms

In the present tense indicative, *are* may occur in third-person singular contexts, usually in existential clauses:

(5)   a.   *They **are** [i.e. There is] another one down the street.*
      b.   *There **are** a big waste in it, you know.*

In the third-person plural, variation between *are* and *is* follows the subject-type rule identified for other verbs (section 2.1.).

(6)   a.   *The rocks **is** still there yet.*
      b.   *I know a lot [of people] that has gone on and lots that **is** a-livin'
           yet.*

With the expletive *there* (commonly pronounced *they*), *is* or *'s* generally occurs whether the subject of the clause is singular or plural:

(7)   a.   *There's lots of mountains.*
      b.   *They's about six or seven guitar players here.*

3.2.   Finite *be*

Although frequently employed by writers of fiction set in Appalachia, finite *be* is obsolescent and extremely rare in the region's speech. It does not express habitual or repeated actions, as in African-American English, and in main clauses it occurs regardless of the number and person of the subject.

(8)   a.   *I **be** too old for such tomfoolery.*
      b.   ***Be** you one of the Joneses?*

More often *be* is found in subordinate clauses introduced by *if*, *until*, or *whether*, contexts that are historically subjunctive.

(9)   a.   *If it **be** barn-cured tobacco, you have a different thing.*
      b.   *He would ... leave [the tobacco] until it **be** so hard when it would
           come out it would never get dry and crumley.*
      c.   *... whether it **be** just providing materials so that you wouldn't have
           to ship cargo from way off.*

3.3.   Past tense forms

In traditional AppE, *was* and *were* may be used for both singular and plural, but there is today and apparently has long been in all persons and numbers a strong preference for *was*, which is far more frequent than *were* with subjects of all types.

(10)   a. *I stayed there from the time I **were** about fifteen years old.*
       b. *There **weren't** even a sprig of fire in his place! The fire **were** plumb out.*
       c. *They **wasn't** doing anything yet.*
       d. *Wherever you went, you **was** welcomed.*
       e. *The older people **was** inclined that way.*

Was may be contracted to *'s* (*I's* 'I was', *they's* 'they was', etc.)

(11)   *I knowed **I's** a new duck.*

3.4.   Negative forms

In negative contexts, contracted forms of *am*, *is*, and *are* are the rule, but these vary from general usage in several ways. The verb form may contract with either the subject (*he's not*) or with *n't* (*he **isn't***; see section 9.6.). In all persons and numbers *ain't* is a common alternative of *am*, *are*, or *is*. Especially in clause-initial position, the variant *hain't* occurs.

(12)   a. *I **ain't** gonna let ye go.*
       b. *It **ain't** half as big as it used to be.*
       c. ***Hain't** no use to tell you anything about my sickness, Dr. Abels. I **ain't** got no money.*
       d. *They **hain't** a-going to do that.*

To negate a verb, *don't* is occasionally added to *be*, especially in an imperative clause with a progressive verb form.

(13)   a. ***Don't be** a-takin' it down till I tell you a little.*
       b. ***Don't be** wearing your good clothes out to play in.*

4.   *Have*

4.1.   Present indicative forms

In the present tense inflected forms of *have* parallel those of *be*. *Have* occurs in the third singular, but apparently only in existential clauses.

(14)   *They've been a big change.*

In the third-person plural, variation between *have* and *has* follows the variable subject-type rule for other verbs (section 2.1.) and for *be* (section 3.1.). *Has* is often used with plural nouns, but not with *they*.

(15)   a.   *The young folks* **has** *left that place.*
      b.   *They* **have** *three sisters that is a-living now, them four babies* **has**.

4.2.   Perfective uses

Has been frequently occurs with adverbials that take the simple past-tense in general usage, especially phrases having the form *ago*.

(16)   a.   *It's* **been** *twenty year ago they offered me a house and land.*
      b.   *That's* **been** *a way back yonder.*

In AppE *have* and *had* may be separated from their past participle by a direct object.

(17)   *We* **had** *all our work* **done** *up and* **eaten** *a good camp supper.*

4.3.   Negative forms

In negative contexts contracted forms of *have* and *has* are the rule, but the verb forms may contract with either the subject (*she's not*) or *-n't* (*she* **hasn't**; see section 9.6.). In all persons and numbers *ain't* is a common alternative of *have* in the present tense and, less often, in the past tense. Especially at the beginning of a clause, the variant *hain't* may occur in a stressed position.

(18)   a.   *I* **ain't** *seen nothin' of him.*
      b.   *They* **hain't** *found it yet.*
      c.   **Hain't** *nobody never set it for any bears since. That's been thirty years ago.*

4.4.   Deletion and addition of *have*

Auxiliary *have* and *had* may be elided or deleted, especially between a modal verb and a past participle.

(19)   a. *I guess it ∅ been five or six year ago maybe.*
      b. *You ought to ∅ seen us all a-jumping and running.*
      c. *Well, they was one on one side of the hill you might ∅ seen the other day.*

Have occurs as a superfluous form after *had* in conditional clauses, probably by analogy with *would have*.

(20)   *Had that not **have** happened, there would have been somebody come in here with a lot of money.*

5.   Modal and semi-modal auxiliary verbs

5.1.   Modal verbs

Except for *mought*, an obsolescent past-tense variant of *might* (*They **mought** have done it*), modal auxiliaries differ from general usage only in usage, not in form. As in other Southern varieties of American English, *might* and occasionally *may* combine with other modals to express conditional force and indirectness.

(21)   a. *You **might could** ask somebody along the road.*
      b. *If you folks don't have a cow barn, you **might ought** to build one.*
      c. *I **might can** go with you tomorrow.*
      d. *If they'd just laid down, the snakebite **might wouldn't** have killed a lot of them.*
      e. *They say I **could might** have lived to make it to the hospital.*
      f. *I **may can** get it out tomorrow.*

Used to may combine with modals and other auxiliaries.

(22)   a. *The drummers **would used** to come from Morristown.*
      b. *You **used to could** look from Grandpa's door to the graveyard.*
      c. *It came out like it **used to did**.*
      d. *The children **used to would** kind of stay in the background, you know.*

5.2.   Semi-auxiliary verbs

In AppE several phrases occur in a fixed position before a verb and modify the principal action or statement of the verb. Some phrases may be inflected for tense, but others are more adverbial in their properties.

(23)   a.   *belong to*
            'to be obligated or accustomed to, deserve'
            *He **belongs to** come here today.*

       b.   *fix to/fixing to*
            'to prepare or get ready to, be about to, intend to'
            (the base form is the source for the progressive, but has become recessive while the latter has gained wide currency throughout the Southern United States)
            *I **fixed to** stay a week to bear hunt; I'm **fixin' to** leave now; It was **a-fixin' to** come a storm.*

       c.   *like(d) to*
            'almost, nearly' (originally *had liked to*, a phrase followed by an infinitive form of the verb, often *have*). Today there is rarely evidence of a following *have* and often only the vestige *'d* of preceding *had*. The final consonant of *liked* is normally elided with *to*:
            *I **like to** never in the world got away; The measles **like to** killed me.*

       d.   *need* (followed by a past-participle form)
            *If you had a job that **needed** finished; That thing **needs** washed.*

       e.   *used to*
            'formerly' (in combination with *could, did, would, didn't*).
            See §7.1.

6.   Miscellaneous verbal features

6.1.   Progressive forms of stative verbs of mental activity or sensation

Such forms may be employed to give a dynamic interpretation.

(24)   a.   *Was you **wantin'** to go to town?*
       b.   We was ***liking*** you just fine.

6.2.   Perfective aspect

Auxiliary *did* and *done* are often used to express completed or emphatic action in two separate patterns. First, *did* may occur in negative clauses with an infinitive form and with *not* (as in general usage), but sometimes with *never* (thus, *I **never did** see* 'I have never seen, I never saw'). The emphaticness of such constructions is shown in that stress is placed on each of the words *never did see* (or other verb phrase elements).

(25)   a. *He **never did say** no more about it.*
        b. *I **never did know** what caused it.*
        c. *I **never did live** in a place where they was no meetin's nor singin's.*

Auxiliary *done* is roughly equivalent to 'already', 'completely', or both. It most often precedes a past participle and may be accompanied by a form of *have* or *be*. Occasionally it is followed by an adjective or *and*.

(26)   a. *I already **done** seed three.*
        b. *We thought Pa and Ma had **done** gone to church.*
        c. *The squirrels was **done** eat.*
        d. *The older ones was **done** through school and married.*
        e. *Uncle John Mingus was **done** dead.*
        f. *She's **done** and brought her second calf.*

6.3.   Ingressive verbs

In addition to constructions found in general usage, the beginning of an action or an action just begun may be expressed by several means involving verb phrases. While these are generally equivalent to 'begin' or 'start', they vary somewhat in sense, some indicating one action that is followed immediately by another.

(27)   a. *begin to* + verbal noun: *Then next day everybody **begin to** wondering what caused the blast to go off.*
        b. *come on to* + infinitive: *I went in the house when it **come on to** rain.*
        c. *commence* + verbal noun: *The dogs come in behind him and **commenced** catching him.*
        d. *commence* + *to* + infinitive: *I **commenced to** train a yoke of oxen.*
        e. *commence* + *to* + verbal noun: *He went back up to the tree and **commenced to** barking.*

f. *fall in to* + verbal noun: *Mr. Huff said to me, "Wiley, **fall in to** eating and eat plenty, for you boys may have to stay out all night."*

g. *fall to* + verbal noun: *Everyone **fell to** eating the corn pone, bacon, and gravy.*

h. *get* + verbal noun: *He said them men **got** hollering at him, and he give them a pumpkin.*

i. *get to* + verbal noun: *A bear **got to** coming into that cornfield.*

j. *go* + verbal noun: *He'd just get a little out of his bottle and just **go** putting that on there.*

k. *go in to* + verbal noun: *[We] all **went in to** skinning that bear.*

l. *go to* + verbal noun: *I **went to** studying for myself.*

m. *let in to* + verbal noun: *Then he **let in to** fussing at me because I let her go over there to spend two weeks with Amy.*

n. *set in to* + verbal noun: *Hit **set in to** raining about dark.*

o. *start in* + verbal noun: *Brother Franklin **started in** telling stories.*

p. *start in to* + infinitive: *I got so I **started in to** read it by heart.*

q. *start in to* + verbal noun: *So we **started in to** fishing near the Chimney Tops.*

r. *start off to* + verbal noun: *They **started off to** hunting.*

s. *start to* + verbal noun: *Then we'd all **start to** shelling [the corn].*

t. *take* + verbal noun: *He made a dive at my brother Richard, and he took running off.*

u. *take to* + verbal noun: *I **took to** raising hogs.*

6.4. Habitual aspect

Habitual aspect is usually not marked in the present tense. The rare exception is the suffix *-s* on verbs, a feature, like uninflected *be*, primarily found in literary dialect.

(28) a. *I **drinks** three and four cups to a meal.*
 b. *Even if it rains, I **sticks** 'em when the sign's in the feet.*

Habitual aspect is expressed in the past tense with *used to* or *would* and also through prepositional phrases (section 14.6.).

6.5. Historical present

In the recounting of events, especially in narrative style, verbs (especially *say*) are made "present" by adding *-s* to indicate vicarious action in the past.

(29)   a. *They **comes** back, and Scott **says** he was a-coming over to their
          house when Lester come back.*

       b. *I **thinks** to myself I'll just slide down there and see if he'd make me
          holler.*

       c. *So she **gets** up and started to go around the house to look for him
          to tell him what she thought.*

       d. *"Father", I **says**, "I'll have to quit eating this meat".*

7.   *A*-prefixing

A prominent feature of AppE is the prefixing of *a-*, especially on present participles of verbs. Historically derived from the Old English preposition *an/on*,
the prefix has little if any semantic content today. It sometimes highlights dramatic action.

(30)   a. *It just took somebody all the time **a**-working, **a**-keeping that,
          because it was **a**-boiling.*

       b. *I got out there in the creek, and I went to slipping and **a**-falling and
          a-pitching.*

The prefix occurs on verbs of all semantic and most structural types, as on compound verbs and on verbs in the middle voice (i.e. active verbs whose subjects
receive the action).

(31)   a. *People will up with their guns and go out **a**-rabbit hunting, **a**-bird
          hunting.*

       b. *... while supper was **a**-fixin'.*

       c. *Something happened to the child when he was **a**-bornin'.*

Less often the prefix occurs on past-tense and past-participle forms of verbs.

(32)   a. *I just **a**-wondered.*

       b. *I would get them **a**-gentled up, and then I put the yoke on them.*

The prefix may also be used on prepositions, on nouns to form adverbs or adverbial phrases of time, place, or manner, on adverbs of position, direction, or
manner, or on adjectives.

(33)   a. *I'll shoot if he comes **a-nigh** me.*

       b. *The bear, it made a pass **a-toward** him.*

       c. *I went back down **a-Sunday**.*

       d. *I didn't do it **a-purpose**.*

    e. *Many preachers would ride **a-horseback** as far as Gregory did from Cades Cove.*

    f. *He was **a-just** tearing that window open.*

    g. *Most of my people lived to be up in years, but I had some to die off **a-young**, too.*

8. The infinitive

8.1. The *for to* infinitive

Especially in older AppE an infinitive may be introduced by *for* + *to* where general usage has only *to*. In some cases this construction expresses purpose or has an intervening noun functioning as the subject of the infinitive.

(34)   a. *They'd turn the sap side up, and they'd use that **for to** spread the fruit on.*

    b. *He's lookin' **for to** quit.*

    c. *We kept [a spot] fenced **for to** grow our potatoes.*

    d. *I like **for** people **to** like me, so I try to get along with everybody.*

    e. *I'd like **for** you **to** advise me if it's too much.*

8.2. Adjective + infinitive

An apparently recent development of the infinitive is its use to express the specification or respect in which something is true. When it follows an adjective (e.g. *He was **bad** to drink*), the subject of the higher clause serves as the subject of the infinitive. *Bad* or *awful* + infinitive usually implies a speaker's judgment that a person spoken of has an unfortunate, excessive, or unhealthy inclination or tendency.

(35)   a. *He was awful **bad to** drink.* (= He was a heavy drinker.)

    b. *He was a **bad man to** drink.* (= He was a heavy drinker.)

    c. *[Bears] were **bad to** kill sheep, but not so **bad to** kill the hogs.*

    d. *He's **awful to** tell stories.*

    e. *The Queen family was all of them **good to** sing.*

    f. *She's an **awful hand to** fish.* (= She loves to fish; she fishes a lot.)

8.3.   Infinitives after *have*

An overt infinitive with *to* may follow *have* and its direct object, to express either causation or the occurrence or experiencing of a condition.

(36)   a. *He **had** my uncle **to** make a road.*
        b. *She'd **have** us **to** stay together all the time.*
        c. *I **had** an uncle **to** witch people.*
        d. *I **had** a sister **to** die several years before I was born.*

8.4.   Elliptical infinitives

Want is often followed by a preposition and has an elliptical infinitive, as *want (to get, go) in, want (to be) out.*

(37)   a. *All I **wanted out** of it was a little bucket of honey.*
        b. *That dog doesn't know whether he **wants in** or **out**.*

9.   Negation

9.1.   Multiple negation

The negative markers *never*, *no*, and *not/n't* are frequently doubled or followed by other words of negative value such as *hardly* in the same clause.

(38)   a. *They **ain't** a-bitin' to do **no** good.*
        b. *I've **not never** heared of that.*
        c. *I **hain't** seen **nothing** of him.*
        d. *Did he **not** get **none** of it?*
        e. *Hit **didn't** scare me **nary** a speck **nor** a spark.*
        f. *The snow **never hardly** got off the ground.*

9.2.   Negative concord

AppE generally follows the rule of negative concord, whereby all indefinite elements in a clause conform in being negative.

(39)   a. *We **didn't** have **no** use for it **noways**.*
        b. *We **ain't** starvin' **none**.*
        c. *There's an old house up here, but **don't nobody** live in it, **not noway**.*

> d. *None of us **wasn't** real singers **nor nothin'** like that.*
> e. *He **wouldn't never** charge **nobody** a dime for **nothing** like that.*

But there are occasional exceptions to this pattern:

(40)   a. *I **never** did go **hardly** any.*
      b. *I **never** did see Grandma do **any** work of **any** kind.*

9.3.   *Never*

AppE uses *never* in two patterns differing from general usage. First, the form may negate a past-tense verb referring to a single event. Accordingly, *never saw* and *never seen* are both equivalent to 'didn't see', and for single events AppE has an alternative to the general pattern of inserting *did* to negate a verb in the simple past tense.

(41)   a. *We **never** seen it then.*
      b. *I **never** saw him while he lived.*
      c. *She **never** died then.*
      d. *We had a drought in here and **never** made nothing.*

In the second pattern, *never* is followed by *did* and the infinitive of a verb. Thus, *never did see* is equivalent to 'didn't ever see' or 'have/had never seen' (see section 6.2.).

9.4.   *Nor*

As in general usage, *nor* follows *neither* in correlative constructions, but it also occurs without *neither*. In these sentences *nor* more often than not follows *not/n't* and may be seen as the negative form of *or* adhering to the rule of negative concord.

(42)   a. *I didn't take any toll off any orphans **nor** widows.*
      b. *She won't bother me, **nor** she won't bother anybody else.*
      c. *Lightning nor thunder **nor** a good sousing **nor** anything else didn't keep him from going.*

9.5.   Negative inversion

A negated verb form such as *ain't*, *didn't*, or *can't* may invert with the subject of a clause. (See also section 17.4.).

(43)   a.   *There's an old house up here, but **don't** nobody live in it.*
      b.   ***Didn't** nobody up in there in Greenbrier know nothin' about it till they run up on it.*
      c.   ***Ain't** nary one of 'em married.*
      d.   ***Hain't** nobody never set [the trap] for any bears since.*

9.6.   Contraction with *not*

A modal verb, a form of auxiliary *have,* and especially auxiliary/copula verb *be* may contract with its subject (most often with a pronoun), preserving the full form of *not.* Thus, *that's not* varies with *that isn't,* etc.

(44)   a.   *Now my memory's **not** as good as it used to be.*
      b.   *We've **not** got around to cooking.*
      c.   *I'll **not** say that I'm going to buck it.*
      d.   *I'd **not** care to drive a car.*

10.   Noun plurals

10.1.   Plural nouns of weight and measure

Plural nouns of weight and measure may lack -*s* when preceded by a numeral or other quantifier. This pattern reflects the partitive genitive from older English. This occurs most often with *mile, pound,* and *year.*

(45)   a.   *There wasn't a church to go to within twenty **mile** of where I lived.*
      b.   *The bear weighed four hundred and seventy-five **pound**.*
      c.   *[We] took that hide offen it and cut it into four **quarter**.*
      d.   *Just after the war a few **year** I was married. I was married at the age of twenty-two year.*

10.2.   Mass nouns

Nouns construed in general usage as mass nouns may be interpreted as plural or treated as count nouns in AppE.

(46)   a.   *These **gravels** are hard on your feet.*
      b.   *We used to make **molasses** and sell 'em.*
      c.   *Have you got any easing **powders**?*
      e.   *We had several **rock** on that trail and nothing to drill those **rock** with.*

10.3.   Plurals for animals

Plurals for animals are noteworthy in several respects. The lack of *-s* on *deer* and other animals of the wild may be extended to other nouns.

(47)   a.   *He hunted **coon**, deer, [and] **bear**.*
      b.   *[There are] lots of **wildcat** here ...*

Second, *-s* may be added to nouns that do not take the suffix in general usage:

(48)   a.   *They used to be plenty of **deers**.*
      b.   *That big old bear had one of Pap's little **sheeps** behind a big log, and it had eaten that little sheep.*
      c.   *I caught a mess of **trouts** today.*

Third, *ox* displays several tendencies. Like *sheep*, its plural may be regularized to form *oxes*. *Oxen* may be interpreted as either plural or singular, in the latter case producing the plural *oxens*.

10.4.   Syllabic plural forms

Nouns ending in *-sp*, *-st*, or *-sk* may preserve the longer syllabic plural form *-es* inherited from earlier English.

(49)   a.   *We had **deskes**, and I remember I'd lay down and go to sleep.*
      b.   *The birds have built **nestes** in the spring house.*
      c.   *I wonder what they aims to do with these pine **postes**.*
      d.   *She taken two **dostes** of medicine. (**dose** + excrescent **t** + plural **-es**)*

10.5.   Associative plurals

The phrases *and all*, *and them* (often reduced to *an' 'em*), and *and those* each mean 'and the rest, and others' and are used usually after a singular noun to include associated people (especially family members) or things.

(50)   a.   *I carried roasting ears, sweet potatoes, Irish potatoes, tomatoes, cucumbers, cabbage, **and all**.*
      b.   *I have a picture of my dad **and them** working their own road.*
      c.   *Helen **and those** were there.*

11.   Pronouns

11.1.   Personal pronouns

Personal pronouns in the nominative or objective case are for the most part the same as in general usage. The main exceptions are forms for the second-person plural (most notably *you'uns*) and *hit* for the third-person singular. AppE has five plural forms of the second-person pronoun (*you, ye, you'uns, you all,* and *y'all*) and two singular forms (*you, ye*). *You'uns* (usually pronounced as two syllables) is a contraction of *you + ones*. *You'uns* is the traditional periphrastic form that has been losing ground to *you all* (less often to *y'all*) for at least three generations.

(51)   a.   *He knows **you'uns** and **you'uns** knows him.*
      b.   *Well, I'll see **you all** later.*
      c.   ***Y'all** come back.*

Ye (pronounced [ji] or [jɪ]) is a variant pronunciation of *you*, not a retention of the Early Modern English plural *ye* found in the Authorized Version of the Bible and elsewhere. It occurs as either singular or plural, usually in such unstressed contexts as a direct object, object of a preposition, or subject in inverted constructions.

(52)   a.   *[Boneset is] bitterer than quinine, and hit'll kill **ye** or cure **ye** one.*
      b.   *I tell **ye**, children, both of **ye**. They got to quit deviling you.*
      c.   *You can see the ski lodge yander, can't **ye**?*

In the third-person singular, *hit* (the historic form of the pronoun) alternates with *it*, occurring most often in stressed positions (usually as a subject).

(53)   a.   Stressed: ***Hit's** been handed down to him, you see, so he's the third or fourth generation.*
      b.   Stressed: *I know positive that **hit** wasn't all true.*
      c.   Unstressed: *They got up with it and they treed **hit**.*
      d.   Unstressed: *They had to raise the young one and take care of **hit**.*

The objective case of singular personal pronouns may be employed in subject position when conjoined with another pronoun or with a noun (in the latter case the pronoun usually comes first). This pattern with plural pronouns is rare, if not non-existent.

(54)   a.   *So **me** and four cousins began right then and there to lay our plans to go.*
      b.   *Ever since **me and her** was engaged, I've been true to her.*

    c. ***Her** and Jess and the girl is all buried there on Caldwell Fork.*

    d. ***Him** and them dogs killed that bear.*

    e. *That mine **you** and Tom Graves found, how can you go to it?*

11.2. Possessive pronouns

Possessive pronouns in attributive position usually conform to general usage. However, in absolute or disjunctive position at the end of a phrase or clause, forms with *-n* may occur instead of forms with *-s*. These developed historically by analogy with *mine* and *thine*.

(55)   a. *I thought **hern** was prettier than mine.*

     b. *My daddy hauled **hisn** to Asheville.*

     c. *[We] generally sold **ourn** to a man on Coopers Creek.*

     d. *The colts is **theirn**.*

     e. *Work them just like they was **yourn**.*

     f. *What did you'uns do with **yournses**?*

11.3. Reflexive pronouns

Reflexive pronouns in AppE differ from general usage in four ways. First, in a construction known as the personal dative, personal pronouns may occur where general usage has forms in *-self/-selves* or no pronoun at all. In many cases the pronouns are optional to one degree or another.

(56)   a. *I had **me** some coal.*

     b. *Git **ye** chairs. (singular or plural)*

     c. *You can catch **you** a mole.*

     d. *You'uns can build **you'uns** back one.*

     e. *He swapped that old steer off and got **him** a jackass.*

     f. *Mary is fixing to make **her** some cotton dresses.*

     g. *We'd just come down and see if we could find **us** a little drink.*

     h. *Well, they'd get **them** a preacher and let him preach a while. Then they'd change and get **them** another.*

Second, following the pattern of *myself* and *yourself*, third-person reflexive pronouns may add *-self* or *-selves* to a possessive rather than an objective form:

(57)   a. *He was just up there by **hisself**.*

     b. *They even carded the wool **theirselves**.*

Third, plural reflexive pronouns may be formed with *-self* or *-selfs* as well as
with *-selves*.

(58) a. *We kept that all to **ourself**.*
      b. *We went by **ourselfs** to the head of Forneys Creek and fished.*
      c. *Dang you ones. If you want them out, get in and get them **yourself**.*
      d. *Step up here, boys, and he'p **you'unsself**.*
      e. *They'd all go and enjoy **themself**.*
      f. *I like to see young people try to make something of **themselfs**.*
      g. *The county went to furnishing them **theirself**.*

Fourth, *own* may be added to form an emphatic reflexive, which is always
based on the possessive rather than the objective form.

(59) a. *Now that was an experience I experienced my **own self**.*
      b. *He has a little kit to give **his own self** a shot.*
      c. *Everybody took care of **their own self**.*
      d. *People doctored **their own selfs**.*

11.4.   Demonstrative pronouns and adjectives

As in many other varieties of English, *them* occurs as a demonstrative pronoun
and adjective as well as a personal pronoun. *This* and *that* and their plural
forms may take *here* or *there* to form compounds.

(60) Demonstrative pronouns:
      a. ***Them** looks a whole lot steeper and taller than they did in my*
          young days.
      b. ***This here** is George Thomas Baxter.*
      c. ***These here** was on the inside there.*
      d. ***That there's** Tom's boy, I guess.*

(61) Demonstrative adjectives:
      a. *I've went up over **them** rocks a many a time.*
      b. *All **this here** poplar went to England across the water.*
      c. *He had one of **these here** hog rifles.*
      d. ***That there** sawmill I worked at was there before I married.*
      e. ***Them there** fellows come through here, stealing horses and things.*

Also the distinction between proximate, intermediate, and distant is maintained
(*this* vs. *that* vs. *yon*). *Yon/yan* and *yonder/yander* most often function as adverbs, but may be demonstrative adjectives as well.

(62)   a. *Middlesboro is on **yan** side of Cumberland Gap.*
       b. *[Y]ou cross the big bridge goin' in **yander** way right there.*

11.5. Indefinite pronouns

Notable usages of indefinite pronouns include *ary/ary'un, nary/nary'un* (see section 12.4.) and *a body* 'one, someone'.

(63)   a. *Could **a body** buy that there dog?*
       b. *About a bushel [is] maybe what **a body** could pretty well carry.*

11.6. Interrogative forms

To introduce a direct or indirect question, AppE has a set of interrogative forms that invert *ever* and the *wh-* element (see also section 15.1.).

(64)   a. *You'd aim at **everwhat** you're shooting at.*
       b. ***Everwhich** one come nigh always come down to the house and stayed full half the night.*
       c. ***Everwho's** higher in seniority gets to keep his job.*

Interrogative pronouns may be combined with *all* to stress the inclusiveness and generality of a statement or question. Thus, *who all* is equivalent to both 'all of whom?' and 'who in general?'

(65)   a. *I don't know **where all** he sold it at.*
       b. *I don't know **what all** we didn't do.*
       c. ***Who all** was there?*

11.7. Personal pronouns + *all*

As suggested in section 10.1., *all* may combine with personal pronouns to emphasize inclusiveness: *theirs all, they all, you all, your all, you'un(s) all*, etc. In all of these the stress falls on the first element, not the second, making these constructions compounds rather than phrases. *You all* is the only combination to have acquired substantial properties of a personal pronoun.

(66)   a. *Cades Cove nearly took **theirs all** to Gregory Bald.*
       b. *Old man Lon and Will all, **they all** went with him.*
       c. ***You-all** may be [needing] it one of these days.*
       d. *Is this table **your all's**?*
       e. ***You'uns all** come to see me.*

11.8.   Unstressed *'un*

One is frequently contracted and reduced to *'un* (occasionally *'n*) when it is unstressed and follows a pronoun (cf. *you 'uns*, section 10.1.) or an adjective.

(67)   a.   ***We'uns*** *come from educated folkses.*
        b.   ***You'uns*** *is talking about rough country.*
        c.   *We'll try **another'n**, being that'un paid off.*
        d.   *The **gooder'ns**'s all gone now!*
        e.   *I don't recollect any of his **young'uns**.*
        f.   *They was all sizes from **little'uns** to **big'uns**.*
        g.   *If he killed **ary'un**, it was before my recollection.*

(See section 17.2. for *one* following *or* in coordinate constructions.)

11.9.   Relative clauses

AppE uses nine forms to introduce restrictive relative clauses: *that, who, ∅, 'at, which, as, what, whose*, and *thats* (of these, *that* is the most common; *what* and *thats*, a possessive, are the least). Four forms introduce non-restrictive clauses: *which, who, that* and *whose* (*whom* is rare, if not non-existent, in colloquial speech).

(68)   a.   *I know the man **that** was lost.*
        b.   *This is Steve Cole, **that** lives in the Sugarlands near Gatlinburg.*
        c.   *And we had some old trained bear hounds **'at** turned off in the roughs.*
        d.   *I came on a party ∅ had been fighting a bear.*
        e.   *They was two wagon loads ∅ went out from there.*
        f.   *Then he handed it down to Caleb, **which** was Eph's Pa.*
        g.   *Tom Sparks has herded more than any man **as** I've ever heard of.*
        h.   *I knowed the White Caps **what** done the murder.*
        i.   *We need to remember a woman **thats** child has died.*

12.   Articles and adjectives
        (for demonstrative adjectives, see section 11.4.)

12.1.   The indefinite article

The indefinite article *a* [ə] rather than *an* may occur before words beginning with a vowel sound.

(69) a. *I had **a** uncle and **a** aunt that moved out there.*
　　 b. *She done our baking in **a** oven.*

12.2. The definite article

The definite article is employed in place names (*the* Smoky = the main ridge of the Smoky Mountains), in the phrase *in the bed*, to indicate possession (*the old lady* 'my wife', *the woman* 'my wife'), with an indefinite pronoun (*the both of them*), and with names of diseases and medical conditions (*the fever* 'typhoid', *the sugar* 'diabetes', etc.)

12.3. *The + other*

The definite article is occasionally reduced to *t'* before *other(s)*. With the function of *t'* as an article having been lost, *t'other* may be modified by *the*.

(70) a. *One or **t'other** of them whupped the other one.*
　　 b. *When one's gone **the t'other's** proud of it.*

12.4. Indefinite adjectives

Ary 'any' (derived originally from *e'er a*) and *nary* 'not any, none' (from *ne'er a*) may occur in negative, interrogative, or conditional clauses. They may take en-clitic *'un* (< *one*) to form the indefinite pronouns *ary'un* ['ærɪən, æɚn] and *nary'un* ['nærɪən, næɚn]. (See also section 10.5.)

(71) a. *We didn't kill **ary** deer then.*
　　 b. *We never seed **nary** another wolf.*
　　 c. *If he killed **ary'un**, it was before my recollection.*
　　 d. *I never seed a deer nor saw **nary'un's** tracks.*

12.5. Comparative forms

The comparative form of adjectives may differ from general usage.

(72) a. *Nothin' [is] **gooder** than crumbled cornbread and milk.*
　　 b. *You're **nearder** to the door than I am.*

Double comparatives are characteristic of AppE:

(73) a. *I'd say I was **more healthier** back then than I am now.*
      b. *I was getting closer and **more closer** with every step I took.*
      c. *I think there are **worser** things than being poor.*

12.6. Double superlative forms

Double superlative forms also occur.

(74) a. *Newport, though, is one of the **most liveliest** towns that I know of.*
      b. *Doc was the **most wealthiest** man [in] this part of the country.*

The suffix *-est* may sometimes be added redundantly, including on adjectives that are historically superlative or absolute.

(75) a. *She could make the **bestest** [sweetbread] in all the country, we thought.*
      b. *Who got there **firstest**?*
      c. *Who growed the **mostest** corn?*

12.7. Present participle + *-est*

Present participles used as attributive adjectives may take the suffix *-est*.

(76) a. *Daddy said he was the gamest and **fightingest** little rascal he ever hunted.*
      b. *He had told somebody she was the **workingest** girl in the country.*
      c. *She's the **aggravatin'est** calf I've ever had.*
      d. *He was the **singingest** man this side of Turnpike.*

12.8. Anomalous comparatives and superlatives

In AppE a form of *big* together with a noun it modifies is equivalent to *most*. *Big* may appear in its positive, comparative, or superlative form and modify any of several nouns, but the meaning of the construction remains 'the most'.

(77) a. *A **big majority** of the people went to church pretty regular.*
      b. *My father did the **big part** of the farming.*
      c. *They done the **bigger majority** of their logging on Laurel Creek.*
      d. *He rode a horse the **bigger part** of the time.*
      e. *The **biggest half** of the people does it.*
      f. *The **biggest majority** down there, they care.*
      g. *The **biggest part** of them was Democrats.*
      h. *[The] **biggest portion** of people didn't have lumber.*

Other unusual superlative forms include *onliest* 'only' and *upperest* 'situated on the highest ground, farthest up' (from *upper* 'on high ground').

(78) a. *She treated it as if it was the **onliest** one she had.*
  b. *Turkey George Palmer was in the **upperest** house on Indian Creek.*

12.9. *All the* + noun phrase

In AppE the adjective phrase *all the* 'the only' may modify singular count nouns or the indefinite pronoun *one* (i.e. not only mass nouns, as in general usage).

(79) a. *I reckon that's **all the** name she had.*
  b. *That's **all the** one they got here.*

12.10. *All the* + adjective

All the may also modify the positive, comparative, or superlative form of an adjective to express extent.

(80) a. *That's **all the** far/farther/farthest I want to go. (= as far as)*
  b. *Is that **all the** best you can do? (= as good as)*

13.   Adverbials

13.1.   Adverbials +-*s*

The suffix -*s* may be added to some adverbs of place and time.

(81) a. *I can rest easier in the woods than **anywheres** else.*
  b. *We learned we had to call him a long time **beforehands**.*
  c. *They keep all over that mountain **everywheres** up there.*
  d. *There's a gold mine in here **somewheres**.*

13.2.   Adverbs without -*ly*

Adverbs (principally ones of manner) without the suffix -*ly* are common.

(82) a. *a **awful** ill teacher (= a very ill-tempered teacher)*
  b. *I think it was a lady, if I'm not **bad** fooled.*
  c. *There's not **near** so many as [there] were at the time we came here.*

   d. *I began stone-cutting at a **powerful** early age.*
   e. *They don't like it **real** genuine. (i.e. very much)*
   f. *Some of that country is **terrible** rough.*
   g. *My family done **tolerable** well.*

By the same token, *good* is a variant of *well* in adverbial contexts:

(83)   a. *He knows [the song] **good**.*
        b. *She could pull a crosscut [saw] as **good** as a boy.*

13.3.   Intensifying adverbs

AppE has many intensifying adverbs to express 'very' or 'quite'.

(84)   a. *That water isn't **bad** cold.*
        b. *Newport's a **mighty** fine place for a young man to go.*
        c. *They said he never was **much** stout after that.*
        d. *I used to trap for 'em [but] never got so **powerful** many.*
        e. *He was **right** young. He was just a boy.*
        f. *It's a **terrible** bad place.*

It also has many ways to express 'all the way' or 'completely'.

(85)   a. *The bullet went **clean** through his leg.*
        b. *My cattle run **clear** to Silers Bald.*
        c. *Uncle John Mingus was **done** dead.*
        d. *They was **plumb** sour, and they would keep **plumb** on till spring.*
        e. *They owned all this, **plumb** up to the gap.*
        f. *I'll be covered **slam** up.*
        g. *We worked till **slap** dark.*
        h. *He was **smack** drunk.*

13.4.   Locative adverbs

AppE has many constructions not found in general usage to indicate position, distance, or direction. These are usually adverbs, but some may function also as adjectives to modify nouns.

(86)   a. *thataway*
           'that way'
           *When you're coming down **thataway**, they ain't many places to stop.*

b. *thisaway*
'this way'
*I'll go around down **thisaway** below him, and you go down in on him.*

c. *yon/yan* (the second form is more common)
'over there'
*I says, "**Yon's** the White Caps now"; She's in the field, up yan, gittin' roughness.*

d. *yonder/yander* (the second form is more common)
'over there'
*They was some trees that stood all up here and **yonder** about in the orchard; I sneaked up in here with a horse from down **yander** where I showed you mine.*

13.5. Other adverbs

Adverbs differing from general usage English include the following:

(87) a. *afore* 'before'
*I done what you told me **afore**, and it holp me some.*

b. *along* (followed by a preposition)
'approximately, somewhere, sometime'
***Along** about Friday we'd have spelling bees.*

c. *along*
'continuously, regularly'
*We'd kill game **along** all the time.*

d. *altogether*
'entirely, exclusively'
*They worked chestnut **altogether**.*

e. *anymore*
'nowadays, at present' (in positive sentences)
***Anymore** they have a hard time protecting things like that.*

f. *anyways*
'to any degree or extent, at all'
*If you was **anyways** near to a bear, he would charge you.*

g. *anyways*
'in any case, at any rate'
*Sometimes you would get more and sometimes less, but **anyways** from ten to fifteen dollars.*

h. *around* (followed by a prepositional phrase)
    'approximately, more or less'
    *The old garden was right **around** up through there.*

i. *edgeways*
    'edgewise'
    *Let's leave time for people to get a word in **edgeways**. (similarly, lengthways 'lengthwise')*

j. *everly*
    'always'
    *He was **everly** going down to the store.*

k. *noways*
    'in any way, at all'
    *We didn't have no use for it **noways**.*

l. *right*
    'immediately, exactly'
    *You find that **right** today.*

m. *sometime*
    'sometimes, from time to time'
    *He'd throw that stick **sometime**.*

n. *someway*
    'somehow, in some manner'
    *The sled got away from him and hurt him **someway**.*

o. *used to*
    'formerly' (placed before the subject of a sentence, in clauses
    having a past-tense verb)
    ***Used to**, you know, there wasn't very much working on Sundays.*

13.6.   Miscellaneous adverbial features

In Appalachia *ago* often occurs with a present-perfect verb rather than one in the simple past (see section 3.2.). *Yet* retains its usage from older English in affirmative clauses (rather than only in negative and interrogative contexts, as in modern English generally). *Yet* is semantically equivalent to, but may co-occur with, *still*, in which case *still* comes first.

(88)   a. *I believe that old good book will do to live by **yet**.*
        b. *The rocks is still there **yet**.*

13.7.   Adverb placement

The qualifying adverbs *about*, *much*, and *nearly* may come after the construction they modify.

(89)   a. *We had all kinds of apples anywhere you went **about**. (i.e. almost anywhere)*
     b. *Well, they were all kinfolks **just about**, you see. (i.e. nearly all)*
     c. *You been sleepin' all day **near about**, and you done broke a sweat, and that's good for you.*
     d. *The weather never got any colder up there **much** than it did here.*
     e. *I'm always at home **nearly**.*

14.   Prepositions and particles

The dialectal character of Appalachian English is conspicuously evident in the use of prepositions.

14.1.   Verbs of mental activity/sensation + *of*

Older AppE uses *of* after *smell*, *feel*, *taste*, or other verbs of mental activity or sensation, but the preposition has little if any semantic content.

(90)   a. *I can recollect **of** him a-going to school.*
     b. *We didn't pay much attention to the fourth of July, as I remember **of**.*
     c. *Smell **of** it*
     d. *He said he tasted **of** everything he had ever killed, every varment, even a buzzard.*
     e. *Feel **of** it now.*

14.2.   Prepositions differing from general usage

(91)   a. *abouten*
       'about'
       *I never knowed a thing **abouten** it.*
     b. *afore*
       'before'
       *I allowed he'd return **afore** this.*

c. *afteren*
   'after'
   *He never give me his check before, just what was left over **after'en** he had been out with the boys.*

d. *against/again*
   'by the time of, before'
   *He'll be in town **against** nine o'clock; He didn't make it back **again** the night.*

e. *anent*
   'close to, beside'
   *I fell back into the river and just took up right up in the water and was wet all over and got up **anent** them.*

f. *being of*
   'because of'
   ***Bein' of** that, Mr. Hood, I just can't take anything from you for the death of Bill.*

g. *beside of*
   'beside'
   *Let me put the bag down **beside of** you.*

h. *enduring*
   'during, through'
   *Did he stay **enduring** the night?*

i. *excepting*
   'except'
   *Faultin' others don't git you nowhere, **exceptin'** in trouble.*

j. *for*
   'because of, on account of'
   *I couldn't see across that log **for** the fog.*

k. *fornent*
   'opposite, beside'
   *He lived over **fornent** the store.*

l. *offen*
   'off, off of'
   *[We] took that hide **offen** it.*

m. *on* (to express an unfortunate or uncontrollable occurrence)
   *My cow up and died **on** me.*

n. *on*
   'of, about'
   *He was never heard **on** no more.*

o. *outen*
   'out of'
   *He frailed the hell **outen** him.*

p. *owing to*
   'according to, depending on'
   *It's **owing to** who you're talking to.*

q. *till*
   'to' (in expressions of time)
   *... quarter **till** five.*

r. *to*
   'at'
   *I belong **to** home with your Ma.*

s. *to*
   'for'
   *That bear was small **to** his age.*

t. *to*
   'of'
   *They were men **to** the community.*

u. *withouten*
   'without'
   *I seed him throw a steer once and tie him up **withouten** any help.*

14.3.   Particles extending or intensifying verbal action

A verbal particle may serve less as an intrinsic element of a phrasal verb than it does to intensify or give durative value to the basic action of the verb. The forms which appear most frequently in such contexts are *up* (as in general usage), *in*, *on*, *out*, and *down*.

(92)   a. *in: We dressed the bear and carried him **in** home.*
       b. *on: [The bear] ran **on** off up the hill.*
       c. *up: The storm scared us **up**.*
       d. *out: Study it **out** [i.e. think it over] while you are bringing in the water.*
       e. *down: I shot the bear in the mouth and killed him **down**.*

14.4.   Combination of forms

A remarkable characteristic of AppE is the combination of two or more locative prepositions to modify the action of the verb.

(93)   a. *I went right **down in on** him and give him another shot.*
        b. *They was several houses **on up around up on** Mill Creek and **up in** there and **on up next to** Fork of the River back **up in** there.*
        c. *The dogs was a-fighting the bear right **in under** the top of Smoky, pretty close **up to** the top.*
        d. *It was just down where that road comes around, **on down in below** where that road comes around.*
        e. *He turned them loose [and] **down through** the sugar orchard they went **out up across over on** Enloe, back **around to** the big branch, **out across** the head of hit **over on** Three Fork.*
        f. *The old tom cat went **up in under** the chair.*

14.5.   Omission of prepositions

Prepositions are occasionally omitted.

(94)   a. *Back (in) old times.*
        b. *She lives over (at) what they call Corn Pone, Cascades.*

14.6.   Prepositional phrases for habitual activity

Temporal prepositional phrases with *of* (especially with a singular indefinite noun as the object) indicate frequent or habitual activity, in one of three patterns equivalent to 'every'.

(95)   a. *of a* + singular noun: *We would have singing **of a night** and **of a Sunday**; We would gather our apples in **of a day** and peel our apples **of a night** and put them out on a scaffold.*
        b. *of the* + singular noun: *They don't have no one to rely on **of the night**.*
        c. *of* + plural noun: *My grandfather was troubled **of nights** in his sleep with what was called nightmares.*

15. Conjunctions

15.1. Subordinating conjunctions

Many subordinating conjunctions either do not occur in general usage or occur with different functions there (see also section 11.6.).

(96) a. *afore*
'before'
*It rained **afore** we had a chance to plow.*

b. *again/against*
'by the time that, before'
*We'd oughta do plenty of fishin' **against** the season closes; I was repairin' the tire **again** you came.*

c. *as*
'than'
*I'd rather work **as** go to school.*

d. *as*
'that'
*I don't know **as** I've been any benefit to the park service.*

e. *as how*
'that, whether'
*I don't know **as how** I can finish it today.*

f. *being, being as, being that*
'because, seeing that'
*We'll try another'n, **being** that'un paid off; **Being as** you weren't at the meeting, you don't get to vote; **Being that** the president was sick, the vice-president adjourned the meeting.*

g. *evern*
'whenever, if ever'
Evern you do that, you'll come home and find a cold supper.

h. *everwhen*
'when'
***Everwhen** we got there, Jack reached for his gun.*

i. *everwhere*
'wherever'
*They just squatted down **everwhere** they were.*

j. *how come* (see section 17.1.)

k. *how soon*
'that ... soon'
*I hope **how soon** he comes.*

l. *iffen*
   'if'
   *Come into the fire **iffen** you-ones wants to.*

m. *lessen*
   'unless'
   *I won't go **lessen** you go.*

n. *like that*
   'like, that'
   *I felt **like that** we needed the power.*

o. *nor*
   'than'
   *[It's] no bigger round **nor** your arm.*

p. *that* (redundant after other forms in *because that, how that*, etc.;
   see section 15.4).

q. *till*
   'so that, with the result that, to the point that'
   *He liked [coffee] so strong **till** you could slice it; My mama had
   rheumatiz, and she got **till** she couldn't walk.*

r. *to where*
   'to the extent that, to the point that'
   *The coons was hung up **to where** they froze up and was alright; He
   got **to where** he was inactive.*

s. *until*
   'so that, with the result that'
   *I've done this **until** they could take and interpret the pictures.*

t. *whenever*
   'of a single event: when'
   *I was just eight **whenever** she died.*

u. *whenever*
   'as soon as, at the earliest point that'
   ***Whenever** you get to Caldwell Fork, it's just across the mountain
   to Hemphill.*

v. *whenever*
   'of a process or extended period: throughout the time that, during
   the time that'
   *My mother, **whenever** she was living, she just told you one time.*

w. *whenevern*
   'of a periodic or intermittent event: when'
   *There were three in the saw crew **whenevern** you cut trees.*

x. *whenevern*
'of a one-time event: as soon as'
***Whenevern** I seen what it was, why I went back to the shack.*
y. *without* 'unless'
*They didn't fish **without** it was just right.*
z. *withouten*
'unless'
*I won't go **withouten** you do.*

15.2. Verbless absolute clauses

AppE has verbless absolute clauses introduced by *and* and interpreted as subordinate to the previous clause. The construction functions as though it has an elliptical form of *be*.

(97) a. *They all wore Mother Hubbard dresses, **and** them loose.*
  b. *That woman is doin' too much work, **and** her in a family way.*
  c. *He would steal the hat off your head **and** you a-lookin' at him.*

15.3. Ellipsis

Ellipsis of the conjunction may occur when introducing the complement of a verb after *want*.

(98) a. *Child, I want ∅ ye should think about it all yer days!*
  b. *They want ∅ you should use the hickory on some of them rough boys.*

15.4. Redundant *that*

A redundant *that* may be used after *where*, *what*, and similar conjunctions:

(99) a. *Not just **because that** I'm born and raised here, but I'm just telling ye what other people tells me.*
  b. *Tell us **how that** you would find and get the sheep in.*
  c. *I don't remember exactly **when that** they started building in White Pine.*
  d. *He brought him out, down to **where that** they could get him in a car.*
  e. *Maybe you can explain then **why that** it does do that.*

16.   Existential clauses

Existential clauses display variation from general usage in three principal respects. First, they are usually introduced by *there*, its related form *they*, or more rarely *it*.

(100) a. ***They*** *is something bad wrong with her.*
     b. *I believe **they** is a cemetery there too, ain't **there**?*
     c. *If you'd have seen what I made it with, **it** would be a lot of people would faint.*
     d. *There was one bedroom upstairs, wasn't **it**?*

Second, *is* (usually contracted to *'s*) and *was* (sometimes contracted to *'s*) are the typical verb forms with both singular and plural subjects. *Are* appears occasionally with singular subjects.

(101) a. *They **is** not so many there now.*
     b. *They's all sizes from little'uns to big'uns.*
     c. *They **are** another one down the street.*

Third, the relative pronoun following the subject is often omitted, regardless of its function.

(102) a. *They is six trees Ø would have made anybody a good dwelling house.*
     b. *They is people Ø gets lost in these Smoky Mountains.*

17.   Miscellaneous patterns

17.1.   *Yes/no* questions

Indirect yes/no questions may take the word order of direct questions, with inversion of the subject and auxiliary verb and with the tense conforming to that of the main clause. Indirect *wh*-questions usually pattern as in general usage, except when *how come* introduces a clause and precedes a noun or personal pronoun in the objective case.

(103) a. *He asked me did I want to work this morning.*
     b. *Somebody asked me was that Jim Ike's truck.*
     c. *We finally asked would they help us.*
     d. *I studied what was the matter.*
     e. *That's **how come** it to be called the Devil's Courthouse.*
     f. *That's **how come** us to leave there, you know.*

17.2. *One*

To specify alternatives, AppE often employs *one* (probably derived from *one or the other*) after conjoined forms or types of phrases, most often nouns.

(104) a. *He was in Tennessee or Kentucky **one**.*
  b. *I'm going home [and] see Emerts Cove or hell **one** before daylight.*
  c. *They had [revival] meeting morning and evening or morning and night **one** all the time.*
  d. *That hearing aid, it's either too high or too low **one**.*
  e. *The first settlers come in here in the eighteen thirties or the forties **one**.*
  f. *They'd set down and climb a tree or pick a fight **one**.*

17.3. Left dislocation

Often a noun or noun phrase is moved from its usual position to the beginning (or left-most position) of a clause, to be replaced by a simple personal pronoun in the original context.

(105) a. *The [hunters] that went the other way into the mountain, they'd killed them turkeys.*
  b. *The bear, it made a pass a-toward him.*

17.4. Interposed pronouns

An indefinite pronoun or pronoun phrase co-referential with the subject of a clause may appear in the verb phrase.

(106) a. *The Queen family was **all of them** good to sing.*
  b. *We don't **any of us** need anything.*
  c. *They can **every one** sing.*
  d. *We don't **nobody** know how long we have.*

The interposed pronoun phrase may appear in an existential sentence, a pattern that may be the basis of clauses with negative inversion (section 9.5.).

(107) a. *They didn't **none of us** ever get snakebit, but their work animal did.*
  b. *There'd **somebody** come around with a truck once in a while.*

Exercises and study questions

1. Is Appalachian grammar more innovative in its prepositions or its conjunctions?

2. Does Appalachian grammar have more irregular/strong verbs than standard written English or less?

3. What are three features of Appalachian grammar that are not attested in the OED after the 18th century?

4. What features of Appalachian grammar are attested also in the writings of Shakespeare?

5. What features of Appalachian grammar might cause a speaker of it to be misunderstood?

6. In what ways might Appalachian grammar be considered more progressive than the grammar of standard written English?

7. What grammatical features does Appalachian English have in common with African-American English?

8. Which possessive pronouns does Appalachian grammar share with southern England but not with northern England?

9. Study the phrases in section 14.4. Is "compound preposition" the best term to describe them, or is there an alternative term that would be better?

Selected references

Please consult the General references for titles mentioned in the text but not included in the references below. For a full bibliography see the accompanying CD-ROM.

McMillan, James B. and Michael Montgomery (eds.)
  1988   *Annotated Bibliography of Southern American English.* Tuscaloosa: University of Alabama Press.
Montgomery, Michael
  1998   In the Appalachians they speak like Shakespeare. In: Laurie Bauer and Peter Trudgill (eds.), *Myths in Linguistics*, 66–76. New York: Penguin.
  2000   The idea of Appalachian isolation. *Appalachian Heritage* 28: 20–31.
  2004   English in Appalachia. In: Tyler Blethen and Richard Straw (eds.), *High Mountains Rising*, 147–164. Champaign: University of Illinois Press.

Montgomery, Michael and Joseph S. Hall (eds.)
  2004   *Dictionary of Smoky Mountain English*. Knoxville: University of Tennessee Press.
Schneider, Edgar W.
  1994   Appalachian mountain vocabulary: Its character, sources, and distinctiveness. In: Wolfgang Viereck (ed.), *Verhandlungen des Internationalen Dialektologenkongresses Bamberg 1990* Volume 3, 498–512. Stuttgart: Steiner.
Wolfram, Walt
  1977   On the linguistic study of Appalachian speech. *Appalachian Journal* 5: 92–102.

Rural and ethnic varieties in the Southeast: morphology and syntax*

Walt Wolfram

1.   Introduction

Notwithstanding the popular stereotype of the American South as a uniform region, the Southeastern US represents one of the most diverse dialect areas in the Unites States. It is an area of robust dialect diversity, including a full range of areal, social, and ethnic variation. At least three major dialect boundaries cut across the Southeastern states of Virginia, North Carolina, South Carolina, and Georgia, including a seaboard region to the east, a highland region to the west, and an intermediate Coastal Plain and Piedmont region. Within the context of dialect diversity in the South is a set of *enclave dialect communities*, that is, communities that have been set apart from mainstream populations and, in some cases, from the major dialect boundaries set forth in dialect surveys such as Kurath (1949), Carver (1987), and Labov, Ash, and Boberg (2006). Admittedly, the notions of "enclave community" and "historical isolation" are difficult to define in a precise, objective manner (Wolfram and Thomas 2002), although these constructs generally involve geographical and/or social remoteness, historical continuity, and communicative disconnection from more widespread populations. Perhaps more important than objectifiable criteria, however, is the fact that these communities usually have a strong sense of local, oppositional identity vis-à-vis other groups.

There are several reasons why enclave dialect communities are significant for the description of language variation in the South. Such communities provide a critical basis for reconstructing the history of vernacular dialects in the US, based on the assumption that enclave dialects will be conservative in language change and that they will be relatively immune to some language changes diffusing throughout the wider population. Enclave communities have, in fact, played an important role in reconstructing the earlier status of prominent social and ethnic varieties such as African American English (Poplack 2000, Poplack and Tagliamonte 2001; Wolfram and Thomas 2002; Mallinson and Wolfram 2002) and Appalachian English (Montgomery 1989; Montgomery and Hall 2004). Another reason is the rapid transformation of some historically isolated dialect communities. Abrupt changes in demographic and socioeconomic conditions during the last half of the twentieth century have threatened these once-insular dialect communities, resulting in rapid dialect dissipation and, in a couple of cases, dialect intensification (Schilling-Estes 1997; Wolfram and Schilling-Estes 2003). The dynamics of dialect change under these circumstances, including the death of some traditional dialects, is of considerable interest to researchers of language variation and change. Finally, the rapid erosion of some of these remote dialect communities has resulted in a sense of urgency to document them before they are lost or drastically restructured. Given the moribund state of many enclave dialects, it seems incumbent on dialectologists and linguists to document the descriptive status of these varieties.

2.　The construction of enclave dialect communities

Like other varieties, enclave dialects in the Southeastern US are a product of founder dialects (Mufwene 2001), language contact, language diffusion, and independent language development. Accordingly, these varieties reveal similar and dissimilar traits with other enclave communities as well as with many other adjacent and non-adjacent dialects. Enclave dialects are typified by a set of structures that are shared not only with each other but also with a relatively wide range of rural dialects in the US. Given the distribution of forms in diverse, rural areas throughout the US and their attestation in earlier varieties of English brought to colonial America, we assume that these communities simply have been conservative in their language change. For example, the use of *a*-prefixing, widely distributed in the earlier English of the British Isles and in the US, is amply documented in enclave communities in the Southeastern US and elsewhere in the rural American South (Pederson 1986–1992), but it is also found in rural contexts in New England (Kurath 1939–1943) and in the Midwestern US. (Allen 1973–1977).

A second type of distribution pattern can be traced to regional dialects of the British Isles. In earlier American English, these patterns might have shown regional distribution as well, as settlers from particular regions of England tended to cluster in particular geographical regions in America. For example, the concord pattern attaching *-s* to verbs with plural noun phrase subjects (e.g. *The dogs barks*) has been attributed to varieties in Northern England and to the dialect of the Ulster Scots immigrants who were a dominant population in the highland areas of Appalachia (Montgomery 1989). In fact, the marking of *-s* on verbs with 3rd plural subjects has now become known as the "Northern Concord Subject Rule", in recognition of its historical regionalization in England (see the chapters by Beal and Filppula, British Isles volume).

The assumed origin of such features in the regional dialects of the British Isles, however, raises important questions about their occurrence in enclave dialects of the Southeastern US. Ulster Scots immigrants and speakers from Northern England were certainly part of the overall mix of English-speaking settlers in the Southeast, but they were much more concentrated in some areas – in particular, the Appalachian mountain range – than they were in others, such as the Southeastern coastal area. Nonetheless, we find traits associated with this assumed regional British dialect founder effect well beyond the original area of settlement. It is possible that the effects of some earlier varieties of English in colonial America diffused to other areas from their original locus, and may even have become part of an earlier American English koiné in the Southeast. If this was the case, then the dialect features might have persisted in enclave varieties that have had no significant contact with each other for a couple of centuries.

In the enclave dialects we survey here, we also find a few structures that are not documented in other regional varieties of American English. In most US varieties, past *be* is usually regularized to *was*, as in *We was home* or *You wasn't there* (Wolfram and Fasold 1974; Wolfram and Schilling-Estes 1998); however, in some enclave communities, we find a pattern in which past *be* is leveled to *was* in positive sentences (e.g. *We was there*) but to *weren't* in negative ones (e.g. *I weren't home*). Within our sample, the *was/weren't* pattern is robust among groups as geographically and culturally disparate as the European Americans of Smith Island and Tangier Island in the Chesapeake Bay (Schilling-Estes 1997; Shores 2000) and the Lumbee Indians of the Coastal Plain of North Carolina (Wolfram and Sellers 1999). At the same time, there is no documentation of this pattern in other current rural dialects in the Southeast.

Although we can only speculate, it does not seem likely that regularization to *weren't* is due to a simple, direct founder effect from the British Isles (where it is very much alive, see Anderwald 2002). The feature was present in some of the varieties brought to regions of the Eastern Seaboard of America, including those varieties that originally came from Southwest England (Orton et al. 1962–1971). From that point, it probably developed into a regional feature of the coastal Delmarva dialect region (Shores 2000; Wolfram and Thomas 2002). As people from the Delmarva region moved to various coastal sites, including islands in the Chesapeake Bay and the Outer Banks, the pattern was apparently diffused along the Mid-Atlantic and Southern coasts. In this case, the earlier development of a regional variety of American English spread to other areas that then became isolated.

Like other varieties, the dialects of enclave communities also change from within. While dialectologists and historical linguists certainly acknowledge the potential for internal linguistic change in peripheral dialect areas, the role of innovation tends to be overlooked in most descriptions of enclave dialect communities. Instead, there seems to be an assumption that dialect forms in historically isolated varieties will be quite conservative with respect to innovation and that relic forms will remain relatively intact in their linguistic composition. Andersen (1988), however, argues that what we conveniently refer to here as *the relic assumption* has led researchers to slight system-internal innovations in favor of hypothetical contact situations that lead to diffusion-based explanations. Andersen (1988: 54) notes: "[…] there are internally motivated innovations which arise independently of any external stimulus. These too have an areal dimension and may appear to spread merely because they arise in different places at different times."

This claim certainly counters the relic assumption that remnant dialect communities will necessarily be conservative in their patterns of change and rarely favor innovation. Our investigation of dialect enclave communities in the coastal US supports the contention that language change can indeed take place fairly rapidly in enclave dialect areas and that dialect intensification – that is, the accelerated development of dialect distinctiveness – can take place through internally based language change, even when a variety is in a moribund state (Schilling-Estes and Wolfram 1999). Wolfram and Schilling-Estes (2003), for example, show that the remorphologization of past tense *be* is an accelerating change taking place currently in at least several unrelated enclave dialects on the mid-Atlantic coast ranging from the islands in the Chesapeake Bay to the Outer Banks of North Carolina.

The rapid rate of change within a relatively compressed time period suggests that we cannot simply assume that dialect change is necessarily slow or fast, or that it takes a unilateral path. Rather, there may be periods of rapidity of change as well as conservatism over the course of centuries of isolation. Even when enclave dialects share a common core of structures vis-à-vis dialects of the wider population, particular communities may indicate selectivity in their retention and development of dialect forms. For example, perfective *be* in sentences such as *I'm been there before* was once a fairly common dialect trait across a broad range of earlier dialects of English, including most of the communities considered here. We know that perfective *have* was a later development in the English language, and that there was widespread fluctuation with perfective *be* well into the seventeenth century. But in one of the enclave communities considered here, we find that the use of perfective *be* is still a robust, productive form, even among younger speakers (Dannenberg 2003). Furthermore, the structure has undergone some independent structural and semantic development that now distinguishes it from other varieties where it is still productive. Though the perfective use of *be* might qualify as a "relic" form given the traditional definition of this notion, it must be understood that such items are hardly static structurally or functionally. Indeed, these forms may undergo independent development within a particular community that sets the community dialect apart from other enclave dialects in subtle but important ways. If we assume that the label "relic" refers to earlier forms selectively preserved intact, then there would be very few forms that qualify; if, on the other hand, we admit that these forms are subject to change just like non-relic features, then we are hard put to show how change in relic forms differs from other types of language change, apart from the fact that relic forms involve changes in items that have receded in more widely distributed, socially dominant varieties of the language.

Finally, change may also involve parallel independent development, or "drift" among unrelated dialect communities due to the operation of the general processes of analogy and universal tendencies to move toward unmarked forms. All of the varieties examined here, for example, show the regularization of irregular plurals (e.g. *two sheeps*), the regularization of past tense forms (e.g. *They growed up*), and negative concord (e.g. *They didn't do nothing*). These general traits are shared not only by these enclave communities but also by a host of other vernacular communities of English that include but are not restricted to American English. The developments are simply part of the natural processes that guide changes quite independently of diffusion or language contact, or, as Chambers (1995: 242) puts it "primitives of vernacular dialects in that they recur ubiquitously all over the world." More than anything, analogical pressures to regularize and generalize linguistic rules distinguish socially subordinate enclave communities from the prescribed standard English norm which is, according to Chambers (1995: 246), "more strictly tightly constrained in its grammar and phonology" due to the social pressures to resist some natural changes. These system-internal processes must be factored into the description and explanation of these varieties as they configure and reconfigure themselves over time in ways that are both uniform and diverse.

Notwithstanding romantic notions about enclave dialect communities existing in splendid isolation apart from all contact with outside dialect communities, we must also consider the role of language contact in the development and maintenance of enclave dialects. Regardless of the situation, there is some inevitable interaction and communication with other groups. The communities represented here are no different in this regard, and each of them has had contact with other groups in their past, as well as varying types of contact more recently. Thus, structural traits may be transferred from other language varieties. However, linguistic accommodation is not necessarily a matter of categorical structural acceptance or rejection. In fact, it is possible that *interdialectal forms* may arise – that is, "forms that actually originally occurred in neither dialect" (Trudgill 1986: 62). In our discussion of the grammatical attachment of third person plural -*s* in one of the communities considered here, Hyde County, we find that the use of -*s* attachment by African American cohorts reflects but does not precisely replicate its use by European Americans, showing a type of overgeneralization characteristic of language contact situations. Donor dialects thus worked in tandem with language contact strategies in the configuration of the earlier African American speech in this isolated, bi-ethnic context. Both intra-community and inter-community contact must be recognized, not only in the formative stages of such dialects, but also as varieties reconfigure themselves over time and as they emerge from insularity. The contact dynamics of different enclave communities must be taken into account along with founder effects, diffusion, and independent development in understanding the structuring and restructuring of enclave dialect communities.

3.   The grammar of enclave dialects

In this section I describe some of the morphological and syntactic traits of a representative set of enclave dialect communities. The description is based on several types of communities. First, we include island communities on the Outer Banks of North Carolina (Wolfram and Schilling-Estes 1997; Wolfram, Hazen, and Schilling-Estes 1999) and the Chesapeake Bay area of Maryland and Virginia (Schilling-Estes 1997; Schilling-Estes and Wolfram 1999; Shores 2000). These mono-ethnic, European American communities represent one of the paradigm types of the Southeastern enclave community. These are complemented by the examination of a couple of bi-ethnic enclave communities, including a longstanding African American and European American community on the coast of North Carolina (Wolfram and Thomas 2002), Hyde County, and a receding bi-ethnic community in the Appalachian mountains of North Carolina, Beech Bottom (Mallinson and Wolfram 2002). Finally, we include the case of a tri-ethnic situation involving the Lumbee Native American Indians (Wolfram and Dannenberg 1999; Dannenberg 2003). The Lumbee, who lost their ancestral language generations ago, have carved out a unique sociocultural variety that symbolizes their unique status as neither white nor black. The location of these communities is given in the map in figure 1.

In describing the structural characteristics of these enclave situations, I attempt to highlight the ways in which they are similar to and different from

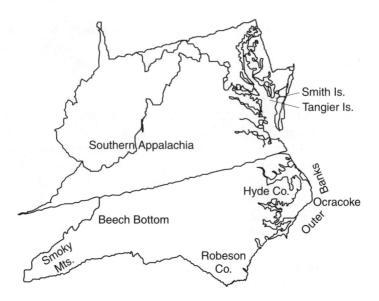

Figure 1.   Rural and ethnic sites of the Southeast United States

each other, as well as from other rural Southern varieties. The description is organized on the basis of major grammatical categories.

3.1.   Verb phrase

Some of the most distinguishing traits of enclave dialect situations involve the verb phrase, including a set of specialized auxiliaries, irregular verbs, and subject-verb agreement patterns. Many of these features unify these varieties with other Southern American vernacular dialects but there are also a couple of cases that seem to be confined to enclave dialect communities.

3.1.1.   *Finite* be

The use of *be* as a finite form in sentences like *That's how it bes* has been attested in selected regions of the South, although its productive use among European Americans tends to be quite regionally restricted (Montgomery and Mishoe 1999). It may occur with a habitual meaning (e.g. *They usually be there*), as it currently does in contemporary African American Vernacular English (AAVE), but it is clearly not restricted to this aspectual reference in enclave dialect communities. It is rare in the enclave communities that we have examined here, excepting Lumbee English in Southeastern North Carolina, where it has become a dialect icon associated with their distinct sociocultural variety. It should be noted, however, that the Lumbee live in a county adjacent to one of the few regions in the United States where finite *be(s)* characterizes the European-American population, Horry County, South Carolina (Montgomery and Mishoe 1999). Older European American residents in Robeson County where the Lumbee reside also show vestiges of finite *be* but elderly European Americans and African Americans in other enclave sites rarely use this form.

A kind of restructuring of *be* in Lumbee English is taking place in the current generation of speakers. This development coincides to some extent with the integration of public schools in the early 1970s, an event that brought Lumbees into increasing contact with African Americans. While the use of finite *be(s)* has come to characterize the Lumbee (Wolfram and Dannenberg 1999), habitual *be* in constructions such as *Sometimes they be acting nice* is a well-known feature of twentieth-century AAVE (see Wolfram, this volume). Among older Lumbee speakers, *be(s)* may be used in habitual contexts, but it is not restricted to this function. Younger Lumbee speakers show the increased use of *be* in v-*ing* constructions with a habitual reading, the contemporary grammaticalized function of *be* in AAVE. At the same time, *be* may have verbal -*s* attachment with 3rd sg. subjects (e.g. *The train bes coming every day at noon*) and, to a lesser extent, 3rd pl. subjects (e.g. *The trains bes coming*). This pattern is unlike its contemporary AAVE use, which does not typically mark verbal -*s*. We thus observe that *be* has partially accommodated the grammaticalization that has taken place in AAVE while retaining distinctive parameters of the concord system of Lumbee Vernacular English.

3.1.2. *Copula/auxiliary absence*

The absence of copula and auxiliary for contractible forms of *is* and *are* (e.g. *She nice* for 'She's nice' or *They acting silly* for 'They're acting silly') is strongly associated with AAVE (e.g. Labov 1972a; Wolfram 1969; Fasold 1972; Rickford 1999), but it is also shared to some extent with Southern white rural vernacular varieties of English. In Southern European American English varieties, particularly those within the former large plantation areas of the South, deletion tends to be limited to contractible forms of *are*; it is also used at reduced frequency levels compared to AAVE. In Southeastern enclave communities, copula absence is associated primarily with African American communities. For example, it is not found in the exclusively white island dialects of the Outer Banks (Wolfram, Hazen and Schilling-Estes 1999) and the Chesapeake Bay (Schilling-Estes 1997) and it is not characteristic of the European American cohort community in Hyde County even though it is found among African Americans there. Deletion is also found among African American speakers in Appalachian enclave communities (Mallinson and Wolfram 2002), where some European American speakers do sporadically exhibit deletion of *are* (Wolfram and Christian 1976). In Lumbee Vernacular English, it is found to a very limited extent (Dannenberg 2003) and used at frequency levels between those for cohort African American and European American speakers. The occurrence of copula absence in enclave communities seems attributable to contact with AAVE speakers rather than to an independent development.

Enclave dialects regularly exhibit the deletion of contracted forms of *have* as in *I been there before* or *He been there*. This is a phonological process involving the deletion of a weak final consonant rather than a morphological process.

3.1.3. Perfective be

Many enclave dialects alternate perfective *be* with the auxiliary *have* as in *I'm been there* for *I've been there* or *You're been there* for *You've been there*. This is no doubt a perpetuation of an earlier pattern that included widespread fluctuation with perfective *be* and *have* well into the seventeenth century. Although perfective *be* is now relatively infrequent in most enclave dialects in the Southeastern US, it remains a robust, productive form in one variety we examined, Lumbee Vernacular English (Dannenberg 2003). Furthermore, its development in this variety distinguishes it from other varieties where it is still found. Perfective *be* is structurally restricted to contracted finite forms (e.g. *I know I'm been here* but not **I know I am been here*), and it has expanded semantically to apply to some simple past constructions (e.g. *I'm forgot the food yesterday*). Though perfective *be* is indicated in a wide range of enclave dialects, its restructuring in Lumbee English illustrates how a particular dialect community may selectively preserve and expand an item to distinguish itself both from other enclave dialect communities and from dialects found in the wider population.

3.1.4. A-prefixing

The use of the prefix or proclitic *a-* with v-*ing* structures, as in *She was a-huntin' and a-fishin'* or *They came a-lookin' for the possum* is a widespread structural trait in enclave dialect communities in the Southeast as well as in other rural vernacular varieties of English. The prefix *a-* may only attach to verbs and verbal complements as in *They went a-walkin'* and *We was goin' up there a-squirrel huntin'*; it is also attached occasionally to *-ed* participles as in *It had a white sheet a-wrapped around it* or *It's supposed to be a-haunted.* It is not generally permissible with prepositions, so that a sentence like *They make money a-fishin'* is well formed but a sentence like **They make money by a-fishin'* is ungrammatical. This restriction is no doubt related to the fact that *a*-prefixing developed historically from a temporal locative as in *Rex was at/on fishin'.* In fact, in some communities, older speakers still occasionally use sentences like *Rex was at fishin' when we got there.* These sentences are remnants from the period when *a*-prefixing alternated with a temporal locative preposition. There are also phonetic restrictions on the current use of *a*-prefixing. *A*-prefixing does not generally occur when the following syllable is unstressed, as in **a-discoverin'* or **a-repeatin'*; this prohibition is no doubt a reflection of the prosodic restriction against words beginning with two unstressed syllables. Furthermore, *a*-prefixing is favored in preconsonantal contexts (e.g. *She was a-drinkin'*) over prevocalic ones (e.g. *She was a-eatin'*) though it is permissible in both types of contexts. All of the varieties we have surveyed exhibit *a*-prefixing to some extent, though they show great variation in their relative levels of usage. Elderly speakers on the Outer Banks use it infrequently and younger speakers rarely use it at all, while some elderly Lumbee speakers use it at high frequency levels and young speakers in more isolated Lumbee communities use it productively as well.

3.1.5. *Completive* done *and* slam

The use of *done* with the past tense of the verb, as in *They done used all the good ones* is a persistent structural trait of enclave dialects that is shared with Southern European American and African American vernacular varieties. On the Outer Banks and among the Lumbee, the variant *slam* is used in much the same way as *done*, so that we may get sentences such as *They slam used all the good ones.* In many respects, completive *done* and *slam* function like a perfect, referring to an action completed in the recent past, but they can also be used to highlight a change of state or to intensify an activity, as in a sentence like *I done/slam told you not to mess up.* It is a stable feature though not used as frequently in enclave communities as it is in some other Southern rural varieties.

3.1.6. *Specialized auxiliaries*

Enclave dialect communities tend to share a set of specialized auxiliaries with surrounding Southern rural vernacular dialects. We find, for example, the generalized Southern form *fixin' to* referring to an immediate future or planned event (e.g. *I'm fixin' to go now*) and double modals such as *I might could do it* in enclave dialect communities. We also find counterfactual *liketa* in *I was so scared I liketa died*, although it may differ subtly from how it is used in more widespread Southern rural varieties. In some varieties of Southern English, its use is restricted to contexts of intensified significance, with a metaphorical rather than a literal reference. In these varieties, a sentence like *They liketa went through the roof when they saw the mess* is well-formed but a sentence with a literal reference of 'almost' such as **They liketa went through the roof but the drill they were using wasn't powerful enough* would not be permissible. In other dialects, including the enclave dialects we have examined here, it may also be used with a literal meaning as well as a metaphorical, intensified sense so that the latter sentence would indeed be permissible. Its more expansive use in different enclave communities suggests that its restriction to counterfactual *liketa* for intensified significance was probably a later development in English. Though *liketa* is derived historically from the phrase *like to have*, it is currently interpreted as an unanalyzable lexical item.

3.1.7. Irregular verbs

Irregular verbs tend to fall well within the vernacular irregular verb patterns set forth in Wolfram and Schilling-Estes (1998: 331). The types of differences are enumerated as follows:

1. past generalized as participle
   I had went down there.
   She may have took the car.
2. participle generalized as past
   He done the work.
   She seen something there.
3. bare root as past
   She run there yesterday.
   They come to my house.
4. regularization of past tense
   Everybody knowed him.
   They drinked the soda.
5. different irregular form
   I hearn something.
   It riz up in front of me.

Enclave dialects are no different from other vernacular varieties of American English in the patterning of irregular verb forms. However, the retention of different irregular forms (Type 5), such as *hearn* for *heard, riz* for *rose, clumb* for *climbed,* or *holp* for *help* is much more characteristic of enclave varieties than most other vernacular varieties of English. Many of these forms are, of course, retentions of an earlier, more expansive set of irregular verb forms in English.

3.1.8. Subject-verb agreement

Several aspects of subject-verb agreement are noteworthy. The concord pattern in which *-s* is marked on a verb with a plural subject, as in *The dogs barks* or *People goes there,* is widely documented as a feature of American English varieties that were influenced by the Scotch-Irish, such as Appalachian English (Wolfram and Christian 1976; Christian, Dube and Wolfram 1988; Montgomery 1989), although its colonial distribution apparently was not limited to the Southern Highland region (Wolfram and Thomas 2002). In fact, we find robust patterns of 3rd pl. *-s* marking in all of the enclave dialect communities we have examined here, extending from European American communities in the Chesapeake Bay and Outer Banks to African Americans in both coastal and mountain locations, as well as in Lumbee Vernacular English in the Coastal Plain. Although it may occur at different levels of usage and is subject to different constraints in its application, it is clearly a widespread feature of enclave dialect communities in the Southeast.

There are several constraints on the incidence of plural *-s* marking, namely, the subject type and the proximity of the subject and the verb. Noun phrase subjects (e.g. *The dogs barks*) favor the incidence of plural *-s* marking over pronoun subjects (e.g. *They barks*), and collective nouns (e.g. *People likes the dogs*) and coordinate noun phrases (e.g. *Me and my dog likes to run*) favor *-s* marking over other types of noun phrases. Some enclave dialects show quite strong subject type constraints whereas others show weaker constraints. For example, the Hyde County European American community shows a categorical prohibition against plural *-s* marking with pronoun subjects whereas cohort African American Hyde County speakers show a relatively weak variable constraint (Wolfram and Thomas 2002).

The second constraint is based on adjacency. Verbs that are not adjacent to the subject because of a heavy NP (e.g. *The dogs in the trucks barks*) or a clausal complement (e.g. *The dogs that barks are hungry*) are more likely to attach a plural *-s* than those that are immediately adjacent to the subject. This appears to be a fairly constant pattern though its application is stronger in some enclave dialect communities than it is in others.

Most of the dialects we have examined show occasional *-s* attachment with subjects other than third person as well, as in *I goes down there* or *You takes* *you a good wife* but this is much more sporadic than 3rd pl. -*s* attachment. Furthermore, the use of -*s* with non-third person subjects tends to be idiosyncratic; a few speakers use it with some regularity but the majority of speakers rarely use it. The attachment of -*s* on 1st person as a type of historical present in personal narratives as in *I goes down there and sees this ghost...* is also found in enclave dialect communities. These communities also use *don't* instead of *doesn't* as a 3rd sg. form, as in *She don't go there* or *The dog don't bark*. This is a widespread characteristic of American English vernacular dialects wherever they are found.

The pattern of 3rd sg. -*s* absence in sentences such as *The dog bark_* has not been documented to any extent in the European American enclave communities we have examined in this survey. At the same time, 3rd sg. -*s* absence is a characteristic of several representative African American enclave communities (Wolfram and Thomas 2002; Mallinson and Wolfram 2002) coexisting with a cohort European American community, revealing a consistent ethnolinguistic boundary in bi-ethnic enclave communities.

3.1.9. Past and present tense *be* agreement

Patterns of subject-verb agreement are both similar to and different from those found in other vernacular dialects of English. On the one hand, enclave dialects participate in the widespread vernacular pattern of *be* regularization for present and past forms of conjugated *be*; *are* and *am* level to *is*, as in *The folks is home* or *Y'all is here* and past tense *be* levels to *was*, as in *The folks was there* or *Y'all was here*. Regularization is much more common in past than in present tense, as it is in virtually all varieties of vernacular English having *be* leveling. The comparison of leveling over time and place indicates that it is diminishing somewhat (Wolfram and Thomas 2002), probably due to the effect of prescriptive norms. Nonetheless, it is still quite robust in some enclave communities.

In most US varieties, past *be* is usually regularized to *was*, as in *We was home* or *You wasn't there* (Wolfram and Schilling-Estes 1998). However, in the Southeastern coastal area extending from Maryland and Virginia to North Carolina, there is an alternate pattern in which past *be* is leveled to *was* in positive sentences (e.g. *We was there*) and to *weren't* in negative sentences (e.g. *I weren't home*). This pattern represents remorphologization of the two past *be* stems on the basis of polarity, such that *was* is now used to mark affirmative rather than singular meaning, and the *were*-stem is now used to mark negativity rather than plurality. In the Southeast, the *was/weren't* pattern is robust among groups as geographically and culturally disparate as the European Americans on the islands in the Chesapeake Bay (Schilling-Estes 1997; Wolfram and

Schilling-Estes 2003) and the Lumbee Indians of the Coastal Plain of North Carolina (Wolfram and Sellers 1999). Furthermore, it is found in both coastal African American and European American enclave communities (Wolfram and Thomas 2002). There is little indication that it is found among cohort rural communities in neighboring Coastal Plain regions or in the Highland South. Although leveling to *weren't* is well-represented in past and present vernacular varieties of English spoken in the British Isles (cf. Anderwald 2002), the coastal Southeastern US is the only region outside of the British Isles where it has been documented.

3.1.10. Other verb phrase structures

A number of traits affecting verbs are restricted to particular lexical items and verb plus complement combinations rather than general categories of verbs. A couple of items involve the use of the complement *to* with the verb. One occurs with v–*ing* constructions as in *He started to running* or *Dad went to driving real fast.* Another involves *have to* with a causative or resultative meaning as in *She'll have him to bring the paper when he comes home.* This trait is shared with most Southern American dialects in general. Enclave dialects are also more prone than other rural varieties to retain *for to* complement constructions as in *I'll have for him to come home* or *I want for her to take it with her.* Many of these uses involve retentions of older forms that have been lost in other varieties of English and are general features shared with surrounding Southern rural varieties of English.

The use of *aim* for 'intend' or 'plan' (e.g. *I aim to do it later*), *hear tell* for 'hear' (e.g. *I heard tell you have a new boat*), *carry* for 'accompany' (e.g. *I'll carry you to the store*), and *reckon* for 'suppose' or 'surmise' (e.g. *I reckon I should leave now*) are widespread features of contemporary or earlier Southern American English that are shared with enclave dialect communities. Particular lexical differences may also characterize specific enclave communities such as the use of *mommuck* for 'harass' on the Outer Banks (e.g. *He mommucked his kids all the time*) or the use of *progging* for 'looking for artifacts' (particularly arrowheads as in *He was proggin' yesterday*) on the islands of the Chesapeake Bay (Shores 2000), but such differences have to be considered on an item-by-item basis for different enclave communities.

3.2.   Adverbs

Several distinctive features of adverbs characterize enclave dialect communities. One is the placement of temporal adverbial phrases. In English, adverbial phrases may occur after the verb phrase as in *We have floods once in a while* or in pre-sentential position as in *Once in a while we have floods*, but some dialects, including the enclave dialects in our survey, also permit placement between the subject and the verb phrase, as in *We once in a while have floods*. We also find the use of *anymore* in affirmative sentences with a meaning of 'nowadays', as in *We have a lot of floods anymore*. These varieties align themselves with regional Midland dialects of American English rather than surrounding Southern varieties in this regard. Although some positive *anymore* varieties permit pre-sentential movement of the adverb as in *Anymore, we have a lot of floods*, it is only found in post-verbal position in the enclave dialects we have surveyed. We also find an expanded reference for the adverb *whenever* in the enclave communities, in which it may be used to refer to a punctual event as in *Whenever I lost my mother a few years ago* or an extended time event in *Whenever she was living she taught me*. It is quite evident in the highland areas of Appalachia, but it is also found to some extent in coastal varieties. In most other varieties of American English, its use is restricted to recurring or conditional events as in *Whenever she goes to the store, she buys fish*.

A set of specialized intensifying adverbs characteristic of Southern dialects is also found in enclave varieties of the Southeast. The intensifier *right* retains its earlier, more unrestricted co-occurrence with general adjectives and adverbs, as in *The dog is right big* or *He hollered right loud*. In most varieties of American English, the intensifier *right* is now limited to location in place or time, as in *She's right around the corner* or *He's right on time*. The intensifier *plumb*, which can alternate with *slam*, refers to a state of completeness, as in *She fell plumb asleep* or *She fell slam asleep*. *Plumb* and *slam* are also restricted to neutral and negative attributes; accordingly, a sentence like *He's plumb ugly* is permissible but as sentence like **He's plumb handsome* is not. In a couple of the coastal dialect communities we have examined, *some* may be attached to an adjective, as in *The meal sure was good-some*. However, we have found it used in contrasting ways; on the Outer Banks island of Ocracoke, *-some* strengthens the degree of the attribute whereas on Smith Island in the Chesapeake Bay it weakens it (Schilling-Estes 1997). Thus, *good-some* in Ocracoke means that the food was very tasty, but on Smith Island it means that it was not very tasty. The adverbial use of *but* with a negative in *He ain't but fifteen* or *There ain't but so much I can do* also is found with a meaning of 'only' or 'no more than'.

Enclave dialects are like most other vernacular dialects of English in their regularization of comparatives, so that multisyllabic words like *beautifulest* or *awfulest* may attach the comparative suffix rather than the lexical comparative forms *more* and *most* that are used in standard varieties. Pleonastic marking in *most beautifulest* and *more older* is also found. Fairly extensive absence of adverbial *-ly* is common in these varieties, so that we find sentences like *I was exceptional scared* or *I'm frightful bad at that*. Again, this is a feature shared by many vernacular varieties of English, though it seems to be more expansively applied in the enclave dialect communities than in some other vernacular varieties (Wolfram and Fasold 1974).

3.3. Negation

Negative patterns in enclave varieties are quite like those in other vernacular varieties of English, including negative concord and the extensive use of the lexical marker *ain't*. Negative concord, or multiple negation, may occur with postverbal indefinites, as in *It wasn't nothing*, with preverbal indefinites, as in *Nobody don't like him* 'Nobody likes him', and with inversion, as in *Don't nobody like him* or *Ain't nobody home*. Cross-clausal negative concord also may occur in sentences like *There wasn't much I couldn't do*, meaning that there wasn't much that the speaker could do. Cross-clausal negative concord, though rare, is shared with other Southern vernaculars (Wolfram and Christian 1976) as well as with AAVE (Labov 1972a).

Like other vernacular dialects, *ain't* is used as a preverbal negative for present tense forms of *be* (i.e. *am not, isn't, aren't* in *She ain't here*) as well as for the present auxiliary *haven't*/*hasn't* in *She ain't been there lately*. The generalized past tense variant *wont* for *wasn't* and *weren't* (e.g. *I wont there yesterday*), found in some mainland Southern vernacular varieties, is not found to any extent in coastal and highland enclave varieties, though it is found in the Coastal Plain and Piedmont regions. Enclave communities still exhibit vestiges of older negative adverbs such as *nary* in *I didn't catch nary a fish last night* or *tain't* in *Tain't a thing that will hurt you*.

3.4. Nominals

Most noun phrase traits found in enclave dialects are shared with a wide range of English vernaculars, although there are also few features that may distinguish these varieties from other dialects. Plural *-s* absence with quantified measure nouns is quite prominent in most of the enclave dialects we have surveyed, as in *I caught 200 pound_ of flounder* or *It's four mile_ from here*. These varieties also share in the regularization of irregular plurals, including items that shift from irregular to regular suffixation (e.g. *oxes, gooses*), the attachment of *-s* to zero marked plural forms (e.g. *three sheeps, two corns*), and the redundant marking of irregular plurals (e.g. *firemens*). In this regard, these varieties are no different from other vernacular dialects of American English.

Some noun phrase differences involve selection restrictions with articles. Certain types of diseases, for example, may routinely take an article (e.g. *the earache, the toothache, the colic*); in most mainstream varieties they do not take an article. Enclave dialect communities also tend to have a small set of unique lexical items referring to local geography (e.g. *up the beach* for 'off the island' in Ocracoke, *on the swamp* for 'neighborhood' in the Lumbee community), terms differentiating locals from outsiders (e.g. *dingbatters* for outsiders versus *O'cockers* for native islanders on the island of Ocracoke) and terms for community-based social distinctions. For example, *swamp Indian* and *brickhouse Indian* are Lumbee designations for high-status and low-status community residents and the term *Lum* is reserved for a person who has a strong sense of Native American identity. Lexical differences of this type must, of course, be catalogued on a community-by-community basis.

Pronominal differences also characterize enclave dialect communities. Most Southeastern US enclave situations participate to some extent in the widespread Southern use of second plural *y'all*. In highland regions of Southern Appalachia, *you'uns* is an alternate form for second person plurals, including some African Americans who live in this highland region. The retention of the -*'n* suffix in *his'n, her'n* in non-attributive position, as in *It's his'n, not her'n* is still found in highland enclave communities, but it is receding rapidly. The use of *me* as a possessive in *I lost me cap* is also found to a limited degree among some elderly speakers in highland and coastal communities.

Enclave varieties share the widespread Southern benefactive dative in sentences like *I got me a new car*, as well as null subject pronouns in embedded sentences such as *It's a man come over here yesterday*. The use of *what* as a relative pronoun in *That's the man what I was talking about* is rarely found, though there are vestiges of it in a few elderly speakers. Elderly speakers may also still show remnants of pronominal attachment in which the *wh*-form follows rather than precedes *ever*, as in *everwhat, everwho*, and *everhow* (e.g. *I do everwhat he says*), though these forms are rarely if ever found among middle-aged and younger speakers.

Enclave dialects share in the widespread vernacular regularization of reflexives *hisself* and *theirselves* as in *He washed hisself* and *They washed theirselves*; the use of objective forms as demonstratives in *I brought them dogs*; and the use of objective forms of the pronoun in coordinates in *Me and him got it*. Finally, we should note the prominence of existential *it* in *It's a new person here* for *There's a new person here*. While a couple of dialects we have examined occasionally use *they* as an existential in *They's a new person here*, existential *it* is much more pervasive.

3.5.   Prepositions

A number of prepositional differences typify enclave dialect areas, but most are lexically specific and therefore have to be discussed on an item-by-item basis. One of the common traits is the use of genitive phrases rather than temporal locatives for times of the day and the seasons, as in *She'll be there of the morning* or *You should plant of the fall*. Island communities regularly use the preposition *to* for static locatives in *She's to the dock* or *She's to the restaurant* where other English dialects use *at*. There are other differences, but they relate to individual lexical items and phrases rather than general patterns, as in *upside the head* for 'on the side of', *agin* for 'against', *across the beach* for *on the beach*, and so forth. Some differences apply to verb + particle combinations rather than prepositions *per se*, as in *bless out* for 'curse' (e.g. *They blessed him out*), *happen in* (e.g. *The happened in on us*), *left out* (e.g. *They left out the house*), and so forth.

4.   Conclusion

We summarize our conclusions in several comparative charts. Descriptive studies of enclave communities include European American island communities on the Outer Banks (Wolfram and Schilling-Estes 1997; Wolfram, Hazen and Schilling-Estes 1999) and in the Chesapeake Bay (Schilling-Estes 1997; Schilling-Estes and Wolfram 1999; Shores 2000); bi-ethnic coastal communities (Wolfram and Thomas 2002) and highland communities (Mallinson and Wolfram 2002); and the tri-ethnic community in which the Lumbee Native Americans reside (Wolfram and Dannenberg 1999; Dannenberg 2003). To situate these varieties in terms of a broader base of vernacular varieties, general Southern rural vernacular English and non-Southern Northern vernacular English are included, based on works such as Wolfram and Fasold (1974), and Wolfram and Schilling-Estes (1998). Separate tables are given for the verb phrase (Table 1), for nominals (Table 2), and for other structures, including negatives, adverbs, and prepositions (Table 3). In the comparison, a check ✓ indicates that the feature is present and parentheses around the check (✓) indicate that the feature is infrequent. The checklist is naturally subject to the usual kinds of limitations associated with qualitative summary inventories of this type.

Table 1.   Comparative dialect profile of the verb phrase

Grammatical Structure	Euro. Am. Coastal	Afr. Am. Coastal	Euro. Am. Highland	Afr. Am. Highland	Lumbee English	Rural Southern (Euro. Am.)	Non-Southern
a-prefixing e.g. *He was a-fishin'*	✓	(✓)	✓	(✓)	✓	(✓)	
3rd pl. *-s* marking e.g. *The dogs barks*	✓	✓	✓	✓	✓		
3rd sg. *-s* absence e.g. *The dog bark*		✓		✓			
Finite *be* e.g. *It bes like that*		(✓)		(✓)	✓		
Copula absence *are*; e.g. *You ugly*		✓	(✓)	✓	(✓)	✓	
is; e.g. *He ugly*		✓		(✓)			
Perfective *be* e.g. *I'm been there*	(✓)	(✓)			✓		
I might be done it					✓		
weren't regularization e.g. *It weren't me*	✓	✓			✓		
Completive *done* e.g. *He done fixed it*	✓	✓	✓	✓	(✓)	✓	
Counterfactual *liketa* e.g. *I liketa died*	✓	✓	✓	✓	✓	✓	
Double modals e.g. *He might could come*	✓	✓	✓	✓	✓	✓	
for to complement e.g. *I want for to get it*	✓	✓	✓	✓	✓		
causative *have…to* e.g. *I have him to do it*	✓	✓	✓	✓	✓	✓	
was/were regularization e.g. *We was there*	✓	✓	✓	✓	✓	✓	✓
irregular verb (1) generalized past/part. e.g. *She had came here*	✓ ✓	✓ ✓	✓ ✓	✓ ✓	✓ ✓	✓ ✓	✓ ✓
(2) generalized part./past e.g. *She done it*	✓	✓	✓	✓	✓	✓	✓
(3) bare root as past e.g. *She give him a dog*	✓	✓	✓	✓	✓	✓	✓
(4) regularization e.g. *She knowed him*	✓	✓	✓	✓	✓	✓	✓
(5) different irregular e.g. *He retch up the roof*	(✓)		✓				

Table 2.   Comparative dialect profile of nominals

Grammatical Structure	Euro. Am Coastal	Afr. Am. Coastal	Euro. Am. Highland	Afr. Am. Highland	Lumbee English	Rural Southern (Euro. Am.)	Non-Southern
-*s*-pl absence, measure nouns e.g. *40 pound_*	✓	✓	✓	✓	✓	(✓)	
Long plural with -*s* + stop e.g. *postes*	✓	(✓)	✓	(✓)	✓		
Regularized plurals e.g. *oxes, sheeps*	✓	✓	✓	✓	✓	✓	✓
2nd pl. *y'all* e.g. *Y'all are a crowd*	✓	✓	✓	✓	✓	✓	
2nd pl. *you'ns* e.g. *You'uns are a crowd*			✓	(✓)			
Absolute –'*n* e.g. *It's his'n*			✓				
Benefactive dative e.g. *I got me a new bike*	✓	✓	✓	✓	✓	✓	
ever + pronoun e.g. *everwhat, everwho*	(✓)		(✓)		(✓)		
Expletive *it* e.g. *It's nothing to do it*	✓	✓	✓	✓	✓	✓	(✓)
Embedded null subject pro e.g. *It's a woman come here*	✓	✓	✓	✓	✓	✓	
Pronominal *what* *The man what I talked to*	(✓)	(✓)	(✓)		(✓)		
Regularized reflexives e.g. *He washed hisself*	✓	✓	✓	✓	✓	✓	✓
Objective demonstratives e.g. *them people*	✓	✓	✓	✓	✓	✓	✓

Table 3.   Comparative dialect profile: Negation, adverbs, prepositions

Grammatical Structure	Euro. Am Coastal	Afr. Am. Coastal	Euro. Am. Highland	Afr. Am. Highland	Lumbee English	Rural Southern (Euro. Am.)	Non-Southern (Euro. Am.)
NEGATION							
Postverbal concord e.g. *It wasn't nothing*	✓	✓	✓	✓	✓	✓	✓
preverbal concord e.g. *Nobody don't like it*	✓	✓	✓	✓	✓	✓	
Affirmative negative inversion e.g. *Didn't nobody like it*	(✓)	(✓)	✓	✓	(✓)	✓	
ain't for *be + not, have + not* e.g. *She ain't there*	✓	✓	✓	✓	✓	✓	✓
nary e.g. *It's nary a fish*	✓	(✓)	✓	(✓)			
ADVERBS							
Verb phrase placement e.g. *We once and a while travel*	✓	✓	✓	✓	✓		
Positive *anymore* e.g. *We watch DVDs anymore*	✓	(✓)	✓	(✓)	(✓)		(✓)
Punctual *whenever* e.g. *Whenever I lost my mother*	(✓)	(✓)	✓	(✓)			
Intensifying *right* e.g. *He's right smart*	✓	✓	✓	✓	✓	✓	
Absolute *plumb* e.g. *They fell plumb asleep*	✓	✓	✓	✓	(✓)	(✓)	
Intensifying *-some* e.g. *The food was good-some*	✓	(✓)					
Regularized comparatives e.g. *It's the most beautifulest*	✓	✓	✓	✓	✓	✓	✓
PREPOSITIONS							
Genitive time and season e.g. *She's there of the morning*	✓	(✓)	✓	(✓)			
Static locative *to* e.g. *She's to the dock*	✓	✓	(✓)				

The comparison reveals that enclave communities in the Southeast share the majority of their dialect structures with other vernaculars of English, particularly Southern rural vernacular varieties. At the same time, there are distinctive traits that set them apart. Some of these traits are shared by all of the enclave varieties we have surveyed but a few structures are unique to a particular enclave dialect community or a subset of communities. Distinctive traits may represent conservative language change and founder effects, but they may also indicate accommodation from language contact and independent language change. The resultant configuration may unite different enclave dialects with each other and with more widespread vernacular dialects, following the principle of *vernacular dialect congruity*, but the constellation of changes may also set apart these varieties from each other and from other dialects. Although dialect surveys of the South and of American English sometimes overlook the role of longstanding enclave dialects, these varieties are clearly an essential part of the unique dialect landscape of the American South.

*   Support for research reported here comes from NSF Grants BCS-0236838 and BCS-9910024, SBR-961633, and SBR-9319577; HHS Grant MCJ-370599, MCJ-370649, and the William C. Friday Endowment at North Carolina State University. Thanks to Becky Childs, Clare Dannenberg, Elaine W. Green, Kirk Hazen, Christine Mallinson, Jeffrey Reaser, Natalie Schilling-Estes, Erik R. Thomas, and Benjamin Torbert for research that contributed to this survey.

Exercises and study questions

1. Discuss the construct "historical isolation" as a factor in describing the development of unique dialects in the American South. What are some the primary social and historical conditions contributing to linguistic insularity, and what are some limitations to the construct "enclave dialect community"?

2. Discuss how different processes in language change function to account for similarities and differences in enclave dialect situations. What kinds of language structures seem to be shared by different enclave communities, and why?

3. Although it is often assumed that "relic forms" are common in enclave dialect situations, we have seen that there is reason to question this assumption. To what extent might this assumption be valid? What are some of its obvious limitations?

4. Listen to several of the speakers representing enclave dialect communities on the CD-ROM. List some of the traits that they seem to share and some of the traits that distinguish them.

5. The perfective use of *be* in sentences such as *I'm been there for a long time now* is not uncommon in different enclave dialect communities. At the same time, its use in these communities may vary considerably. How does this variance reflect the dynamic development of retentive forms in historically isolated dialect communities?

6. In the US today, the use of *weren't* regularization in sentences such as *It weren't me* seems to be found only in isolated dialects along the Southeastern coast. How might this regional dimension of *weren't* regularization have developed to begin with, and why does it appear to be intensifying in some communities along the Southeastern coast?

Selected references

Please consult the General references for titles mentioned in the text but not included in the references below. For a full bibliography see the accompanying CD-ROM.

Andersen, Henning
    1988   Center and periphery: Adoption, diffusion, and spread. In: Jacek Fisiak
              (ed.), *Historical Dialectology*, 39–83. Berlin/New York: Mouton de
              Gruyter.
Chambers, J.K.
    1995   *Sociolinguistic Theory*. Malden/Oxford: Blackwell.
Dannenberg, Clare
    2003   *Sociolinguistic Constructs of Identity: The Syntactic Delineation of a
              Native American English Variety*. (Publication of the American Dialect
              Society No. 87.) Durham: Duke University Press.
Mallinson, Christine, and Walt Wolfram
    2002   Dialect accommodation in a bi-ethnic mountain enclave community: More
              evidence on the development of African American Vernacular English.
              Language in Society 31: 743–775.
Montgomery, Michael
    1989   The roots of Appalachian English. *English World-Wide* 10: 227–278.
Montgomery, Michael and Margaret Mishoe
    1999   "He bes took up with a Yankee girl and moved up North": The verb bes in
              the Carolinas and its history. *American Speech* 75: 240–281.

Montgomery, Michael B. and Joseph S. Hall
   2004   *A Dictionary of Smoky Mountain English.* Knoxville: University of
            Tennessee Press.
Schilling-Estes, Natalie
   1997   Accommodation vs. concentration: Dialect death in two post-insular is-
            land communities. *American Speech* 72: 12–32.
Schilling-Estes, Natalie, and Walt Wolfram
   1999   Alternative models of dialect death: Dissipation vs. concentration.
            Language 75: 486–521.
Shores, David L.
   2000   *Tangier Island: People, Place, and Talk.* Newark: University of Delaware
            Press.
Wolfram, Walt, and Natalie Schilling-Estes
   1997   *Hoi Toide on the Outer Banks: The Story of the Ocracoke Brogue.* Chapel
            Hill/London: The University of North Carolina Press.
Wolfram, Walt, and Jason Sellers
   1999   Ethnolinguistic marking of past *be* in Lumbee Vernacular English. *Journal
            of English Linguistics* 27: 94–114.
Wolfram, Walt, and Clare Dannenberg
   1999   Dialect identity in a tri-ethnic context: The case of Lumbee American
            Indian English. *English World-Wide* 20: 79–116
Wolfram, Walt, and Natalie Schilling-Estes
   2003   Language change in 'conservative' dialects: Evidence from Southern
            American enclave communities. *American Speech* 78: 208–227.

Newfoundland English: morphology and syntax

Sandra Clarke

1.   Introduction

The corresponding chapter on Newfoundland phonology of this volume (see Clarke, this volume) provides a brief sociohistorical introduction to the English spoken in the easternmost Canadian province of Newfoundland and Labrador (NfldE). As outlined therein, the distinctiveness of NfldE was shaped by a number of factors: fairly homogeneous founder populations that originated almost exclusively in southwest England and southeast Ireland; the region's peripheral geographic location, which promoted linguistic conservatism; and the general lack of economic incentives for substantial in-migration. Another important factor was the time-depth of British settlement of the area. As Kirwin (2001: 444) points out, "Newfoundland English, especially its common and folk varieties, began its development well before many English speakers had settled in the present area of Canada and at least 200 years before the United Province of Canada was created in 1841 or the Dominion of Canada in 1867".

World War II and union with Canada in 1949 played crucial roles in building and strengthening Newfoundland's ties with mainland North America. The effects on local speech varieties have been substantial – particularly with respect to the accents of younger urban speakers and younger females in general, who are increasingly adopting supralocal pronunciations, particularly in their more formal interactions. Apart from a few shibboleths of pronunciation, local non-standard grammatical features tend to be more stigmatized than local phonological features, and more subject to overt commentary and correction (as witnessed, for example, by their general absence from the Newfoundland English taped samples which accompany this volume). Yet these features – which typically represent morphosyntactic patterns inherited from source varieties in the West Country and southeast Ireland (cf. the chapters by Wagner and Filppula, British Isles volume), with possible reshaping in the Newfoundland context – have survived remarkably well as markers of local identity, especially in the many tiny fishing communities which dot the coastline. The English and the Irish founder groups for the most part settled different areas of the island, and a number of these features continue to distinguish the speech of descendants of these two groups, though some have diffused across the ethnolinguistic boundary.

For the most part, the features documented in this chapter are associated with the vernacular grammars of working-class rural residents of Newfoundland. Today, some are fairly recessive, and would have been much more common a generation or two ago. The grammatical systems of educated and urban middle-class Newfoundlanders closely resemble those of their counterparts elsewhere in Canada, with some small exceptions. Since a number of the features outlined below diverge markedly from features associated with the grammars of most North American native English speakers of European origin, the range of grammatical diversity is considerably greater in Newfoundland than in much of the North American mainland. The parallels between vernacular NfldE and both African American and Caribbean Englishes are, however, at times quite striking – an observation that is less surprising than it might first appear, given the time-depth of settlement in all three cases, as well as similarities in the geographical origins of the European founder populations of Newfoundland, parts of the American South, and the Caribbean.

This chapter draws on a number of sources of information on NfldE grammatical features, among them Noseworthy (1971), Paddock (1981), Halpert and Widdowson (1996), Clarke (1997a,b), as well as the vernacular taped corpus collected in the south coast community of Burin by Catherine Lanari, phonological aspects of which are reported on in Lanari (1994). Much valuable information has also been obtained from tape recordings of older, rural and conservative speakers held by the Memorial University Folklore and Language Archive (MUNFLA). The majority of examples presented below were obtained from these recordings, as well as the sources named above, in particular Halpert and Widdowson (1996). Unfortunately, space generally does not permit mention of the precise source of each example cited. In order to convey some flavour of the actual pronunciations used, these examples often include eye-dialect representation, in particular *d* for *th* (e.g. *dey*), and indication of loss of syllable-initial *h* (e.g. *'ouse* for *house*).

The works cited in both Newfoundland chapters of this volume, as well as in the general bibliography, provide many further details on particular features, as well as illustrations of them. Information on the history and development of NfldE is also to be found in a number of these sources, in particular Kirwin (1993, 2001).

2.   The verb phrase

Like English varieties in general, vernacular NfldE – understood as the conservative casual speech styles associated primarily with older, working-class, rural residents of the province – displays a simple verbal morphology. Temporal representation is based on a bipartite tense system which opposes past and non-past (present), and is encoded for the majority of verbs via a suffixal inflectional morphology. With the exception of several suffixes (notably *-ing*, representing an event in progress), aspect and modality are encoded via a set of preverbal markers which often surface – as in other spoken varieties – in reduced phonological form, e.g. *I'll* (< *will*) *do it, I'd* (< *would*) *like to*, both of which represent irrealis modality. Vernacular NfldE, however, is characterized by its degree of phonological reduction of pre- and post-verbal morphology; as outlined below, a frequent outcome is the apparent absence of overt surface morphological marking. The verbal system of vernacular NfldE differs from that of standard English in several principal areas: its aspectual system, in particular the representation of habitual and perfect aspect; the regularization of irregular past forms; and non-past subject-verb agreement.

2.1.   Habitual aspect

As in Standard English, the simple forms of verbs (e.g. *I see/saw her; They run/ran every day*) represent a range of aspectual meanings, notably habitual, durative/continuous and punctual. Like other varieties, NfldE displays the past habitual marker [justə] (e.g. *We used to go there all the time*), with preverbal (*woul)d* an alternative option (*Whenever we saw it we'd shout out*). Unlike most varieties, however, vernacular NfldE displays use of the suffix *-s* throughout the entire non-past paradigm (e.g. *we/they goes*). While suffixed verbs carry the same range of aspectual meanings as do non-suffixed forms (*we/they go*), they are most frequently associated with habitual meaning (see Clarke 1997a) – just as in a number of other dialects in which they have been investigated, among them diaspora African American English varieties, as well as conservative Devon English (Poplack and Tagliamonte 2001).

The verb *be* stands out in terms of aspectual representation. This verb has two sets of non-past stems: a standard set (i.e. *am/is/are*); and the stem *be*, which represents habitual, and occasionally durative, aspect. Though it is categorically marked with the suffix *-s* in NfldE, the latter closely resembles invariant *be* in conservative African American Vernacular English (AAVE) in terms of semantic function – see for example Wolfram (on AAVE, this volume). This yields oppositions such as *They bees sick* (*all the time, often*) vs.

They're sick (right now). Habitual *bees* – today fairly recessive – is most associated with areas of the province settled by the southwest English. Though this form is also attested on the Irish-settled Avalon peninsula in the southeast corner of the province, Irish-settled areas are characterized by a competing habitual variant, unstressed periphrastic *do* [də] *be*, as in *He do be sick some lot*. Today, however, the *do be* variant is highly recessive. Since in the negative and interrogative habitual *be* requires *do*-support, just as in AAVE, *bees* and *do be* are indistinguishable in such contexts, where their frequency is perhaps greater than in affirmative declaratives (e.g. *Do he be sick a lot?*; *They don't be here that often*). The *be* stem is also fairly frequently encountered in *don't be* V-*ing* constructions, particularly in negative imperatives conveying disapproval (e.g. *Don't be goin' on like that*); apart from the Irish-inherited idiom *Don't be talkin'*, these typically permit a habitual reading in addition to that of a single-event-related durative.

2.2.   The perfect: competing variants

As in standard varieties of English, the NfldE perfect consists of *have/had* + past participle; an older form of the latter, involving the prefix *a-*, occurred variably among Newfoundland vernacular speakers born prior to 1900, particularly in areas of the province settled by the southwest English, as in *(they've) abeen, acome, adrinked, ahung, aput, atried*. The *have*-perfect is however in competition with a number of other variants in NfldE, and is often not the form of choice to represent past events with present relevance, even on the part of educated speakers. As in North American English in general, these variants include the simple past form (e.g. *I just saw her*). They also include forms constructed with the (non-past) auxiliary *be* rather than *have*, an option restricted to verbs which involve a change of state: thus *They're already left*; *You're come again*; *They're turned in (i.e. gone to bed) now*; *Are you finished?*; *Times are changed*.

Three other perfect forms in NfldE are inherited from source regional varieties in the British Isles and Ireland (for more details on each, see Clarke 1997b). The first, often termed the "resultative" or "accomplishment" perfect, reflects an earlier perfect construction in which the past participle follows rather than precedes the direct object of a transitive verb (as in *I got a lot of it forgot, see*; *After he had the two of 'em killed*; *They got money enough sove up*, the latter two from Halpert and Widdowson 1996). This construction regularly occurs in NfldE, as in other varieties for which it has been documented, with dynamic rather than stative verbs, e.g. *they('ve) got it built (already)*, but not *they('ve) got it loved*.

The second is the Irish "*after* perfect" *be* + *after* + V-*ing*, as in *I'm (al-ready) after doin' that*, which though most frequent on the southeastern, Irish-settled Avalon peninsula area is by no means limited to this portion of the province. The *after*-perfect displays the full semantic range associated with the *have*-perfect, including the representation of a long-standing event with present relevance, e.g. *I'm after havin' eleven rabbits eaten (by dogs) this last three months*; *I'm after burning now (in the sun) about three times*. The NfldE *after*-form is thus not restricted, as apparently it may be in some varieties of Irish English, to a "hot news" representation of a very recent event. For deep vernacular or basilectal speakers in Irish-settled areas of the province, the *af-ter*-perfect constitutes the usual variant in affirmative statements, though it is less commonly found in negatives and interrogatives. Even speakers who do not use the form regularly may have recourse to it to emphasize the negative consequences of an event (e.g. *She's after gettin' some fat*; *Now you're really after doin' it* – i.e., 'You're in real trouble now').

While both the accomplishment perfect and the *after*-perfect are frequently encountered in present-day NfldE, this is not the case of the third inherited variant, which likewise occurs in Irish-settled areas of the province. This is the use of a simple non-past form to represent an event that began in the past and continues through the moment of speech, as in the example *I'm off* ('not employed') *a year now*, from Lanari's Burin corpus.

The most striking perfect variant in NfldE is a highly localized one, docu-mented to date only on the south coast Burin peninsula area of the island. This is a form consisting of the auxiliary *been* (pronounced [bɪn]) plus past parti-ciple, as in the following examples, from Noseworthy (1971: 69): *I been heard it* ('I heard it'); *Have 'ee (< dee, i.e. 'thee') been eat?* ('Have you eaten?'); *been* + past participle also appears after *ain't* ('haven't'), as in *I ain't been done it*. According to Noseworthy, these forms appear to represent an event that occurred further in the past than an event represented by the *have*-perfect. There are obvious parallels here with AAVE – indeed, this NfldE usage may possibly constitute the only documented case of "remote *been*" outside African American varieties.

2.3.   Irregular verbs: past forms

Like other vernacular varieties of English, vernacular NfldE displays extensive reg-ularization of its irregular (i.e. "strong" or "mixed") past forms, those in which the past tense and past participle are based primarily on vowel change (e.g. *drive, drove, have driven*; *catch, caught, have caught*) rather than the regular pattern of suffix -*ed* addition (e.g. *like, liked, have liked*). As outlined below, three basic patterns of regularization are in evidence: the first involves incorporation of irregular verbs into the regular *-ed* paradigm; the second and third, morphological levelling through generalization of either the past tense or past participle as a single past form. Some verbs display more than one pattern of morphological levelling; regional and social correlates for individual verb usage have yet to be described in any detail.

(1) Irregular verbs regularized by addition of the *-ed* suffix to the non-past stem, resulting in such past tense/participle forms as *blowed, comed, dealed, drinked, falled (down), freezed (up), goed, growed, heared, knowed, leaved, lied (down), maked, runned, seed, teached, throwed.*

(2) Past tense generalized as a single past form, replacing the past participle, as in *Have they drove home already?*; *He haven't went there yet*; *Have she tore her jacket?*; *They've took it back*; also *drank, wore.*

(3) Past participle with or without the suffix *-(e)n* generalized as a single past form, as in *They done/seen/sung/rung it (already)*; *He swum across the pond*; *It riz* (rather than *rose*) *up good*; past tense *become, begun*. These cases may involve verbs in which the vowel of the past participle coincides with that of the non-past form, giving the appearance of generalization of the bare root (e.g. *She come here last week*; *He already eat it*; *They give 'im a good talking-to*).

Minor regularization processes also characterize NfldE, among them the double marking of past forms (e.g. *drownded, ownded, bursted, beated*, as well as *frozed*). Many past participles in *-en* lose the participle marker (e.g. *I haven't forgot*; *Have the bread riz yet?*). At the same time, new irregular past forms have appeared, including *scrope* for *scraped*, and *sove* and *wove* rather than *saved* and *waved* (cf. general North American *dove* instead of *dived*). Some irregular verbs exhibit past forms that differ phonetically from those of standard: these include *sot* instead of *sat* as the generalized past of *sit* (*They sot down*), *bet* as the past of *beat*, and [mɛd] as the past of *make*. An extremely recessive variant of the regular verb past suffix /əd/ contains a tense vowel ([id]), and has been attested in such verbs as *fittied, loadied*, and *wan(t)ied.*

2.4.   Subject-verb agreement

As noted earlier, the *-s* suffix occurs readily throughout the non-past lexical verb paradigm. This is the case no matter what the person and number of the subject (*I likes, we eats, they runs, the dogs barks*). Suffixation is not constrained in vernacular NfldE, as in a number of varieties, by the nominal vs. pronominal nature of the grammatical subject: *-s* marking is as common with adjacent personal pronoun subjects as with other subject types (see Clarke 1997a). The *-s* suffix thus serves as a generalized (though variable) non-past tense marker for lexical verbs. Though it is confined to casual speech styles, it none the less commonly occurs in both rural and urban NfldE. Cross-dialect comparison rates (see Godfrey and Tagliamonte 1999) suggest that verbal *-s* is more frequent in NfldE than in other vernacular varieties in which it has been documented (e.g. Devon English, diaspora AAVE).

Have and *do* exhibit special status in vernacular NfldE. As in southwest England, there is a morphological distinction between their function as lexical verbs and as auxiliaries: among conservative speakers, the former are marked with *-s* for all grammatical subjects, while the latter take a zero suffix. In addition, analogical levelling may affect the verb stem, yielding *haves* and *doos* [duz] throughout the non-past lexical verb paradigm (see Table 1).

Table 1.   Have and *do* in vernacular NfldE

Have/do as lexical verb	*Have/do* as auxiliary
She does/doos lovely drawings.	*He don't want to leave*; *Do she want to see you?*
They does/doos a lot of good work.	*Don't they want to go tomorrow?*
He has/haves a new car.	*He haven't got no fire*; *Have she left already?*
They has/haves their dinner early.	*They haven't seen her yet*

Though (non-habitual) *be* does not display a parallel suffixal contrast between auxiliary and non-auxiliary function, its paradigm is characterized by analogical levelling of the verb stem, in both the non-past and past tenses. Thus 1st singular *am* (*'m*) may generalize to all other persons, i.e. *we'm, you'm, they'm,* (*s)he'm*; more rarely, 3rd singular *is* (*'s*) is extended to the 1st and 2nd persons, as well as the 3rd plural (*I's, we's, you's, they's*). However, these regularized non-past auxiliary and copula forms are now extremely recessive. In the past tense, *was*-levelling is considerably more common, e.g. *We was down there*; *They was some mad*; *I knowed you waddn('t)* ('wasn't') *happy*. Third singular indicative *were*, e.g. *he were(n't) sick*, has also been attested, though very rarely; its occurrence in the subjunctive is more common in NfldE, particularly in standard varieties (e.g. *I wish she were here*), along with non-past subjunctive *be* (e.g. *They requested that he be there tomorrow*). A century ago, highly conservative forms of (indicative) *be* were in evidence, including the 2nd singular *dee* (< *thee*) subject forms *dee bis(t)* ('you are'), *bain't (d)ee* ('aren't you?').

2.5. Absence of surface marking

Vernacular NfldE is characterized by a number of phonological processes, notably assimilation and consonant cluster reduction, which may result in loss of overt morphological marking. Most striking here is final /t/ and /d/ deletion, which affects the past tense and participle not only of historically regular verbs that form their pasts through addition of *-ed*, but also the many irregular verbs which have been absorbed into this class. To the untrained ear in particular, there often appears to be no phonetic difference between bare (non-past) and past forms in such verbs as *slip, live, happen, as(k)* (e.g. *He live there for years*), as well as in regularized verbs like *begin, drink, fall, run, see, throw*, etc. (e.g. *She fall down and broke her leg*; *They begin to eat*). While the /t/ or /d/ of the suffix is more likely to be articulated before a vowel, it may be absent even in pre-vocalic environment. The suffix may also be deleted in verbs ending in an alveolar stop (e.g. *invite, start, persuade, pound*) where standard varieties require the /əd/ allomorph, resulting in such past forms as *He pound on the door*; *They start back to the road*; *De woman want me 10 years longer and I wouldn' stay* .

Likewise, preverbal aspect and modality markers, notably *'ll* (< *will*), *'d* (< *would*), *'ve* (< *have*) are subject to deletion, particularly but by no means solely in pre-consonantal position. This gives rise to such apparently unmarked surface strings as the following, all from an older rural female speaker:

(*Woul*)*d* deletion	*Father p'raps bring over one in de spring when he go fishin'.*
	The name of it be cobe I believe. (speaking of the best-quality flour)
(*Ha*)*ve* deletion	*How long de sacks been gone?*

Rapid speech processes may also result in deletion of unstressed auxiliaries and even occasionally copula *be*, as in *... when dey (were) up dere*.

Deep vernacular speakers are characterized by a high rate of application of the phonological processes noted above. The overall effect is that of a minimally marked, almost creole-like verbal system containing two principal suffixes, non-past *-s* and progressive/continuative *-in'* (*-ing*). Since unmarked surface forms carry a range of verbal functions (past tense, past participle, "future", past habitual, etc.), disambiguation is often context-dependent.

2.6.   Other verb phrase structures

Vernacular NfldE contains many verb + particle constructions. These may correspond to simple verbs in standard varieties, but may also offer a more succinct representation of an event than the standard provides. They include *pass out* ('die'); *kill up* (e.g. *he killed it up wit' de gun*); *sing out* 'call [out]'); *come in* (e.g. *when de trawlers come in*, i.e. 'were first introduced'); *go out* (*I ain't made much in jars since de molasses wen' out*, i.e. 'since they stopped getting molasses'). At least one of these has undergone nominalization, and occurs in the common phrase *(the) last goin'-off*, meaning 'finally, at the end'.

A number of verb phrases common in NfldE are not generally found in standard varieties. Among these are counterfactual *had liketa* ('had like to'), as in *I had liketa lose all my money*, as well as *hear tell of* in the sense of 'hear of'.

3.   Negation

Negation patterns in vernacular NfldE are similar to those found in other vernacular varieties of English. Negative concord is commonplace, and usually involves double negative marking, as in *(He) couldn't get no further*, *I don't want no dinner* (Halpert and Widdowson 1996 contains many such examples). A clause-initial negative indefinite may be followed by a negated verb, as in *Nobody don't recognize him* ('Nobody recognizes him'). *Never* is commonly used as a generalized negator instead of *not*, whether on its own (*That time she never come up so far*) or in combination (*Nobody never came*). As in other varieties, preverbal *ain't* is used to negate both non-past *be* and auxiliary *have*. The latter is illustrated by the following examples from a traditional rural speaker, the second of which displays multiple negation: *You ain't asked me about makin' butter yet*; *I don't have no breakfast when I ain't got none* (i.e. 'cereal'). However, the use of *ain't* appears to have declined considerably in recent years; an alternative variant of *haven't* – *(h)an't* – has all but disappeared. Negatives may also occur with *only* or *but*, as in *We couldn' have 'em only once a day*, meaning 'It was only once a day that we could have them'.

Several fairly common vernacular NfldE negators exhibit a distinctive phonetic form. *(T)iddn'* '(it) isn't' and *(t)waddn'* '(it) wasn't' derive from sibilant assimilation (see Clarke, this volume), yielding examples like *Tiddn' no good if tiddn' good is it?* ('It isn't good if it isn't good is it?') and *I waddn'* ('I wasn't') *getting' enough to eat*. Negative *weredn'(t)*, presumably an analogical form, is also attested, though much less frequently. *Neither*, typically realized as *nar* or *ne'er* [nɛɹ], has the generalized indefinite meaning of 'no' or 'none', as in ...

couldn' get nar drink; *There's nar one of 'em livin' in dat 'ouse* (i.e. 'None of them is living in that house'). Its affirmative counterpart is *ar* (< *either*), meaning 'any', as in *Ar water in that?*.

4. The noun phrase

While vernacular NfldE exhibits several nominal features that distinguish it from standard varieties, distinctions are particularly marked with respect to pronominals.

4.1. Noun plurals

In NfldE, nouns follow the regular pattern of *-s* plural marking, outside of a phenomenon often attested in vernacular varieties: the absence of a plural suffix in phrases involving a numerical quantifier (e.g. *three ton of bricks, ten mile*). Even when the quantified noun displays plural marking, it may be processed as a notional singular, as indicated by the singular determiner agreement in a phrase like *this last three months*.

NfldE makes frequent use of the associative plural *and* (*th*)*em*, to designate family, friends, or habitual associates. Though this feature has been claimed to be of creole origin, its appearance in a number of vernacular varieties of English suggests a regional British ancestry. In NfldE, *and they* occurs as a less frequent associative plural variant, along with possessive *and their*(*s*): *How's Joan and them makin' out?*; *Mr. Edwards and they teached our Pad*; *He went for Bob's and their sister* (all from Lanari's 1994 Burin corpus). A corresponding *and that* form is also found as an inanimate pluralizer.

4.2. Determiners

In NfldE, the definite article is often used as a proximal demonstrative with measures of time, e.g. *the fall, the year*, meaning 'this (past or coming) fall, year'. *Them* is frequent as a distal demonstrative meaning 'those' as in *them days* 'times past', *them sheep over there*; an alternative variant is *they*, e.g. *for to lanch* ('launch') *one o' dey schooners*. In generic NPs, *the* may occur in more conservative varieties of NfldE in instances where present-day standard English would opt either for no article (e.g. *in the bed*; *with the fright*; *he was fond of the gun*) or else for indefinite *a*(*n*), e.g. *when they'd get the cold*; *lots o' times when I had de cow*.

4.3.   Noun + prepositional phrase

Vernacular NfldE is characterized by a number of noun + PP constructions in which the prepositional phrase is often redundant, among them *the spring/fall of the year, a meal of food, a job of work*. Similar to this is the following now recessive construction, from a speaker born before 1900: *There was tree* ('three') *brothers of 'em*; *There was tree sisters o' we*.

4.4.   Pronominals

The pronominal system of vernacular NfldE exhibits a number of features inherited from southwest England, which have continued for the most part to be restricted to areas of the province that were settled by the English rather than the Irish. Though today these features are stereotypically associated with conservative rural working-class speech, many are in common use among younger residents of rural communities. They include grammatical gender for inanimates; the object pronoun *en/un*; and pronoun exchange. In addition, both Irish- and English-settled areas of the province display a number of inherited second person pronouns, while all NfldE vernacular varieties are characterized by several pronominal features that occur in many parts of the English-speaking world. The latter include reflexives based on a possessive stem (e.g. *hisself, theirselves*); the unstressed possessive determiner *me* (e.g. *me book*), which also appears in *meself*; and the somewhat less common existential *it*, as in *'Cause 'tis a big beach down Little Harbour where de caplin rolls in*; *Lot o' guys through here this year, is it?*; *There should be more people coming though, I thinks, than it do*. Finally, Pro-drop, or the deletion of a subject personal pronoun, is extremely common in vernacular NfldE.

4.4.1.   *Grammatical gender*

In the conservative NfldE pronominal system found in English-settled areas of the province (see, e.g., Paddock 1981, 1988), the pronoun *it* refers exclusively to non-count nouns (e.g. *rain, frost, truth*). Count nouns are classified on the basis of mobility: those with non-mobile referents are represented as masculine (*he, his*), and with mobile referents, as feminine (*she, her*). The latter grouping includes ships and vehicles (e.g. *boat, sleigh, car*), as well as such moving objects as waves or the tide, e.g. *In she come again*. The former represents the unmarked or default category, ranging from flora to buildings to computers, e.g. *(H)e's bad*, said of a cut hand, or *(H)e looks good on ya*, said of a coat. Occasionally, feminine gender is found with a wider semantic range than that of mobile object. Though often difficult to gloss, *she/(h)er* in many such examples refer to 'the situation at the time', as in a reference to the economic depression of the 1930s: *Depression, whatever you might call 'er.* Compare the common expression *She's gone, boy, she's gone* (i.e., 'the economic situation is really bad') and an example from Lanari's Burin corpus describing a night out drinking: *Every now and then I gets out and lets 'er go, right, when I get there...* Wagner (2003) contains an excellent overview of gender distribution in NfldE, as well as in its source varieties in southwest England.

4.4.2.　Third person object forms

While standard English uses *him* as both a direct and indirect object pronoun for masculine animates, an alternative variant is common in English-settled areas of Newfoundland, just as in southwest British English. This is the object pronominal *en* or *un* ([ən]), which derives from the historical direct object form (cf. Old English *hine*) rather than the indirect object *him.* In vernacular NfldE, the *en* form is used regularly, in both direct and indirect object contexts, for non-mobile count nouns as well as masculine animates: *He got a half tub o' coal for to carry home with en*; *I fell down and cut en* (i.e., 'hand'); *Why don't ya buy en* ('a coat')? Rarely, the *en* form designates a feminine referent.

4.4.3.　Pronoun exchange

Also inherited from southwest England is the use of subject-like pronouns in stressed object position, as in *... for we fellas*; *And dere was 'Melier* ('Amelia') *next to she* (i.e., 'in age'); *I had to give dey* (i.e., 'oats') *to de hens, once a day*; *Dis doctor (who) was to we* (i.e., 'our doctor'). Though this is a highly salient feature that is subject to overt commentary, it is surprisingly frequent in English-settled rural communities today: Newhook (2002) found it used in approximately one quarter of the stressed object contexts she examined in a small southwest-coast fishing community, with significantly greater usage by males than females. Considerably more rare today is the use of an object-like pronoun in unstressed subject position, as in *Where's 'em* ('them') *to*?

4.4.4.　Second person pronouns

The 2nd singular subject pronoun (*d*)*ee*, from the historical object form *thee* (e.g. *Did 'ee see en*? 'Did you see him/it'?) is nowadays highly recessive in those English-settled areas of the province where it was in common use in former centuries. While *you* (unstressed *ya*) is the usual form in both singular and plural, *yous* (unstressed version [jəz]) is an alternative plural variant in some areas of the province. *Yous* is not however typical of the Irish-settled Avalon, where the usual (stressed) vernacular plural is *ye* [ji], with corresponding possessive form *yeer(s)*. Within a single community, there may be a number of competing variants: among the 2nd person plural forms observed by Noseworthy (1971) in the small English-settled south coast community of Grand Bank are *yous*, *ye all*, *'ee all*, *y'all* and *all yous*.

5.   Other lexical categories

5.1.   Intensifiers

Vernacular NfldE is characterized by a number of adverbial intensifiers that are adjectival in form – that is, intensifiers that have resisted the *-ly* adverbial marker, as has *real* in most vernacular varieties, e.g. *real good*. Among these intensifiers are *wonderful*, *terrible*, and *ugly* (*She was a wonderful smart lookin' girl*; *Them times was terrible bad*). As Paddock (1981) notes, *-ly* is not a productive derivational suffix in vernacular grammar for adverbs in general; rather, *-like* fills this role, e.g. *Foolishlike, I went and stepped on the gas instead of the brake*.

Two adjectivals in present-day standard English are commonly used as adverbial intensifiers in Newfoundland: *right*, and the very frequent *some* as in *He was right strange*; *It was some nice party*. Likewise, forms functioning as adjectives of degree in vernacular NfldE may differ from their standard counterparts, as shown by *all* and *every bit* in the following examples, from a conservative rural speaker: *When we was growin' up sir we had to drink all molasses*; *'Twas every bit fresh butter* (the sense in both is 'nothing but' or 'completely'). A sequence of two adjectives of similar meaning is occasionally used for intensification, as in (*a*) *little small* (*book*). Finally, as in many vernacular varieties, comparatives and superlatives may be doubly marked, e.g. *more handier*, or marked in a non-standard fashion, e.g. *beautifullest*.

5.2.   Prepositions

A common feature among urban and rural Newfoundlanders of all social classes and regions is the use of *to* as a stative as well as a dynamic preposition. Thus *to* may correspond to standard English *at* (e.g. *He sat to the table*; *They knocked to the door*; *Next thing I was to the rock*), or to a zero preposition (*Stay where you're to*). *Into* with a stative meaning (e.g. *This bottle has a cork stopper into it*) is somewhat more restricted in its social distribution. *To* and *in* are frequently absent after directional prepositions like *down*, *up*, *over*, e.g. *down Little Harbour*. Also noteworthy is the Irish-like use of *on* to signify negative impact, as in *It broke on me*; *she* ('a boat') *blowed around twice on he*.

6.   Syntactic patterns

6.1.   Relativization

Relativization strategies in NfldE are similar to those in standard North American English. Ongoing changes include the increased use of *that* with animate referents, to the detriment of *who* (e.g. *the people that's been displaced from their jobs*); and the extension of possessive *whose* to inanimate referents (*a book whose pages were stuck together*), along with innovative *that's* (*an item that's use is declining slightly*). In addition, vernacular NfldE exhibits two non-standard relativization strategies which it shares with other vernacular varieties. The first is the use of *what* as a relative pronoun, as in *red one* ('potato') *what you don't see now very often*; *They couldn't put the milk away ... what come out the cows*. This usage is highly recessive today. The second is much more common, namely, the tendency to delete subject relative pronouns, as in *There's no one pays any attention to that*; *Couple o' fellas got der boats wrecked up in Cow Head is here.*

6.2.   Complementation

Among the features NfldE shares with other vernacular varieties is subject-auxiliary inversion in embedded clauses that would otherwise be introduced by *if* or *whether*, in particular embedded questions (*They asked me did I do that*; *... to see would he meet anybody*). Infinitival phrases of purpose may retain the *for to* [fɚdə] complementizer, which lost out in standard English to the competing variant *to*: *Not a bit o' collection* ('money for the collection plate') *if I want* ('wanted it') *for to carry to church*; *... piled in a lump for to drain out de lye*. The *for to* construction is occasionally found in other types of infinitival complement, as in *I managed for to do it.*

6.3.   Other embedded clauses

Vernacular NfldE makes use of a number of inherited subordinating conjunctions that either belong to a different lexical category in standard English, or else exhibit a somewhat different meaning. These include *(ac)cordin'* (*as*) ('while'), *(a)fraid* ('so that... not, in case'), *till* and *where* (both in the sense of 'so that') and *without* ('unless'):

> *The woman got to watch her steps where she won't go down between*
> *and break her leg*   (Paddock 1981)

> *Bake me (a) cake mother ... till I goes off to see where Tom is*
> (Halpert and Widdowson 1996)

> *And she got to keep her eye on him 'fraid he's going to go off... and fall down...*   (Paddock 1981)

> *The women isn't satisfied now without they'm goin' around stark naked*   (MUNFLA tape C186)

At least one embedded clause type has been inherited from Irish English, and occurs, though infrequently today, in Irish-settled areas of the province. This is the subordinating *and* construction that represents a concessive clause (e.g. *She went out for a walk and it raining*). A present participle may also correspond to a temporal clause introduced by *when*, as in *We comin' along (de) shore, de squalls was dat hard she blowed aroun' twice on he.*

7.   Lexicon

The morphosyntactic structure of vernacular NfldE displays many conservative features inherited from its regional source varieties in southwest England and southeast Ireland. As the *Dictionary of Newfoundland English* (Story, Kirwin and Widdowson [1982] 1990) attests, the same observation may be made of its word stock, which contains numerous lexical and semantic retentions largely unknown in mainland Canada, though some are shared with the Canadian Maritime provinces and to a lesser degree, New England. The Irish Gaelic substratum has given rise to lexical borrowings some of which are in common use today (e.g. *sleveen* 'rascal', *scrob* 'scratch'), and language contact is reflected in a small number of borrowings from French (e.g. *caplin* 'a salt-water smelt') and Inuktitut (e.g. *komatik* 'sleigh'; see Kirwin 2001 for an overview). Other common lexical items were originally nautical terms that have undergone semantic generalization: these include *clew up* in the sense of 'finish' (*They clewed up their work*), *fair* (meaning 'straight' or 'even'), and *rig(-out)*, in the sense of 'clothing'. Some lexical items in frequent use in fishery-related contexts have undergone a more subtle broadening of meaning, such as the verbs *haul* and *hoist* in the examples *haul out a chair* or *hoist a picture up on the wall*. A number of NfldE items represent neologisms, or at least cannot be traced to a precise historical source with any degree of certainty.

8. Conclusion

This brief survey of the salient grammatical features of vernacular NfldE provides some indication of the degree of divergence of this variety from standard North American English. As noted above, a striking characteristic of the grammatical system of NfldE is its conservatism, in the sense of retention of features transported to Newfoundland by early settlers from the British Isles and Ireland. NfldE displays a number of noticeable parallels with other regional and non-standard varieties that have early roots in the New World, among them African American English (e.g. habitual *be*, remote *been*, verbal *-s*, associative noun plurals). Yet though the features documented in this chapter have survived for several centuries, in the past fifty or so years they have come under the increased threat of encroaching supralocal norms. Extensive out-migration to mainland Canada from rural fishing communities – coupled with generally negative attitudes among many younger Newfoundlanders towards overt linguistic symbols of local identity – suggests that these traditional features may play a diminished role in the grammars of future generations.

Exercises and study questions

1. A number of varieties of English use *she* and *her* to refer to inanimate objects, at least in casual styles. Collect some data either on your own, or by investigating what others have written on the subject, and compare your findings to the NfldE system.

2. In vernacular NfldE, what would the sentence *She was ugly pretty* mean? A recent Newfoundland music group known for its traditional repertoire had the name *Wonderful Grand Band*. "Translate" this name into a Standard English equivalent.

3. In NfldE, final /t/ and /d/ are regularly deleted after homorganic nasals and liquids, as in *ground* and *wild*, particularly in pre-pause and pre-consonantal environments. Explain how hypercorrection might lead to such doubly marked past forms as *ownded* instead of *owned* and *drownded* instead of *drowned*.

4. As shown, processes of assimilation and deletion affect many preverbal markers in NfldE. Relate this to the ongoing change in the grammatical status of *better* that is apparent in many varieties of English today (e.g. *You better do it*; *This better work*).

5. Along with other dictionaries as necessary, use the *Dictionary of Newfound-land English* (Story, Kirwin and Widdowson [1982]1990) – or its online version at www.heritage.nf.ca/dictionary – to determine the original mean-ing of the nautical terms mentioned in section 7. Use the same sources to trace the origins and meaning of the following words, which are common in NfldE today: *gig* (e.g. *There's not a gig in her*, said of an engine); *barachois/ barasway* 'shallow lagoon sheltered by a sandbar'; *streel* 'a slovenly person, especially female'; *fousty* 'mouldy, having a bad smell'; *emmit/immit* and *pismire* 'ant'; *bedlamer* 'a young seal'.

Selected references

Please consult the General references for titles mentioned in the text but not included in the references below. For a full bibliography see the accompanying CD-ROM.

Clarke, Sandra
    1997a   English verbal *-s* revisited: The evidence from Newfoundland. *American Speech* 72: 227–259.
    1997b   The role of Irish English in the formation of New World Englishes: The case from Newfoundland. In: Jeffrey Kallen (ed.), *Focus on Ireland*, 207–225. (Varieties of English around the World, 21.) Amsterdam/Philadelphia: Benjamins.
Godfrey, Elizabeth and Sali Tagliamonte
    1999   Another piece for the verbal *-s* story: Evidence from Devon in southwest England. *Language Variation and Change* 11: 87–121.
Halpert, Herbert and J.D.A. Widdowson
    1996   *Folktales of Newfoundland*, Volumes I and II. (Publications of the American Folklore Society.) St. John's, Newfoundland: Breakwater.
Kirwin, William J.
    1993   The planting of Anglo-Irish in Newfoundland. In: Clarke (ed.), 65–84.
    2001   Newfoundland English. In: Algeo (ed.), 441–455.
Lanari, Catherine E. Penney
    1994   A sociolinguistic study of the Burin region of Newfoundland. M.A. thesis, Department of Linguistics, Memorial University of Newfoundland.
Newhook, Amanda
    2002   A sociolinguistic study of Burnt Islands, Newfoundland. M.A. thesis, Department of Linguistics, Memorial University of Newfoundland.
Noseworthy, Ronald G.
    1971   A dialect survey of Grand Bank, Newfoundland. M.A. thesis, Department of Linguistics, Memorial University of Newfoundland.

Paddock, Harold
  1981   *A Dialect Survey of Carbonear, Newfoundland.* (Publications of the American Dialect Society 68.) Alabama University: University of Alabama Press.
Paddock, Harold
  1988   The actuation problem for gender change in Wessex versus Newfoundland. In: Jacek Fisiak (ed.), *Historical Dialectology*, 377–385. Berlin/New York: Mouton de Gruyter. (Revised version in Trudgill and Chambers [eds.], 29–46.)
Story, G.M., W.J. Kirwin and J.D. A. Widdowson
  [1982] 1990   *Dictionary of Newfoundland English.* Toronto: University of Toronto Press. (Online version at www.heritage.nf.ca/dictionary)
Wagner, Susanne
  2003   Gender in English pronouns: Myth and reality. Ph.D. dissertation, Albert-Ludwigs-Universität, Freiburg im Breisgau.

Urban African American Vernacular English: morphology and syntax*

Walt Wolfram

1. Introduction

Although the roots of contemporary African American Vernacular English (AAVE) were no doubt established in the rural South, its twentieth century development as a sociocultural variety is strongly associated with its use in non-Southern urban areas. Descriptive studies of AAVE that helped launch the modern era of social dialectology concentrated on Northern metropolitan areas (Labov et al. 1968; Labov 1972; Wolfram 1969; Fasold 1972), and this urban focus has continued up to the present (Spears 1982; Baugh 1983; Rickford 1999; Dayton 1996; Labov 1998). A tradition of descriptive studies of rural Southern AAVE now complements the urban focus (Wolfram 1974; Wolfram and Thomas 2002; Bailey 2001; Bailey and Maynor 1985, 1987, 1989; Cukor-Avila 2001), but large metropolitan areas continue to be at the center of many of the linguistic, social, and educational concerns attendant to AAVE.

The emergence of urban AAVE was certainly a by-product of the Great Migration in which African Americans moved from the rural South to large metropolitan areas of the North in the early and mid-twentieth century, though demographic movement *per se* is not a sufficient explanation for the cultural shift in which urban areas became the contemporary norm for AAVE. In 1910, almost 90 percent of all African Americans in the US lived in the South and 75 percent of that number lived in communities of less than 2,500. According to the Census definition, rural residents generally live in unincorporated places of less than 2,500 and metropolitan areas are counties of 100,000 or more with central cities of more than 50,000 people. Census-based definitions do not, however, consider social and cultural factors that may defy demographic criteria. Starting with World War I and continuing through World War II and beyond, there was a dramatic redistribution of African Americans as they left the rural South for northern cities. By 1970, 47 percent of African Americans lived outside of the South, and 77 percent of those lived in urban areas. More than a third of all African Americans lived in just seven cities – New York, Chicago, Detroit, Philadelphia, Washington, DC, Los Angeles, and Baltimore (Bailey 2001: 66). The large influx of African Americans in these metropolitan areas led to intensified racial isolation and, along with other social and cultural ramifications of such de facto segregation, a social environment conducive to the maintenance of ethnolinguistic differences.

Population movement among African Americans has shifted somewhat in the last several decades, as the influx of Southern in-migrants slowed and more African Americans move from the inner city to suburban areas, but this has hardly affected inner-city segregation. The 2000 US census indicates that approximately 60 percent of all African Americans now live in the non-South and that approximately 6 million African Americans live in the large metropolitan centers mentioned above. Some of these cities have become even more densely populated by African Americans than they were several decades ago. For example, the city of Detroit is now 83 percent African American (2000 US Census); in the mid-1960s, when the author conducted his fieldwork, it was only 37 percent African American (Wolfram 1969: 21). Furthermore, a half-century ago, the vast majority of middle-aged and elderly African Americans living in Northern urban areas were born in the South. In the 1960s, less than 10 percent of African Americans in Detroit over the age of 40 were born in the North; today the majority of African Americans were born there or in another metropolitan area. At the turn of the twenty-first century, the population demographics of non-Southern urban areas reveal the continued existence of well-established, largely segregated African American populations, especially for those living in poverty.

There are several reasons for the earlier and current interest in urban AAVE, ranging from personal and practical reasons to descriptive and theoretical interests. To begin with, most linguists who worked on AAVE in the 1960s lived near Northern metropolitan areas, where the contrast between African American speech and the varieties of the surrounding European Americans was most salient. During the launching period for AAVE studies (Labov et al. 1968; Shuy, Wolfram, and Riley 1967; Wolfram 1969; Fasold 1972), there was also an apparent link between AAVE and significant social and educational problems in American society, including urban poverty and racial disparity in school performance. These problems were acute in metropolitan areas, where they affected large numbers of a rapidly growing African American population. In fact, early studies of AAVE such as Labov's landmark study of AAVE in Harlem (Labov et al. 1968) and Shuy, Wolfram, and Riley's study of Detroit speech (1967) were funded by the US Office of Education because of the concern for an apparent correlation between vernacular speech and low educational achievement. Early sociolinguistic studies often addressed prominent educational issues such as literacy and educational achievement in addition to their focus on dialect description (Labov 1972a; Fasold and Shuy 1970).

As the study of AAVE progressed and encompassed rural Southern varieties of AAVE (Wolfram 1974; Bailey and Maynor 1985, 1987, 1989; Cukor-Avila 2001; Wolfram and Thomas 2002), questions about language change within African American speech emerged, largely subsumed under the *divergence hypothesis* (Labov 1987; Bailey and Maynor 1989; Poplack 2000; Poplack and Tagliamonte 2001). This hypothesis maintains that contemporary AAVE is evolving independently in ways that increase the difference between AAVE and other vernacular dialects of English. The debate over the nature and extent of innovation continues, but most researchers (Bailey and Maynor 1987, 1989; Dayton 1996; Poplack 2000; Labov 1998; Poplack and Tagliamonte 2001) agree that the locus of independent innovation within AAVE is largely urban and that change within AAVE is diffusing from urban to rural contexts.

The significance of urban versions of AAVE is also connected to the establishment of contemporary language norms related to African American youth culture. Morgan (2001) observes that there is a new urban language ideology that relies, among other behaviors, on the differential use of linguistic features. As Morgan (2001: 205) puts it: "Thus, urban African American life is not simply represented in relation to in-group intersubjectivities, but through cultural symbols and sounds, especially linguistic symbols, which signify membership, role, and status so that (…) words, expressions, messages circulate as commodities".

The center of African American youth culture today is primarily urban, and many norms and models of behavior, including language, seem to radiate outward from these urban cultural hubs as the norms of contemporary, supraregional AAVE follow the lead of speakers in these urban areas.

2.   The construction of urban AAVE

Historically, urban AAVE was established on the basis of transplant dialect communities of Southern rural speakers who moved to non-Southern cities during the early waves of the Great Migration in the first half of the twentieth century. There were patterns of interregional movement in which African American residents from coastal Southern states such as Virginia, the Carolinas, and Georgia tended to move northward to cities such as Washington, DC, Baltimore, Philadelphia, and New York and residents of Mississippi, Tennessee, Alabama, and Texas tended to move to cities such as St. Louis, Chicago, Cleveland, and Detroit, as well as westward to Los Angeles, but most urban neighborhoods were mixed in terms of their Southern regional roots. The increasing number of African American in-migrants in these urban contexts, the shared Southern rural cultural heritage, the segregated living conditions, and the bi-racial ideology characteristic of most Northern urban cities certainly provided an ideal context for nurturing ethnolinguistic distinction.

The contrast between urban AAVE and the speech of the surrounding European American cohort communities is hardly at question; there is ample descriptive and subjective sociolinguistic evidence for this division. The intriguing questions about urban AAVE relate to issues of dialect leveling, accommodation, and innovation. To what extent are these urban varieties similar to and different from the rural AAVE varieties that were brought to the area originally? Which features of their Southern regional founder dialects have been retained and which have been lost? How have these varieties accommodated to the regional dialect forms of the benchmark European American regional varieties in these urban contexts? What types of linguistic changes now differentiate urban AAVE from its Southern rural counterparts? And what is the significance of such differentiation? These are questions that must be addressed in a comprehensive examination of AAVE as it has developed during the twentieth century. Although most of the discussion of urban AAVE since the 1980s has centered on the extent to which it shows independent development and divergence from European American vernaculars (e.g. Labov 1987; Bailey and Maynor 1985, 1987, 1989; Dayton 1996), the sociolinguistic construction of urban AAVE is much more complex than the issue of independent innovation within AAVE.

There are several different kinds of language change that need to be considered in the comparison of contemporary urban AAVE and the Southern rural roots that provided the founder input (Mufwene 2001). First, there is a kind of dialect leveling in which traditional, localized Southern features may be reduced or lost. For example, in urban Northern AAVE there is no evidence of 3rd plural -*s* in *The dogs barks* even though this trait was a characteristic of some earlier regional varieties in the South (Schneider 1989; Montgomery and Fuller 1996; Wolfram and Thomas 2002). Similarly, past tense *be* leveling to *weren't* based on polarity (e.g. *I weren't there*), a regional trait of earlier African American varieties spoken in the Mid-Atlantic coastal region (Wolfram and Thomas 2002), is not found in Northern urban AAVE.

Earlier, generalized traits of Southern rural AAVE may also be lost, such as *a*-prefixing in *She was a-fishin'* or the use of *for to* complement as in *I want for to go now*. Although earlier studies of urban AAVE (Labov et al. 1968) recognized this type of change, it has become more evident with the expansion of studies of AAVE in the South (Cukor-Avila 2001; Bailey and Maynor 1985, 1989; Wolfram and Thomas 2002).

As already noted, change in urban AAVE may also derive from independent language innovation. Studies of *be* + V-*ing* as a 'habitual' marker (Bailey and

Maynor 1985, 1987, 1989; Dayton 1996; Rickford 1999; Cukor-Avila 2001) suggest that it is largely an innovation of the post-World War II era and that the change has spread from an urban locus outward. While independent studies (Bailey and Maynor 1987, 1989) confirm this pattern of innovation and diffusion for habitual *be*, the status of other structures, such as the resultative-conditional *be done* in a sentence such as *If you leave it in the tub the chicken be done jumped out the tub by the time you get back* and narrative marking *-s* attachment in *He goes and sit down* is more disputable (Rickford 1999).

One type of sociolinguistic process associated with urban AAVE is *linguistic camouflaging*, in which a vernacular form resembles a standard or different vernacular form so closely that it is simply assumed to be identical to its apparent structural counterpart. However, this similarity may disguise the fact that the form carries a distinctive semantic-pragmatic meaning or is constructed in a subtly different way. Spears (1982) shows that the use of a semi-auxiliary *come* in the sentence *They come talking that trash about him* seems quite similar to the standard English use of *come* with movement verbs as in *They came running when they heard the news*. Close examination of the use of *come* in the former sentence, however, indicates that it fills a unique semantic-pragmatic role indicating speaker indignation. In an analogous way, camouflaging may also involve syntactic expansion based on a shared semantic-pragmatic reading, as in sentences like *They call themselves dancing*. While counterfactual *call oneself* is quite common with noun phrases in most English dialects (e.g. *They call themselves linguists*) or adjective phrases (e.g. *They call themselves intelligent*), its structural expansion to include V-*ing* complements sets AAVE apart from most other American English dialects. Some camouflaged structures, especially those involving grammaticalized semantic-pragmatic forms (Spears 1982; Baugh 1984), seem to be characteristic of subtle changes within urban AAVE, though it is of course possible that these structures simply may have been overlooked in rural varieties.

Thus far, we have discussed urban AAVE only in relation to its change from Southern founder dialects and its independent development, but part of its uniqueness may be found in its relationship to surrounding European American varieties. One of the distinctive traits of Northern Urban AAVE appears to be its relative immunity to the linguistic changes taking place in cohort white communities. Although this exclusion tends to be more salient in phonology than in morphology and syntax, a similar pattern of resistance may be found for regional grammatical patterns. Many AAVE speakers in Midland dialect regions such as Pittsburgh, Pennsylvania, do not adopt regional morphosyntactic traits such as positive *anymore* (*e.g. We watch a lot of DVDs anymore*), *need* + past participle (e.g. *The car needs washed*), and 2nd plural *youns* or *yous*.

Part of the construction of AAVE as an ethnic variety in its urban context is certainly related to its apparent lack of regional accommodation.

Up to this point, we have treated rural and urban AAVE as if it were an obvious binary distinction, but this does not necessarily match the reality of contemporary African American culture and language. Such a distinction cannot simply be based on demographic statistics such as the size of the metropolitan area or population density, as one might be apt to do if relying solely on census data. Furthermore, the distinction between urban and rural may not be as relevant for contemporary AAVE as it once was. Thus, Cukor-Avila (2001) and Wolfram and Thomas (2002) show that traits formerly associated with urban AAVE are present among younger African American speakers in remote rural areas of the South. At the same time, African Americans in these regions may be abandoning local regional traits, showing a movement away from local dialect traits as they acquire traits associated with urban AAVE. For example, Wolfram and Thomas (2002) show a trajectory of change in which regional dialect features recede and structures associated with urban AAVE intensify over four generations of speakers in Hyde County, North Carolina, a sparsely populated, outlying coastal region of North Carolina. Figure 1, an adaptation of the figure given in Wolfram and Thomas (2002: 200), shows an idealized change slope for four generations of speakers divided on the basis of different sociohistorical periods: speakers who were born and raised in the early twentieth century up through World War I; speakers born and raised between World War I and school integration in the late 1960s; speakers who lived through the early period of school integration as adolescents, and those who were born and raised after integration.

The trajectory of change shows that African American speech has shifted rather dramatically over time, both in its intensification of features associated with urban AAVE and in its divergence from the local regional dialect norms. Can we truly say that African Americans in this remote region are now urban when they reside in a county inhabited by less than 10 people per square mile and having no public transit system, no shopping centers or malls, and no fast food stores? Wolfram and Thomas (2002) suggest that contemporary AAVE is characterized by a movement towards supraregional AAVE norms and a movement away from, or lack of accommodation to, local regional norms so that the urban-rural distinction is dissipating. At the same time, we recognize that current change is radiating from urban centers outward. Given the current status of AAVE, the use of the urban-rural distinction in this description must be interpreted in terms of its historical context and the current pattern of diffusion within AAVE rather than in terms of a strict, demographically based dichotomy between urban and rural African American populations.

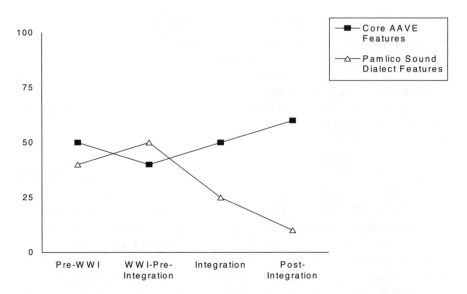

Figure 1.   Idealized model of change for African Americans in Hyde County

3.   The grammar of urban AAVE

In this section, I outline some of the major structures of urban AAVE grammar. Given the historical connection to rural varieties of AAVE, the existence of supraregional norms, and current patterns of diffusion, there are many traits of urban AAVE that are shared with non-urban varieties. In fact, the shared core of AAVE structures is an essential part of the unique linguistic story of AAVE. Nonetheless, there are ways in which Southern-based, rural and non-Southern, urban varieties differ. In describing the characteristics of urban AAVE in the following sections, I attempt to highlight some of the ways in which contemporary urban AAVE is similar to and different from other varieties, including rural Southern African American and European American varieties, non-Southern vernacular European American varieties, and standard English. For convenience, the description is organized on the basis of grammatical category.

3.1.   Verb phrase

The most noteworthy traits of AAVE have typically been associated with the verb phrase, including the use of tense, mood, and aspect. For several decades now, researchers (Fasold 1972; Labov 1972a, 1998; Dayton 1996; Baugh

1983; Rickford 1999) have acknowledged that these dimensions distinguish AAVE from other varieties of English, although there is no consensus on its distinctive aspectual parameters. Although there are a number of distinguishing traits, the most prominent features are a distinct set of preverbal particles or auxiliaries.

3.1.1. Copula/auxiliary absence

The absence of copula and auxiliary for contractible forms of *is* and *are* (e.g. *She nice* for 'She's nice' or *They acting silly* for 'They're acting silly') has been one of the most often described structures of AAVE (e.g. Labov et al. 1968; Wolfram 1969; Fasold 1972; Baugh 1983; Rickford 1999). Although there are a number of descriptive and explanatory dimensions of copula absence that remain in dispute, including whether it is derived through a grammatical or phonological process (Fasold 1976), there is general agreement about its ethnolinguistic status. Wolfram (1974) and Feagin (1979) note that AAVE shares copula absence with some Southern white rural vernacular varieties of English, but that there are some qualitative and quantitative differences in the respective varieties. Copula absence is quite pervasive in urban AAVE but is not found at all in Northern urban benchmark European American varieties. In Southern European American English varieties, mostly the former large plantation areas, it tends to be limited to forms of *are* and used at reduced frequency levels compared to AAVE. Studies of copula absence in apparent time and in different regions (Bailey and Maynor 1985, 1987, 1989; Cukor-Avila 2001; Wolfram and Thomas 2002) show that the process has been quite stable in AAVE for some time now, and that differences in urban and non-urban use are quantitative rather than qualitative.

3.1.2. Invariant be

Invariant *be* in sentences such as *Sometimes they be playing games*, also referred to as non-finite *be*, habitual *be*, and *be$_2$*, is probably the most salient grammatical trait of AAVE, to the point of becoming a stereotype. Its structural and functional properties have now been studied in a number of different urban (Labov 1972a; Labov et al. 1968; Wolfram 1969) and rural settings (Wolfram 1974; Bailey and Maynor 1985, 1989; Cukor-Avila 2001), as well as its development and diffusion over time and place. Although there is disagreement as to how *be$_2$* might be represented in the grammatical system of AAVE (e.g. Fasold 1972), most analyses agree that *be$_2$* marks a unique aspect referring to an intermittent activity, hence the reference to 'habitual *be*.'

To begin with, the use of 'habitual' *be* or *be*₂ needs to be distinguished from several other uses of *be*, including those derived through phonological processes that affect contracted forms of *will* and *would*. In constructions such as *She be there in a minute*, the *be* comes from the loss of /l/ before a labial (*she'll be* → *she be*) (see Edwards, this volume), whereas in a construction like *If they get a DVD player they be happy*, the form is derived from the loss of /d/ (*they'd be* → *they be*), since /d/ before a labial may geminate to the /b/ and then be lost in a general phonological process of degemination (e.g. *good bye* → *goob bye* → *goo'bye*). The difference βετωεεν the phonologically derived forms, represented in (1) and (2) and the use of *be* in (3) is readily apparent in tag forms (1a, 2a, 3a) and negatives (2a, 2b, 3b).

(1)   *She be here in a minute.*
   a. *She be here in a minute,* **won't she**?
   b. *She* **won't** *be here in a minute.*

(2)   *If they get a DVD player, they be happy.*
   a. *If they get a DVD player, they be happy,* **wouldn't they?**
   b. *If they get a DVD player, they* **wouldn't be** *happy.*

(3)   *Sometimes they be playing tag.*
   a. *Sometimes they be playing tag,* **don't they?**
   b. *Sometimes they* **don't be** *playing tag.*

Sentence (3) illustrates the fundamental syntactic and morphological properties that distinguish *be*₂ from its counterpart in other varieties of English; it does not alter its form in finite uses and takes *do* support in a way that is comparable to main verbs. Over the last half century, the habitual reference of *be*, particularly with V-*ing*, has grammaticalized in a change that has been spreading from urban centers outward. Practically all studies of AAVE show that younger vernacular speakers use *be* V-*ing* more than older speakers (Wolfram 1969; Cukor-Avila 2001; Bailey and Maynor 1987, 1989), and that urban speakers are more likely to use it than non-urban speakers (Cukor-Avila 2001; Wolfram and Thomas 2002). It is also possible that the use of habitual *be* may be age-graded, and that younger speakers who use it frequently will reduce its use as they get older, since it now has a strong association with black youth culture.

A more recent aspectual change is the semantic expansion of invariant *be* beyond its reference to habituality. Alim (2001), for example, notes that *be* is commonly used in hip-hop equative sentences such as *I be the truth* or *Dr. Dre be the name* in a way that seizes upon its iconic status as a marker of black speech. Under earlier analyses (e.g. Fasold 1972; Wolfram 1969), such stativity would have been considered ungrammatical, since it is incompatible with a habitual reading. Dayton (1996) proposes that highly affective utterances such as these may signify shift towards intensified stativity, or super-real status, rather than habituality. As with the original grammaticalization of *be* V-*ing,* this most recent change appears to be taking place in more urban versions of AAVE and spreading outward from that point.

3.1.3. Completive done

The use of *done* with the past tense of the verb, as in *They done used all the good ones*, is a persistent structural trait of AAVE that is shared with Southern European American vernacular varieties of English. Although the verbal particle *done* also occurs in Caribbean creoles, its syntactic configuration in AAVE and its semantic-pragmatic function differ somewhat from its creole counterparts. In AAVE, *done* occurs only in preverbal auxiliary position with past tense forms whereas it occurs with a bare verb stem (e.g. *They done go*) and can occur in clause-final position in some creoles (Holm 1988: 162). In many respects, it functions in AAVE like a perfect, referring to an action completed in the recent past, but it can also be used to highlight the change of state or to intensify an activity, as in a sentence like *I done told you not to mess up.* It is a stable feature, but it is more frequently used in Southern rural versions of AAVE than in urban AAVE.

3.1.4. Sequential be done

AAVE may also show a combination of *be* and *done* together in sentences such as *My ice cream be done melted by the time we get there,* marking a resultative or a future conditional state. On one level, this construction seems to function like a future perfect similar to standard English *will have melted* in the example given above. Dayton (1996) suggests that a newer use of this form functions more like a future resultative-conditional, referring to an inevitable consequence of a general condition or a specific activity, as in a sentence like *If you love your enemy, they be done eat you alive in this society.* According to Dayton (1996) and Labov (1998), the resultative-conditional meaning, which is often associated pragmatically with threats or warnings, is a newer semantic-aspectual development. This meaning, like some of the other nuanced meanings of auxiliaries discussed in the following sections, seems to be characteristic of urban AAVE. Although Dayton (1996) documented numerous examples of this type during her years of participant observation with AAVE speakers in Philadelphia, it still seems to occur rather infrequently in most varieties of AAVE.

3.1.5.   Remote béen

The stressed use of *béen* with a past tense form of the verb may denote a special aspectual function that marks an activity that took place in the distant past. In sentences such as *I béen had it for about three years* or *I béen known him*, it refers to an event that took place, literally or figuratively, in a distant time frame. In some contexts, the form may be interpreted as the deletion of a contracted form of the perfect (e.g. *She's béen married*), thus camouflaging some of its subtle semantic difference from other varieties. For example, Rickford (1975) showed that European Americans and African Americans, when given the stimulus utterance *She béen married,* had quite different responses to the question *Is she still married?* European Americans interpreted the stressed *béen* as a deleted perfect form (e.g., *She's been → She been*) and as implying that the referent is no longer married, whereas African Americans interpreted it as a distinctive aspectual marker indicating that the referent had been married a long time. With the exception of the phrase *I béen known* or *I béen knowin'* (phonetically quite similar if not identical to *known* [noun]) in casual speech, the use of remote *been* in urban areas appears to be receding.

3.1.6.   *Simple past* had + *verb*

One of the newer features of AAVE is the narrative use of the auxiliary *had* with a past or perfect form of the verb (see the section on irregular verbs) to indicate a simple past tense action, as in *They had went outside and then they had messed up the yard...* . This use is equivalent to the use of the simple past (e.g. *They went outside and then they messed up the yard*) in Standard English. Whereas earlier descriptions of AAVE (Labov et al. 1968; Fasold and Wolfram 1970; Fasold 1972) do not mention this feature at all, recent descriptions (Cukor-Avila 2001; Rickford and Théberge-Rafal 1996) observe that this construction may be quite frequent in the narratives of some preadolescents. Descriptions of AAVE document the narrative use of *had* + verb in both urban (Rickford and Théberge-Rafal 1996) and rural AAVE settings (Cukor-Avila 2001). The fact that this feature is so frequent among preadolescents raises the possibility that it may be age-graded, and that AAVE speakers will diminish its use as they become adults, although this interpretation is discounted in some of the data from Cukor-Avila (2001). Of course, age-grading and language change are not necessarily incompatible notions, and it may be that it is a newer feature that shows some degree of age-grading.

3.1.7. Specialized auxiliaries

Several auxiliaries fill specialized semantic-pragmatic roles that subtly set apart AAVE from other vernacular varieties of English. Among these auxiliary-like constructions are the use of *come* to indicate a state of indignation, the use of *steady* to mark a continuative intensifying activity, and the use of *finna* to indicate an immediate future or planned event. The use of *come* with V-*ing* in the sentence *He come walkin' in here like he owned the damn place* (Spears 1982: 852) indicates a speaker's annoyance about the action or event. Structurally, this use closely resembles the use of *come* with movement verbs (e.g. *She came running*) in other varieties, and is thus a camouflaged form.

Another apparent camouflaged form is *steady* in sentences such as *Ricky Bell be steady steppin' in them number nines* (Baugh 1983: 86), where the adverb *steady* indicates an intensified, persistent activity. The specialized auxiliary *finna* in *I'm finna go*, related to the generalized Southern form *fixin' to* (also *fixta*, *fitna*, and *fidda*), refers to an immediate future or planned event. Camouflaged forms such as indignant *come* seem to be more recent developments concentrated in urban varieties, although it may be the case that these forms simply have not been noticed in Southern varieties because of their relative infrequency and structural similarity to related forms in benchmark European American varieties.

At the same time, the use of other auxiliaries in urban AAVE seems to be receding when compared with their use in Southern vernacular counterparts. Whereas double modals such as *I might could do it*, counterfactual *liketa* in *I was so scared I liketa died*, and causative *have to* in *I'll have him to do it* can be found in contemporary urban AAVE, they tend to be much more robust in rural Southern versions of this variety.

3.1.8. Irregular verbs

The irregular verbs of urban AAVE follow those found in other vernacular varieties of English, in particular, rural Southern white varieties. These include the extension of past as participle (e.g. *I had went down there*), the participle as past (e.g. *They seen it*), the bare root as past (e.g. *They run there yesterday*), and regularization of past tense (e.g. *Everybody knowed him*). Unlike rural Southern varieties, it does not tend to retain some of the older different irregular forms (e.g. *hearen* for *heard* or *clumb* for *climbed*).

3.1.9. Subject-verb agreement

Two aspects of subject-verb concord are prominent in urban AAVE, one re-lating to the attachment of the verbal suffix *-s* and the other relating to the conjugated forms of past and present *be* forms. Practically all studies of urban (Labov et al. 1968; Wolfram 1969; Fasold 1972; Rickford 1992) and rural AAVE (Cukor-Avila 2001; Wolfram and Thomas 2002) have documented the current-day pattern of 3rd sg. *-s* absence in sentences such as *She walk* for *She walks* and *She have money* for *She has money*. The incidence of 3rd sg. *-s* absence is so high for younger AAVE speakers in some sociolinguistic studies of core vernacular adolescents – reaching levels of between 75–100 percent for some speakers – that it has prompted several researchers (Labov et al. 1968; Fasold 1972) to speculate that contemporary urban "AAVE has no concord rule for verbal *-s*" (Fasold 1972: 146). This extensive pattern of ab-sence seems to contrast with earlier Southern rural versions of AAVE, which are more prone to have variable attachment of verbal *-s* with 3rd sg. subjects. Furthermore, in some cases, Southern rural AAVE had verbal *-s* attachment with subjects other than 3rd sg., particularly 3rd pl. subjects as in *The dogs barks a lot* (Cukor-Avila 2001; Wolfram and Thomas 2002) but also with 1st and 2nd subjects (Schneider 1989; Cukor-Avila 1995). Evidence (Cukor-Avi-la 2001; Wolfram and Thomas 2002) indicates that 3rd sg. *-s* absence is shared by urban and non-urban verbal AAVE varieties, with some intensification of this pattern in core urban vernaculars taking place over the past half-century. Although it has been suggested that a specialized narrative use of verbal *-s* oc-curs in constructions such as *She takes your clothes and lend them to people* in one urban variety of AAVE (Labov 1987), this pattern has not been confirmed in other studies (Rickford 1999), and has been disputed as an innovation in AAVE (Wolfram and Thomas 2002).

The second concord pattern affecting urban AAVE is the regularization of present and past forms of conjugated *be*. AAVE is much like the vast majority of other vernacular varieties of English in its use of *be* leveling; in the present tense, *are* and *am* level to *is*, as in *The folks is home* or *Y'all is here,* while past tense *be* levels to *was*, as in *The folks was there* or *Y'all was here.* Past tense *be* leveling is much more common than present tense leveling in AAVE, as it is in virtually all varieties of vernacular English having *be* regularization. The comparison of leveling over time and place indicates that the incidence of *be* leveling is diminishing somewhat (Wolfram and Thomas 2002), probably due to the effect of prescriptive norms. Nonetheless, *be* leveling, particularly with past tense, remains an integral and robust pattern within urban AAVE.

3.1.10. Other verb phrase structures

There are other types of verb structures that distinguish AAVE, but these are restricted to particular lexical verbs and their complements. For example, the verb *beat* in AAVE may function as an intransitive verb, as in *We beat* for 'won', whereas it is required to co-occur with an object in other varieties of English as in *We beat the team*. This use of intransitive *beat* is quite common in urban versions of AAVE. Or, a verb plus particle may function together lexically as in *blessed out* for 'scold' or 'swear at' in *She blessed him out*. This use is common in both urban and rural contexts and is shared with Southern European American English. The use of *say* to introduce a quote, as *She told him, say, "Where you been?"* is similar to its use in some creoles, prompting speculation that it is a vestige of creole influence (Rickford 1999: 9). *Say* may also be extended in AAVE to refer to non-human and inanimate objects, as in *The rock say "boom"*, which distinguishes its use in AAVE from other varieties using the general quotative *go*, as in *The rock went "boom"*. The verb *go* in the construction *Here go the house* functions as a static locative in AAVE, distinguishing it from benchmark European American varieties that use it only as a dynamic locative. There are a number of differences of this type that distinguish AAVE from other varieties but they are related to individual lexical items or phrasal complements and not to the overall grammatical configuration of AAVE.

3.2.   Negation

The formation of negation in AAVE is not particularly distinct from other vernacular varieties of English in the US and beyond. To begin with, it participates in negative concord, or multiple negation, in which a single negative proposition may be marked both within the verb phrase and on postverbal indefinites, as in *It wasn't nothing* or *They didn't do nothing about nobody having no money or nothing like that*. In this respect, it is no different from the majority of vernacular dialects of English (Wolfram and Schilling-Estes 1998). In urban areas, the incidence of negative concord is sharply stratified; some low-status speakers show the categorical realization of negative concord while middle-class speakers often show very low frequency levels or no negative concord at all in their sociolinguistic interviews (Wolfram 1969: 156).

AAVE also participates in a type of negative concord that involves a pre-verbal indefinite and verbal negative as in *Nobody don't like him*, which is equivalent to the standard sentence *Nobody likes him*. In standard varieties of English, it is possible for the two negative propositions to cancel each other, as in the longstanding American TV advertisement phrase, *Nobody doesn't like Sara Lee* [pastries], which of course implies that everyone likes the product. Although some isolated sentences of this type might be syntactically ambiguous, the intent of most sentences is readily apparent from the context in which they are uttered.

Related to the preverbal negative pattern is a type of inversion of the negative auxiliary and indefinite subject, as in *Don't nobody like him*, meaning 'Nobody likes him' or *Ain't nobody home* for 'Nobody is home'. Constructions like these are often used for emphasis, especially if the indefinite is stressed, as in *Don't nobody like him*.

Negative concord can also be transferred across clauses, as in a well-know example cited by Labov (1972: 130), *It ain't no cat can't get in no coop,* referring to the fact that cats are not able to get into the bird coops built on the roofs of apartment buildings. Although it has been speculated that this type of cross-clausal negation might be unique to AAVE, Southern-based European American vernaculars (Wolfram and Christian 1976: 113) also use cross-clausal negative concord. This type of concord is quite infrequent in AAVE, as it is in other varieties where it is found, and there are lingering questions about the default interpretation of cross-clausal negatives.

Like other vernacular dialects, AAVE uses *ain't* as a general preverbal negative for present tense *be* (*am not, isn't, aren't*) and for the perfect auxiliary *haven't/hasn't* as in *She ain't here* or *She ain't been there lately*. In this respect, AAVE is no different from other vernacular varieties of English. However, AAVE is unlike most European American vernacular varieties in generalizing the use of *ain't* for *didn't* as well, as in *She ain't do it*. This distinctive use is fairly widespread in urban varieties of AAVE, although it is camouflaged by other, shared uses of *ain't*. The generalized past tense variant *wont* for *wasn't* and *weren't* in *I wont there yesterday*, found in some Southern vernacular varieties, is not typical of urban AAVE. Finally, *ain't* and *don't* may be used with *but* to indicate 'only' or 'no more than' as in *She ain't but three years old* or *He didn't take but three dollars*. As with most other aspects of negation in urban AAVE, this is shared with Southern rural African American and European American vernacular varieties.

3.3.   Nominals

Although many of the characteristics of the noun phrase in AAVE are shared with a wide range of English vernacular varieties, there are also a few traits that set it apart from European American vernaculars in the US. Perhaps the most noteworthy of these is the absence of inflectional *-s* on possessives and plurals. The absence of possessive *-s* in sentences like *The dog_ tail was wagging* or *The man_ hat was old* are rare among other American English vernaculars. This is a relatively stable feature in AAVE wherever it is found in the US, though Rickford (1999: 271) suggests that it may be subject to age-grading since it is more frequent among younger speakers.

The formation of plurals in AAVE is noteworthy for several reasons. First, there is the pattern of *-s* absence related to measure nouns with quantifiers, as in *I got 50 cent _* and *It's four mile_ from here.* The absence of the plural *-s* with measure nouns is a characteristic of a number of Southern-based varieties of English as well as some Northern rural vernacular varieties (Wolfram and Schilling-Estes 1998; Wolfram and Christian 1976), and is probably more robust in Southern-based, rural varieties than it currently is in urban AAVE. However, AAVE may also have a more generalized absence of *-s* plural unrestricted by the type of noun, as in *some dog* or *two boy.* Although generalized plural *-s* absence is a trait of urban AAVE, it is relatively infrequent, with typical absence levels less than 10 per cent out of all the cases where it might occur. Older, more rural versions of AAVE show a higher incidence of generalized plural *-s* absence, with some speakers showing levels up to one-third of all potential cases. Another type of plural marking involves the regularization of irregular plurals, including shifts in word class status from irregular to regular (e.g. *oxes, gooses*), the attachment of plurals to forms that have zero marking in other varieties (e.g. *three sheeps, two corns*), and redundant marking of irregular plurals (e.g. *two firemens, childrens*). In this regard, it is like other vernacular varieties of English, apart from some differences in frequency levels.

It has been suggested (Labov et al. 1968) that a type of associative plural *an 'em* in AAVE, as in *Jerome an 'em* for 'Jerome and his friends', is more similar to English creoles than to other varieties of English, but this type of associative plural is not unusual in other varieties of American English, including Southern and Northern European American varieties. The use of the second person plural *y'all* in *Y'all done now* or *It's y'all ball* is quite common in both Southern and Northern versions of AAVE and therefore contrasts with second person plural formation in regions that are characterized by variants such as *youse, you guys,* or *youns.*

A couple of distinctive traits of AAVE are found in the possessive pronouns. The use of the possessive pronoun *they* in *It's they book* is quite robust in most urban and rural regions of the US, and it usually distinguishes AAVE from benchmark European American vernaculars. The regularization of *mine* to *mines* in *The book is mines* is quite robust in most varieties of AAVE, though it appears more typical of preadolescent speakers than older speakers.

AAVE shares a number of pronominal traits with other vernacular varieties of English, including the regularization of the reflexive *hisself* as in *He washed hisself*, the extension of the objective form *them* for attributive demonstratives such as *She likes them apples*, and the use of objective forms in coordinate subjects as in *Me and him got style*. It shares benefactive datives as in *I got me a new car* with Southern dialects. Urban AAVE also shares null subjective relative pronoun in embedded sentences such as *It's a man come over here talking trash*. The use of *what* as a relative as in *That's the man what I was talking about*, found in some forms of earlier AAVE, is no longer found to any extent in urban AAVE.

3.4.   Question formation

There are two aspects of question formation that distinguish AAVE syntax, both involving subject auxiliary inversion. First, questions may be formed without subject-auxiliary inversion, as in *Where that is?* or *Why I can't go?*. These non-inverted forms tend to occur with *wh-* questions and syntactically simple sentences. While the productive use of simple non-inverted question order may be receding, it is still quite common in some fixed phrases such as *What it is?* or *Who that is?* At the same time, embedded questions may retain subject-auxiliary inversion, as in *I asked her could I go with her*, contrasting with the standard pattern in which *if* or *whether* is used with non-inverted order, as in *I asked him if I could go with him*. This is a stable pattern shared with a number of vernacular varieties.

4.   Conclusion

The descriptive profile of urban AAVE grammar given in the above sections indicates a robust, dynamic sociocultural variety that maintains continuity with its historical Southern rural roots while becoming the locus of current innovation within AAVE. At this stage of development, factors of social class, speech community, identity, and language ideology are probably as essential as the rural-urban dichotomy but the historical role of this relationship cannot be disputed. Large metropolitan areas appear to be the current sociocultural centers for innovation and the establishment of supraregional norms in AAVE, with change diffusing from these urban locations into more rural regions (Cukor-Avila 2001; Wolfram and Thomas 2002).

In tables 1–3, we summarize the status of the major grammatical structures surveyed in this description: Table 1 summarizes innovative and intensifying features of urban AAVE; table 2 summarizes receding features; and table 3 summarizes stable features. Our primary basis for comparison is rural AAVE during the period of the Great Migration, simply labeled Southern AAVE, but we also compare urban AAVE with earlier AAVE (the nineteenth century), Southern European American vernacular English, and Northern European American vernacular varieties. In the comparison, a check ✓ indicates that the feature is present and parentheses around the check (✓) indicate that the feature is infrequent. The checklist is naturally subject to the usual kinds of limitations associated with qualitative summary inventories of this type. In this case, the limitation includes our differing levels of knowledge about the status of some structures in earlier AAVE and benchmark European American varieties.

Table 1.   New and intensifying structures in urban AAVE

Structure	Urban AAVE	Rural AAVE	Earlier AAVE	Southern EAVE	Northern EAVE
habitual *be* + V-*ing* e.g. *I always be playing ball*	✓	(✓)			
intensified equative *be* e.g. *She be the diva*	✓				
preterit *had* + V e.g. *Then had tripped*	✓	✓			
resultative *be done* e.g. *She be done had her baby*	✓				
indignant *come* e.g. *They come talkin' that trash*	✓				
3rd sg. -*s* absence e.g. *She run everyday*	✓	✓	✓		
ain't for *didn't* e.g. *I ain't go yesterday*	✓	(✓)	✓		
counterfactual *call oneself* e.g. *He calls himself dancing'*	✓	✓		(✓)	

Table 2.   Receding urban AAVE features

Structure	Urban AAVE	Rural AAVE	Earlier AAVE	Southern EAVE	Northern EAVE
remote *béen* e.g. *I béen ate it*	(✓)	✓	✓		
double modals e.g. *I might could do it*	(✓)	✓	(✓)	✓	
a-prefixing e.g. *I was a-huntin'*		✓	✓	✓	
leveling present *be* to *is* e.g. *We is here*	(✓)	✓	✓	(✓)	
3rd pl -*s* e.g. *The dogs barks*		(✓)	✓	✓	
counterfactual *liketa* e.g. *I liketa died*	(✓)	✓	(✓)	✓	
causative *have…to* e.g. *We'll have him to do it*	(✓)	✓	(✓)	✓	
wont for past *be* e.g. *I wont there yesterday*		(✓)		✓	
different irregular forms e.g. *It riz in front of me*		✓	✓	✓	
for to complement e.g. *I want for to bring it*		✓	✓	✓	
what as a relative pronoun e.g. *The man what took it*		(✓)	✓	(✓)	
non-inverted simple questions e.g. *What that is?*	(✓)	✓	✓		

Table 3.   Stable urban AAVE features

Structure	Urban AAVE	Rural AAVE	Earlier AAVE	Southern EAVE	Northern EAVE
copula absence e.g. *She nice*	✓	✓	✓	(✓)	
completive *done* e.g. *She done did it*	✓	✓	✓	✓	
negative concord e.g. *She didn't do nothing'*	✓	✓	✓	✓	✓
preverbal indefinite e.g. *Nobody don't like it*	✓	✓	✓	(✓)	
negative inversion e.g. *Didn't nobody like it*	✓	✓	(✓)		
ain't for *be + not have + no* e.g. *I ain't been there*	✓	✓	✓	✓	✓
regularized *was* for past *be* e.g. *We was there*	✓	✓	✓	✓	✓
irregular verbs					
past for participle e.g. *I had went*	✓	✓	✓	✓	✓
participle for past e.g. *I seen it*	✓	✓	✓	✓	✓
bare root past form e.g. *Yesterday I run fast*	✓	✓	✓	✓	✓
regularized past form e.g. *I knowed it*	✓	✓	✓	✓	✓
different past e.g. *It riz up in front of me*		✓	✓	✓	
finna quasi auxiliary e.g. *I finna do it*	✓	✓	(✓)	✓	
quotative *say* e.g. *He told him say, "Leave"*	✓	✓	✓		
stative locative *here go* e.g. *Here go the pencil*	✓	✓	(✓)		
Plural					
measure noun pl. abs. e.g. *three mile*	✓	✓	✓	✓	

Table 3. (continued)   Stable urban AAVE features

Structure	Urban AAVE	Rural AAVE	Earlier AAVE	Southern EAVE	Northern EAVE
generalized -s abs. e.g. *three boy*	(✓)	✓	✓		
regularized irregulars e.g. *oxes*	✓	✓	✓	✓	(✓)
subject relative pro deletion e.g. *It's a man took it*	✓	✓	✓	✓	
benefactive dative e.g. *I got me a new car*	✓	✓	(✓)	✓	
possessive -s absence e.g. *the girl hat*	✓	✓	✓	✓	
regularized *mines* e.g. *It's mines*	✓	✓	✓	(✓)	
regularized *hisself* e.g. *He shaved hisself*	✓	✓	✓	✓	✓
possessive *they* e.g. *It's they book*	✓	✓	✓		
2nd pl. *y'all* e.g. *Will y'all be there*	✓	✓	✓	✓	
demonstrative *them* e.g. *I love them shoes*	✓	✓	✓	✓	✓
associative *an 'em* e.g. *Derek an' em will be there*	✓	✓	✓	(✓)	(✓)
existential *it* e.g. *It's a J Street in DC*	✓	✓	✓	✓	
existential *they* e.g. *They's a J Street in DC*	✓	✓	(✓)		
inverted embedded questions e.g. *I asked could I go*	✓	✓	✓	✓	(✓)

By far, the largest inventory of structures is represented in table 3, which lists the stable structures of AAVE. These traits were present in the Southern rural varieties of AAVE originally transplanted to urban non-Southern areas, thus showing the historical and current continuity of AAVE as it now transcends regional boundaries. There is certainly innovation and intensification as shown in table 1, as well as recession as shown in table 2, but these inventories are not nearly as exhaustive as the stable core of AAVE regardless of region. Notwithstanding some regional variation, there is strong support for a supra-regional core of AAVE, affirming the primary sociocultural and ideological basis for the construction of present-day AAVE.

It is also noteworthy that the non-Southern, urban context of AAVE tends to stand in stark opposition to benchmark European American varieties in these metropolitan areas. In an important sense, urban AAVE is more, though not isomorphically, aligned with Southern rural European American vernacular varieties than it is with surrounding European American Northern vernaculars. This dynamic is probably a reflection of the bi-racial ideology that defines most urban areas in the US and the developing oppositional identity that has developed in African American youth culture. As Fordham and Ogbu (1986) observe, young African Americans in urban areas do not want to 'act white'. In this context, 'speaking white' is the most salient indicator of white behavior. Although the notion of 'talking black' is constructed in such a way that it cannot be reduced to a simple inventory of structural traits as described here (Morgan 2001), linguistic features are certainly a part of this construction, and provide support for the perpetuation of ethnolinguistic distinctiveness. Urban AAVE may change and redefine itself over time and with changing social conditions, but it seems certain that it will remain the most prominent and significant sociocultural variety of American English for some time to come.

* Support for the research reported here comes from NSF Grand 0236838 and NSF Grant 9910024, HHS Grant MCJ-370599, MCJ-370649, and the William C. Friday Endowment at North Carolina State University. I'm grateful to Erik Thomas, Becky Childs, Christine Mallinson, Jeffrey Reaser, Daniel Schreier, and Benjamin Torbert for comments on an earlier version of this paper.

Exercises and study questions

1. What are the primary sociohistorical reasons for the emergence of urban AAVE as the locus for the development of this variety in the twentieth century?

2. Describe some of the features of AAVE that most likely developed or intensified in the twentieth century.

3. AAVE shares many features with other versions of vernacular American English dialects. How might these similarities best be accounted for?

4. Describe how camouflaging may be responsible for some subtle but significant traits of AAVE.

5. Why would AAVE intensify its linguistic traits at the same time that institution desegregation was taking place in American society?

Selected references

Please consult the General references for titles mentioned in the text but not included in the references below. For a full bibliography see the accompanying CD-ROM.

Alim, H. Sammy
    2001   I be the truth: Divergence, recreolization, and the equative copula in Black
            Nation Language. Paper presented at NWAV 30, Raleigh, NC. October,
            2001.
Bailey, Guy
    2001   The relationship between African American Vernacular English and White
            Vernaculars in the American South: A sociocultural history and some pho-
            nological evidence. In: Lanehart (ed.), 5–92.
Bailey, Guy and Natalie Maynor
    1985   The present tense of *be* in Southern Black folk speech. *American Speech*
            60: 195–213.
    1987   Decreolization? *Language in Society* 16: 449–474.
    1989   The divergence controversy. *American Speech* 64: 12–39.
Baugh, John
    1984   *Steady*: Progressive aspect in Black Vernacular English. *American Speech*
            59: 3–12.
Cukor-Avila, Patricia
    1995   The evolution of AAVE in a rural Texas community: An ethnolinguistic
            study. Ph.D. dissertation, Ann Arbor: University of Michigan.
    2001   Co-existing grammars: The relationship between the evolution of African
            American and Southern White Vernacular in the South. In: Lanehart (ed.),
            93–128.
Dayton, Elizabeth
    1996   Grammatical categories of the verb in African American Vernacular
            English. Ph.D. dissertation, Philadelphia: University of Pennsylvania.
Fasold, Ralph W.
    1976   One hundred years from syntax to phonology. In: Sanford Steever, Carle
            Walker and Salikoko Mufwene (eds.), *Papers from the Parasession on
            Diachronic Syntax*, 79–87. Chicago: Chicago Linguistics Society.
Fasold, Ralph and Walt Wolfram
    1970   Some linguistic features of Negro dialect. In: Fasold and Shuy (eds.),
            41–86.

Feagin, Crawford
    1979   *Variation and Change in Alabama English: A Sociolinguistic Study of the White Community*. Washington, DC: Georgetown University Press.

Fordham, Signithia and John Ogbu
    1986   Black students' school success: Coping with the burden of "acting white." *Urban Review* 18: 176–206.

Labov, William
    1987   Are black and white vernaculars diverging? Papers from the NWAVE XIV panel discussion. *American Speech* 62: 5–12.
    1998   Coexistent systems in African-American vernacular English. In: Mufwene, Rickford, Bailey and Baugh (eds.), 110–153.

Labov, William, Paul Cohen, Clarence Robins and John Lewis
    1968   *A Study of the Non-Standard English of Negro and Puerto Rican Speakers in New York City*. U.S. Office of Education Final Report, Research Project 3288.

Montgomery, Michael M. and Janet Fuller
    1996   Verbal $-s$ in 19th century African-American English. In: Schneider (ed.), 211–230.

Morgan, Marcylienna
    2001   "Nuttin but a G thang?" Grammar and language ideology in hip hop identity. In: Lanehart (ed.), 187–209.

Rickford, John R.
    1975   Carrying the new wave into syntax: The case of Black English *bin*. In: Fasold and Shuy (eds.), 162–183.
    1992   Grammatical variation and divergence. In: Marinel Gerritsen and Dieter Stein (eds.), *Internal and External Factors in Linguistic Change*, 175–200. The Hague: Mouton.

Rickford, John R. and Christine Théberge Rafal.
    1996   Preterit *had* + V-ed in narratives of African-American preadolescents. *American Speech*: 227–254.

Shuy, Roger W., Walt Wolfram and William K. Riley
    1967   *Linguistic Correlates of Social Stratification in Detroit Speech*. USOE Final Report No.6–1347.

Spears, Arthur K.
    1982   The Black English semi-auxiliary *come*. *Language* 58: 850–872.

Wolfram, Walt
    1974   The relationship of Southern White Speech to Vernacular Black English. *Language* 50: 498–527.

Earlier African American English: morphology and syntax

Alexander Kautzsch

1. The sociohistorical background for the evolution of AAVE

This section briefly summarizes the socio-historical context under which AAVE might have emerged. What is responsible for the extent to which slaves learned approximations of white dialects or restructured the English they used is likely to depend on the nature of the contact between black and white. Regional differences in and temporal change of settlement patterns, demographics, and economics of the US South suggest varying conditions for the slaves' language acquisition within the former colonial area of the US South (Rickford 1997; Winford 1997; Mufwene 2000). From a temporal perspective four "phases" need to be considered (Winford 1997: 314): the seventeenth century, the eighteenth century, the nineteenth century until reconstruction, and the post-reconstruction period.

At the beginning of colonization in the seventeenth century "Africans were scattered and integrated within a European majority" (Mufwene 2000: 237). This refers both to Virginia (founded in 1607) and South Carolina (founded in 1663). Nothing suggests the development of a pidgin or creole (Mufwene 2000: 237), although Winford (1997: 315) assumes that "creolized forms of English" (from the Caribbean or Africa) "existed side by side with the English dialects in at least some areas". Caribbean influence at this early stage is disputed (con: Mufwene 2000; pro: Rickford 1997; Winford 1997).

In the eighteenth century a regional distinction between the coastal areas of South Carolina and Georgia (founded in 1733) and the remaining area is necessary. In coastal South Carolina and Georgia, slave labor became more and more important because of the growing cultivation of rice and indigo (Winford 1997: 315). As a result a setting emerged that is similar to the one in the Caribbean, and it was likely that this context gave rise to Gullah (Mufwene 2000: 243; Winford 1997: 315). On the other hand, the slaves in the piedmont areas of Virginia, South Carolina and North Carolina may have continued to learn the settlers' dialects on small farms of Scotch-Irish settlers (Winford 1997: 315), on which the contacts between blacks and whites were probably fairly close. It is likely that "various second-language varieties" existed at this stage, which ultimately provided "the broad base on which AAVE continued to evolve" (Winford 1997: 315–316).

Due to increasing demands for cotton for the evolving textile industries (Mufwene 2000: 247), the nineteenth century sees an "expanding settlement of the Lower South, particularly the Gulf states" (Winford 1997), i.e. Alabama, Mississippi and Arkansas, in particular. This movement resulted in a relocation of about 250,000 slaves (Winford 1997: 316), which obviously contributed heavily to the spread of the "relatively stable AAVE vernaculars" (Mufwene 2000: 247) that had evolved by that time.

The Civil War (1861–1865) and the abolition of slavery brought only little economic improvement for former slaves. Due to the Jim Crow Laws (1877) in the southern states, which "disfavored African-Americans in the competition for jobs and for welfare entitlements" (Mufwene 2000: 248), segregation increased and reduced interaction between African and European Americans. As a consequence, thousands of African Americans started migrating to the North and West in the 1870s. This tendency continued when during the Great Migration (1910–1930) almost one million African Americans left the South. Finally, by the 1970s about 6 million had "outmigrated" (Mufwene 2000: 250). Of those who had left, a large majority had to live in urban ghettoes, socializing among themselves, and interacting "with other populations only at work" (Mufwene 2000: 250). This might indeed be the temporal starting point for the distinction between present-day urban and rural AAVE (cf. Wolfram, this volume), and it is likely that in this context some linguistic patterns, namely those primarily associated with AAVE today, emerged as signs of identity or "ethnic markers" (Mufwene 2000: 251) within the relatively homogeneous urban African American communities all across the US.

I am aware of the fact that this is a very sketchy description of the sociohistorical background, but it will meet the present needs. Note, however, that it is

> important to recall that each colony developed at different times along different lines, with different settlement patterns and demographic ratios between whites and blacks. Moreover, different types of agricultural activity made for different community settings both across colonies and within each colony, resulting in rather different kinds of contact between Africans and Europeans, and hence different linguistic outcomes. (Winford 1997: 319).

2.   Sources for the historical reconstruction of AAVE

The linguistic description of a historical variety is first and foremost dependent on the quality of the sources used in the reconstruction process. Early studies of the history of AAVE have relied upon "literary representations of the dialect in earlier centuries, travelers' reports, diaries, letters, newspaper announcements, and the like" (Schneider 1989: 2–3); but these types of sources are regarded as problematic today, especially because one of the main concerns in the study of Earlier AAVE is the quantitative description of this highly variable variety.

In the last two decades, however, quite a number of sources have been unearthed that provide us with various types of material that have turned out to be reliable sources for a valid reconstruction of Earlier AAVE on an empirical basis. Since the evaluation of sources in this field has become a very prominent and important issue, I will discuss the types of evidence that have been used in turn. (Bibliographical details of the source texts appear on the CD-ROM.)

2.1.   Written accounts of Earlier AAVE speech

Apart from those mentioned in the quotation above, the first source used were the WPA ex-slave narratives (ESN; Rawick 1972), on selections of which, e.g., Schneider (1989) is based. The reliability of Rawick (1972) has been disputed because of severe cases of editing, but Rawick's *Supplement* (1977/79) – a collection of the earlier unedited narratives – does lend itself to linguistic investigations (Kautzsch 2002: 12–19). An offshoot of ESN, namely the narratives conducted in Virginia and published separately by Perdue, Barden and Phillips (1976), has been shown to be a valuable source due to the proficiency of one interviewer in particular (Kautzsch 2002: 20–22). A further precious source are Harry Middleton Hyatt's (1970–1978) interviews with hoodoo doctors, which come very close to modern socio-linguistic interviews. (cf. Kautzsch 2002, amongst others). What is necessary when using these kinds of sources as linguistic evidence is a careful selection of samples with special reference to the quality of the fieldwork.

2.2.   The ex-slave recordings (ESR)

The only extant audio-samples of Earlier AAVE have been discovered by Guy Bailey and his associates (Bailey, Maynor and Cukor-Avila 1991) and have been analyzed in a variety of publications (e.g., all articles in Bailey, Maynor, and Cukor-Avila 1991; most articles in Poplack 2000; Schneider 1989; Kautzsch 2002). Although doubts have been raised about the representativeness of this relatively small sample, they remain an invaluable starting point for the evaluation of any new "written" source.

2.3. Diaspora varieties and insular communities

A research group around David Sankoff and now especially Shana Poplack and Sali Tagliamonte aims at describing the language of the African American Diaspora. They discovered fairly isolated African American communities both in Samaná (in the Dominican Republic; Samaná English, SE) and Nova Scotia (Canada; African Nova Scotia English, ANSE). The assumption that isolated communities are likely to preserve older stages of a variety due to lack of contact to outsiders makes these sources a valuable part of the reconstruction process. Having produced a fairly large body of research (e.g., all articles in Poplack, 2000; Poplack and Tagliamonte 2001), the central aim of this research group is to pin down the English heritage of (Earlier) AAVE.

Walt Wolfram and associates (e.g. Wolfram, Thomas and Green 2000; Wolfram and Thomas 2002) use data from a "longstanding, relatively isolated, bi-racial community" (Wolfram, Thomas and Green 2000: 316) in Hyde County, North Carolina. The English(es) spoken there by different generations of both black and white residents should "provide insight into the extent to which earlier AAVE shared in local dialect patterning" (Thomas and Green 2000: 316).

The third group in this category are former slaves who were sent to Liberia in the 19th century. John Singler (e.g. Singler 1989) analyzes their descendants' speech (Liberian Settler English), assuming that they have preserved some traits of Earlier AAVE up to the present. What is interesting in this context is that this variety of Earlier AAVE has the strongest resemblances to creoles.

2.4. Private correspondence

The last group of sources are collections of letters written by African Americans in the eighteenth and nineteenth centuries. Although it is likely that there is a multitude of letter collections slumbering in US archives, the linguistic analysis of this type of source has been fairly limited.

The sources analyzed so far are samples from the Federal Bureau Letters (FBL) published in Berlin et al. (1982, 1985, 1990, 1993), letters of former slaves who had been freed to Liberia (Wiley 1980) and of a slave family from Alabama, who partly migrated to Liberia (Miller 1978). (Letters from the latter two sources will be referred to as LAL in this article). Finally, there is a collection of letters from freed blacks who settled in Sierra Leone (Fyfe 1991; Sierra Leone Settler English, SLSE).

Especially when using letters as linguistic data some caution is necessary because literacy was the exception with African Americans at that time. Montgomery (1999) suggests that only writers who are obviously struggling with the written medium should be used as linguistic informants. Nonetheless, it is likely that certain linguistic features do not occur in written correspondence, either because of the limited size of the respective sources or because of norms that prevent or reduce non-standard forms in writing (cf. Kautzsch 2002: 253).

3.   Core issues in Earlier AAVE morphology and syntax

This section surveys the features of Earlier AAVE studied most intensively, as well as a selection of less prominent realms of the grammar useful for cross-variety comparison. Although this handbook seeks to provide primarily qualitative information on morpho-syntax, it is hardly possible to describe (Earlier) AAVE without mentioning quantitative distributions of linguistic features because it is mainly the proportional occurrence of variants that distinguishes (Earlier) AAVE from other varieties of English. From a merely qualitative point of view, Earlier AAVE has to offer only a few unique items, such as zero copula or *ain't* for *didn't*. The most prominent "distinctive" features of present-day AAVE – such as remote *been*, habitual *be* + V-*ing*, or the camouflaged forms *come* and *steady* – seem to be innovations established in the 20th century (cf. 1; Wolfram, this volume).

The whole section will show that on the one hand AAVE has come a long way in terms of internal diachronic evolution, on the other it needs to be kept in mind that at every stage there was a considerable amount of synchronic internal variation, implying that Earlier AAVE cannot have been a monolithic whole at any stage, but rather consisted of a bundle of varieties ranging from more or less creolized ones to fairly close approximations to white dialects. (cf. Kautzsch and Schneider 2000 for a detailed account of "differential creolization" in Earlier AAVE exemplified by ESN data from South Carolina).

3.1.   Verb morphology and tense/aspect

At the center of present tense morphology there is the highly variable presence of verbal -*s*. It occurs in all persons, but is never required. The primary grammatical person for verbal -*s* is 3rd singular, but it might also occur frequently in 1st and 3rd plural, with hierarchies of the plural contexts changing from source to source. (cf. Poplack and Tagliamonte 2001: 186; Schneider 1989: 69). What is more, even the constraints on or the conditions for its appearance differ widely. As far as phonological conditioning is concerned, some sources (e.g. ESN) revealed that after sibilants verbal -*s* tends to be omitted (*he wish*), while vowels and other consonants don't show a pattern, in others (ANSE, SE) vowels tend to favor verbal -*s* (*he goes*) and consonants tend to disfavor it (*she run*) (Schneider 1989: 70; Poplack and Tagliamonte 2001: 188–190). The type of subject might also have an effect on the occurrence of verbal -*s*. Noun phrase subjects – as opposed to pronoun subjects – sometimes favor verbal -*s* (*the woman speaks, he speak*) (SE, ANSE, FBL; Poplack and Tagliamonte 2001; Montgomery and Fuller 1996, FBL), however, this effect can be irrelevant, too (Hyde County elderly African Americans [Wolfram, Thomas, and Green 2000: 336–337]). In some varieties of earlier AAVE verbal -*s* is more likely to occur when the respective subject does not immediately precede the verb (i.e. when the two are non-adjacent; *the man who is ... speaks*). Sometimes this effect can be seen with pronoun subjects only, sometimes also with noun phrases (Montgomery and Fuller 1996; Poplack and Tagliamonte 2001). Finally, in some sources (SE and ANSE; not: FBL) verbal -*s* is favored in habitual context (*she always speaks*) (Poplack and Tagliamonte 2001; Montgomery and Fuller 1996).

Past-reference verbs in Earlier AAVE can either be morphologically marked for past tense or appear as stem forms. On the whole, scholars agree that the majority is in fact overtly marked, either by the attachment of the past tense suffix -*ed* – sometimes involving nonstandard regularization as in *knowed* – or by means of irregular past tense forms. (Schneider 1989: 81, ESN; Poplack and Tagliamonte 2001: 118, ANSE; Montgomery 1999: 11, SLSE).

Here, the conditions for explicit past marking are again quite variable. SLSE, in the first place, does not display clear conditioning effects at all (Montgomery 1999: 11). In those sources which do, the major constraint seems to be the phonetic context: before and after consonants the unmarked stem is clearly favored (*she talk to ... yesterday*) (Poplack and Tagliamonte 2001: 125–126; Schneider 1989: 81). In addition, in some varieties (SE and ANSE; not ESR) habitual aspect might have promoted -*ed* deletion (*my dad chop wood every...*) (Poplack and Tagliamonte 2001: 124, 127).

The second group of past-reference verbs are those which do not (only) form the past tense by means of the suffix -*ed*. There is a large number of nonstandard forms that involve consonant cluster reduction (*kep'*, *tol'*), devoicing of final /d/ (*killt*, *turnt*), double marking (*stoled*), invariable base form (*run* as past tense), past and participle switch (*drunk* as past tense), and nonstandard vowel change (*brung*) (Schneider 1989: 90–91).

Again, it seems that the majority of past-reference irregular verbs appear in their marked form. SLSE has only 12% of zero past tense marking (Montgomery 1999: 11). Poplack and Tagliamonte's (2001: 118) figures for stem forms in past contexts with strong verbs range from 23% (ESR; Samaná; North Preston, Nova Scotia) to 27% (Gaynesborough Enclave, Nova Scotia). When unmarked forms are used with past reference, however, they are likely to appear either with verbs that use their stem forms as participles (*come*), or in habitual contexts (Poplack and Tagliamonte 2001: 132).

The formation of present perfect and past perfect by means of *have/had* + past participle is basically identical to other varieties (Schneider 1989: 114, 117). Earlier AAVE can also delete *have* in structures like *have been* + V-*ing/* past participle (*I been making ... / I been hit by ...*). One somewhat striking but rare phenomenon in this section is that *been* + Vinf (*he been stay in de swamp*) can be used for past reference – equivalent to Standard English past tense or past perfect. From a structural point of view, this feature is similar to present-day AAVE's remote stressed *been*, but in Earlier AAVE the action denoted does not have to be remote (Schneider 1989: 114–120). In addition, perfective aspect can be expressed by *done* + past participle (or rarely V*inf*) as in *I done told you, She done write* with both present and past as reference points. *Done* can also be preceded by a form of *be* or *have* to mark present or past tense, respectively (*He is done gone / I had done quit*) (Schneider 1989: 121–124).

Progressive aspect in Earlier AAVE has not received wide attention, but seems to be identical to Standard English. In connection to this, prefix *a-* before V-*ing* (*I'm a-huntin'*) is a fairly stable feature, which only occurs on a very limited basis in present-day AAVE (Schneider 1989: 143–148).

What we know about the expression of future events in Earlier AAVE so far is that both *will* and *going to* (*gonna*) future are the two main variants of about equal frequency, while present simple and progressive have only minority status (Poplack and Tagliamonte 2001: 218–234; SE and ANSE). As far as constraints on the usage of *will* vs. *going to* are concerned, it seems that the latter is favored in future-in-the-past and in subordinate clauses, is avoided with verbs of motion, and does not imply proximity of future action, as is the case in other varieties of English (Poplack and Tagliamonte 2001: 227).

Finally, it needs to be mentioned that three of the four features that play a central role in the description of present-day AAVE are clearly innovations of the 20th century, namely the high frequency of invariant *be* before V-*ing* (*he be waking up at nine*) and the infamous aspectual markers *come* (for indignation; *they come talking that trash*) and *steady* (continuative; *she be steady stepping in there*). The existence of the fourth feature, habitual *be* (*We be here every day*), in Earlier AAVE is somewhat disputed. Some data, but definitely not all, suggest that habitual uses of *be* might have developed in or before the 19th century.

3.2. The copula in Earlier AAVE

This section surveys the most prominent type of auxiliary of Earlier AAVE: the copula *be*. In principle, this variety of English has the choice between using an overt form of the copula, *viz.* the full forms *am, are, is* or the contracted forms *'m, 're, 's,* or not (zero Ø).

Since zero copula is relatively rare (< 15%) with first person singular subjects, copula analyses mostly deal with the forms of *are* and *is*. Comparing a variety of sources, zero *is* seems to be quantitatively stable in spoken Earlier AAVE (13%–24%), while zero *are* has relative wide margins across sources (31%–71%). In letters the copula is rarely absent (< 2%), and in fact occurs near-categorically in its full form (Montgomery 1999: 9; Kautzsch 2002: 238).

The varying degree of copula absence is closely connected to the type of subject preceding it and the type of grammatical item following it, but also to the phonetic context. As far as subject type is concerned, personal pronouns favor copula absence over noun phrase subjects, at least in spoken sources (*she running; the woman's/is running*). (cf. Kautzsch 2002: 242-243 on letters). The grammatical categories that can follow after the copula are *gonna*, V-*ing*, adjectives, locatives and noun phrases. In most sources copula absence is most frequent with the two verbal complements *gonna* (*he gonna go to...*) and V-*ing* (*he running*) and least likely with noun phrases (*he's/is a man*). Adjectives (*she's/is/Ø pretty*) and locatives (*he's/is/Ø in the house*) are intermediate and their relative impact on copula absence varies greatly across sources. (For details see Rickford 1998; Kautzsch 2002; amongst others). In addition, the phonetic environment has some influence on the form of the copula, too: a preceding consonant favors the full form of *is* (*the cat is ...*), a preceding vowel promotes contraction (*she's...*). A following consonant favors zero *is* (*he Ø bad*), while a following vowel equally favors full and contracted *is* (*this man 's/is awful*) (Kautzsch 2002: 133–134).

The copula in past tense environments is overtly realized as *was* or *were* in most cases. Past tense copula absence ("... hadn' bought his check, I'd car'y him free, 'cause he Ø so sca'ed.' I like ter vomited." Simon Hare; Rawick 1977: 921) is the exception (Kautzsch 2002:93).

As regards the usage of *was* and *were*, some varieties of Earlier AAVE (e.g. ANSE) exhibit *was* leveling, i.e. *was* is the predominant form in standard *were*-contexts. Moreover, elderly African Americans in Horry County, NC, for example, level *was* (*you was ...*) in positive constructions and *weren't* (*he weren't ...*) in negative ones, which is clearly a reflex of the white vernacular in that region (Wolfram, Thomas and Green 2000).

3.3.   Negation

Negation in Earlier AAVE is in principle very similar to other non-standard varieties of English. Full verb negation is mostly achieved by means of *don't/ doesn't/didn't*. The norm for present tense copula negation is clearly *ain't*, although some sources also display some amount of *am/are/is* + *not*. The past tense copula forms are mostly *wasn't/weren't*. Present tense perfectives can be negated both by *ain't* and to a lesser degree by its standard counterpart *haven't/ hasn't*. Notice, however, that differences across sources can be great. With past tense perfectives *had't* seems to occur categorically (Kautzsch 2002: 44).

What is special about Earlier AAVE is the (rare) usage of *ain't* as a full verb negator, i.e. as an alternative for both *don't/doesn't* ("I hop' ya ain't wanna kno' much mo' 'cause I 'bout through." [Perdue, Barden and Phillips 1976: 210]) and *didn't* ("...but ah have went all ovah the house. An' ah ain't see nothin'. Like no kinda machine or nothin'." [Hyatt 1970–1978: 4565]) (cf. Schneider 1989; Kautzsch 2002). Moreover, *ain't* + past participle can also occur in non-perfective past tense contexts ("Marse Fleming ain't cared how much we dance, but ole overseer would raise de debbil." [Perdue, Barden and Phillips 1976: 224]) (Schneider 1989: 201–202; Kautzsch 2002: 44). Interestingly, in letters (LAL, FBL) *ain't* does not occur at all, which might be a reflex of the impact of some amount of literacy on writing (Kautzsch 2002: 226).

Of course, in combination with indeterminate items like *anything/nothing/ never* and the like, Earlier AAVE makes use of all kinds of negative transfer (negative concord, negative attraction, negative postposing). Negative concord (or multiple negation), where a negative element is present both in the predicate and in an indeterminate item (*I don't know nothing*), is clearly preferred over the standard pattern (*I don't know anything*) (Schneider 1989: 192; Kautzsch 2002: 62). In letters, however, the reverse is true (LAL, FBL; Kautzsch 2002: 227).

In negative attraction the negative is transferred from the predicate to a preverbal indeterminate (*Nobody knows it*; *I never saw...*). This pattern is the norm in Earlier AAVE, but its nonstandard counterpart, where the negative indeterminate is followed by a negated predicate ("No white folks didn't leave me nothing but de wide world." [Perdue, Barden, and Phillips 1976: 77] "A dirt dauber got a wisdom dat yo' an' yore mother nevah ain't learnt." [Hyatt 1970–1978: 1329]), also occurs, though only as a minority variant (Kautzsch 2002: 78). Personal letters only contain the standard patterns (LAL, FBL; Kautzsch 2002: 230). A peculiar construction in connection with preverbal *never*, is the usage of *did* + Vinf sometimes replacing the past tense form of the predicate ("We never did pay him, 'cause we ain't never had nothin'." [Perdue, Barden, and Phillips 1976: 14; Kautzsch 2002: 81]).

Finally, negative postposing is also very frequent, with negation being expressed in a postverbal indeterminate ("In wah times a man wuz no more den a varmint." [Rawick 1977: 1347]). In instances with preverbal *never* the negative element tends to be repeated in an indeterminate, resulting in something like a mixture between negative attraction and negative postposing ("He never had no children." [Hyatt 1970–1978: 912; Kautzsch 2002: 82]).

3.4. Relativization

Earlier AAVE has basically the same relativizers as Standard English: *who, which, whom, whose, that,* and zero (i.e. relative marker deletion) when it is not the subject of the relative clause (*the man Ø I saw; the man Ø I gave the book to*). In spoken sources, however, the *wh*-relativizers – especially *whom* and *whose* – occur only to a very limited extent. In addition, there are two frequent non-standard usages, namely zero in subject position (*The man Ø came round the corner was my daddy*) and *what* (*The man what came around the corner...*). Interestingly, the latter is virtually absent from written correspondence. Finally, some sources contain the (marginal) usage of *that which* ("But these, these little fellahs that which had stayed befo' God prayin', they didn't go an' drink the wine ..." [Hyatt 1970–1978: 4718]) and non-spatial *where* as relative markers ("My father was one o de founders o' de Underground Railroad where help de slaves to run way to de North ..." [Perdue, Barden, and Phillips 1976: 17; cf. Kautzsch 2002: 172]).

As all other kinds of variables, relative marker choice can also be due to a variety of factors. The number one criterion obviously is the syntactic function of the relative marker. It appears that – at least in spoken sources – zero and *that* tend to be preferred in non-subject (*The man Ø I saw*) and subject position (*The man that came ...*), respectively, while *what* is not favored in either. In written sources of private correspondence *that* is first choice both as subject and non-subject (Kautzsch 2002: 244).

Further constraints are the humanness or non-humanness of the antecedent as well as its grammatical category (such as pronoun, definite or indefinite noun phrase), and also the adjacency or non-adjacency of the relative marker to its referent. Table 1 (cf. Kautzsch 2002: 210, 252) surveys these for spoken sources. Items printed in bold type are those on which spoken and written sources agree.

Table 1.   Constraints on the choice of *that, what* and *zero*

subject *that*	adjacent, **non-human, definite NPs/pronouns**
subject *what*	adjacent, human, definite NPs/pronouns
subject zero	**non-adjacent, human, indefinite NPs**
non-subject *that*	adjacent, **human**
non-subject *what*	non-adjacent, non-human, (definite/indefinite) NPs
non-subject zero	**adjacent pronouns**

3.5.   Noun morphology: plurals and possessives

In principle, plural marking is very similar to Standard English. There is regular pluralization by means of the suffix -*s* and irregular plural marking.

What is special here, again, is that the plural suffix -*s* is variably present in regular nouns. Interestingly, rates for plural marker absence have a fairly wide range from 2% to 40% across sources. And the conditions for unmarked plurals are also highly variable. What seems to be a very important constraint are other indications of plurality in the noun phrase. Numerals and other types of quantifiers, such as plural demonstratives (*these*) or items like *all* or *many* might have a favoring effect on zero plural (ESN, Schneider 1989; SE, ANSE, ESR, Poplack, Tagliamonte and Eze 2000; SLSE, Montgomery 1999). The phonetic context may also play a role, with slight tendencies towards zero plural before and after consonants. But variation is still considerable (SE, ANSE, ESR, Poplack, Tagliamonte and Eze 2000: 83).

What is definitely at work in Earlier AAVE is a tendency for particular lexemes to remain unmarked for plural. But again, different sources have different preferences: *head, mile,* and *year* are on top of the ESN list for non-marking (Schneider 1989: 153), and so are *time* and *day* for ANSE, SE and ESR, where *year*, on the contrary, favors overt plural marking.

As regards plural formation of Standard English irregular nouns, there are three possibilities in Earlier AAVE. The first is to use a regularized form instead of an irregular one (*mans*), the second to attach plural -*s* to the irregular form (*mens*), which is called double marking, or finally to use the unmarked form (*man*), with the latter possibly being the most popular amongst the nonstandard forms. On the whole, there is a high degree of variation once more, ranging from the occurrence of very few isolated standard forms (*goose* and *ox* in ESN, Schneider 1989: 159) to a relatively stable standard majority (59% in SLSE, Montgomery 1999: 16).

The second inflectional suffix on nouns in Earlier AAVE is genitive *-s*. It has only been studied by Schneider (1989: 162–167), who reports that its absence is rare both in ESN (9,3%) and ESR (10,3%). The only favoring effect for zero genitive seems to be a preceding sibilant.

3.6.   Pronominal system

Personal, possessive and reflexive pronouns are briefly surveyed in Table 2 (ESN, reproduced from Schneider 1989: 170–174).

Table 2.   Personal, possessive and reflexive pronouns of Earlier AAVE

pronouns	singular	plural
personal		
1st person	*I, me* (rare)	*we, us, we'uns, we-all*
2nd person	*you, you all* (very rare)	*you, you all, youse all, you'uns*
3rd person	masc: *he, him, hims* (the latter two are rare) fem: *she, her* (rare) neuter: *it, hit*	*they/dey*
possessive		
1st person	*my, me*	*our, us*
2nd person	*your* (orth. variation)	*your, you* (very rare), *you's* (very rare)
3rd person	masc: *his, he, him, hims* fem: *her, she* (very rare) neuter: *its, hits*	*their, they*
absolute forms		
1st person	*mine*	*our'n, ours*
2nd person	*yourn*	
3rd person	*hisn, his, hern, hers*	
reflexive		
1st person	*myself*	*ourselfs, ourself, us ownse'fs*
2nd person	*yourself*	*youahseves*
3rd person	*himself, hisself, his own self, hese'f, herself, itself*	*theyselves, dey ownse'fs, theirselves, themselves* (very rare)

In some sources it might be likely to encounter isolated cases of creole forms, such as *he* with female reference, or *we* both as personal (subject and object) and possessive pronoun (ESR, Schneider 1989: 175; note, however, that the informant is Wallace Quarterman, a native speaker of Gullah.).

Demonstrative pronouns are *this* and *these* for near reference, sometimes used in combination with *here*. For distant reference *that* and *them* are the norm. *Those* occurs only rarely (Schneider 1989: 174–175).

A very widespread pattern in the realm of pronouns is pronominal apposition, in which a noun phrase is immediately followed by a pronoun (*Marse Peter he makes a speech.*). This feature seems to be favored by definite human noun phrases in subject position and is almost exclusively restricted to 3rd person contexts (Schneider 1989: 186–191).

4.   Major issues in current research

The three main interests in current research are the discovery and validation of sources that might represent earlier stages of AAVE (see section 2 above), quantitative analyses to prove or disprove creole and/or British dialect connections, and – closely related to this – the investigation of the divergence claim. This section surveys the latter two.

The origins of AAVE "loom large in the discussion of the development of African-American Vernacular English" (Rickford 1998: 154). Traditionally, creolists and dialectologists had opposing views. The former held that AAVE started out as a full-fledged creole similar to the ones spoken, for example, in the Caribbean today, while the latter saw AAVE just as a dialect of English which the newly arrived slaves acquired from their masters or the white people they worked with. (References for both views appear on the CD-ROM.) This dichotomy is, however, not a categorical one. The dialectologists have never "excluded the possibility of a previous creole stage of Black English, especially with respect to the initial stages of slavery, nor have they denied the existence of African or creole remnants in the present-day dialect" (Schneider 1989: 25). On the contrary, most creolists admit that some influence of white speech on black "is clearly to be expected, but the degree and importance of this influence is thought to be relatively limited" (Schneider 1989: 25).

The topicality of this debate is exemplarily reflected in two recently published volumes: Rickford (1999) represents a moderate version of the creolists' view, Poplack (2000) and associates aim at documenting the "English History of African-American English". It seems that varying opinions towards the development of AAVE are strongly a matter of degree and largely depend on the focus of the respective investigation. Rickford (1998: 189) argues "that *at least some* of the predecessors of modern AAVE arose from a restructuring process similar to that which produced the English-based creoles" (my emphasis). Quite differently, the group around Poplack emphasizes that the development of the grammatical core of present-day AAVE is entirely English. To some extent, the two approaches are complementary. Taken together, AAVE developed out of an English grammatical core, but has been steadily reshaped – at least in fringe sections of its grammar – by creole or substrate influences from outside or by creolization or imperfect second language learning from within.

What is necessary to put at the center of the discussion, however, is to realize that AAVE used to be much more heterogeneous in its early days than it is today (cf. Mufwene 2000; Kautzsch and Schneider 2000); and an integrative approach that takes into account both sides is most likely to deliver the most accurate assessment of the status and the evolution of AAVE.

The second big issue is the claim that present-day AAVE is structurally becoming more and more different from other varieties of English, which is usually referred to as the "divergence hypothesis" (For references see CD-ROM.) From a socio-political point of view, divergence means that, although attempts have been made to integrate black people into mainstream US society, the segregation of the ethnic groups in the US is still great. On the other hand, this tendency can also be seen as "part of a symbolic statement of today's young people of awareness and pride of their African American identity" (Rickford 1999: Preface xiii). The central linguistic features that are assumed to be divergent – which means that they are proportionally increasing in number – are invariant *be*, the deletion of third singular and possessive *-s* and of the copula. On the contrary, some features are also reported to remain stable or in fact converge with the white ones, as for example plural and past marking. (For a tabular survey of stable, converging and diverging features cf. Wolfram's survey in this volume.)

As far as methods are concerned, it is necessary to "go back in time, both to the historical records and as far as possible to all of the other available evidence to see what was going on" (Rickford 1997: 60). This brings us back to one of the central statements of this article: what we can learn about Earlier AAVE is only as good as the sources we use.

Exercises and study questions

1. Judging from a socio-historical perspective, is it likely that today's African American English has one homogeneous ancestor? Include the relationship between settlement patterns / demographics and language contact in your answer.

2. Describe the two opposing views on the historical evolution of African American English.

3. What does the "divergence hypothesis" claim?

4. Which grammatical features can be omitted (zero forms) in Earlier African American English? Which are the conditions that favor the respective zero forms?

5. Corpus analyses (good for class assignments or in-class group work):
   The accompanying CD-ROM contains samples of Earlier African American English letters and of transcribed interviews (some accompanied by speech samples from the ex-slave recordings).
   a) Read the sample texts on the CD-ROM and identify (i.e. analyze qualitatively) all (or a selection of) nonstandard linguistic features mentioned above. Is there a difference between letters and interviews?
   b) Take any linguistic feature discussed in the article above (e.g. verbal -*s*, past tense formation, copula usage, negation patterns, relative markers, etc.) and make quantitative analyses on the basis of the sample texts.
   For verbal -*s*, take all present tense predicates and count the absence or presence of the morpheme in all persons and enter your findings in a table like the one below. Compare the results for each text. Is there individual variation across speakers/writers? Then combine the results for the interviews and the results for the letter. Is there a difference between the two source types?

Sample table for quantification

person	verbal -*s* present	verbal -*s* absent
1st sing.		
2nd sing.		
3rd sing.		
1st pl.		
2nd pl.		
3rd pl.		

Selected references

Please consult the General references for titles mentioned in the text but not included in the references below. For a full bibliography see the accompanying CD-ROM.

Berlin, Ira, Joseph R. Reidy and Leslie S. Rowland
  1982   *Freedom. A Documentary History of Emancipation, 1861–1867*. Series II.
            The Black Military Experience. Cambridge: Cambridge University Press.
Berlin, Ira, Barbara J. Fields, Thavolia Glymph, Joseph R. Reidy and Leslie S.
  Rowland
  1985   *Freedom. A Documentary History of Emancipation, 1861–1867*. Series
            I, Vol. I. *The Destruction of Slavery*. Cambridge: Cambridge University
            Press.
Berlin, Ira, Thavolia Glymph, Steven F. Miller, Joseph R. Reidy, Leslie S. Rowland and
  Julie Saville
  1990   *Freedom. A Documentary History of Emancipation, 1861–1867*. Series I,
            Vol. III. *The Wartime Genesis of Free Labor: The Lower South*. Cambridge:
            Cambridge University Press.
Berlin, Ira, Steven F. Miller, Joseph R. Reidy and Leslie S. Rowland
  1993   *Freedom. A Documentary History of Emancipation, 1861–1867*. Series I,
            Vol. II. *The Wartime Genesis of Free Labor: The Upper South*. Cambridge:
            Cambridge University Press.
Fyfe, Christopher (ed.)
  1991   *"Our Children Free and Happy": Letters from Black Settlers in Africa in
            the 1790s*. Edinburgh: Edinburgh University Press.
Hyatt, Harry Middleton
  1970–1978 *Hoodoo – Witchcraft – Conjuration – Rootwork*. Vol. 1.–5.
            Washington: The Alma Egan Hyatt Foundation.
Kautzsch, Alexander
  2002   *The Historical Evolution of Earlier African American English. An
            Empirical Comparison of Early Sources*. Berlin/New York: Mouton de
            Gruyter.
Kautzsch, Alexander and Edgar W. Schneider
  2000   Differential creolization: Some evidence from Earlier African American
            Vernacular English in South Carolina. In: Neumann-Holzschuh and
            Schneider (eds.), 247–274.
Miller, Randall M.
  1978   *"Dear Master." Letters of a Slave Family*. Ithaca and London: Cornell
            University Press.
Montgomery, Michael
  1999   Eighteenth-Century Sierra Leone English: Another exported variety of
            African American English. *English World-Wide* 20: 1–35.
Montgomery, Michael and Janet M. Fuller
  1996   What was verbal -*s* in 19th century African American English? In: Schneider
            (ed.), 211–230.

Mufwene, Salikoko
   2000   Some sociohistorical inferences about the development of African
             American English. In: Poplack (ed.), 233–263.
Perdue, Charles L., Thomas E. Barden and Robert K. Phillips
   1976   *Weevils in the Wheat: Interviews with Virginia Ex-slaves.* Charlottesville:
             University Press of Virginia [Reprinted 1992].
Poplack, Shana, Sali Tagliamonte and Ejike Eze
   2000   Reconstructing the source of Early African American English plural mark-
             ing: A comparative study of English and Creole. In: Poplack (ed.), 73–
             105.
Rawick, George P. (ed.)
   1972   *The American Slave: A Composite Autobiography.* 19 vols. Westport,
             Connecticut: Greenwood.
Rickford, John R.
   1997   Prior creolization of African-American Vernacular English? Sociohistorical
             and textual evidence from the 17th and 18th centuries. *Journal of
             Sociolinguistics* 1: 315–336. [Reprinted in Rickford and Romaine (eds.),
             233–251.]
   1998   The creole origins of African-American vernacular English: Evidence
             from copula absence. In: Mufwene, Rickford, Bailey and Baugh (eds.),
             154–200.
Singler, John V.
   1989   Plural marking in Liberian Settler English, 1820–1980. *American Speech*
             64: 40–64.
Wiley, Bell I.
   1980   *Slaves No More. Letters from Liberia 1833–1869.* The University Press of
             Kentucky.
Winford, Donald
   1997   On the origins of African American Vernacular English – A creolist per-
             spective. Part I: The sociohistorical background. *Diachronica* 14: 305–
             344.
Wolfram, Walt, Eric R. Thomas and Elaine W. Green
   2000   The regional context of earlier African American speech: Evidence for
             reconstructing the development of AAVE. *Language in Society* 29: 315–
             355.

Gullah: morphology and syntax[*]

Salikoko S. Mufwene

1. Introduction

Gullah is one of the offspring of English spoken primarily among descendants of Africans on the coastal marshlands and islands of South Carolina and Georgia in the United States. Like its speakers, it has also been identified by the derogative name *Geechee*. Linguists have characterized it as a creole, and even stipulated it to be a separate language, but to its native speakers and this author, it is as much English as other nonstandard dialects that evolved concurrently with it. These include African American vernacular English (AAVE, spoken among African Americans elsewhere), Appalachian English, and Old Amish English, among others which are also socially stigmatized.

A reason commonly invoked to set Gullah apart from other North American English varieties is that it is not intelligible to speakers of other English varieties. However, mutual intelligibility is not a reliable criterion for determining whether a particular language variety is a dialect of a language or a separate language. Besides, there are numerous English dialects that are not intelligible to many other speakers, including the classic case of Cockney, which nobody has ever claimed to be a separate language.

Another reason is that Gullah is contact-based, as is putatively made evident by the several structural features it shares with Caribbean English creoles, as illustrated in section 2. However, the history of European immigrations to English North America suggests that all English varieties that developed in the relevant colonies are contact-based (Mufwene 2001). It is also highly debatable whether creoles can be characterized as a special type of languages based on their typological features alone and whether, in the first place, the features they share are due primarily to the non-English contributions to their developments.

Linguists have generally professed to following the sentiments of native speakers in determining whether a particular variety is a dialect or a separate language. Ironically, the same principle has not been followed in the case of creoles (and pidgins). Linguists have typically disregarded the fact that most of their users say they speak English (albeit a nonstandard and stigmatized variety) or any other relevant European language. Gullah and the like can very well be considered disfranchised varieties of Germanic and other Indo-European languages.

Unlike its sister AAVE, whose origins can be associated with the tobacco and cotton plantations of the American southeast, Gullah developed on the large South Carolinian and Georgian coastal rice fields of the early 18th century, a few decades after the first British colonists and their African slaves settled in Charleston, from Barbados, in 1670. The earliest written attestations of it date from the early 19th century, in William Gilmore Simms' *The book of my lady* (1833), although there are reports in 18th-century colonial newspapers of some runaway slaves speaking "broken" English, especially those who had been on the plantations for a few months only.

Given all the negative attitudes toward Africans since the beginnings of the American colonization by the English, the fact that Gullah remained undocumented for so long—although it must have started diverging from other American Southern English varieties in the early 18th century—reflects a number of factors, including the following:

(1) American English has always been spoken variably among (descendants of) Africans, as among (those of) Europeans. Interpreted as a continuum of basilectal and lower mesolectal varieties relative to the national or some regional standard variety, Gullah is not spoken by all the native coastal African Americans identified by the same name, not any more than AAVE can be associated with all African Americans in other parts of the USA, or southern English with all White Southerners.

(2) During the earlier colonial times, especially during the 17th century, most of the locally-born African Americans must have spoken like the locally-born White Americans with whom they grew up and interacted regularly in the same homestead. Before major plantations had developed, the Africans were generally minorities, the societies were not rigidly segregated, and all adults joined efforts to survive the harsh challenges of life in their new physical ecology. Note that the earliest forms of colonial English must have been as proletarian as most of their European speakers, who were often destitute and from the lowest ranks of the European societies.

(3) As observed in Mufwene (2001), Gullah as an ethnolect spoken by a significant proportion of locally born descendants of Africans was probably not identifiable as a distinct variety before the second quarter of the 18th century, after the rice plantations increased in size and number. Then, their slave labor increased more by importation than by birth (Wood 1974; Edgar 1998), the population turnover was rapid, and language was being transmitted to learners more from non-native than from native speakers. This fostered

more and more room for substrate elements to influence Gullah's divergence away from other American southern varieties, although in many, if not most, cases the influence meant favoring particular variants of colonial English that would be disfavored in the other varieties. For instance, this appears to have been the case in the selection of preverbal *duhz/does* [dəz] as a marker of habitual activities, as in *how you duhz cook hog maw?*, of preverbal *duh* [də] as the durative marker, and of the pronunciations of *bear* and *carry* as [bʰɛ] and [kʲaː] respectively.

Specifics about how the divergent restructuring proceeded away from other varieties remain as controversial as regarding the development of creoles in general. The traditional explanation in terms of language contact raises more interesting questions than it provides conclusive answers to them. The attribution of its divergence to the particular influence of the Black African languages that had been spoken by the slaves who developed it (Turner 1949) would be less controversial if the African languages were typologically homogeneous and if one did not have to account for the competition and selection mechanisms that favor some particular substrate influences over other competitors. While substrate influence seems obvious, determining how it prevailed, and whether it could have done so if there had not been particular congruent features in colonial English itself remain open questions (Mufwene 2001).

2.   Gullah and Atlantic Creoles

Gullah has been identified as a Creole for a number of reasons, chiefly because it evolved under socio-economic conditions similar to other new nonstandard vernaculars of the Atlantic and Indian Oceans called creoles. As noted above, it also shares several structural features with these vernaculars. Moreover, its primary speakers are of African descent, just like those of the other vernaculars previously identified as creoles. However, the term *creole* itself is unknown to its speakers and has not been used locally in the histories of South Carolina and of Georgia to designate either the locally born populations of non-indigenous stock or this new language variety. It was assigned to Gullah, as to other such English vernaculars, by linguists, on the mistaken assumption that creoles have evolved by nativization from erstwhile pidgins. This assumption is supported by no shred of evidence from the socio-economic histories of the territories where creoles and pidgins developed, viz., settlement and trade colonies, respectively (Mufwene 2001).

Among the features that Gullah shares with other Atlantic English creoles are the following, some of which are discussed more informatively in Part 3: 1) extensive use of preverbal free morphemes, rather than verbal inflections for tense and aspect (e.g. *bin* for past or past of past, *go/ga* [gə] for future, *duh* [də] for progressive, and *done* 'finish' for perfect); 2) partial gender and case distinctions in the pronominal systems (thus *him* is used for all three genders and is used both as object and subject); 3) use of *say* not only as in English but also as a complementizer (e.g. *we hear say you gone to da city* 'we heard that you [were] gone to the city'); 4) use of *fuh* [fə] (from English *for*) as a non-factive complementizer (as in *we tell um fuh come* 'we told him to come'); 5) modal use of *fuh* (as in *Fonzo bin fuh come* 'Fonzo had/was expected to come'); 6) extensive use of serial verb/predicate constructions (as in <u>come kyah</u> me to d'hospital 'come and take me to the hospital'); 7) use of an invariant relativizer *weh* derived from *what* (and perhaps also relativizer uses of *where*) in nonstandard English; 8) nonindividuated nouns for generic or mass reference (as in <u>kyat</u> don eat **raw tato** 'a cat does not eat raw potato' or 'cats don't eat raw potato'); 9) common usage of the associative plural (as in *Sara <u>dem</u> very nice people* 'Sara and her family/friends/associates are very nice people'); 10) predicate cleft (as *duh talk he duh talk!* 'he is really talking!'); and 11) similar pronunciations of words such as *oil* [aʸl], *cat* [kʸat], *fair* [fʸɛː], variable stopping of interdental fricatives, and variable [b] or [β] pronunciations of /v/ and /w/ (as in [βɛrɪ βɛl] 'very well').

Some of these similarities are only partial and in fact there is no fixed set of features that a vernacular must have of necessity to be identified as a creole. For instance, 1) Gullah has an indefinite article *a* (pronounced only as [ə]) where other English creoles use the singular quantifier *one*; 2) it actually has a schwa (which is not attested in Caribbean creoles); 3) it uses prenominal *dem* (as in *dem boy*) both with the meaning 'those boys' and the meaning 'the boys', whereas Jamaican Creole uses prenominal *dem* for the plural demonstrative meaning only and has *di* + Noun + *dem* for definite plural; 4) it has a wider set of negators (*aint, don*, and narrow-scope *no* within a noun phrase) where Jamaican Creole, for instance, uses only *no*; 5) it has a special habitual marker *duhz*, which only Guyanese Creole has been reported to have (in the form of *doz*, because it has no schwa); and 6) it also has the option of using *tuh/to* [tə] (often voiced to [də]) to introduce non-factive verb phrases (e.g., *Uh start duh run* 'I started to run'), as well as 7) that of omitting the complementizer *fuh* or *tuh* after the verbs *want, start,* and *try* (as in *Uh try tell um* 'I tried to tell him').

Gullah shares some of these features that distinguish it from other English creoles with AAVE and neighboring White English vernaculars, for instance uses of: 1) prenominal *dem* for plural demonstratives; 2) *aint* as a negator in contexts where standard English would use *did not* or *have/has not* in full or contracted form; 3) an indefinite article *a* which need not become *an* when the noun starts with a vowel; 4) *yall* as a more common second person plural pronoun (instead of *unu/una* which is not the dominant variant in other Atlantic creoles either); and 5) invariant *be* for repeated states of affairs (as *he be so sick/ staring at me*). One can actually also argue that Gullah is a subvariety of African American English spoken where there used to be rice fields, or that it is a separate ethnolect that is structurally between AAVE and Caribbean English creoles. There is no clear structural boundary between Gullah and AAVE. Mufwene (2001) claims that both can be considered regional varieties of African American English, with the former confined to coastal South Carolina and Georgia. In more or less the same spirit, Kautzsch and Schneider (2000) argue for a geographical continuum in which "creole" features decrease as one proceeds inland. Similarities and differences between AAVE, Gullah, and Caribbean creoles have hotly been debated since the 1960s.

Differences between Gullah and other Atlantic/Caribbean English creoles have been used to argue that Gullah has "decreolized," in the sense of losing some illusory common basilect of all English creoles, in the direction of American middle class English. AAVE would putatively be farther along on this trajectory. However, the evolution of English in North America has not been uniform, largely reflecting variation in the patterns of earliest settlements (Founder Effect) and in later population growth.

Further, heeding Labov and Harris (1986), some linguists have concluded that since the early 20th century AAVE has been diverging from White Southern English, with which it shares origins (e.g., Bailey and Cukor-Avila forthcoming). Recent forceful arguments for the English origins of several African American English features can be found in, for instance, Poplack (2000). The ongoing divergence is due to decreasing social contacts between White and African Americans and the fact that language also functions as a marker of identity within both ethnic groups. In other words, Gullah and AAVE seem to have emerged as distinct varieties from other American (nonstandard) English vernaculars in the way hypothesized by Chaudenson (2001) and Mufwene (2001) for creoles in general, viz., basilectalizing away from their colonial kin varieties spoken by (descendants of) Europeans, to which they were structurally closer in the earlier stages.

Thus the above similarities and differences, as well as others not discussed here or in the literature, suggest the following conclusions: Gullah developed from English varieties similar to those that evolved into Caribbean English creoles. The family resemblance between them, as among all creoles that developed from the "same" European language, are attributable to ecological differences that favored varying selections into each creole's system from similar pools of competing variants. The ecologies include, among other factors: the times of settlements, the rates of population growth, the extent of ethnolinguistic diversity and the demographic strengths of particular groups at various colonial stages (especially within the substrate population), inter-group relations, proportions of Europeans and non-Europeans, and time of segregation since the founding of the colony (Mufwene 2001). A number of recurring elements from one setting to another, compounded with convergent shifts to (varieties of) the same language, account for the similarities.

3.   Gullah's structures

This part focuses on various morphosyntactic features that have been discussed by various scholars, mostly myself, since Turner's (1949) pioneering and seminal linguistics study. Unfortunately none of them will be cited here. More interested readers can consult dissertations and publications since the 1970s by Irma Cunningham, Patricia Jones-Jackson, Patricia Nichols, Katherine Mille, Tometro Hopkins, Tracey Weldon, and myself (listed in the comprehensive bibliography on CD.) Space limitations naturally constrain both the number of grammatical peculiarities discussed below and the depth of the discussions themselves. Examples are from my own fieldwork data, some cited with informant initials and the year of fieldwork.

There are many ways in which Gullah has preserved structures that are English, for instance, the basic major constituent order in a sentence is Noun Phrase (NP) + Verb Phrase (VP), although the rule that inverts the order of the subject NP and an auxiliary verb in interrogative main clauses does not apply. Questions are typically marked by intonation, especially those starting with a *wh*-phrase or *aint* ([ɛʸn(t)], [ɛ̃], [ɪnɪ] < *aint it*), as in *Ain/Inni you see Al yes'day?* 'Didn't you see Al yesterday?' (literally, 'Isn't it true/the case that you saw Al yesterday?'). In such a sentence *aint/inni* has scope over the whole sentence, in more or less the same way as the French *n'est pas que* does, as in *N'est-ce pas que tu as vu Al hier?* The other kind of negative question, which happens to have the same surface structure in non-creole English would be *You ain see Al yes'day?* The wider scope *aint/inni* can co-occur with another *ain* or any other negator inside the sentence, as in *Ain you ain see Al yes'day?* 'Isn't it true/the case that you didn't see Al yesterday?' or *Aint you don buy grits?* 'Isn't it the case that you don't buy grits?'.

The object NP still follows the verb, and within the NP, the order is still Det(erminer) + Adj(ective) + N(oun) + Modifying clause. Gullah strands prepositions and does not pied-pipe them, just like nonstandard English dialects, in which constructions such as *the boy* **to whom** *I spoke* are not typical. And indeed it has prepositions and no postpositions. It has also preserved the category Adj, though adjectives are used without a copula in the predicative function, as in *Robert very tall* or *Robert taller 'n Faye* or *April more puhty* 'April [is] prettier'. Substrate influence can be identified in some details of the grammar, such as the complete obliteration of Subject + Verb Concord, uses of the same pronominal forms in subject and possessive functions, and uses of *done* pre- or post-verbally to mark nuances of perfect (see below), although such influence must be more from Kwa-like languages than from Bantu (in which the possessive pronoun is clearly marked as such and follows the head noun). Overall substrate influence in Gullah is the strongest where there was at least partial congruence between the feature of some colonial English dialect and its counterpart in some African languages. There is little in Gullah's structural system that does not have a (partial) model in some nonstandard English dialect.

Though the following discussion will focus on those respects in which Gullah differs from other English dialects, one need not jump to the conclusion that these domains of divergence justify identifying it as a creole. As noted above, creoles differ among themselves in regard to the structural features that make them different from other offspring of the same European languages they have evolved from. The identification of some new colonial vernaculars as creoles seems to have had to do more with who their speakers are than with the particular kinds of restructuring that have produced them.

3.1. The noun phrase

One of the things that first caught my attention about Gullah's structures is the use of nouns in non-individuated form (i.e., without a determiner and number suffix) not only for mass reference, as in *he don eat* **hog maw** 'he/she does not eat hog maw', but also for generic or non-specific reference as in the following examples:

(1)   a. *you gwine cut it with* **knife**?
          'Are you going to cut it with **a knife** (not assumed known to the addressee)?'
   b. *all he do is chase* **ooman**
          'all he does is chase **women**/all he did was chase women'
   c. *You ever see cat eat raw tato skin*?
          'Have you ever seen a cat eat raw potato skin?'

Worth noting in this connection is also the fact that Gullah marks nominal plural sometimes as in other English varieties, by attaching the plural suffix {S} to the noun. This practice, which has nothing to do with decreolization, is common in the mesolect, which is the variety spoken by the vast majority of its speakers, a phenomenon that is true of other creole-speaking territories, as observed by Rickford (1990). However, in the basilect, nominal plural is marked by preposing *dem* to the noun, as in *dem boy*, with the ambiguous meaning 'the boys' or 'those boys'. Co-occurrence with the plural suffix {S} is also common, making Gullah similar to other American nonstandard English varieties on the particular parameter of nominal pluralization. The plural marker is typically missing when the noun is modified by a numeral quanti- fier, as in *four boy(s)*, though constructions such as *four chillun* 'four chil- dren' and *four people* (with suppletive plural forms) are common. Evidence that nominal *dem* is a portmanteau morpheme for both plural and definite is provided by the ill-formedness of **four dem boy(s)*, as opposed to *dem four boy(s)*. Gullah is also well known for its associative plural, in which a proper name or a definite NP is followed by *(an') dem* or *(an') nem* to associate the definite referent with a specific group, such as family, friends, and colleagues. When the head noun is a proper name, *an* 'and' is often omitted, as in *Sara (an') dem/nem*.

Regarding personal pronouns, Gullah's basilect diverges from its Jamaican and Guyanese counterparts in particular. For the first person singular, it has the subjective form *Uh* [ʌ], the objective form *me*, which also alternates in the possessive function with the more common variant *muh* [mʌ] (English *my*). The second person pronoun is *you*, which remains the same in all syntactic functions. It commonly assumes the form *ye* [yi] in the possessive function, as in *ye buba* 'your brother'. The unmarked pronominal form for the third person singular is *(h)e*, regardless of gender. It becomes *(h)im* or *um* [ʌm] in the ob- jective function but remains *he* in the possessive. When used as the object of the verb *see*, *um* fuses with it in the stereotypical form *shum* [ʃʌm]. There is, however, also the gender-specific pronoun *she*, which remains the same in all syntactic functions. In addition, the pronoun *it* behaves more or less like *she*, except that it seems to merge with *(h)e* in the possessive function. It is thus partly inaccurate to claim that Gullah's pronominal system is gender-less in the third person singular. Only *(h)e* and *(h)im/um* are gender-neutral. *She* and *I(t)* are gender-specific.

In the first person plural, *we* occurs in the subject function but alternates in the object function with *us*. In the possessive function the allomorph *our*, typically pronounced [aʷ] is used. Although the variant *you* is also used for second person plural (with the same distribution as the singular), the more common one is *yall* [yɔ:l], as in other American South nonstandard English varieties, with *yall's* as the possessive. There is also the celebrated variant *(h)una* [(h)ənə] ~ [unə], which I have encountered only in stereotypical discourse produced in performances. The third person plural pronoun is *deh* [dɛ:], attested in the subject and possessive functions, and *dem* [dɛm] which occurs in the subject and object functions. Its weaker variant *em* [ɛm] is attested only in the object function.

With the exception of *yall's*, all the above pronouns combine with *own* to express possession elliptically, viz., *my/muh own* 'mine', *you own* 'yours', *he/she own* 'his/hers/its', *we/ou' own* 'ours', and *deh own* 'theirs'. To form the reflexive, the morpheme *se(l)f* is added to whatever form also occurs in the possessive function, except *yall's*, viz., *meself/muhself, youself/yeself, heself/sheself, weself/ourself*, and *dehself/demself*.

3.2.   Relative clauses

It is useful to distinguish between factive and non-factive/purposive relative clauses. The latter are introduced by the complementizer *fuh*, as in *a book fuh da chillun (fuh/tuh) read* 'a book for the children to read'. Factive relative clauses are introduced by a null complementizer or by *weh* [wɛ], from English *what*, pronounced [wæt] in some dialects and also used as a relativizer in some nonstandard English varieties, as in *everything what Alison said* 'everything that Alison said'. This example corresponds to *everything (weh) Alison say* in Gullah. Moreover, *weh* also occurs in more or less the same form as an interrogative, as in *Weh/Way he tell you?* 'What did he tell you?'.

The relativizer *weh* seems to function as a complementizer. When the relativized noun is the object of a preposition, this must be stranded, never pied-piped, as illustrated below:

(2)   a.   *a knife fuh cut da meat wi'*
            'a knife to cut the meet with'
        a'. **a knife wi' weh fuh cut da meat*
            'a knife with which to cut the meat'
        b.   *da gyal (weh) Clinton duh look at*
            'the girl (that) Clinton is looking at'
        b'. **da gyal at weh Clinton duh look*
            'the girl at whom Clinton is looking'

When the relativized noun has a possessive function, a resumptive pronoun is needed in the construction:

(3)   a. *da man (weh) he wife die laas week*
           'the man whose wife died last week'
       b. *da ooman (weh) Uh meet he son*
           'the woman whose son I met'

On the other hand, the relativized noun is gapped, along with the preposition *than*, as in other syntactic contexts, when it is the object of a comparative. The preposition *than* can be retained only when there is a resumptive pronoun.

(4)   a. *T's only ting weh covetin happier*
           'It's [the] only thing that coveting is happier than'   (AS, 1986)
       b. *Teddy da man (weh) everybody taller than *(him)*   (AS, 1986)

The relative pronoun can also be omitted when the relativized NP is a subject, thus producing a contact relative clause, as in *Dis da young man come 'eyah las' week* (MI, 1986) 'This is the young man [who/that] came here last week'. Such facts underscore the fact that Gullah has evolved from nonstandard English, rather than from a standard variety.

3.3.   Tense, mood, and aspect

Like other English varieties, Gullah expresses mood through modal verbs or the absence thereof. The verbs are the same, except that some of them are pronounced differently and have their own morphosyntactic peculiarities. The modal *can* is often pronounced as [kin] and its negative as [kɛ̃:]. In past contexts, it becomes *could, couldn'*, or *coulda* (< *could've* < *could have*). Its syntax is the same as in other English varieties.

The modal *must* works in basically the same way as in other English varieties too (with the negator following it, in a contracted form). When it is used epistemically, it is often followed by *be* as in (5), where *must be* either precedes the main verb or occurs sentence-initially:

(5)   a. *Deh must be put um deh.*
           'They must have put it there.'
       b. *Must be deh put um deh.*

The combination may well be interpreted as an adverb, like *maybe*, but it has not been subjected to any syntactic tests. There are some cases in which the subject is repeated after *must* as in the following sentence:

(6)   *When Uh first start buyin chicken, e mus' e bin about two cents*
       a pound.
       'When I first stated buying chicken, it must have been about two cents
       a pound.'   (MI, 1986)

There are also combinations of *must be* and *could(a)* in my data, as in:

(7)   *Dem gata must be coulda go fast.*
       'Those alligators must have been able to go/move fast.'   (EL, 1988)

Such a combination suggests that Gullah may not have an infinitive or a clear-cut finite/nonfinite distinction. The modal *can* certainly does not have an infinitival alternative. The negation in the above example would be *must be coudn' go fast* 'must not have been able to go/move fast'. If *must be* is treated as a phrasal or compound modal, then this example also illustrates a double modal use (so far hardly investigated in Gullah).

The modal *will* is seldom heard, because the future marker is *ga* [gə] (see below). On the other hand, *would* and *woulda* 'would have' are used, as in other English dialects. It is also negated as *wouldn'*, as in *Uh wouldn tell a damn lie* (JR, 1988). The auxiliaries *may* and *might(a)* are also attested in Gullah, with no particular idiosyncrasies to report here. Noteworthy are also attestations of the modal *have*, often in the form [hæ] 'have, had' followed by the complementizer *fuh* or *tuh*. Perhaps what distinguishes this vernacular the most from other American English vernaculars is the modal use of *fuh* as below:

(8)   *Jean bin fuh come yes'day*
       'Jean was to/had to/was expected to come yesterday.'

In this respect it is more akin to Caribbean English creoles, in which a similar construction is attested.

Gullah is also closer to Atlantic English creoles in the preverbal morphemes it combines with to mark tense and aspect. When the verb combines with no tense marker, reference is to the past or to a habit if it is non-stative but most likely to the present if it is stative, especially when the contextual domain does not suggest otherwise. The preverbal *bin* denotes anteriority, either past or past of past, depending on the contextual domain of its use. *Bin* is seldom used to express past, as the stativity parameter and the contextual domain provided by the ongoing discourse makes this redundant. Only at the beginning of some discourses would it be required. Future is expressed with the preverbal marker *ga* or *gwine*. This is negated by preposing *ain* to the verbal construction. It is also a relative tense, because it can be used in some contexts to express future of past, translated by *would* in English (an option also available in Gullah).

Gullah diverges the most from other American (southern) English counterparts by the way it marks aspect. As with tense, the marker is a free preverbal morpheme. The progressive, also known as durative in creolistics, is expressed with *duh* [də] followed by a verb stem or by a present participle. The latter can also be used alone for the same purpose. Thus one can ask 'How are you doing' in three different ways: *How you duh do? How you duh doin?* or *How you doin?* (However, the phrase *Uh duh tell you!* 'I am telling you the truth!'/'I am not lying!' occurs only in this idiomatic form.) The verb phrase is understood in this case as stative and the tense can be present or past, depending on context. It is negated with *ain*, as in *he ain duh talk at all* 'he is not talking at all'. The origin of the marker seems to lie in Southwestern British English, in which periphrastic *do*, deeply rooted since Middle English and also pronounced unstressed as [də], appears to have been used similarly for both progressive and habitual states of affairs (Pargman 2002).

But Gullah is unlike most American English varieties and even some Caribbean creoles in having a specific habitual marker *duhz* [dəz], as in *How you duhz cook hog maw* (EL, 1988) 'How **do you/did you use to** cook hog maw?' It is also negated with *ain*, as in *You ain duhz make no hog cheese?* (EL, 1988) 'Didn't you make any hog cheese?'. Its tense may be universal or past, depending on the discourse context of its use. This feature, also attested in Newfoundland English, has the same origins as *duh*, though its selection may clearly have been influenced by the semantics of many black African languages which delimit verbs with different morphosyntactic devices for habits and non-habits. Like other creoles, Gullah can thus be a useful window into colonial English, from which it developed. This habitual construction should not be confused with the consuetudinal *be* + V-*in'*/Adj/PrepP construction, *Faye be eatin'/sick every time I visit*, which does not denote repeated activities but repeated states of affairs, which can be states or processes. The consuetudinal is used in the same way as in AAVE.

Gullah shares with Atlantic English creoles and some nonstandard American English varieties (such as Appalachian English: Christian, Dube and Wolfram 1988) the use of perfect *done* [dʌn], as in *Uh done eat dat one (already)* 'I ate/have eaten that one (already)'. As in other nonstandard English varieties, it conveys some emphasis on the completion of the activity or its relevance to the reference time. Unlike in other nonstandard English dialects, it is not necessarily followed by a verb in the past tense or past participle. It often combines with the verb stem for exactly the same meaning. It also combines with stative verb phrases as in *he brother done dead* 'his brother is already dead' and *Uh kin tell you wha I done been tru* (JR, 1988) 'I can tell you what I have been through'. It can also modify a verb phrase already delimited with the tense marker *bin* as in *Uh done bin finish* 'I finished a long time ago'. Unlike in white nonstandard English varieties, there is no particular evidence in Gullah that would suggest deletion of an underlying *have* or *be* in contexts where *done* is used. The interpretation of its tense is also relative, depending on the discourse context. Another interesting peculiarity is that *done* can be used post-verbally, as in *Uh eat/talk done* 'I have eaten/spoken [and I don't intend to do so again]'. It implicates completion with no intention on the part of the subject to re-engage him/herself in the activity.

The grammatical behavior of *done*, which is a cognate of English participial adjective *done* 'finished' (not the auxiliary *do*), is made possible by the fact that Gullah does not require that all predicate phrases be headed by a verb in the surface structure. It is also in the same way that the purposive preposition *for/fuh* could develop a modal use, as illustrated above in (8). In overtly anterior contexts, they can also be modified by *bin*, as in *Peter bin done dead when I come back* 'Peter had already died when I came back'.

3.4.   Negation and focus

Another interesting aspect of Gullah's morphosyntax is its strategies for negation. Not counting the frozen negative forms of modal auxiliaries (discussed above), it differs from Caribbean creoles in having more than one basic negator: *ain, don, didn*, and *no*. Unlike in Jamaican and Guyanese Creoles, for instance, *no* has only two functions: 1) a wide-scope negator in elliptical, or at the beginning of, answers to *yes/no* questions; and 2) a NP-internal narrow-scope negator, as in *no hog cheese*. *Didn* is used in PAST contexts, where Jamaican Creole favors *neba* with the non-emphatic meaning 'did not'. *Don* is used in two contexts: 1) in imperative sentences, as in *Don le' da' bread get cold on you* (ER, 1988) and *we tell um fuh don come* 'we told him/her not to come'; 2) in habitual sentences, as in *da' duh som'um Uh don buy* (JR, 1988) 'that's something I don't buy'. In all other cases, the sentence, wide-scope negator is *ain*, as in the following examples:

(9)   a. *She ain tell um*
           'She did not tell him/She has not told him.'
       b. *Uh ain ga go nowhere*
           'I won't go anywhere.'   (JR, 1988)
       c. *Uh ain bin a take no chance on da' road*
           'I didn't take any chances on that road.'   (JR, 1988)

d.   *People ain duh plant no tato now*
'People **weren't planting/didn't plant** any potatoes now/then.'

(JR, 1988)

e.   *Yall ain duhz make no hog cheese?*
'Didn't you make any hog cheese?'   (EL, 1988)

Like other nonstandard English varieties, it has negative concord, as in *Uh ain go nowhere*, and *nobody ain go nowhere*. *Aini* also functions as an invariant tag question marker, similar to colloquial English *right?*, London Jamaican *init?*, French *n'est-ce pas?*, and German *nicht wahr?*. Examples include the following:

(10)   a.   *Yall didn buy no clothes from town, inni?*
'You didn't buy (any) clothes from the city, did you?'   (EL, 1988)

b.   *You ain know Harry, inni?*
'You didn't/don't know Harry, did/do you?'   (JR, 1988)

c.   *You be cookin up all kine o' ting, inni?*
'You would be cooking all kinds of things, wouldn't you?'
'You've been cooking all kinds of things, haven't you?'

(EL, 1988)

Finally, *ain* also functions as a negative focus marker in the following examples:

(11)   a.   *Ain nobody ga worry wid you*
'**There's nobody/There isn't anybody** that will worry with you.'

(JR, 1988)

b.   *Ain Sara we duh talk 'bout; duh Faye we duh talk 'bout.*
'It's not Sara we are talking about; it's Faye we are talking about.'

A sentence such as (12) is ambiguous between a negative concord interpretation and double-negation interpretation. Only the discourse context can clarify such ambiguities.

(12)   *Ain nobody ain go deh*
a.   'There isn't anybody/There's nobody who went there.'
b.   'There isn't anybody/There's nobody who has not gone there.'

Positive focus constructions are marked with sentence-initial *duh*, as in *duh Sara we duh talk 'bout* 'it's Sara we are talking about'. This is similar to its translated English cleft construction. The only difference is that it allows bare verb stems in the cleft-focus position, as in *duh talk he (bin) duh talk* 'he/she was really talking (in an unusual kind of way)'. VPs are not acceptable in the cleft-focus position: **duh talk to me he de talk*. This constraint is similar to the restriction of preposition phrases from such constructions: **duh 'bout Sara we duh talk* is also ill-formed. The focused verb appears to occur in this position as a NP derived with a zero suffix (by simple category shifting). A similar construction is attested in several substrate languages, both Kwa and Bantu. Moreover, English allows similar verbal clefts, which must be nominalized through the gerund, as in *it's singing he prefers to playing a musical instrument*. The name Verb/Predicate Clefting by which the construction is identified in creoles is thus a misnomer which suggests misguided contrasts between English and Gullah in this respect, though there are some having to do, for instance, with how the verb is nominalized.

3.5.   Serial verb constructions (SVCs)

Far from being a misnomer is the combination of verbs identified as serial verb/predicate construction. It consists of verb or predicate phrases concatenated without connectives between them and sharing an argument whose function can be the same (typically subject) or different (typically object of the head verb and subject of the second, serial verb). Examples include:

(13)   a. *Uh **run go home**.*
           'I ran home.'   (JM, 1987)
        b. *He **up deh duh hammer** on da' leg.*
           'He [was] up there, hammering on that leg.'   (PR, 1987)
        c. *Uh **tell um stop**.*
           'I told him [to] stop.'   (LW, 1987)
        d. *Uh **ga see d' doctor fix medicine fuh me**.*
           'I will see the doctor to fix [some] medicine for me.'   (JM, 1987)

In (13a-b), the two predicate phrases share the subject; the only differences are that the head predicate in (13b) is a preposition, which Gullah grammar allows to head a predicate phrase, the second predicate phrase is modified by a progressive marker. There are no participial forms, with uses similar to the English translation, in Gullah's basilect. In (13c-d) the object of the head verb functions as the subject of the serial verb. This construction also illustrates the fact that tense is indicated only once in a serial predicate construction. It functions as a syntactic unit which can be modified only by one negator, as in *Uh ain know fix da bread with water* (JM, 1987) 'I don't know how to bake bread with water'.

This is an aspect of creoles' grammars where substrate influence has been considered incontrovertible since Turner (1949). However, English also has constructions such as ***go get*** *the paper* and ***come play*** *with me*. The role of partial congruence between, on the one hand, the African SVCs and, on the other, this infinitival construction and the gerundive ones in, for instance, *go fishing* and *start working*, should not be discounted a priori in the development of this grammatical characteristic. The fact that most verbal inflections were lost during the development of creoles must have contributed to the wider attestations of SVCs. In any case, English varieties which evolved in settings without a significant presence of African languages do not have the wide range of SVCs attested in Gullah and its creole kin of the Caribbean, including the complementizer use of *say*, as in *she **answer say** she mama ain come* or *we **hear say** Bill ain ga come* discussed in Mufwene (1989, 1996).

4.   Conclusions

The above information in section 3 gives us a glimpse of a subset of Gullah's structures, highlighting both differences and similarities between it and other nonstandard English varieties in the United States. Most comparisons have been in relation to Standard English and have given the unjustified impression that Gullah has diverged from English almost beyond recognition. Compared to other nonstandard English varieties, it is hard to determine which variety has diverged the most; nor is it certain that one can measure the extent of divergence in ways suggested by the creolistics literature.

Colonial English was variable and also contained xenolectal features, even among the European speakers. One must remember that Ireland, which provided a lot of indentured servants, was just beginning to become an Anglophone country in the 17th century, as it was becoming geographically the closest of England's settlement colonies. Besides, the other colonists came from outside the British Isles and also spoke English as a second language. The Africans who were shifting to English as their vernacular, and those acquiring it natively, were not always able to tell which European linguistic models were native and which ones were not. One can simply imagine a setting, such as in colonial Africa and Asia, in which learners appropriate a language from other non-native speakers and the European speakers are somewhat privileged. Moreover, there were no English language classes and the target language was being "acquired" only naturalistically, by immersion in the society. Even the native models varied among themselves, representing diverse dialects from the British Isles.

From a language evolution perspective, some important questions arise: 1) What are the mechanisms that regulated the competition of features between

English and the other languages with which it came in contact, within English itself, and among the other languages? 2) Was competition always resolved? 3) Why isn't Gullah more different from the other American English varieties than it is? This question is significant because race segregation was institutionalized the earliest on the coastal rice plantations, to protect the Europeans from the black majority which obtained already in the first quarter of the 18th century (Wood 1974). 4) What is the actual nature of substrate influence in Gullah and how extensive is it?

The answer to the first question cannot be formulated straightforwardly and succinctly in the space available here. Nor can our current understanding of the mechanisms of competition and selection within a language contact feature pool answer it exhaustively. Suffice it to note that ecology-based principles of markedness, population structure, and relative degree of entrenchment of some features (having to do with the founder population) seem to have played important roles during the gradual development of this new vernacular (Mufwene 2001). The answer to the second question is obvious. Current variation in Gullah's system suggests that the competition was not always resolved.

As for the third question, the fact that Gullah's structures have remained so English(-like) despite its divergence can be explained in part by the growth pattern of the African population relative to the European population. The homestead phase produced a critical mass of non-European native speakers who would become the transmitters of the colonial vernacular even after the institutionalization of race segregation. Many of the locally-born slaves had access to varieties diverging the least from those spoken by the Europeans. They continued to offset the extent of non-native influence that the bozal slaves exerted on the local colonial vernacular. One can imagine this by simply comparing Gullah to varieties such as Sarmaccan and Sranan in Surinam, where contact with native speakers of the colonial vernacular was significantly reduced, if not completely severed, quite early in its history.

Regarding the fourth question, we should start by noting that substrate influence is made difficult to deny because all over the world any language appropriated by a different ethnolinguistic group has changed under the influence of the language(s) previously spoken by its new users. European-American English varieties are a function of how competition and selection were resolved in the various communities, although, as noted by Kurath (1928), regional differences in waves of settlement had a role to play in the process. Thus varieties that developed among groups of Africans necessarily reflect influence from African languages. The structural data suggest that most of the influence may have consisted more in (dis)favoring particular variants in colonial English than in introducing non-lexical materials in the system.

We must bear in mind that favoring some variants also entailed modification of the relevant grammatical principles in ways that made them more similar to those of some substrate languages. Identifying those particular principles and the extent of modification has remained controversial, in part because Gullah's structures, like those of other creoles, have been compared to Standard English rather than to nonstandard varieties. One must also remember that a global comparison of two or more dialects in all grammatical respects is unwarranted, because knowledge of a language is developed piecemeal and selectively, with materials originating in different sources (be these idiolects or dialects). More work and scholarship is thus needed to answer the third question.

While Gullah makes a good case for studying language divergence, the role of race segregation in its development also makes it an informative window into structural features of colonial English. This statement is not intended to support the claim by Krapp (1924) and several other dialectologists of the same period that African Americans have retained the English formerly spoken and now presumably abandoned by the low-class Europeans with whom their ancestors interacted before Emancipation. Gullah is not an archaic conservative variety of colonial English, not any more than any other nonstandard American English dialect is. It only contains features that were current in the varieties spoken during the colonial period, some of which can also be identified today in some white nonstandard varieties.

Sample Gullah text from Mufwene's field records (1980s) transcribed in eye dialect:

JR *You trow way... trow way wha? En one day, Uh gone down deh... en talk bout something bin a bite! Uh bin on dat flat, en Uh had me line, Uh done ketch couple a whitin... Uh say, Uh ga put up da drop net... when Uh look up, duh look from yah to you cah deh, Uh see sompin on da damn side da shoulder comin, like a damn log. Uh watch um, en when Uh see him gone down...*

'You throw away... throw away what? And one day, I went/had gone down there... and talk[ing] about something biting! I was on that flat, and I had my line, I had caught a couple of whiting... I said, "I'll put up the drop net"... when I looked up, [I] was looking from here to your car there, I saw something on the damned side of the shoulder coming like a damned log. I watched it, and when I saw it gone down...'

EL *Hm hm!*

JR *En dat tide bin a comin in... en dat sucker swim close, closer en closer, den Uh look en Uh see dat alligator open e damn mouth!*

'And that tide was coming in... and that sucker swam close, closer and closer, then I looked and saw that alligator open its damned mouth!'

* Field research on which this chapter is directly or indirectly based was sponsored
in the 1980s by the National Endowment for the Humanities (Independent Study
and Research Fellowship 1982, and Summer Stipend 1988) and by the National
Science Foundation, grant BNS 8519315, for which I am very grateful.

Exercises and study questions

1. Discuss the following comment on African-American speech. Derive some
   of your arguments from this chapter and from whatever you know about language acquisition and transmission. If you have access to Mufwene (2001),
   you may benefit from his discussion of the notions 'language acquisition'
   and 'language transmission'.
   *The English of African Americans is different from European-American
   English varieties simply because of any or all of the following reasons: 1)
   the African slaves were too lazy to learn English like everybody else; 2) they
   did not have enough exposure to English and had to invent new forms and
   constructions for those parts of English they did not learn; 3) their minds
   were too traumatized by the experience of slavery to learn English well; 4)
   they were handicapped by their anatomical features to articulate English
   like European Americans do; and/or 5) it is just too difficult for speakers of
   non-European languages to acquire European languages perfectly.*

2. One can argue that recent immigrants to the United States have exerted less
   influence, if not a negligible one, on today's American English varieties.
   While one can make a good case for European, African, and Anglophone
   Caribbean immigrants, the position may be harder to defend about other immigrants, especially Latin Americans. Can you explain why and what this
   non-uniform impact of immigrants on the local language suggests about the
   development of Gullah and the like?

3. Go over the sample Gullah text published with this chapter. Tally in two
   separate columns the features that it shares with English (standard and nonstandard) and those that is does not. Comment on the following passage in
   the present chapter:
   *Gullah and the like can very well be considered disfranchised varieties of
   Germanic and other Indo-European languages.*

4. Listen to the audio version of the same text, without concurrently reading
   the transcription. Do you think that the position that Gullah is a creole and
   a separate language from English is empirically justified? Think about what

counts as "empirical" evidence and whether your conclusion is supported by other sample texts of "varieties of English" (e.g., Cockney, Appalachian English, Australian nonstandard English, Scots English) that you have listened to.

5. Compare the grammar of Gullah as described in the article to the grammars of Earlier African American English (see the article by Kautzsch in this volume), Bahamian Creole (see the article by Reaser and Torbert in this volume) and Jamaican Creole (see the article by Patrick in this volume). Identify areas of similarities and differences. Find out something about possible historical explanations for the relationships that you have identified.

Selected references

Please consult the General references for titles mentioned in the text but not included in the references below. For a full bibliography see the accompanying CD-ROM.

Bailey, Guy and Patricia Cukor-Avila
  fc.   *The Development of African American English*. Cambridge: Cambridge University Press.
Chaudenson, Robert
  2001   *Creolization of Language and Culture*. London: Routledge.
Edgar, Walter
  1998   *South Carolina: A History*. Columbia: University of South Carolina Press.
Kautzsch, Alexander and Edgar W. Schneider
  2000   Differential creolization: Some evidence from earlier African American vernacular English in South Carolina. In: Neumann-Holzschuh and Schneider (eds.), 247–274.
Krapp, George Philip
  1924   The English of the Negro. *The American Mercury* 2: 190–5.
Kurath, Hans
  1928   The origin of dialectal differences in spoken American English. *Modern Philology* 25: 385–395.
Labov, William and Wendell Harris
  1986   De facto segregation of black and white vernaculars. In: David Sankoff (ed.), *Diversity and Diachrony*, 1–24. Amsterdam/Philadelphia: John Benjamins.
Mufwene, Salikoko S.
  1989   Equivocal structures in some Gullah complex sentences. *American Speech* 64: 304–326.

1996   Creolization and grammaticization: What creolistics could contribute to research on grammaticization. In: Philip Baker and Anand Syea (eds.), *Changing Meanings, Changing Functions: Papers Relating to Grammaticalization in Contact Languages*, 5–28. London: University of Westminster Press.

Pargman, Sheri
2002   Internal and external factors in language change. Ph.D. dissertation, University of Chicago.

Rickford, John R.
1990   Number delimitation in Gullah: A response to Mufwene. *American Speech* 65: 148–63.

Turner, Lorenzo Dow
1949   *Africanisms in the Gullah Dialect*. Chicago: University of Chicago Press.

Wood, Peter
1974   *Black Majority: Negroes in Colonial South Carolina from 1670 through the Stono Rebellion*. New York: Knopf.

Chicano English: morphology and syntax[*]

Robert Bayley and Otto Santa Ana

1. Introduction

Latinos are the largest minority group in the United States, numbering 37 million in 2000. They are not evenly distributed across the nation, but concentrated in the urban centers of a few states. For example, Latinos make up 32 percent of the population of Texas, and over 59 percent of San Antonio. In Texas, Latinos are overwhelmingly of Mexican origin. For a second example, Latinos comprise 45 percent of Los Angeles County's 9.5 million people. The national origins of Los Angeles Latinos are more varied. In Los Angeles County, for example, 76 percent are of Mexican origin, according to the 2000 census. Although many Mexican-origin Latinos claim English as their sole or dominant language, the varieties of English spoken by Mexican-Americans have received relatively little scholarly attention. More than 20 years ago, Peñalosa observed that "the most obvious discrepancy in the field of Chicano sociolinguistics is that between the extensive use of English in the Chicano community and the paucity of serious studies concerning the varieties of English used by Chicanos" (1980: 115). The situation has improved in recent years with the appearance of a number of dissertations and articles dealing with phonological and grammatical features of Chicano English (see Mendoza-Denton 1999 for a review). Nevertheless, the study of English varieties spoken by Mexican Americans remains a relatively neglected area of sociolinguistic research.

The neglect of Chicano English (henceforth ChcE) may be in part a consequence of the difficulty of defining the limits of the dialect, as well as other questions that do not figure in accounts of English varieties spoken in predominantly monolingual communities. Among these questions are the extent and nature of the influence of the Mexican Spanish substrate, the distinctions between the learner varieties spoken by immigrants and the native varieties spoken by U.S.-born Chicanos and by those who immigrated as young children, and the relationships among the varieties of English spoken by Chicanos and other vernacular dialects. In this chapter, we define ChcE as an ethnic variety of English spoken by people who acquired English as their first language, who acquired English and Spanish simultaneously, or who began to acquire English when they enrolled in elementary school, usually around the age of 5, well before the end of the critical period for second language acquisition. Speakers of ChcE are concentrated primarily in the urban *barrios* of California and the southwestern United States. However, given the spread of the U.S. Mexican-origin population in recent years, ChcE speakers may also be found in other urban centers, particularly in cities such as Chicago that have long drawn large numbers of Mexican immigrants. Speakers of ChcE may or may not speak Spanish as well as English. Nearly all ChcE speakers, however, live in communities where Spanish is widely spoken and most have at least some passive knowledge of Spanish. Indeed, many ChcE speakers come from families where Spanish is used to varying degrees in the home. Excluded from the definition are people of Mexican ancestry who have fully assimilated into the dominant culture and who speak varieties of the standard language that are indistinguishable from those of middle and upper-middle class Anglos in the same regions.

Our definition of ChcE distinguishes this native-speaker dialect from interlanguages, or the varieties of learner language spoken by native-speakers of Spanish who immigrated to the United States as adolescents or adults. Although we recognize that the widespread use of Spanish in Chicano communities may well influence the English spoken by native English-speaking Chicanos, we reject the notion of interference that has been used to attempt to explain so many of the features of ChcE. In second language acquisition, interference, or transfer, is a psycholinguistic construct that attempts to explain how features of a learner's first language inhibit the acquisition of features of a second language. Such a construct has no relevance for describing a language variety that is the sole or dominant variety of a group of speakers. Since there are ChcE speakers who do not speak any Spanish, Spanish cannot be the proximate source of their native English dialect. Nevertheless, because ChcE speakers are often in daily contact with fluent speakers of Spanish and because many ChcE speakers live in communities where they have only minimal contact with speakers of Anglo varieties, we acknowledge the possible influence of the Spanish substrate on features of ChcE grammar.

In this chapter, we outline the grammatical features of ChcE, many of which are common to other vernacular dialects. Then, because sociolinguistic research has shown that differences or similarities between dialects are determined not so much by the presence of absence of particular forms or grammatical features, but rather by the patterning of constraints on those variants, we discuss two variables, negative concord and relative pronoun choice, that have been systematically investigated using standard sociolinguistic methodology.

2.   Grammatical features common to ChcE and other dialects

The majority of ChcE grammatical and syntactic features that diverge from prescriptive norms are also found in other vernacular dialects, including those spoken in non-contact situations. In this section, we summarize the morphological
and syntactic features that diverge from Anglo norms and provide examples
of each. Wherever possible, we illustrate the different grammatical features
discussed with examples from our own data sets. The San Antonio (SA) and
northern California (NC) examples were collected by Bayley and colleagues
between 1991 and 2001 in three separate projects. Except where indicated, the
Los Angeles (LA) examples were collected by Santa Ana between 1987 and
1991 during several fieldwork projects. In addition to providing information
about the area where the examples were collected, we also provide information
about speaker gender and age after each example.

2.1.   The verb phrase

ChcE shares a number of features of the verb phrase with other vernacular dialects, including African American Vernacular English (AAVE). Among these
are regularization of irregular verbs, variable absence of 3rd sg. -*s*, and variable use of *is* and *was* with plural subjects:

(1)   Regularization of irregular verbs:
       *When I was little and that teacher hit my hand on my- my upper side
       of the hand- that when she **striked** me with that, that just blew my
       mind ...* (SA, f, 30)

(2)   Absence of 3rd sg. -*s*:
       *If somebody **come** up and **push** me then I'll just probably have to push
       em back or something.* (SA, f, 12)

(3)   *is* with plural subject:
       *And the people that live here **is** ....* (SA, f, 33)

(4)   *was* with plural subject:
       *They **was** like, you know little girls, "what are you doing?"* (SA, f, 29)

In addition to the structures illustrated in (1) through (4), ChcE also exhibits
variable absence of past-tense marking:

(5)   *I saw some girl, she, she **look** pretty.* (SA, f, 12)

(6)   *By like the first grade I was already, you know, catching on like **de
       volada** then after that I **talk** English.* (SA, m, 15)

(7)   *This girl you know she hated me and everything and she was in a different gang than I was, and she had, you know, she went up to the principal go- she **tell** him that I had an illegal weapon.* (SA, f, 15)

Note that (5) and (6) contain examples of unmarked regular past-tense verbs. The absence of past-tense marking of *look* (in 5) and *talk* (in 6) might well be a result of consonant cluster reduction, a phonological process that we have investigated in detail among both California and Texas Chicanos (Bayley 1994; Santa Ana 1996). In fact, Bayley (1994: 310) found that -*t/-d* was absent from 24 percent of regular past-tense verbs produced by a sample of San Antonio Chicanos. Moreover, unlike many non-contact varieties of English, ChcE does exhibit a fairly high rate of cluster reduction before vowels. In Bayley's study, prevocalic clusters were reduced at a rate of 21 percent (1994: 310). Thus, it seems reasonable to attribute the absence of past-marking in (5) and (6) to a phonological process that is common to virtually all dialects of English. Unmarked past reference *tell* in (7), however, indicates that a frequently-studied phonological process is not the only cause of the variable absence of past-tense marking in ChcE. Clearly, the abundance of past tense forms in the examples throughout this chapter provides evidence that the ChcE speakers, in contrast to English language learners, usually mark past reference verbs. However, as with many other ChcE variables, the possible constraints on past marking have yet to be systematically investigated.

In addition to the features discussed thus far, ChcE also exhibits occasional use of zero copula:

(8)   *... they Ø like, "you speak a little bit weird"* (SA, f, 12)

(9)   *I see so many people dying of diseases and I Ø just like tired of it ...* (SA, f, 12)

The two speakers who provided the examples above lived in the overwhelmingly Latino west side of San Antonio and attended a school with a Latino enrollment of 97 percent. Aside from an African American boy with whom they attended school for a year – with whom they did not socialize – neither girl had direct contact with African Americans, who in any case constitute only seven percent of the population of San Antonio.

Like AAVE, ChcE, at least as spoken in Los Angeles, exhibits use of habitual *be*, although at a much lower rate, as in (10):

(10)   *Her name was Sister Dorothy. I used to hate her because it's the same reason. You **be doing** a classwork in class, and she used to tell me: "Do this".* (LA, f, 18)

Also, like many other vernacular dialects, ChcE provides examples of auxiliary deletion:

(11)   *I Ø been doing dancing for a long time, for eight years already.*
        (SA, f, 12)

In both Los Angeles (Fought 2003: 97–98) and San Antonio, ChcE exhibits variable use of the past perfect where standard English would use a simple past, as well as generalization of past tense irregular verb forms to the past participle:

(12)   *I don't know if it was my son or my nephew that **had** told me.*
        (SA, f, 36)

(13)   *It was in the apple that the witch had **gave** Snow White that wasn't poisonous.* (SA, f, 11)

2.2.   Negation

Like nearly all vernacular dialects of English, ChcE speakers frequently use negative concord:

(14)   *You really **can't** do **nothing** about it because you're on welfare right, and you live here, and you barely make it, right?* (SA, f, 30)

(15)   *I **didn't** see **nothing no more**. I **didn't** have that dream **no more**.*
        (LA, m, 19)

This feature is one of the few ChcE grammatical structures that has been investigated quantitatively. We describe it in greater detail in section 4 below.

Like negative concord, other aspects of ChcE negation are not especially distinct from those found in other vernacular dialects. Thus, *don't* is variably used with both singular and plural third person subjects, as in (16):

(16)   *She **don't** like it here in the courts and my dad well I'm not sure 'cause he **don't** live with us.* (SA, f, 15)

The acquisition of English negation was one of the earliest topics investigated in modern second language acquisition research (see, e.g., Schumann 1978). To simplify a bit, research has shown that English language acquirers move from NO + V to unanalyzed DONT + V to analyzed DON'T + V. At first glance, then, it might be possible to attribute the type of negation illustrated in (16) to an incomplete acquisition of English negation. However, other data from the same speaker indicate that Spanish interference or incomplete English language acquisition are unlikely explanations for the non-standard use of *don't*. In contrast to what we see in transcripts from language learners, the transcript from this speaker contains numerous instances of conjugated DO+N'T, including both present and past tense forms, as in (17):

(17) *It **doesn't** matter what color you are but in God's eyes, you know, people should be treated the same.* (SA, f, 15)

Finally, as in other vernacular dialects, ChcE speakers use *ain't* as a negative with present tense *be* and *have*:

(18) *You fight back 'cause you know they touched you and they **ain't** supposed to do that.* (SA, f, 12)

2.3. Direct object absence

ChcE vernacular exhibits occasional use of zero direct objects:

(19) *He took a bath. I gave him Ø to eat.* (LA, f, 52)

(20) *I just told [my three year old daughter who surprised her mother by laughingly hanging out of the tailgate window of a moving car]: "Patricia, get inside the car". Yea. You know I didn't wanna scare her. I wanted her to get in the car. Then I told my boyfriend: "Close that back window. If you ever open Ø again I'm gonna kill you!"* (LA, f, 40)

Like many of the features exemplified here, this feature has not been studied in detail.

2.4. Quotative *go, be like, be all*

Among younger speakers, the innovative quotatives *go, be like,* and *be all* are common in informal speech, a development that parallels changes in other vernaculars spoken in the United States and elsewhere (Daily-O'Cain 2000). The following examples, which contain numerous tokens of *go, be like,* and *be all*, are from two early adolescents and an adult who live in a San Antonio *barrio*. The speakers, who are bilingual in Spanish and English, were born in Texas and attended Texas schools beginning at the age of 5. Aside from teachers or supervisors at work, none has had extensive contact with Anglos:

(21) *When people wanna fight me **I'm like** "well okay, well then I'll fight you."* (SA, f, 12)

(22)   *Like at the exact moment that we're supposed to take off, he'll [her ex-husband] **go** like, "I'm not taking you nowhere".* (SA, f, 36)

(23)   *Then some girl **goes** "eh they jumped you right?" And I **was like**, "Oh, my god, you had to say that!" And I **was like** "No they didn't" And she [the speaker's mother] **was all** "what, what happened? **I was like**, "uh nothing". **She's all**, "J., you better tell me". And I had to tell her. And **I go** "well don't, don't go to my school. If I have to fight then I'll take care of it, I'll fight them by myself." And **she goes** "Well they gave you a ticket J." And I, **she goes**, "Does Miss A. [the school principal] know?" So **I was like**, "Yes".* (SA, f, 12)

Fought (2003) also discusses the prevalence of *be all* and *be like* among young Chicanos in Los Angeles and provides a number of examples. Although innovative quotatives have yet to be fully investigated in ChcE, preliminary analysis of our data suggests that quotative *go* is used frequently by older and younger speakers and *be like* and *be all* are common among younger speakers in California and Texas. The widespread use of these innovative forms suggests that even speakers whose social networks are restricted to other Latinos may be more open to linguistic influence from Anglo varieties than previously supposed.

2.5.   Focuser *like*

The quotatives *be like* and *be all* are used primarily by younger speakers. Focuser *like*, however, is common among ChcE speakers of all generations, as illustrated in the following examples taken from sociolinguistic interviews with speakers ranging in age from 18 to 54.

(24)   *I talk to people a lot and a lot of times they're **like** trying to get a word in edgewise.* (SA, f, 18)

(25)   *She was **like** a real thin lady.* (LA, m, 52)

(26)   *So Nora like she was kind of **like** free, independent.* (N CA, m, 54)

As in the case of quotative *be like* and *be all*, in the popular mind, focuser *like* is strongly associated with the speech of young Anglo women in California (Dailey-O'Cain 2000). However, examples such as those above indicate that the one-dimensional popular conception fails to capture the reality.

2.6.   Pronouns

In ChcE, *it* is sometimes used in place of *there* as an empty subject pronoun:

(27)   *They were saying that they had a lot of problems at Garner because **it** was a lot of fights and stuff.* (SA, m, 35)

Although we have no examples from Texas, Fought (2003: 95) observed a number of non-standard pronouns in Los Angeles ChcE, including *theirselves* in place of *themselves* and *hisself* in place of *himself*. Finally, resumptive pronouns can be found occasionally in the speech of Los Angeles and San Antonio Chicanos, as in (28) and (29):

(28)   *I don't think I had a teacher that I didn't really like **him**.* (LA, m, 16)

(29)   *I know this lady that **she** used to live here.* (SA, f, 36)

3.   Features specific to Chicano English

3.1.   Reported speech

Wald (1987) investigated reported speech among ChcE speakers in East Los Angeles. He observed three distinctions between ChcE and other vernacular dialects. First, speakers in Wald's study as well as other studies, used *tell* to introduce questions:

(30)   *I **told** Elinore: "Is that your brother?" She goes: "I don't think so mom".*   (LA, f, 52)

Second, the East Los Angeles speakers, in contrast to speakers of other vernacular dialects, sometimes extended complementizer *that* to direct speech following *tell*:

(31)   *I told him **that** "I can't go out with you no more ..."*
        (Wald 1987: 58)

Third, again in contrast to speakers of other dialects, the East Los Angeles speakers Wald studied used inversion only with *wh*-questions and never with *yes/no* questions:

(32)   a. *He asked me where did I live.*
        b. *He asked did I live there.*   (Wald 1987: 60)

3.2.   Modals

More recently, Wald (1996) studied modals in East Los Angeles ChcE. Among other issues, Wald examined the use of *would* in *if*-clauses with both stative and non-stative verbs, as in (33):

(33)   *If he'd be here right now, he'd make me laugh.*
        (Wald 1996: 520)

Owing to the relative rarity of the construction in his data, Wald was only able to analyze a small number of tokens. In the 39 tokens that he did examine, he found that *would* was used much more frequently with non-stative than with stative verbs (Wald 1996: 521–522) and suggested that use of *would* with hypothetical clauses might be more common in ChcE than in other varieties as a result of substrate influence.

   Fought (2003) also briefly discusses the use of modals in Los Angeles ChcE. She notes the extension of *could* rather than *can* to mean competence:

(34)   *Nobody believes that you **could** fix anything.*
        (Fought 2003: 100)

Fought states that this particular usage was very common in her data. She further notes that it has not been documented for AAVE, does not appear to have any relationship to Spanish syntactic patterns, and is not found in the speech of the Anglos she interviewed. Thus, this would seem to be an independent innovation in ChcE.

3.3.   Prepositions

The use of prepositions is one area of ChcE grammar where Spanish influence seems likely:

(35)   *And we used to go stand **in** the porch cause they never used to let*
        *us in the house. You used to go stand **in** the porch and look at the t.v.*
        through the window. (LA, f, 52)

(36)   *We start **on** July.* (SA, m, 17)

The nonstandard use of *in* in (35) and *on* in (36) appears, superficially at least, to originate in the fact that in Spanish both meanings are expressed by *en*. However, the majority of prepositions in our data are used as they are in standard English, as in (37) and (38):

(37) *I have a sister named Rachel that's **in** eighth grade.* (SA, m, 12)

(38) *I don't like um, what's it called, being **in** clubs and all that.* (SA, f, 12)

To fully understand the use of nonstandard prepositions in ChcE, we need more systematic studies to identify which prepositions are involved and whether particular contexts favor the use of forms that diverge from the surrounding dialect.

3.4. Zero subject pronouns

As is well known, Spanish is a pro-drop language. That is, personal subject pronouns may be expressed overtly, as in *Yo quiero...* (I want) or they may be omitted, as in *Quiero...* ([I] want). Zero subject pronouns are also occasionally found in ChcE as well, e.g.

(39) *I tried that door. Over and over and over. I moved the lock. Ø locks from the inside.* (LA, m, 34)

Compared to the Mexican Spanish substrate, in which most pronominal subjects are realized as null, zero pronoun use in ChcE is very rare. Without further investigation, it is premature to attribute the relatively infrequent absence of subject pronouns in ChcE to Spanish influence.

4. Quantitative studies of Chicano English

Thus far, we have outlined morphosyntactic features where ChcE differs from prescriptive norms and noted that many of these features are common to a range of English vernacular dialects. In fact, Chambers (2003: 265–266) refers to a number of these features, such as conjugation regularization and negative concord, as "vernacular primitives" because they are pervasive in vernacular dialects and because they result from processes that we may expect to find in nonstandard varieties of other languages as well. However, sociolinguists have long considered as axiomatic the proposition that similarities and differences among language varieties are best investigated not simply by listing features and noting which ones are shared, but by systematically investigating the patterning of constraints on the use of those features. Indeed, in his classic definition of the speech community, Labov gives "the uniformity of abstract patterns of variation which are invariant in respect to particular levels of usage" (1972b: 121) as one of the two main criteria by which membership in a speech community may be judged. Thus, to understand the relationship between ChcE and other English vernaculars with which Chicanos are in contact, we need systematic quantitative studies of ChcE. However, in contrast to many other varieties of English, there have been very few quantitative studies of ChcE morphology and syntax that use standard sociolinguistic methods. In fact, aside from the cases of negative concord (Fought 2003), and relative pronoun choice (Bayley 1999), we do not yet have the quantitative evidence that would allow us to determine whether ChcE patterns are similar to or different from other vernacular dialects. Even in the cases of negative concord and relative pronoun choice, we are limited to a results of two fairly small-scale studies. In this section, then, we will discuss the two variables that have been systematically studied with standard methods of multivariate analysis.

4.1. Negative concord

Negative concord is one of the most persistent features in vernacular English dialects (Labov 1972a; Wolfram 1969, 1974; Wolfram and Schilling-Estes 1998). As in other vernacular dialects, multiple negation, or negative concord, is common in ChcE, as illustrated by the following examples collected from working class speakers in Los Angeles and San Antonio:

(40)   *You guys **don't** like me **no more**. You guys **don't** come visit me **no more**.* (LA, f, 18)

(41)   *I **can't** take it **no** more, you know.* (SA, m, 42)

(42)   *I **wouldn't** go much **nowhere**.* (SA, f, 36)

Note that all of the speakers who provided examples (40) through (42) are fully proficient in English and began to acquire the language by the age of 5, if not from birth. There is no reason to assume a priori that the type negative concord seen in these and many other examples that we could have provided represent instances of interference from Spanish, although in Spanish, negative concord is obligatory, e.g.

(43)   *No*   *sabe*   *nada.*
       NEG   know-3 sg present   nothing
       'He doesn't know anything.'

Although most studies of ChcE have commented on the presence of negative concord, only Fought (2003) has investigated the variable in detail, and her study is limited to a relatively small number of tokens from adolescent and young adult speakers in the Los Angeles area.

In order to examine the constraints on ChcE negative concord, Fought extracted all of the negative sentences from 28 sociolinguistic interviews, for a total of 323 tokens. She analyzed these tokens to test for the effect of one linguistic and four social factors: syntactic category, social class (middle, working, low income), gang status (gang member, gang affiliated, non-gang member, tagger), bilingualism, and sex. The results of multivariate analysis showed that among the social factors, gang status, social class, and bilingualism all significantly affected speakers' choices between standard and non-standard negation. Overall, the speakers in Fought's study used negative concord at a rate of 49 percent. As might be expected, the highest incidence of use was by taggers and gang members and low-income speakers. Bilinguals also favored negative concord. In this respect, the results contrasted with the results for the phonological variables that Fought investigated, where bilingualism had no significant effect. Bilingualism, however, was the least important of the factor groups that achieved statistical significance in the study of negative concord. In contrast to the results of studies of other communities (e.g. Wolfram 1969 on Detroit AAVE), sex was not significant. Women were just as likely to use negative concord as were men.

Fought's (2003) results for syntactic type are shown in Table 1. The table includes the results of statistical analysis after non-significant factor groups had been removed from the model, percentages of occurrence in each environment, and examples of each syntactic type. Fought analyzed the data with VARBRUL, a specialized application of the statistical procedure of logistic regression that has long been used in sociolinguistics. This statistical method allows the researcher to consider simultaneously all of the factors that may potentially influence the use of a specific linguistic form.

Table 1. Negative concord in Los Angeles Chicano English (source: Fought 2003: 147)

Factor	Example	VARBRUL weight	%
neg aux + adv	*I won't do it no more/any more.*	.80	74
neg aux + pronoun	*I can't say nothing/anything.*	.65	64
neg in lower clause	*I don't think he did nothing/anything.*	.42	25
neg aux + det	*They didn't have a/any/no car.*	.35	37
neg adv + other (incl. *not*)	*I never dated nobody/anybody black.* *...ticket for not having no/any/Ø/ headlights.*	.21	23
neg subj + pro, adv, or det	*Nobody said nothing/anything.*	.15	22
neg in outside clause	*She's not dead or nothing/anything.*	.14	15

Fought's (2003) results suggest that negative concord in ChcE is subject to systematic linguistic conditioning. As the results in Table 1 show, the syntactic environments considered differ greatly in their effect on speakers' use of negative concord, ranging from a low of 15 percent for a negative outside the clause to a high of 74 percent for a negative auxiliary plus adverb.

In addition to reporting on the results of her study of negative concord in ChcE, Fought also compared the results with AAVE. Although she noted many similarities, including use of negative concord outside the clause, she also found differences. Overall, the incidence of negative concord in Fought's data was much lower than reported by Labov (1972a) in his study of Harlem in New York City, where some speakers used negative concord almost categorically, or by Wolfram (1974) in his study of Puerto Rican English in East Harlem, where speakers used negative concord at a rate of 87.4 percent. Finally, Fought (2003: 142–143) observed a number of qualitative differences between negative concord in AAVE and in ChcE. In contrast to previous studies of AAVE, she found no instances of negative inversion (e.g. *Didn't nobody play in the sandbox*). In addition, negative concord with a negative auxiliary was extremely rare in Fought's data. She found only one example, produced by a 17-year-old woman:

(44)   ***None** of the girls **don't** like her.*   (Fought 2003: 143)

Fought's results are clearly valuable, particularly given the rarity of quantitative studies of ChcE syntactic variables. However, more work needs to be done if we want to understand the relationship between negative concord and other ChcE variables on one hand and between the patterning of negative concord in ChcE and other vernacular dialects, particularly AAVE, on the other. Studies of AAVE have revealed remarkable similarities in that dialect in cities across the United States. As yet we lack comparable work that would allow us to understand whether the patterns of syntactic variation in ChcE as spoken in cities across the United States are similar to one another or whether they differ from one another as a result of the varieties with which ChcE speakers are in contact.

4.2.   Relative pronoun choice

Relative pronoun choice is the second syntactic variable that has been investigated in ChcE using standard sociolinguistic methodology. In ChcE, as in other varieties of English, a relative pronoun may be realized as a *wh*-form, *that* or zero:

(45)   *This is the house **which/that/Ø** I told you about.*

Although speakers' choices among the three options shown in example (45) have received less attention in working class and regional American English vernaculars than in standard varieties, a number of scholars have focused on relative pronoun use in vernacular dialects and included working class speakers in their samples (see e.g. Wolfram and Christian 1976 on Appalachian English). Research has documented a number of ways in which vernacular dialects differ from one another with respect to relative pronoun use. However, several general tendencies have emerged that differentiate relative pronoun choice in U.S. vernacular dialects from the more standard varieties. For example, the vernaculars studied to date typically exhibit a high percentage of use of *that*, particularly with human subject head nouns. In addition, vernacular dialects usually exhibit a higher percentage of zero in all grammatical categories in the embedded clause, including subject position (e.g. *I have a friend Ø did that*).

Bayley (1999) investigated 895 relative clauses, extracted from 37 interviews with children, adolescents, and adults in San Antonio and northern California. The data were coded for a range of linguistic factors that previous studies had indicated might influence speakers' choices among a *wh*-form, *that*, or zero. These included whether the antecedent was human, whether the relative pronoun and the antecedent were adjacent or separated by another relative clause or another element, the syntactic function of the relative pronoun in the relative clause, the grammatical category of the subject of the relative clause (pronoun, noun, or relative pronoun), and a number of other features of the antecedent. In addition, Bayley investigated the effects of age, geographical region, immigrant generation, and social class.

Overall results showed a number of differences between ChcE and other dialects. ChcE speakers tended to use *that* as a relative pronoun at the very high rate of 71 percent, compared to 60 percent reported by Berni (1995) for predominantly Anglo speakers in Oklahoma and 44 percent reported by Guy and Bayley (1995) for upper-class Anglo males. The overall rate of use of *wh*-forms, at only 11 percent, was correspondingly low, as was the rate of use of the zero option, 18 percent, compared to the 35 percent reported in Berni's study of Oklahoma English.

Statistical tests with VARBRUL revealed that ChcE relative pronoun choice was constrained by a complex array of linguistic and social factors. Among the social factors, only social class and age reached statistical significance. As might be expected, middle class speakers were more likely to use a *wh*-form than were working class speakers, particularly with a human antecedent, although both middle and working class speakers used *that* more frequently than any other option. The results for age present a more complex picture and suggest that younger speakers are converging both with standard and vernacular norms. On the one hand speakers younger than 25 were more likely to use *wh*-forms. On the other hand, they were also more likely to use zero. These results suggest that the younger speakers have been influenced both by the prescriptive norms taught at school and by features of Anglo or African American vernaculars.

Among the linguistic factors, perhaps the most interesting results of Bayley's (1999) study of relative pronoun choice concern the use of *that* with human antecedents as in (46):

(46)   *Some guys I find that I can't trust them. There's like one like about one that I find **that** I could.* (SA, f, 15)

These results, shown in Table 2, indicate that like speakers of other English dialects, ChcE speakers favor *wh*-forms for human antecedents and tend to use *that* or zero for non-human antecedents. However, even though ChcE speakers favor *wh*-forms for human antecedents relative to *that* or zero, the speakers in Bayley's study still used *that* for 80 percent of all human antecedents.

Table 2.   Human and nonhuman antecedents: VARBRUL weights and percentages for *that*, and *wh*-, and zero (source: Bayley 1999: 129)

	that		*wh*-		zero	
	VARBRUL weight	%	VARBRUL weight	%	VARBRUL weight	%
+Human	.41	80	.74	12	ns	8
–Human	.58	63	.16	10	ns	28
Input	.75		.11		na	

In the cases of both negative concord and relative pronoun choice, research has shown that constraints in ChcE function much as they do among non-Chicano populations. For example, although Fought (2003) found that not all of the types of negative concord in AAVE were present in ChcE, examples of negative concord in the environments where it does occur in ChcE may be found in AAVE and other vernacular dialects. Bayley (1999) also found that most of the linguistic constraints on ChcE relative pronoun choice operated in a similar manner for speakers of other vernacular dialects and even for upper-class Anglo speakers, although the actual percentages of use of variants differed substantially. Given these results, the view that ChcE grammatical features are due to simple interference from Spanish is untenable. Interference cannot explain the kind of orderly variation observed in Fought (2003) and Bayley (1999), particularly when we consider the fact that some speakers in those studies were monolingual in English.

5.   Chicano English as an ethnic dialect

The preceding sections of this chapter have shown that most of the features of ChcE morphology and syntax that diverge from prescriptive norms are shared by other vernacular English dialects. However, as we have noted, very few of these features have received the kind of systematic study required to determine if they pattern in the same way as they do in other English dialects. Such studies have the potential to contribute greatly to our understanding of everyday language use in Chicano communities as well as to our understanding of the processes of language maintenance and language shift. Speakers in communities undergoing language shift do not merely shift from one language to another. Rather, they move from one specific variety of a language to a specific variety of another language and, in some cases, create a new variety through which they may express their identity. A recent survey of Latino adults reported that 61 percent of U.S.-born respondents regarded themselves as English-dominant and 35 percent considered themselves bilingual (Brodie et al. 2002: 13). Fully 78 percent of third generation and higher respondents considered themselves English-dominant and only 22 percent considered themselves bilingual (Brodie et al. 2002: 16). While this information is useful in combating the popular misconception that Latinos are unwilling to learn English, broad surveys of self-reported language dominance tell us nothing about the kinds of English that U.S.-born Latinos speak. To answer that question, we need the kind of careful sociolinguistic work that has enriched our understanding of African American speech (see Wolfram, this volume).

The issue of possible Spanish influence presents a different but related question. As indicated in the introduction to this chapter, early accounts of ChcE were based on the outdated notion that interference from the first language was the primary cause for divergences between the speech of learners and native-speakers of the target language. Given such an assumption, researchers had no need to do more than compare features of ChcE with features of Spanish. When they found a match, they believed that they also found a cause for the divergence. Clearly such a procedure is inadequate. Rather, before we can understand fully the possible influence of Spanish, we need to understand both the linguistic and social constraints on ChcE. Fought's (2003) finding that bilingual speakers were more likely to use negative concord than were monolingual speakers is intriguing in this regard and suggests that the obligatory nature of negative concord in Spanish may have some effect on ChcE speakers' choices of a widespread English vernacular pattern. However, we need to know whether bilingualism also influences speakers' choices of other nonstandard morphosyntactic variants. Only then we will be in a position to evaluate empirically the possible influence of Spanish and to provide a sociolinguistically adequate description of Chicano English.

*   Research on this chapter was supported by a University of Texas at San Antonio faculty development leave to Robert Bayley and by a Rockefeller Foundation fellowship at the University of California, Santa Barbara Chicano Studies Center to Otto Santa Ana. We thank Carmen Fought for generously sharing an advance version of her book on Chicano English (Fought 2003).

Exercises and study questions

1. Chicano English speakers live in close proximity to African Americans in many areas of the U.S. On the basis of the information presented in this chapter and in Wolfram (this volume), which grammatical features does ChcE share with AAVE? Which features are not shared by AAVE and ChcE? What explanation can you provide for why the two dialects share some features but not others?

2. The following excerpt is from an interview with a 15 year old Chicana from Texas. Identify the vernacular grammatical features that are shared with other vernacular dialects:

   Ever since I've been here, you know, me and him, when I was with that other guy … you know, me and him would talk and everything, me and him got to know each other, and once I broke up with that other guy, me and him was still talking and everything and we just got together all of a sudden. And then, next day I flew to Dallas without letting him know … and, you know, he was in the penitentiary, just recently he got out you know, but, he don't do drugs or anything. He may drink a beer once in a while but he don't really get drunk.

3. Examine the relative pronoun data in Table 2. Notice that in ChcE, *that* is used with both human and nonhuman antecedents, although a *wh-* form is used more frequently with human than it is with nonhuman antecedents.

What explanations can you provide for the spread of *that*? How does the ChcE use of *that* as a relative pronoun resemble other dialects? How does it differ?

4. Consider the negation patterns described in the article and summarized in Table 1, and compare it to negation in standard English. How strongly are these two grammatical subsystems related? Point out areas of overlap and differences.

5. Which features of the morphosyntax of Chicano English appear to be influenced by Spanish? If you compare Spanish traces in the morphosyntax and the phonology of Chicano English, do you see differences in the amount of transfer?

Selected references

Please consult the General references for titles mentioned in the text but not included in the references below. For a full bibliography see the accompanying CD-ROM.

Bayley, Robert
    1994   Consonant cluster reduction in Tejano English. *Language Variation and Change* 6: 303–326.
    1999   Relativization strategies in Mexican-American English. *American Speech* 74: 115–139.
Berni, Mary
    1995   Restrictive relative pronouns in the Survey of Oklahoma Dialects. Paper presented at NWAVE 24, University of Pennsylvania.
Brodie, Mallyann, Annie Steffenson, Jaime Valdez, Rebecca Levin and Roberto Suro
    2002   *2002 National Survey of Latinos*. Menlo Park, CA and Washington, DC: Henry J. Kaiser Family Foundation and the Pew Hispanic Center.
Dailey-O'Cain, Jennifer
    2000   The sociolinguistic distribution of and attitudes toward focuser *like* and quotative *like*. *Journal of Sociolinguistics* 4: 60–80.
Fought, Carmen
    2003   *Chicano English in Context*. Houndmills/New York: Palgrave Macmillan.
Guy, Gregory R. and Robert Bayley
    1995   On the choice of relative pronouns in English. *American Speech* 70: 148–162.
Mendoza-Denton, Norma
    1999   Sociolinguistics and linguistic anthropology of U.S. Latinos. *Annual Review of Anthropology* 28: 375–395.

Peñalosa, Fernando
   1980   *Chicano Sociolinguistics: A Brief Introduction.* Rowley, MA: Newbury
            House.
Santa Ana, Otto A.
   1996   Sonority and syllable structure in Chicano English. *Language Variation
            and Change* 8: 63–90.
Schumann, John H.
   1978   *The Pidginization Process: A Model for Second Language Acquisition.*
            Rowley, MA: Newbury House.
Wald, Benji
   1987   Spanish-English grammatical contact in Los Angeles: The grammar of re-
            ported speech in the East Los Angeles contact vernacular. *Linguistics* 25:
            53–80.
   1996   Substratal effects on the evolution of modals in East LA English. In:
            Jennifer Arnold, Renée Blake, Brad Davidson, Scott Schwenter and Julie
            Solomon (eds.), *Sociolinguistic Variation: Data, Theory and Analysis*, 515–
            530. Stanford, CA: Center for the Study of Language and Information.
Wolfram, Walt
   1974   *Sociolinguistic Aspects of Assimilation: Puerto Rican English in New York
            City.* Washington, DC: Center for Applied Linguistics.

Bahamian English: morphology and syntax[*]

Jeffrey Reaser and Benjamin Torbert

1. Introduction

Given the discontinuous settlement of the Bahamas by various groups, one would expect a great deal of linguistic diversity. The geophysical separation of the islands and imposed racial boundaries have prevented the formation of a homogeneous, pan-Bahamian speech variety. Some research has noted similarities between Afro-Bahamian English (AfBahE) and African American Vernacular English (AAVE) (Holm with Shilling 1982; Shilling 1978), while other research has drawn comparisons between Gullah and AfBahE (Holm 1983). Despite this attention to potential donor sources for the Afro-Bahamian population, little attention has been paid to the linguistic status of the Anglo-Bahamian population, a group that further complicates efforts to describe "Bahamian English". Hypothesized relatedness of Gullah, AAVE, and AfBahE, especially on southern out islands, is supported by historical settlement records that indicate a number of slaves brought to Exuma, Cat Island, and Crooked Island were likely from Gullah-speaking areas, whereas slaves or freed slaves on other islands may have come from non-Gullah speaking areas of the North American mainland. Given the range of varieties originally brought to the Bahamas during the early settlement, which (potentially) included colonial Bermudian English, British Cockney, RP, Scots English, an earlier African American variety, and Gullah, it should be no surprise that there remains a great deal of grammatical diversity in the Bahamas today.

Urban varieties spoken in Nassau and Freeport, as described by Hackert (2004), differ from those spoken in the Southern Bahamas and those on other out islands (cf. Childs, Reaser, and Wolfram 2003). Further, various researchers have noted an ability of Bahamians to style-shift between acrolectal and basilectal varieties, and an ability to imitate, at least to some degree, symbolic Jamaican indicators, depending on the discourse environment. Thus, describing all the grammatical variation in Bahamian English (BahE) would require a much more rigorous survey of islands and communities than has been done and remains outside the scope of this study.

The description found here represents the compilation of observations by many researchers, drawing especially on the work of John Holm, Alison Shilling, and Stephanie Hackert, who have contributed greatly to the knowledge of the grammatical system of BahE. This description also draws on more than 80 interviews conducted by various members of the North Carolina Language and Life Project with the residents of Cherokee Sound and Sandy Point, on Abaco Island. These speakers tend to be more acrolectal than the varieties described in other studies, which may be a reflection of skilled style-shifting on the part of our informants. It is worth noting that Abaco has a much larger percentage of Anglo residents (roughly 50%) than other islands in the Bahamas (roughly 15%) and therefore, Afro-Bahamian residents may not have undergone the same degree of basilectalization as areas with higher concentrations of Afro-Bahamian residents, including Nassau and Freeport. It appears that basilectalization may be a largely urban phenomenon, and not an active process in the formation of out islander speech.

2.   The linguistic status of Bahamian varieties

The linguistic diversity found in the Bahamas makes labeling the variety problematic. In Ian Hancock's (1971: 509–525) original survey of pidgin and creole languages, BahE is not included as a creole variety, although he later revised this assessment. While it seems that the general consensus, based on the inclusion of Bahamian English in the work of Holm (1988–1989) and Wells (1982) as well as other publications, is that BahE (or at least AfBahE) is a creole variety, existing somewhere between AAVE and more creolized varieties such as Jamaican Creole (JamC). As Holm (1983: 314) concludes, since "such a great variety of overlapping linguistic features is involved that even within a given community one simply cannot say – except with total arbitrariness – where Gullah leaves off and black English begins". AfBahE exists somewhere in this range, with some speech communities more clearly creolized (or basilectalized) than others. Discerning whether AfBahE is a creole or not, however, is not the goal of this chapter. For this reason, we will refer to varieties spoken in the Bahamas collectively as "Englishes" rather than "Creoles". Further, while it is established that there is overlap of linguistic features between ethnic varieties (Holm 1980), and that locally, ethnicities and ethnic labeling is far more complex than a binary taxonomy would suggest, for clarity and concision, we will refer to the varieties of English spoken by the white or light-skinned Bahamians as *Anglo-Bahamian English* (AnBahE) and the varieties spoken by the black or mixed Bahamians as *Afro-Bahamian English* (AfBahE). Even so, we acknowledge that there are often no clear racial boundaries in the Bahamas, which include British,

American, African, American Indian, Haitian, and mixed heritages of all combinations.

Given the fairly well documented history of settlement (Albury 1975; Holm 1980, 1983, 1988–1989; Craton and Saunders 1992) and the sociohistorical dynamics that have shaped the communities, linguistic data from the Bahamas may provide substantive insight into social and linguistic processes in terms of language divergence from and convergence to American, British, or Caribbean creole norms, issues of creolization and decreolization, and ethnolinguistic de-marcation and accommodation.

Skilled register shifting has been noted in other varieties of English includ-ing both creole and non-creole varieties. This shifting alone makes discerning the status of AfBahE difficult, and makes the question: "what is true Bahamian English", a difficult or impossible question to answer. Complicating this ques-tion are differences between urban and non-urban varieties; ethnic segregation; different levels of exposure to tourism; and more and more, immigration from non-English speaking areas such as Haiti. However, much can be learned from BahE and its relation to other varieties in the Americas and beyond. What fol-lows is a grammatical profile of prototypical AnBahE, mesolectal AfBahE, and basilectal AfBahE, organized by grammatical category.

3.   The grammar of Bahamian English

3.1.   Verb phrase structures

3.1.1.   Copula absence and leveling

The copula has been studied extensively in American vernaculars (e.g., Wol-fram 1969; Fasold 1972; Labov 1972a; Baugh 1983; Rickford 1999) in vari-eties spoken in transplant communities (e.g., Walker 2000: 35–72), in creole varieties of English (e.g., Rickford 1999; Patrick 1999) and in BahE (Shilling 1978; Hackert 2004). Generally, Anglo vernaculars tend to align more closely with prescriptive norms than do Afro varieties, both quantitatively and qualita-tively. It is more difficult to generalize about Creole varieties, as many creoles have alternate forms such as JamC's *da* (Holm 1984, 1988–1989) or a redis-tribution of standard forms. Shilling (1980: 136) reports that in the AfBahE basilect, "there is only the form *is*, with *am* and *are* very seldom appearing". In more acrolectal Bahamian varieties, including AnBahE, leveling to *is* (*they's nice*) occurs but at a drastically reduced rate, and present tense copula forms generally coincide with StE full and contracted forms.

Both AfBahE and AnBahE varieties conform to AmE patterning, whereby Afro varieties exhibit more extensive absence than Anglo varieties, and *are* is more prone to absence than *is*. Despite this similarity, important differences exist between these and other Caribbean and American varieties. Our own observations on mesolectal AfBahE reveal an unusual pattern, whereby *am* is more prone to absence than *is*, a pattern not attested elsewhere in the Caribbean. While other creole varieties have demonstrated significant absence of first-person copula forms, these creoles typically do not utilize prescriptive *am, is,* and *are* forms, making this attribute somewhat of an anomaly.

AnBahE is characterized by high rates of copula absence preceding adjectival phrases (*She_ nice*). Elevated conditioning rates of predicate adjectives are associated with creole varieties including Gullah and JamC (Holm 1984). Shilling (1978: 27) suggests that this pattern persists "because in the basilect these [adjectives] are stative verbs". However, while this pattern is also attested in basilectal and mesolectal AfBahE, the persistence of this pattern in AnBahE should not be considered evidence that AnBahE is a creole variety.

Absence of past tense copula is another feature often associated with creole varieties. Though relatively limited, absence of *was* (and *was* and *were* in the AfBahE mesolect) is a feature of AfBahE. This feature, however, is ethnically distributed in the Bahamas and past tense copula forms are almost categorically present in AnBahE (Shilling 1980). Like present tense leveling to *is*, leveling of the past tense verb paradigm to the single form *was* is common in varieties around the world. Wolfram and Schilling-Estes (1998: 336) note that "[v]irtually all vernacular varieties show" this pattern. It is not surprising, therefore, to find leveling to *was* in both AfBahE and AnBahE. More basilectal varieties exhibit elevated rates of leveled and reduced forms (/(ə)z/) (Shilling 1980). Positive leveling to *were* is also weakly attested. As with present tense forms of *be*, more acrolectal varieties, such as those found on Abaco, more closely approximate StE norms for *was/were* distinctions.

3.1.2.   *Finite* be

One of the most salient features of AAVE is the finite use of the verb *be* as a habitual marker (e.g. *Sometimes my ears be itching*). Shilling (1980) reports the related form *bes* for all grammatical subjects to signify habitual or durative status in AnBahE. Interviews with AnBahE speakers in Cherokee Sound included the habitual, *She bes home nearly all the time* and the durative, *He bes out in the yard. Bes* in Cherokee Sound is limited to third person subjects, while *be* occurs with both third person and other grammatical subjects.

Shilling (1980) found that finite forms of *be* are more frequent in AfBahE than AnBahE. AfBahE speakers almost categorically favor *be* over *bes* for all grammatical subjects, closely resembling the AAVE usage of this form. She reports that finite forms of *be* often occur in a *does+be+*Verb-*ing* pattern and can reference present *We does be reading play every time* or past tense, *She know two people does be sleeping in this bed* (Shilling 1980). In these contexts, the auxiliary sometimes appears in reduced forms realized as /əz/ or /z/, resulting in utterances such as *They think they's be actin' sharp but they's just be looking tired* (Shilling 1980). The commonness of this feature in AfBahE may provide evidence for Rickford's (1974) hypothesis that habitual *be* in AAVE is derived from a *does+be+*Verb-*ing* pattern found in earlier AAVE. Habituals in other Caribbean creoles such as JamC typically require alternate copula forms such as *a* or *de*, further distancing BahE from other Creoles (Winford 1993; Patrick 1999).

Recent interviews on Abaco Island suggest that *be* can be used even in non-habitual or non-durative constructions, such as the perfective *be* in *you must be ate some sometime*, produced by elderly AnBahE speaker. The AfBahE speakers from Abaco also exhibit variation with respect to widespread Bahamian patterns including the example *where the boats's be now* for 'where the boats does be now'. The form *bes* also appears in mesolectal AfBahE, but is not attested in studies of the basilect, suggesting potential accommodation to the Anglo population, which is, demographically, more numerous on Abaco (roughly 50%) than elsewhere in the Bahamas (roughly 15%).

3.1.3. *Perfective* I'm

Widespread during the seventeenth century, the use of inflected forms of perfective *be* (*I'm been there* for 'I've been there') has been relegated to infrequent use in varieties in the American Southeast; most notably as an ethnic marker in Lumbee English in Robeson County, North Carolina (Wolfram and Schilling-Estes 1998). Interviews with AnBahE speakers from Abaco Island reveal alternation between perfective *be* and standard *have* constructions, with older residents favoring the former.

This form does not appear to be a part of AfBahE. Constructions that typically take "I'm" in AnBahE such as __got or __been are realized occasionally with a full form (*have*), but more typically with a contracted form ('*ve*), or most often without an auxiliary as in *I __ been to the doctor in Marsh Harbour.* Perfective *you're* (*You're been there*) has been observed in AnBahE, though its use is infrequent and much less salient than perfective *I'm*.

3.1.4. *Auxiliary* done

Wolfram and Schilling-Estes (1998) note that completive *done* is found in both AAVE and in Southern American English (SAmE). Many creoles differ from the AmE pattern, lacking tense marking with this form, leading to utterances such as *She's done send the photographs.* Hackert (2004) attests extensive use of the creole *done*+bare root pattern for irregular verbs in urban AfBahE though only sparse use in AnBahE. Shilling (1980) also suggests that non-urban basilectal AfBahE tends to lack past tense marking, though she does not control for consonant cluster reduction, as in the example *I done ask forgiveness for that.* Our own observations of monoethnic enclaves on Abaco Island reveal that both AfBahE and AnBahE speakers use completive *done* frequently in interviews though they favor the non-creole form, *She done sent the photographs.* The fact that in the United States, completive *done* in Anglo varieties is restricted to the South may help establish a historical connection between research communities on Abaco Island and the Southern United States, while the lack of completive *done* in other white Bahamian enclaves may help establish a historical connection with settlers from the Northern United States, again, calling to mind the sundry groups responsible for shaping the history of the Bahamas. The subtle differences between realizations of this feature again demonstrate the range of linguistic varieties spoken in the Bahamas.

3.1.5. *Irregular verbs and past tense*

The taxonomy of six distinctive alternate forms of irregular past tense, identified by Wolfram and Christian (1976) can be summarized as follows: (1) ambiguous verbs such as *come*, which may be either a past participle substituted for preterit, a perfect whose auxiliary has been deleted, or a bare root; (2) substitution of the preterit for the past participle; (3) past participle substituted for the preterit; (4) unambiguous bare root forms; (5) regularization; and (6) different strong forms. Not surprisingly, Hackert (2004) reports significant past tense zero in urban areas of the Bahamas. Mesolectal AfBahE from Abaco exhibits lower, but still robust rates of zero inflections; AnBahE informants seldom stray from StE forms of past tense. *Have* and *do*, whether main verb or auxiliary, are seldom unmarked. By comparison, rates of past tense unmarking are not as robust in the ex-slave Recordings (Bailey, Maynor, and Cukor-Avila 1991) or in Samaná, Dominica, and North Preston and Guysborough, Nova Scotia (Poplack and Tagliamonte 2001). Additionally, AfBahE features a variety of periphrastic marking with *did* and *used to* (Hackert 2004). Other irregular forms of preterit and past participle, widespread in other areas (e.g. Appalachian English [AppE]) are weakly attested in all these studies.

Unmarked past tense is one of the clearer indicators of a creole residue in AfBahE. Though standard preterits and past participles are plentiful among many speakers, and past tense variation fluctuates from individual to individual, Bahamian unmarking does not approach speakers of Trinidadian Creole (TrnC) or JamC whose speakers exhibit near-categorical past tense zero (Winford 1993; Patrick 1999). Hackert (2004) discusses the ramifications of AfBahE past tense variation for aspectual systems, but detailed discussion of this topic is beyond the scope of this chapter. The popular conception of BahE past tense marking, according to *More Talkin' Bahamian,* is "Very simple! Just get rid of all those superfluous '-ed's' from your verb endings and use the present tense form" (Glinton-Meicholas 1995: 10). This simplified version, which may be an epiphenomenon of consonant cluster reduction, leading to elevated levels of surface unmarking of weak verbs, seems to be most descriptive of basilectal speakers. Albury (1981: 21) provides a more detailed hierarchy known as the 'flip-flop rule':

Basilectal:	zero
Mid-mesolectal:	zero with variable overt past
marking	
Upper-mesolectal:	t/d/ɪd with variable zero marking
Acrolectal:	t/d/ɪd

3.1.6. Subject-verb concord

Subject-verb concord patterns in StE reflect redundant and non-productive reflexes of the Old English inflectional system such as verbal *-s* attachment following third singular subjects, as in, *the woman walks.* Often, Southern AmE, especially AppE, will attach *-s* to verbs following third person plural noun phrases, as in *people walks* (Wolfram and Christian 1976). With the exception of finite *be,* the pattern of attaching *-s* to verbs following collective nouns is not found in AnBahE, despite the potential for historical ties between Southern AmE and BahE. AnBahE seems to follow prescriptive norms, attaching an *-s* only when following third singular subjects. This is to be expected, as third singular *-s* absence is generally not a part of Anglo-American vernaculars in North America (Wolfram and Thomas 2002).

Mesolectal AfBahE exhibits more *-s* variation. The same AfBahE speaker produces an *-s* with a collective (*Some people lays down for nine months*), and with a singular pronoun subject, often first person (*I buys fireworks from over there* or *I goes in the water*), as well as utterances that follow prescriptive norms (*the men work hard*). It should be noted that *-s* attachment following first singular *I* is not limited to historical present in narratives, but can be found with some regularity in more general conversational styles. Third singular *-s* absence appears variably, and speakers tend to exhibit both *-s* absence and *-s* attachment with third singular subjects (*Our daughter live_ in Brunswick, Georgia ... she works over there*). Whether the subject is a pronoun or a noun phrase seems to matter little, if at all. Instead, it appears as though the attachment or absence of verbal inflectional *-s* is an optional process in AfBahE. The variable presence of morphological *-s* in AfBahE distinguishes the variety from JamC and basilectal TrnC (Patrick 1999).

3.1.7. Questions

Shilling (1978: 50) notes that basilectal AfBahE speech lacks "inversion for questions" a prototypical creole feature. Holm's (1980: 62) sole white informant from Inagua Island lacks subject-verb inversion, suggesting possible creole or African influence on AnBahE. Our own observations reveal a good deal of individual variation with respect to question formation. While some speakers categorically invert questions, and others have categorically non-inverted question formation, the vast majority of speakers alternate between constructions. This co-occurs with auxiliary deletion, occasionally making it difficult to determine the position in which the auxiliary would exist (e.g. *you going?* may be inverted *are you going?* on non-inverted *you are going?*). Alternation between standard and non-standard constructions can be found in speakers of all ages and in both communities, perhaps suggesting that there is limited accommodation of this feature by AnBahE, while simultaneously reaffirming that AfBahE speakers do have access to StE interrogative formation. Of course, the alternation between inverted and non-inverted forms is not necessarily atypical as, even in StE, a speaker can signal a question through rising intonation, thus, *Have you been there?* may be just as easily be asked as *You've been there?*, which lacks the subject-verb inversion but productively asks the same question.

One notable aspect of question formation in the AnBahE variety of Cherokee Sound is the use of perfective *be* in questions elicited during conversational speech, as in *How long I'm been in Cherokee?*

3.1.8. Adverbs

AnBahE has preserved some now (in mainstream English) archaic intensifiers. Most common is the use of *right* as an intensifier in expanded contexts such as *that's right nice of you*, a form found as early as Middle English but now restricted to temporal and locative contexts in StE.

3.2. Noun phrase structures

3.2.1. Plurals

Poplack, Tagliamonte and Eze (2000) provide a classification system of noun types and patterns of plurals in English-based creoles and AAVE. Many vernacular varieties do not require an *-s* following measure nouns premodified by a numeral, as in *I walked four mile_ yesterday*. Others exhibit regularization of irregular plurals (e.g. *two deers, four fishes*) and even, occasionally, double-marked plurals where StE vowel alternation is preserved (e.g. *three mens*). Creole languages, like JamC, often mark plurals by inserting *dem* either before or after a noun or through extensively leveled patterns of pluralization (Patrick 1999).

Although BahE pluralization has not been studied as rigorously as the varieties in Poplack, Tagliamonte and Eze (2000), various publications have commented that BahE plurals are extremely irregular. Glinton-Meicholas (1995: 10) sums up BahE plurals as follows: "You don't have to add a plural ending at all – 'I had four husband'. Or you can add the ending '-dem'; e.g. 'De boy-dem playin' hockey'; Or you can have yourself a ball and add 's' and '-dem'; e.g. 'De boys-dem playin' ball'." Glinton-Meicholas' observation that there are multiple manifestations of plurals in BahE seems consistent with other observations of BahE. Shilling's (1980) examples seem to suggest an ethnic division whereby AnBahE speakers tend to have standard plural *-s* attachment while Af-BahE speakers tend to have variable marking of plurals. However, the basilectal speakers do not have categorical unmarked plurals, but instead alternate between marked and unmarked forms. Even Shilling's basilectal speakers (1978: 56–57) tend to exhibit at least some standard plural *-s* attachment, including following count nouns, an environment that often does not take plural as in *I think he bout two months now*. Traditional creole *dem* is not attested in her data, and standard realizations of irregular plurals suggest that even basilectal AfBahE may not align closely with creole patterns of pluralization.

3.2.2. Possessives

Possessive *-s* inflection also reveals a strong ethnic division. Generally, in AnBahE, possessive pronouns are most common, favored over constructions that require morphological possessive *-s*. *Me* and *my* seem interchangeable in AnBahE but not in AfBahE, as in *me children and grandchildren. That's my grandson*. Cases in which possessive inflection would be required in StE typically have standard *-s* inflection, as in *I used to keep my truck ... down at a friend's [house]*. AfBahE speakers occasionally use *they* or *theys* in place of *their* or *theirs,* as in *They bring they own equipment, it's theys boat*, or *what's* *ours is ours and what theys is theys.* The StE possessive *-s* is almost categorically absent from even mesolectal AfBahE, where possession is marked either by a pronoun or by syntactic proximity, as in *My son_ truck.*

3.2.3. Pronouns

Present-day English lacks a distinction between singular and plural *you*, while some varieties have innovated forms to distinguish between these subjects, including Southern AmE *y'all*, AppE *you'uns*, and Northern AmE *youse*. Holm (1983: 308), drawing on the work of the folklorist Elsie Clews Parsons, reports that the Gullah second plural pronoun *oonah* is restricted to the island of San Salvador, but that the related form *yonner* is found on Andros and that the most frequent form today is *yinna*. Holm notes that *yinnuh* and *yunnah* are both found in Gullah, and uses this as evidence of the relatedness of these varieties. Glinton-Meicholas (1995) reports that both *yinna* and *y'all* can be found in the Bahamas for second plural subjects. The data from Abaco fail to strengthen the Gullah connection, however, as standard *you* occurs in every utterance except one – which features *y'all* – in AnBahE and every instance in AfBahE.

   One of the most salient features of AnBahE, and the feature that Shilling (1980: 137) claims offers "the clearest difference between [AnBahE] and [Af-BahE]" is the use of existential *it* in sentences like *it's not many people around here* or *It was Indians that probably lived here.* While AnBahE uses *it* for existential *there* far more frequently (categorically for some speakers) than Af-BahE, existential *it* does occur in AfBahE. Shilling (1978) claims that this only occurs when an Afro-Bahamian community is near an all-white settlement, but it is found with some frequency in both the older and younger speakers from Sandy Point, a monoethnic community more than thirty miles from the nearest all-white (or even mixed) settlement. Mesolectal AfBahE speakers alternate between *it* and *there* for existential constructions, while Shilling's (1980: 138) basilectal speakers often lacked existential markers altogether as in *wasn't nothing to do then like today.*

   Other pronouns in AnBahE also exhibit variation. *What* can be used as a relative pronoun for both human and non-humans, in utterances such as *The road what they got there* and *My auntie what's dead.* This can be found in AfBahE, but less frequently than in AnBahE or in Gullah (Mufwene 1986).

3.2.4. Negation

Like many vernacular varieties of English, both AnBahE and AfBahE exhibit negative concord and frequent use of *ain't*. Negative concord seems to be the typical negation pattern, although still variable in BahE, as is *I didn't have no parents and he didn't have any parents*, which features both variants in the same utterance. Negative concord occurs most commonly in post-verbal position (*I don't have none here*) but occasionally in a preverbal position (*nobody don't have none here*), and is often inverted (*Didn't want to stay no longer than I had to*). Cross-clausal negative concord differs semantically in Bahamian speech from enclave varieties in the Southeast U.S. and AAVE (cf. Labov 1972a; Wolfram and Christian 1976). Instead, tokens that exhibit this pattern, such as *ain't much Bahamians can't do* would be interpreted not as 'there isn't much Bahamians can do', but rather that 'Bahamians are capable of doing most things'.

In BahE, *ain't* functions in much the same way as it does in most vernacular dialects. *Ain't* can be used instead of negative forms of *be* as in *ain't no tennis court around here*, as well as in place of negative forms of *have/has* (i.e., 'haven't,' 'hasn't') as in *I ain't never been there*, a domain that in BahE alternates with *don't* as in *she don't/ain't got no husband*. Mesolectal BahE does not use *ain't* in place of 'didn't' as AAVE does, although it does appear in the basilect.

3.2.5. Prepositions

Among the more salient variants in prepositional phrases is static locative *to*. While AfBahE exhibits variable use of *to* and standard forms, AnBahE uses *to* nearly categorically in constructions such as *She's down to the long dock*. *To* can also be found in place of a number of other prepositions in BahE, including *on*, as in *Put them to your feet*; *in*, as in *He lives to Marsh Harbour*; *from*, as in *they do it to Marsh Harbour more than they do from here* ('they hunt more from Marsh Harbour'); and *over/during*, as in *my granddaughter been here to Christmas*. Occasionally, *to*, or another preposition, will be absent in AfBahE speakers, such as *They go __ Marsh Harbour*; this absence, also noted by Glinton-Meicholas (1995: 11), does not seem to be a part of AnBahE.

3.3.   Lexical items

The Bahamian lexicon may be the most documented aspect of BahE. Collections of common Bahamian usages have been compiled in various places such as the *Dictionary of Bahamian English* (Holm with Shilling 1982) and *More Talkin' Bahamian* (Glinton-Meicholas 1995). Lexical evidence has been used to attempt to establish the provenience of Bahamian settlers. Holm (1980: 50) cites a number of lexical items that occur on out islands and in Gullah, but not other creoles such as *"hoe-cake* 'cornmeal cake,' *gutlin,'* 'greedy,' *sper-rit,* 'ghost,' *Hoppin' John* 'beans and rice,' and *ninny* 'breast'". Holm (1983) cites these and other lexical items shared by BahE and Gullah in an attempt to establish the relatedness of these varieties, though it should be noted that these terms are not known in all areas of the Bahamas. Further, some Bahamian lexical items, such as *obeah,* 'witchcraft', *gumbay,* 'social gathering', and *jumbey,* 'spirit', have African origins.

One lexical dimension worth noting is the taxonomy of ethnicity. While individuals from certain communities have specific labels such as *Crabs* (people from Hope Town) or *Cigillians* (people from Spanish Wells), more general labels are used to describe broad demographic groups in the Bahamas (Holm 1980). The term *white* is used to cover a broad spectrum that entails racially mixed locals and even some "light-skinned American blacks" (Holm 1980: 54). *Conchy Joe* or *Conky Joe* is the term locally used to describe what Americans would classify as "white". The term can carry a derogatory connotation in the Bahamas, and locally, this group tends to describe themselves as *white* and the rest of the Bahamas as *black,* or *Negro.* Afro-Bahamians locally refer to themselves as *black* or simply as *Bahamians.*

Like other marine-based communities, the Bahamas have noteworthy lexical items describing aspects of the ocean and marine life, though few are unique to the islands. One of the principal sources for money in many non-tourist based Bahamian economies is *crawfishing* for what are more commonly called (Caribbean) spiny lobster or *Panulirus argus.* Additionally, eels are called *morays*: a semantic broadening of the term. Bahamians have also adapted topographical terms to describe the subtleties of the islands, including the British definition of *creek* to mean an inlet or recess of the sea and *spit* for a point of land extending into the sea. Many more nautical and geotopical terms vary from community to community, and may be referenced in the sources mentioned above. One slightly unusual usage that is not documented in these sources that is found on Abaco is the use of *quit* in place of *leave* or *left.* This form has only surfaced in the speech of elderly AfBahE speakers in examples such as, *some of the people quit during hurricanes*; *they asked them to quit. They didn't quit, I mean the storm come. The storm kill everybody but one man and a dog there*; and *only was just a few colored people, we quit and come out here.*

4.   Conclusions

The various histories of individual islands and groups are reflected in the extensive linguistic variation of features between basilectal speech, acrolectal speech, and ethnically demarcated varieties. The various Englishes of the Bahamas do not align isomorphically with any U.S., British, or Caribbean creole variety. Bi-dialecticism and style-shifting may further complicate potential comparisons. Linguistic processes such as decreolization, accommodation, potential basilectalization, and social factors such as segregation, integration, and more recently, tourism and Haitian immigration further complicate questions regarding linguistic inputs to various islands.

Despite the complexities involved in describing a pan-Bahamian variety and the elusiveness of documenting the sociohistorical and linguistic explanations for current of linguistic features, there is a clear indication that there is bilateral accommodation between both AnBahE and AfBahE. Nonetheless, there exists a persistent qualitative and quantitative ethnolinguistic division. Further, the varieties currently spoken at both the basilectal and acrolectal extremes remain uniquely Bahamian with respect to lexical and grammatical features and pseudo-ethnolinguistic marking, as can be seen in the comparative Tables 1 through 3.

Linguistic preservation, innovation, decreolization, basilectalization, and accommodation, have created unique patternings of linguistic varieties in the Bahamas. Research on these varieties can help researchers better understand linguistic processes, as well as adding important information with respect to documenting and explaining the forces that have given birth to modern varieties of English in the Caribbean, the U.S., and around the world.

Table 1.   Comparative dialect profile of the verb phrase

Grammatical Structure	Anglo-Bahamian	Mesolectal Afro-Bahamian	Basilectal Afro-Bahamian	Jamaican Creole	Gullah	AAVE
Agreement						
3rd pl. -s marking e.g. *The dogs barks*	✓	(✓)				
3rd sg. -s absence e.g. *The dog bark*		(✓)	✓	✓	✓	✓
Be						
Finite *be* e.g. *It bes like that*	✓	✓	✓	✓	✓	✓
Perfective *be* e.g. *I'm been there*	✓					
Is leveling e.g. *They's home*	(✓)	(✓)	✓	✓*	✓	(✓)
was leveling e.g. *We was there*	✓	✓	✓	✓*	✓	✓

Table 1. (continued)   Comparative dialect profile of the verb phrase

Grammatical Structure	Anglo-Bahamian	Mesolectal Afro-Bahamian	Basilectal Afro-Bahamian	Jamaican Creole	Gullah	AAVE
Copula						
are absence	✓	✓	✓	✓*	✓	✓
e.g. *You ugly*						
is absence	(✓)	✓	✓	✓*	✓	✓
e.g. *He ugly*						
am absence		✓	✓	✓*	(✓)	
e.g. *I ugly*						
Past tense copula absence		(✓)	✓	✓	(✓)	
e.g. *She [was] here*						
Alternate forms			(✓)	✓	(✓)	
e.g. *da*						
Questions						
Non-inverted questions	(✓)	(✓)	✓	✓	✓	(✓)
e.g. *They are home?*						
Other auxiliaries						
Double modals				✓	✓	✓
e.g. *He might could come*						
Completive *done*	✓	✓	✓	✓	✓	✓
e.g. *He done fix(ed) it*						
Stressed remote *bin*			✓	✓	✓	
e.g. *He bin go*						
Irregular past tense						
(1) ambiguous forms	✓	✓	✓	✓	✓	✓
e.g. *He come over here*						
(2) pret. for past part.	✓	✓	(✓)		(✓)	✓
e.g. *She had went*						
(3) past part. for pret.	✓	✓	(✓)		(✓)	✓
e.g. *I seen her*						
(4) bare root	✓	✓	✓	✓	✓	✓
e.g. *He run yesterday*						
(5) Regularization	✓	✓	(✓)		(✓)	✓
e.g. *He growed up tall*						
(6) different strong form	✓	✓	✓	(✓)	✓	✓
e.g. *He retch up the roof*						

*   JamC uses few standard copula forms in the basilect, and therefore there is not extensive *is*-leveling or *are* absence per se, but there is extensive leveling to and absence of other non-standard forms or where Standard English would have these copula forms.

Table 2. Comparative dialect profile of nominals

Grammatical structure	Anglo-Bahamian	Mesolectal Afro-Bahamian	Basilectal Afro-Bahamian	Jamaican Creole	Gullah	AAVE
-s-pl. absence e.g. *40 pound_*	(✓)	(✓)	✓	✓	✓	✓
Plural *dem* e.g. *The dem-boy playing*			✓	✓	✓	
Regularized plurals e.g. *Oxes, sheeps*		(✓)	✓		✓	✓
2nd pl. *y'all* e.g. *Y'all are a crowd*		(✓)			(✓)	✓
2nd pl. *Yinnah* or related form e.g. *Yinna are a crowd*			✓	✓	✓	
Existential *it* e.g. *It's no place to go*	✓	✓	✓		(✓)	✓
Embedded null subject pro e.g. *It's a woman come here*	✓	✓	✓	✓	✓	✓
Pronominal *what* e.g. *The man what I talked to*	✓	(✓)	(✓)	(✓)	✓	✓
Possessive *'s* absence e.g. *My Son_ truck*		(✓)	✓	✓	✓	✓

Table 3. Comparative dialect profile: negation, adverbs, prepositions

Grammatical structure	Anglo-Bahamian	Mesolectal Afro-Bahamian	Basilectal Afro-Bahamian	Jamaican Creole	Gullah	AAVE
Negation						
Postverbal concord e.g. *It wasn't nothing*	✓	✓	✓	✓	✓	✓
Preverbal concord e.g. *Nobody don't like it*	(✓)	(✓)	(✓)	✓	✓	✓
Inverted concord e.g. *Didn't want to stay no longer than I had to*	(✓)	✓	✓	✓	✓	✓
Affirmative cross-clausal e.g. *Ain't nothing nobody had*				✓	✓	✓
ain't for *be+not, have+not* e.g. *She ain't there*	✓	✓	✓		✓	✓
ain't for *did+not* e.g. *I ain't go*			✓		✓	✓

Table 3. (continued)   Comparative dialect profile: negation, adverbs, prepositions

Grammatical structure	Anglo-Bahamian	Mesolectal Afro-Bahamian	Basilectal Afro-Bahamian	Jamaican Creole	Gullah	AAVE
Adverbs						
Intensifying *right* e.g. *He's right smart*		(✓)	(✓)		✓	✓
Prepositions						
Static locative *to* e.g. *She's to the dock*	✓	✓	✓	✓	✓	✓
to for other prepositions e.g. *Put them to your throat*	✓	✓	✓		✓	
Deleted prepositions e.g. *They go __ Florida*		(✓)	✓	✓	✓	

*   The research in this analysis was supported by NSF Grant No. BCS-9910224 and the William C. Friday Endowment at North Carolina State University. We would like to thank Walt Wolfram, Peter Patrick, and Tracy Weldon for their help with this chapter.

Exercises and study questions

1. What traditionally creole grammatical features can be heard in the speech of Afro-Bahamians?

2. Which morphosyntactic features are shared by AAVE and African BahE but not with White BahE?

3. Which morphosyntactic features of Afro-Bahamian English most likely have been accommodated by White residents of the Bahamas? (i.e., what's a part of White BahE but not Southern AmE).

4. Which morphosyntactic features were most likely accommodated by the Afro-Bahamian speakers from Colonial overseers?

5. The speakers in the audio sample(s) claim the "Carolinas" as the place their ancestors came from. What features would support this claim? Which features would weaken this claim? Evaluate this claim in terms of linguistic innovation, accommodation, and (de)creolization.

6. In what ways are the speech samples similar to Gullah, in what ways different?

7. Evaluate the notion of Pan-Caribbean identity based on the Bahamian and Jamaican speakers. What features are viewed by outsiders as pan-Caribbean linguistic features? Is this accurate?

8. Evaluate the notion of Pan-Bahamian English. To what extent can Afro-Bahamian Englishes be considered a homogeneous variety of English?

Selected references

Please consult the General references for titles mentioned in the text but not included in the references below. For a full bibliography see the accompanying CD-ROM.

Albury, Anne
    1981   The status of the *-ed*-suffix in Black Bahamian English. M.A. thesis, University College London.
Albury, Paul
    1975   *The Story of the Bahamas*. London: Macmillan.
Childs, Becky, Jeffrey Reaser, and Walt Wolfram
    2003   Defining ethnic varieties in the Bahamas: Phonological accommodation in black and white enclave communities. In: Aceto and Williams (eds.), 1–28.
Craton, Michael and Gail Saunders
    1992   *Islanders in the Stream: A History of the Bahamian People,* 2 Volumes. Athens: University of Georgia Press.
Glinton-Meicholas, Patricia
    1995   *More Talkin' Bahamian*. Nassau: Guanima Press.
Hancock, Ian
    1971   A map and list of pidgin and creole languages. In: Hymes (ed.), 509–525.
Holm, John
    1980   African features in white Bahamian Speech. *English World-Wide* 1: 45–65.
    1983   On the relationship of Gullah and Bahamian. *American Speech* 58: 303–318.
    1984   Variability of the copula in Black English and its creole kin. *American Speech* 59: 291–309.
Holm, John with Alison Shilling
    1982   *Dictionary of Bahamian English*. Cold Spring, NY: Lexik House.
Mufwene, Salikoko S.
    1986   Restrictive relativization in Gullah. *Journal of Pidgin and Creole Languages* 1: 1–31.
Poplack, Shana, Sali Tagliamonte and Ejike Eze
    2000   Reconstructiong the source of Early African American English plural marking: A comparative study of English and Creole. In: Poplack (ed.), 73–105.

Shilling, Alison
    1978   Some non-standard features on Bahamian Dialect syntax. Ph.D. disserta-
              tion, Department of Linguistics, University of Hawaii.
    1980   Bahamian English – a non-continuum? In: Day (ed.), 133–145.
Walker, James A.
    2000   Rephrasing the copula: contraction and zero in Early African American
              English. In: Poplack (ed.), 35–72.

Jamaican Creole: morphology and syntax

Peter L. Patrick

1. Introduction

Jamaican Creole (JamC, known to its speakers as Patwa) is a language of ethnic identification for roughly two and a half million people in the island of Jamaica, and overseas for many thousands of native speakers (and non-natives, see British Creole (BrC) chapters in the British Isles volume). JamC is a canonical example of an Atlantic Creole. One of the first Caribbean English-lexicon Creoles to be described using modern linguistic methods (Loftman 1953; Cassidy 1961), it remains among the best-researched. The first generative grammar of a Creole was Bailey's *Jamaican Creole Syntax* (1966). The first comprehensive etymological dictionary of a Creole was Cassidy and Le Page's *Dictionary of Jamaican English* (1967, hereafter *DJE*).

1.1. History

JamC owes little or nothing to either the indigenous Arawaks or Spanish invaders, starting with Columbus in 1494, who settled the island in 1509, bringing the first African slaves. By 1601 only a handful of Arawaks remained alive alongside 1,000 Africans. When the British arrived in 1655 with 9,000 troops, they met 6,000 inhabitants, 1,500 of African descent and the rest mostly Spanish; after 1660, a few dozen Spanish remained, while 300 Maroons fought from the mountains. The Maroons today, custodians of African culture, still preserve a distinctive speech form, Maroon Spirit Language. Their ranks were supplemented by runaways under slavery, and they maintained their independence by treaty, defeating the British in 1739 and 1795.

However, the origins of JamC postdate 1660, in the interaction of British colonists and African slaves. The language did not yet exist in 1658, when the 7,000 settlers and soldiers in the island from Britain, Ireland and the Americas outnumbered Africans 5 to 1; but between 1677, when there were about 9,000 each of whites and blacks, and 1703, when the white population had slightly declined but the numbers of enslaved Africans had risen to 45,000, the roots of JamC were planted. Many key features were in place before 1750, though others can only be documented from the early and mid-19th century (Lalla and D'Costa 1990).

Jamaican language and its place in society reflects the brutal history of Jamaica as a British sugar colony until Independence in 1962. Creolization in the broadest sense led to emergence of new cultural and social institutions, including language, but the subordination of JamC to English – the native tongue of a tiny minority – has persisted to the present day, with consequences for education, economy, and psychological independence. The collapse of the plantation economy between the two world wars brought on mass urbanization, making Kingston the largest "English-speaking" city in the Americas south of Miami (Patrick 1999). Yet only in the 21st century has the Jamaican government seriously begun to explore language planning and recognition of JamC as a national language.

Jamaican Creole's dramatic genesis in British slavery, imperialism and the African diaspora to the Americas has focused creolist research on language contact, especially the influence of African languages (Akan and Kwa families, along with Bantu), and to a lesser extent British English dialects (West of England, Irish and Scots), as well as universals of language acquisition and creation. Over 90 percent of Jamaica's population are of African origin. Other groups claim Indian, Chinese, Syrian and European heritage; of these, only Europeans were present before 1845 and contributed to the formation of JamC. For all these Jamaicans, JamC is a shared marker of ethnic and national identity which serves to distinguish them from other peoples, and to unite them in possession of a rich, diverse set of discursive resources.

1.2.   The Creole continuum

Social stratification in Jamaica is crucial to understanding the extreme variability of contemporary Jamaican speech. The complex linguistic situation can be related to an equally intricate web of social relations, using the model of the creole continuum. This is opposed to discrete multi-lingual or multi-dialectal descriptions such as community bilingualism, standard-plus-dialects, and diglossia. The inapplicability of classic diglossia to Jamaica motivated De-Camp to invent the (post-)creole continuum model: "There is no sharp cleavage between Creole and standard (...) [but] a linguistic continuum, a continuous spectrum of speech varieties, ranging from (...) 'broken language' (...) to the educated standard" (DeCamp 1971: 350), i.e. from basilect to acrolect.

JamC is natively available to nearly all Jamaicans, but Standard Jamaican English (StJamE), the acrolect, is not – it is a home language for a small minority, and learned as a second language of school, literacy, mass media and work by others. This is the direct result of the colonial distribution of power in earlier centuries, which worked to create and maximize the norms that still devalue JamC and elevate StJamE. Many Jamaicans, and even many linguists (Creole-speaking and other), still maintain this contrast in prestige as a base component of their attitudes towards Jamaican language, and it surfaces in many linguistic descriptions.

In truth, both poles of the continuum are idealized abstractions, a collection of features most like standard Englishes (the acrolect) or most distant from them (basilect). Yet between these poles lies the continuum of everyday speech: a series of minimally differentiated grammars with extensive variation – an apparently seamless web connecting two idealized varieties which arose in the same place and time-frame and share distinctive features, yet cannot be genetically related.

The descriptive problem is thus to reconcile genetic descent and non-genetic, contact-induced language change within a finely-graded continuum. While StJamE is recognized as an English dialect, descended by normal transmission from 17th- and 18th-century British input dialects, creolists agree that the grammar of basilectal JamC differs radically from native English dialects, due to extensive language contact resulting in structural mixing. There is less agreement on whether this process took the form of abrupt creolization, whether a pidgin developed in the island first, or whether a prior pidgin existed – e.g. on the African coast – and was relexified (Cassidy 1971; Alleyne 1980; Lalla and D'Costa 1990). The prevailing opinion is that this sharp contrast makes it impossible to relate JamC genetically to English – or indeed to its African input languages, with which there is also a radical structural break (Thomason and Kaufman 1988; Thomason 2001) – though it bears obvious historical links to both.

1.3. The Jamaican mesolect

As linguists since Bailey have preferred to focus on these extremes, most research concentrated on basilectal JamC, until the recent emergence of studies on StJamE (e.g. Shields 1989). (Patrick 1999 is the only study of the mesolect.) Yet in purely social and demographic terms, the most important variety in Jamaica is the intermediate one known as the mesolect; its broad limits include the speech uttered by most Jamaicans, in most situations. Although empirical data for language description of JamC are nearly always drawn from points within the continuum (i.e. the mesolect), it remains under-theorized and underdescribed.

This may be because most linguistic treatments of JamC adopt a categorical perspective (Chambers 1995), seeking to explain away inherent linguistic variation by attributing it to the random mixing of so-called invariant grammars, viz., the basilect and acrolect. Thus, Bailey (1971: 342) tried to model mesolectal speech as "standard with incursions from the creole, or creole with incursions from the standard" through "borrowing and interference", while Akers (1981: 4) believed it was due to a failure of acquisition by speakers who "incompletely control their code". Both views portray Jamaicans as less than competent in their everyday language, and the mesolect as grammar-less.

Such an approach fails to reach descriptive adequacy: the mesolect cannot be reduced to interference between two discrete, polar systems, and no such detailed description has ever been attempted. The existence of language ideologies and attitudes (resembling those commonly found in bilingual communities) which do not explicitly grant the mesolect autonomy, should not mislead as to its systematic internal organization. Although highly variable, it comprises a grammar describable via both qualitative linguistic generalizations and quantitative constraints, which has evolved over three centuries, arriving at a set of socially-evaluated patterns with their own historical and cultural ecology. Its post-creolization development is broadly similar to that of other, non-creole, speech communities, to which variationist theory and descriptive methods have been profitably applied (Chambers, Trudgill and Schilling-Estes 2002). Earlier speculations that the creole continuum might be so variable as not to constitute a speech community at all proved unfounded. In the most detailed account of the mesolect, Patrick (1999) concludes that it is characterized by the systematic presence and integration of English forms and rules in a partial and variable, but non-random, manner. On this view, mesolectal grammar does not result from improvised mixing or code-switching between two polar varieties, nor are its speakers fossilized learners. Rather, the mesolect is an organized, distinctive collection of elements with a long history and its own complex norms, structures and social patterning. Many choices and variants are possible within it, but many are not. Ways of speaking are not accidental but conventionalized; borrowing occurs, but is not the sole source of variation; grammatical rules exist and interlock; and it is transmitted through normal language acquisition. Though change occurs, the mesolect contrasts with newer and less stable varieties such as BrC.

Despite the defining presence of English elements, which mark it off clearly from the basilect, the mesolect shares with the latter many constraints, structures and organizing principles which are not generally characteristic of native dialects of English. Insofar as creoles are defined through such contrasts (Mühleisen 2002), the mesolect is thus Jamaican Creole, and not Jamaican English (i.e. it cannot be genetically related to English). Indeed, it probably appeared earlier than the basilect (Alleyne 1971). English-like surface forms (some exclusive to the mesolect, e.g. *did*, others shared with the acrolect, e.g. *neva*, or even the basilect, e.g. *ben* – all three tense-markers are discussed below) characteristically alternate with zero, governed by constraints shared with basilectal JamC but not with native Englishes. This pattern is found in both earlier Jamaican texts and contemporary speech.

The mesolect is naturally the primary object of description here, with frequent reference also to basilectal structures. Though there is a clear dividing line between these two grammars (Patrick 1999), there is none between mesolect and acrolect, since the partial presence of English forms and constraints merges indistinguishably into the possession of full competence in StJamE. While the many structures shared with the basilect provide a firm linguistic basis for treating the mesolect as JamC, there is no such structural warrant for restricting "English" only to the high acrolect – it is strictly the power of social convention which influences speakers, and therefore linguists, to do so.

In practice, this lack of a sharp upper boundary creates difficulties in analysing some speakers or texts. The search for a single point, a linguistic and social division, where StJamE starts and JamC ends, is the misguided product of colonial language ideologies. Below, however, illustrative contrasts are drawn. This coincides with the symbolic value speakers attach to fine, or even illusory, distinctions between "proper English" and Patwa (a term broad enough to encompass, at times, everything but the high acrolect).

1.4. The data and orthography

Much data below is cited from written records. Cassidy's phonemic orthography (1961) has served as a model for many other Creole writing systems, but is little-followed by Jamaican writers. Uncredited data are by the author (as are most translations) or by recorded informants, and generally follow Cassidy. While creolists generally prefer a diachronic perspective, and seek out "pure" basilectal forms as evidence of earlier stages of language development, the description below is synchronic and does not privilege the basilect. This may affect some analyses, e.g. whether to treat *se* 'say' under complementation or verb serialization.

2. Tense, mood and aspect marking

2.1. A Creole TMA system?

All descriptions of basilectal JamC agree that it combines invariant pre-verbal particles with unmarked verb stems to express these grammatical categories, where native Englishes typically use verbal auxiliaries, inflectional suffixes and agreement-marking. It is also generally argued that contrasting linguistic categories and semantic values underlie and constrain these formal differences.

The most influential account is given by Bickerton (1975, 1981) for creoles in general. Three main categories – anterior tense, irrealis mood, and non-punctual aspect – each have a principal pre-verbal marker, which must combine in the order T-M-A. In creoles, Bickerton argued, states, habitual situations and progressive events can all be described as having non-punctual aspect. Further, verb stativity is said to crucially affect the occurrence and interpretation of markers of past-reference: bare non-stative verbs receive a default past-reference reading, while statives are non-past unless preceded by a tense-marker. These claimed syntactic and semantic properties together describe a grammar that "clearly bears no relation to the system of English" (Bickerton 1975: 47). This gives the following paradigm:

	Stativity	**Pre-V Marker**	**Meaning**	**Examples**
(1)	+stative	none	present, habitual	*Mi Ø lov im*
(2)	-stative	none	past	*Mi Ø run*
(3)	+stative	*(b)en/did*	past	*Mi ben lov im*
(4)	-stative	*(b)en/did*	past-before-past	*Mi ben ron*

with the translations:
(1)   'I love her' (now) / 'I love her' (habitually)
(2)   'I ran'
(3)   'I loved her'
(4)   'I had run' (before some other past event or action)

Bickerton argued that creole basilects, including JamC, do not have an absolute past tense, but rather a relative anterior tense. Instead of taking the moment of speaking as an absolute reference point (with past tense required for events before it, and future for events after), this point is relative. For stative verbs it is the moment of speaking, but for verbs of action it is some relevant earlier moment. Thus when they are preceded by a past marker (*ben* in 5), they refer to a past-before-past action, sometimes called *remote past*.

(5)   *Father Manley fight and mek black pickney go a St Hilda's school,*
       where no black pickney couldn't ben go first time.
       'Manley fought so that black children could go to St Hilda's school,
       where no black children had been able to go in the old days.'
                                                              (Sistren 1987: 105)

While Bickerton's description often matches JamC utterances at surface level, the analysis is flawed. It is widely conceded that this scheme fails to account for the full range of facts over many Creoles, and articulates poorly with general TMA and typological studies. However, it is rarely noted that, as a categorical analysis assuming private oppositions, it misconceives the nature of creole grammars, including JamC. That is, it predicts a strict form-meaning isomorphism which does not hold: e.g., in order to convey a past-before-past meaning, a nonstative verb must be marked with an anterior marker (basilectal *ben* and variants *wen, en, min*; mesolectal *did*); and when so marked, it must receive such a reading. In reality, exceptions occur in both directions. The prediction is worth refuting because many other linguists give such idealized accounts of Creole grammars.

2.2. Habitual, progressive and completive aspect

Progressive aspect is uniformly signalled by pre-verbal *a* (6–7), while habitual aspect is often unmarked (1), though at an earlier stage both were marked alike in a single imperfective category with *(d)a* (*da* and *de* persist in western Jamaica, Bailey 1966: 138). It is still possible to mark habitual with *a + Verb*, just like the progressive. Aspectual *a* is tense-neutral in JamC, and may be preceded by tense-markers (*ben + a, did + a, ben + de, was + a* etc.).

| (6) | -stative | *a, de* | progressive | *Mi a ron* |
| (7) | -stative | *ben/did + a/de* | past progressive | *Mi ben a ron* |

(6) 'I'm running' / 'I was running' / 'I (used to) habitually run'
(7) 'I was running' / 'I used to habitually run'

Completive aspect is signalled by *don*, which unlike other TMA markers may occur not only pre-verbally but also after the verb phrase (8–9), or even both.

(8) *Him lucky we never nyam him too, for we did done cook already.*
'It's lucky we didn't eat it too, for we had already cooked.' *[of a chicken]* (Sistren 1987: 30)

(9) *Dem deh-deh, till she cook and we nyam done.*
'They stayed there until she had cooked and we had finished eating.'
(Sistren 1987: 82)

2.3.   Anterior tense

In both basilectal and mesolectal JamC, anterior markers occur more rarely than Bickerton's analysis predicts, and occur in environments where they are not predicted. Bare verb forms are very common, and do not have a single necessary interpretation. Instead of being precisely regulated by syntactic or semantic factors, the occurrence of anterior markers is inherently variable, correlated with such discourse features as provision of background information. JamC is thus governed by a principle of wider application:

> Mark past-tense more often when temporal organization of the discourse is disrupted, and less often when it is predictable.

This principle also operates in other variable discourse contexts, such as the English historical present. JamC is much less often constrained by concord than English, but where both are variable, similar pragmatic constraints apply. Furthermore, the tense interpretation of bare verbs interacts with the specificity of the noun-phrase (section 10.3).

In urban mesolectal JamC today *ben* is infrequent (though recognized, in fact stereotyped as rural, by all). Pre-verbal *did* occurs instead (10). This *did* cannot be confused with the English emphatic auxiliary, which does not exist in JamC (past *did* cannot be stressed). Tense-marking *did*, popularly identified with urban speech and positively valued, appears most commonly among older speakers, and is receding among the young (Patrick 1999). Infrequently, non-concord *was* occurs to mark past-reference – typically in progressive *was + a + Verb*, more rarely with nominal or locative complements, and not at all with perfective meaning (i.e., ...*was du* in 10).

(10)   *If yu luk pan we Itla did du ina Jaamani*
        'If you consider what Hitler did in Germany'

Linguists analyzing creole languages often create grammars for them which are neat, efficient and functional, claiming they do not formally mark information which is recoverable from context – thus contrasting with older natural languages in which redundancy is a design feature. Comrie (1985: 31) argues that JamC "omit[s] tense markers when an overt adverbial of time location is present". Again, this constraint is not categorical but a tendency, often over-ruled: not only do unmarked past-reference forms occur in the absence of ad-verbials, but mutual co-occurrence is also common:

(11)   *Ten tauzin yiers ago dem did penichriet aal dem ting.*
        'Ten thousand years ago they already understood all those things.'

The negative past form is *neva*. While in the acrolect and upper mesolect it is adverbial, like English, lower on the continuum it is a tense-marker. Thus for acrolectal speakers, presence of *neva* is not correlated with verb-inflection, time-reference is absolute, and *neva* may be used predictively. For lower mesolectal speakers, inflection is prohibited after *neva*, as after other pre-verbal particles (12), while time-reference is relative past; perfective meaning is the norm, as for many vernacular English dialects (Cheshire 1982), and predictive use does not occur. (Rarely, it redundantly combines with *did* in *neva did*, parallel to basilectal *no ben*.) *Neva* co-exists with tense-neutral pre-verbal negator *no*, which is more common in the basilect (13). *Neva*, like *did*, is preferred among older urban speakers.

(12)   *Dat manggo chrii dier, notn neva du it.*
       'Nothing (has ever) happened to that mango tree.'

(13)   *Im no biznis huu it kyach.*
       'He didn't care who got shot.'

3.   Verb forms

3.1.   Verb inflection

The common mesolectal occurrence of variable, English-like verb inflection with *-ed* is a striking contrast with the basilect. Variable inflection appears to be a general feature of Caribbean English Creole grammars, holding true as well in Barbados Creole (BbdC) and Bahamian Creole (BahC). Despite earlier linguists' belief that it results from error or dialect mixing, regularization and hyper-correct insertion of *-ed* are extremely rare. Patrick (1999) found that fully one-third of past-reference verbs in urban speech were inflected for tense on the surface, with a wide range of individual variation (though speakers who used *did* or *neva* were least likely to inflect verbs). Bare, uninflected verbs occurred well over half of the time, and pre-verbal past-markers made up only 10 percent; only a single possibly hyper-correct form was found in 15 hours of speech.

Strong verbs are the least-often inflected. In this, JamC resembles the creoles just mentioned, but differs from other varieties of English which variably mark the past, such as AAVE and African American Diaspora varieties in Samaná, Nova Scotia and Liberia (Fasold 1972; Poplack and Tagliamonte 2001): in these varieties, as well as for English second-language learners, irregular verbs are overwhelmingly marked more often than regular verbs. For a number of strong verbs in JamC, the stem corresponds to an English past form: *los* 'lose', *marid* 'marry', *gaan* 'go away, leave', *bruk* 'break', *lef* 'leave' – at least the last two being widely shared with Creoles from West Africa to the Carolinas to Guyana. Upper-mesolectal speakers do inflect irregular verbs, but this marks a very salient distinction between them and other JamC speakers.

Just as with *did* and *neva*, in the mesolect the variable use of English inflectional *-ed* is governed not by absolute past tense but by anteriority – understood as a general discourse principle – and/or stativity. However, the tendency for stativity to favor past-marking is not a general syntactic constraint as Bickerton originally proposed, but the effect of a handful of very common stative verbs such as *have*, combined with the tendency for statives to appear in background clauses, e.g. in narration (Patrick 1999; confirmed for BahC by Hackert 2004).

It is not clear how far the basilect can be described as morphologically invariant, but verb inflection in mesolectal JamC is common and significant, despite being discounted in traditional descriptions. Yet while inflection may resemble English, when it occurs it is governed by classic creole constraints. Only at the upper reaches of the continuum do English grammatical principles apply, for speakers who inflect the great majority of their past-reference verbs.

3.2.   Person and number agreement

Person and number are not marked on finite verbs in all forms of JamC. That is, present-tense verbs with third-person singular subjects never show inflection with *-s*, and the verb paradigm is perfectly regular (14).

(14)   *Dis wan swiit im.*
        'This one pleases her.'

This is linked to two other facts about JamC discussed below: (subject) pronouns are not distinguished for case, and auxiliary inversion does not occur (15). All three properties co-occur in some regional dialects of British English too, either for a subset of agreement-less finite verbs, or more generally. Many Jamaicans are aware of the existence of verbal *-s* in English, and may use it when "cutting English" or talking "speaky-spoky" (Russell in Lalla and D'Costa 1990: 189; Patrick 1997).

Radford analyzes this, in the terms of minimalist syntax, as an indication that "only interpretable head-features survive" in JamC (1997: 183), i.e. only elements which contribute to meaning. Following this line, rather than say that there is no verbal agreement in JamC, one might say that there are no uninterpretable agreement features – thus it automatically satisfies the Principle of Full Interpretation in this respect. This focus on the importance of meaning-bearing elements in the grammar might be one respect in which JamC could be characterized as "simpler" than StE, where earlier broad-brush efforts to say that creoles e.g. lack morphology or derivational depth have proven incorrect (though see section 9 below). The venerable project of finding simplicity in creole structures is however a questionable, ideologically-motivated mission.

3.3. (Modal) auxiliaries and past participles

JamC lacks the primary auxiliary verbs present in most English dialects: forms of *be, do, have* (though it possesses main-verb counterparts of *do* and *have*). The functions they normally perform are either absent (e.g. subject-inversion in questions, 15) or carried out by other elements (e.g. the invariant particles marking TMA). There is no distinction between simple past and present perfect verb forms in JamC (*iit* 'eat, eaten'), and neither of them requires an auxiliary or pre-verbal marker; distinct participial forms do not occur, and thus cannot be generalized, nor substituted by preterite (e.g. AAVE *had went*). Ellipses like English *They do*, without a main verb, are not possible with JamC modals.

(15)   *Im no lov dem ting?*
        'Doesn't she like those things?'

However, JamC does have a full complement of modal auxiliaries. Bailey (1966) divides them syntagmatically into two groups:

(16)   Mod-1:   *mos(-a, -i)*   'must'
                    kuda   'could'
                    wuda   'would'
                    shuda   'should'
                    mait(-a)   'might, may'
                    wi   'will'

(17)   Mod-2:   *kyan*   'can'
                    fi   'ought'
                    hafi   'must'
                    mos(-a, -i)   'must'

As in English, modals show no agreement; as in regional British and American varieties, double modals occur in JamC. In fact, over a dozen combinations are possible, and even triple modals may occur. (Mod-1) (Mod-2) are followed by a Tense marker (if any), an Aspect marker (if any), and a main verb. This gives the order M-T-A, as in *Im shuda-M en-T a-A ron* 'He should have been running.' Triple modals involve interpolation of *mos* between other forms. Thus, simplifying away the T and A components, one finds:

(18)   Mod-1 Verb: *Dem mosi nuo.*
                                   'They must (have) know(n)/They
                                   certainly knew.'

(19)   Mod-2 Verb: *Mi hafi gaan.*
                                   'I must leave.'

(20)   Mod-1 Mod-2 Verb: *Dem kuda kyan bai a bred.*
                                   'They would be able to buy a loaf of
                                   bread.'

(21)   Mod-1 *mos* Mod-2 Verb: *Wi wuda mos hafi riich soon!*
                                   'We really ought to arrive soon!'

A mesolectal past modal not mentioned by Bailey (1966), *had was*, occurs only with infinitival *to* (not the typical JamC *fi*), with the meaning 'had to' (22). This appears to be sometimes extended to purposive clauses with the verb *wanted* (23). Interestingly, *was* here is redundant in its tense-marking function. Alongside main-verb *sapuoz* 'suppose', there is also semi-auxiliary *sapuosi* with epistemic modal force, as in *sapuosi kyan kom* 'ought to be able to come'.

(22)   *My stepfaada had was to tell him not to come back to our yard.*
        'My stepfather had to tell him not to come back to where we lived.'
                                                        (Sistren 1987: 270)

(23)   *Him do it because him wanted was to control di people living in di
        Underworld.*
        'He did it because he wanted to control the people living in the
        Underworld.'   (Sistren 1987: 263)

4.   Negation

4.1.   Sentential negation

The simplest and most common structure in JamC sees a single, invariant negator *no* (reducible to /na/) before the verb (13, 15); adverbs may intervene. It combines with the basilectal tense marker as *no ben*, which is functionally equivalent to *neva* (see above).

Most speakers also have tense-neutral *duont*. *Duont* is typically non-past or imperfective (24), but may occur with any time-reference or aspect, including perfect (25), and with untensed clauses (26). It is not restricted to psychic state or habitual verbs (25), contra Bailey (1966: 54).

(24)   *She don't fight woman; a pure man she fight.*
        'She doesn't (didn't) fight women; she only fights (fought) men.'
                                                            (Sistren 1987: 271)

(25)   *Up to now, Spangler don't come back in di area.*
        'Until this day Spangler has not come back into the area.'
                                                            (Sistren 1987: 279)

(26)   *Him may leave today to go out to all di countryside, far district, and*
        don't come back tomorrow.
        'He may leave today to go out all over the countryside, and not come
        back tomorrow.'   (Sistren 1987: 25)

4.2.   Negative tags and negative imperatives

No and *duont* also occur as interrogative tags on either negative or affirmative declaratives (and *no*, but not *duont*, as imperative tag, on affirmative requests only). However, it is not always clear whether tags with *na* are related to negative *no*. *Duont* may also be preposed (28, 29). Negative imperatives may occur with either negator; the typical basilectal form requires an expletive verb *bada* (< *bother*, 29) while *duont*, being verbal, requires none. As a rhetorical question or interjection, *no mos* indicates that something is expected or obvious (30).

(27)   *Shut unu ai, na!*
        'Shut your (pl.) eyes, won't you?'   (Roberts 1973: 37)

(28)   *A di bridj im a taak, duont? Duont a di bridj im a taak?*
        'It's the bridge he's talking about, isn't it? Isn't it the bridge he's
        talking about?'   (Roberts 1973: 20)

(29)   *No bada gwaan bad. / Duon gwaan bad, yaa?*
        'Do not misbehave (you hear?).'

(30)   *'Den yu a go kom tinait?' 'No mos!'*
        'Then you're going to come tonight?' 'Of course!'

4.3.   Negative concord and other negative forms

Negative concord is the norm in JamC: as in many dialects of English, negative adverbials and nominals (e.g. *nontaal* 'not (at all)', *nombadi* 'nobody') may agree with a sentential negator, without contributing additional negative force. In contrast with some analyses of AAVE however, in JamC such sympathetic negation need not apply on every possible occasion. Thus (31) might as well have concluded with negative *nomo* as positive *again*. Since auxiliary inversion does not occur, there is no negative inversion. The form *ain't* does not occur in JamC, nor does negative tag *innit* (though both do in BrC).

There is coalescence of *no* with progressive particle *a*, giving pre-verbal *naa*, which is used both for progressive and for periphrastic future (32). Most modals have negative forms (33), except *wi*. Negative *kyàan* is differentiated from positive *kyán* by the former's low tone and vowel length, and is much less likely to contain a palatal glide, especially in formal speech (34).

(31)   *Don't me done tell yuh seh me na go do nutten again?*
       'Haven't I told you already that I'm not going to do anything further?'
                                                          (Sistren 1987: 70)

(32)   *Nabadii na a kom ina mai aus.*
       'Nobody is going to come into my house.'   (Roberts 1973: 36)

(33)   Mod-1:   *kudn*   Mod-2:   *no fi*
                      wudn   *naafi* (< *no hafi*)
                      shudn   *mosn*
                      maitn

(34)   *If I kyán only get word to him ... Mama kyàan catch us because we run.*
       'If I could only get word to him ... Mama couldn't catch us because we ran.'

Finally, copular forms of *be* from StJamE appear first in the mesolect in negated form, e.g. *wasn't*. Another mesolectal form, *nat*, alternates with *no* most often in structures corresponding to English *be + not + Complement* or *be + not + Verb-ing*, though frequently without an overt *be*-form.

5. Word order, focus and copular structures

5.1. Word order

JamC word order is head-initial: in verb phrases the order is thus [V-NP], while prepositions occur in [P-NP] order, determiners appear as [Det-N], and adjectives as [Adj-N]. It is uniformly Subject-Verb-Object, like most Atlantic English-lexicon Creoles. Lacking auxiliary inversion, as noted, it also lacks negative and question inversion. *Yes-no* questions differ from declaratives only in having a final-rise intonation contour. The main deviation from surface SVO order occurs in focus structures.

5.2. The copula: Functions and significance

JamC has no single copular verb matching English *be*, but employs a range of forms differentiated by function. These verbs are tense-neutral and uninflected, combining with pre-verbal TMA markers; some alternate with zero-forms, others are necessarily overt. Alternation with non-concord (but tense-specific) forms of *be* also occurs in the mesolect. However, full forms of *be* are the norm, while contracted forms are surprisingly uncommon compared to AmE and BrE.

There is sharp contrast with native English varieties in the distribution of forms and functions; possibilities of alternation and absence; and relative frequencies of copula presence by syntactic environment. The exceptions are African American Diaspora varieties of English, with which significant resemblances have been observed. The distribution of JamC copular forms has figured importantly in debates concerning historical linkage between AAVE and Caribbean English Creoles.

5.3. The copula in progressive forms

Progressive *a* + Verb is discussed above (6, 7); an alternating mesolectal form is Ø + Verb + *in*. Tense-specific variation of zero with *is/was* also occurs here, though *a* itself is incompatible with both *be*-forms and with the *-in* suffix. Contrary to notions of neat separation according to forms, the so-called basilectal *a* + Verb form is used at all levels of the mesolect, while predominantly basilectal speakers are familiar with the supposedly mesolectal Ø + Verb-*in* form. Several main verbs which are semantically continuative typically take *a* + Verb complements: *kipaan* 'keep on', *gwaan* 'go on', *depan* 'be engaged in an action or activity; in a state of continuing or repeated action' (lit. locative *de* + *pan* 'upon, on, in, at').

5.4.   The copula in equative forms

In equative contexts, a subject and a nominal complement are joined by the verb *a*. In older JamC, the form was *da* (35). This varies mesolectally with non-concord *is/was*. Zero copula does occur, but Rickford's (1996: 225) quantitative data show an overt copula more than 80 percent of the time.

(35)   *Ebry day da fishing day, but ebry day no fe catch fish.*
        'Every day is a day for fishing, but you won't catch fish every day.'
                                                        (DJE: 141, from 1873)

Bailey treats *niem* 'name' as a distinctive verb (1966: 33) in constructions such as *Mi niem Piita* 'My name is Peter/I am named Peter'. They do not allow an overt copula in JamC; in her analysis, they are not equative but predicative.

5.5.   Focus structures: Predicate clefting

The same form *a* serves to focus a wide range of fronted or clefted constituents, both predicative and non-predicative. The fronted item receives stress and emphatic or contrastive meaning. Only predicative elements are copied in the original sentence position when clefted; they include verbs (36, 38), adjectives (37) and, uniquely among modals, *mos* (38). Variation of *a* with *is* occurs, giving present or perfect meaning, but no other *be*-form appears in this structure.

(36)   *A swel it swel, luk da. A bigfut dem gi mi.*
        'It certainly **swelled** up, look there. Someone gave me the bigfoot.'

(37)   *Luk hou a krievm im krievm.*
        'See how **greedy** she is!'

(38)   *A mos im mosi gaan aredi.*   or   *A gaan im mosi gaan aredi.*
        'He **must** have left already.'   'He must have **left** already.'

5.6.   Focus structures: Other types of clefting

Non-predicative elements may be clefted similarly but are not copied. These include pronouns and nouns (28, 36, 39), locative phrases (40), temporal phrases (41), manner adverbials, and question-words (42). *Wh*-questions are normally clefted, and have a falling intonation contour; they may be introduced by *a*, *is*, or zero. Even Louise Bennett, the paragon of basilectal folk-poets, shows such variation as *A noh sintin ... Is sintin ...* 'It's not something that... It's something that...' (Bennett 1966: 126).

(39)   *She waan mi fi come back cause a she one deh-deh and she fraid.*
       'She wanted me to return for **she alone** was there and she was afraid.'
                                                                   (Sistren 1987:77)

(40)   *A wisaid unu a go go luk fi im? A wichpaat im de ya?*
       'Where are you (pl.) going to look for him? Where is he?'

(41)   *Afta it kom oot a di fut, a chrii die schriet hit bon mi.*
       'After it came out of my foot, it burned me for **three days straight**.'

(42)   *Lord God! A weh a go tell me madda seh?*
       'Lord God! What am I going to tell my mother?'   (Sistren 1987: 69)

(43)   *Yes, Brer Puss, all di weddin' you was a come a yahso, you was a*
       come come eat out di butta!
       'Yes Brother Puss, even the "weddings" you were coming to here, you
       were only coming to finish eating the butter!'   (Dance 1985: 19)

Other focus constructions are common in JamC as well. Pseudo-clefts occur
with initial *aal* 'all', which may have either quantitative force or intensive, or
both (43). Non-restrictive relatives often use an identificational left-dislocation
structure (72).

5.7.   The copula with adjectives and locatives

Zero copula is normal before bare predicate adjectives in JamC (Rickford 1996
finds it to be near-categorical). Predicate adjectives in JamC may be negated by
no, may follow pre-verbal TMA markers (44), and may be the complement of
a modal. Progressive *a* conveys a processual interpretation (45) with semantically appropriate nonstative verbs (Winford 1996); this also happens with the
comparative (*deh-deh a colder*), or with the simple adjective plus the process
verb *get* (*deh-deh a get cold*). Bailey notes that the quantitative adjectives *likl*
'little', *nof* 'much, many; abundant' and *tumoch* 'too many' have predicative
functions, and thus do not require an overt copula (1966: 43).

When adjectives modify a following noun complement (Adj-N is the order
of modification in JamC), i.e. when they are attributive, the equative copula is
required, as expected.

(44)   *Mi ongl se im did shaat!*
       'I only said he was short!'

(45)   *Yuh wife cook yuh dinner and it deh-deh a cold.*
       'Your wife cooked your dinner and it sits there getting cold.'
                                                                   (Sistren 1987: 72)

(46)   *Dem musn kom ko nobadii no di de an tiicha no da ya.*
        'They mustn't come because nobody is there and Teacher is not here.'

                                                                    (Roberts 1973: 37)

(47)   *Yu hav wan sinting __ niem Ruolin Kyaaf.*
        'There is something __ called Rolling Calf.'

A distinct, tense-neutral verb *de* 'be there' occurs with locatives (45, 46), either taking a prepositional complement or question-finally; it is homophonous with *de* 'there'. Studying a text "replete with basilectal or 'deep creole' elements", Rickford finds verbal *de* "the most persistent of the creole copulas" (1996: 221, 227), occurring in about two-thirds of all locatives. However, even here he finds in nearly 20 percent of cases *iz/waz* are used; these *be*-forms occur before locatives throughout the mesolect as well.

Returning to the significance of comparisons made between creoles (JamC in particular) and AAVE, Baugh (1980) was the first to look for separate patterning of *be*-forms before adjectives and locatives in AAVE, theorizing that they might confirm its creole ancestry. While the AAVE data on this point remain complex and equivocal (Rickford 1996), there is no doubt of the dramatic contrast between these structures within JamC: overt copula forms of any sort are rare before predicate adjectives, but zero copula is rare before locatives.

Existential meaning in JamC is expressed by the verb *hav*, often with an indefinite pronoun subject *yu* or *dem* (47; here and in other examples containing a relative clause the gap site is marked "__").

6.   Complementation and subordination

JamC clause structure contrasts with English dialects in several ways. Non-finite complements use the verb stem only: there are no gerund forms with *-in(g)*. More radically, JamC like other Atlantic Creoles possesses serial verb constructions (SVCs, below), due to the substrate influence of West African languages.

6.1.   Nonfinite clauses

JamC does not always require a particle (e.g. English *to*) to precede non-finite clauses (48); as in StE, some verbs optionally select bare infinitive clauses. The default infinitive marker is *fi* (not to be confused with modal *fi*), but *tu* alternates for upper mesolectal speakers. *Fi* often occurs with purposive clauses (49), and as the complement of the desiderative verb *waan* 'want'. Impersonal subjects of adjectives also take *fi*-complements (50), as do animate subjects (51–52). Structures like *Mi glad for see you* are attested as early as 1774 (Lalla and D'Costa 1990: 89). Unlike StE, constructions like **John is easy to cry* are acceptable (51). Imperatives can be formed with *Pliiz tu* + Verb (e.g. *Pliiz tu kom dis said* 'Come over here').

(48)   *Him start tell di cousins all sort a someting.*
      'He started to tell the cousins all kinds of things.'   (Sistren 1987: 103)

(49)   *She only do half day work fi come fi follow him go a airport.*
      'She only worked a half day in order to come here to follow him to the airport.'   (Sistren 1987: 103)

(50)   *I hard fi kraas di riba.*   or   *Di riba haad fi kraas.*
      'It's hard to cross the river.'   'The river is hard to cross.'

(51)   *Jan iizi fi krai.*   or   *I iizi fi Jan fi krai.*
      'John cries easily.'   'It is easy for John to cry.'
                                               (Bailey 1966: 125)

(52)   *Him fraid fi grab it, for him fraid me tear it.*
      'He was afraid to grab it, for he was afraid I would tear it.'
                                               (Sistren 1987: 103)

6.2.   Finite clauses

JamC declarative complementizers include *se* 'say' and the all-purpose *dat* 'that'; both take finite complements and alternate with zero, so that in general it is possible for no complementizer to appear before a subordinate clause. *Se* is restricted to following verbs of speech (53), thought (e.g. *biliib* 'believe', *nuo* 'know', *fain* 'realize'), perception (*sii* 'see', *yier* 'hear') or emotion (*sari* 'sorry', *shiem* 'shame'); it probably derived from a serial construction for speech alone. It may serve as complement to predicate adjectives, and can be stranded by clefting of *wh*-items (42). Complementizer *se* cannot follow main-verb *se* 'say', thus testifying to its incomplete grammaticalization. Some psychic-state verbs however typically take zero complementizers, such as *biznis* 'care'. In (54), we might equally have found *Dat mean dat ...* or *Dat mean se ...* All these forms are very common; examples (48–49, 52–54) occur on a single page of dialogue, randomly chosen.

(53)   *Him all swear seh him was going to tell me.*
      'He even swore that he was going to tell me.'   (Sistren 1987: 103)

(54)   *Dat mean him deh go tek set pon me.*
'That means (that) he is going to become malignly fixated upon me.'
(Sistren 1987: 103)

6.3.   Subordinating conjunctions

JamC uses several subordinating conjunctions which are either absent, or now archaic, in StE. (The coordinating conjunctions *an, bot, ar, nar* function similarly to their StE counterparts *and, but, or, nor*.) These include conditional forms such as *wais* 'whilst, if, provided' and *sieb* 'except, unless' (55, from *save*), causal *sieka* 'because of' and *tru* 'because' (from *for the sake of* and *through*; 56), temporal *wen(eva)taim* 'when(ever)' (57), concessive *no kya* 'no matter' (58, from *no care*) and manner *laka se* 'as if' (59, from *like say*).

(55)   *Yu kyaan kom iin-ya siev yu pie yu fier.*
'You can't come in here unless you pay your fare.'   (*DJE*: 394)

(56)   *She just tell him dat tru him leggo di secret.*
'She just told him that because he let out her secret.'
(Sistren 1987: 184)

(57)   *Weneva taim dat im kom, im gwain plie a trik.*
'When she comes she is going to play a prank.'   (*DJE*: 469)

(58)   *No kya we yu go yu naa fain non.*
'No matter where you go, you won't find any.'   (Bailey 1966: 58)

(59)   *Him ron laka se dem set daag ata im.*
'He ran as if they had set dogs after him.'   (*DJE*: 270)

7.   Serial verb constructions

Serial verb constructions have been topics of extensive research by creolists (Alleyne 1980). Though they resemble both coordination and subordination structures, there are strong arguments against both analyses. It has been suggested that they are natural products of first- or second-language acquisition under certain conditions, but this seems unlikely. Not all creoles have SVCs; they appear to be a legacy of substrate languages, especially the Kwa family in the JamC case. Besides, Lalla and D'Costa (1990: 71) note "Serial verbs are not attested in the earliest texts"; appearing only in the later 19th century.

SVCs involve two or more verbs brought together without a complementizer, conjunction or infinitive marker, and with no pause. If TMA or negation are marked, the marking on all verbs agrees, and typically only occurs on the first. There is normally a single expressed subject, and one direct object (if any); these are often shared across the verbs, but there is cross-linguistic variation here. SVCs are commonly categorized as directional, instrumental, dative (62), benefactive, comitative, comparative etc. Creoles may be grouped according to how many of these functions occur. Most types occur in JamC, except possibly benefactive. Direction away normally employs *go*, and towards uses *come*; (60) recalls the indignant semi-auxiliary *come* of AAVE. Instrumental with *tek* 'take' (61) is a typologically important function, grouping JamC with deep creoles such as the Surinamese languages, Krio and Haitian. The comparative serial (63) is now infrequent in JamC. When three serial verbs occur together, one is always directional (64); here the third verb has a different subject.

(60) *Dis naga man come come collar me de same like a say me da him sexis.*
      'This black man comes and collars me just as if I were the same sex as he.'   (1877, quoted in *DJE:* 116)

(61) *Im tek naif kot mi.*
      'He cut me with a knife.', lit. 'He took knife cut me.'
                                                        (Alleyne 1980: 93)

(62) *Kya di buk kom gi mi.*
      'Bring the book for me.'   (Alleyne 1980: 94)

(63) *Manggo de a yaad paas plenti.*
      'A great many mangoes are in the yard.'   (Cassidy p.c.)

(64) *Im waan mi fi go kya im kom.*
      'He wants me to bring it', lit. 'He wants me to go carry it come.'
                                                        (Alleyne 1980: 91)

8.   Relativization

The general structure of relative clauses in Atlantic Creoles follows their lexifier languages. JamC is no exception. Christie (1996) closely examines JamC relatives which are simultaneously the subject of emphatic focusing strategies (left-dislocation, pseudo-clefting); she finds this co-occurrence very common, and gives a developmental account.

JamC relative markers are *a, we, wa(t), huufa, dat* and *huu*; in many cases a null relativizer is also possible. The non-pronominal relativizers originated in deictic elements (*a, dat < that*), while the relative pronouns originated in interrogative pronouns, e.g. *wa < what*. Christie assumes the most general basilectal pronoun, *we*, to have derived from *where* and expanded from an original locative use, but the *DJE* gives a NW England dialectal etymon *wha* for both *wa* and *we*, which are indistinguishable today except in locative relatives (*we* only). *Huu* is the acrolectal and mesolectal form, following English in its restriction to [+human]; so too does *huufa* (< *who* + *for* via possessive pronoun *fi-huu*), but its use is basilectal; it does not alternate with zero.

Three types of relativization can be distinguished, involving overt relativizers, null relativizers, and resumptive pronouns. The one closest to StE involves a relative marker introducing a clause in which there is a corresponding structural gap (65, where the gap is in subject position of the relative clause; 10, 66, in object position with *we*; 13 with *huu*; 71 with *huufa*; and 67, the object of a stranded preposition). The gap results from movement of the *wh*-item.

(65)   *Yu miin him a ___ wena mek naiz mam?*
        'Do you mean the one that ___ was making noise, ma'am?'

(66)   *We have a place weh we call ___ Atom Hole.*
        'There is a place that we call ___ Atom Hole.'   (Dance 1985: 94)

(67)   *Mi rispek ar tu di dort we shi waak pan ___, Mada.*
        'I respect her to the ground that she walks on ___, Mother.'

Pied-piping is not possible in JamC (in 67, * ... *pan we shi waak*). In general prepositions and other post-verbal particles are tightly bound to the verb. The only apparent exception to this is *fi-* in the interrogative pronoun *fi-huu*.

Null relativizers are the norm in existential sentences when the relativized noun-phrase is indefinite, and the subject of the clause (47 above, but not 66), and also occur in other sentence types (23, 68). Christie argues for "deletion of the coreferential NP within the relative clause" (1996: 54), rather than *wh*-fronting. She also includes some purposive *fi*-clauses here (69), though *fi* does not vary with zero and in other ways is not a typical relativizer.

(68)   *Him say me one one hog me have ___ me fi give you ___.*
        'He said I should give you (___) the only hog I have ___.'

(Dance 1985: 21)

(69)   *Mi bring kluoz fi di uman put aan __.*
     'I've brought clothes for the woman to put on __ .'
(Christie 1996: 55)

In the third type resumptive pronouns occur inside the relative clause. Christie suggests this "more usually occurs ... where the co-referential NP is possessive ... [and] an overt relativizer is necessary" (1996: 58), (70). Resumptive pronouns also occur outside the relative clause, most commonly in non-restrictive relatives (72). Both types occur in non-standard English dialects. Interestingly, resumptive pronouns are also common in acrolectal Jamaican English relatives.

(70)   *Di uman we dem tiif **ar** biebi gaan a stieshan.*
     lit. 'The woman that they stole **her** baby has gone to the station.'
(Christie 1996: 58)

(71)   *Di uman huufa biebi dem tiif __ gaan a stieshan.*
     'The woman whose baby they stole __ has gone to the station.'
(Christie 1996: 56)

(72)   *Mi yu si ya, **mi** kyaan bada wid dem.*
     'I (whom) you see here, **I** can't bother with them.'
(Bailey 1966: 108)

9. Pronouns

The pronominal system of JamC makes few distinctions of case or gender, and is not characterized by agreement in these dimensions. It does however make systematic distinction of person and number, in fact more so than StE. Even at the most basilectal level JamC distinguishes case in the possessive pronoun *huufa* if nowhere else, though Christie suggests it is a late 19th-century innovation (1996: 56–57). Mesolectal speakers typically possess some gender- and case-specific forms, but are not consistent in their use. The system is therefore not simpler than StE, either in the sense of possessing fewer dimensions of contrast, or in being grammatically regular as English is (Mühlhäusler 1997: 234–236). Little work has been done to explore conditions for variation.

Setting aside *huufa*, Radford finds a case-less system of pronouns further evidence that JamC lacks "uninterpretable case-features; those which have been retained are interpretable person-, number- and gender-features" (1997: 182–183). Thus JamC would share common ground with native child acquisition of English, in which uninterpretable features are acquired later. Radford argues JamC distinguishes "between overt and covert forms ... the minimal case distinction we should expect to find in any language" (1997: 206–207).

9.1.   Personal pronouns

The personal pronouns are given in (73). *Im* 'he, she, him, her, it' is the default gender- and case-less form (14), sometimes used for impersonal or non-human referents (8), but *i* 'it' is not used for human ones (50); animacy is a distinction native to JamC. English-like forms enter in 3rd person singular; though common in the mesolect, they are not fully integrated into the grammar of JamC. *Shi* is the first gender-marked form to appear; *ar* cannot be focused (**A ar mi lov*, 'It's her I love'), indicating that it is a marked form. Mesolectal speakers use gender- and case-marked 3sg pronouns (when they do use them) in appropriate ways (24, 67), without hyper-correction. Use of *ii* 'he' and *shi* 'she' for oblique cases does not occur in JamC.

(73)	**Person**	**Singular**	**Plural**
	1	*mi, a (ai)*	*wi*
	2	*yu*	*unu*
	3	*im, i (ii) (shi) (ar)*	*dem*

The 2nd pl. form *unu* (27, 40) is traced to Igbo (*DJE*; Allsopp 1996; Parkvall 2000), or to convergence among e.g. Wolof *yena*, Kongo *yeno*, Kimbundu *yenu*, and Common Bantu **nu* (Holm 2000). Lalla and D'Costa (1990: 78), however, find it "only in the middle and later 19th century". *Unu* is also used as an indefinite pronoun, like AmE *you* or BrE *one* (74), while *yu* sometimes has non-singular reference.

Ai is a distinctive feature of Rastafarian speech, with productive compounding in *I-man, I-an-I, I-dren* (Pollard 1994). These metaphorically and ideologically motivated uses cannot be confused with everyday standard usage, where it is strictly acrolectal. As an element of Rasta Talk accessible to a general audience for a variety of discourse purposes, *ai* is a regular, if specialized, component of the JamC pronominal system. However, as creative use is a hallmark of this register, *ai* and its compounds cannot be exclusively assigned a single number, case or person (75).

(74)   *Unu kudn bloodbat gi i man chrii onjrid dala.*
          'Nobody could even give the man three hundred damn dollars.'

(75)   *Ai an ai taakin tu di ai ier.*
          'I have been talking to this man.'   (Pollard)

First- and second-person pronouns (and 3rd sg. *i*) have final short lax vowels, and even *ai* may be reduced to /a/ (42). As this is quite common in West African languages and other Atlantic Creoles, but not permitted by the phonotactics of most English varieties, it is clearly African-derived.

9.2.   Possessive pronouns

Possessive pronouns are simply derived in JamC by prefixing *fi-* to the personal pronouns *mi, yu, im, ar, wi, unu* or *dem* (76). *Fi-huu* serves as possessive interrogative, and the probable source of *huufa*. Though it is not necessarily stressed, the *fi-* prefix may receive primary stress here (77); this is also true when it operates as a possessive adjective, i.e. modifies rather than replaces a noun (78). Lalla and D'Costa (1990: 75) note "the absence of *fe* + Noun as a possessive marker in the earliest texts".

(76)   *Black bud lef' fe 'im ticks fe pick fe go pick cow own.*
       'Black bird leaves his own ticks to go and pick **Cow's**.'

(Watson 1991: 37)

(77)   *Mi nuo di fuor touzin mi mek a fi-mi!*
       'I know the four thousand I make is **mine**!' *[=dollars]*

(78)   *Den no fi-me work me put yuh inna?*
       'Then wasn't it **my** job I got for you?'   (Sistren 1987: 126)

The emphatic or contrastive possessive adjective *uon(a)* 'own' usually follows a possessor noun (76), but may appear with just a pronoun (79), or even the combination of *fi* + proper noun (80). When *uon(a)* does appear, the possessed noun may be present – e.g. (77) might as well have terminated (...) *a fi-mi uona ting!*, with stress on *uona* – but is more often absent, in which case the complex functions as possessive pronoun (i.e. *ar uon* = 'hers', *fi-wi uon* = 'ours'). In these constructions stress generally falls on the preceding possessor (pro)noun, unlike English, where stress usually falls on *own*.

It is also possible to have only bare personal pronouns with possessive force (*unu* in 27, *yu* in 55, the first *me* in 68), i.e. possession by juxtaposition (possessor + possessed); this structure is not restricted to pronouns, but occurs also with full nouns, including proper nouns (e.g. *di uman biebi* 'the woman's baby', *Rabat buk* 'Robert's book'). English-like forms alternate in the mesolect, especially in the first person (*mai, owa*), as in (81).

(79)   *Me did a carry a pan a water from di next door yard for dem did lock off fi-we own again.*

'I used to carry a pan of water from the yard next door, for they had shut off ours again.' [a standpipe]   (Sistren 1987: 187)

(80)   *Jos bikaaz evribadi wena go luk pan fi-Patsi uon...*
        'Just because everybody was looking at Patsy's ...' [=frock]

(81)   *Mek wi go ina owa pakit an bai di lika oot a wi pakit!*
        'Let's reach in our pockets and buy the liquor out of our own pockets.'

9.3.   Interrogative pronouns

Interrogative pronouns include the *wh*-items *we, wa, huu* and *huu-fa* (above). These function similarly to adjectives *wich* 'which', adverbs *wa mek* 'why', *hou* 'how, why', *wen* 'when', and *homoch* 'how much/many' in terms of a preference for *a*-clefting. In the mesolect *wai* 'why' occurs, but it cannot be clefted. Several interrogative pronouns are semantically transparent compounds, e.g. *huufa* and *homoch* above, but also *wen-taim* 'when' (57), *wich-paat* 'where, wherever' and *wi-said* 'where' (40), which may be relative pronouns too. This strategy also occurs in prepositions such as *batam-said* 'below' (82).

(82)   *Mi waak kom dong a dis ais kriim plees, likl bit batamsaid di hoos.*
        'I walked down to this ice-cream place, a little below the house.'

(83)   *So wen she go long, she see so-so head in de road.*
        'As she went along, she saw just a head in the road.' [without a body]
                                                                    (*DJE:* 417)

(84)   *Dem miit op (dem) wan aneda pan di ruod.*
        'They met each other on the road.'

9.4.   Indefinite, reflexive and reciprocal pronouns

Indefinite pronouns are transparently derived from English, but may combine several functions, e.g. *somting* 'something; thing' (usually reduced to [soʔm]), *smadi* 'somebody; person; human being; one'. They may also take determiners and be quantified or counted, e.g. *wan smadi* 'someone, a person', *chrii smadi* 'three people', *evri smadi* 'everyone'.

While JamC does follow an English model for reflexive pronouns, suffixing number-neutral *-sef* 'self' to make *misef, yusef, imsef, arsef* – as well as *wisef, unusef* and *demsef* – other forms also serve similar functions, e.g. *so-so* 'only, by itself' (83). Reciprocals in any person may be formed on the model *(Pron-pl) wan aneda* 'each other', with an optional preceding personal pronoun (84).

9.5.   Demonstratives

Demonstratives in Atlantic English Creoles generally derive from superstrate forms and syntax, given the normal word order of modification by demonstrative adjectives: European lexifier (Dem-N), but West African substrate (N-Dem). Indeed, superstrate demonstratives are also generally thought to be the source of the definite articles in many Creoles (below), given the prominence of deictic terms in language contact situations, plus their strong forms and likelihood of bearing stress, compared to articles.

JamC demonstrative pronouns are singular proximal *dis* 'this', singular distal *dat* 'that', and plural *dem* 'these, those'. The demonstrative adjectives are the same, and always appear in pre-N position. They are supplemented by singular *da* 'this, that', which may only occur before nouns suffixed by the locative particles *-ya* 'here' or *-de* 'there'. However, the main forms are not only compatible with this structure, but also with direct suffixing of the locatives, giving the paradigm in (85).

		Proximal	**Distal**
(85)	**Singular**	*dis-ya ting* *dis ting-ya* *da ting-ya* 'this thing'	*dat-de ting* *dat ting-de* *da ting-de* 'that thing'
	Plural	*dem-ya ting* *dem ting-ya* 'these things'	*dem-de ting* *dem ting-de* 'those things'

JamC demonstratives are [+definite] and occupy the same syntactic slot as articles, thus may not co-occur with them. However, they may co-occur with all other available components of the noun-phrase (including plural suffix *-z*) except, apparently, post-nominal plural-marker *-dem*. In over 3,600 tokens of semantically plural noun phrases, I found only one case of demonstrative *dem* with plural *-dem*, i.e. *dem* N*-dem* (86).

(86)   *So, dem bwai-dem kom an dem fling tuu brik an tuu bakl.*
        'So those guys came and threw a few bricks and a few bottles.'

(87)   *Hou dem spiik da wie de an wii spiik da wie ya?*
        'How come they speak that way, and we (only) speak this way?'

(88)   *A dis yah kind a life yuh want? Look pon yuh!*
        'Is this the kind of life you want? Look at you!'   (Sistren 1987: 123)

(89)   *If we did ever see yuh dat deh night, we wuda mek police beat yuh.*
        'If we had seen you that night, we would have let the police beat you.'

10.   Noun phrase structure

10.1.   Possession

Several aspects of noun-phrase structure have been treated above. In particular, possessive structures are generally similar regardless of whether they are headed by a possessor pronoun or noun. In StE there are three types of possessive structures:

i)   [possessor pronoun – possessed noun], e.g. *my book*
ii)   [possessed noun + *of* + possessor noun], e.g. *books of Michelle*
iii)   [possessor noun + *-s* + possessed noun], e.g. *Michelle's books*

The structures equivalent to (i) were described above; (ii) is rare, and does not differ from StE except in the preposition, *a* 'of' (90). The third type, suffixing possessive *-s*, does not occur in JamC, and is a salient marker of StJamE. However, JamC has another common structure which does not occur in StE:

iv)   [possessor noun – possessed noun], e.g. *Jien pat* 'Jane's pot'

Complex possessive phrases also occur mixing patterns: (91) utilizes (i) and (iv). This order also occurs in non-possessive noun-noun compounding, e.g. kin-terms such as *biebi-madda* (92, 93); the pattern is well-established in StJamE, e.g. (93), which also uses the possessive *-s* suffix.

(90)   *Wel natchrali! Mi fiil di anz a dopi, man.*
        'Well, naturally! I have felt the hands of ghosts, man.'

(91)   *Me aunty never like we to mix wid we faada family.*
        'My aunt didn't like us to mingle with our father's family.'
                                                        (Sistren 1987: 164)

(92)   *She never like we fi go down to mi Granny, me faada-madda.*
        'She didn't like us to go visit my Granny, my father's mother.'
                                                        (Sistren 1987: 164)

(93)   *Betty's baby-father came to the dress rehearsal.*   (Sistren 1987: 292)

10.2. Noun classification

Nouns are divided into the same classes traditional in English grammars, namely mass, count and proper nouns. Their properties are largely the same as StE. Mass nouns (e.g. *rais* 'rice'), being non-count, cannot take a plural marker or the singular indefinite article *wan* 'a, an', though they may be either semantically definite or indefinite. Proper nouns have similar restrictions, except that when they refer to humans, they may take the associative plural. Count nouns may receive any determiner or plural marker; only count nouns can properly be generic. Bailey (1966: 21–26) further identifies a class of abstract nouns (94), which may take the definite article (*di*, 'the') where StE does not allow it, or an indefinite quantifier (*no, aal, tumoch* 'too much', etc.). However, there are counter-examples to her claim that they may not take the demonstrative (95).

Noun class membership is not the same as in StE. In particular, some nouns that are mass in StE are count in JamC (96, 20).

(94)   *Di honggri ena wip me.*
       'Hunger was whipping me.'   (Bailey 1966: 25)

(95)   *Dat lov, dat ziyl, wa wi did av fors taim, yu don hav it agen.*
       'That love, that zeal, we had in the old days, you don't find it
       anymore.'

(96)   *If me sista want a money, she would have to go and meet him.*
       'If my sister wanted money, she would have to go and meet him.'
                                                              (Sistren 1987: 165)

10.3. Articles

JamC has a singular indefinite article *wan* 'a(n)', and a number-neutral definite article *di* 'the', which appear deceptively similar to StE in function. *Wan* is transparently derived from the numeral *one*. In JamC, specificity rather than definiteness directly motivates article use. A striking reflection of this is the influence of noun-phrase specificity on the tense interpretation of bare non-stative verbs (section 2.3).

		Spec	Def	Past	Non-past
(97) a.	*Di uman sel di manggo.*	+	+	+	
b.	*Di uman sel di manggo-dem.*	+	+	+	
c.	*Di uman sel manggo.*	−	−		+
d.	*Di uman sel mangoes.*	−	−		+
e.	*Di uman sel wan manggo.*	+	−	+	

The default interpretation for (97) a. and b., with object noun-phrases that are both definite and specific, is past-tense. In contrast, the default interpretation for (97) c. and d., with object noun-phrases that are neither definite nor specific, is non-past. For (97) e., however, the specific but indefinite noun phrase forces a past-tense reading, just like the other [+specific] cases. This interaction has been described for Haitian Creole, and interpreted as evidence that while stativity is useful in accounting for tense interpretation, other *aktionsart* properties (e.g. telicity) are also important.

Bickerton (1981) proposed for creoles in general the following pattern:

- The definite article is used for presupposed/specific NPs (98);
- the indefinite article is used for asserted/specific NPs (99); and
- no (zero) article for non-specific NPs (100).

This account describes much JamC data (98–100), though a number of non-Atlantic creoles do allow a definite interpretation of bare nouns (Holm 2000: 214; i.e., cases resembling 97 c. behave like 97 a.).

(98)   *Lef dem chiljren op a di hoos.*
        '[I] left those kids up at the house.'

(99)   *Y'av a glas choch op de.*
        'There's a glass[-fronted] church up there.'

(100)   *Bad man dem taim-de!*
        '[There were] bad guys around in those days.'

Furthermore, generic noun phrases, which are utterly non-transparent in the StE article system, are systematically rendered with no article in JamC. The subjects of the StE sentences in (101–104) are all generic, but each exhibits a different determiner structure. In their JamC equivalents, each subject noun phrase would be rendered simply *Man* (except 104, *Wiel a mamal*, with the equative copula *a*).

(101)   *A man should have a dog.*

(102)   *Man is a mammal.*

(103)   *Men are mammals.*

(104)   *The whale is a mammal.*

(105)   *Police shoot Starman inna dance ... Dem rain down gunshot pon him.*
        'The police shot Starman at a dance ... They rained down gunshots on him.'   (Sistren 1987: 192)

However, in JamC a bare noun may also receive an indefinite, specific reading (*gunshot* in 105), suggesting that at least some sentences like (97) c. behave like (97) e. Thus bare noun phrases, just like bare verb forms, do not have a single necessary interpretation. This is another piece of evidence that categorical analyses based on privative oppositions misrepresent creole grammars, including JamC: strict form-meaning isomorphy does not hold for bare, unmarked forms.

From a historical perspective, this is unsurprising: unstressed, non-transparent elements like the English articles might well have gone missing early in language contact, leaving bare forms subject to a range of interpretations and contextual constraints. Subsequent conventionalization over three centuries has not essentially altered this situation. Though the reconstituted article system of JamC operates along simpler, more regular lines than that of StE, it is not the sort of perfectly neat, idealized system which linguists prefer to construct for creole grammars (but which is alien to other natural languages).

10.4.   Number marking

In contexts where Standard English requires plural number to be categorically marked with allomorphs of {plural -s}, JamC attaches post-nominal affix -*dem*, historically derived from the third-person plural pronoun *dem* 'they'. Plural -*dem* only occurs on definite nouns, and there is a strong tendency for it to be preceded by *di* 'the', while it is very rarely found in the *dem* + Noun-*dem* construction (86 above). Plural -*dem* is only available for third-person referents, not first-person or direct address (* *Aal yu bwai-dem!* 'All you boys!'') – no doubt owing to its pronominal origin.

Yet the mesolect shows frequent use of *s*-marking, and JamC also allows zero-marking of plural nouns (*pieren* in 107), which occurred 45 percent of the time in a Kingston study. In fact, both -*s* and zero-marked forms, and variation between the two, are attested in 17th- and 18th-century JamC – far earlier than -*dem*, which has only been found from the latter half of the 19th century (Lalla and D'Costa 1990). All are present in basilectal speech as well as mesolectal (106).

Though it is relatively rare, it is perfectly acceptable for -*dem* and -*s* to co-occur (107–109): -*s* is always more closely attached to the noun (i.e. *Noun-s-dem*), while -*dem* may attach to the right edge of the noun phrase (109).

(106)   *Tings noh bright, bickle noh nuff!*
          'Things aren't easy, there's not much food!'   (Bennett 1966: 121)

(107)   *Afta a no iivn rimemba di nuots-dem agen.*
          'I don't even remember the *[musical]* notes any more.'

(108) *Fi-dem pieren mait muor richa dan mai pieren, so dem mait av muor*
       – beta fasilitiz-dem.
       'Their parents might be richer than mine, so they might have more
       – better facilities.'

(109) *Frenz an a uol-dem, neva falo frenz an a uol.*
       'Friends in general, never follow friends in general.'

Possessives, demonstratives and definite articles all mark a noun-phrase as
definite; *-dem* cannot easily appear without them. While indefinite quantifiers
freely occur with *-dem* in partitive phrases (110, 111), the very few instances
of definite quantifiers (e.g. cardinal numerals) plus Noun-*dem* are often interpretable as indefinite (note the first use of *two* in 112). Furthermore, *di* + Noun-
dem phrases are compatible with a definite but non-specific reading (113).

(110) *Some a di woman dem is single woman.*
       'Some of the women are single women.'   (Sistren 1987: 49)

(111) *None a di member dem no do notten bout it.*
       'None of the members did anything about it.'   (Sistren 1987: 87)

(112) *Me pack up me two sinting dem inna two big barrel.*
       'I packed up my few possessions into two big barrels.'
                                                           (Sistren 1987: 192)

(113) *Di man dem in my district is not easy.*
       'The men of my district can be truculent.'   (Sistren 1987: 89)

-Dem is only allowed to occur in definite NPs. In StE, of course, this require-
ment does not apply to *-s* at all, but in JamC, these environments also favor
-s. Determiners that mark number (quantifiers, numerals and demonstratives)
disfavor *-s*, while *-dem* practically does not occur with them at all. This can
be characterized as a functional pattern, where markers tend to appear in
cases that would otherwise not bear surface signs of their plural meaning.

Both markers are favored by the presence of a [+human] head noun. Similar
constraints apply in Liberian and Nigerian English Creole varieties, possibly
related to *-dem*'s history of grammaticalization from a pronoun with primarily
human reference.

Number marking in JamC grammar is thus characterized by intricate, coexisting constraints on competing forms from English (*-s*) and Creole (*-dem*).

10.5. Associative plurals and other phenomena

In JamC, as in a number of Atlantic Creoles and African substrate languages, an associative plural using *-dem* may attach to a person's proper name with the meaning 'X and her customary associates' (e.g. friends, family members, co-workers, etc.). While this construction resembles coordinate structures in vernacular Englishes (e.g. *John an' dem* in AAVE, see Wolfram, this volume), there is no conjunction in the JamC cases (114).

(114) *Miss Waaka dem laaf afta im.*
     'Miss Walker and the others laughed at him.'   (Roberts 1973: 18)

(115) *Mi faati-plenti aredi!*
     'I am well over forty already!'

JamC possesses several indefinite quantifiers which contrast with StE, and typically co-occur with *-dem*, other than those given by Bailey (1966: 30). A near-obsolete one is *pempeny* 'plentiful' (*DJE:* 345, < Twi *mpempem* 'thousands'); common today is *uol-iip* 'many, a lot' (< *whole heap*). *Wan-wan* may either mean 'occasional(ly), sporadic' or 'one at a time'. The word *-plenti* may be suffixed to a numeral (115), but this normally only happens with a bi-syllabic stem. Finally, measure words of weight, distance, currency etc. occur in JamC much as in StE but unlike other many British dialects which have *three mile*, *four pound*, they show no tendency to disfavor plural marking with *-s* – in fact, there is a small tendency to the contrary.

11.   Conclusion

Compared to many creoles, and indeed many vernacular dialects of English, a great deal is known about JamC morphology and syntax – but this basic description of morphology and syntax suggests further exploration is needed. I have barely mentioned sociolinguistic and applied linguistic research. I conclude by calling for research into poorly-explored areas, encouraging the empirical use of language corpora to shed light on JamC by looking at new and little-studied sources. Linguists often rely too much on their own, or other people's, intuitions, or on a handful of well-known texts or sources of data (e.g. Emmanuel Rowe's stories, transcribed by DeCamp in Le Page 1960; Beryl Bailey's native intuitions in Bailey 1966). JamC is a vital language, continually producing new data, both innovative and traditional, for linguists to attend to. Recent useful examinations include the study of ordinary vernacular writing, mass media, style and register, vernacular orthography, translation to and from JamC, academic writing, and institutionally-defined speech and literacy. There can be little doubt that a great deal more remains to be discovered.

Exercises and study questions

1. In what ways – social and linguistic – does JamC resemble the textbook model of a typical Creole language? What aspects of its structure and history, described above, create difficulties for fitting it into this type? (Further information on the history of JamC can be found in Alleyne 1988 and Lalla & D'Costa 1990, while an overview of Creoles can be found in Holm 2000.)

2. Compare negation in JamC with a non-Creole, non-standard dialect of English, e.g. AAVE, pointing out similarities and contrasts. Which features of JamC negation are specifically Creole structures? Which features are more general in non-standard varieties of English? Do any features resemble common patterns from child-language or second-language acquisition?

3. Using data in this chapter, construct a 4-line dialogue between two speakers, which contains two sentences in basilectal Jamaican Creole and two in mesolectal JamC.

4. This chapter illustrates both mesolectal and basilectal JamC structures. In each there is some inherent variability (e.g., alternation of *did+Verb* with *V-ed* for past reference). Do you think JamC basilect and mesolect constitute two separate, complete grammars? Support your position with data and arguments from the chapter.

5. Compare the pronoun system of JamC to that of Standard English, taking into account the dimensions of case, person, gender and number. Is one more regular, or more elaborate, than the other? Is there evidence that the genesis of JamC in language contact has simplified the pronoun system? Support your position with data and arguments from the chapter.

6. Using the materials in the chapter, translate the following English sentences into JC. Some other words you may need are provided below.
   (a) I want the mango.
   (b) She ran the race. ('race' = *ries*)
   (c) I wanted the mango.
   (d) She was running the race.

(e) In those days, I trusted him. ('In those days'= *Dem taim de*; 'trust'= *trus*)

(f) I told the man I had sold it already.

(g) While I was waiting, he stole the mango. ('While' = *wails*, 'wait' = *wiet*, 'steal' = *tiif*)

(h) The horse is resting after it raced. ('horse' = *haas*, 'rest' = *res*, 'after' = *aafta*)

Selected references

Please consult the General references for titles mentioned in the text but not included in the references below. For a full bibliography see the accompanying CD-ROM.

Akers, Glenn
    1981   Admissibility conditions on final consonant clusters in the Jamaican continuum. In: Pieter Muysken (ed.), *Generative Studies on Creole Languages*, 1–24. Dordrecht: Foris.

Alleyne, Mervyn C.
    1971   Acculturation and the cultural matrix of creolization. In: Hymes (ed.), 169–186.

Bailey, Beryl Loftman
    1971   Jamaican Creole: Can dialect boundaries be defined? In: Hymes (ed.), 341–348.

Baugh, John
    1980   A re-examination of the Black English copula. In: Labov (ed.), 83–106.

Bennett, Louise
    1966   *Jamaica Labrish*. London: Collins.

Cassidy, Frederic G.
    1971   Tracing the pidgin element in Jamaican Creole. In: Hymes (ed.), 203-221.

Cheshire, Jenny
    1982   Linguistic variation and social function. In: Suzanne Romaine (ed.), *Sociolinguistic Variation in Speech Communities*, 153–166. London: Edward Arnold.

Christie, Pauline
    1996   Jamaican relatives in focus. In: Pauline Christie (ed.), *Caribbean Language Issues Old and New*, 48–60. Mona JA: University of West Indies Press.

Comrie, Bernard
    1985   *Tense*. Cambridge: Cambridge University Press.

Dance, Daryl C.
    1985   *Folklore from Contemporary Jamaicans*. Knoxville: University of Tennessee Press.

DeCamp, David
  1971   Towards a generative analysis of a post-creole speech continuum. In: Hymes (ed.), 349-370.
Loftman, Beryl
  1953   Creole languages of the Caribbean area. M.A. thesis, Columbia University.
Patrick, Peter L.
  1997   Style and register in Jamaican Patwa. In: Schneider (ed.), 41–56.
Pollard, Velma
  1989   The particle *en* in Jamaican Creole: A discourse-related account. *English World-Wide* 10: 55–68.
  1994   *Dread Talk: The Language of Rastafari*. Kingston: Canoe Press.
Radford, Andrew
  1997   *Syntax: A Minimalist Introduction*. New York: Cambridge University Press.
Rickford, John R.
  1996   Copula variability in Jamaican Creole and African American Vernacular English: A reanalysis of DeCamp's texts. In: Guy, Feagin, Schiffrin and Baugh (eds.), 357–372.
Roberts, Peter
  1973   Speech of 6-year-old Jamaican children. *Society for Caribbean Linguistics Occasional Paper No. 1*. Mona, JA: University of the West Indies (Caribbean Language Research Programme).
Russell, Thomas
  1868   *The Etymology of Jamaica Grammar*. Kingston: DeCordova, MacDougall. [Reprinted in full in Lalla and D'Costa (eds.), 184–201.]
Shields, Kathryn
  1989   Standard English in Jamaica: A case of competing models. *English World-Wide* 10: 41–53.
Sistren, with Honor Ford-Smith
  1987   *Lionheart Gal: Life-stories of Jamaican Women*. Toronto: Sister Vision.
Watson, G. Llewellyn
  1991   *Jamaican Sayings: With notes on Folklore, Aesthetics and Social Control*. Tallahassee, FL: Florida A&M University Press.
Winford, Donald
  1996   Verbs, adjectives and categoriality in Caribbean English Creoles. In: Pauline Christie (ed.), *Caribbean Language Issues Old and New*, 12–26. Mona, JA: University of West Indies Press.

Eastern Caribbean English-derived language varieties: morphology and syntax

Michael Aceto

1. Introduction

The syntax of the Anglophone Eastern Caribbean is only marginally better documented than the phonology of this region. Consult the chapter on the phonology of the Eastern Caribbean by Aceto (this volume) for a discussion of this region's frequent absence from research programs in creolistics and for a map of the region; see Aceto (2002a) who designates specific islands of the Eastern Caribbean (among other areas of the Americas as well) as neglected sites for future research. Aceto and Williams (2003) fills in some of the research gaps noted in Aceto (2002a).

Syntax has often been considered at the heart of Creole studies as it is within the discipline of linguistics in general. Many theoretical issues in creole studies (e.g. the locus of creole emergence, whether creole languages offer unique insights into internal language or cognitive constructs, the nature of variation in creole-speaking communities, etc.) rely largely on syntactic data in order to support their claims. This chapter is largely based on Holm (1988–1989), Winford (1993), Aceto and Williams (2003), various specific articles referenced below, and the author's own notes from fieldwork whose results have not yet appeared in published articles.

2. Some general syntactic features of Eastern Caribbean English-derived languages

2.1. Introduction

In this chapter, I discuss some syntactic features found in the general Eastern Caribbean (while making reference to features believed to be representative of the Western Caribbean as well), and then discuss specific islands and their English-derived varieties. It should be acknowledged that we do not have much research on many of these varieties, at least when compared to the impressive amount of research carried out on, say, Jamaica and the Surinamese Creole languages (and thus they are largely ignored in this discussion). See the chapter on the phonology of the Eastern Caribbean by Aceto (this volume) for a discussion of English varieties heard by Africans in the Western Hemisphere and for the linguistic motivations for separating Caribbean restructured Englishes into broad Western and Eastern varieties.

2.2.   Preverbal markers

2.2.1.   Past

There are several overt preverbal past tense markers in the Caribbean in general, and nearly all of them have been documented in the Eastern Caribbean, though there is a preference for reflexes of *mi(n)* in many locations (e.g. Antigua, Barbuda, Dominica). It is important to remember that dynamic or [-stative] verbs (and sometimes even [+stative] verbs as well) often have a default "past" interpretation even if there is no overt past tense marker stated. (The terms *past* and *future* with regard to tense, instead of *anterior* and *irrealis*, are used along the lines suggested in Winford 1993.)

(1)   a. [luk mɪŋ go a skul] 'Luke went/has gone to school.'

(Barbuda; Aceto 2002b)

   b. [tri a hi frɛn wʌz de] 'Three of his friends were there.'

(St. Thomas; Hancock 1987: 283)

   c. [trii a hi frɛn bɪn dɛ dɛ] 'Three of his friends were there.'

(St.Vincent; Hancock 1987: 283)

   d. [mi waak kras de yɛside] 'I walked along there yesterday.'

(St. Kitts/Nevis; Hancock 1987: 292)

   e. [onli wan boi kʌm] 'Only one boy came.'

(St. Eustatius; Aceto 2006)

The past tense marker *bin* is commonly heard in Jamaica and even in the Eastern Caribbean as is the marker *di(d)*, which is often considered an intermediate or so-called mesolectal form and is probably the most widely distributed form throughout the Caribbean. Forms related to *mi(n)* are found in both Western and Eastern Caribbean Englishes but seem to have emerged more strongly in the Eastern Caribbean. In several fieldwork locations (e.g. Barbuda, Dominica) I have extensively documented *mi(n)* but not a single instance of *bin*, though Hancock (1987) reveals several instances of preverbal *bin* in Eastern Caribbean locations such as St. Vincent and St. Kitts/Nevis. Preverbal *woz* is heard in the Western Caribbean, specifically within creole-speaking areas of Panama (Aceto 1996), but has not been documented, to my knowledge, for any area of the Eastern Caribbean. The US Virgin Islands reveal preverbal past tense *di(d)* or *had*; Whitehead (1932) reveals the use of *bin* as a past tense marker.

No researcher, to my knowledge, has yet explored why [mɪn] and its related forms emerged so strongly as past tense markers in the Eastern Caribbean as opposed to some form of [bɪn] as is more common in Jamaica and Suriname. Clearly, the word-initial onset [m-] in [mɪn] may be transparently viewed as a nasalization of the word-initial [b] in [bɪn], or, from a diachronic point of view, as a weakening of the word-initial [b-] segment as it assumes the feature of nasality. Is this feature due somehow to the native languages spoken by African slaves? Is it a local innovation? If so, from where did it emerge and spread? Furthermore, the reflexes [mɪŋ] and [mi] have no correspondences (e.g. [bɪŋ] or [bi]) in areas that display high usage of past tense [bɪn]. What factors are responsible for the emergence and persistent use of [mɪn] and its reflexes in specific areas of the Caribbean? These questions are beyond the scope of the present chapter but I will try to provide answers in the future.

Several islands in the Anglophone Eastern Caribbean such as Saba and St. Eustatius have no overt past tense markers. The past is indicated by default, several strong verb forms (e.g. *gaan* 'gone/went'), suppletive forms (e.g. *woz* 'was') or by context (e.g. *yesterday*, *last week*, etc.).

2.2.2. Future

The general future tense marker in the Eastern Caribbean is *go* and sometimes *goin*, but these are not exclusive to the region.

(2) a. [mo go du am tumara] 'I'm going to do it tomorrow.'
     b. [ʃi a go siŋ] 'She is going to sing.'
                                    (Barbuda; Aceto 2002b: 234)
     c. [ʃiz gooɛn tu sɛiŋ] 'She is going to sing.'
                                    (Saba; Hancock 1987: 301)
     d. [ʃɪ go sɪŋ] 'She is going to sing.'
                                    (Carriacou; Hancock 1987: 301)
     e. [a go dʌn fɪks ɪt pɔn dɛ bai tomaro] 'I will have fixed it on there before tomorrow.'
                                    (Grenada; Hancock 1987: 304)

The future tense marker *gwain*, which is so prevalent in the Western Caribbean, seems not to have emerged with anywhere near the same distribution in the Eastern Caribbean. In many fieldwork locations (e.g. Barbuda, St. Eustatius, Dominica among Kokoy speakers) *gwain* was rejected as a local form, and I did not record it either. The marker *a go* is also heard in the Eastern Caribbean. Winford (1993: 58–60) states that the semantic difference between *go* and *a go* is generally that the former indicates volition and the latter intention. However, I was unable to elicit these purportedly different meanings explicitly through interviews with informants in Barbuda who use both forms, though the meanings Winford ascribes may still be productive in other locations. Guyanese Creole English reveals the form *sa* as a future tense marker (as well as *go*). This form is most likely derived from Dutch *zal* 'shall, will'. Dutch-derived varieties were spoken in the general area of Guyana and Suriname historically; *sa* is also documented for Sranan, Saramaccan, Negerhollands, and Berbice and Skepi Dutch.

2.2.3. *Progressive aspect*

There is a preference for preverbal *a* or sometimes *da* in the Eastern Caribbean, though in the same location preverbal *de* may occur to some degree as does the common verbal suffix *-in* as well (*da* is documented in some western varieties such as Jamaican as well), which sometimes can co-occur with preverbal *a*.

(3)   a. [wi a taak] 'we are talking'
       b. [so waa mi a traiın fu se] 'So what am I trying to say?'
                                        (Barbuda; Aceto 2002b: 232)
       c. [nɔtn nʌ de apm] 'Nothing's happening.'
                                        (Antigua; Hancock 1987: 287)
       d. [hi mama a kaal ɔm] 'His mother is calling him.'
                                        (St. Vincent; Hancock 1987: 290)
       e. [a traın tu sii] 'I'm trying to see.'
                                        (St. Eustatius; Aceto 2006)

Often *a* is associated with the Eastern Caribbean and *de* with the western group of English-derived languages, but *de* is documented for Barbuda and Antigua as well as among Kokoy speakers in Dominica (more below) who exclusively use *e* as a progressive marker (e.g. *mi e nyam* 'I'm eating'). In the US Virgin Islands, Whitehead (1932) reveals the use of *(d)a* as progressive markers.

2.2.4. *Completive aspect*

As in many Anglophone Caribbean communities (as well as in North American varieties of English), preverbal *done* [dʌn] is the completive marker (e.g. *she done eat* 'she's finished eating/she's already eaten'). See Hancock (1987: 296–

297) for a list of English-derived varieties that exhibit reflexes of this broad pattern. Post-verbal or clause-final [dʌn] is often considered to be the older pattern but nevertheless it appears to be highly restricted (if occurring at all) in the Eastern Caribbean. Completive aspect can be signaled by an adverbial such as [aredi] 'already' as well, e.g. *she eat already.*

2.2.5. Habitual aspect

Often preverbal *doz* is considered a habitual marker that characterizes Eastern Caribbean varieties. However, it is restrictively heard in the Western Caribbean as well, though its occurrence there may be related to intra-Caribbean migration in the last century. Many Eastern Caribbean varieties also use the preverbal progressive aspectual marker *a* (and sometimes *de*) as a habitual marker.

(4) a. [wi doz traiin fi gɛt di haus finiʃ nau] 'We have been trying to finish the house (for some time).'

  b. [ʃi du om aal taim ~ ʃi doz aalweiz a du om] 'She does that all the time/she's always doing that.'

  c. [bout a kam ɪn bai nait] 'Boats arrive by night.'

              (Barbuda; Aceto 2002b: 236)

  d. [i de si i brɛda] 'she sees her brother (on weekends).'

            (Antigua; Hancock 1987: 288)

  e. [ʃi dʌz si ʃi brɛda] 'she see her brother (on weekends).'

     (St. Kitts/Nevis/Carriacou; Hancock 1987: 288)

Western Caribbean varieties often leave the verb phrase unmarked (e.g. *she go by im haus* 'she stops by his house [regularly]', which is reminiscent of similar habitual strategies in lexifier dialects. However, some areas of the Anglophone Eastern Caribbean such as Saba and St. Eustatius exhibit the same grammatical pattern.

In some areas of the Eastern Caribbean, V(erb)+-*in* can express either habitual or progressive action, whereas it typically only expresses progressive action in the Western group. However, V+-*in* as a marker of habituality seems limited to the Windward Islands that reveal a joint Francophone/Anglophone history (e.g. St. Lucia, Dominica, Grenada).

(5) [de gooin in toun evri sonde] 'They go to town every Sunday.'

                  (Garrett 2003: 167)

This strategy seems related to the similar grammatical marker *ka* in the earlier French creole that also has both functions.

In the Bahamas (which is often considered part of the North American group of Englishes but geographically proximate to the Eastern Caribbean as well), habitual *be* is used with verb forms, e.g. *they just be playing* or *they be walk right up*, in a manner similar to that found in African American Vernacular English (AAVE). However, *doz* indicates habitual action in the Bahamas as well, as is noted for much of the Eastern Caribbean in general.

For habitual actions exclusively in the past, *yustu* (< *used to*) appears in a range of Englishes in the Caribbean and North America, though other markers described above can also be interpreted in past contexts.

2.3.   Copula

Copula forms and their distribution are not usually features that typologically define Eastern English-derived varieties vis-à-vis Western varieties. In general, the nominal or equative copula is often [a] but [ɪz] and [bi] are also found in most consultants' repertoires as well. The attributive form is often [de] or zero, as is also common in general English-derived Atlantic creoles. The locative copula is often [de] or [ɪz]. In addition, in Barbuda, *tap* (historically < *stop*) functions as a kind of copula (e.g. [wai ya tap so] 'Why are you like that?'). The form *tan* (historically < *stand*) as in [dɛm no tan so] 'they're not like that' is reported for Antiguan (Hancock 1987: 287). (Bastimentos Creole English in Panama displays the use of [stie] in a manner similar to [tap] and [tan].)

(6)   a. [di waadɪn a di man dat kontrol di ailan] 'The warden is the man who controls the island.'
       b. [hi a ma paatna/hi a mi bʌdi] 'He's my partner/friend/buddy.'
       c. [we i de] 'Where is he/she?'
       d. [ʃi/i aarait] 'She's doing fine.'
       e. [natn a hapɪn] 'Nothing's happening.'

(Barbuda; Aceto 2002b: 239)

According to Hancock (1987: 284), the following islands of the Eastern Caribbean exhibit reflexes of *is* [ɪz] in nominal copula forms: St. Thomas, St. Eustatius (confirmed by Aceto 2006), Saba, Carriacou, and Grenada. St. Kitts/Nevis exhibit a zero form in the nominal construction, e.g. [hi mi paadna] 'he's my partner', which is similar to constructions found in AAVE.

2.4.   Plurality

The post-nominal plural marker [an dɛm] is generally diagnostic of the Anglophone Eastern Caribbean, though simple post-nominal [dɛm], the form generally associated with Western Caribbean varieties, is heard as well. Hancock (1987: 305) lists pluralizing [an dɛm] forms for Antigua, St. Vincent, and Carriacou; and simple post-nominal [dɛm] forms for St. Thomas and St. Eustatius (confirmed by Aceto forthcoming a) as well as bound inflectional morphology for Saba and Grenada. The unique post-nominal plural form [an de] is heard in Barbuda as well. There is as yet no research examining why the post-nominal form [an dɛm] (or [an de] in Barbuda), as opposed to simple [dɛm], emerged so strongly in the Eastern Caribbean.

(7)   a.   [di ʃiip an dɛm] 'the sheep'
      b.   [luk pan maavin an de a troubl dɪ ʃiip] 'Look at Marvin and his
           friends bothering the sheep.'
      c.   [di artoritiz an dɛm gat rait doŋ tu di elbo in de] 'The
           authorities are up to their elbows in there (the drug trade).'
      d.   [de hɛd fo amerɪka bika dɛm plɛnti gat kruz ʃɪp an de] 'They
           head for America because they have a lot of cruise ships.'
      e.   [stap tʃesɪn dɪ ʃip dɛm] 'Stop chasing the sheep!'

                                    (Barbuda; Aceto 2002b: 238)

A further plural strategy is also found in many Caribbean varieties, including many English-derived dialects in several locations: prenominal [dɛm] (i.e. [dɛm diplomatɪk paasport] 'their diplomatic passports') indicates not only possession but plurality as well. Hancock (1987: 305) also records this strategy for St. Kitts/Nevis. In instances of this nature, a redundant post-nominal plural marker is rarely if ever heard.

(8)   [an dɛn de kieri in dɛm sut bika dɛm gat dɛm diplomatɪk
      paasport] 'And then they carry (drugs) in their suits because they
      have diplomatic passports'

                                    (Barbuda; Aceto 2002b: 238)

The co-occurrence of these forms in the Eastern Caribbean may be due to intra-Caribbean migration in the last 150 years, or they may indicate a long standing point of variation since English-derived restructured varieties began to emerge in the Caribbean during the period of slavery. It is difficult to be certain, even if creolists in general feel more comfortable with the highly questionable assumption that earlier varieties of creole languages were monolithic and contemporary synchronic variation is a more recent (i.e. post-emancipation) phenomenon.

2.5.   Pronouns

It is in the pronominal systems that we can see what may be the most transparent and robust split between Eastern and Western Caribbean English-derived varieties. The following pronominal forms are heard in the Eastern Caribbean. All forms should be considered to have multiple functions as subject, object and possessive pronouns unless otherwise indicated.

Table 1.   Pronouns in Anglophone Eastern Caribbean varieties

	Singular
1ˢᵗ person	a (subject), mi
2ⁿᵈ person	yu
3ʳᵈ person	(h)i 'he/she/it' (subject/possessive)
	ʃi 'she' (subject/possessive)
	om, am, im 'he/she/it' (object)

	Plural
1ˢᵗ person	aawi
2ⁿᵈ person	aayu/unu
3ʳᵈ person	de (subject), dɛm

Many Eastern Caribbean varieties, as reported in Hancock (1987: 298), lack the second person plural form [unu] or any of its reflexes that are so common in Western Caribbean English-derived varieties (however, Barbados reveals [wuna]). Instead, Eastern varieties reveal the common regional form [aayu] or [alyu] or some reflex of those forms. Reisman (1964: 64) states that forms for the second person plural pronoun [hunu ~ unu] are reported by some Antiguans to be more closely associated with Barbuda and largely absent from Antigua. Though the form is occasionally heard in Barbuda (I recorded [unu] specifically), it is far less common than [aayu], etymologically 'all of you'. The former form is more associated with exasperation or anger with a group of persons, often children who are misbehaving.

Diagnostically, *unu* is often considered more Western Caribbean and *a(l)yu*, which is rarely heard in western varieties, more Eastern Caribbean. The common English-derived dialect form [y(u)aal] is heard to some degree as well. Other pronouns that seem to be typologically diagnostic of this eastern-western split are *(h)im* (as both subject and object pronouns) in Western varieties, which are nearly always *(h)i* (as a subject pronoun) and *om* (as a third person singular object pronoun 'he/she/it') in Eastern Caribbean varieties; see Williams (2001) who argues that the source of this pronoun is restructured varieties of Dutch. Finally, *wi* is often the first person plural pronoun (as both subject and object pronouns) in Western varieties, and the corresponding form is *aawi* in the Eastern Caribbean; some of the Leeward Islands (Antigua, St. Kitts, Nevis, Montserrat, Anguilla, Barbuda) reveal [aabi] (Holm 1988-1989: 451).

3.   Some features of specific Eastern Caribbean Islands

3.1.   The Turks and Caicos Islands

The Turks and Caicos Islands are often considered part of North American varieties of English. However, they are included in Aceto and Williams (2003) due to the fact that these islands are geographically proximate as well as under-researched. Cutler (2003) examines the English spoken on Grand Turk Island among the Turks and Caicos chain of islands. She concludes that Turks Island English (TIE) has more in common with AAVE (as well as Gullah and Bermudian) than with other varieties of English spoken in the Caribbean. For example, in TIE plurality is variably marked by the suffix *-s*, its allomorph *-z*, or Ø. The post-nominal plural marker [dɛm], found in many Atlantic Creoles (e.g. [di boi dɛm] *the boys*) did not occur in Cutler's corpus. Also, possession is variably expressed by a suffix *-s* or Ø. TIE speakers exclusively use the first person singular nominative pronoun *I* [ai] unlike many English varieties in the West Indies that display [mi] or [a]. Lastly, all the speakers in her corpus used the third person singular verbal suffix *-s* variably. Future tense is marked by *gon* [gən] and *will* [βil] in TIE as are common strategies in AAVE (e.g. *he gon build my house* 'he's going to build my house' (Cutler 2003: 68). Furthermore, there is no overt pre-verbal past tense marker; the past is indicated by verbal forms (both regular and irregular) found in lexifier varieties. Lastly, no examples of completive forms such as *done* appear in her corpus. Cutler believes that studying the language of the Caicos Islanders, most of whom are descended from American-born slaves, may provide some insight into earlier forms of AAVE spoken in the USA.

3.2.   Virgin Islands

Sabino, Diamond and Cockcroft (2003) examine plural marking in several of the Virgin Islands, both American and British. Their consultants reveal intra-systemic variation in that they all display the Standard English strategy of using

-*s* (or one of its variants), the creole strategy of post-nominal *dem*, and a noun that is unmarked for number. They provide a valuable longitudinal perspective of 51 years from 1933 to 1984 and represent speakers from four of the Virgin Islands: St. Thomas, St. John, Anegada, and Tortola. They conclude that audience is a crucial factor in predicting which forms their consultants select and that "in over four decades there has been no appreciable shift towards Standard English" (Sabino, Diamond and Cockcroft 2003: 92).

3.3.   Anguilla

Williams (2003) examines the Webster dialect of Anguillian English, a variety spoken among the island's population of European descent in Island Harbour. See the discussion of Anglophone Eastern Caribbean phonology by Aceto (this volume) for a discussion of Williams' research and the importance of understanding Euro-Caribbean varieties for creole and dialect studies.

Many of the features of the Webster dialect are common throughout the Caribbean. For example, all varieties of Anguillian English follow the general Anglophone Caribbean pattern of not inverting subjects and auxiliary verbs in question forms (e.g. *you did go?*). The determiners are similar to those found in other varieties of English in the Eastern Caribbean. The indefinite article alternates between the more vernacular form *one* [wan ~ an] and the more formal form *a* [e ~ ə]. Possession is indicated by simple juxtaposition of two nominals in the order possessor-possessed (e.g. *my mother father ... my daddy father were brothers*), as is common in the Caribbean and in AAVE, but suffixation is used as well (e.g. *in my father's time*). Negation is often indicated by *ain't/tain't/tisn't*, and doubly marked forms are typical of the Webster dialect of Island Harbour as they are in many English-derived varieties in the Americas.

Pronouns heard in the Webster dialect are: *I* [ai ~ ə] for first person singular, and *he/she* [hi]/[ʃi] for third person singular human males and females respectively. Speakers also use [awi] 'all we' as the first person plural pronoun.

Several features of the Webster dialect are different than common forms heard in the general Anglophone Eastern Caribbean and in other English-derived varieties spoken on Anguilla. For example, the second person plural form [ɑyu] 'all you' is not part of the grammar of Island Harbour. Furthermore, the Webster dialect does not reveal any use of the postposed plural marker [dɛm] that is so common in many Anglophone Caribbean creoles, and this form is not part of the grammar of Anguillian English Creole in other villages on the island as well.

Habitual aspect is often indicated by the third person present verbal suffix -*s* (e.g. *I goes there every Sunday*). This strategy is often used in the Webster dialect and is heard across the island beyond Island Harbour. This feature is common in many of the English dialects of the British Isles (see, for example, Anderwald, British Isles volume). Preverbal *do* [də] or the use of the third-person singular present tense form (verbal -*s*) to indicate habituality are documented as features of the English varieties historically spoken in the southwestern counties of England. Other strategies for marking habituality are: [də] (e.g. *Those rooms* [də] *come hot*), [də bi] (e.g. *From noon 'til three o'clock, it* [də bi] *hot*), and [dʌz] (e.g. *I* [dʌz] *send it always*). Past habitual forms are typically marked with [yuustu] 'used to'.

Some forms in Island Harbor seem similar to AAVE forms, but Williams does not suggest language contact as the explanatory factor. For example, using past perfect forms associated with standard varieties to indicate simple past is a feature that has been widely associated with AAVE and its assumed influence. In Anguillian Englishes, the form is common both in black and white varieties on the island (e.g. *my friend, Eddie, he had call*). The presence of this strategy in the Webster dialect provides preliminary evidence that the form most likely does not derive from a North American source, and instead, likely has a source, or sources, in English dialects brought to the Caribbean by settlers and colonists. Similarly, the future is marked with the preverbal marker /gɔn/ in Webster dialect (e.g. *Someday I* [gɔn] *call you too, you know*). Similar forms are found in other varieties of Anguillian English throughout the island.

Progressive aspect in the Webster dialect is marked via three strategies: 1) *a* [ə] + V+-*in* (e.g. *the new ones did now start* [ə-] *comin in*), 2) V+-*in* (e.g. *she is goin college in Maryland*), and 3) *do be* + V+-*in* (e.g. *February, March corn do be comin*). The first and third strategies appear to be archaic in that they are heard among the oldest Websters, and are often considered to be examples of the way that the older Websters spoke, especially in the times when there was no formal education. Completive aspect is indicated by the common preverbal form *done*, e.g. *I done gone*, though it is limited in the Webster dialect to older folks who are thought not to have had much education.

3.4.   Barbuda

Aceto (2002b) describes some of the general grammatical features associated with Barbudan Creole English (BCE). BCE reveals no fewer than four different present progressive aspectual constructions: *a* + V (e.g. [wi a taak] 'we are talking'), *de* + V (e.g. [yu mada de kaal yu] 'your mother is calling you'), V-*in* (e.g. [yu mami kaalin yu] 'your mother is calling you'), and *a* + V-*in* (e.g. [so waa mi a traiin fu se] 'So what am I trying to say?'). This last strategy is reported for Anguilla (Williams 2003), the Bahamas (McPhee 2003), and the Appalachian area of the USA (Wolfram and Christian 1976).

The simple past tense marker [min] (e.g. [de min a inglisʃman (a inglisʃman dem bi)] 'they were Englishmen') is also realized as [mɪŋ] (with a velarized nasal) (e.g. [luk (mɪŋ) go a skul] 'Luke went/has gone to school') or as the reduced form [mi] (e.g. [an de mi hab plenti gol] 'and they had a lot of gold'). The widespread Caribbean form [di(d)] is heard as well (e.g. [a inglisʃman di bi tʃif a polis] 'an Englishman was the chief of police').

Habitual aspect is indicated by preverbal *doz* (e.g. [wi doz traiin fi get di haus finiʃ nau] 'We have been trying to finish the house for some time') and an unmarked verbal form used with an adverbial (e.g. [ʃi du om aal taim] 'She does it all the time'). Progressive forms may also be interpreted as habituals as well (e.g. [buot a kam in bai nait] 'Boats often arrive at night'). In BCE, the future can be marked by either *go* (e.g. [yu ʃut wan dir an de go brɪŋ yu in] 'you shoot a deer and they're going to bring you in') or *a go* (e.g. [ma sisa a go antiga tumara] 'My sister is going to Antigua tomorrow'). In several instances, *gan* arose, as did *wil*, but not *gwain*.

BCE reveals a seemingly unique post-nominal pluralizing marker: [an de] (e.g. [luk pan maavin an de a troubl dɪ ʃiip] 'Look at Marvin and his friends bothering the sheep'). This plural marker is considered more "Barbudan" by many of my consultants than the typical Antiguan or general Eastern Caribbean form [an dɛm] or simple post-nominal [dɛm], which is occasionally heard.

Reisman (1964: 114) reveals [an dɛm], [dɛm], and [ɛm] for geographically proximate Antiguan Creole English, which is just two dozen miles to the south of Barbuda; Farquhar (1974: 43) only mentions "*-andem*" for Antiguan. None of these sources reveals post-nominal [an de] as is heard in Barbudan Creole English.

3.5.   Carriacou

Kephart (2000) sketches many of the basic grammatical features of Carriacou Creole English (CCE). Several CCE features have been rarely documented in the literature. For example, the general grammatical function of *an* within the verbal complex in both future and past verbal constructions (e.g. [a gouin an pik mango] 'I'll pick mangoes [perhaps tomorrow]' [2000: 94] and [wi bin an pik mangou] 'we picked mangoes' [2000: 93]) has not been explored, to my knowledge, in any research (see Aceto 1998 for a similar occurrence in Panamanian Creole English).

The morpheme classes exhibited by CCE and other English-derived varieties in the Caribbean (2000: 64–65) (e.g. [fas(t) + -a] 'faster', [wikid + -nis] 'wickidness') raise the issue of when diachronically this aspect of morphology emerged in the creole's grammar. The issue of whether Creoles manifest bound inflectional or derivational morphology is a subject of some current debate in creole studies (see McWhorter 1998; Plag 2001). Also, the preference of CCE in using [finiʃ] as a completive marker (e.g. [a finiʃ it] 'I'm done eating'; [dʌn] seems to be rarely heard in this creole) is one of several interesting and/or unique features of this English-derived language (2000: 90–91), and it seems to point towards the hypothesis that CCE may be significantly influenced by the chronologically earlier French Creole.

Some other general features found in CCE are as follows. As with several creoles in the Eastern Caribbean (e.g. Barbudan, Antiguan), the post-nominal plural marker is *an dem* in CCE (e.g. [wi ting an dem] 'our things') not simple *dem* as is common in the Western Caribbean. Progressive aspect is signaled by V+-*in* (e.g. [rein komin] 'rain is coming') or preverbal *(d)a* (e.g [we yu a go] 'where are you going?'). The past tense marker is *di(d)* (e.g. [shi di dei in skul] 'she was at school') and the future marker is *gou* (e.g. [yu gou reivn] 'you will be greedy'). The stressed form *bín* only appears as the past of *be* (e.g. [we yu bín] 'where have you been/where were you?') or in limited past tense constructions (e.g. [wi bín gouin houm] 'we were going home'; [a bín an pik mangou] 'I was picking mangoes'). Negation is indicated by placing *no*, *dou*, or *en* before the predicate (e.g. [a en go dans wit yu] 'I won't dance with you'; [de no spikin patwa gi yu] 'they won't speak Patois for you').

3.6.   St. Lucia

Garrett (2003) is the most comprehensive examination of St. Lucian Vernacular English (SLVE) to date. Garrett argues that SLVE is *not* a creole but instead a vernacular variety that has emerged relatively recently (in the late 19th and 20th centuries) due to contact in educational institutions between English-speaking teachers and students who were/are native speakers of Kwéyòl, a French-lexified creole that dates back to the island's French colonial period (1642–1803). Thus, SLVE's greatest influence (phonologically, semantically, and, above all, syntactically) has not been English-derived creoles spoken in the Caribbean but St. Lucia's Kwéyòl instead. Some of the features that SLVE does not share with other creoles of the Eastern Caribbean are the following: anterior/past *mi(n)* (or *bin*); continuative/progressive *(d)a*; habitual *(d)a*; anterior/past *did*; completive *don*; the use of *en*, *na*, and *no* as negative preverbal markers; and pluralizing/deictic *dem*.

SLVE has several unique features usually not found in most English-derived language varieties in the Caribbean. For example, past tense is indicated by preverbal *had* (e.g. [hii had iit do bred biifoh hii goo tuu skuul] 'he ate the bread before he went to school'), habitual aspect is indicated by V+-*in* (e.g. [dee gooing in toun evrii sondee] 'they go to town every Sunday'), and the negative imperative is formed by preposing *naat tu* preverbally (e.g. [naat tuu toch dat] 'Do not touch that!'; [naat] and [doo] are the usual negative markers). The adverb *again* [ogen] has been broadened to include the meanings 'still', 'anymore', and 'else', probably on the model of Kwéyòl *ankò* (< French *encore,* e.g. [yuu hav moh klooz tuu waash ogen] '[do] you still have more clothes to wash?'). Prepositions have different meanings in this language than in other English-derived varieties (e.g. [muuv **in** do reen] 'get out **of** the rain'; [hii sending stoon **biihain** piipl] 'he is throwing stones **at/after** people'). In other instances, no overt prepositions are used in SLVE where they would typically appear in other English-derived varieties (e.g. [hii lafing mii] 'he is laughing at me'). The completive marker is *already* [oredii] and not *done* in SLVE (e.g. [yoh modo riich oredii] 'your mother has arrived').

4.   Conclusion

Aceto (2002a) pointed out that many research locations in the Eastern Caribbean have not yet been the focus of any piece of published research: St. John, St. Thomas, Tortola, Virgin Gorda, Anegada, St. Eustatius, the Grenadine Islands of St. Vincent (Bequia, Mustique, Canouan, Union Island, and Mayreau). Furthermore, the following research locations have been the subject of only a single publication in linguistics or creole studies: Grenada, Montserrat, St. Croix, Nevis, St. Martin, and St. Vincent. More work by more fieldworkers would greatly improve our understanding of specific linguistic and sociohistorical features which one lexically-related Creole or English variety may or may not share with another. See Aceto (this volume) on the phonology of the Anglophone Eastern Caribbean for more concluding remarks.

Exercises and study questions

1. Explain the range of past tense markers in the Anglophone Caribbean and which markers generally occur in which locations.

2. Which future tense markers generally occur in the Eastern Caribbean? Which marker that is typically found in the Anglophone Western Caribbean is highly restricted in the Eastern Caribbean?

3. What are the progressive aspectual markers for the Anglophone Caribbean and which ones are more common in the Eastern area versus the Western area?

4. Explain the different habitual aspect markers heard in the Eastern Caribbean. Which islands reveal strong patterns of usage for which markers?

5. Which pronouns are generally considered diagnostic of the Anglophone Eastern Caribbean? How are they different from the ones typically heard in the Western area?

Selected references

Please consult the General references for titles mentioned in the text but not included in the references below. For a full bibliography see the accompanying CD-ROM.

Aceto, Michael
    1996   Syntactic innovation in a Caribbean creole: The Bastimetos variety of Panamanian creole English. *English World-Wide* 17: 43–61.
    1998   A new Creole future tense marker emerges in the Panamanian West Indies. *American Speech* 73: 29–43.
    2002a   Going back to the beginning: Describing the nearly undocumented Anglophone creoles of the Caribbean. In: Gilbert (ed.), 93–118.
    2002b   Barbudan Creole English: Its history and some grammatical features. *English World-Wide* 23: 223–250.
    2006   Sation Creole English: An English-derived Language emerges in the Dutch Antilles. *World Englishes* 25: 411–435.
Aceto, Michael and Jeffrey P. Williams (eds.)
    2003   *Contact Englishes of the Eastern Caribbean.* (Varieties of English Around the World. G30) Amsterdam/Philadelphia: John Benjamins.
Cutler, Cecilia
    2003   English in the Turks and Caicos Island: A look at Grand Turk. In: Aceto and Williams (eds.), 51–80.
Garrett, Paul B.
    2003   'An English Creole' that isn't: On the sociohistorical origins and linguistic classification of the vernacular in St. Lucia. In: Aceto and Williams (eds.), 155–210.
Hancock, Ian
    1987   A preliminary classification of the Anglophone Creoles, with syntactic data from thirty-three representative dialects. In: Gilbert (ed.), 264–334.
Farqhuar, Bernadette
    1947   A grammar of Antiguan Creole. Unpublished Ph.D. dissertation, Cornell University.

Kephart, Ronald
    2000   *Broken English. The Creole Language of Carriacou*. New York: Peter
            Lang.
McPhee, Helean
    2003   The grammatical features of TMA auxiliaries in Bahamian Creole. In:
            Aceto and Williams (eds.), 29–49.
McWhorter, John
    1998   Identifying the creole prototype: Vindicating a typological class. *Language*
            74: 788–818.
Plag, Ingo
    2001   The nature of derivational morphology in creoles and non-creoles. *Journal
            of Pidgin and Creole Linguistics* 16: 153–160.
Reismann, Karl
    1964   'The isle is full of noises': A study of creole in the speech of patterns
            of Antigua, West Indies. Unpublished Ph.D. dissertation, Harvard
            University.
Sabino, Robin, Mary Diamond and Leah Cockcroft
    2003   Language variety in the Virgin Islands: Plural markings. In: Aceto and
            Williams (eds.), 81–94.
Whitehead, H.S.
    1932   Negro dialect of the Virgin Islands. *American Speech* 7: 175–179.
Williams, Jeffrey P.
    1987   Anglo-Caribbean English: a study of its sociolinguistic history and the
            development of its aspectual markers. Unpublished Ph.D. dissertation,
            University of Texas, Austin.
    1988   The development of aspectual markers in Anglo-Caribbean English.
            Journal of Pidgin and Creole Languages 3: 245–263.
    2001   Arguments against a British dialect source for UM in Bajan English Creole.
            Journal of Pidgin and Creole Languages 16: 355–363.
    2003   The establishment and perpetuation of Anglophone white enclave com-
            munities in the Eastern Caribbean: The case of Island Harbor, Anguilla. In:
            Aceto and Williams (eds.), 95–119.

The creoles of Trinidad and Tobago: morphology and syntax

Winford James and Valerie Youssef

1. Introduction

In the words of Allsopp (1996: 1, emphasis original), "[t]he vocabulary of Caribbean English comprises the whole active *core vocabulary of World English* as may be found in any piece of modern English literature, together with all *Caribbean regionalisms produced by the ecology, history and culture* of the area". In keeping with the character of that vocabulary as well as of the vocabulary of Creole languages generally, the vocabulary of the Creoles spoken in Trinidad and Tobago is shaped by a partially autonomous phonology, as described in our companion chapter in this volume, with considerable differences, particularly in the vowel system, from the phonologies of metropolitan (i.e. non-creole) English varieties. It is supported, in varying degrees, by a variety of morphological and semantic processes as summarily reported on by Ian Hancock (1980) and Richard Allsopp (1980), and is characterised by far more derivational than inflectional morphology.

Various aspects of the syntax and morphology have been described earlier. The following works, and others (see the full bibliography on the accompanying CD), describe aspects of Tobagonian morphosyntax, both basilectal and mesolectal: James and Youssef (2002); Winer (1993); Winford (1993). And the following describe aspects of Trinidadian morphosyntax, both basilectal and mesolectal: Solomon (1993); Winford (1993); Winer (fc., 1993); James and Youssef (2002). In presenting the description of Tobagonian and Trinidadian morphosyntax, we draw on insights in (some of) them.

Because of their low affixation, the Creole languages rely mainly on syntactic relationships between non-affixal grammatical and lexical morphemes in various subsystems of the grammar. In normal speech in Trinidad and Tobago, the grammars in contact are related to one another in the grammars of individuals which display different levels of varilingual competence (James and Youssef 2002). That is to say, people mix basilectal, mesolectal, and acrolectal grammars in the stream of speech in accordance with their degree of control of the individual grammars, and in accordance with the sociolinguistic demands of each situation in which they find themselves.

But, as the varietal labels suggest, the different grammars can be isolated. The syntax of basilectal Tobagonian speech as well as of mesolectal Trinidadian and Tobagonian speech can therefore be separated out of the speech to a fair extent, although, as detailed in Youssef (1996), there has been a level of merger through close contact which renders exclusive assignation of certain lexical and grammatical items to particular lects problematic. By and large, the mesolectal varieties are shared. However, the very fact that there are two contact systems in Trinidad (mesolect and a local variety of Standard English) and three in Tobago (basilect, mesolect, and a local Standard English) (cf. James and Youssef 2002) means that the norms for usage of the forms in contact vary from one island to the next, mesolectal features being more prestigious in the Tobagonian speech community, where they represent a mid-level variety as opposed to representing a lower-level variety in the Trinidadian speech community where no English Creole basilect has been described. As discussed elsewhere in relation to pre-verbal *don* in African-American and in Guyanese (Edwards 1995, 2000), different levels of contact between varieties make for a different range of semantic usage in one variety as distinct from another, and this applies equally to Trinidadian and Tobagonian. In addition, factors such as socio-economic background and level of education will determine the relative usage of semantically related markers, for example, StE Present Perfect *have* + -*en* versus Creole Ø and *done* (cf. Winford 1994).

All in all, Tobago and Trinidad are separate speech communities in some senses, while sharing understandings to a large extent; these issues have been discussed further in our companion chapter.

In this chapter, we will do the following. First, we will illustrate most of the lexico-morphological processes identified above. Secondly, we will illustrate typical sentence structures. Thirdly, we will describe the most common affixal morphemes as well as a variety of non-affixal grammatical morphemes, and illustrate their use in sentences. Finally, we will describe the major systems in the syntax, i.e., the pronoun, verb (including negation), and noun systems. In the process of making these presentations, we will be distinguishing between those forms and structures that are typically (basilectal) Tobagonian and those that are common to the mesolectal varieties of both Tobagonian and Trinidadian (as a convenient shorthand, we thus speak of *mesolectal Trinbagonian* in the following sections)

In the illustrations, a phonemic spelling system is used in which each letter symbolises a particular sound or phoneme. The system is straightforward except for two letters – *ē* and *ō*. The first is meant to represent a tense monophthongal pronunciation of the vowel in words like *face*, which would be [feis] in RP, but [fes] in our Creoles. The second is meant to represent the tense monophthongal sound in words like *nō*, which would be [nəʊ] in RP, but [no] in our Creoles.

2. Lexical expansion/progression

Hancock (1980) identifies twelve processes of lexical progression, dividing them up equally as morphological and semantic. The six morphological ones are: coining (including onomatopoeia and ideophony), incoining or blending (including portmanteaux words), back-formation (including abbreviation), tautology or redundant extension, reduplication, and calquing; and the six semantic ones are: (eight kinds of) extension, shift, convergence (including folk etymology), divergence, tonalising (including tone and intonation), and adoption. Allsopp (1980) discusses Hancock's categories and provides clarifications that are more in keeping with the Trinidadian and Tobagonian realities. He also adds the following six processes, separately categorising some that Hancock subsumes in more general categories, and without making Hancock's morphology-semantics distinction: misascription, functional shift, folk etymology or phonological shift in transmission, code overlap, attraction, and free compounding.

Table 1 below displays Trinidadian and Tobagonian examples of the products of some of the processes identified by Hancock and Allsopp. For a fuller listing of examples, see Allsopp (1996) and Winer (fc.).

Table 1. Illustration of lexical expansion processes

WORDS & GLOSSES	PROCESS	DEFINITION OF PROCESS
Bubulups (n) 'fat lady'; *badam* 'sound of a blow or fall'	Coining	Spontaneous creation in display action
Komesiv (adj.) 'meddlesome and interfering'; *bodarēshon* (n) 'trouble or calamity'	Incoining/ blending	Combination of established lexemes/morphemes to make new words
ai-woota (n) 'tears'; *ōnwē* (adj.) 'wayward'; *dō-mowt* 'threshold'	Calquing or relexification	Literal translation of substrate words by English words
Kyã (modal) 'can'; *kyã* (neg. modal) 'cannot'; *TĒ*.la (n) (HL) 'tailor' / *tē*. LA (surname) (LH) 'Taylor'	Semantic pitch differentiation	Use of epimorphic pitch/tone (without necessarily changing the stress) to differentiate the meaning of homophones

Table 1. (continued)   Illustration of lexical expansion processes

WORDS & GLOSSES	PROCESS	DEFINITION OF PROCESS
Basi-basi (n) 'confusion'; *krai-krai* (v) 'cry constantly'	Reduplication	Repetition of a base word for intensity
Puuja 'prayer meeting'; *seke-seke* (adj./adv.) 'random and arbitrary' / 'at random and arbitrarily'	Retention	Survival, more or less intact, of substrate words
Ōva (prep. & v) 'be finished/dismissed'; *fiftiin* (v) 'turn fifteen'	Functional shift	Increasing the number of word-classes of a word
Gloori siida 'gliricidia'; *fōr-an-a-haaf* 'fore-and-aft'; *tek iin* 'take ill, be taken ill'; *bati manswell* 'bati mamzel' (French Creole), 'dragon fly' (English)	Phonological shift in transmission	Pronouncing a word that is not well heard on the pattern of already-known others that are close in sound
Sik-owt (n) 'sick-out' (on the pattern of 'sit-in' and 'lock-out)	Attraction	Formation of phrases by false analogy with a slot in English phrase
Kyaa-du-dis-kyaa-du-dat (n); *neva-si-kom-si* (n)	Free-compounding	'Spontaneous nominalising (also adjectivalising) of any short phrasal item that has a strong descriptive or allusive thrust'
Long (L)-ai (H) 'covetousness'; *dog (L)-mowt* (H) 'dog's mouth'; *jroma (LL)-man* (H)	Compounding	Formation of compound words out of two words by placing a high tone (H) on the last syllable of the last word, but a low tone (L) on the syllable(s) of the preceding word
Vup, bodōw, budup, blaw	Ideophony	Creation of words to match sound of event, action, etc.

3.   Typical sentence structure

The typical structure of a declarative Creole sentence is SUBJ + PRED, where:

SUBJ → {DP, NP, QP, AP, PP, LOCP}
PRED → {VP, PP, ADVP}
DP → D NP
D → {demonstrative specifiers, non-demonstrative specifiers, singulariser}
NP → (N) N
QP → Q N
AP → A N
PP → P NP
LOCP → (P) LOCADV (locative adverb)
VP → {V (SUF/PCL) (COMP), (PCL) V (PCL) (COMP)}
V → {adjectival verb (e.g., *sik*, *gud*), main verb, copula (e.g., *a*, *de*)}
ADVP → ADV {A, V}
COMP = SUBJ

In the notations above, SUF, PCL, and COMP are respectively short forms for suffix, particle, and complement. In particular, COMP is used here to include the notions of complement and object. N, V, and A are lexical categories, while D, Q, P, LOCADV, SUF, and PCL are grammatical categories. The following sentences illustrate the most typical arrangements of syntactic categories:

(1) *Di man iit (di fuud).*
     D N   V (D N)
     'The man ate the food.'

(2) *Lochri tikit koos chrii dolaz.*
     N   N   V   Q   N
     'A lottery ticket costs three dollars.'

(3) *Red mango don.*
     A   N   V
     'The red mangos are finished' / 'No more red mangos.'

(4) *Onda da chrii de   gud tu shēd.*
     P   D N   SUF V I V
     'That tree there is good to shade under.'

(5) *Ōva-so   hav plenty bush.*
     P   LOCADV V   Q   N
     'There's plenty bush over there.'

(6) *Di bēbi sik.*
     D N   V
     'The baby is sick.'

(7)   *Hi a dakta.*
        D V N
        'He's a doctor.'

(8)   *Hi a   sliip.*
        D PCL V
        'He's sleeping.'

(9)   *Hi sliipin.*
        D V-SUF
        'He's sleeping.'

(10)   *Hi bai lochri tikit.*
        D V N   N
        'He has bought {a lottery ticket / lottery tickets}.'

(11)   *Shi laik red mango.*
        D V   A   N
        'She likes red-mango.'

(12)   *Shi swiip op   onda di tēbu.*
        D V   PCL P   D N
        'She swept [that part of the floor] under the table.'

(13)   *Hi kliin ōva-de.*
        D V   P   LOCADV
        'He cleaned [that part] over there.'

(14)   *Hi ōva   faas.*
        D ADV A
        'He is too meddlesome.'

(15)   *Hi maasta oparēt di kompyuuta.*
        D ADV   V   D N
        'He is versed in the operation of the computer.'

Apart from the declarative relational structure of SUBJ PRED, there are also the following two structures: a) PRED (only), where there is no subject and the constituents are COP(ula) *a* (basilectal Tobagonian) and COP *iz* (mesolectal Trinbagonian) followed by COMP; this PRED can be structurally independent; and b) PRED SUBJ PRED, where the first PRED may also be composed of *a/iz* and COMP, in which case it is structurally independent, or may be composed of *a/iz* and unsuffixed V, in which case it cannot stand apart from the typical structure SUBJ PRED; in both cases, however, it highlights particular constituents from SUBJ PRED which have moved into it as full phonetic forms or as copies of (parts of) such forms. The following sentences illustrate:

(16)   *A/Iz di tiicha.*
       COP D N
       'It's the teacher.'

(17)   *A/Iz ōva-de/dyee.*
       COP P   LOCADV
       'It's [that place] over there.'

(18)   *A   di tiicha*₁ *hi a   taak tu t*₁.
       COP D N   D PCL V   P DP
       'It's the teacher he's talking to.'

(19)   *Iz   di tiicha*₁ *hi took-in   tu t*₁.
       COP D N   D V   SUF P DP
       'It's the teacher he's talking to.'

(20)   *A   ōva-de*₁   *hi gaan t*₁.
       COP P   LOCADV D V   LOCP
       'It's over there he's gone.'

(21)   *Iz   ōva-dyee*₁   *hi goon t*₁.
       COP P   LOCADV D V   LOCP
       'It's over there he's gone.'

(22)   *A   kom hi a   kom.*
       COP V   D PCL V
       'He's COMING.'

(23)   *Iz   kom hi kom-in.*
       COP V   D V   SUF
       'He's COMING.'

Sentences (16-17) feature independent PRED. In (18-21), the DP and LOCP are analysed as moving in full phonetic form from one COMP position to another, leaving bound traces in the process. In (22), a copy of V, rather than the original form itself, moves from COMP to COMP. And in (23), a copy of V, but not of SUF, moves to pre-subject position. The reason why only a copy of V (and not the whole original constituent itself) moves is that the imperfective PCL *a* is strictly pre-verbal, that is, it must come before a phoneticised verb.

In brief, then, our Creoles are 'SVO' (or, more accurately, SVC(OMP)) languages, with special sentences without subjects and with highlighted constituents that have moved in full phonetic form or as copies.

In both interrogative and exclamative sentences, the declarative order is maintained, only that the intonation differs. The declarative sentence is produced with a relatively falling or low tone on the final constituent of PRED, the interrogative with a relatively rising or high tone, and the exclamative with a tone just lower than the interrogative tone.

The fact that the interrogative order is the same as the declarative means that there is no subject-verb/auxiliary inversion. More specifically, to the extent that AUX is a movable category, there is no AUX in the Creoles, and, consequently, no *do*-support. What the Creoles have instead are immovable pre-verbal particles:

(24)   a. *Hi doz tiich yu?*
        b. **Doz hi tiich yu?*
            'Does he teach you?'

(25)   a. *Hi a kom?*
        b. **A hi kom?*
            'Is he coming?'

(26)   a. *Yu laik it?*
        b. **Duu yu laik it?*
            'Do you like it?'

Indeed, by comparison with Standard English, there is little movement of constituents in these languages.

The unavailability of inversion is directly responsible for non-inverted acrolectal speech like the following sentences, which users generally do not realise is not Standard English:

(27)   *Evriwon kud sii?*
        'Can everyone see?'

(28)   *Yuu-ool hɜd dhat?*
        'Did you all hear that?'

4. Derivational morphology

Some of the most common derivational affixes on metropolitan English nouns, verbs, and adjectives (but not adverbs) have been retained and are productive. There is no productive adverb affix, not even *-li*, essentially because no morphological distinction is made between descriptive, gradable words that are used adjectivally and adverbially (e.g., *priti, swiit*). Tables 2–4 display examples of productive affixes.

Table 2. Productive noun affixes

Noun Affix	Words
-nis	*chupidnis, hongrinis*
-sh{o~a}n	*salvēshan, badarēshan*
-yan	*Chrinidaadyan, Tubēgōnyan*
-ment	*betament, govament,*
-{o, a}-(man/wuman)	*tiicha(wuman), honta(man)*
-iiz	*chainiiz, japaniiz*
-ful	*beliful, spuunful*

Table 3. Productive verb affixes

Verb Affix	Words
ri-	*ripēnt, ribil*
ova-	*ōvadu, ōvaiit, ōvakuk*
dis-	*dislaik, disapoint*
mis-	*misondastan, mistēk, misbihēv*
on-	*ontai, onrap*

Table 4. Productive adjective affixes

Adjective Affix	Words
-abl	*ējabl, nolijabl, riidabl*
-iv	*aktiv, comesiv*
-ish	*redish, likrish, swiitish*

5.   Inflectional morphology

The languages have very few inflectional morphemes, which may be divided into two groups: 1) those that are only bound forms, and 2) those that function in both bound and free-standing capacities. The first group comprises the imperfective suffix (IMPERFV SUF) *-in* (which subcategorises as progressive suffix (PROG SUF) and habitual suffix (HAB SUF)); the attributive suffix (ATTRIB SUF) *-i* (usually on adjectives or nouns denoting colour, fruit, and size); and the adverbial suffix (ADV SUF) *-iin*. The second group comprises the morphemes *se(l)f, ya/hyee, de/dyee, so/sō, ōn*. Table 5 characterises the inflectional suffixes by syntactic category and phrasal syntax.

Table 5.   Inflectional suffixes by syntactic category and phrasal syntax

Inflectional Morpheme		Syntactic Category	Phrasal Syntax
BASILECT	**MESOLECT**		
	-in	IMPERFV SUF (PROG SUF, HAB SUF)	VP
-i		ATTRIB SUF	DP, AP
-iin		ADV SUF	VP
so	*sō*	ASSOC SUF	ADVP, DP
sef	*self*	RECI(PROCAL) SUF	DP, ADVP
ōn	*ōn*	POSS SUF	DP
ya, de	*hyee, dyee*	LOC SUF	DP, PP

The following sentences, phrases, or words illustrate the morphemes.

(29)   *Shi   tiich   -in*   *di klaas now.*
            V   PROG SUF

(30)   *Shi   kool   -in   mi evri nait.*
            V   HAB SUF

(31)   *A   griin   -i   /a   staach   -i   /a big -i.*
        A   SUF   /   N   ATTRIB SUF/   A   ATTRIB SUF

(32)   *Shi luk sik   -i   sik   -i.*
            A   ATTRIB SUF A   ATTRIB SUF

(33) *Mami gaan -iin*   /   *Mami gaan *iin di ruum.*
            V   ADV SUF

(34) *A   den   -sef   mi ge maad.*
             ADV   RECI SUF

(35) *Hii   -se(l)f   tel mi.*
           DP   RECI SUF

(36) *Iz   di dokta   -self   tel mi.*
               DP   RECI SUF

(37) *A   Kandia –se(l)f   tel mi.*
               DP   RECI SUF

(38) Dis   **-ya**   /Dat   **-de**
           DP   LOC SUF   /DP   LOC SUF

(39) *Dem   -ya*   /   *Dem   -de*
           DP   LOC SUF   /   D   LOC SUF

(40) *Dem bwai   -ya*   /Dem bwai -de
           DP   LOC SUF   /DP   LOC SUF

(41) *Ōva   -so*
           P   ASSOC SUF

(42) *Ten laik   hii   -so   kyãã priich tu mii.*
                        DP   ASSOC SUF

(43) *Iz   mai   -ōn.*
           DP   POSS SUF

6.   Non-affixal grammatical morphemes

6.1.   Preverbal markers

Verbs (including adjectival ones such as *swiit* and *sik*) are preceded by grammatical markers which variously carry aspect, tense, mood, and emphasis meanings, and which may be stressed (or high-toned) or unstressed (or low-toned). Tables 6 and 7 display these markers and their meanings. (The grave accent represents low stress/tone; the acute accent represents high stress/tone.)

Table 6.   Unstressed or low-tone pre-verbal markers in Tobagonian and Trinidadian

Grammatical Category	Basilectal Tobagonian	Mesolectal Trinbagonian
Imperfective (aspect)	*a*	
Future Habitual Modal (tense-aspect-mood)	*(g)o, àgò*	*(g)o;* *gō* (Trinidadian only*)*
Present Habitual (tense-aspect)		*doz (*and variants *do, oz, s)*
Remote Past (Tense)	*bin (*and variants *in, bi, bĩ, ĩ, min)*	*di(d)*
Past Imperfective (tense-aspect)	*bìnà (*and variants *ina, mìnà)*	*woz…in*
Contrafactual	*bìnà (*and variants *inà, mìnà), bìn(à)gò (*and variants *in(à)gò, mìn(à)gò)*	*di(d)…in, wòzgò, wùdà*
Modal of Intention	*fu, bìn-/mìnfù*	*tu, wòzgò, wòztù*

Table 7.   Stressed or high-tone pre-verbal markers in Tobagonian and Trinidadian

Grammatical Category	Basilectal Tobagonian	Mesolectal Trinbagonian
Past Completive/Perfect (tense-aspect)	*don*	*don*
Emphatic	*duu*	*duu*
Past Imperfective (tense-aspect)		*yuuz(z)tu*
Modal of obligation	*(h)áfù, bóngtù*	*(h)ávtù, bóngtù*

It is worth noting that these tables of pre-verbal markers are not complete overviews of the system because of the major role which the zero marker plays in the mix. The role of zero in Creole verb systems has been much debated and the full oppositional subset is discussed further under the section 7 below.

6.2.   (Pre)nominal markers

Nouns are modified by markers which participate in a semantic opposition of specificity vs. non-specificity. In that opposition, only demonstratives are stressed (with H tone). Tables 8 and 9 display the markers.

Table 8. Non-specific pre-nominal markers

Grammatical category	Basilectal Tobagonian	Mesolectal (Trinbagonian))
The unmodified bare (count) noun	*kyat (i.e., ø)*	Same
Quantifier	*Som~faiv kyat*	Same
Adjective	*Priti kyat*	Same
Noun	*Pusi kyat*	Same

Table 9. Specific prenominal markers

Grammatical category	Basilectal Tobagonian	Mesolectal (Trinbagonian)
Non-demonstrative specifiers	*(e.g., di, mi)*	Same
Demonstrative specifiers	*Da...ya, da...de, dem, dem...ya, dem...de*	*Dis...hyee, da(t)...dyee, dem, dem...hyee, dem...dyee*
Singulariser	*wãã*	Indefinite *a*
Name	*Anjela*	Same

6.3.   Pronouns

In both varieties, the pronouns generally both are opaque for case and participate in an unstressed-stressed opposition. Tables 10 and 11 categorise and list them. Unstressed pronouns can't stand alone in discourse, that is, by themselves outside a normal sentence (e.g., **Mi! *Shi! *De!*), but their stressed lengthened counterparts (*Mii! Shii! Dem!*) can.

Table 10. The basilectal Tobagonian pronoun paradigm

Category	Unstressed		Stressed		
	Subject	Object	Subject	Object	Disjunctive
1st per. sg.	*mi*	*mi*	*mii(so)*	*mii(so)*	*mii(so)*
2nd per. sg.	*yu/o*	*yu/o*	*yuu(so)*	*yuu(so)*	*yuu(so)*
3rd per. m sg.	*(h)i*	*am, om*	*(h)ii(so)*	*(h)ii(so)*	*(h)ii(so)*
3rd per. f sg.	*shi*	*am, om*	*shii(so)*	*shii(so)*	*shii(so)*
3rd per. n sg.	*i*	*om, am*			

Table 10. (continued)   The basilectal Tobagonian pronoun paradigm

Category	Unstressed		Stressed		
	Subject	Object	Subject	Object	Disjunctive
1ˢᵗ per. pl.	*wi*	*wi*	*wii(so),* *aawi(so)*	*wii(so),* *aawi(so)*	*wii(so),* *aawi(so)*
2ⁿᵈ per. pl.			*aayu(so)*	*aayu/o(so)*	*aayu/o(so)*
3ʳᵈ per. pl.	*de, dèm*	*dèm*	*dém(so)*	*dèm(so)* *dém(so)*	*dém(so)*

per. = person; *m* = masculine; *f* = feminine; *sg.* = singular; *n* = neuter; *pl.* = plural; *the grave accent* = low tone; *the acute accent* = high tone.

As can be seen in the basilectal paradigm, all the categories except the third person singular ones are opaque for case and participate in an unstressed-unstressed opposition; also the third person singular *dèm* (but not *de*) is ambivalent for case. In respect of the third person singular ones, there are the forms *am/om* which are used only as generalised objects (that is, they refer to masculine, feminine, and neuter referents). In addition, the unstressed neuter pronouns have no stressed counterparts. It is only the stressed pronouns that are used disjunctively.

Table 11.   The mesolectal Trinbagonian pronoun paradigm

Category	Unstressed		Stressed		
	Subject	Object	Subject	Object	Disjunctive
1ˢᵗ per. sg.	*a*	*mi*	*ai*	*mii(so)*	*mii(so)*
2ⁿᵈ per. sg.	*yu/o*	*yu/o*	*yuu(so)*	*yuu(so)*	*yuu(so)*
3ʳᵈ per. m sg.	*hi*	*im*	*hii(so)*	*hii(so)*	*hii(so)*
3ʳᵈ per. f sg.	*shi*	*shi,*	*shii(so)*	*shii(so)*	*shii(so)*
3ʳᵈ per. n sg.	*i*	*it*			
1ˢᵗ per. pl.	*wi*	*wi*	*wii(so)*	*wii(so)*	*wii(so)*
2ⁿᵈ per. pl.			*oolyu/o(so)*	*oolyu/o(so)*	*oolyu/o(so)*
3ʳᵈ per. pl.	*de*	*dèm*	*dém(so)*	*dèm(so)* *dém(so)*	*dém(so)*

In the mesolectal system, there are two specifications absent from the basilectal system. First, there is no general third person object; rather, each of the three genders has its own object. But of the three, only the third person feminine is opaque for case since the exponent, *shi*, also functions as subject. Secondly, in the third person plural category the subject is distinguished from the object in not having the coda *m*; that is, *dèm* is not a mesolectal subject. And, again, it is only the stressed pronouns that are used disjunctively.

Although we have treated these forms as if they are only pronouns, it must be pointed out that they also function as possessive adjectives.

6.4.   Prepositions

Both varieties make use of the English inventory of prepositions, but there are at least six prepositions – five basilectal and one mesolectal – that deserve to be highlighted as they are strictly Creole in phonology or syntax or semantics. They are given in Table 12.

Table 12.   Basilectal and mesolectal prepositions

Basilect	Mesolect	English
a		in, on, at, to, into, from
iina		in, inside
ton (plus DP)		according to
pan		on
pantap		on (top of)
laka		like
	in	to

Basilectal *pan*, *pantap*, and *laka* are used exactly like their English counter-parts, but not *a*, *iina*, or *ton*. The (unstressed) preposition *a* is the most seman-tically economical of the lot, encompassing the spatial meanings of location, source, and goal of various English prepositions, as in (44) below:

(44)   a. *Hi kom owt [a Delafōd]* (source).
            'He's come from Delaford.'
        b. *Hi hit mi [a mi jabōn]* (location).
            'He hit me on the jaw.'
        c. *Aa, Kiini bwai, yu kom [a wool]* (location).
            'Ah, Kini boy, you've come into the world.'
        d. *Hi de [a Shaalotvil] a mek schraif* (location).
            'He is in/at Charlotteville stirring up trouble.'

    e. *Mi a go [a shap]* (goal).
      'I am going to the shop.'

Iina, a combination of *iin* and *a*, is a stressable version of *a* (with H tone on *iin*) and covers only the spatial notion of location. It appears in sentences such as (45) where it allows the translations 'in', 'into', and 'in(side)':

(45)   a. *Mi no hav no pat$_i$ fu put am **iina**___$_i$.*
        'I don't have any pot to put it in.'
    b. *Hi daiv **iina** di riva.*
        'He dove into the river.'
    c. *I de **iina** di jakit pakit.*
        'It's in(side) the jacket pocket.'

In (45a) in particular, it licenses gapping, and is able to do so because its *iin* component is stressed in final position, unlike *a* which is always unstressed, and which cannot occur sentence-finally as a free-standing morpheme (*Mi no hav no pat$_i$ fu put am ***a***___$_i$*).

    Ton (< *turn*) is a perspectival preposition that is followed typically by speech-capable DPs, as in (46):

(46)   ***Ton** Aava, dat an God fẽs hi no go si.*
        'According to Ava, that and God's face he will not see.'

Mesolectal *in* functions as a goal preposition, as in:

(47)   a. *A gō-in in tong.*
    b. *Shi gō-in **in** big skuul now.*

However, to express movement to a goal, it is typical to leave out the prepositions *a*, *in*, and *tu*, as in:

(48)   *A gō-in {tong, San Fanandō, Amerika}.*

6.5.   Interrogative/relative words

There are certain words which deserve comment. Tables 13 and 14 distribute them between basilect and mesolect, with Table 13 displaying the interrogative list and Table 14 the relative list.

Table 13.   Selected Trinbagonian interrogative words

Basilect	Mesolect	English
wa	*wo*	what
huu (-person N) *(singular)*	*huu* (-person N) (singular)	who
huu-an-huu (plural)	*huu*	who
wich-wan (singular)	*wich-won* (singular)	which
wich-paat	*wich-paat, we*	where
({*wa-, we-*})*mek*)	*wo* + *mēk as V*	why

Table 14.   Selected Trinbagonian relative words

Basilect	Mesolect	English
we	*we*	that, who, which, where
wich-paat	*wich-paat*	where
({*wa-, we-*})*mek*)	*why*	why

The tables reveal some interesting facts by comparison with analogous concepts in English. There are more interrogative than relative words. The basilect has a plural form (*huu-an-huu*) for the person interrogative. Both basilect and mesolect have a bi-morphemic word for the singular non-person interrogative: they combine *wich* with *wan/won*. The basilect has a bi-morphemic word for the location and reason notions (*wich-paat, wa/we mek*), while the mesolect has one only for the location notion (*wich-paat*) but two separate words for the reason notion (*wo* plus the verb *mēk* heading a clause). In both basilect and mesolect, there is only one form (*we*) for relating to person, non-person, and place subjects.

The listed words are illustrated below:

(49)   *{Wa, Wo} yo woont?*
       'What do you want?'

(50)   *Huu-man yo tookin bowt?*
       'What man are you talking about?'

(51)   *Huu-an-huu woz in di kaa?*
       'Who are the persons that were in the car?'

(52)   **Wich-wan** *yo want?*
'Which do you want?'

(53)   **Wich-paat** *yu put di buk?*
'Where did/have you put the book?'

(54)   **(We-)mek** *yu tel am dat?*
'Why did you tell him/her that?'

(55)   **Wo mēk** *yo tel im dat?*
'Why did you tell him/her that?'

(56)   *Da iz di man* **we** *fain mi wolet.*
'That is the man who found my wallet.'

(57)   *Shi put shi bag on di ting* **we** *doz spin rong.*
'She put her bag on the thing that spins around.'

(58)   *Da iz di skuul* **we** *mi chail doz gō tu.*
'That is the school that my child goes to.'

(59)   *Da iz di plēs* **wich-paat** *de keri shi.*
'That is the place where they took her.'

(60)   *Da iz di riizn* **mek** *mi tel yu.*
'That is the reason why I told you.'

6.6.   Post-subject adverbs

Both varieties have a number of adverbs that fill a syntactic slot just after the
subject of a sentence, or just before the main negators *no/ē*, much like the slot
that an IP adverb like *certainly* fills in a language like English. Because of the
inflectional poverty of the varieties, we will use the label *post-subject adverbs*
in preference to IP adverbs. Common examples of these adverbs are bolded in
the illustrations below:

(61)   *A* **taiyad** *tel im not tu kiip baad kompani.*
'I am fed up telling him not to keep bad company.'

(62)   *Hi* **mosi** *no a kom agēn.*
'He probably is no longer coming.'

(63)   *Hi* **maad** *kom tel mii dat?*
'He isn't crazy enough to come and tell me that!'

(64) *A **don** ẽ di laik shi.*
      'I already don't like her.'

(65) *Hi **maasta** plē gēmz on di kompyuuta.*
      'He's fond of playing games on the computer.'

(66) *Shi **wel** kos op shi hozban.*
      'She roundly cursed her husband.'

(67) *Yo **gud** iit mi fuud laas wiik.*
      'You ate a lot of my food last week.'

(68) *Da gyal de **huu** feel shi nice!*
      'That girl thinks she is really beautiful!'

(Incidentally, of the adverbs highlighted *huu* (68) is the only one peculiar to Tobagonian speech.)

6.7.   Reportive particles

By *reportive particle*, we mean a word that introduces reported information in clauses. There are three such particles – basilectal *se* and mesolectal *dat* and *dat-how*. *Se* is used optionally with a translation like 'that' after reporting and belief-expressing verbs like *tel* and *biliiv*, as in (69) and (70):

(69) *[Hi tel mi] (**se**) [hi naa kom agēn].*
      'He told me that he wasn't coming any longer.'

(70) *[Mii no beliiv] (**se**) [hi ago marrid shi].*
      'I don't believe he's going to marry her.'

In these sentences, it is substitutable by *dat* and *dat-how*. After other kinds of verb, however, it is obligatory:

(71) *[Hi de a hi ruum] **se** [hi a stodi].*
      'He is in his room ostensibly studying.'

(72) *[Hi gaan hōm] **se** [hi a go du hi hōmwok].*
      'He's gone home ostensibly to do his homework.'

6.8.   The particles *fu, fo, fa*

Fu, fo and *fa* are grammatical items that divide up infinitive, possessive, and interrogative functions amongst themselves. *Fu* and *fa* are basilectal, with *fu* functioning as an infinitive and possessive marker, and *fa* only as an interrogative marker. *Fo* has infinitive and interrogative functions and is mesolectal Tobagonian in respect of both, but mesolectal Trinidadian in respect of the interrogative function only, the Trinidadian infinitive marker typically being *tu*. As a possessive marker, *fu-* is an emphatic prefix; as a possessive marker, *-fa* is a suffix; and as interrogative markers, *-fa* and *-fo* are discontinuous suffixes. Table 15 captures these facts.

Table 15.   Varietal distribution of the particles *fu*, *fo*, and *fa*

Basilect	Mesolect	Function
fu	*fo, tu*	infinitive
fu		possessive
-fa	*-fo*	interrogative

The following sentences illustrate how the particles are used:

(73)   *Mi waant {fu, fo, *fa} sliip.*
        'I want to sleep.'

(74)   *Hi kaal mi {fu, fo, *fa} tel mi no bada].*
        'He called me to tell me not to bother....'

(75)   *{Fu-mii, *Fo-mii, *Fa-mii} pērans an dem] no bina biit.*
        'MY parents did not beat (us).'

(76)   *{Fu-huu, *Fo-huu, *Fa-huu} pikni dat?*
        'WHOSE child is that?'

(77)   *We yu du dat {-fa, -fo, *-fu}?*
        'Why did you do that?'

(78)   *We yu a bada mi {-fa, fo, *fu}?*
        'Why are you bothering me?'

(79)   *{Huu-fa, *Huu-fo, *Huu-fu} dat?*
        'Whose is that?'

6.9.   Existentials

The existentials in the two varieties are displayed in Table 16.

Table 16.   Basilectal and mesolectal existentials

Semantic Category	Basilect	Mesolect	English
Location	*it ge(t)*	*it ha(v)*	there is/are (even stress on both kinds of words)
Possession	*fu ge(t)*	*tu hav*	to have
Existence	*Luk…!*	*Luk…!*	Here is/are…, There is/are…! (stress on 'there')
Existence	*Luku…!*	*Luk at…!*	Expression introducing abundance
Location	*fu de*	Absence of copula	to be

The following sentences illustrate their use:

(80)   *{It ge(t), It hav* chrii kow iina di yaad.*
'There are three cows in the yard.'

(81)   *Ōva hyee {get, hav} tumoch bush.*
'There's too much bush over here.'

(82)   *Ōva hyee {get, hav}.*
'There is some over here.'

(83)   *Luk shi kom-in.*
'Look! She's coming.'

(84)   *{Luku, Luk at} piipu!*
'What a large crowd of people!'

(85)   *Luku wuman!*
'What a large number of women!'

(86)   *Luku flowa!*
'What an abundance of flour!'

Location *it get/hav* and possession *fu get/hav* may or may not be followed by a DP complement; location *fu de* must be followed by a locative word or phrase (e.g., **Hi de*); and existence *luk, luku,* and *luk at* must be followed by a DP (e.g., **Luku!; *Luk at!*). *Luku* and *luk at,* in particular, must be followed by mass nouns or plural count nouns (e.g., *Luku wãã jombi!*). *Luk* is the item that must precede singular count nouns (e.g., *Luk a jombi!*). *Luku* therefore seems to have a generic suffix in its final *-u.*

6.10.   Preclausal warning particles

In both basilect and mesolect, there are at least two forms, *main* and *tikē,* that are used before clauses, which must be positive, to alert the hearer to danger. Obviously phonological restructurings of English *mind* and *take care,* they are used as in (87-90),where the clause is bracketed:

(87)   ***Main** [yu brēk di glaas].*
        'Be careful not to break the glass.'

(88)   ***Main** *[yu no/ē brēk di glaas].*

(89)   ***Tikē** [yu brēk di glaas].*
        'Be careful not to break the glass.'

(90)   ***Tikē** *[yu no/ē brēk di glaas].*

7.   The verb system

In the verb system, there are three main types of structure: main verb structure (e.g., *Shi kuk di fuud*), copula structure (e.g., *Shi de a tong*), and copula-less structures (e.g., *Shi sik*). As suggested in our treatment of sentence structure above, the system is one in which main verbs (e.g., *kuk*), adjectival verbs (e.g., *sik*), and copulas (e.g., *de*) are modified by pre-verbal tense, aspect, and mood (TAM) markers (and, in one case, the aspect suffix *-ing*), with the aspect ones having the greatest frequency of usage. These markers are distributed in discourse in relation to their denotation of background time, focus time, and different kinds of mood. Tables 17 and 18 display the basilectal and mesolectal TAM distribution respectively.

Table 17. The basilectal TAM distribution in discourse

Background time		Focus time						Mood		
T	T-A	A				A-T	T	Confac	Past	Focus
Rem Past	Past Impfv	Past Compl/ Perf	Pfv	Impfv	Hab	Impfv Fut	Fut			
										(h)áfú,
bìn	bìnà	dón	Ø dúú	à	gò	àgò	gò	bìnà bìnàgò bìngò	bìnfù	bóngtù gò kyằ, kù fù

(*Rem = Remote; Impfv = Imperfective; Compl = Completive; Perf = Perfect; Pfv = Perfective; Hab = Habitual; Fut = Future; Confac = Contrafactual*)

Table 18. The mesolectal TAM distribution in discourse

Background time		Focus time						Mood		
T	T-A	A				T-A	T	Confac	Past	Focus
Rem Past	Past Impfv	Past Hab	Past Compl/ Perf	Pfv	Impfv	Pres Hab	Fut			
										(h)ávtù, bóngtù
dìd wòz	dìd...ìn wòz...ìn	yúúztù	dón	Ø dúú	-ìn	dòz gò	gò	wòzgò wùdà	wòztù	gò k(y)ã, kù tù

The markers occur in different sequences in the different types of verb structure. In main-verb and copula-less structures, typical maximal sequences are *bìnàgò, dón bìnà, dón dìd...ìn, dón wòz...ìn, bìn háfù, dìd bóngtù, yúúztù, wòzgò, wòztù, wùdà, bìnfù, dòz k(y)ắắ,* and *gò k(y)ắắ*. There are markers that do not co-occur with any others; they are perfective emphasiser *dúú*, habituals *dòz* and *yúúztù*, and modals *k(y)ằ* and *kù*.

In copula structures, the copulas select pre-verbal particles depending on their (own) semantics. There are three copulas – equative *a*, locative *de*, and naming *nēm*. Equative *a* is basilectal and it maximally selects the sequence *dón bìn*. Locative *dè* is also basilectal and it selects *dón bìnà, dón bìn, bìn háfù, bìn bóngtù, bìngò, bìnàgò* and *bìnfù*. *Nēm* is both basilectal and mesolectal. Basilectally, it selects *dón bìnà, dón bìn, bìnàgò, bìngò,* and *bìnfù*. Mesolectally, it selects *dón dì(d), wòzgò, wòztù, dìd (h)ávtù, dìd bóngtù,* and *wùdà*.

In a recent analysis of Caribbean Creole markers as they have been variously ascribed different labels, Youssef (2002) synthezises past analyses (e.g., Solomon 1993; Winford 1993) of the oppositional systems of labelling. The paper ascribes a comprehensive perfective label to the zero marker as a key marker in the perfective-imperfective opposition, which label holds across the board in the tense-aspect system and stands against imperfective marking in *bin, bina* and *a* (basilectal) and in *did, woz* + *-in* and *-in* in the mesolect. The following sentences, reproduced from mesolectal Tobagonian data in Youssef and James (1999: 609), support this analysis:

(91)   *Hi hyee wel kot. It **luk** gud.*
        'His hair is well cut. It looks good.' (Reference time present; focus immediate; state seen as a whole)

(92)   *Hi **skoo** a gōl.*
        'He scored a goal.' (Reference time past; focus immediate; event seen as a whole)

(93)   *Yestadē hi **tek** a 2-liita batl an hi **kari** it to skuul.*
        'Yesterday he takes a 2-litre bottle and he carries it to school.'
        (Reference time past; focus immediate; events seen as wholes)

Whatever the most precise tense-aspect label for events/states, perfective marking links them all and covers their different reference times, in addition to the immediate focus of the speaker – that which, from a discourse perspective, defines the foreground role in narrative. This usage of Ø may be ranged in opposition to that represented by, for example, preverbal *bin*, a marker which affirms both the anteriority of an event to another reference-time event and the background status of that event, as in:

(94)   *Ting **bin** chiip. Di moni **bin** smaal rēli, bot yu kuda mek am dō. An den mi kom an mi get marid.*
        'Things were cheap. The money was small, really, but you could have made it though. And then I got married.'

The example discourse above provides the opportunity to consider an interesting narrative structure – *kom an* + *verb. Kom an* seems to have the function of introducing an important event (such as a marriage) in a narrative.

8.   Negation

Basilectally, there is one negator – free-standing *no*; mesolectally, there are four – free-standing *ẽ*, *dõ*, *din*, and the clitic *-n*. *No* occurs before main verbs, the copulas *de* and *nēm* (but not the copula *a*), and all the basilectal pre-verbal markers except *don*. *Ẽ* occurs before main verbs, the copula *nēm* (but not the copula *iz*), and only the markers (*g*)*o* and *tu*. *Dõ* occurs only before main verbs. *Din* occurs only before *yuuztu*. And *-n* attaches only to the mesolectal forms *doz*, *di*(*d*), *wu*(*d*), and *ku*(*d*). Table 19 displays their association with the relevant markers.

Table 19.   The association of negators with basilectal and mesolect preverbal markers

Grammatical Category	Basilect Marker	Negator	Mesolect Marker	Negator
Imperfective (aspect)	*a*	*no* (before)	*-in*	*NA*
Past Completive/ Perfect (tense-aspect)	*don*	*no* (after)	*don*	*ẽ, dõ, din* (after)
Future Habitual Modal (tense-aspect-mood)	(*g*)*o, ago*	*no* (before)	(*g*)*o*	*ẽ* (before)
Present Habitual (tense-aspect)			*doz* (and variants *do, oz,* but not *z*)	*-n*
Emphatic	*duu*	*NA*	*duu*	*NA*
Remote Past (tense)	*bin* (and variants *in, bi, bĩ, ĩ, min*)	*no* (before)	*di*(*d*), *woz*	*-n*
Past Imperfective (tense-aspect)	*bina* (and variants *ina, mina*)	*no* (before)	*yuuztu*	*din* (*before*)
Contrafactual	*bina* (and variants *ina, mina*), *bin*(*a*)*go* (and variants *in*(*a*)*go, min*(*a*)*go*)	*no* (before)	*wozgo, wuda*	*-n* (after *woz*) *-n* (after *wu*(*d*))
Modal of Intention	*fu, bin-/minfu*	*no* (before)	*tu* *woztu*	*ẽ* (*before*) *-n* (*after woz*)
Modal of Possibility / Ability	*kyà̃*	*no* (before)	*ku*(*d*)	*ku*(*d*)*-n* (past meaning)

In the syntax of negation, the markers *don*, *doz*, *go* and *k(y)à/k(y)ã̃́* and the absence of negators before the copulas *a* and *iz* require special comment. *Don* is the only marker that is not preceded by a free-standing negator; indeed, all such negators can occur immediately after it. *Doz* and *go* are the only markers that are negated by a modal, namely post-posed *k(y)áắ*, apart from the clitic *-n* (in the case of *doz*) and the pre-occurring negators *no* and *ẽ* (in the case of *go*). So that we have *doz k(y)áắ* (which translates as 'cannot' but combines the meanings habituality and negative possibility / ability); and we have *go k(y)áắ* (which translates as 'cannot' but combines the meanings future and negative possibility/ability). The pair *kyà/kyáắ* are differentiated by contrastive vowel tone and vowel length, with low tone and shortness denoting possibility / ability and high tone and length denoting negative possibility / ability. Finally, the absence of negators before the copulas *a* and *iz* is more accurately expressed as the phonetic disappearance of the copulas in negative sentences, as in {*Hi a dakta*; *Hi iz dokta*} versus {*Hi no dakta*; *Hi ẽ dokta*}. The copulas seem to be incorporated in whatever negators apply; intuitively, the latter seem to be *no* and *ẽ*.

Double negation occurs in both basilect and mesolect (e.g., *mi no nō notn*; *a ẽ nō notn* 'I don't know anything'), as indeed in many varieties of English. But there is an emphatic type of double negation that has hardly been described in the literature, as is illustrated in mesolectal sentences below:

(95)   *Shi ẽ nō priti.*
        'She is NOT pretty.'

(96)   *Shi ẽ nō dokta.*
        'She is NOT a doctor.'

(97)   *Shi ẽ nō laik im; shi jos doz took tu im, da iz ool.*
        'She DOESN'T love him; she only talks to him, that's all.'

As sentences (95–97) show, the normal mesolectal clause negator *ẽ* (basilectal *no* functions in the same way too) comes immediately before another negative word (*nō*) before an adjective (95), a noun (96), and a verb phrase (97). The critical observation is that *nō* emphasises the proposition in the normal negative phrase (e.g., not being pretty in *shi ẽ priti*), and it does so by having the long tense vowel *ō* and interposing itself between the normal negator and the content part of the phrase.

9.   The noun system

The noun system is one in which the bare (i.e., unanalysed) noun is modified by a number of (mostly) grammatical words. The typical linear surface representation is as follows:

> *[determiners] [numerals] [adjectives, nouns] bare noun [plural suffix]*
> *[pluraliser] [phrases]*

A phrase which illustrates this representation is:

(98)   *[Di] [faiv] [priti] kyat[s] [(an) dem] [we de iina di kowch]*

Some typical phrases are:

(99)   Unmodified bare noun (N) (e.g., *kyat*)

(100)   NP (e.g., *moda kyat*)

(101)   AP (e.g., *hongri daag*)

(102)   NUM(eral)P (e.g. *faiv kyat*)

(103)   DP (e.g., *di kyat; wãã kyat, dem kyat*)

(104)   PL(ural)P (e.g., *di kyat (an) dem*)

The grammatical (or non-lexical) categories of modifier are illustrated in Table 20.

Table 20.   Basilectal and mesolectal grammatical noun modifiers

Modifier	Basilect	Mesolect
Determiner		
Specifying articles	*di, mi, shi, aayu*	*di, mi, shi, ool-yu*
Non-specifying articles	*som*	*som*
Name	*Kandia, Akini*	*Kandia, Akini*
Singulariser	*wãã*	*a*
Demonstratives	*da...ya / (de), dem...ya / de, dem*	*dis...(hyee), da...(dyee), dem...hyee / dyee, dem*
Numeral	*tuu, faiv*	*tuu, faiv*
Pluraliser	*-dem, -de*	*-(an) dem, de*

A word on the unmodified bare noun, determiner phrase, and plural phrase. Just as the main verb (V) is bare or unanalysed, so is the noun. Unmodified, it allows the inference of non-specific reference where both count and mass nouns are concerned. But the count noun in particular encodes non-individuated non-specific reference; it refers to a class of referents, not to specific members of the class. In the determiner phrase, the singulariser and demonstratives deserve further comment. The singulariser, *wãã*, lacks the generic value of Standard English *a(n)*; it is wholly specific in its denotation, meaning only 'one member of the class of referents'. Where the demonstratives are concerned, basilec-tally, discontinuous *da...ya/(de)* is singular while discontinuous *dem...(de/ya)* is plural. The mesolectal counterparts are typically *dis...(hyee), da(t) (dyee)*, and *dem...(hyee/dyee)*. The plural phrase is specially interesting because the pluraliser *(an) dem* is discontinuously tied to pre-nominal specifying articles; no pluralized noun can stand apart from a specifying article or a (specifying) name (e.g., *di **kyat** (an) dem* vs **kyat* (an) dem*; *Kandia (an) dem*). The pluralis-er comes in an emphatic-non-emphatic pair, with *(an) dem* being the emphatic item and *de* being the non-emphatic one. The former occurs in both subject and object position while the latter is limited to subject position, as in:

(105)　a.　***Kandia dè / (an) dém** gaan a maakit.*
　　　　b.　*M'aa go bai **Ava *dè / (an) dém**.*
　　　　c.　*Hi stap taak to **Ava *dè / (an) dém**.*

The noun system is underlain by a basic semantic opposition between the fea-tures *specificity* and *non-specificity*, as illustrated in Table 21 below. In this, it may be distinguished from the opposition of *definite* versus *non-definite* estab-lished for the Standard.

Table 21.　The semantics of the Tobagonian noun phrase

SPECIFICITY	NON-SPECIFICITY
di (faiv) (priti) kyat(s) an dem (a specific group of cats; *an dem* pluralises *kyat*; *s* confirms that it is referents of the same class)	*(priti) kyat* (reference unspecified)
	faiv (priti) kyat (five unspecified cats, i.e., any five cats)
dem (priti) kyat(s) (an dem) (plural; a specific group of cats; *an dem* is a reflex retention and provides emphasis)	*som (priti) kyat* (unspecified number of cats)
shi (priti) kyat (a specific cat)	*Kandia an dem* (a specific Candia with unspecified associates)
wãã (priti) kyat (a specific cat)	
da (priti) kyat (ya) (a specific cat)	
da (priti) kyat (de) (a specific cat)	

Table 21. (continued)   The semantics of the Tobagonian noun phrase

SPECIFICITY	NON-SPECIFICITY
dem (priti) kyat (ya) (specific cats)	
dem (priti) kyat (de) (specific cats)	
Kandia (a specific person)	
di Kandia (a specific person)	
di Kandia an dem (specific persons each named Candia)	

10.   Conclusion

In an overview chapter of this nature, it is impossible to either describe all the lexical and morphosyntactic patterns and processes in the varieties being reported on or show the social patterning of lexical and grammatical items. What we have done is to present the essential parts of the lexical and morphosyntactic system, identifying in the process signature forms, uses, and processes. We have presented the basilectal system, which sets the Tobagonian community apart from the Trinidadian community, as well as the mesolectal system, which is substantially shared by both communities. The Trinidadian and Tobagonian speech community has its own Standard variety, but the main burden of everyday public interaction is carried by the mesolect, with private interaction conducted typically also in the mesolect in Trinidad but typically in the basilect in Tobago.

It is important to note that particular forms in the mesolect are distributed differently both between Tobago and Trinidad and between particular groups of speakers in both islands, depending on factors such as socio-economic background and level of education. But unfortunately, there is very little sociolinguistic work on Tobago and Trinidad, and such work has focused on distributional differences in respect of the verb system. Youssef (2001) is an example of such work, and it found, for instance, that there was a significantly lower usage of *does* by older rather than younger speakers and, further, that the form *does be* + *-in*, which, like basilectal *a*, links both habitual and continuous functions, was used specifically by younger people who argued, in interview, for a strong Creole identity.

Future research needs to focus on the distributional difference of the full range of morphosyntactic forms between Tobago and Trinidad, as well as between different social groups in both islands as the varieties continue to evolve in time. It would improve our understanding of the social development of the peoples who speak them, in particular, and about language development and change, in general.

Exercises and study questions

1. Compare the inflectional morphology of Tobagonian with that of another basilectal English-lexicon Creole. Pay particular attention to the notions denoted by the inflections.

2. Show how the syntax of the Creoles of Trinidad and Tobago compensates for their paucal inflectional morphology.

3. Discuss five ways in which the Tobagonian basilect is morphosyntactically distinguishable from the mesolect of Trinidad and Tobago.

4. Discuss the relationship between preverbal particles and non-inverted questions in the Creoles.

5. Using focaliser structures as a basis, examine whether there is constituent movement in the Creoles.

6. From the information provided in this chapter on morphemes distinguished by stress/tone and rhyme length, analyse which discourse categories of message take stressed elements and which do not. (You may have to define stress as subcategorising high tone and long vowels, in part.)

7. The basilectal preposition *iina* is presented as the stressed version of *a*. Is the argument adduced convincing?

8. *Huu-an-huu* is presented as the plural form of interrogative *huu*. Research other Creoles for its occurrence.

9. Is 'post-subject adverb' an appropriate label for the phenomena it is claimed to describe? Or is another term such as 'IP adverb' more suitable?

10. Investigate the functional distribution of *fu*, *fo*, and *fa* (or their analogues) in other Creoles.

11. Are the sequences of preverbal particles in basilectal Tobagonian typical of other basilects? What interesting things do they tell us about TAM structure in universal grammar?

12. In what other varieties of English is *n* an emphatic negator after the normal negator in double negation structures?

13. How valid is it to hold that the Creoles of Trinidad and Tobago are underlain by a semantic opposition of *specificity vs non-specificity* in the noun system but that StE is underlain by one of *definiteness vs non-definiteness*?

Selected references

Please consult the General references for titles mentioned in the text but not included in the references below. For a full bibliography see the accompanying CD-ROM.

Allsopp, Richard
  1980   How does the creole lexicon expand? In: Valdman and Highfield (eds.), 89–107.
Edwards, Walter
  1995   A sociolinguistic exploration of the usage of the aspectual marker *don* in AAVE in Detroit. Paper presented at the 24th NWAVE conference, University of Pennsylvania, October 1995.
  2000   Aspectal *don* in AAVE and its relation to Guyanese Creole *don* + V. Paper presented at the 13th Biennial Conference, Society for Caribbean Linguistics, 16–19 August, UWI, Mona, Jamaica.
Hancock, Ian
  1980   Lexical expansion in Creole languages. In: Valdman and Highfield (eds.), 63–88.
James, Winford and Valerie Youssef
  2002   *The Languages of Tobago: Genesis, Structure, and Perspectives.* School of Continuing Studies: University of the West Indies, St. Augustine, Trinidad.
Solomon, Denis
  1993   *The Speech of Trinidad: A Reference Grammar.* School of Continuing Studies: University of the West Indies, St. Augustine, Trinidad.
Valdman, Albert and Arnold Highfield (eds.)
  1980   *Theoretical Orientations in Creole Studies.* New York: Academic Press.
Winer, Lise
  fc   *Dictionary of the English/Creole of Trinidad and Tobago.* Toronto: University of Toronto Press.
Winford, Donald
  1994   Variability in the use of perfect *have* in Trinidadian English: A problem of categorical and semantic mismatch. *Language Variation and Change* 5: 141–187.

Youssef, Valerie
    1996   Varilingualism: The competence underlying code-mixing in Trinidad and Tobago. *Journal of Pidgin and Creole Languages* 11: 1–22.
    2001   Age-grading in the Anglophone Creole of Tobago. *World Englishes* 20: 29–46.
    2002   How perfect is perfective marking? An analysis of some terminological problems in the description of some tense-aspect categories in creoles. *Journal of Pidgin and Creole Languages* 18: 1–24.
Youssef, Valerie and Winford James
    1999   Grounding via tense-aspect in Tobagonian Creole: Discourse strategies across a creole continuum. *Linguistics* 37: 597–624.

Surinamese creoles: morphology and syntax[*]

Donald Winford and Bettina Migge

1.   Introduction

The creoles of Suriname diverge to a considerable extent from English, their primary lexifier language, and are therefore often referred to as "radical" creoles. They include Sranan, Aluku or Boni, Kwinti, Matawai, Ndjuka or Okanisi, Pamaka, and Saamaka. Sociohistorical and linguistic evidence suggest that they all have their origins in the early creole varieties that emerged on the plantations of Suriname in the late 17th to early 18th century. Modern Sranan is a direct continuation of this early contact language while the other creoles, also referred to as maroon creoles, split off from it as a result of their founders' flight from the Surinamese plantations. Sranan is spoken both as a first language and as a lingua franca for inter-group communication throughout the country and in western French Guiana. The other languages used to be spoken only in the interior of the rain forest in socio-politically semi-autonomous communities founded by escaped slaves in the early to mid 18th century. The Aluku, Ndjuka and Pamaka reside in the eastern part of Suriname and western French Guiana along the Marowijne river (Aluku, Ndjuka, Pamaka) and its tributaries, the Tapanahoni river (Ndjuka) and the Lawa river (Aluku). Their community languages are entirely mutually intelligible but differ somewhat in phonology and lexicon. They are best viewed as dialects of a common language that we refer to as the Eastern Maroon Creole (EMarC). Saamaka and Matawai are also highly mutually intelligible. They are spoken in communities with the same name, which are located in the western part of Suriname along the Suriname river (Saamaka) and the Saramaka river (Matawai). The Kwinti reside on the Coppename river. Their language is linguistically intermediate between the two main clusters. With the increase in migration towards the coast, due to socioeconomic considerations, these varieties are today also well represented in the coastal urban centers of Suriname (Paramaribo, Albina, Mongo) and, with the exception of Matawai and Kwinti, in the urban centers of French Guiana (St. Laurent, Kourou, Cayenne, Mana) (see also Smith and Haabo, this volume). The Saamaka and Ndjuka each number about 50,000 people while the Aluku, Matawai and Pamaka each number roughly 6,000. The Kwinti are the smallest group, they count roughly 500 members. Unless otherwise indicated, the sample sentences come from recordings of natural conversations and formal elicitations carried out by the authors.

2.   Tense, mood and aspect

Categories of tense, mood and aspect, as well as negation (see section 3.4.), are expressed by invariant preverbal forms. The Surinamese creoles share a common set of TMA categories, though some of the forms that express them vary across the creoles.

2.1.   Tense

Categories of tense include a (relative) Past, expressed by *ben* (Sranan), *be* (EMarC), *bi* (Saamaka), and a Future, expressed by *o* (< *go*) (see also Veenstra 1996: 12–14):

(1)   EMarC | *Alen* | *be* | *kai.* |
|---|---|---|
| Rain | PAST | fall |

'It rained.'

(2)   Saamaka | *Mi* | *o* | *sikiifi* | *wan* | *biifi.* |
|---|---|---|---|---|
| I | FUT | write | a | letter |

'I'll write a letter.'

2.2.   Aspect

Categories of aspect include Imperfective, expressed by (*d*)*e* in Sranan and the EMarC, and by *ta* (< *tan* 'stay') in Saamaka. They mark situations as habitual, progressive or continuous. Completive (Perfect) aspect is expressed by VP-final *kaba* (< Port. *acabar* 'finish'). It indicates that a situation is completed or it marks the result of a process. The unmarked verb conveys perfective aspect, and can be interpreted in various ways, depending on the context.

(3) | Saamaka | a. | *Mi* | *tá* | *wáka.* |
|---|---|---|---|---|
| EmarC | b. | *Mi* | *e* | *waka.* |
| | | I | IMPFV | walk |

'I'm walking.' or 'I usually walk.'

(4)   EMarC | *A* | *nyan* | *kaba.* |
|---|---|---|
| she | eat | COMPL |

'She's already eaten.'

(5) Sranan   *A*   *kownu dede.*
                      DET (sg) king die
                      'The king has died.'

2.3. Modality

The Surinamese creoles also have a rich system of modality, covering a range of meanings associated with types of possibility (i.e., the senses of 'can') and necessity (i.e., the senses of 'must').

2.3.1. Possibility

Deontic senses of possibility include learned ability, physical ability, permission and general ability (ability constrained by social or moral law). Learned ability is expressed by the form *sabi* 'know' (< Portuguese *sabir* 'know') in all the creoles.

(6) Sranan   *A*   *pikin*   *sabi*   *swen* *bun.*
                      DET (sg) child   know swim good
                      'The child can swim well.'

There are some significant differences among the creoles in the way they express the other types of root possibility. Physical ability, permission and general ability are all expressed by the modal *sa* (< Dutch *zal* 'will') in the EMarC and Saamaka.

(7) Pamaka   *A*   *taanga. A sa   opo wan ondo   kilo.*
                 He   strong he MOD lift one hundred kilo
                 'He's strong. He can lift a hundred kilos.'

(8) Saamaka *Aaii, di*   *mii sa   fika   duumi ku   mi.*
                 Yes DET (sg) child MOD remain sleep with me
                 'The boy can stay here tonight.'

By contrast, Sranan uses *kan* or *man* for (positive) physical ability, *kan* or *mag* (< Dutch) for permission, and *kan* for general ability.

(9) Sranan a. *A*   *pikin kan/man opo ondro   kilo.*
                    DET (sg) child can/can lift hundred kilo
                    'The child can lift a hundred kilos.'
         b. *A*   *boi mag tan   dya tide   neti.*
                    DET (sg) boy may stay here today night
                    'The boy can stay here tonight.'

Under negation, all types of ability (except learned ability) are expressed by *sa* in Saamaka, whereas the EMarC uses *man* or *poi* (Ndjuka).

(10)   Saamaka   *Di   mujee   dɛ   woyo   booko. Á   sa   si.*
                   DET (sg) woman   there eye   break   NEG can   see
                   'That woman is blind. She cannot see.'

(11)   Pamaka   *A   boi á   man tan   ya   tide   neti.*
                   DET (sg) boy NEG can stay   here today night
                   'The boy cannot stay here tonight.'

Sranan never uses *sa* to express any kind of negative ability, choosing *kan* or *mag* for permission, and *kan* or *man* for the other types.

All of the creoles use *sa* to express epistemic senses of possibility, that is, the sense of 'maybe' or 'perhaps' (though *sa* seems to be more restricted in this function in Sranan). Other strategies include the use of adverbials like *kande* 'perhaps', or expressions such as *A kan de* (*taki*) 'it can be (the case) that'.

(12)   Sranan   *Jan   sa   de   na   oso   nownow.*
                   John   MOD   be   LOC   house now
                   'John may be at home now.'

(13)   Pamaka   *Kande   den   pikin   e   siibi   nounou.*
                   perhaps   DET (pl) child   IMPFV   sleep   now
                   'The children may be asleep now.'

2.3.2. *Necessity*

Meanings associated with necessity are expressed by *musu* (*fu*) or by the reduced form *mu* (< *musu*), which express weaker or stronger obligation.

(14)   Sranan   *Wan pikin musu arki   en   bigi sma   alaten.*
                   a   child must listen its big   people always
                   'A child must always obey its parents.'

(15)   Pamaka   *I   mu   kiibi a   moni   fi   i.*
                   you   must keep   DET (sg) money for you
                   'You should save your money.'

The same forms are used to express epistemic necessity, that is the sense of 'It must be the case that', based on the speaker's inference. Alternatively, the expression *A musu de* (*taki*) 'It must be the case that' can be used.

2.3.3. Need and desire

Finally, the senses of need and desire are conveyed by the expression (*abi*) *fanoudu* (*fu*) 'have need of' and the main verb *wani* 'want' respectively.

(16) Sranan *A pikin abi furu lobi fanoudu.*
　　　　　　 DET (sg) child have full love need
　　　　　　 'The child needs a lot of love.'

2.4. Auxiliary ordering

The usual ordering of auxiliaries is as follows:

　　TENSE > MODALITY > ASPECT

This is illustrated in the following example from Sranan:

(17) Sranan *Jan ben sa e sribi.*
　　　　　　 John PAST MOD IMPFV sleep
　　　　　　 'John would have been sleeping.'

However, the canonical ordering shown above is by no means the only one found. In Sranan, for example, the Imperfective marker can precede the modality marker.

(18) Sranan *A ben e musu e taki nanga unu.*
　　　　　　　　　　　　　　　　　　　　　　　　　　 (elicited)
　　　　　　 he PAST IMPFV must IMPFV talk with us
　　　　　　 'He usually had to be talking with us.'

3. Basic clause structure

Like all languages, the Surinamese creoles have three basic sentence types, declaratives, yes/no interrogatives and imperatives. All of these have SVO ordering, with interrogatives employing rising intonation as distinct from the other two types, which have falling intonation.

3.1. Declarative sentences

Verbs may be intransitive or transitive, the latter being divided into various subclasses depending on the number of arguments they can take.

　　Intransitive verbs include general movement verbs such as *go* 'go', *ko(n)* 'come', *kai* 'fall', *lon* 'run', *waka* 'walk', etc. The subclasses of transitive verbs include those that take a compulsory object, those whose object is optional, and those that require both a direct and an indirect object.

(19)   EMarC   *L.   puu   a   kumalu.*
               L.   pull   DET (sg)   type of fish
               'L. removed the fish.'

(20)   EMarC   *Mi   e   wasi.*
               I   IMPFV   wash
               'I am washing (myself).'

In sentences with di-transitive verbs the direct object precedes the indirect one.

(21)   EMarC   *Den   mu   gi   mi   wan   pisi   doti.*
               they   MOD   give   me   one   piece   land
               'They have to give me a piece of land.'

Prepositional phrases and adverbs generally follow the verb or its object. Note that the maroon creoles have a special class of adverbs, so-called ideophones, which specify more closely the meanings of verbs.

(22)   EMarC   *A   go   na   a   sabana.*
               he   go   LOC   DET   savannah
               'He went to the savannah.'

(23)   Saamaka   *A   bi   djombo viiin   te   a   wata   djuubu.*
               He   PAST   jump   QUICKLY   till   LOC   water   SPLASH
               'He jumped quickly, splash! in the water.'

                                           (Bakker, Smith and Veenstra 1995: 174)

Other semantic roles are introduced by so-called serial verbs (see section 6.2.).

Many verbs are ambi-transitive, that is, they can be used both transitively and intransitively.

(24)   Sranan   a.   *A   batra   broko.*
                     DET (sg)   bottle   break
                     'The bottle broke.'   (Winford 1997: 265)

          b.   *A   pikin   broko   a   batra*
                     DET (sg)   child   break   DET (sg)   bottle
                     'The child broke the bottle.'

3.2.   *Yes/no* questions

The Surinamese creoles also have certain variations of yes–no questions, such as alternative (either–or) questions, and tag questions.

(25)   Sranan   *Oh,   you   e   meki   bestelling, o   yu   e*
                   Oh   you   IMPFV   make   orders   or   you   IMPFV

                  meki   gewoon   fu   yu   oso?
                  make   only   for   your   house?
                  'Oh, do you take orders or do you make [cakes] only for yourself?'   (Winford 2000a: 426)

(26)   EMarC   *Da   a   te   a   bilo   u   komoto?*
                  Then   FOC   till   LOC   down-river   you (pl)   leave
                  'So you come (all the way) from the coastal area?'

In tag questions, Sranan and modern varieties of maroon varieties use the Dutch particle *tog*, while EMarC uses *no*.

(27)   Sranan a.   *Oh, ma   dan   a   ben   kan kon   taki   now, tog?*
                  Oh, but   then   he   PAST   can   come   talk   now, right?
                  'Oh, but then he can come and chat now, right?'
       EMarC b.   *Ma   a   gi   i   a   moni,   no?*
                  But   he   give   you   DET (sg)   money   right
                  'But he gave you the money, right?'

3.3.   Imperative sentences

Imperatives are the only sentences that do not require an overt singular subject, but when addressed to several people, they require the plural pronoun *u* or *unu*.

(28)   EMarC a.   *Tapu   mofu!*
                  close   mouth
                  'Shut up!'
          b.   *U   kon   njan   nou!*
                  you (pl)   come   eat   now
                  'Come eat!'

Hortatives are introduced by *meki* 'make', or *kon* 'come'.

(29)   Sranan   *Meki/kon   unu   libi   a   tori   dati   yere.*
                  make/come   we   leave   DET (sg)   story   DEM   hear
                  'Let's forget that story, okay?'

3.4.   Clause negation

Negative sentences in the creoles are mere variants of the basic sentence types
sketched earlier. Each of these may be negated in the same way, by placing the
negator, *no* in Sranan and *ná/á(n)* (31) in the EMarC/Saamaka, immediately
before the first element of the VP, no matter how many TMA particles appear
before the verb.

(30)   Sranan *Yu   no   ben   man   taki leki fa   den yungu sma   now.*
                You NEG PAST MOD talk like how DET young person now
                                                                   (pl)
                'You couldn't talk [to an adult] the way young people [do] now.'

The creoles also employ sentence level negators. In the EMarC, these include
the items *èéé*, *nono* 'no', *noiti* 'never' and *kwetikweti* 'not at all'. They either
precede or follow a sentence or they occur in isolation as responses to contributions of another speaker.

(31)   Pamaka a. T: *U   ná   a   wan sani fu   taki.*
                            We   NEG have a   thing for   say
                            'We do not have anything to say.'
                    P: *Kwetikweti*
                            'not at all'
                b.   *A   taki   "eée disi án   bun   gaaman"*
                        He   say   no   this NEG good   king
                        'He said "no king, this isn't good".'

Finally, negative structures are characterized by negative concord (multiple
negation).

(32)   Sranan *Noyti   mi   no   sii   en   dya   a   Coronie.*
                Never   I   NEG see   him   here   LOC Coronie
                'I've never seen him here at Coronie.'

There are various other strategies of negation in these creoles, involving inherently negative quantifiers (*ná/no wan sani* 'nothing', *ná/no wan sama/sma*
'nobody' etc.), adverbs (*ná/no wan peesi/presi* 'nowhere') and other polarity
items, which are beyond the scope of this summary.

3.5.   Copular-type sentences

The Surinamese creoles, like other New World Creoles, have a distinctive set
of copular–type constructions (so called because they require a copula in the
lexifiers). They employ the copula *na/da* for present time nominal predication,

and *de* for locative/existential constructions, adverbial expressions and for nominal predication under other TMA specifications. They use no copula at all in attributive (adjectival) predicate constructions, in which the predicative property items behave like intransitive verbs, being directly preceded by TMA markers.

(33) Sranan a. *Sranan   liba   na   wan bun   bradi   liba.*
                   Suriname   river   COP   a   good   broad   river
                   'The Suriname river is a really broad river.'

           b. *A   watra   ben   faya.*
                 DET (sg)   water   PAST   hot
                 'The water was hot.'

           c. *Den   pikin   musu   de   ini   a   oso.*
                 DET (sg)   child   must   COP   in   the   house
                 'The children must be in the house'

           d. *Gado   de.*
                 'God exists.'

3.5.1. Equative copular predication

The syntactic behavior of equative copula *na* suggests that it is not (fully) verbal. Unlike verbs, it precedes the negator and past tense marker.

(34) EMarC *En   na   be   basi.*
             she   COP   PAST   boss
             'She was the boss.'

(*N*)*a* is replaced by *de* after any TMA marker and optionally also in constructions with past time reference or negative polarity.

(35) Sranan *Mi   prakseri   a   boi   disi   nanga a*
               I   think   DET (sg)   boy   DEM   with   DET (sg)

               man   dati   musu de   brada.
               man   DEM   must COP   brother
               'I think this boy and that man must be brothers.'

Saamaka makes a distinction between identificational and attributive (class inclusive) equative structures, employing *da* and *de* respectively.

(36) Saamaka a. *Me da/*dɛ   Gadu.*
                 I   COP   God
                 'I am God.'

b. *Me   dɛ   wã   kabitẽ*
   I   COP   DET   captain
   'I'm a captain.'

(*N*)*a* cannot appear in final position. In cases of movement such as *wh*-questions and predicate clefting the copula *de* is used. In sentences with future time reference it may also be replaced by a verb meaning 'turn' or '(be)come'.

(37) Sranan   *Na   leriman   a   man   de.*
                FOC   teacher   DET(sg)   man   COP
                'A teacher is what the man is.'

(38) EMarC   *A   sa/o   toon   fetiman.*
                He   MOD/FUT   become   fighter
                'He may/will become a troublemaker.'

Equative constructions probably arose from topic-comment structures in which *da/na* functioned as a resumptive pronoun. The latter differ from regular equative constructions in having a pause or comma intonation after the topic NP.

(39) Sranan   *Hertoch,   na   koniman.*
                Hertoch,   PRE   intelligent-man
                'Hertoch is an intelligent man.'

3.5.2. Locative/existential copular constructions

The copula *de* may be freely preceded by TMA markers and the negator.

(40) Sranan   *Den   pikin ben/sa/o   de   na   skoro.*
                DET (pl)   child PAST/MOD/FUT   COP   LOC   school.
                'The children were/may/will be at school.'

It is generally agreed that the source of copula *de* is adverbial *de* < *there*, as used in earlier existential and locative constructions.

(41) Sranan   *Masra,   soopie   de.*
                Master,   drink   there
                'Master, here is your drink.'
                                    (Van Dyk 1765, in Arends and Perl 1995: 170)

3.5.3. Attributive (adjectival-like) predication

There has been a great deal of debate as to whether the property items (corresponding to English adjectives) that appear in creole copular-like structures are adjectives.

(42) Sranan *A*   *liba*   *bradi*
                    DET (sg)   river   broad
                    'The river is wide.'

The property items in question also function as modifiers of nouns, and their adjectival status in this function is not under dispute. In their use as predicators, however, there is good evidence that such items are in fact verbal in the Surinamese creoles (Alleyne 1987; Winford 1997; Migge 2000).

First, we find the following parallels between the syntactic behavior of such predicates and that of intransitive verbs:

– They are immediately preceded by TMA markers.
– They undergo predicate cleft, leaving a copy *in situ*.
– Adverbial modifiers typically follow them.
– They appear in comparative serial verb constructions.

The following Sranan examples from Winford (1997: 257-259) illustrate:

(43) Sranan a. *A*   *pikin*   *e*   *bigi.*
                          DET (sg)   child   IMPFV   big
                          'The child is getting big.'
             b. *Na*   *langa*   *a*   *pikin*   *langa.*
                          FOC   long   DET(sg)   child   long
                          'The child is really tall.'
             c. *A*   *watra*   *faya*   *tumsi.*
                          DET (sg)   water   hot   too-much
                          'The water is too hot.'
             d. *A*   *pikin*   *bigi*   *pasa*   *yu.*
                          DET (sg)   child   big   pass   you
                          'The child is bigger than you'.

Most property items also function as transitive verbs in the Surinamese creoles, similarly to ambi-transitive verbs like *broko/booko* 'break' and *priti/piiti* 'split'.

(44)   Sranan   *Sidon   tumsi   e   fatu   y.*
               sit   too-much   IMPFV   fat   you
               'Sitting too much fattens you.'

4.   Variations on basic clause structure

4.1.   Passive constructions

Passive constructions do not display characteristics associated with the analytic passives found in English. In particular, they lack a "be" auxiliary, morphological marking on the verb, and an agentive prepositional phrase.

(45)   Sranan   *Kande   den   suma   disi   ben   kweki   tra   fasi*
               Perhaps   DET (pl)   person   DEM   PAST   raise   other   fashion
               'Perhaps these people were raised differently.'
                                          (Winford 2000b: 95)

(46)   EmarC   *Sopi   ná   e   diingi   a   ini   boto!*
              Rum   NEG   IMPFV   drink   LOC   in   boat
              'Rum is not consumed in the boat!'

There are greater restrictions on the class of verbs that can undergo passivization, by comparison with English. For instance, stative verbs such as *love, know, believe* etc., and perception verbs like *see, hear,* etc., generally resist passivization in these creoles, except in certain discourse contexts. In general, activity verbs tend to passivize more readily. Passives involving verbs with animate subjects (e.g. *eat*) tend to be avoided in favor of impersonal constructions, in order to avoid ambiguity (see Winford 1988 for further discussion).

4.2.   Left-dislocation, topicalization and focus

In addition to passives, there are two other types of construction in which constituents are moved to sentence-initial position. The first type includes cases of left-dislocation and topicalization, both of which involve the fronting of an NP followed by some comment on it. The distinction between the two lies in the fact that a resumptive pronoun (or sometimes a copy of the moved NP) appears in left-dislocations but not in topicalizations. The second type includes cleft constructions.

4.2.1. Left-dislocation and topicalization

The following Sranan example illustrates left-dislocation.

(47) Sranan *Den   siki   di   de   now   a   fosten*
               DET (pl) sick   REL   COP   now   DET (sg)   former-time

            den   no   ben   de.
            they   NEG   PAST   COP
            'The diseases that there are nowadays weren't around long
            ago.'   (Winford 2000b: 72, 93)

Topicalization is illustrated in the following:

(48) Sranan *Oh,   wan   kronto   srefi   oom   N.   no   man   kapu.*
               oh,   one   cocnut   self   uncle   N.   NEG   can   chop
            'Oh, even a coconut Uncle N. can't cut?'

In the EMarC, topics are frequently introduced/marked by *dati*.

(49) EmarC   *Mi   dati   án   de   a   ini.*
               I   TOP   NEG   COP   LOC   inside
            'As for me, I am not part of it.'

4.2.2. Focus in cleft constructions

Cleft constructions are very similar to topicalizations, except that the former introduce the focused element with a focus marker. The latter is identical in shape to the equative copula in all the Surinamese creoles except Samaaka, which employs the postposed focus marker *wɛ* retained from Fongbe.

Two distinct types of focus are involved in these constructions – presentational or information focus and identificational or contrastive focus. Presentational focus constructions usually present some new topic, and usually involve the fronting of an NP.

(50) Sranan *A   wan piki pikin boi e moksi smenti drape.*
               FOC ART little little boy IMPFV mix   cementthere
            'It's a little boy that mixes cement there.'

In identificational or information focus, the fronted element may be any major constituent of the sentence, including NPs, PPs, and adverbs. The function of such constructions is to identify some participant, entity, etc. that is presumed to be unknown to the hearer, as the actual one involved in the situation described.

(51) EMarC *Na   nounou den   e   njan fu   mamanten oo.*
             FOC   now   they IMPFV eat   for   morning   EM
             'It's NOW that they eat for morning, i.e. breakfast.'

(52) Saamaka *Di   mujee wɛ   mi bi   bel,   naa di
                womi.*
                DET (sg) woman FOC I   PAST phone NEG the man
                'It was the WOMAN I phoned, not the man.'

                                                (Smith 1996: 118)

4.2.3. Predicate clefting

Closely related to the contrastive focus constructions is so-called predicate clefting, in which verbs and predicative property items can undergo fronting. In such cases, however, a copy of the fronted element remains *in situ*.

(53) EMarC *Na   booko a   booko a   wagi fu   mi.*
             FOC   break he   break DET (sg) car   for me
             'He BROKE my car.'

When NP predicates are fronted, a copula appears in the place of the fronted NP.

(54) Sranan a. *Na   leriman Jan   de.*
                    FOC   teacher Jan   COP
                    'John's a TEACHER.'
                b. **Na   leriman Jan   leriman.*

4.3. *Wh*-questions

Information (*wh*-) questions do not allow auxiliary inversion. Moreover, they employ a range of *wh*-expressions that are quite different from those in English, as shown in Table 1.

Table 1. *Wh*-forms in the Surinamese creoles

Gloss	Sranan	EMarC	Saamaka	Early Sranan
'who'	*suma*	*sama*	*ambɛ*	*o suma (< somebody*
'what'	*san*	*san*	*andi*	*o sani (<something)*
'where'	*pe*	*pe*	*unse*	*o pe (<place)*
'how'	*fa*	*(on)fa*	*(um)fá*	*o fasi (<fashion)*
'why'	*(fu) san ede*	*(fu) saide*	*(fu) andi mbei* ('for what make')	*fu san ede* ('for what head=reason')

Except for Saamaka *ambɛ* 'who' and *andí* 'what', which derive from Gbe, all other *wh*-forms appear to derive from earlier compounds indicated in the last column in Table 1.

(55) Saamaka   *Andí*   *de*   *féni*   *límbo?*
                  What   they   find   clean
                  'What did they find clean?' (Veenstra 1996: 69)

(56) Sranan   *San*   *yu*   *bo*   *taki?*
                  What   you   PAST + FUT   talk?
                  'What were you going to say?'

5. Complex constructions

This section briefly surveys a number of multi-clause constructions, including cases of coordination, verb serialization, and subordination.

5.1. Coordination

Coordinate structures may be divided into three main types: simple coordination with *and*; adversative coordination with *but*; and disjunctive coordination with *or*.

Sranan uses *nanga*, EMarC *anga* (< English *along*) and Saamaka *ku* (< Gengbe) all meaning 'with' for simple coordination of noun phrases. To conjoin clauses, they employ a different conjunction, *dan* 'then' or *en* 'and' in Sranan, *da* or *neen* in the EMarC and *hen* or *noo* in Saamaka.

(57) Sranan a. *Tyari a   karaaf nanga wan kan gi   mi.*
                    carry   DET (sg) pitcher with   one can give me
                    'Fetch the pitcher and a can for me.'

      Sranan b. *yu e   go na   a   mma   dan yu o   taki.*
                    You IMPFV go LOC the mother then you FUT speak
                    'You'd go to the mother and then you'd speak.'

      EmarC *Eside,   den wasi osu   neen den kaabu(den) ganda.*
                Yesterday 3pl wash house then 3pl weed(the-pl) outside
                'Yesterday, they cleaned the house, then cleaned/weeded the
                outside.'

For adversative coordination, all the creoles employ *ma* (< Dutch *maar* 'but').

(58) Saamaka *Mi bi   musu yasa wan kuku tide ma mé   bi   a*
                  I   PAST must bake a   cake today but I-NEG PAST have

                tin   fu   yasa en   moo.
                time for bake it   more
                'I should have baked a cake today, but I did not have time.'

For disjunctive coordination at both phrasal and sentential levels, Sranan employs the form *of* 'or' (< Dutch); the EMarC uses *efu*. Samaka, on the other hand,
employs the form *na so* (which is also found in more conservative Sranan).

(59) Sranan a. *Den e   taki wan dipi sortu fasi   of den*
                    They IMPFV take one deep sort fashion or they

                    e   gi   ala sortu agersi fasi.
                    IMPFV give all sort parable fashion
                    'They'd talk in a deep way or use all kinds of parables.'

      Saamaka c. *Di womi ta   wooko na so hen   mujee ta*
                      The man IMPFV work   not so 3-poss wife   IMPFV

                      wooko.
                      work
                      'Either the man is working or his wife is.'
                                              (Park, Glock and Rountree 1981: 77)

5.2.   Serial verb constructions

Like other New World Creoles, the Surinamese creoles employ a variety of
sentence structures that contain two or more verb phrases linked together with

no overt markers of coordination. These serial verb constructions (SVCs) can be divided into several types, depending on the function performed by the serial verb, which is usually, but not always, the second verb (V2). The main types include directional, dative/benefactive, and comparative serials, though there are others more difficult to classify.

5.2.1. Directional serial verb constructions

In directional SVCs, the serial verb (V2) indicates the direction of the motion expressed by the main verb (V1). For example, *go* as V2 indicates direction away from the point of reference, while *kon* 'come' indicates motion towards it. They are highly productive in the Surinamese creoles, which possess by far the widest range of directional serial verbs of all New World Creoles.

(60) *Sranan Yu   musu go na   kownu go aksi en   wan wroko.*
            You   must go LOC   king   go ask   him   one work
            'You must go to the king to ask him one favor.'

(Sebba 1987: 61)

5.2.2. Dative/benefactive serial verb constructions

Another common SVC is one in which a verb meaning 'give' functions as V2, and introduces a recipient or a benefactive argument. The recipient type SVC involves a V1 expressing some kind of transfer such as 'sell', 'send'.

(61) Sranan *Mi   seri   a   oso   gi   en.*
             I   sell   DET (sg)   house give   her
             'I sold the house to her.'

The Surinamese creoles also employ 'give' to introduce several other types of arguments or thematic roles, including "substitutive", "experiencer", and "source"; see Migge (1998).

5.2.3. "Comparative" SVCs

Comparison is expressed by an SVC in which the V2 is either *pasa* '(sur)pass' or *moro* (Sranan) and *moo* (EMarC) 'exceed' (< English *more*). The latter is the more frequently used.

(62) Sranan *Amba   tranga   moro/pasa   Kofi.*
             Amba   strong   exceed/pass   Kofi
             'Amba's stronger than Kofi.'

Sranan has adopted more Dutch-like comparative structures, though not all native speakers accept these.

(63) Sranan *A   man   moro   gridi   leki   a   uma.*
                The   man   more   greedy   than   DET (sg)   woman
                'The man is more greedy than the woman.'

5.2.4. Other types of SVC

The Surinamese creoles also employ a wide variety of SVCs in which *teki* 'take' functions as the V1, introducing arguments of various types. The following is an example in which 'take' introduces an instrumental argument.

(64) Sranan *Kofi   teki   a   nefi   koti   a   brede.*
                Kofi   take   the   knife   cut   the   bread
                'Kofi took the knife and cut the bread.'

We also find so-called resultative SVCs, in which the V2 expresses a result stemming from the action of the V1.

(65) EMarC *A   naki   a   bata(a)   booko.*
                She   hit   DET (sg)   bottle   break
                'She broke the bottle by hitting it.'

There are various other kinds of SVCs found in these creoles, which are more difficult to classify, because there is freer selection of verbs. They include sentences like the following:

(66) Sranan *Amba   go   na   wowoyo bai   nyan.*
                Amba   go   LOC   market   buy   food
                'Amba went to the market and bought food.'

6.   Subordination

6.1.   Complement clauses

Sentential complements can be divided into two types: indicative (*that*-type) and non-indicative or subjunctive (*for*-type). These complements may appear as full sentences, or may be "reduced" in some way (e.g. lacking overt subjects, TMA marking, etc.). Each type can be further differentiated.

6.1.1. Indicative complements

Indicative-type complements include the following:

– arguments of predicates like *seem*;
– complements of assertion verbs (*say*, *tell*, etc.); of psyche state verbs (*know*, *believe*, etc.); and of perception verbs (*see*, *hear*, etc.).
– complements of causative *make*

Complements to *seem* and to evaluative predicates like *true* are always extra-posed sentential subjects. Such complements are clearly full (finite) sentences.

(67) Sranan   *A   gersi   taki   den   kuli   wani   teki   a*
             It   seem   COMP   DET (pl)   Hindustanis   want   take   the

             kondre   now   op.
             country   now   up
             'It seems that the Hindustanis want to take over the country
             now.'   (Winford 2000b: 96)

6.1.2. Complements to verbs of saying, etc.

The verb *taki* 'talk' also introduces complements to a variety of verbs, including verbs of assertion (*say*, *tell*, etc.), desideratives (*wish*, *hope*, etc.), verbs of psychological state (*believe*, *know*, *think*, etc.), and perception verbs (*see*, *hear*, etc.).

(68) EMarC   *A   man   á   be   sabi   taki   na   so   wan*
            DET (sg)   man   NEG   PAST   know   COMP   FOC   so   one

            sani   be   o   du   en.
            thing   PAST   FUT   do   him
            'The man didn't know that such a thing would happen to him.'

In Sranan *taki* is often replaced by *dati* (< Dutch *dat*) or by a zero complementizer.

(69) Sranan   *En   mi   hoop   dati   a   kondre   o   kon*
            and   I   hope   DEM   DET (sg)   country   FUT   come

            bun   yere.
            good   hear
            'And I hope that the country will get better, right.'
                                  (Winford 2000b: 115)

6.1.3. Perception verb complements

Perception verbs take two types of complement, a finite type introduced by 'talk' as well as a reduced (small clause) type without 'talk'. Veenstra (1996) demonstrates this distinction for Saamaka with examples like the following:

(70)   Saamaka a. *De*   *sí*   *táa*   *dí*   *ógi*   *wómi*
                    They   see   talk   (DET) sg   bad   man

                    bì   disá   dí   kónde   gó.
                    PAST   leave   DET (SG)   village   go
                    'They saw that the wicked man had left the village.'

            b. *De sí dí   ógi   wómi   disá dí kónde gó.*
               'They saw the wicked man leave the village.'

As Veenstra points out, the "reduced" type involves events that are simultaneous with the time of the matrix verb, while the finite type does not.

6.1.4. Complements to causative 'make'

Complements of causative *make* are also finite sentences, which can function as both subject and object arguments.

(71)   Saamaka   *Egber bebé daán hía   pói   mbéi a   fiká   a*
                  Egber drink rum   much spoil   make 3-subj stay   LOC

                  wósu   síki-síki.
                  house   sick
                  '[The fact that] Egber drank too much rum made him stay
                  at home sick.'   (Veenstra 1996: 101)

6.2.   "For" complements

Non-indicative complements in these creoles are introduced by the preposition *fu* 'for', which can also function as a modal auxiliary. For convenience, we will refer to these collectively as "for" complements.

These complements express potential events or states. The predicates that take them include desideratives (verbs of desire, intent, request and command), "aspectual" verbs like *start* and modal predicates like *have, able, obliged*, etc. *Fu* also introduces adverbial clauses of purpose and reduced relatives.

"For" complements may be either reduced or full clauses. The following are examples of the former type. Note that, when matrix and complement subjects are co-referential, *fu* may be omitted.

(72) Saamaka a. *A$_i$ ke   (fu)Ø$_i$ go   a   di   wosu.*
               s/he   want   (for)   go   LOC DET (sg) house
               S/he wants to go to the house.' (Caskey 1990: 703)

        b. *Kofi$_i$ ko   a   wosu   fu ø$_i$ sikifi di   lete.*
           Kofi   come   LOC   house   for   write   DET (sg)

letter

           'Kofi came to the house to write the letter.'
                                (Caskey 1990: 700)

Note also that an overt subject may appear in the complement clause, and may refer either to the matrix subject or some other party, as in the following:

(73) Saamaka *Kofi$_i$ ko   a   wosu   faa$_{i/j}$ skikfi di   lete.*
               Kofi   come   LOC   house   for-him   write   DET (sg) letter
               'Kofi came to the house (for him/her) to write the letter.'
                                  (Caskey 1990: 700)

When the matrix and subordinate clause subjects are clearly different, the latter is always overtly expressed.

(74) Sranan   *Wan pikin aksi a   man fu a   man rij*
              A   girl   ask   DET (sg) man for DET (sg) man ride

              a   laatst rij.
              DET (sg) last   ride
              'A girl asked the guy to take one last ride.'
                            (Winford 2000a: 433)

A corollary to this is that complements to desiderative verbs are interpreted quite differently when they have null pronominal subjects as opposed to overt pronominal ones. The following is an example from Caskey (1990: 701).

(75) Saamaka a. *Di   mujee$_i$ hakisi da   di   womi$_j$*
               DET (sg)   woman   ask   give   DET (sg)   man

            fu PRO$_i$ go   a   di   wenke.
            for   go   LOC   DET(sg)   store
            'The woman asked the man [permisssion] to go to the store.'

        b. *Di mujee$_i$ hakisi da di womi$_j$ faa$_j$ go a di wenke.*
           'The woman asked the man to go to the store [requested that he go].'

These few examples will serve to illustrate the complexity of control relationships in such complements. Caskey (1990: 694) suggests that these relationships depend largely on the inherent meaning of matrix predicates.

6.3.   Relative clauses

Relative clauses in these creoles include both restrictive and non-restrictive types. We will confine our attention to the former, which are the more common ones. The main relativizer is *di* 'who, that, which' (< *disi* 'this'), an item that also has a variety of other subordinating functions, being interpreted as 'where, when, because', etc. (see discussion below).

(76)   EMarC   *Luku a   uman di   e   weli a   buuku.*
                 Look DET (sg) woman REL IMPFV wear DET (sg) trousers
                 'Look the woman who is wearing the trousers.'

Other types of relative clauses in ACs include "for" relatives (similar to infinitival relatives in English), reduced relatives (similar to small clauses); and place relatives. "For" relatives follow the pattern of other "for" subordinate clauses that we discussed earlier.

(77)   EMarC   *A   feni   kwaka   fu   bai.*
                 She   PAST   search-manioc for   buy
                 'She found baked manioc to buy.'

Place relatives are among a few types in which the Surinamese creoles use a *wh*-form as a relativizer.

(78)   EMarC   *Na   a   konde   pe   a   e   tan.*
                 FOC   DET (sg)   country   where   she   IMPFV stay
                 'It's the village where she lives.'

Interestingly, Sranan is increasingly employing its interrogative pronouns, particularly *suma* 'who' and *san* 'what' as relativizers, perhaps on the model of *pe* 'where', which is long established in place relatives.

(79)   Sranan   *Den ben   bigin ferteri yu   wan sani san   yu*
                  they PAST   begin tell   you   one thing REL   you

                  musu   ben   sabi.
                  must   PAST   know.
                  'They started to tell you things that you had to know.'
                                                              (Winford 2000b: 74)

In general, noun functions such as subject and object, which are high on the Noun Phrase Accessibility Hierarchy (Keenan and Comrie 1977), lend themselves more readily to relativization of the type that leaves a gap in the site of the relativized noun. When nouns lower on the scale (e.g., objects of prepositions, possessives, objects of comparison) are relativized, a resumptive pronoun must occupy the position of the relativized NP.

(80)   Sranan   *Dan   a   man   di   mi   nanga   en   e*
                Then   DET (sg)   man   REL   I   with   him   IMPFV

       taki,   a   man   taki,   "yu   kan   go".
       talk   DET (sg)   man   talk   you   can   go.
       'Then the man who I was talking with said, "You can go."'

6.4.   Adverbial clauses

We find once more a marked difference between the Surinamese creoles and English varieties in their repertoire of subordinators that introduce adverbial clauses. Some of these are reflexes of English conjunctions, e.g., *bikasi* < *because*. However, the Surinamese creoles have also developed their own peculiar set of subordinators, including *di/te* 'when', *pe* 'where', *fa* 'how', and others. Several of these are identical to the *wh*-forms we discussed earlier.

6.4.1.   Temporal clauses

The creoles employ several temporal subordinators, the chief of which are *di* and *te*, both meaning 'when'. *Di* is used in cases where a specific (usually past) situation is referred to, while *te* is used for irrealis (future or speculative) or non-specific, including habitual and non-realized, situations.

(81)   EMarC   *Di   mi   be   yonku,   te   u   be   go   a*
                when   I   PAST young   when   we   PAST   go   LOC

       foto   u   bai   tjaipi   sani.
       town   we   buy   lots   thing
       'When I was young, whenever we used to go to town, we bought lots of things.'

Other temporal conjunctions include *fosi* 'before' and compounds like *baka di/te* 'after'.

(82) Sranan   *Baka di   a   dringi a   dresi,   a   koso*
                After REL he   drink DET (sg) medicine, he cough

      wan   heri   yuru.
      one   whole   hour
      'After he drank the medicine, he coughed for a whole hour.'

(83) EMarC   *Fosi   a   njan   a   diingi   wan   bii.*
                Before she eat   she drink   a   beer
                'Before she ate she drank a beer.'

We also find complex forms such as *vanaf di* (Sranan), *fanafu di* (EMarC)
'since', which combine a Dutch loan *vanaf* 'from' with (*fu*) *di*.

(84) Sranan   *Vanaf   di   a   oto   naki   mi   dan   mi*
                Since   REL   DET (sg) car   knock   me   then   I

      no   kan   hori   wan   owru
      NEG   can   hold   one   machete.
      'Since the car struck me I can't hold a machete.'

6.4.2. Clauses of reason

Clauses of reason generally fall into two types, the first introduced by a subor-
dinator meaning 'because' *bikasi* (Sranan), *bika* (EMarC) and *biga* (Saamaka)
and the second introduced by *fu di*. All creoles also use Dutch-derived subordinators such as *want(i)* and *omdat(i)* 'because'.

(85) EMarC   *Mi   o   bai   en   bika   a   moi.*
                I   FUT   bay   it   because it   nice
                'I'll buy it because it is nice.'

(86) Sranan   *Someni   ben   dede   fu   di   den   no   ben*
                So-many PAST   die   for   that they   NEG   PAST

      kisi   wan   bun   yepi.
      get   one   good   help
      'Too many died because they didn't get a good helping hand.'
                                        (Nickel and Wilner 1984: 27)

6.4.3. Conditional clauses

There are two kinds of condition – real and unreal. The former refer to actual events, whether present, generic or past. In these cases, the speaker leaves open the possibility that some state of affairs does or did exist.

(87)   Sranan   *Efu   mi   no   ben   wroko   mi   no   nyan.*
          If   I   NEG   PAST   work   I   NEG   eat
          'If I didn't work, I didn't eat.'
       (Winford 2000b: 108)

Unreal conditions may be divided into predictive (future) and imaginary types (Thompson and Longacre 1985: 191). Predictives are somewhat like real conditions in that the speaker adopts an "open" or neutral stance toward the state of affairs. The Surinamese creoles in fact treat both types as the same, syntactically.

(88)   EMarC   *Efu   a   feni   en,   da   a   o   boo.*
          If   she   find   it   then   she   FUT   breathe
          'If she finds it (French papers), she'll be happy/relieved.'

Imaginary conditions include hypotheticals and counterfactuals, both of which have a strong element of epistemic modality. Both of these types are conveyed by the use of the past tense in the *if*-clause and by combinations of past plus modal or future in the consequent clause. This applies to both present and past situations.

(89)   Saamaka   *Yee di   wagi bi   naki mi, mi bi   o*
          dede.
                  If   DET (sg)   car   PAST   hit   me   I   PAST FUT   die
                  'If the car had hit me, I would have been dead.'

(90)   Sranan   *Efu mi ben   abi   moni   mi bo   bai wan oto.*
          If   1sg PAST have   money   1sg PAST+FUT   buy ART car
          'If I had money, I would buy a car.'

The combination of past and future is also used in hypothetical statements like the following:

(91)   Sranan   *Kande   a   no   bo   sabi   mi   moro.*
          Perhaps   she   NEG   PAST+FUT   know   me   more
          'Perhaps she wouldn't have recognized me.'

6.4.4. Concessive clauses

Concessive clauses may be divided into three types: concessive conditionals conveying the sense of 'even if'; indefinite concessives (the sense of 'whatever', 'no matter what'); and "definite" concessives (the sense of 'although') (Thompson and Longacre 1985: 196–198).

Concessives conveying the sense of 'even if' are quite similar to open conditions, and have been referred to as concessive conditionals (Thompson and Longacre 1985: 196–198). They are introduced by the conjunction (*a*) *winsi* (source unknown).

(92)   Sranan   *Wins i   yu   no   wani   nyan moro tog   yu*
                Even-if you NEG   want   eat   more TAG   you

                e   nyan.
                IMPFV   eat
                'Even if you don't want to eat any more, right, you keep eating.'
                (Winford 2000b: 119)

The same conjunction is used to introduce indefinite concessives.

(93)   Sranan   *A   winsi   san   e   pasa   a   plan*
                FOC no-matter what IMPFV happen DET (sg)   plan

                fu   a   Masra   e   go   doro.
                of   DET (sg)   Master   IMPFV   go   through
                'Whatever happens, the Lord's plan continues.'

Definite concessives fall into two sub-types: those that convey the sense of 'although' or 'in spite of', and those that convey the stronger sense of 'no matter how much'. The former are introduced by *ala di*, or *ala fa*.

(94)   Sranan   *Ala   fa   mi   bari   a   meisje, toku   a*
                All   how   I   shout   DET (sg)   girl   still   she

                teki   waka   nanga   a   boi.
                take   walk   with   DET (sg)   boy
                'In spite of the fact that I warned that girl, she still went with that guy.'

To convey the stronger sense of 'no matter how much', the creoles employ a type of concessive involving predicate clefting.

(95) Sranan   *Ala*   *di*   *na*   *kosi*   *den*   *kosi*   *en,*   *a*   *no*
               All   that   FOC   curse   they   curse   him,   he   NEG

               piki   *den*   *noti.*
               answer   them   nothing
               'No matter how much they cursed him, he did not answer
               them.'   (John Wilner, pc. 5/03)

6.4.5. Clauses of purpose

Purpose clauses are introduced by the preposition *fu* 'for'. The subject of the purpose clause may be overt, even when it is coreferential with the matrix subject.

(96) Sranan   a.   *A*   *no*   *ben*   *abi*   *moni*   *fu*   *a*   *ben*
                  he   NEG   PAST   have   money   for   he   PAST

                  kan   *seni*   *pai*   *mi.*
                  can   send   pay   me
                  'He didn't have money so he could send it to pay me.'
                                         (Winford 2000b: 80)

       EMarC   b.   *Mi*   *ná*   *a*   *moni*   *fu*   *seeka*   *mi*   *tifi.*
                  I   NEG   have   money   for   fix   my   teeth
                  'I don't have money to fix my teeth.'

Like desiderative clauses, discussed earlier, 'for' purpose clauses express unrealized situations, and may be contrasted with purposive 'go/come' clauses like the following, which usually express realized goals.

(97) Sranan   *A*   *pikin*   *waka*   *go*   *na*   *wowoyo*   *go*   *bai*   *aleisi.*
                ART   child   walk   go   PREP   market   go   buy   rice
               'The child walked to the market to buy rice (and did so).'
                                       (Sebba 1987: 61)

Bickerton (1981) in fact claimed that this contrast was diagnostic of "prototypical" creoles, though this claim is not generally accepted.

7. Morphology

The creoles of Suriname lack inflectional (bound) morphology. Grammatical relationships such as agreement are not overtly expressed at all, while categories such as number and possession in nouns and tense/aspect in verbs are expressed by free forms.

7.1.   Nouns

7.1.1. Definiteness in nouns

The Surinamese creoles distinguish among definite, indefinite and generic nouns, but the way they mark these distinctions differs subtly from the way English marks them. Definitiveness is marked on singular nouns by the preverbal determiner *a* (Sranan , EMarC) and by *di* in Saamaka while plural nouns are marked by plural forms of these articles, namely, *den* (EMarC, Sranan) and *dee* (Saamaka).

(98)   EMarC a. *A   minisiti   e   kisi   diitenti   dunsu*
              DET (sg) minister   IMPFV get   300   thousand

              wan   mun.
              one   month
              'The minister is getting 300.000 guilders per month.'

      Saamaka b. *Dee   sembɛ,   dee   bi   go   a   foto.*
              DET (pl) people   they   PAST   go   LOC   town
              'The people, they went to town.'

Indefinite nouns are marked by preverbal *wan* (< *one*), while unmarked nouns are either generic or abstract in character.

(99)   EMarC a. *A   tja   wan   bii   kon   gi   mi.*
              she   carry a   beer come   give   me
              'She brought me a beer.'

             b. *Di   mi   go   ape,   mi   si   pikin   a   ini*
              when   I   go   there   I   see   child   LOC   in

              a   osu.
              DET (sg)   house
              'When I went there, I saw children in the house.'

7.1.2. Demonstratives

Sranan has a distinct class of (definite) demonstrative modifiers. The proximate demonstrative modifier is expressed by *disi* and the distal demonstrative modifier is *dati*, both of which occur post-nominally.

(100) Sranan *Den*   *ten*   *disi*   *a*   *son*   *e*   *faya.*
                DET (pl)   time   DEM   DET (sg)   sun   IMPFV   fire
                'These days it is hot.'

In the maroon creoles a demonstrative meaning is expressed by placing the definite article before the noun and a locative adverb after it. In this combination, the proximate locational adverbs *ya* (EMarC) and *aki* (Saamaka) 'here' express the meaning 'this', and the distal adverbs *de* (EMarC) and *dɛ* (Saamaka) 'there' convey the meaning 'that'. *Anda* (EMarC) and *ala* (Saamaka) 'over there' refer to an entity that is even further removed from the point of reference.

(101) Saamaka *Di*   *mii*   *dɛ*   *sá*   *wata*   *bunu.*
              DET (sg)   child   there   know   water   well
              'That child can swim well.'

7.1.3. *Number, gender and case*

As noted above, plurality in nouns is indicated by plural forms of articles. Gender distinctions are sometimes expressed through compounds with *man-* and *uma-* (*womi-* and *muyɛɛ-* in Saamaka), e.g. *manpikin* 'boychild' vs *umapikin* 'girlchild', but in general gender is not marked. Possession is conveyed either by juxtaposition, with the possessor preceding the possessed noun, or by the preposition *fu*, (*u* in Saamaka) which introduces the possessor. Possessive pronouns precede the noun.

(102) Saamaka *Di*   *boto*   *u*   *gaama.*
              DET (sg)   boat   for   chief
              'The chief's' boat.'

(103) EMarC   *A*   *kabiten*   *osu*
              DET (sg)   capitain   house
              'the lineage head's house'

(104) EMarC   *mi sutuu*
              'my chair'

7.2. The pronominal system

7.2.1. *Personal pronouns*

The three creoles organize their pronominal systems quite similarly, and in ways that differ in three important respects from the English system. First, subject, object, and possessive meanings are generally expressed by the same form. The only exception to this are the third person singular forms, where the subject form is distinct from an oblique (object and possessive) form. Second, the creole third person singular pronouns are not gender-differentiated. Third, the creoles have special pronouns that are used for emphasis. Table 2 presents an overview.

Table 2.   Strong and weak forms of pronouns in the creoles of Suriname

Saamaka	EMarC	Sranan	Meaning
mi	*mi*	*mi*	1. person singular subject, object, possessive pronoun
mii	-	-	1. person singular emphatic pronoun
i	*i* and *yu* (Ndjuka)	*yu*	2. person singular subject, object, possessive pronoun
i, yu	*i, yu*	*i, yu*	2. person singular emphatic pronoun
a	*a*	*a*	3. person singular subject pronoun
ɛn	*en*	*en*	3. person singular object and possessive pronoun
hɛn	*en*	*en*	3. person singular emphatic pronoun
u	*u, wi*	*unu*	1. person plural subject, object, possessive pronoun
un, unu	*u, wi*	*unu, wi*	2. person plural subject, object, possessive pronoun
de	*de(n)*	*den*	3. person plural subject, object, possessive pronoun

Emphasis on subject and object pronouns may also be indicated by putting special stress on the pronoun or by combining it with the emphatic marker *seefi* (EMarC), *srefi* (Sranan) or *seei* (Saamaka). Emphasis may also be conveyed through focus (see section 5.2.2.).

(105)   Saamaka   *Mi   seei   du   ɛn.*
                    I   self   do   it
                    'I did it myself.'
        (Rountree 1992: 51)

In the maroon creoles, several of the subject pronouns change phonological shape when they are combined with vocalic or vowel-initial markers of negation, tense and aspect.

(106) Pamaka   *U*   *án*   *si*   *en*   *ete.*
                       [wá]
                       we   NEG   see   it   yet
                       'We haven't seen it yet.'

Reflexivity is expressed by *seefi* (EMarC), *srefi* (Sranan) and *seei* (Saamaka) 'self, same' placed after the personal pronoun.

(107) Ndjuka   *A*   *e*   *taki*   *anga*   *en*   *seefi.*
                   she   IMPFV   speak   with   her   self
                   'She's talking to herself.'   (Huttar and Huttar 1994: 278)

7.2.2. Demonstrative pronouns

In Sranan and the EMarC, *disi* 'this' and *dati* 'that' also function as demonstrative pronouns. They may be pluralized by combining them with the plural determiner and in the EMarC they may co-occur with the locative adverbs *ya* and *de*.

(108) EMarC   *A*   *dati*   *o*   *kii*   *en.*
                FOC   DEM   FUT   kill   her
                'That will kill her.'

(109) EMarC   *Den*   *disi ya*   *án*   *hogi enke den*   *disi de.*
                DET (pl)   DEM here   NEG   bad   like   DET (pl)   DEM there
                'These ones here [cassava bread] are not as bad as these ones there.'

7.3.   Derivational morphology (word formation)

Three kinds of word formation process are attested in the creoles of Suriname: reduplication, affixation, and compounding.

7.3.1. Reduplication

Reduplication creates a new word by copying all or part of a base form. It can be divided into five major types, each yielding words that share some common meaning.

– Intensive or emphatic reduplication;
– Attributive-forming reduplication;
– X-like reduplication, forming verbs denoting an X-like quality, where X refers to the meaning of the base;

– Deverbal noun-forming reduplication;
– Distributive reduplication, conveying a sense of 'scattered, here and there'.

The first two of these types are highly productive in the Surinamese creoles, the other three less so. (For other minor types of reduplication, see Huttar and Huttar [1997].)

Intensive reduplication yields words that augment the meaning of the base. It usually involves full reduplication, that is, the entire base is copied, and may apply to adjectivals (property items), nouns or verbs. It adds a sense of "more of X", where X is the base. With property items, it conveys an emphatic or intensive meaning, that is, the sense of 'very'. With nouns, the resulting word conveys augmentative sense ('many'), while with verbs the result conveys the sense of recurrence or continuation.

(110) Sranan   a. attribute *bruya* 'confused' *bruya-bruya* 'very confused'
                 b. noun   *saka* 'sack, bag' *saka-saka* 'many sacks/bags'
                 c. verb   *tai* 'to tie; bind' *tai-tai* 'to tie repeatedly'

Attributive-forming reduplication, sometimes referred to as stative reduplication, also involves full reduplication, and takes verbs as its input, creating items that refer to (unusual) states. In general, verbs referring to an activity that results in a visible or ascertainable state, or verbs referring to concepts of human propensity, may function as inputs.

(111) EMarC   a. *booko* 'to break'   *booko-booko* '(in a) broken
       (state)'
                b. *baaka* 'to blacken'   *baaka-baaka* '(in a state of) black'
                c. *giili* 'to make greedy' *giili-giili* '(in a) greedy (state)'

The resulting elements are not verbal, but function as predicative and attributive adjectives. In the former function, they are introduced either by the copula *de* or the verb *tan* 'stay'.

(112) EMarC   *E*   *uwii*   *de*   *lusulusu*   *kaba.*
                his   hair   COP   loose-loose   already
                'His hair is in an loosened/unbraided state.'

They also function as postposed modifiers of NPs.

(113) Saamaka   *De*   *mbéi*   *hen*   *límbo-límbo*
                 they   make   it   clean-clean
                 'They made it clean.'
                 (Veenstra 1996: 158)

X-like reduplication forms verbs denoting an X-like quality, where X refers to the meaning of the base. Certain nouns and (most kinds of) verbs can be inputs to this process. The verbs derived thus convey diminutive, approximative and similar senses, and can be either intransitive or transitive.

(114) EMarC   a. *A   dagu   ya   fatu-fatu.*
                  DET (sg) dog   here   fat-fat
                  'This dog is/has gotten fattish.'

          b. *A   baakabaaka   den   buuku.*
             she   black-black DET (pl)   trouser
             'She made the trousers blackish.'

It would appear that, in general, the same items that undergo attributive reduplication can also undergo X-like reduplication. The precise relationship between the two kinds of reduplication is still in need of further research.

De-verbal noun-forming reduplication, as the name implies, creates nouns
from verbs, and may be full or partial. The nouns produced may refer to instru-
ments, results and various other unpredictable interpretations. This process is
no longer productive, though.

(115) all   a. *nai* 'to sew'   *nanai* 'needle'
      Sranan   b. *dyompo* 'to jump'   *dyompo-dyompo* 'grasshopper'

Distributive reduplication is somewhat similar to X-like reduplication, but
Gooden (2003) argues that this is a separate type in Jamaican Creole, distinguished by a different pitch pattern. Whether the same distinction holds for
the Surinamese creoles is still to be determined. It creates words that convey
senses such as 'scattered, here and there', and so on. Verbs, adjectivals (property items) and nouns can all undergo this process.

(116) EMarC   *Den   piiti-piit   a   impi.*
                they   rip-rip   DET (sg)   shirt
                'They ripped the shirt in several places/kind of ripped it.'

According to Huttar and Huttar (1997: 397), nouns reduplicated in this way
may express "variety", that is, "the sense of several groups or kinds, or actions
dividing things into groups or kinds".

(117) EMarC   *Den   wataawataa   fu   libi   sama   sikin.*
                DET (pl) water-water   for   live   person   body
                'the various liquids of the body'

7.3.2. *Affixation*

The creoles of Suriname have two suffixes, *-man* and *-pe*. The former is productively used to derive agentive nouns from verbs and nouns, nomina posses-
siva or agentive nouns from nouns, and the notion of "inhabitant or member of
a particular place, group" from place names and names of groups (e.g. ethnic
group or other organizational units). The base may be a simple noun or verb or
a complex NP or VP.

(118) Saamaka   a. *hondi-ma*   < hunter+AG 'hunter'
                 b. *pali-ku-mujee-ma* < give-birth-with-woman-AG
                                         'midwife'
                                        (Bakker, Smith and Veenstra 1995: 173)

       EMarC   c. *wenkiman*   < shop+AG 'shop owner, person
                                         working in a shop'
       EMarC   d. *soolanman*   < St. Laurent+AG 'person of St.
                                         Laurent'

Nouns derived with the suffix *-man* can, in most cases, refer to both men and
women. There are some terms that are only used to refer to either men or wom-
en. They denote activities that are generally only performed by the members of
one sex.

(119) Ndjuka   *Den   umanpikin   de   na   beeman.*
                 DET (pl)   woman   DEM   COP   belly-person
                 'Those women are pregnant (women).'

In these compounds referring to the "inhabitant or member of some group", the
suffix *-man* is often replaced with *uman* 'woman' when specifically referring to
a female member. Nouns involving *uman* often have either a pejorative meaning and/or they distinguish women's activities from men's.

(120) EMarC   *A   tou   anga   wan   soolanuman.*
                 he   marry   with   a   St. Laurent-woman
                 'He married a woman from St. Laurent.'

The suffix *-pe* is used to derive place names from verbs.

(121) EMarC   a. *tanpe*   < stay+place 'domicile'
                 b. *wookope* < work+place 'location where one works'
                 c. *belipe*   < bury+place 'cemetery'

7.3.3. Compounding

The most productive process of word formation in the creoles of Suriname is compounding. The overwhelming majority of compounds are NN compounds.

(122) EMarC   a. *mata tiki* 'pestle'   < *mata* 'mortar' + *tiki* 'stick'
                 b. *maka sii ain futu* 'ankle'   < *make* 'thorn' + *sii* 'grain'
                                                    + *ain* 'eye' + *futu* 'leg/
                                                    foot'

But there are also compounds involving a verb and a noun, a numeral and a noun, a preposition/adverb and a noun, and an adjective and a noun.

(123) EMarC   a. *keeosu* 'mortuary'   < *kee* 'cry' + *osu*
                                                              'house'
                 b. *dii futu* 'tripod for balancing pots'   < *dii* 'three' + *futu*
                                                              'leg, foot'
                 c. *fositin* 'former times/flight time'   < *fosi* 'before' + *tin*
                                                              'time'
                 d. *gaansama* 'elder'   < *gaan* 'big,
                                                              important' +
                                                              sama 'person'

7.4.   Prepositions and location

The structure of locative and directional phrases (cf. section 6.2.1.) in the Surinamese creoles differs quite substantially from those in English. Locative phrases are typically headed by a general locational marker, (*n*)*a*, which selects location-denoting NPs that express location, direction, or origin. *Na* itself is neutral in meaning, and the kind of spatial meaning it expresses depends on the nature of the predicate.

(124) EMarC   *A   puu   en   ne   en   ana.*
                he   pull   her   LOC   his   hand
                'He took her from him.'

The locational marker also heads complex phrases that express a variety of spatial relationships. In these phrases, the location-denoting NP is modified by locational specifiers that function as nouns. In Sranan and the EMarC they are either derived from English prepositions, such as *ini* 'inside' (< *in*), *ondro/ ondoo* 'underside' (< *under*), etc., or from English nouns *tapu* (< *top*), *baka* (< *back*), *se*(*i*) (< *side*) etc. In Saamaka some of the specifiers have a different (possibly Portuguese) origin, e.g. 'top, on' is conveyed by *liba*, and 'in' by

dendu. These specifiers are either juxtaposed to the NP, thus creating a possessive construction, or are connected to it by a possessive marker, *fu*.

(125) EMarC   a. *A   e   taampu   na   a   tafa*
tapu.

         It   IMPFV   stand-up   LOC   DET (sg)   table   top
         'It is standing on the table.'

         b. *A   uku   fika   na   a   se*
           DET (sg)   fishing-rod   leave   LOC   DET (sg)   side

         fu   mi   osu.
         POSS   my   house
         'The fishing rod was left behind/remains at the side of
         my house.'

8.   Conclusion

This summary provides only a rough overview of the syntactic phenomena
of the Surinamese creoles. Many of these phenomena remain relatively under-researched, and many questions remain unanswered. The issue of origins
continues to attract most attention, particularly the relative contributions of
superstrate and substrate languages, and the role played by universal principles
of acquisition, as well as internally motivated changes. Besides descriptive
studies, a significant amount of work on the creoles of Suriname has therefore
focused on analyzing textual sources from early Sranan, investigating the sociohistorical matrix of creole formation, comparing creole grammar and lexicon
with those of their possible input languages and with universals of language acquisition. The interaction among these factors explains many of the similarities,
as well as the differences, found among the Surinamese creoles. At the same
time, issues like these cannot be fully explored in the absence of sound empiri-
cally-based analyses of the grammar of these creoles. There is need of more
research on complex constructions such as subordination and relativization, as
well as co-ordination. There is also much that needs to be done on areas that
have only been partly explored, such as passivization and focus constructions.
Finally, while a great deal of attention has been paid to Sranan, and to a lesser
extent to EMarC and Saamaka, the other varieties have not been explored in
any detail. Future research will no doubt reveal much more about the workings
of their grammar, and its sources. It is also hoped that future research will de-
vote attention to sociolinguistic issues since practically nothing is known about
the sociolinguistic makeup of these communities.

* Part of the research on which this paper is based was funded by NSF Grant # BCS-0113826, for which the authors would like to express their sincere thanks.

Exercises and study questions

1. Transcribe part of the recordings of Sranan Tongo or Pamaka and do a comparison of tense-aspect marking in the two creoles.

2. Compare word formation processes in Sranan Tongo and any other Surinamese creole.

3. What kinds of morphological or syntactic evidence can you find to support the claim that Gbe languages played a prominent role in the emergence of the Surinamese creoles?

4. Compare and contrast the ways in which location and spatial relationships are expressed in the Surinamese creoles, with how they are expressed in English.

5. Discuss the structure of NPs in the Surinamese creoles, with special reference to the system of determiners they use. Compare and contrast the structure of NP in English, or in any other English-lexicon creole.

6. Compare the structure of relative clauses in Surinamese creoles with their structure in English or another English-lexicon creole.

7. Compare the structure of *wh*-questions with that of focus constructions in the Surinamese creoles. What similarities do you find? Do you find similar parallels between these two types of construction in other Caribbean creoles?

8. Discuss the similarities and differences between copula predication in English and copular predication in the Surinamese creoles.

9. What do you understand by the term *serial verb constructions*? Find examples of different types in the Surinamese creoles. What similarities or differences can you see in their structure?

Selected references

Please consult the General references for titles mentioned in the text but not included in the references below. For a full bibliography see the accompanying CD-ROM.

Alleyne, Mervyn
    1987   Predicate structures in Saramaccan. In: Mervyn Alleyne (ed.), *Studies in Saramaccan Language Structure*, 71–88. Kingston, Jamaica: Folklore Studies Project, University of the West Indies, Jamaica.
Arends, Jacques and Matthias Perl
    1995   *Early Creole Texts: A Collection of 18th Century Sranan and Saramaccan Documents*. New York: Lang.
Bakker, Peter, Norval Smith and Tonjes Veenstra
    1995   Saramaccan. In: Jacques Arends, Pieter Muysken and Norval Smith (eds.), *Pidgins and Creoles: An Introduction*, 165–178. Amsterdam/Philadelphia: Benjamins.
Caskey, A. F.
    1990   Controlling into purpose clauses the Creole way. *Linguistics* 28: 689–712.
Gooden, Shelome
    2003   Reduplication in Jamaican Creole: semantic functions and prosodic constraints. In: Silvia Kouwenberg (ed.), *Twice as Meaningful: Reduplication in Pidgins, Creoles and other Contact Languages*, 93–104. London: Battlebridge.
Huttar, George and Mary Huttar
    1994   *Ndyuka*. London/New York: Routledge.
Huttar, Mary and George Huttar
    1997   Reduplication in Ndyuka. In: Spears and Winford (eds.), 395–414.
Keenan Edward L. and Bernard Comrie
    1977   Noun phrase accessibility and universal grammar. *Linguistic Inquiry* 8: 63–99.
Migge, Bettina
    1998   Substrate influence in creole formation: The origin of *give*-type serial verb constructions in the Surinamese Plantation Creole. *Journal of Pidgin and Creole Languages* 13: 215–265.
Migge, Bettina
    2000   The origin of property items in the Surinamese Plantation Creole. In: McWhorter (ed.), 201–234.
Nickel, Marilya and John Wilner
    1984   *Papers on Sranan*. Paramaribo, Suriname: Summer Institute of Linguistics.
Park, James, Naomi Glock and S. Catherine Rountree
    1981   *Discourse Studies in Saramaccan*. (Languages of the Guianas Vol. III.) Suriname: Summer Institute of Linguistics.

Rountree, S. Catherine
    1992   *Saramaccan Grammar Sketch*. Paramaribo: Summer Institute of Linguistics.

Sebba, Mark
    1987   *The Syntax of Serial Verbs*. Amsterdam/Philadelphia: Benjamins.

Smith, Norval
    1996   Focus-marking *wε* in Saramaccan: Grammaticalization or substrate. In: Philip Baker and Anand Syea (eds.), *Changing Meanings, Changing Functions: Papers Relating to Grammaticalization in Contact Languages*, 113–128. London: University of Westminster Press.

Thompson, Sandra and Robert Longacre
    1985   Adverbial clauses. In: Timothy Shopen (ed.), *Language Typology and Syntactic Description*. Vol. II: *Complex Constructions*, 171–234. Cambridge: Cambridge University Press.

Veenstra, Tonjes
    1996   *Serial Verbs in Saramaccan. Predication and Creole Genesis*. Dordrecht: ICG Printing.

Winford, Donald
    1988   Stativity and other aspects of the creole passive. *Lingua* 76: 271–297.
    1997   Property items and predication in Sranan. *Journal of Pidgin and Creole Languages* 12: 237–301.
    2000a   Tense and aspect in Sranan and the creole prototype. In: McWhorther (ed.), 383–442.
    2000b   Irrealis in Sranan: Mood and modality in a radical creole. *Journal of Pidgin and Creole Languages* 15: 63–125.

Belize and other central American varieties: morphology and syntax

Geneviève Escure

1.   English in Central America

In the 15th and 16th centuries, the Spanish empire subjugated the Amerindian population from the Caribbean to Central and South America, ruling from the island of Hispaniola, but in the 17th century other European powers started disputing Spanish supremacy in the New World. Thus, the Central American region has been subjected to multiethnic and multilingual influences over the last centuries. I will specifically address the lingering linguistic effects of England's encroachment on Central American territories whose colonial histories are similar to that of the Caribbean. They include, from North to Southeast, Belize, Honduras, Nicaragua, Costa Rica, Panama, and the offshore islands. The location of English speakers in Central America reflects the tumultuous conflicts that opposed Spain and England between the 17th and the 19th centuries. All English-speaking regions are located on the Caribbean coast of Central America, and except for Belize, they are part of overwhelmingly Spanish-speaking republics. The goal of this overview is therefore to describe the use of English-based varieties spoken by minority groups, in particular by the Creoles, i.e. the Afro-Caribbean descendants of transported African slaves, but also by some whites who have settled at various times in coastal areas. The primary emphasis is on Belize, which includes the highest percentage of English speakers, but I will also refer to other English-speaking communities, specifically those of the Bay Islands of Honduras, the Miskito Coast of Nicaragua, the Puerto-Limón area of Costa Rica, and the Bocas del Toro province of Panama. The English-based creoles spoken in these areas include Belizean Creole (BelC), Bay Islands Creole (BIsC), Miskito Coast Creole (MisC), Limón Creole (LimC), Panamanian Creole (PanC), as well as varieties spoken in the islands of Providencia (ProC) and San Andres (SanC) (See map 1).

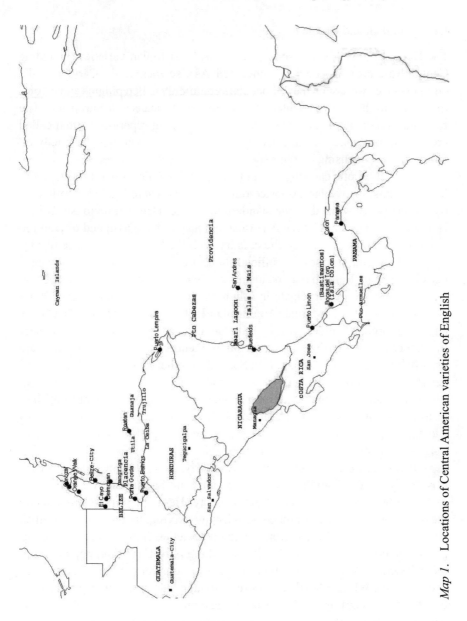

Map 1. Locations of Central American varieties of English

1.1.   English and Creole

The label "English" is a misnomer as far as West Indian varieties (including Central American varieties) are concerned. As elsewhere in the Caribbean, the circumstances were such that vernaculars commonly called pidgins and creoles developed in the course of interactions between Africans and Europeans. The resulting linguistic phenomena include wide ranging repertoires often called creole continua. The special relation of creoles to English must be briefly examined before focusing on their specific morphosyntactic aspects.

Two varieties, one carrying overt prestige, and the other covert prestige, typically co-exist or overlap in postcolonial societies where English is officially or nationally recognized as the standard language. Belize (previously British Honduras) is the only Central American country to have assigned official recognition to English. It is also the country with the highest percentage of English speakers. But in spite of its official status, English in Belize is not anyone's native language. English may be unanimously recognized as the language that one must acquire to participate in official government activities, but it is not commonly used in its external (American or British) standard form. This fact is largely ignored, or unidentified by both language users and language planners. In other countries, English has vernacular or identity value, and its speakers are usually bilingual or multilingual (in Spanish or other languages). The isolated geographic location of Afro-Caribbean groups and their neglect by local Spanish governments contributed to the maintenance of native forms of English in historically remote areas. Thus, on Roatán (one of the Bay Islands of Honduras, a territory that was for ten years a Crown colony), English-based varieties have long been the primary language of the Creole segment of the black population, as well as of some early white settlers. Similarly, the Limón area of Costa Rica was totally cut off from the rest of the country until a railroad was completed in 1975 after a twenty-year construction delay (Herzfeld 2003). Consequently, the different areas to be examined will display varying, though related English structures that are different from standard varieties. Table 1 presents an approximate comparison of the English-speaking Afro-Caribbean population in the five Central American countries based on various census sources, estimates, and websites. When official sources refer to language use, they pay little attention to minority groups and their languages, providing vague combined numbers for the black / West Indian / mixed group, thus not differentiating between Creoles, Miskitos, or Garinagu (Afro-Indians; note that the singular form is Garifuna). Some of them speak only Spanish, and others may speak Creole or English as L1 or L2. Belize and Honduras figures – checked on location in 2003 – are fairly accurate.

Table 1.   Creole/English speaking population in Central America

	Total population	Creole/English speakers (%)	Est. pop. ('Black' West-Indian)	Other ethnic groups
Belize	240,204	67,480 (28.1%)	35%	Mestizo, Maya, Garifuna, other
Honduras	6,560,608	80,000 (1.2%)	5%	Mestizo, Garifuna, Miskito, Pech
Nicaragua	5,023,818	40,000 (0.8%)	9%	Mestizo, Miskito, Rama, Garifuna
Costa-Rica	3,344,934	55,000 (1.6%)	3%	Mestizo, Bribri, Cabecar, other
Panama	2,882,329	100,000 (3.5%)	14%	Mestizo, Cuna, Chiriqui, other

In Belize, where English is the educational medium while the creole variety (BelC) has strong vernacular value, the continuum is extensive, ranging between two poles: the creole vernacular is the basilect, whereas the official English norm is the acrolect. Intermediate varieties constitute the mesolect. The persistent legacy of colonialism is still reflected in the widespread belief that any variety that does not conform to English canonical norms is *brokop* (broken English) a term that often denotes basilects as well as mesolects. In countries in which no official English model is available, English varieties may have a more limited range; they may be more conservative, or on the contrary may be the result of contact with dialectal forms of English that may, or may not, have been exposed to African influences.

1.2.   Lectal shifts

The examples presented below to illustrate the morphosyntax of 'English in Central America' are meant as a summary representation of the complex systems available to speakers of English. For example, although the basilect is the norm in Belize, it is not the only variety used by Belizeans. Thus, it would be misleading to solely illustrate Belizean varieties exclusively with creole forms. Furthermore, each individual controls a wide-ranging repertoire. Consequently, I will adduce structures commonly used in daily natural situations that require shifting up or down depending on the context, setting, topic, or participants. Lectal shifts also regularly occur within conversations, or even within sentences, as represented in the two short samples below that I collected in Placencia, Belize. This means that there are no strictly basilectal, mesolectal, or acrolectal speakers. In the examples shown, simple English orthography is used to denote an acrolect, in spite of numerous phonetic differences from Standard English. For mesolects and basilects, I use a broad phonetic transcription of the type generally accepted in creole studies. In this case a general translation is also provided (more specific glosses are used in the second part of the section when necessary).

Text 1: In this sample, an elderly lady, Tina, 80, uses the acrolect when addressing a little girl, Betty, with occasionally intruding mesolectal features. She switches to a consistent mesolect to address a friend [the author]. It is not unusual for older women to select acrolects when addressing children. This choice appears to reflect the nefarious consequences of the traditional colonial shame associated with the use of the creole.

[Tina admonishes Betty, 7, who tries to drink out of a glass containing stale water]

(1a)   *I say, what is this? It's hot now, that is not cool again, it isn't cool again, that isn't cool again, it's hot, it isn't nice again. Don't do it! Don't! Tell me something: you had your supper already? No? Let me see your mouth. Mani no give you your supper today? What you eat tonight, child?*

[to me, continuing conversation]:

(1b)   *Mai hosban waz a mada ankl, ha gramada ankl. A deliva aal ha chidrn, nayn a em, dey aal kaal mi 'aanti.' Po, i had kensr, kensr a di lang.*

'My husband was her mother's uncle, her grandmother's uncle. I delivered her children, all nine of them, they all call me 'auntie.' Paul, he had cancer, lung cancer.'

[to girl]

(1c)   *Betty Jane, what are you doing now?*

[to me]

(1d)   *Smok an drink. Finally, tri o for yaz i stap di drinkin, i yuztu tek wan o tu bia wen i kom hom i se i bonin op insaid.*
'(Paul used to) smoke and drink. He finally quit drinking in the last three or four years (before he died) he was down to one or two beers. When he would come home, he would say that he was burning up inside.'

(Escure 1997: 101)

The lectal variation represented in Text 1 illustrates the astonishing adaptability of creole speakers to varying interlocutors, topics and moods. Acrolectal forms can be characterized by the frequent use of the copula/auxiliary, as well as – phonetically – by the occasional use of interdentals. The shift to a basi-/mesolectal structure with preverbal negative and absence of the *do* auxiliary, as in *Mani no give you?[...] What you eat?* within the context of a generally acrolectal discourse is not unusual. It signals a move away from the admonishment mode to a friendlier inquiry. When switching back to the topic of her dead husband's illness, Tina eventually reverts to another lect, a more natural vernacular for her: no possessive case, agreement or tense marking, but no creole morphemes either – typically a mesolect, often considered appropriate when addressing serious topics in an informal context. This variable behavior is indeed typical: A Belizean speaker fluidly shifts from one set of forms to another, combining an acrolectal form such as *was* or *is* with the zero-possessive *he was her mother uncle*. Such combinations are no evidence of 'imperfect' acquisition of the standard. They merely represent the natural options available to creole speakers.

Text 2: The following short sample represents a more basilectal, and animated version of the speech genre we may call 'admonishment.' This type of remonstrance, usually delivered in a lively and humorous fashion, is a common mode of address when parents or elders disapprove of younger people's behavior, and the admonished typically listen respectfully (though this does not necessarily entail behavior modification). In this case Cara, 65, upbraids her son Raul, 40, for being an alcoholic, and she does so by occasionally addressing me, referring to him in the third person (although he is present). Raul accepts his mother's disapproval, though he tries to 'up' her by arguing that her watching television is just as bad an addiction, then by pointing out that he is now drinking water. Note the frequent use of the preverbal morpheme *de*, which is a marker of imperfective [IMPFV] (both progressive and iterative/habitual):

(2)   C=a. *Dada an mi sit down watch tivi i de   drink evriday.*
            Dad and me sit down watch TV he IMPFV drink everyday

      b. *dey en   nayt, so a biliv   i   naw*
          day and night, so I believe it now

         de   afek yo   breyn.
         IMPFV affect your brain

     R=c. *Samtaym   tivi da   di   bad ting*
          Sometimes TV that the bad thing

C=d. *bot   di   layf   we   yu   liv   wid   alkohol   da*
    But   the   life   that   you   live   with   alcohol   that

    notin   gud   in   dat
    nothing   good   in   that

R=e. *da   lown   wata   a   de   drink   yu   now.*
    That   only   water   I   IMPFV   drink   you   know

C=f. *yu   now   wat   a   taak   a   no   taak   bawt   di   wata*
    You   know   what   I   say   I   NEG   talk   about   the   water

g. *yu   now   we   a   kom   from*
    you   know   where   I   come   from

h. *yu   destray   yuself   bway   di   ting   dat   yu   de   sey*
    you   destroy   yourself   boy   the   things   that   you   IMPFV   say

i. *Raul   mos   awta   yo   rayt   mayn*
    Raul   must   out of   your   right   mind

'C=While father and I watch TV, he [Raul] drinks everyday, day and night, so I believe that it is now affecting your brain
R=It's watching TV that is a bad thing (simultaneous speech)
C=But it's awful, the way you live under the influence of alcohol
R=It's just water I'm drinking now
C=You know what I'm talking about, I'm not talking about (this glass of) water, you know what I mean; you are destroying yourself, my boy. And the (stupid) things that you say (when you are drunk), Raul, you must be out of your right mind' [dialogue partly included in Escure 1997: 114].

The short texts presented above suggest that the selection of a representative sample of English in Central America presents a real challenge because of the variability available to speakers. Methodological scope is crucial, since explanations are directly dependent on the kind and range of speech data collected. A brief sociolinguistic overview of each region provides an essential perspective illustrating the differential reasons for language use in various parts of Central America.

2. Belize: Sociolinguistic and demographic background

Belize, the former British colony of British Honduras, is a complex society in spite of its small size: it has the lowest population density in Central America (240,204 according to the 2000 Population Census) for a territory covering barely 13,000 square kilometers. Because of its pivotal geographical position at the juncture of Central America and the West Indies, and its complicated history, it exhibits both multiculturalism and multilingualism. It is also the Central American country with the highest percentage of English speakers, since the Creole group currently amounts to almost one third of the total population.

When the Spaniards arrived in the Bay of Honduras in the 16th century, the great Mayan cities had already been deserted. The Spanish used the area for the extraction of the precious woods favored in Europe, but did not dwell there. This remote coast, its long reef, and outlying islands were thus a favorite retreat for pirates throughout the 17th century (Placencia natives trace their ancestry to French, Dutch and English pirates). Some say that the name *Belize* was derived from *Wallis,* the name of a Scottish buccaneer. The diverse Belizean population results from waves of immigrants who supplemented the indigenous Amerindian population of Mayas and Kekchis. After the English snatched Jamaica from Spain in 1655, African slaves were brought to the Bay settlement to work on logging camps, and Miskito Indians joined them a century later after the English colonists were forced (by the Spanish) to evacuate the British settlement of the Mosquito Coast (now Nicaragua) in 1787. On September 10th, 1798, the British defeated the Spanish armada near St George's Caye, just outside Belize City. Subsequently, England took possession of British Honduras as a colony (1862), then a Crown colony (1871) until 1981, at which time Belize became independent, and acquired its new name. Belize's ethnic diversity was enriched by the emigration of a small Garifuna population (or Black Caribs, deported by the British from St Vincent to Honduras in 1797), by Mestizos (Spanish/Indian refugees of the Indian Caste War in Mexico), and by indentured servants from India. More recent immigrants include Mennonites, and Hispanic refugees or laborers. The current population is generally identified as including four major groups: Amerindians, Creoles, Mestizos, and Garinagu. All speak different native languages as shown in Table 2. As Latinos move in from El Salvador, Guatemala and Honduras (they almost exclusively constitute the labor force on the banana and citrus plantations), the Mestizo community has increased by at least 15% since the 1991 census (Escure 1997: 29). Consequently, English speakers (Creoles) would seem to amount to no more than 29%, and are amply surpassed by Spanish speakers. In 1991, the Creole and

Mestizo population co-existed in roughly equal numbers, about 32%. However, Belizean Creole English is now gaining new native speakers as Garinagu are losing their native Garifuna language.

Table 2.   Ethnic groups in Belize in 2000: Total=240,204

Ethnic group	Language	Population	%
Mestizo	Spanish	112,935	47.0
Creole	Belizean Creole	67,480	26.1
Maya	Maya	24,400	10.2
Garifuna	(Garifuna)* BelC	15,685	6.5
Mennonite	German	8,125	3.4
East Indian	Belizean Creole	8,020	3.3
Other	Chinese, Arabic	3,559	1.5

[*indicates that the Garinagu are losing their language and acquiring BelC as L1]

As is the case everywhere in Central America, a large segment of the population has emigrated abroad, mostly to the United States, in search of better economic opportunities. The number of emigrants over the last 30 years may have reached as much as 150,000. High emigration patterns are reflected in the relative youth of the Belizean population: 65% is under age 24, whereas the most productive segment of the population (age 25-54) amounts to 28%, and individuals over 54 constitute only 8% of the population. This generational distribution suggests that the breadwinners live abroad (sending home regular checks), and that they have only limited influence on the linguistic and behavioral development of the younger generation.

Ethnic groups are not evenly distributed all over the country, but on the contrary, ethnic enclaves are still very clearly segregated from each other across the six districts that make up Belize, as shown on Table 3. The Creole population is primarily located in the Belize District that includes the main city (Belize-City), and the administrative capital of the country, Belmopan (much less populated than Belize-City), and neighboring districts to the West (Cayo) and the South (Toledo).

Table 3. Ethnic groups in the Six Districts of Belize (1991)
[northern to southern geographical locations] (Escure 1997: 31)

Districts	**Creole**	**Garifuna**	**Mestizo**	**Maya**
Corozal	7.6%	1.3%	74.1%	5.0%
Orange Walk	7.4	1.2	71.7	9.1
Belize	**67.9**	5.3	18.7	1.2
Cayo	**23.0**	1.7	58.0	8.7
Stann Creek	**25.1**	36.2	23.7	8.0
Toledo	5.7	10.0	11.9	62.8

In Table 3, the districts including the highest Creole population are shown in bold characters. I conducted fieldwork primarily in the Stann Creek District, and in particular in the village of Placencia, located on the coast. Although Belizean structure has been linked to Jamaican influence, its morphology differs significantly from that of Jamaican Creole; for example, its imperfective morpheme is *de – a* in JC, and its past/anterior morpheme is *me – bin* in JamC. BelC is more similar to Nicaraguan varieties (Miskito Coast, Providencia Creole, and San Andrés Creole), and that is due to frequent migrations in the 18th century across the British settlements of the Miskito Coast and Belize. Various aspects of BelC have been documented by Greene (1999), Hellinger (1972), and LePage and Tabouret-Keller (1985).

3. Other Central American countries

There is a minority English-speaking population in each of the four remaining Central American nations located south of Belize (Honduras, Nicaragua, Costa Rica, and Panama). Guatemala is not discussed because it has no substantial Creole population. However, the creole is spoken on the narrow coastal strip separating Belize from Honduras, especially in the busy port of Puerto-Barrios, and there are several Garifuna communities (e.g., Livingston) that almost certainly include speakers of English Creole as L2 because of frequent interactions with Belizean and coastal Honduran populations. Spanish is the dominant and increasingly encroaching language in each of those countries. Some form of English is spoken by only 1 to 3% of the overall population, but it is still the primary language in some areas. There are also a few speakers of English Creole in the islands of Providencia, San Andrés, and St. Catalina. Those islands politically belong to Colombia, a South American nation, but they have close historical and cultural ties with the Caribbean coast of Central America, and they are thus included in this description.

As England assumed control of Jamaica in 1655, the island became a major holding port for African slaves, who were then sent to various logging camps or settlements all along the Central American coast. All Central American countries gained independence from Spain in 1821, but many did not achieve complete independence from England until the end of the 19th or the beginning of the 20th century.

3.1.   Honduras

All speakers of English or Creole English reside primarily in the Bay Islands (Roatán, Utila, and Guanaja), and a few along the coast, in Tela, and other communities reaching into Guatemala, and then Belize. Until the 1980s, the Honduran government had neglected the Bay Islands. The identification of English/Creole speakers in Honduras is complicated by the fact that Creoles and Garinagu (Afro-Indians) are often counted together as *morenos* (blacks), or *población negra de habla inglesa* (English-speaking black population). The Creole population has been estimated to be 20,000 but often excluded from the discussion of Honduras's seven ethnic groups. However, more recent figures obtained in Honduras in 2003 (*Fiscalia especial de etnia y patrimonio cultural, Ministerio público Honduras*) give much higher and separate figures for English speaking blacks (80,000) and Garinagu (250,000) (Escure 2004). There is some general confusion as to the origin, history and demography of the Garinagu as differentiated from that of the Creoles. Whereas the Garinagu inhabit remote villages on the east side of the island, at or around the original landing site of Punta Gorda, the Creole population mostly lives on the western part of the island (in Sandy Bay, West End, Flowers Bay, and Coxen Hole), but also in older settlements in Oak Ridge, and in French Harbour, that used to be an active commercial center. The Spanish never stayed on the Bay Islands, and the English attempted to settle the islands at various times, but the Spanish/British conflicts constantly interfered with long-term settlements. The first permanent settlement was established in the 1830s after emancipation, when freed slaves and former slave owners emigrated to Roatán from the Cayman Islands, Belize, or the Mosquito Shore. They brought with them the variety of Creole/English spoken elsewhere along the coast. By 1855, the Bay Islands harbored 1,600 blacks and 200 whites (mostly on Utila). After a brief stint as a Crown colony, the Bay Islands were ceded to the Republic of Honduras, but the islands remained isolated from the mainland.

Until the late 80s education was strictly in English and provided 'sparsely' by private religious schools. By then, the Honduran government realized the economic potential of the Bay Islands, and began to develop a tourist industry on Roatán, as well as a basic educational and social infrastructure. Education in Spanish is now obligatory, which means that individuals under 40 grew up with a consistent external Spanish model. The increase in the Hispanic population from the Honduran mainland seeking work on the island contributes to the spread of Spanish. In addition, there are recent incentives – especially among younger people – to learn American English because of the developing tourist industry (mostly upscale diving groups in a few select hotels) that provides jobs for local people. Young adults are increasingly socialized in outgroup cultural and linguistic systems.

It has been claimed that the variety of English spoken on the Honduran Islands (BIsC) is not a creole. The smallest islands, Utila and Guanaja (Bonacca), have a dominant white population that appears to speak mesolectal varieties, or perhaps English dialects (Graham 1997; Warantz 1983). *Wellerism* – the merger of /w/ and /v/ – is identified as a typical 'white' feature, which is also a characteristic of Cayman Islands English. There is also a very small white minority on the largest island of Roatán that may have been established on the island before Africans moved in (Graham 1997), though Evans accurately says that they are more likely to be light-skinned Creoles. This succinctly documented variety also appears to be a mesolect: it is said to include *doz* and *don* as habituals, and *had* as preverbal past. However, the black Creoles speak a more basilectal variety. My personal observations (2000-2003) indicate that, in spite of the development of the western part of the island, and the construction of a paved road that facilitates access to Sandy Bay, West End and West Bay – Bay Island Creole (BIsC) is still used by young people in informal conversations. It is also heard in villages located toward the eastern side (in particular Politilly Bight and Oak Ridge). A variety of creolized English is spoken by those older Garinagu (over 50), who grew up on the island at a time where BIsC was the dominant language. Those people are truly trilingual in Garifuna, BIsC and Spanish. Creoles also control some variety of acrolectal English, and increasingly so due to the tourism and diving industry, and frequent emigration to the United States. In this sense Roatán is not unlike the situation in Belize on a smaller scale.

3.2.   Nicaragua

Two creole varieties have been identified along Nicaragua's Atlantic Coast, Miskito Coast Creole (MisC), spoken by Creoles and Afro-Indians (Miskitos) around the Bluefields, and Pearl Lagoon areas, as well as on the Corn Islands (Islas de Mais), and Rama Caye Creole (RamC), spoken by the Rama Indians on a small island whose population is no more than 500 (Assadi 1983). 9% of the population of Nicaragua is of African descent, 69% is Mestizo, and 5% indigenous, but only about 1% (or less) speak MisC. O'Neil (1993: 280) claims that "indeterminate numbers of nearly 70,000 Miskito Indians have Nicaraguan English as their native language."

The Puritans who had settled on Providencia Island in 1630 probably traded with the Indians on the Miskito Coast, and a form of contact English may have developed there, then submitted to other influences as African slaves, maroons and English buccaneers, loggers and planters interacted with local Indians. The Miskitos intermarried with the Africans, and now most Miskitos are Afro-Indians, and many live in Honduras (Gracias de Dios province, just north of the border with Nicaragua). Africans were brought from other parts of the Caribbean in the mid 18th century when the coast was a British Settlement from 1740 to 1787, at which time the English were forced to leave the area to the Spanish. Some moved to Belize with their African slaves and their Miskito allies, but many also remained along the coast. Other groups migrated there by the mid 19th century, including Garinagu who had moved down the coast from Honduras. Native Miskito and Rama Indians (many of them are now Afro-Indians like the Garinagu) have mostly lost their native languages. It is likely that Spanish has now spread as surface communication between Managua and the coast has improved since the Sandinista revolution in 1979. Consequently, the use of English is probably receding (not unlike the situation in Costa Rica) in spite of efforts to encourage cultural pluralism, and literacy campaigns to preserve English on the Atlantic coast.

It is claimed that RamC is distinct from MisC, mostly because of the influence exerted by German missionaries in the 19th century. However, this influence appears to be primarily lexical, as the two varieties share a similar morphology.

3.3.   Providencia and San Andrés islands (Colombia)

The Old Providence Island (Providencia) was the site of one of the earliest English settlements in the New World, as a small group of Puritans settled there in 1630. Their experiment lasted only ten years, as the Spanish forced them to move to the Bocas del Toro area, now in Panama (see 3.5). San Andrés was settled later in the 18th century, but in 1786, the Miskito Shore and the offshore islands were ceded to Spain. English settlers were allowed to stay on San Andrés, and it is generally considered that the variety (*Islander*) spoken on

San Andrés (SanC) is more basilectal than the variety spoken on Providencia (ProC), and the smaller St Catalina (Washabaugh 1975, 1983). Recent forays show that in spite of Spanish dominance, Caribbean English has continued to exert an influence in Providencia and St Catalina, resulting in continuum maintenance.

3.4.   Costa Rica: Limón Creole

There is a population of English Creole speakers in the Limón area along the Atlantic coast, estimated to be around 55,100 (Herzfeld 1983a, 1983b, 2003).

Spain claimed Costa Rica from native Indians in the 16th century, and imported a small number of African slaves – about 200 during the colonial period. When slavery was abolished in 1824, there were no more than 100 Africans. Jamaicans and others were brought in large numbers in the 19th century to build the railroads, and work for the United Fruit Company until 1942, and they primarily resided in the Puerto-Limón area. This part of Costa Rica has long been isolated, both geographically and culturally, until the 1970s, which has probably contributed to the survival of Limonese Creole (LimC), commonly known as *mekaytelyu*, from Jamaican Creole *let me tell you*. Since the construction of a highway connecting the coast to the rest of the country in 1975, population movements have been facilitated, and Spanish has become dominant, but the creole is still associated with an extensive continuum (Herzfeld 1978, 2003). However, Afro-Costa Ricans have acquired negative attitudes toward their native language, and LimC is often restricted to family contexts. Calypso lyrics may be the last bastion of LimC, usually presented in its mesolectal form. Some calypso songs preserve Anansi stories, and others reflect the nostalgic loss of Creole identity.

3.5.   Panama

Panamanian English Creole (PanC) is spoken as a first language in the Caribbean coastal areas, in parts of the two major cities – the capital Panama, and Colón – and in the province of Bocas del Toro in the northwest of the country. In addition, it is reported that there is a Creole community in Puerto Armuelles on the Pacific coast, although this creole remains undocumented (Herzfeld 1983a: 150). The creole, commonly known as *wari wari*, is a purely oral language. Speakers claim that there are different varieties of PanC spoken across the nation. However such variation has yet to be studied.

During Spanish colonization in the 16th century, Panama was an important transition zone for the placement of slaves, including as many as 30,000 Africans, but this early wave had acculturated by the time Panama was liberated from Spanish domination in 1821. Thus, most Afro-Panamanians or Mestizos speak only Spanish. A second wave of immigrants arrived in the early 17th century as 500 English puritans emigrated with their 450 African slaves (originally imported from Barbados and other parts of the Eastern Caribbean) from the island of Providence, as mentioned above. They settled in the remote Bocas del Toro area, and PanC probably developed there. Most other West Indians came from Jamaica to work on the banana plantations, or to build the railway and the canal in the late 19th century. Consequently, the English varieties spoken in Panama may have been influenced both by Eastern and Western Caribbean varieties. It is estimated that 14% of the Panamanian population are blacks of African or mixed origin, while 65% are Mestizo, and the rest Amerindian, but half of the coastal population is claimed to speak PanC (Herzfeld 1983b: 25). Spanish is of course the medium of instruction and of all public functions, as in other Central American countries, thus Creole English is waning as it is elsewhere. A standard variety of English is probably spoken because of the long US involvement in Panama affairs (Panama only regained control of the canal in 1999).

The creole spoken on the islands of Colón and Bastimentos (Bocas del Toro province) has been more particularly studied (Aceto 1996; Herzfeld 1978, 1983a, b, 2003). Exposure to metropolitan varieties of English is extremely restricted in the islands, so one might expect to find that PanC is a more conservative variety, and perhaps less likely to have developed acrolectal features than others, such as Belizean Creole. However, this does not seem to be the case. On the contrary, PanC – perhaps because of Barbadian influence – appears to include more mesolectal features than the current basilectal features found in BelC. For example, PanC uses *did* and *waz/woz* as preverbal past morphemes besides *ben,* whereas *me, men* are found in Belize, Nicaragua, and the offshore islands.

This does not mean that PanC is totally deprived of basilectal features found in other creoles. PanC includes the widespread preverbal imperfective *de,* but also the variation between *de-, Ø* and *iz-* (Aceto 1996: 52), a typical basilectal-mesolectal-acrolectal variability found elsewhere in the West Indies.

4.   The verb phrase in Central American creoles

There is no unified Central American Creole (CAmC), but rather several partially overlapping varieties, as illustrated with the Belizean samples shown above. All show some evidence of a lectal continuum stretching between formal and informal varieties, although some appear to be deprived of a true basilect (Utila English for example). This section examines briefly the verb phrase across CAmC varieties, and across lects, including only major categories, such as unmarked verbs, TMA markers, adjectival or copular predicates, serial constructions, passives, and negation, and some aspects of the noun phrase. The noun phrase is also illustrated in the following samples, and will be briefly discussed. Abbreviations used below include: IMPFV=imperfective; PA=past; FUT=Future; LOC=locative; TOP=topicalizer, topic particle; REL= relative pronoun; INDEF=indefinite determiner; DET=determiner and POSS=possessive.

4.1.   Tense, aspect, modality system

4.1.1.   *Unmarked past*

This feature is shared by all creoles, including CAmC, and it is widely illustrated across the samples provided, thus only one example is shown here. There are several preterites relexified as unmarked verbs (e.g., *lef* 'leave', *brok* 'break'). The same applies to *ku* 'can' which functions as a tense-neutral modal, not 'could'. Note, however, the use of *gaan* 'went', only used in past contexts (*gwain* in present contexts).

(3a) *So   i   **hapn**   dat   i   **hia**   bawt   wan   ledi*
      So   it   happen   that   he   hear   about   a   lady

(3b) *we   **ku**   kyur   eni   kaynda   siknes*
      who   can   cure   any   kind of   sickness

(3c) *So   di   fela   **gaan** tu   di   owl   ledi   en   i   **tell**   a[...]*
      so   the   fellow go   to   the   old   lady   and   he   tell   her[...]

      'He happened to hear about a woman who could cure any disease, so the fellow went to see that woman and he told her: "..".'

                                              (BelC, Escure, collected in 1981)

4.1.2.   *Imperfective (IMPFV)*

In CamC, the imperfective refers to continuative (progressive) functions as well as to iterative (habitual) functions. They are often marked by the same preverbal morpheme, which can be *de* (in BelC, MisC, PanC, and ProC), and sometimes *a* (in LimC, and occasionally ProC). But in varieties closer to English, the progressive and habitual functions may be split. Thus, PanC uses *de* as progressive marker (7), but *doz* as habitual marker (10). Other morphemes can also function as iterative or progressive markers. For example, *stodi* in ProC (13), *stedi* in BelC (17b), or *wuda* in BelC (14) are common non-past habituals. In mesolectal varieties (as in BIsC, Utila or Roatán), the morphemes *bi/biz* and *doz bi* (11, 12) function as habitual markers. Habitual past is frequently marked with *yuztu/yuwsa* 'used to' (15, 16).

(4) *i   gat   mora wan   ting   we   a   **de**   tink   baut*
     it get   more one   thing   REL   I   IMPFV   think   about
     'There's more than one thing that I am thinking about'
                                        (BelC, Escure, collected in 1987)

(5) *wen a **de**   work lang di ki   ya   hia wan li   'kiling kiling'*
     when I IMPFV work along the caye you hear a   little 'kiling-kiling'
     'When I work on the caye, you can hear a noise'
                                        (BelC, Escure 1983: 34)

(6) *a **de**   dɛd*
     I IMPFV   die
     'I am dying.'   (BelC, Escure, collected in 1985)

(7) *ay **de**   tahk kriol   tahk [. .]   ay   **de**   tahk   it*
     I   IMPFV   talk Creole talk [..]   I   IMPFV   talk   it

     from   mi   hed
     from   my   head
     'I am speaking Creole, it comes naturally.'
                                        (PanC, Herzfeld 1983a: 152)

(8) *a   siy   litl   modi   wahta   **de**   kom*
     I   see   little muddy   water   IMPFV   come
     'I saw some muddy water coming out.'
                                        (ProC, Washabaugh 1983: 159)

(9) *if   im   **a**   kom   mi   gan   owm   ron*
     if   he   IMPFV   come   I   go   home   run
     'If he is coming, I run home.'   (LimC, Herzfeld 1983a: 135)

(10) *in de rekreo taym yu   **doz**   kowm owt eniy   taym*
      in the break time you IMPFV   come out   any   time
      'During the break, you come about any time.'
                                        (PanC, Herzfeld 1983b: 30)

(11) *hi   alveyz   **biz**   **telin**   mi   abaw   da   gorlz   owva*
     he   always   IMPFV   telling   me   about   the   girls   over

     der   in   seyba
     there   in   Ceiba
     'He is always telling me about the girls in La Ceiba.'
     (BisC-Utila, Warantz 1983: 84)

(12) *shi   sik   shi   **doz**   **bi**   havin   som   bad   spelz*
     she   sick   she   IMPFV   IMPFV   having   some   bad   spells
     'She is sick, she often has bad spells.'
                           (BisC-Roatan, Graham 1997: 356)

(13) *a sen   it   gens   i   howl   we   a   siy   im   **stodi**   pahs   tru*
     I send   it   in   its   hole   REL   I   see   it   IMPFV   pass   through
     'I sent [the line) in the hole where I see it (a fish) regularly passing.'
                               (ProC, Washabaugh 1983: 159)

(14) *soma   dem   bway   **wuda**   go   awt   an[..]   luk   bawt   di   mangrurut-de*
     Some   the   boy   would go   out   an   look   about   the   mangrove-root
     'Some fishermen usually look around the mangrove roots (for items
     from shipwrecks).'   (BelC, Escure 1983: 36)

(15) *wat   geym   yu   **yuztu**   pley   wen   yu   smahl?*
     what   game   you   IMPFV   play   when   you   small
     'What games did you play when you were small?'
     (LimC, Herzfeld 1983a: 135)

(16) *i   **yuwsa**   layk   fishin   an   evar   dey   hi   gowz   awt   fishin*
     he   used to   like   fishing   and   every   day   he   goes   out   fishing
     'He used to like fishing and he would go fishing every day.'
     (MisC, Holm 1983: 112)

4.1.3. Past and anterior morphemes (PA)

Although simple past time reference is not marked on the verb, as seen above, all CAmC varieties also use at least one preverbal morpheme to refer generally to some anterior past event. Although some creoles seem to assign different meanings to the use of that morpheme before stative verbs (it would then mean simple past), the variation is not systematic, as seen in the examples below. The basilectal past morpheme is *me* (in BelC, RamC, MisC and SanC), but variants occur as well: *men, wen*, and *we* in SanC, and ProC, or *ben* in PanC and BIsC. The negative equivalent of *me* is invariably *neva*, which does not mean 'never,' but simply negates a past event (18, 22a, 26). Other CAmC varieties, especially those that are less basilectal, include other preverbal markers such as *did,* and *woz* in LimC, PanC and BIsC. Note again that several morphemes can co-occur in a single variety (for example *ben/did* in PanC, BisC, and *me/did* in MisC).

(17a) *wen a da* **me** *wan grup lida de a now dem gyal*
       when I TOP PA a group leader DET I know the girl

(17b) *dey layk* **stedi** *go run go tell run go tell pan dis girl*
       they like IMPFV go run go tell run go tell on this girl
       'When I was group leader, I knew that the girls [office workers]
       always liked to gossip about this girl.'
                                (BelC, Escure, collected in 1987)

(18) *him* **me** *mek di kyar gwayn* [..] *bika i* **neva** *siy di kenip*
     he PA make the car go because he NEG see the guinep

     triy
     tree
     'He kept the car going because he didn't see the guinep tree.'
                               (SanC, Washabaugh 1983: 166)

(19a) *yu no haw ay* **we** *de prey fi im kom howm*
      you know how I PA IMPFV pray for him come home
      'You know how much I prayed for him to come home.'
                             (SanC, Washabaugh 1983: 167)

(19b) *we sayd dem* **wen** *de?*
      What side they PA LOC
      'Where were they?'   (SanC, Washabaugh 1983: 167)

(20) *ay* **ben** *gat mowr intris in dis howl man an yu* **ben** *gat*
    I PA got more interest in this old man than you PA got
    'But I had more interest in the old man than you did.'
                         (PanC, Herzfeld 1983a: 152)

(21) *an him pey de moni? Wel im* **did** *hav tu pey it*
    And he pay the money? Well he PA have to pay it
    'And he paid the money? Well, he did have to pay it.'
                         (LimC, Herzfeld 1983a: 153)

(22a) *i se: 'a* **did** *tayad an* **neva** *kom'*
     he say: I PA tired and NEG-PA come
     He said: 'I was tired so I didn't come.'   (MisC, Holm 1983: 103)

(22b) *a se: 'yu   **me** drinkin da   way   yu   no   **me wan** kom   ya"*
　　　 I say 'you   PA   drink   that   why   you   no   PA FUT   come   here'
　　　 I said: "you were drinking, that's why you wouldn't come here.'

(MisC, Holm 1983: 103)

(23) *shi   hir   that   it   **was**   come   through*
　　　she   hear that   it   PA   come   through
　　　'She heard that it had arrived.'

(BisC-Roatan, Graham 1997: 367)

(24) *Dem aks   mi   if   a   **woz** want   it*
　　　they ask   me   if   I   PA   want   it
　　　'They asked me if I wanted it.'　　　(PanC, Aceto 1996: 54)

(25) *ay **bin had**   it   redi   ay   weytin   an   yu*
　　　I   PA PA   it   ready   I   waiting for you
　　　'I've had it ready, I'm waiting for you.'

(BIsC-Roatan, Graham 1997: 367)

4.1.4. Past-Imperfective (IMPFV + PA morphemes)

The combination *me de+Verb* (or *men de+Verb*) is representative of basilectal progressive past aspect. Some varieties combine morphemes generally attributed to different lects, such as *di(d)+de* and *woz+de* (in PanC, in 28, 29), but there is an occasional *me+V+ing* – only in MisC, see (22b) above. Those 'mismatches' may indicate a mesolect, or may indicate that the basilect is unstable. Such combinations have not been observed in BelC, which suggests that it is a more vigorous creole.

(26) *dat da   we   dey   **me de**   du riper pan   we   dey*
　　　that TOP REL   they PA + IMPFV   do repair on   REL   they

　　　neva   *du gud*
　　　NEG-PA   do good
　　　'That's what they were repairing, and they did not do it well.'

(BelC, Escure, collected in 1987)

(27) *a   klowz   i   **men de**   wash*
　　　TOP clothes he   PA+ IMPFV   wash
　　　'That's clothes he was washing.'

(SanC, Washabaugh 1983: 168)

(28) *yu* **di** **de**   *waak hier ar yu* **di** **de**   *ron de*
you PA+ IMPFV walk here or you PA IMPFV run there
'Were you walking or running (to get here)?'

(PanC, Aceto 1996: 55)

(29) *mi* **woz** *jos* **de**   *taak*
I   PA   just IMPFV talk
'I was just talking.'

(PanC, Aceto 1996: 55)

4.1.5. Future (FUT)

Several creoles have grammaticalized the volition verb *want* into the preverbal future marker *wan*. This is the case in BelC, but also in RamC. Others use *go, gwain*, or *wi/wil*. Aceto (1996) claims that a new future marker *gwainan* is developing in PanC.

(30a) *a tel dem pipl   da nobadi els* **wan** *de   da   kamp*
I tell the people that nobody else FUT LOC that camp
'I told them that nobody else will be at the camp.'

(30b) *a* **wan** *mek im   nou   dat wen a gaan dat dey kant du dat*
I FUT let him know that when I leave that they can't do that
'I will let him know that when I'm gone, they can't do that.'

(BelC, Escure, collected in 1998)

(31) *di man go tu   moch ina di   kol   an   no* **wan** *lisn*
the man go too much in the cold and NEG FUT listen
'Theman goes out too much in the cold, and won't listen.'

(RamC, Assadi 1983: 119)

(32) *bot diz   bastad* **wi** *milk yu dey* **wi** *milk yu ontil yu gow*
but these bastards FUT milk you they FUT milk you till   you go
'But those bastards will exploit you, they will exploit you until you leave.'

(MisC, Holm 1983: 103)

4.1.6. Counterfactual [anterior + future combination] (PA+ FUT)

The combination of the anterior marker and the future marker is often used to capture an irrealis modality that refers to an unrealized event, often con-ditional to another. Thus in (33a) a hypothetical situation is evoked (if you can see some rope on top of the mangrove, it's no good). This presupposes a prior event ('someone would have picked it up if it was good rope'). This reconstructed event is represented in BelC by the *me wan* combination. In (34) the irrealis situation is somewhat different: the use of '*me wan kum in*' refers to uncertainty, or a simple putative event. (35) represents also an unrealized situation, specifically negating the possibility of an event. In some varieties (LimC), a past marker alone can function as irrealis (36). There is no mesolectal counterpart (**did will*).

(33a) *If yu si   an hay pantap a   mangru   no go luk   i   gaan*
       If you see it high on top of mangrove no go look it gone

       lang   taym
       long   time

(33b) *sambadi   **me**   **wan** pik   it   in*
       somebody IMPFV   FUT   pick it   up
       'If you see [some rope] on top of the mangrove, don't even look, it's
       no good, somebody would have picked it up already.'
                                                    (BelC, Escure 1983: 36)

(34)   *Toni kaal mi tel   mi dey me   gat tu   pipl   we   **me***
       Toni call me tell me they IMPFV get two people that IMPFV

       ***wan** kum in*
       FUT   come in
       'Toni called me to tell me that they had two people who might come
       in.'   (BelC, Escure 1997: 101-2)

(35)   *yu   me drinkin das way yu   no   **me wan** kom   ya*
       you PA drinking that why you NEG   PA FUT come here
       'You were drinking, that's why you couldn't have come here.'
                                                    (MisC, Holm 1983: 103)

(36)   *we   **did** hapn   if aal dowz pipl..*
       what PA   happen if all those people
       'What would have happened if all those people...'
                                                    (LimC, Herzfeld 1978: 205)

4.1.7. Completive aspect (COM)

A preverbal completive marker is present in all varieties, and it is usually *don*, regardless of the lectal level. This morpheme can be combined with other aspectual functions.

(37)   *shi se shi did **don** giv sombodi els di skalaship*
       she say she PA COM give somebody else the scholarship
       'She said that had already given the scholarship to somebody else.'
                                         (LimC, Herzfeld 1978: 223)

4.1.8.   *Locative verb (LOC)*

All creoles have a distinctive locative verb, whereas in English the copula is used in locative as well as in equative contexts. The most frequent creole locative verb is *de* [dɛ] (probably derived from *there*). This is clearly a verb, because, like all creole verbs, it can be preceded by TMA markers such as *me, neva,* or *wan* (30a).

(38)   *only di lida **de***
       only the leader LOC
       'Only the leader is there.'   (BelC, collected by Escure)

(39)   *elektrisite neva **de***
       electricity NEG-PA LOC
       'There was no electricity.'   (BelC, collected by Escure)

(40)   *We im wok **de** naw?*
       Where he work LOC now
       'Where is he working now?'   (MisC, Holm 1983)

(41)   *di biebi **de** onda tri*
       the baby LOC under tree
       'The baby is under the tree.'   (LimC, Herzfeld 1978: 193)

4.2.   Adjectival predicate or copular predicate

The English copula has no clear equivalent in basilectal CAmC, but acrolects and sometimes mesolects have acquired some forms of *be* – either *is, are,* or both. An adjectival predicate need not contain a verb per se, thus adjectives are verbal categories. This is confirmed by the fact that predicate adjectives can be preceded by TMA markers, such as *me,* or *did.* In some cases (especially in mesolects), the English copula *iz* functions as a topicalizing particle. For example, the first clause of (43) has zero copula, but the second clause includes *iz* – clearly for emphasis, and the same applies to (44). See 4.3. below.

(42)   *Da* **me**   **wan** **propaganda** **ting** *an* *I* *kom* *wan* *taym*
       TOP IMPFV DET propaganda thing and it come DET time

       wen   *dis*   *Guatemala*   *kwesion*   **me**   **kaynda** **hat.**
       when this Guatemala question IMPFV kind of hot
       'That was pure propaganda, and it occurred when Guatemala was a
       hot issue.'   (BelC, Escure 2001: 69)

(43)   *Omar* *i* **brayt** *i* **iz** **veri** **bray**
       Omar he bright he is very bright
       'Omar is bright, he is indeed very bright.'
                                            (BelC, Escure, collected in 1999)

(44)   *di* *baibl* *now*   *wat* **gud** *fa* *yu* *rayt* *so* **iz** *haad.*
       The bible knows what good for you right so is hard.
       'The bible knows what's good for you, right? So it is hard.'
                                            (BelC, Escure, collected in 1999)

4.3.   The pseudo-copula or topicalizer (TOP)

Since a morpheme *da* (with occasional variant *a*) frequently occurs in the
copular position in basilectal sentence, it has been assumed that *da* is a creole
copula. This is unlikely because the same morpheme also occurs in sentence
initial position (including a question) as a highlighter or pragmatic particle.
This element is probably derived from English 'that', and is often repeated
– *da(t) (d)a* as in (46). Mesolects clearly transfer this topicalizing function to
iz (49, 50). Like the locative verb *de*, *da* can be accompanied by an aspect particle in basilects, but in the order *da me,* contrary to the regular sequence *me
de.* This confirms that *da* is not a verbal item, though it occurs at the beginning
of the predicate:

(45a) **da**   *den*   *bad* *ting*   *hapn.*   **da**   *him* *mek*   *a*
       TOP then bad things happen. TOP him make it
       'That's when bad things happen, it's him who causes that.'
                                            (BelC, Escure, collected in 1983)

(45b) **da**   *Tatabuende* *mek*   *yu*   *get* *chap*
       TOP Tatabuende make you get hurt
       'It's Tatabuende (a mythical Boogeyman) who hurts you.'
                                              (BelC, Escure 1983: 42)

(46) ***da*** *hu* *fo* *hu* ***da*** *fu bleym?*
      TOP who to who TOP to blame
      'Who is it who is to blame?'   (RamC, Assadi 1983: 119)

(47) *dat no riva dat **a** siy*
      that no river that TOP sea
      'That's not a river, that's the sea.'   (LimC, Herzfeld 1978: 194)

(48) ***da*** *elba giv wi wan*
      TOP Elba give we one
      'It's Elba who gave us one.'   (RamC, Assadi 1983: 119)

(49) *Yu no now **iz** huu*
      you not know TOP who
      'You don't know who it really is.'   (MisC, Holm 1983)

(50) ***iz*** *da vuman hi sey dat bringz ya da nuwz*
      TOP the woman he say that bring   you the news
      'He says that it's the woman who brings you the news.'
                                                     (BIsC-Utila, Warantz 1983: 79)

4.4. The passive

Since there is no auxiliary such as *be* in basilects, there is no passive structure in those varieties, although English-style passivization is introduced in
acrolects. However, the passive meaning is derived from the context in spite
of apparent ambiguity, for example in *a disgas* 'I am disgusted', and *i tich* 'he
teaches/he taught', or 'he is taught /he was taught' (51).

(51) *yu aks im bawt wat i **tich** doz nayt i downt*
      you ask him about what he teach those night he don't

      ivn   rimemba
      even   remember
      'When you ask him [5-year old son] what he was taught in evening
      school, he doesn't even remember.'   (BelC, collected by Escure)

(52) *No fret baw dat pleys dat gon **kliyn** a gon kliyn i*
      No fret about that place that going clean I going clean it
      'Don't worry about that place, it's going to be cleaned, I'm going to
      clean it.'   (MisC, Holm 1983: 102)

(53a) *yu put it in di woven tu byek en yu sidon*
      you put it in the oven to bake and you sit down

(53b) *an   wyet ontil i **beyk***
   and wait till it bake
   'You put it in the oven to bake, then you sit down, and wait till it is
   baked.'   (LimC, Herzfeld 1978: 188)

4.5. Non-declarative sentences (imperative, interrogative, and negative)

Imperative, interrogative and negative sentences typically use the declarative
order, with preverbal negative *no* or *neva* (in past contexts). As indicated above,
a question is often – but not necessarily – introduced by the particle (*da, a* or
iz). The auxiliary *do* is only introduced in mesolects, typically without agreement marker, such as *don't* in (51).

(54) *may ticha   **neva**   yuzta   liv   dat fa*
   my teacher NEG-PA IMPFV live that far
   'My teacher didn't live that far.' (BelC Escure, collected in 1999)

(55) *we   hapn? yu   **no**   tel im   bawt di   layt?*
   What happen? you NEG tell him about the light?
   'What happened? You didn't tell him about the light?'
            (BelC Escure, collected in 1999)

(56) *den   da haw yu   ga   dem dat?*
   Then T how you give them that?
   'Then, how did you give it to them?'
            (BelC, Escure, collected in 1999)

4.6. Serial verbs

Series of adjacent verbs are frequently found in creoles. In some cases they
look like English structures without coordinating elements (especially in mesolects and acrolects), but basilectal sentences display a distinctly different
breakdown of the semantic structure of verbs. See for example (17b) above *dey
layk stedi go run go tell run go tell pan dis girl* 'they always gossip about this
girl'; or (34) *Toni kaal mi tel mi.*='Toni called to tell me.'

(57) *samtaim   di bebi **wan** **gu** **wak***
   sometimes the baby want go walk
   'Sometimes the baby wants to walk.'
            (BelC, Escure, collected in 1999)

(58a) *dey **pas** **kum** **don**   dey me de   meyt*
   they pass come down they PA IMPFV mate

(58b)   *en   dey   pas   klos   alang   al   di   kos*
     and they pass close along all the coast
     'They (manta rays) came close to the coast to mate.'

(BelC, Escure 1991: 183)

4.7.   Existential structures (expletives)

There is a variety of structures equivalent to 'there is/are', ranging from *ga/gat/ i gat* to *hav/i have,* and *it's* that overlap often with clefting/focusing constructions. So, topicalizers such as *da, dat,* and *iz* often fulfill the role of expletives in existential structures.

(59)   ***ga*** *li   aystaz   we   grow pan   dem*
     got little oysters REL grow on   them
     'There are small oysters growing (on the mangrove trees).'

(BelC, Escure 1983: 35)

(60)   ***dey hav*** *tu   difren   tayp af obia*
     they have two different type of obeah
     'There are two different types of obeah.'   (BelC, Escure 1997: 96)

(61)   ***hav*** *no wan tu teyk ke   af dem*
     have no one to take care of them
     'There is nobody (no teacher) to take care of them.'

(BelC, Escure 1997: 97)

(62)   ***iz*** *meni yang   men rawn   hia dat pik dis habit op*
     is many young men around here that pick this habit up
     'There are many young men here who get addicted to it.'

(Graham 1997: 380)

5.   The noun phrase

The structure of the noun phrase is amply illustrated in the above examples, so few additional sentences are provided here. As indicated above, English morphology is acquired in acrolects, but basilects and mesolects variably present idiosyncratic features. The most prominent include the use of the numeral 'one' as indefinite article (INDEF) (65), and the use of pronominal as well as postnominal determiners (DET) – usually in the objective form – as plural markers, as in (63). There is also a distinctive second person plural pronoun *unu/una* clearly derived from West African sources (66). There is a widespread merger of the English objective and subjective pronominal forms. Thus the creole counterpart of the English objective pronoun can be used in subject position, and the subjective in object position, as in (64). Basilects typically do not have distinctive gender marked pronouns – *i* is the universally unmarked pronoun for third person singular, but there is frequent variation and co-occurrence of *shi* and *i* in mesolects (67). We could say then that there are simply no number or case morphemes in creoles. Possession is marked by simple juxtaposition, but there is also a periphrastic possessive construction with *fi* (POSS) (65).

(63) *gi   dem   di   wom   pilz   **dem***
      give them the worm pills DET
      'Give (the dogs) the worm pills.'

(64a) *if enitin   tu stodi a hav   tu ripit   dat   tu **shi***
      if anything to study I have to repeat that to her

(64b) *bifa   a gu tu may bed*
      before I go to my bed
      'If (she had) homework, I had to repeat it to her before going to bed.'
                                    (BelC, Escure, collected in 1997)

(65) *da   **wan**   nays sayz papi   **dog pa**   **fi**   **dem   pap***
      TOP INDEF nice size puppy dog father POSS DET pup

      *da   **wan**   big dog*
      TOP INDEF big dog
      'That a good size puppy; those pups' pa is a big dog.'
                                    (BelC, Escure, collected in 1999)

(66) *hu   **unu**   me gat da   trip fa*
      who 2-PL PA got that trip for
      'Who did you do that trip for?'   (BelC, Escure 1999: 174)

(67) *Elvita **shi** no   kom   we   **i**   de   we   **shi** de?*
      Elvita she NEG come where she LOC where she LOC
      'Elvita hasn't come? Where is she? Where is she?
                                    (MisC Holm 1983: 104)

6.   Conclusion

Central America is a linguistic and ethnic *masala* that reflects multiple influences originating from various continents. Varieties of English spoken along the Central American Atlantic coast cover a broad lectal range. Some display similarities to Western Caribbean creoles (especially Jamaica), others to East Caribbean creoles (especially Barbados), and still others to British dialects.

Only Belizean Creole appears to be thriving. In spite of the growing encroachment of Spanish, it has even gained popularity with young people from different ethnic backgrounds, but BelC functions primarily as a marker of black identity. In other countries, Spanish seems to be gaining the linguistic battle as Afro-Caribbeans are no longer isolated, and are concurrently getting more acculturated to Hispanic dominance. However, it was observed that in the Bay Islands (especially Roatán) increased tourism may lead to the maintenance of English-based varieties. But this renewed interest may in fact be geared toward the acquisition of a standard variety of American English rather than to the preservation of creolized forms. This situation may be symptomatic of future trends in Central America, featuring the usual conflict between allegiance to native identity and the need for external communication.

7.   Speech samples

The speech samples include Anansi stories (basilectal Belizean Creole) told by a 60-year old woman, a conversation (basilectal-mesolect) between three Belizean women (ages 50, 60 and 80), a story told in Roatán Creole/English (mesolect) produced by a trilingual Garifuna woman (55), and a sample of Limonese Creole produced by a man (35) (mesolect) kindly contributed by Anita Herzfeld.

Exercises and study questions

1. Locative [dɛ] and imperfective [de] are quite similar phonetically in natural fast speech. They are therefore shown with the same orthographic representation. Can you identify the two types of *de* in the Belizean texts (Anansi stories, or conversations)? Justify your choices, and in the case of the imperfective specify the aspectual function of *de*: does it mark habituality or continuing (progressive) action?

2. Topicalization plays an important role in animated Creole discourse. Identify strategies that help achieve salience or emphasis.

3. Note how past events are presented. Try to determine under what conditions preverbal markers (*me* or *ben/bin/wen*) are used in creole varieties. It has been claimed (Bickerton 1975) that this morpheme marks anteriority before action verbs but regular past tense with stative verbs. Is this claim validated in the speech samples or other examples included in this chapter?

4. Copula or zero-copula? Find in the texts reflexes of the English copula. For example, how do you explain the difference between: *Bra Fayaflay **de** da bo* ('Brother Firefly was at the bow') and *if **da** wan small wan* ('If **that was** a small one')? Both examples are drawn from 'Anansi stories' (BelC). Note: *da* in *da bo* is a locative preposition 'at'.

5. Escure (1983b, 1988, 1993a) thinks that *da* is never a copula in Creoles, but (when it's not a preposition) a pragmatic particle marking topic or focus. Find examples in the texts or examples that either support or contradict this claim.

6. You may note in the various texts and examples the occurrence of English lexical items that are unusual, or very specialized in contemporary varieties of Standard English: see for example *ive* [heave] for 'toss' and *baal* [bawl] for 'wail, cry out, cry'. To what influence might such lexical usage in creoles be attributed?

Selected references

Please consult the General references for titles mentioned in the text but not included in the references below. For a full bibliography see the accompanying CD-ROM.

Aceto, Michael
    1996   Variation in a variety of Panamanian Creole English. Ph.D. dissertation, University of Texas, Austin.
Assadi, Barbara
    1983   Rama Caye Creole. In: Holm (ed.), 115–123.
Escure, Geneviève
    1983   Belizean Creole. In: Holm (ed.), 29–70.
    1991   Serialization in Creole oral discourse. In: Francis Byrne and Thom Huebner (eds.), *Development and Structures of Creole Languages. Essays in Honor of Derek Bickerton*. Amsterdam/Philadelphia: John Benjamins.

1997   *Creole and Dialect Continua: Standard Acquisition Processes in Belize and China (PRC)*. Amsterdam/Philadelphia: John Benjamins.

2001   Belizean Creole: Gender, Creole, and the role of women in language change. In: Marlis Hellinger and Hadumod Bussman (eds.), *Gender across Languages. The Linguistic Representation of Women and Men*, I, 53–84. Amsterdam/Philadelphia: John Benjamins.

2004   Garifuna in Belize and Honduras. In: Geneviève Escure and Armin Schwegler (eds.), *Creoles, Contact and Language Change: Linguistics and Social Implications*. Amsterdam/Philadelphia: John Benjamins.

Graham, Ross

1997   Bay Islands English: Linguistic contact and convergence in the Western Caribbean. Ph.D. dissertation, Department of Linguistics, University of Florida.

Greene, Laurie

1999   *A Grammar of Belizean Creole: Compilations from two Existing United States Dialects* . New York: Peter Lang Publishing.

Hellinger, Marlis

1972   Aspects of Belizean Creole. *Folia Linguistica* 6: 118–35.

Herzfeld, Anita

1978   Tense and aspect in Limón Creole: A sociolinguistic view towards a creole continuum. Ph.D. dissertation, Department of Linguistics, University of Kansas.

1983a   The creoles of Costa Rica and Panama. In: Holm (ed.), 131–56.

1983b   Limón Creole and Panamanian Creole: Comparison and contrast. In: Carrington, Craig and Dandare (eds.), 23–37

2003   *El Mekaytelyuw: El Inglés Criollo de Limón*. San Jose, University of Costa Rica.

Holm, John

1983   Nicaragua's Miskito Coast Creole English. In: Holm (ed.), 95–114.

O'Neil, Wayne

1993   Nicaraguan English. In: Charles Jones (ed.), *Historical Linguistics. Problems and Perspectives*, 279-318. New York: Longman.

Warantz, Elissa

1983   The Bay Islands English of Honduras. In: Holm (ed.), 71–94.

Washabaugh, William

1975   Variability in decreolization on Providence Island, Colombia. Ph.D. dissertation, Department of Language and Literature, Wayne State University.

Washabaugh, William

1983   Creoles of the off-shore islands: Providencia, San Andrés and the Caymans. In: Holm (ed.), 157–180.

Synopsis: morphological and syntactic variation in the Americas and the Caribbean

Edgar W. Schneider

1. Introduction

Varieties of English spoken in North America and in the Caribbean share a number of structural phenomena with other Englishes world-wide, but there are also several distinctive traits with regional extensions. Of course, the most obvious question that stands behind a comparison of varieties in this region is that for typological differences between the dialect grammars of the mainland and the "creole" grammars of the Caribbean and its vicinity. In approaching this question I have tried to steer a compromise between categorizations reported in the literature and more recent lines of thinking which accept blurred boundaries. The following discussion categorizes morphosyntactic features into broad grammatical categories, largely as suggested to authors in the original project phase. In summarizing the variability found I started out from the feature lists provided by authors as input for the interactive map display on the CD-ROM. Subsequently, I have supplemented these categorizations extensively with data drawn from the papers (to which the reader is primarily referred as the sources of the statements made below) and, occasionally, from further references. It should be noted that such a synopsis unavoidably needs to abstract from many details, i.e. it tends to overgeneralize and ignores some facts. Otherwise, no broader picture, the goal of such a survey, would emerge. Readers interested in specific phenomena and their exact diffusion patterns are warned to be cautious, to take the statements below with a grain of salt, and to consult the original sources for details.

2. Tense, aspect and modality

Most grammars of English analyze the language as realizing two distinct aspectual categories, the perfect (expressed by the auxiliary *have* plus a past participle and expressing something like 'current relevance of an earlier action or state') and the progressive (formally marked by the auxiliary *be* plus a present participle and expressing an inside perspective of an activity, viewing it as ongoing or inconcluded). Broadly, AmE dialects share this system, with some slight modifications, while creoles mark a wider range of aspectual relations but pay less attention to tense marking.

In AmE, a clear-cut functional distinction between the **perfect** and the past tense is typically not upheld as consistently as it is in the grammar of British standard English; such a difference is reported as missing in CollAmE, OzE, ChcE and NfldE (as well as in a few of the creoles) and as weakened in a few other varieties [feature list no.25]. The auxiliary *have* may be omitted in several dialects of AmE. AAVE has recently developed a new formal variant, *had* with a past participle, with a simple past or perfect (rather than a past perfect 'past-before-past') reading; this is now also reported for some varieties of ChcE as well as for the English of Anguilla in the eastern Caribbean. A formal variant found elsewhere in the English-speaking world, the use of the auxiliary *be* with the perfect, is rare in the Americas, restricted to a few conservative dialects where close historical ties with a British origin can be hypothesized (NfldE, SEAmE, AnBahE); however, in Lumbee English in the Southeast this feature has been restructured as a distinctive ethnic marker [26]. AppE and NfldE allow a direct object to be placed between *have* and the past participle; AppE also has a perfective *never did* construction. The originally Irish *after*-perfect is documented for NfldE only, though with fewer functional restrictions than in Ireland proper [33]. NfldE also allows a perfective reading for simple non-past verb forms. A sequence-of-tenses rule is weak in AmE and generally fails to apply in Caribbean creoles [30].

An extension of the uses of the **progressive**, e.g. to stative verbs (*be wanting*, *was liking*), characterizes the conservative dialects of AmE (AppE, OzE, SEAmE, NfldE) and CollAmE in general; it occurs occasionally in ethnic varieties (ChcE and AAVE); and extends to the closest kin of AAVE in the Caribbean region, BahE; but it is not found in the Caribbean creoles proper [21]. The pattern *was stood* with progressive meaning [32] characterizes NfldE only. AppE and SE enclave dialects display several "**ingressive**/incipient" constructions (e.g. *got to coming, took to raising, went to driving*). For the formal variant of "*a*-prefixing", see the section on verb morphology.

On the other hand, a wider range of aspectual categories characterizes creoles in particular (though not exclusively), and these languages tend to express them in formally different ways, typically by analytic **preverbal markers** (at least in basilectal varieties) – presumably this is their most distinctive, certainly their most widely cited, structural trait.

The choice of a **habitual** marker distinguishes individual varieties. A habitual *be* is found in North America (AAVE, Gullah, BahE, also NfldE, where the form, recessively used, is also *do be*, and some, apparently regional, varieties of ChcE). BahE and BIE have the formal variant *does be*, sometimes reduced to *'s be* in the Bahamas. Invariant *be* followed by a verbal *-ing* form with a habitual meaning (*he be playin'* 'he always plays') has been documented to be a vigorously spreading innovation of urban and adolescent varieties of AAVE. A form derived from *do* in this function is noted for Gullah (*duhs/does*), PanC, the eastern Caribbean (*doz*) and mesolectal TrnC and TobC, while other forms predominate in other Caribbean creoles (zero or *a*, with *da/de* as possible regional variants, in JamC). [23, 24] AppE, AAVE, NfldE and the dialect of Anguilla may mark actions as habitual by a verbal *-s* suffix. The habitual category cannot always be distinguished from **durative** / **continuative** / **progressive** events; in some varieties these fall together under one form as **imperfective** (as in the SurCs, expressed by *(d)e* or *ta*). For this function Gullah employs *duh/do*, JamC has *a*, less commonly also *de* (with Ø + *Vin'* occurring in the mesolect), and other creoles also have either *a* (eastern Islands, TobC, LimC), *de* (most CAmCs) or *e* (Dominica). The form *Vin* is stated to express habituality only in the Windward Islands but habituality or progressivity in the entire eastern Caribbean. In Anguilla, the progressive aspect can be expressed by *do be Vin*.

A **perfective** or 'completive' *done/don* is extremely widespread; it occurs both in most AmE dialects (most notably in AAVE and southern varieties) and in the Caribbean creoles [28]. AAVE has also a "sequential" *be done*. A pattern with perfective *done* preceded by a primary (tense-marked) auxiliary (e.g. *He is done gone, I had done quit*) seems restricted to earlier AAVE, however. Some SEAmE dialects (notably on the Outer Banks and among the Lumbee in North Carolina) have a functionally similar form, *slam*. With respect to *don*, some Caribbean creoles behave differently from North American dialects by allowing not only a preverbal but also a postverbal position (JamC; with the latter being restricted and considered an older variant in the eastern Caribbean). The corresponding form in SurCs, Portuguese-derived, is *kaba*, in VP-final position.

A form *been/ben* as a marker of **anteriority** is found in practically all creoles as well as, with restrictions, in AAVE (with reference to a distant past) and NfldE (where it is strictly localized and precedes a past participle verb form, not a bare root form) [29]. In JamC and Tob/TrnC *ben* is considered rural and basilectal, corresponding to *did* in the mesolect (a form also found in some eastern Caribbean locations). Variants of this form appear to be regionally distributed in the Caribbean, with *ben* being the western, mostly JamC, form (also in SurCs) but a variant form *mi(n)* predominating in the chain of eastern islands, e.g. in Antigua, Barbuda (locally also as *ming*), Dominica and TobC (also *in*). SurCs have *be/bi* as formal variants; BelC and other CAmCs have predominantly *me* but also *men* / *wen* / *we* in this function, as well as, in mesolects, *did* and *woz*. St. Lucian CE has *had* before bare root verb forms for anteriority. It should be noted that a realistic and more comprehensive account of these markers (and similar ones) needs to go beyond distributional patterns of forms, as pointed out here, to take into account finely-graded functional usage conditions, like co-occurrence restrictions with the stativity of the following main verbs (nonstative verbs tend to receive a default past time interpretation even without overt marking) or the discourse flow of time orientation in a given context. In general, *ben* tends to be used less frequently than expected in Caribbean creoles, marking a change or disruption of temporal organization rather than a global time orientation.

To mark **future** events, creoles have a wide range of preverbal markers, including *ga* (Gullah), *gwine* (Gullah, JamC, CAmC), *go/goin'* (eastern CarCs, TobC, TrnC; reduced to *o* in SurCs), *gon* (Turks Island, Anguilla), *wi* (Turks, CAmC), *sa* (GuyC, SurCs), and *wan* (BelC and other CAmC). Combinations of anterior and future markers in CarCs typically mark a counterfactual proposition, as in BelC *me wan*.

The most unusual phenomenon concerning the uses of **modal verbs** in the Americas is the occurrence of "**double modals**", considered a hallmark of Southern AmE (and here reported for all conservative dialects, in weak form also in Gullah) and found also in JamC [34]. In OzE, the first element of a double modal is predominantly *useta*; in SAmE and AppE it tends to be *might* (with *might could* being particularly common). An epistemic meaning of *mustn't* to mark a statement which is probably not true is reported for NfldE and Gullah (where epistemic *must* tends to associate with *be*) as well as, in weaker form, for south-eastern US dialects and ChcE. SAmE dialects, in particular OzE, AppE, and SE enclave dialects have developed **new quasi-modals**, in particular a 'counterfactual' *liketa* (cf. *had liketa* in NfldE) and the forms *supposeta, useta,* and *fixin' to* (for an immediate future action; sometimes reduced to *finna*). Innovative auxiliaries in AAVE include *come* (to express indignation) and *steady* (for a persistent activity). Caribbean creoles display a range of modals which have some distinctive syntactic and semantic properties. For JamC, for instance, we get *mosi, cuda, wuda, shuda, wi, kyan, hafi, fi,* and others. It seems worth noting that JamC modals are reported not to allow elliptical constructions. For TobC, *bina, fu, binago, (h)afu, bongtu* and others are listed. Distinctive modals in the SurCs include *sabi* (from Portuguese, expressing learned ability), *kam, man, mag, sa* (from Dutch, all for ability), *musu/mu* (necessity), and others.

3. Verb morphology and syntax: Auxiliaries, agreement, verb forms, serialization

It is not uncommon for nonstandard dialects to violate the **concord** rules that govern the choice of forms of the **verb *be*** in StE, e.g. to generalize the form *is* to grammatical persons other than the third singular (e.g. *The rocks is still there*, AppE; similarly in AAVE, ChcE, and some forms of BahE). In NfldE the form *am/ 'm* may generalize in similar ways. In existential sentences in particular, the form *there's* with plural subjects is common in all North American dialects and weakly reported for BahC and Belize as well [55]. Similarly, in the past tense the generalization of *was* (called "default singulars" by Chambers 2003: 266; less commonly *were*) is practically universal [59]. For the emergence of a polarity distinction with past tense copula forms, see the section on negation.

An invariant, or **finite**, use of the form *be*, frequently with habitual meaning, characterizes AAVE, some enclave dialects of SEAmE, BahE, and NfldE, and is obsolescent (without functional specifics) in AppE. Occasionally the form accepts a verbal suffix, yielding *bes/bees* (a distinction which largely sets off AnBahE from AfBahE, for example).

The deletion of the **copula *be*** characterizes Caribbean creoles as well as AAVE and Gullah in the USA and is also found, with restrictions, in AppE, rural AmE dialects, ChcE and BahE. In addition, the basilectal creoles of the Caribbean are characterized by a considerably wider range of distinctive uses of the copula, depending upon the grammatical environment, respectively: Typically, before adjectives there is no copula form at all (so that in that respect adjectives behave like stative verbs, and they may be preceded by the plain pre-verbal negator, e.g. *no*). Distinctive copula forms occur before noun phrases, e.g. *a* (with *da* as an older variant) in JamC (also TrnC, TobC, eastern CarCs, with *be, is* or zero as variants; SurCs have *na/da*), and before locatives, mostly *de* (e.g. in JamC, TobC, TrnC, eastern CarCs, CAmCs, SurCs). Minor, regional copula-like forms include *tap* (Barbuda), *tan* (Antigua) and *stay* (Panama). A copula-like form frequently serves as a topicalizer as well (see section 8).

The deletion of the auxiliary *have* is reported, and mapped accordingly, for some American varieties (SEAmE, AppE, AAVE, BelC, JamC), but essentially this process is difficult to diagnose, as its output is identical with a widespread morphological phenomenon, the confusion of past and past participle forms (see below) [58].

The variability of the **verbal suffix -*s*** is conditioned by structural, social and regional factors. Creoles are marked by invariant verb forms, so typically (except for intermediate forms like BahC and uses approaching the acrolect, where a suffix may appear variably) there are no verbal suffixes. In North America, invariant verb forms are primarily associated with AAVE (and, of course, also found in Gullah, its close kin), but they are also found variably in a number of North American dialects (ChcE, OzE and CollAmE in general) [53]. Conversely, a suffix-*s* may appear in persons other than the third singular in a number of varieties, notably the conservative ones (freely in NfldE and OzE, and, frequently with conditions and limitations, several others, including BahE, especially AfBahE; in AAVE this feature marked earlier forms but seems to have largely disappeared by today) [54]. NfldE has "regularized" forms of *have* and *do*, viz. *haves* and *doos* [duz]. The so-called "Northern Subject Rule", where in the third person plural an-*s* ending is promoted by a full noun phrase subject (*dogs barks*) but avoided after the pronoun *they* (*they bark*) or after words intervening between subject and predicate (*dogs that bark*), characterizes a few south-eastern varieties (where historical continuity from Britain, notably through the so-called "Scotch-Irish" or Ulster Scots, can justifiably be hypothesized), namely SEAmE, AppE and BahE [60]. A possible habitual function associated with -*s* in some varieties was mentioned earlier.

Past tense and past participle forms of verbs show a great deal of variability in nonstandard dialects; some of this is lexically idiosyncratic, but parts of it can be described as structurally systematic processes. Preterites and past participles are frequently leveled. The target of this leveling process can be a regularized form, i.e. one regularly derived by means of an -*ed* suffix from the base form of a verb which in standard English shows irregular forms (e.g. *catched, knowed*); to varying extents this occurs in all dialects of North American English, including Gullah, AAVE and BahE [36]. The same applies to the uses of unmarked verb forms in past and past participle functions (e.g. *give, run*); in addition, this pattern also corresponds to the Caribbean creole tendency for verbs to occur without morphological variation [37]. Furthermore, there are the possibilities of a standard past form functioning as the past participle in nonstandard varieties (e.g. *He had went*) , and vice versa (e.g. *He gone*); again, both patterns are to be found throughout most of North America and the Caribbean, at times subject to certain (mostly lexical) restrictions [38, 39]. The lack of a past tense -*ed* morpheme on regular verbs is found in all Caribbean creole basilects, including Gullah and JamC, and it occurs variably in some dialects as well (CollAmE, OzE, ChcE, AAVE, NfldE, AfBahE) [40]. Mesolectal Caribbean varieties tend to have variable past tense marking.

Finally, the **prefixing of *a*-** before verbal -*ing* forms, as in *he come a-runnin'*, sets off a tightly circumscribed group of conservative North American dialects (AppE, OzE, SEAmE, and NfldE) [41] (and this tendency to prefix *a*- may also extend to other parts of speech, e.g. *a-back*). In NfldE this is also found but recessive with past participles (*acome*).

Serial verb constructions (*I run go home*) are typical of creoles (BelC, TrnC, TobC, JamC, Gullah, SurCs, CAmCs), with conditioned variants occurring in other contact varieties (ChcE, AAVE) [74].

4.   Negation

Multiple negation is practically universal in the varieties under consideration; only for ChcE restrictions on its occurrence are reported [44]. In AAVE and southern dialects the effect of negative copying may in fact cross a clause boundary and affect an indefinite constituent of a subordinate clause as well.

The form ***ain't*** to represent negations of either *be* or *have* is also regularly used in all North American varieties and in some of the Caribbean ones (BahE, T&TC) [45, 46]. On the other hand, as a generic main verb negator, equivalent to *didn't*, *ain't* is reported as generally occurring only in Gullah and the T&T creoles as well as, with limitations, in ChcE, AAVE (where this use is documented rarely in earlier sources but has been spreading), and basilectal BahE – but not for European American dialects [47].

A morphologically **invariant** use of ***don't/don*** for all grammatical persons in the present tense is also found everywhere (except for Suriname) [48], though the precise conditions of its use vary: in Gullah, for example, this is restricted to imperative and habitual sentences; in ChcE, it is considered a transitional phenomenon. The use of ***never*** to negate single events in the past is equally widespread (with limitations in SEAmE dialects, Gullah and AAVE, and BahE) [49]. In earlier AAVE (and occasionally in mesolectal JamC) a pattern with *never did* plus a verb occurs, with unclear conditions of usage. In most Caribbean creoles *neva/neba* is considered a general past time negator (e.g. JamC).

On the other hand, the **preverbal negator** *no/na* characterizes the Caribbean creoles exclusively (with limitations in BahE) [50]. In JamC it may coalesce with the progressive marker *a*, yielding *naa*. Another possible form of an invariant negator in some CarCs is *en* (e.g. in some eastern CarCs) or a nasalized *ẽ* (TrnC).

As to **past tense copula** forms, a morphological split between a positive form *was* as against a different negative form, i.e. *weren't*, is unique to SEAmE dialects [51]. Invariant tags, like *innit*, are also relatively rare, being reported for Gullah (with the forms reported as *aini/inni*) and the T&T creoles as well as, with restrictions, JamC (*no/na* or *duont*) and BelC. For distinctive "negative inversion" patterns, see section 8 below.

5.   Subordination: relativization, complementation

In the American context, the only nonstandard **relativizer** that occurs fairly regularly is *what*; it occurs in CollAmE and OzE, recessively or with restrictions also in SEAmE dialects, AppE and NfldE, as well as, regularly and formally reduced to something like *we(h)*, in creoles (Gullah, BelC, TrnC, TobC, BahE and JamC) [61]. In AAVE, relative *what* was found in earlier forms but has largely disappeared from the modern dialect; earlier AAVE also shows traces of *that which* and non-spatial *where*. The use of *that* or *what* in non-restrictive contexts is reported for some Caribbean creoles as well as CollAmE, NfldE, and, with limitations, rural AmE dialects and ChcE [62]. On the other hand, the relative particles *as* and *at* are rare, occurring only occasionally in AppE and in the south-east [63, 64]. The SurCs have a relativizer *di* or *disi*, derived from *this*, and Sranan increasingly uses relativizers derived from interrogatives. Analytic possessives, like *what's* or *that his*, are reported for BelC and BahC, and occasionally for SEAmE and AAVE [65]. In contrast, the possibility of omitting a subject relativizer is much more widespread; it is documented in JamC and BelC as well as in Gullah and AAVE, AppE and SEAmE, NfldE, and, in weaker form, ChcE [66].

Resumptive pronouns are reported for JamC, BelC, AAVE, Gullah, and SEAmE dialects, also for ChcE and SurCs [67]. Using a pronoun copy of a subject NP (so-called "pronominal apposition", "left dislocation", or "double subject" constructions; e.g. *My brother, he did ...*) is almost a universal strategy in spontaneous spoken language, presumably a focusing device. In contrast, ChcE is the only variety for which the possibility of omitting a direct object is reported, and this dialect sometimes also features zero subject pronouns in main clauses (presumably a transfer feature reflecting the pro-drop parameter of Spanish).

The use of *would* in *if*-clauses is regularly reported for NfldE only; with restrictions it is also found in SEAmE dialects, ChcE, AAVE and BelC [31]. Variants of *there* as the dummy subject in existential clauses (including *they* or *it*) are common throughout the region, except for SurC, JamC and ChcE [56]. In Caribbean varieties forms of *get* and *have* occur as predicates in existentials (e.g. JamC, TobC, TrnC, CAmCs).

Some American dialects have distinctive **subordinators**, like *whenever* meaning 'as soon as' (AppE, Midlands and SE dialects), *'fraid* 'so that ... not' in NfldE, or a "redundant *that*" (*because that*, *where that*; a conservative feature with familiar roots in Early Modern English) in AppE. NfldE also shows the IrE subordinating *and* for concessives. A complementizer form derived from *say* (often spelled *se*) and introducing object clauses after speech act verbs characterizes the Caribbean and creole-related varieties (JamC, TrnC, TobC, BelC, AAVE, Gullah; *taki* in the SurCs) but not, except for traces in ChcE, the North American dialects [68]. ChcE has some distinctive reported speech patterns (*tell* 'ask'; *tell that* with direct speech).

The use of *for to* in infinitival purpose **clauses** is common in conservative and ethnic North American dialects (SEAmE, OzE and NfldE, weaker in AppE, ChcE and AAVE). The distribution of *as/than what* in comparative clauses is similar (regular in CollAmE, SEAmE, OzE, NfldE, AAVE and also JamC; under conditions in ChcE and Gullah) [73]. Midwestern CollAmE has a distinctive pattern of quasi-modals followed by past participle verb forms (e.g. *The car needs washed, The cat wants petted, The baby likes cuddled.*)

Caribbean creoles (like JamC) have **non-finite clause complements** with bare root verb forms (not necessarily with the marker *to*, and in basilects normally not as -*ing* forms). The form *fi* is a widespread infinitive marker or complementizer, sometimes (though not necessarily) expressing a purpose (JamC). Similarly, in the SurCs *fu* introduces non-factive complement clauses.

6.   Noun phrase structure

Throughout North America and the Caribbean after numerals and in nouns of measure the lack of a **plural** marker is common [14]. In AAVE, and even more so earlier variants of this dialect, this restriction is less effective, i.e. the omission of a plural marker is possible in other contexts as well. In creoles, the plural typically remains unmarked morphologically; if needed, it tends to be expressed by a form *dem*, which can be preposed to the noun, as in basilectal Gullah (*dem boy* 'those boys'; also in some eastern Caribbean locations), postponed (*di bwai-dem*, JamC, similarly TobC or CAmCs), or also co-occurring with an inflectional suffix, as in BahE (*de boys-dem*) or, rarely, JamC. In the eastern Caribbean *an dem* predominates as a variant of the plural marker (also T&TCs); *an de* is unique to Barbuda. A plural suffix -*s* in creolized varieties remains restricted to mesolectal forms (e.g. mesolectal Gullah). Regularized noun plural forms (*deers, corns*) as well as, less widely, double plurals (*firemens*) occur with regional and social restrictions. AppE has syllabic plural forms (*deskes, postes*). Group plurals are also quite common, being reported for CollAmE, SEAmE, OzE, AAVE, BelC and the T&T creoles as well as, less regularly, ChcE, NfldE and BahE [15]. The same applies to group genitives (regular in CollAmE, SEAmE, OzE, AppE, NfldE and JamC; with restrictions in ChcE, AAVE, and BahE) [16]. AppE, NfldE, AAVE, Gullah and CarECs (JamC) display "associative" plurals after a noun form to suggest a collective reading (*and them*, *and all, dem*), designating the family or associates of the person referred to.

A tendency to omit or insert **articles** in unusual ways, at varying degrees of regularity, occurs both in AmE dialects and in CarECs, though this seems difficult to generalize, given that many of these phenomena are lexically bound (for instance, SE enclave dialects use articles with diseases, as in *the toothache*) [17]. In terms of article uses, Caribbean creoles differ quite fundamentally from North American dialects in having different forms and expressing different functional distinctions (like specificity rather than definiteness); most notably, a indefinite but specific form *wan* is common (like in JamC, BelC and CAmCs, the SurCs, or, with a nasalized vowel, TobC).

Contrary to zero plural forms, the omission of a genitive suffix (*my daddy brother*) is only rarely found among European American dialects, so this feature sets off AAVE from related varieties in North America. In the Caribbean, this pattern is fairly widespread, however (e.g. JamC, Anguilla, SurCs). Postnominal *for*-phrases to express **possession** are a conditioned possibility in most North American dialects, also found in the Caribbean (e.g. in SurCs; see below for corresponding pronoun forms) [18].

Both double **comparatives** and **superlatives** (*more cheaper*, *bestest*) and regularized comparison strategies (*gooder*, *the regularest*, *most pretty*) occur in most of the varieties under discussion, regularly or to some extent [19, 20]. AppE, and to some extent CollAmE elsewhere, allow comparatives and, especially, superlatives of participles (*fightingest*, *singingest*).

7.   Pronominal systems

Interestingly enough, loosened conditions for uses of **gendered pronouns** are more widely reported for the North American dialects than for the Caribbean creoles. In particular, *she* for inanimate referents is fairly common (general in CollAmE, SEAmE, OzE, and NfldE; conditioned in AppE, ChcE, AAVE, and BahE), while generic *he* seems somewhat more restricted to NfldE and contact varieties (unconditioned also in Gullah, where gender-neutral *he* co-exists with gender-specific *she* and *it*, JamC, BelC and SurCs, with the form *a*; with limitations in ChcE and AAVE) [7, 8].

A functional conflation of **subject and object forms of pronouns** is also considered more characteristic of creoles (e.g. JamC, eastern Caribbean) than of English dialects, though to some extent is does occur in the latter as well. "Pronoun exchange" seems robust in NfldE in particular. Both subject pronoun forms in object function and vice versa can occasionally be observed in NfldE and in a few of the CarCs (notably, BelC and, in the former case, also TrnC and TobC) [12]. On the other hand, most varieties, including creoles, have retained a distinction between subject and object forms of pronouns (like *(h)e* vs. *(h)im/um* in Gullah).

In the third person singular, AppE has preserved a conservative neuter form *hit* and, in the possessive, *hit's*. In NfldE a distinctive third person object form *en/un* has been retained from British sources.

Nonstandard uses of *us* are found in AAVE, NfldE, BelC, and occasionally in SEAmE dialects [11]. Gullah has object *we* in addition to *us*. In general, *we* is claimed to be a western Caribbean subject and object form, distinguished from *aawi* (with a variant *aabi* in some islands) in the eastern region. In the Rastafarian variety of JamC the element *I/ai* is widely productive.

Remarkably, all of the varieties in our area, whether or not creolized, have developed distinct **second-person plural** pronoun forms [3]. The southern hallmark *yall* has found a corresponding *you guys* elsewhere in CollAmE. The form *you'uns* is found in the South Midlands and western Pennsylvania and in AppE. Further options are *yous* (NfldE) and *ye* (AppE, NfldE). Creoles have an African-derived form *una/unu*, which occurs marginally in Gullah (in performance discourse) and normally in JamC, CAmCs or SurCs. Variant forms of this type include *yinna/yunna* (reported for BahE). A regional split separates the western Caribbean, where *unu* and its variants occur, from the eastern Caribbean, where the predominant forms are *aal-you* or, less commonly, *you-aal*.

With respect to **possessives**, the form *me* for *my* marks most creoles (Gullah, SurCs, TrnC, TobC, JamC) and NfldE and can be found under certain conditions in SEAmE and BahE (in AfBahE but not normally AnBahE) [2]. Similarly, some varieties, like Gullah, have the second-person singular possessive form *ye*. The possessive of southern *yall* is *yall's*. A possessive form *they* seems strongest in AAVE, but it is also documented in AfBahE. In Gullah, all possessives may add the form *own*. Basilectal Caribbean creoles allow for a productive formation of possessives by means of a prefix *fi-* with personal pronouns, e.g. *fi-mi* 'my', *fi-im* 'his, her' and also *fi-huu* 'whose' in JamC (similarly in TobC and TrnC). Possession may also be expressed by bare juxtaposition, both of pronouns and of nouns (e.g. *di uman biebi*, JamC).

Some AmE dialects (mostly southern and Midland ones) have variant forms of the absolute possessive pronouns (*hisn, ourn*; AAVE also has *mines*). A benefactive "personal dative" construction (*I got me something*) may also be found, mostly in southern and related dialects, including AAVE.

The paradigm of **reflexive** pronouns tends to be regularized somehow everywhere [4], with object forms forming the basis of reflexives mostly (though not exclusively) in the creoles [5] and the number distinction being given up generally or variably in a wide number of dialectal and creole varieties as well [6].

The use of a non-reflexive *meself/myself* characterizes all North American dialects as well as some contact varieties (Gullah, AAVE, SurCs, ChcE, the T&T Cs) [9]. In AppE an emphatic reflexive with *own* (*my own self*) may be formed. In coordinate subjects, *me* rather than *I* is the regular choice everywhere [10].

Demonstrative *them* for *those* is almost universal in North America and the Caribbean [1]. In CollAmE of the South and the Midlands and AppE demonstratives may be reinforced morphologically, yielding *this here* and *them there*, a pattern also documented in earlier AAVE and, in a similar fashion, in JamC (*dis-ya*, *dat-de*). In the SurCs demonstrative meaning is also achieved by a combination of prenominal determiners and postnominal locative adverbs (*di ... ya/aki/de*). Traces of a system with a third (distant as against intermediate) demonstrative, *yon/yonder*, can be observed in AppE. AppE also has interrogative pronouns with *ever-* (*everwhich*, *everwho*). NfldE uses the article as a proximal demonstrative with measures of time (*the* 'this' *fall*).

8.   Adverbs

Adverb forms without the *-ly* suffix are widespread everywhere, both for degree adverbs and for others [41, 42]. Southern dialects (in particular, AppE, OzE and SE enclaves) have a characteristic set of intensifying adverbs (*right, plumb, mighty, powerful, slam*); the same applies to NfldE (*right, some, wonderful, terrible*) and AnBahE (*right*). In AppE, a characteristic set of place and time adverb forms occurs (*anywheres, beforehands; thataway; yon*).

The use of *anymore* in non-interrogative clauses has spread from AppE and OzE to CollAmE in wider regions of the Midlands. SE enclave dialects have a vestige negative adverb *nary*.

9.   Word order and discourse organization

Many of the Caribbean creoles are characterized by a "topicalizer", which morphologically is mostly equal to a copula form (frequently *is* or *a*), placed in sentence-initial position immediately before the highlighted constituent (which may be repeated in the following clause structure). Gullah has *duh* as such a sentence-initial focus marker but, unlike many other creoles, fails to accept VPs in the following, clefted position. In JamC this focus marker is *a*, and it may also mark "predicate clefting" (e.g. *A swell it swell* 'it certainly swelled up'). In TrnC, TobC and SurCs the form *a* is also attested in this function. In CAmCs it tends to be *da*, with *iz* as a mesolectal equivalent.

An inverted V-N word order in indirect questions, unlike in standard English, is common in all North American dialects, including AAVE, and also found in some creoles (Gullah, BelC) [69]. In main clauses, both in *wh*-questions and in *yes/no*-questions uninverted question patterns are practically universal [70, 71]. Some North American varieties (notably OzE, AppE and AAVE) have "negative inversion" patterns with sentence-initial inverted negative auxiliaries, as in *Didn't nobody show up*; Gullah has such a structure with *Ain't* as a negative focus marker.

One of the new functions that the word *like* has developed, that of a focusing device, is reported for a few dialects and creoles (strongly for AppE, NfldE, ChcE and BelC; weakly for SEAmE dialects and the T&T creoles) [75]. More commonly, however, *like* occurs as a quotative form – generally in North American dialects (though not in Gullah), also in BahE, and less regularly in BelC and T&T [76].

Exercises and study questions

1. Which of the dialects covered in this volume have a verbal -*s* ending, and in which functions? Attempt a systematic survey of the distribution of this ending in the Americas and the Caribbean, looking into geographical and functional aspects. Do you have any historical explanation for the patterns that you find?

2. Which forms in the verb phrase can be employed to refer to events in the past in North America and in the Caribbean? Select three of them and explain the specific meaning that they express.

3. Define what is meant by "progressive" and "habitual" in the verb phrase. Which formal realizations may the progressive have in the Americas and the Caribbean? Where does the category "habitual" have a distinct realization, and which one? Discuss the relationship between both categories, considering regional and functional patterns.

4. Compare patterns of negation in nonstandard varieties of American English with Caribbean creoles. Which differences do you find with respect to the uses of the forms *ain't* (and its corresponding realizations) and *never* (including its variants)?

5. The forms *dem* and *de* occur in different dialects both of North America and the Caribbean, but they are highly multifunctional, i.e. in different regions they can mean different things. Systematize their functions and their regional patternings. Which of these functions are typical of creole languages?

6. Provide a systematic survey of ways of forming the plural of nouns in the Americas and in the Caribbean, quoting examples from the articles. How widespread and common are the different options? Account for the forms that you discuss historically, i.e. explain their origins. Which of these forms are typical of creole languages?

7. Draw a map of North America and the Caribbean and enter different forms of second-person plural pronoun forms where they are used. Provide a structural description of the constituents of these forms in a comparative perspective. Develop hypotheses on the origin and formation of these pronoun forms.

8. Compare patterns of relative clause formation in nonstandard varieties of American English with Caribbean creoles. In which functions do you find zero forms in both regions? How do you account for the function of *what* (and its derivatives) in both regions?

Index of subjects

NORTH 44, 47, 55, 59, 62, 64, 70, 73, 76, 78, 81, 90–91, 102, 105, 119, 121–122, 131, 132, 140, 141, 153, 154, 164, 170, 185, 194, 196, 198, 204–205, 212, 221, 243, 260, 267, 316–317, 328, 331, 344, 366, 371, 387–388, 393

Northern Cities Shift/Northern Cities Chain Shift [NCS, NCSS] 30, 45, 56, 58, 80–84, 86, 132, 140–141, 155–156, 184, 189, 384–385, 387

Northern Subject Rule (see *agreement*)

noun
count 26, 206, 234, 412, 444, 453, 502–503, 548, 599, 637, 673, 682–688, 693

mass 23, 157, 239, 272, 444, 453, 554, 557, 567, 610, 637, 642, 682, 688

measure 37, 252–253, 285, 322, 326–327, 444, 483, 487, 525, 529, 566, 599, 641, 771

noun phrase [NP] 5, 263, 453, 465, 469, 479, 483–484, 501, 514, 524, 539, 541, 543–544, 546, 554, 556–558, 560, 565, 597–598, 599, 623, 630–631, 635–636, 638–640, 665, 687–689, 702, 704–707, 715, 724, 726–729, 747, 758, 767–768, 770–771

nucleus 56, 59, 71–73, 78, 87, 90, 95, 98–102, 104, 116, 124, 137, 140, 154–155, 169, 197–198, 223, 244–245, 259–265, 275, 278–280, 314

number
absence of 314
agreement (see *agreement*)
associative plural 445, 501, 525, 554, 558, 637, 641
distinction
lack of number distinction 314, 774
group plural 407, 771
plural (marking) 176, 301, 501, 525, 544, 558, 637, 641, 651, 653–654, 656–657, 758, 771

NURSE 44, 46, 55, 70, 72, 76, 81, 91, 97, 102–103, 106–107, 131, 153, 164, 171, 185, 194, 196, 204, 211–212, 243, 260, 267, 316, 328, 331, 344, 352, 353, 371, 388

O

object (see also *case, objective*) 335, 408, 421, 446, 460, 502–503, 523, 546, 554, 556, 558–560, 565, 577, 613, 630, 638, 652–653, 665, 673–675, 688, 698, 712, 715, 722, 759, 770, 772–773
direct 435, 442, 446, 495, 503, 577, 629, 698, 764, 770
indirect 503, 698
oblique 632, 722

obstruent 78, 81, 85, 97, 100, 123, 132, 137, 140, 163, 169, 175, 184, 187, 252, 276–277, 280, 296, 314, 394

offglide (see *glide/gliding*)

onset 48, 56, 163, 167, 169, 174, 228, 248, 264, 273–277, 279, 281, 283, 296, 332–333, 376, 387–391, 647
cluster, 274, 277, 279

oral 165, 176, 256, 259, 274–275, 324, 332, 745

orthography 272, 287, 402, 613, 642, 736

P

palatal 48, 61, 174, 183, 200, 272–274, 281, 376, 622
/l/ (see /l/)
alveo- 165–166, 175, 277

palatalization 305, 330, 372, 376, 394

PALM 44–45, 55, 57, 64, 70, 72–73, 76, 80, 82, 91, 98, 131–132, 152–153, 164, 168, 185, 194, 196, 204, 211, 221, 243, 260, 267, 316–317, 328, 331, 344, 355, 387

participle 403–404, 406, 415, 419, 423, 452, 477–478, 496–497, 499, 521, 529, 539–540, 596, 768, 772
past 228, 403, 414, 435–436, 438, 495–497, 499, 514, 540, 542, 562,

Index of varieties and languages